The Brussels Effect

The Brussels Effect

How the European Union Rules the World

ANU BRADFORD

OXFORD
UNIVERSITY PRESS

OXFORD
UNIVERSITY PRESS

Oxford University Press is a department of the University of Oxford. It furthers the University's objective of excellence in research, scholarship, and education by publishing worldwide. Oxford is a registered trademark of Oxford University Press in the UK and certain other countries.

Published in the United States of America by Oxford University Press
198 Madison Avenue, New York, NY 10016, United States of America.

© Oxford University Press 2020

Library of Congress Cataloging-in-Publication Data
Names: Bradford, Anu, author.
Title: The Brussels effect : how the European Union rules the world / Anu Bradford.
Description: New York : Oxford University Press, 2020. | Includes bibliographical references and
    index.
Identifiers: LCCN 2019031328 (print) | LCCN 2019031329 (ebook) | ISBN 9780190088583 (hardback) |
    ISBN 9780190088606 (epub) | ISBN 9780190088590 | ISBN 9780190088613
Subjects: LCSH: Law—Mobility. | Law—European influences. | Law—European Union countries. |
    European Union—Influence.
Classification: LCC K590.5 .B73 2020 (print) | LCC K590.5 (ebook) | DDC 341.242/2—dc23
LC record available at https://lccn.loc.gov/2019031328
LC ebook record available at https://lccn.loc.gov/2019031329

5 7 9 8 6 4

Printed by Sheridan Books, Inc., United States of America

Note to Readers
This publication is designed to provide accurate and authoritative information in regard to the subject matter covered. It is based upon sources believed to be accurate and reliable and is intended to be current as of the time it was written. It is sold with the understanding that the publisher is not engaged in rendering legal, accounting, or other professional services. If legal advice or other expert assistance is required, the services of a competent professional person should be sought. Also, to confirm that the information has not been affected or changed by recent developments, traditional legal research techniques should be used, including checking primary sources where appropriate.

*(Based on the Declaration of Principles jointly adopted by a Committee of the
American Bar Association and a Committee of Publishers and Associations.)*

Äidille ja isälle

For mom and dad

Contents

Preface   ix

Introduction: The Brussels Effect   xiii

PREFACE TO PART ONE: *Theory*

1. How the EU Became a Global Regulatory Power   7

2. The Brussels Effect   25

3. The Brussels Effect in Context   67

PREFACE TO PART TWO: *Case Studies*

4. Market Competition   99

5. Digital Economy   131

6. Consumer Health and Safety   171

7. Environment   207

PREFACE TO PART THREE: *Assessment*

8. Is the Brussels Effect Beneficial?   235

9. The Future of the Brussels Effect   265

Notes   289

Index   387

Preface

THE IDEA FOR this book was born as a reaction to the nearly constant public commentary about the European Union's demise or global irrelevance that permeates modern popular discourse. That narrative contradicted the data and patterns I observed in my own academic research, which provided many profound examples of the EU's global regulatory power and influence. Accurately examining these examples affirms the EU's continuing, even growing, global relevance to the conduct of international regulatory affairs. These conflicting narratives sparked the idea to initially write an article about the mechanisms driving the EU's regulatory influence in an effort to correct the misperceptions about the EU's decline, and to advance a more informed view of the EU's role in the world. In that article, published in 2012 in *Northwestern University Law Review*, I coined the term the "Brussels Effect"—to capture the origins of the EU's power that stems from its Brussels-based institutions and to pay tribute to, and to build on, David Vogel's pathbreaking work on the California Effect.

Encouraged by the debate the article generated, I accepted the Oxford University Press's invitation to expand the article into a book. Much has happened since 2012, yet the EU's influence over global markets has only grown, despite the seemingly constant series of crises that the EU has continued to face. This book seeks to advance a considerably more detailed and nuanced theory of the EU's global regulatory clout than the one initially articulated. It also broadens the scope of the inquiry into new areas of regulation, new industries, and new countries while also asking new questions, such as whether the Brussels Effect is welfare-enhancing and whether it will endure into the future.

The main contribution of the book is descriptive. It explains how and why the EU has become the global regulatory hegemon unmatched by its geopolitical rivals, without endorsing or criticizing the EU for the regulatory power it possesses. Like anyone, I hold my own normative views about the EU, and deeply care about its destiny. My pride of the EU's many accomplishments is as profoundly felt as are my frustrations about its repeated failures. Toward the end of the book and for the purpose of simulating discussion, I propose a normative stand on the Brussels Effect. However, the core argument and the overall contribution of the book does not turn on my own views on the EU. The Brussels Effect exists whether one likes it or not, and ultimately, I leave it for the reader to decide whether the Brussels Effect is a phenomenon that advances the state of the world or presents a cause for concern.

With this book, my hope is to engage supporters and detractors of the EU alike. It challenges the critics' view that portrays the EU as a powerless global actor, and shows how such a criticism focuses on a narrow and outdated vision of what power means today. For the most ardent supporters of the EU, the book gives comfort that the EU matters, but also undermines the narrative that further integration is needed for the EU's revival and relevance. Even in the absence of a European federation, the EU is already able to advance its interests, both within and beyond its borders, through the Brussels Effect. Similarly, this book is written for European and non-European audiences alike. It hopes to speak to the Brussels policy insiders as well as to foreign governments, companies, and citizens with little direct experience with the EU as such—until they notice how pervasively and persistently the EU regulations reach their shores and affect their daily lives.

As a result of my personal and professional journey from Europe to the United States, today I have the benefit of observing the EU at the same time as an insider and as an outsider. For nearly two decades, I have studied the EU as a European living in the United States. Being part of the American scholarly and public conversation creates a certain distance to the debates taking place in Brussels, affecting the way I perceive and write about the EU. Yet I will never be a genuine outsider: I grew up in Finland; studied and worked in Belgium, France, and Germany before moving to the United States; and wrote the bulk of this text while living in Spain and traveling throughout Europe. When I write about the EU regulations and institutions today, I write about something deeply familiar. To me, EU law remains domestic law, not foreign law.

Throughout the writing process, I benefited from rich and varied conversations with an incredible group of individuals, both in the United States and Europe. The manuscript improved immensely as a result of those conversations—yet all errors and deficiencies are mine alone. The book made its greatest leaps in two manuscript conferences that took place in New York in 2018 and Madrid in 2019. I am deeply grateful to an amazing group of scholars who took the time to read the manuscript and share a daylong conversation about it. Warmest thanks to Alberto Alemanno, George Bermann, Katja Biedenkopf, Adam Chilton, Marise Cremona, Grainne De Burca, Piet Eeckhout, Dan Kelemen, Suzanne Kingston, Katerina Linos, Abe Newman, Mark Pollack, Tonya Putnam, Anne-Lise Sibony, Thomas Streinz, David Vogel, Maria Weimer, Jan Wouters, and Tim

Wu for putting aside your own projects and lending your brilliant minds to discuss the Brussels Effect with me. This is a very different and a much-improved book because of those conversations.

I had the opportunity to present drafts of the manuscript in various conferences in Europe and the United States, including at the Council for European Studies 26th International Conference of Europeanists in Madrid; Trade Lecture Sessions at the WTO in Geneva; Observatory of the European Union at the IE School of Global and Public Affairs and Universidad Carlos III de Madrid in Madrid; 10th Forum of Trans Europe Experts in Paris; EU Law Workshop at the European University Institute in Florence; Global Governance Colloquium in the Graduate Institute of Geneva; European Union seminar series at Princeton University; Faculty Workshop at Columbia University; Workshop on Modeling Convergence of the EU with the World at The City Law School, City, University of London; and at the Duke-Yale Foreign Relations Law Roundtable at Duke University. I am deeply grateful for the excellent feedback I received.

I also greatly benefited from generous reading and invaluable insights from many of my trusted colleagues. Special thanks to Rachel Brewster, Tom Ginsburg, Katharina Pistor, Eric Posner, Dave Pozen, and Matt Waxman for your thoughtful read and astute feedback, and to the anonymous reviewers at the Oxford University Press who offered numerous insights that pushed the argument further. Warm thanks also to Jessica Bulman-Pozen, Stavros Gadinis, Kathryn Harrigan, Bert Huang, Olati Johnson, Ben Liebman, Florencia Marotta-Wurgler, Sophie Meunier, Joanne Scott, Alex Wang, Jonathan Wiener, and Angela Zhang for helpful conversations and reading suggestions. I owe deep gratitude to numerous EU officials, legal and policy experts, and representatives of governments and corporations for sharing their perspectives with me and directing me to the right questions or sources. Of course, the arguments advanced in this book are mine alone and cannot be attributed to these individuals or their organizations. In particular, my sincere thanks go to Julia Backmann, Matthew Bye, Riccardo Falconi, John Frank, Tony Gardner, Bruno Gencarelli, Hans Ingels, Cyril Jacquet, Sabine Juelicher, Michael Kefi, Esther Kelly, Nicholas Levy, Guillaume Loriot, Patrick Robinson, Jessica Schonberg, James Stevens, Emiliano Tornese, Nicolas Veron, Peter Zapfel, and Karolina Zazvorkova.

This book would not exist without my incredible team of research assistants. Teaching and working with such an immensely talented and dedicated group of students is an enormous privilege and makes this the best job in the world. My sincere thanks to Phil Andriole, Bruna Barletta, Kelly Benguigui, David Blackman, Andrew Brickfield, Sami Marouf Cleland, Marie-Marie De Fays, Pap Diouf, Haley Flora, Hui Zhen Gan, Jonah Garson, Rohan George, Rossana Gonzalez-Munoz, Julia Grabowska, Isabella Harris, Emily Hush, Lear Jiang,

Janet Kanzawa, HyunKyu Kim, Deul Lim, Yu-teng Lin, Ravi Kumar Mahto, Marie Menshova, Kevin Minofu, Peter Neuboeck, Julie-Irene A Nkodo, Liuyi Pan, Neeraj RS, Aakanksha Saxena, Elvira Sihvola, Eric Sliva, Alastair Smith, Sreenidhi Srinivasan, Julia Szinovatz, Laura Weinblum, and Mitra Yazdi. Without them, this book would have taken years more to write and would never have its current reach. Their research allowed me to bring examples of the Brussels Effect across Asia, Africa, and Latin America and discuss many regulations or industries I discovered only through their research. Thank you for sharing my ambition and going out of your way repeatedly for me. I also want to extend my warmest thanks to my fantastic editor, Chris Lura, whose utmost care, dedication, and professionalism made this a far more readable book.

I want to acknowledge with gratitude the funding by various centers and institutes at Columbia University whose support made this research possible: Jerome A. Chazen Institute for Global Business; Millstein Center for Global Markets and Corporate Ownership; and Richard Paul Richman Center for Business, Law, and Public Policy. The research also benefited from the support of the Erasmus + Programme of the European Union.[1]

Finally, my family. My heartfelt thanks to my three children—Oliver, Sylvia, and Vivian—whose patience extended to Saturday mornings over the past two years. My 12-year-old Oliver can articulate the Brussels Effect as well as anyone. As a bicontinental citizen who is concerned for the future, he takes comfort in how the Brussels Effect reaches him in New York City every day. My deep gratitude to my husband Travis, who never grew tired of discussing the Brussels Effect or reminding me how much this insight mattered. Thank you for reading and rereading every word of the draft manuscript and gifting me with both uncompromised honesty and unwavering support. You helped me see further and think deeper, and many of the most important insights of the book can be traced to the numerous conversations we shared.

This book is dedicated to my parents, Riitta and Lauri, who deserve my most profound gratitude. The key elements of this book were developed while working from my childhood home in Finland. Thank you for the countless hours of child care, which gave me the vital space to think and write. Thank you for your tireless support, for this project and for every past endeavor on which this project builds. You always encouraged me to chase my own dreams, not yours or anyone else's. All my accomplishments, including this book, I owe to that.

Madrid, Spain
June 2019

Introduction

THE BRUSSELS EFFECT

READING THE CURRENT news or any of a steady stream of policy analyses by think tanks and government agencies, it is easy to discern a deeply held assumption that Europe's best days are over. Policy experts, scholars, and journalists writing about Europe observe how "The Continent's grand unity project is failing, and its global influence is fading."[1] They describe "The European unraveling"[2] or document "The EU's Fall and Decline: The Struggle Against Global Irrelevance."[3] They refer to "The coming erosion of the European Union"[4] or explain "Why Europe no longer matters."[5] Some regret the decay of Europe, noting how "The decline of Europe is a global concern,"[6] while others remind how Europe's decline is a result of its own making given that "Europe Paves the Way for Its Decline."[7] A narrative that emerges from this commentary is one portraying the European Union (EU) as an aging and declining power that is struggling to remain relevant.

There are several elements to the EU's perceived weakness. A united Europe has never been a military power, making it unfit to respond to global threats with hard power. Its economic power is now waning as Asia's is rising. The lingering effects of the Euro crisis have further weakened the public's confidence in the European project. Aggravating these structural challenges, the EU is now facing new threats and pressures stemming from a more assertive Russia; the rise of economic populism and Euroskepticism; increased terrorism; the refugee crises; and, of course, the United Kingdom's Brexit vote to leave the EU. The multitude and the gravity of these crises may easily leave even the most ardent supporter of the EU convinced of the inevitability of its decline.

This book advances an alternative and opposite view of the EU's role in the world. It argues that notwithstanding all its challenges, the EU remains an influential superpower that shapes the world in its image. The persistent narrative of the EU's decline overlooks an important dimension of its power that remains unaffected by the recent crises—the EU's unilateral power to regulate global markets. The EU today promulgates regulations that influence which products are built and how business is conducted, not just in Europe but everywhere in the world. In this way, the EU wields significant, unique, and highly penetrating power to unilaterally transform global markets, be it through its ability to set the standards in competition policy, environmental protection, food safety, the protection of privacy, or the regulation of hate speech in social media. Therefore, this book argues, regardless of any financial and political shortcomings it may possess, the EU is, and is likely to remain, a major force in the global economy for a long time to come.

Today, few Americans are aware that EU regulations determine the default privacy settings on their iPhone or the type of speech that Twitter will delete as unacceptable. Americans are hardly alone in this regard. Examples of EU's regulatory influence abound across global markets. EU laws determine how timber is harvested in Indonesia, how honey is produced in Brazil, what pesticides cocoa farmers use in Cameroon, what equipment is installed in dairy factories in China, what chemicals are incorporated in plastic toys in Japan, as well as how much privacy is afforded to internet users in Latin America.

These are but a few examples of a phenomenon this book describes as the "Brussels Effect." The Brussels Effect refers to the EU's unilateral power to regulate global markets. Without the need to use international institutions or seek other nations' cooperation, the EU has the ability to promulgate regulations that shape the global business environment, leading to a notable "Europeanization" of many important aspects of global commerce. Different from many other forms of global influence, the EU does not need to impose its standards coercively on anyone—market forces alone are often sufficient to convert the EU standard into the global standard as companies voluntarily extend the EU rule to govern their worldwide operations. Under specific conditions, the Brussels Effect leads to "unilateral regulatory globalization," where regulations originating from a single jurisdiction penetrate many aspects of economic life across the global marketplace.

Unpacking the determinants of unilateral regulatory globalization also reveals why the EU—as opposed to another great power such as the United States or China—has become the predominant regulator of global commerce, and why the EU can successfully export certain regulations but not others. The EU has a large consumer market, supported by strong regulatory institutions. Trading with the EU requires foreign companies to adjust their conduct or production to EU standards—which often represent the most stringent standards globally—or else forgo the EU market entirely. Rarely, however, is the latter an option for multinational companies. In addition, these companies cannot circumvent EU rules by moving regulatory targets to another jurisdiction because the EU primarily regulates inelastic consumer markets as opposed to more elastic capital markets like in the United States. While capital may flee when faced with a constraining regulatory environment, inelastic consumers will not. Further, even though the EU regulates only its internal market, multinational corporations often have an incentive to standardize their production globally and adhere to a single rule as opposed to customizing their production to each individual market. This is a key factor for how an EU regulation becomes converted into a de facto global regulation. Of course, other large economies could also exercise unilateral global regulatory influence. However, the United States, for example, effectively cedes this power to the EU by choosing to promulgate less-stringent regulatory standards across most policy domains, relegating the regulation of key areas such as data protection largely to the markets.

By providing both a theoretical and empirical account of the EU's unilateral regulatory power, this book provides a corrective to the current discourse that portrays the EU as a weak and declining power. The goal of this book is not to deny the various criticisms of the EU's weaknesses or argue that such criticism lacks merit. The goal is to show that the full story is much more balanced, and that in some very fundamental ways, the EU remains a powerful actor in the global economy. In addition, this book also challenges the prevailing narrative that views the EU as a champion of multilateral cooperation and universal norms,[8] painting a stark contrast with the United States' unilateralism in international affairs. The Brussels Effect shows that the EU's commitment to multilateralism and universalism must be qualified. Like any great power, the EU is willing to shape the international order to ensure that international norms reflect its regulatory preferences—often multilaterally but at times even more effectively unilaterally.[9] The United States is also typically associated with the pro-market views while the EU is seen as distrusting the markets and relying on government institutions instead. However, through the Brussels Effect, it is the EU, and not the United States, which best deploys the market forces to unleash its unilateral global regulatory power. Consequently, this book demonstrates that the EU's greatest global influence may not be through multilateral mechanisms and political institutions, but instead through unilateral actions, facilitated by markets and private corporations.

Through numerous examples across different regulatory policies, this book not only shows that the Brussels Effect exists but also that it matters. In the global contest for influence, regulatory power is highly relevant. EU regulations penetrate numerous aspects of people's everyday lives around the world. The Brussels Effect affects the food they eat, the air they breathe, and the products they produce and consume. While many traditional tools of influence have waned in importance, the regulatory power of the EU remains more durable, more deployable, and less easily undermined by other states. It is increasingly difficult today to exert raw military power or even rely on economic sanctions or conditional incentives embedded in trade or loan agreements.[10] Economic power is no longer an exclusive domain of a few relatively homogenous players such as the United States, the EU, and Japan. Today, China and other emerging economies are growing in affluence. In a world of multiple powers and heterogeneous interests, exercise of unilateral economic power is rarely possible. The persisting inability to conclude the World Trade Organization (WTO) trade talks is one reminder that in the world where many are powerful, no country is powerful enough to get anything done alone. Economic sanctions are rarely successful today because embargoed nations have an easier time finding alternative suppliers or markets for their products. Trade wars can easily throw the world markets into disarray, breeding grave uncertainty and often leading to significant economic losses to all parties, including to the nation waging such wars. Conditional aid and other rewards traditionally used as means of leverage by powerful nations and institutions such as the World Bank and the International Monetary Fund are decreasingly effective as countries such as China are prepared to extend aid even to rogue countries—often with no strings attached. Therefore, in contrast to these traditional channels to wield influence, regulatory power is one of the few areas where unilateralism still works.

This book's thesis is also particularly relevant today given the growing concerns over the future of international cooperation and global institutions. It offers a new perspective that differs in subtle and gross ways from the prevalent view that globalization is in retreat. While international cooperation may be in crisis, the Brussels Effect shows how we can continue to generate international rules to govern global markets even in the absence of multilateral cooperation. For example, while President Trump can withdraw the United States from international treaties and institutions, there is little that the current US administration can do to roll back EU regulations and curtail the EU's ability to export those rules through the Brussels Effect—to the United States or elsewhere. Similarly, this book will argue that Brexit will not liberate the United Kingdom from the EU's regulatory leash. Roughly half of UK exports are destined for the EU, with little expectation of change. The United Kingdom will therefore continue to need access to the EU's large consumer market long after Brexit. While UK companies could, in principle, adopt one set of standards for Europe and multiple other sets of standards for the rest of the world post-Brexit, the Brussels Effect makes this unlikely. This shatters the illusion of the regulatory freedom that Brexit is meant to deliver to the United Kingdom. The Brussels Effect therefore mitigates the declining globalization and keeps the United Kingdom tightly connected to the EU market long after leaving the EU.

The Structure of the Book

This book proceeds in three parts. Part I, consisting of chapters 1–3, develops the theoretical foundation for the Brussels Effect. It explains how the EU evolved into a global regulatory power and discusses the conditions under which the Brussels Effect occurs. Part II, consisting of chapters 4–7, offers concrete evidence of the Brussels Effect across different policy areas, industries, and jurisdictions. Part III, consisting of chapters 8 and 9, examines the desirability of the Brussels Effect and offers predictions on whether the EU's regulatory hegemony will last. Each part of the book also includes a short preface to help orient the reader and transition across the book's three parts. The preface to Part I provides an introductory definition of the Brussels Effect and a comment on the book's theoretical positioning and contributions to the literature. The preface to Part II briefly discusses the structure of the case studies and the rationale for their selection, and highlights some key takeaways that emerge from them. Finally, the preface to Part III introduces the key issues to consider when assessing the desirability and the endurance of the Brussels Effect in the final two chapters.

Chapter 1 sets the stage by discussing the EU's emergence as a global regulatory power. It introduces key EU institutions and describes their role in the regulatory process. It then explains how regulation has become a key tool to advance European integration, giving these institutions a powerful motivation to pursue an ambitious regulatory agenda. It also argues how the creation of the single market was always the primary concern for the EU institutions. For a long time, the Brussels Effect was an ancillary and largely unintended by-product of a regulatory agenda that was driven by internal motivations. Only more recently, a conscious external agenda has emerged alongside this internal agenda.

Chapter 2 forms the conceptual heart of the book by laying out the conditions under which a single jurisdiction exerts global regulatory authority, and shows why the EU today is in a unique position to assume the role of a global regulatory hegemon. These conditions explain the emergence and prevalence of the Brussels Effect. A country's *market size* is a well-understood proxy for its ability to exercise regulatory authority over foreign corporations and individuals. But market size alone does not guarantee global regulatory influence. The state must also have the *regulatory capacity* as well as the political will to generate *stringent rules*. Moreover, the Brussels Effect only occurs when the EU regulates *inelastic targets*, such as consumer markets as opposed to capital. Unlike capital, consumers are not able to flee to less-regulated jurisdictions, compromising the EU's regulatory clout. Finally, EU standards become global only when companies' production or conduct is *non-divisible*—in other words, when a company's benefits of adhering to a single standard exceed the benefits of taking advantage of laxer standards in other markets. These conditions, taken together, explain why the EU is the only regulatory regime that can wield unilateral regulatory influence across global markets today.

Chapter 3 places the EU's unilateral regulatory influence in context of the EU's broader external influence. The Brussels Effect is not the sole manifestation of the EU's global regulatory power. Instead, the EU wields norm-setting power through a number of different channels such as trade agreements and participation in international institutions and transnational government networks. This chapter reviews these alternative channels of the EU's regulatory influence in an attempt to provide context for the Brussels Effect within the broader set of tools that the EU has at its disposal. It then compares the relative advantages and disadvantages of those alternative methods when contrasted with the Brussels Effect, and discusses when these other channels of influence are likely to complement or, alternatively, substitute the Brussels Effect.

In Part II, the book turns to the empirical evidence of the Brussels Effect. Chapters 4–7 illustrate the Brussels Effect by reviewing several areas of regulatory policy where companies are converging their global production and conduct to EU regulations (the de facto Brussels Effect) or where foreign governments are emulating EU regulations domestically (the de jure Brussels Effect). These case studies include the EU's regulation of market competition (chapter 4), digital economy (chapter 5), consumer health and safety (chapter 6), and the environment (chapter 7). The goal is to explain why and how the EU has emerged as the most prominent global regulator in these policy areas, and to provide concrete examples of the manifestations of the Brussels Effect.

Part III, consisting of chapters 8 and 9, considers the normative implications and reflects on the future of the Brussels Effect. Chapter 8 asks whether the Brussels Effect is beneficial in terms of advancing people's welfare, both in the EU and abroad. In examining this question, the chapter engages with economic and political criticism leveled against the Brussels Effect. It asks if the global reach of EU regulations is costly and capable of hindering innovation, or driven by protectionist motives. It also queries if the Brussels Effect should be viewed as a manifestation of regulatory imperialism, undercutting the power of foreign sovereigns to make critical decisions regarding their economies and serve their citizens in accordance with their democratically established preferences.

Chapter 9 concludes this book by looking into the future. It addresses both external and internal challenges to EU's regulatory hegemony and examines whether and how the Brussels Effect will persist, given these challenges. The impending departure of the United Kingdom from the EU may appear to weaken the EU's regulatory power. The growing concerns over the future of multilateral institutions and international cooperation may also challenge the EU's ability to shape the global regulatory environment. Additional challenges loom on the horizon. These include the rise of China and other emerging powers that will gradually erode the relative market power of the EU. Technological change may revolutionize industrial processes, allowing for greater customization and thereby reducing the need to produce to a single global (often European) standard. Finally, the EU's internal political struggles may compromise its ability to engage in effective rule-making as the anti-EU sentiment grows. This chapter will consider each of these challenges in turn, offering an account of not just the EU's regulatory power but the persistence of that power. In doing so, it also invites a question as to whether this book will be read as describing the history or the present in the decades to come.

PREFACE TO PART ONE

Theory

Part I of this book lays the theoretical foundation for the Brussels Effect and sets it in the context of the EU's broader external influence. Chapter 1 discusses the EU's emergence as a global regulatory power. It explains how regulation has offered a key tool to advance European integration, giving EU institutions a powerful motivation to pursue an ambitious regulatory agenda. Chapter 2 shows how market forces have externalized this regulatory agenda through the Brussels Effect, leading to a significant de facto globalization of EU regulations. Specifically, it outlines the conditions under which the Brussels Effect occurs and shows how the EU is in a unique position to exert unilateral regulatory influence globally today. Chapter 3 situates the Brussels Effect in the broader context of the EU's global regulatory influence. It reviews alternative channels of the EU's regulatory influence and discusses when and how these channels complement or, alternatively, substitute the Brussels Effect.

Before proceeding with Part I, however, it will be useful to take a moment to define the "Brussels Effect" and distinguish it from other mechanisms of global regulatory influence. Following that definition , the rest of this preface situates the Brussels Effect within the current scholarly debates on regulatory politics and regulatory races as well as the EU's external relations and its global role—while also showing how the Brussels Effect relates to, and builds on, the influential scholarship on the California Effect.

What Is the Brussels Effect?

The term the "Brussels Effect" refers to the EU's unilateral ability to regulate the global marketplace. The Brussels Effect can be unintentional, arising from a set of enabling conditions sustained by markets rather than from the EU's active efforts to export its regulations. While acknowledging that other forms of the EU's global influence exist, this book generally reserves the term the Brussels Effect to capture the phenomenon where the markets are transmitting the EU's regulations to both market participants and regulators outside the EU. In these instances, the EU does not have to do anything except regulate its own market to exercise global regulatory power. The size and attractiveness of its market does the rest. Thus, in essence, the Brussels Effect emerges from market forces and multinational companies' self-interest to adopt relatively stringent EU standards globally. At the same time, the Brussels Effect is not only the result of private power: it is the interplay between EU regulations and the market forces' ability to externalize those regulations in different markets that give rise to the Brussels Effect.

Further, there are two variants of the Brussels Effect: the "de facto Brussels Effect" and the "de jure Brussels Effect." The de facto Brussels Effect explains how global corporations respond to EU regulations by adjusting their global conduct to EU rules. No regulatory response by foreign governments is needed; corporations have the business incentive to extend the EU regulation to govern their worldwide production or operations. The de jure Brussels Effect—which refers to the adoption of EU-style regulations by foreign governments—builds directly on the de facto Brussels Effect: after multinational companies have adjusted their global conduct to conform to EU rules, they have the incentive to lobby EU-style regulations in their home jurisdictions. This ensures that they are not at a disadvantage when competing domestically against companies that do not export to the EU and that, therefore, have no incentive to conform their conduct or production to costly EU regulations.[1]

This kind of situation—where the de facto Brussels Effect changes the incentives of foreign multinational companies and leads them to lobby for regulatory adjustment in their home markets—illustrates the strict definition of the "de jure Brussels Effect." Sometimes this process alone can lead to the formal adoption of EU-style regulations by foreign governments. However, often the decisions of foreign governments to emulate EU regulations will be the result of multiple factors that may only partially have their origins in the de facto Brussels Effect. As a result, the term "de jure Brussels Effect," less-strictly defined, can also be used to describe a broader set of mechanisms that transmit EU rules to foreign jurisdictions. For example, the EU often exports its regulations to foreign jurisdictions through various economic and political treaties and via international organizations and governmental networks. EU regulations can also mobilize foreign consumers to support regulatory reforms at home. These other instruments and mechanisms can facilitate, amplify, or otherwise interact with the Brussels Effect, but they can also lead to the diffusion of EU regulations on their own. Empirically, it is often difficult to separate the various motivations that lead a foreign government to adopt an EU-style law. For this reason, this book adopts the less-strict definition of the de jure Brussels Effect and discusses the various empirical examples that stem from these varying motivations.

Between the two variants of the Brussels Effect, the de facto Brussels Effect is the primary focus of this book and the core of the theoretical discussion in chapter 2. The de jure Brussels Effect has been conceptually developed elsewhere: the strict definition of the de jure Brussels Effect—the regulatory adjustment that follows from the lobbying efforts by firms that have experienced the de facto Brussels Effect—was developed by David Vogel in his work on the California Effect and will therefore not be revisited in detail in this book. The broader definition of the de jure Brussels Effect—including the diffusion of EU norms through international treaties and institutions—has similarly been extensively discussed in prior literature. However, empirical evidence of the de jure Brussels Effect has not been extensively examined except in narrow policy areas and with respect to selected jurisdictions. Thus, in addition to its theoretical and empirical contribution to the understanding of the de facto Brussels Effect, the objective of this book is to show how pervasive the de jure emulation of EU regulations is and how the de jure Brussels Effect complements and interacts with the de facto Brussels Effect. Together, this will hopefully offer a more comprehensive picture of the EU's influence.

This book's primary focus within regulatory theory is market regulation—typically as applicable to consumer markets. The Brussels Effect is not inherently limited to product regulation but extends to the regulation of production processes as well. This "product versus process" distinction is common in the literature on trade and economic regulation but analytically less central to the Brussels Effect, which accommodates both.[2] Several examples of the Brussels Effect deal with product regulation—such as personal data that is available online, the presence of certain chemicals in a product, the inclusion of hazardous material in electronics, or certain software package that is offered by a developer. Other examples of the Brussels Effect deal with process regulation—such as the process of storing data, a particular testing method (such as animal testing) of cosmetics, or the regulation of greenhouse gases emitted as part of a production process. Thus, there is nothing that inherently limits the applicability of the Brussels Effect to the regulation of products as opposed to production methods. Instead, the conditions for the Brussels Effect, described in detail in chapter 2, delineate the types of regulations that can be subject to the Brussels Effect. For example, the Brussels Effect is typically limited to "inelastic targets" and therefore rarely applicable to financial regulation given the elasticity of capital. Similarly, corporations' conduct or production needs to be "non-divisible" for the Brussels Effect to occur, leaving many labor standards such as minimum wage typically outside the phenomenon. Moreover, the Brussels Effect is tied to the EU's ability to leverage its "market size," making it rarely applicable to constrain, for example, human rights violations that occur abroad and that are typically not subject to EU's market access.

Further, while this phenomenon is labeled the "Brussels Effect" herein and used to explain the EU's role as a global regulatory hegemon today, the conditions for this phenomenon are generic as opposed to EU-specific in nature. They are designed to explain any jurisdiction's ability to unilaterally supply rules for the global marketplace with the help of market forces. In this sense, they are independent from and should outlive the EU's regulatory hegemony, explaining if and when such a hegemony would diminish or be displaced by another unilateral global regulator when the similar conditions might arise elsewhere. Consequently, the Brussels Effect is more a theory of unilateral regulatory power that any jurisdiction may derive from the interplay of its size, behavior and market forces—the EU's ability to do so in current times is only a powerful and underappreciated application of that theory.

How the Brussels Effect Challenges the Regulatory Debate

This book seeks to contribute to several scholarly debates in law, political science, and economics. It builds on theories of regulatory competition and convergence,[3] including the pathbreaking work by David Vogel on the California Effect. In addition, this book provides a corrective to the debates that portray the EU as a weak and declining player that has acquiesced its global role to a preoccupation with numerous existential crises. Within these debates, the Brussels Effect also invites us to reconsider the relative roles that governments and markets play in shaping economic outcomes. It also aims to bring a new perspective to discussions on international cooperation by highlighting the power of unilateral rule-making to transform both global markets and global politics.

The Brussels Effect challenges the critics of globalization who claim that trade liberalization undermines domestic regulation.[4] These critical voices fear that globalization leads to a "race to the bottom" where countries lower their regulatory standards in order to improve their relative competitive position in the global economy.[5] Recently, many of the assumptions driving this influential literature have been discredited.[6] For example, fears of businesses relocating to pollution havens or capital flights following higher levels of corporate taxation have generally not materialized. Scholars have instead shown that international trade has frequently triggered a "race to the top," whereby domestic regulations have become more stringent as the global economy has become more integrated.[7] Still, the race-to-the-bottom paradigm remains influential, shaping the debates among scholars and policy makers alike. The Brussels Effect adds to this literature by showing how the benefits of uniform production across the global marketplace incentivizes companies to adjust their regulatory standards upward rather than downward.

The discussion on global regulatory races mirrors the debates on regulatory outcomes in federal systems. The "Delaware Effect" has been used to explain the race to the bottom in corporate law within the United States: since corporations can incorporate in any state irrespective of where they do business, all states have an incentive to relax their chartering requirements in order to attract corporate tax revenues. Delaware has won this race by being the most attractive place to incorporate, either from the perspective of management, shareholders, or both.[8] The "California Effect" captures an opposite phenomenon: due to its large market and preference for stringent consumer and environmental regulations, California is, at times, effectively able to set the regulatory standards for all other states.[9] Businesses willing to export to California must meet its standards, and the benefits from uniform production give these firms an incentive to apply this same (stringent) standard to their entire production.[10]

This book builds on the California Effect yet goes beyond it in some critical ways. First, the Brussels Effect expands the dynamics of the California Effect from a US federal system to a global context.[11] In doing so, it uncovers and explains perhaps the most significant example of the California Effect—its global occurrence—which has been undertheorized and underestimated as an empirical phenomenon. Second, the Brussels Effect outlines the precise conditions that allow an upward regulatory convergence to emerge. The theory underpinning the California Effect recognizes the importance of market size and scale economies as a source of a jurisdiction's external regulatory clout. Yet it fails to acknowledge factors such as regulatory capacity and inelasticity as key components of the theory, and overlooks factors other than scale economies that can prevent a company from producing different varieties for different markets. Thus, the discussion of the Brussels Effect provides a more nuanced theory of the conditions under which a single jurisdiction can exert regulatory influence outside its borders. This more accurate and complete understanding of the conditions underlying the Brussels Effect explains why the EU, as opposed to any other large economy, can unilaterally supply global standards. It also makes the theory more generalizable. Assuming the specific conditions outlined by the theory are met, what today amounts to the Brussels Effect may one day be described as the "Beijing Effect."

Finally, the literature on regulatory competition—including the California Effect—focuses on a dynamic where a lax foreign regulator formally adopts the stringent rule of the lead regulator.[12] This attention to "de jure regulatory convergence" fails to account for regulatory convergence that takes place in the absence of formal changes to legal rules. In reality, this type of formal "trading up" often fails to occur. Instead, we typically see only a "de facto regulatory convergence" whereby much of global business is conducted under unilateral EU rules even when other states continue to maintain their own rules. This is true, for instance, with respect to US competition laws, privacy laws, and rules on food safety. Unilateral regulatory globalization does not need to elicit a formal regulatory response from another nation. The EU law governs whether other countries follow suit or not.

Seen in this light, the Brussels Effect is more about one jurisdiction's ability to over-ride others than it is about triggering an upward regulatory race.

The Brussels Effect also departs from the existing scholarship on the relation-ship between regulatory convergence and regulatory power. Daniel Drezner has argued that great-power consensus leads to regulatory convergence whereas great-power disagreement leads to regulatory divergence and the emergence of rival stan-dards.[13] Which rival standard trumps the other depends on the regulatory powers' relative ability to seek allies supporting their respective regulatory preferences.[14] In contrast to Drezner, this book shows that de facto convergence can take place in the midst of a great-power disagreement. When the conditions for the Brussels Effect exist, rival standards between two equal powers fail to materialize. Instead, the out-come of the regulatory race is predetermined: the more stringent regulator prevails.

Prevailing theories on regulatory globalization explain the emergence of regula-tory convergence as a result of either cooperation or coercion. The Brussels Effect adds to this theoretical discussion but differs from it because it falls between coop-eration and coercion. It can be distinguished from political cooperation where convergence results only after a consensus is reached between states or regulatory authorities. It is also different from unilateral coercion, where one jurisdiction imposes its rules on others through threats or sanctions. In contrast, unilateral reg-ulatory globalization occurs when the law of one jurisdiction migrates into another in the absence of the former actively imposing it or the latter willingly adopting it.

Finally, Part I's contribution to the regulatory debate is descriptive. It shows that the Brussels Effect is pervasive and relevant, without endorsing or criticizing the phenomenon. The broader normative questions of whether the Brussels Effect is desirable or not will be discussed in Part III. Part I puts this normative question aside for the moment and focuses on articulating a descriptive theory on when and how the Brussels Effect takes place—and when it fails to do so.

I

How the EU Became a Global Regulatory Power

SINCE THE 1990s, the EU has embarked on an ambitious project to build a European regulatory state. Through regulation, EU institutions have integrated the common market by adopting common standards to protect the health and safety of consumers and the environment, to foster competition, and to safeguard the integrity of personal data. An important motive behind these regulations has been to build a single market that allows for a harmonized regulatory environment and thereby frictionless trade across the member states. Over the years, this internal goal of pursuing European integration through regulation has gained an increasingly external dimension—driven by the Brussels Effect—establishing the EU as the global regulatory hegemon. For a long time, the Brussels Effect was an ancillary and largely unintended by-product of a regulatory agenda that was driven by internal motivations. Only more recently, a conscious external agenda has emerged alongside this internal one.

This chapter discusses the EU's evolution into a global regulatory power. First, it briefly introduces key EU institutions and their role in the regulatory process. It then explains how regulation has been developed to advance European integration, giving these institutions a powerful motivation to pursue an ambitious regulatory agenda, while catering to the European Commission's bureaucratic interests in the process. Finally, it considers the internal and external motives that have guided the EU's regulatory rule-making.

The Key Institutions Generating EU Regulations

The EU institutions involved in the legislative and regulatory process are comprised of three primary players: the Council of the European Union (Council), the European Parliament (EP), and the European Commission (Commission),

The Brussels Effect. Anu Bradford, Oxford University Press (2020). © Oxford University Press.
DOI: 10.1093/oso/9780190088583.001.0001

representing the interests of the individual EU member states, the European citizens, and the EU as an institution, respectively. In addition, European courts play a crucial role in the interpretation and enforcement of EU treaties, regulations, and directives.[1]

The Council brings together the executive branches of the member states and is composed of the government ministers of each member state. It forms the legislative arm of the EU and meets in different configurations, depending on the policy area being discussed. For example, when the Council considers an environmental regulation, each member state sends its environmental minister. Similarly, when the Council legislates on agricultural policy, the minister responsible for agriculture represents each member state. These representatives are authorized to vote on behalf of their member state, binding their respective countries to the decisions the Council makes collectively. The Council makes decisions in accordance with a simple majority, qualified majority, or unanimous vote, depending on the subject matter.

The EP represents the EU citizenry and exercises legislative authority in conjunction with the Council in this capacity. The EP consists of 751 members (MEPs) who are directly elected by European citizens. Each member state is afforded representatives in the EP roughly proportionate to its population. For example, while Germany, as the most populous nation in the EU, is allotted 96 MEPs, Malta, Estonia, Cyprus, and Luxembourg each have 6 MEPs. The MEPs organize themselves into political groups and typically vote with their political group as opposed to along national lines. For example, Spanish center-right parties align themselves with MEPs representing center-right parties in all other member states (European People's Party) while the Spanish socialists align themselves with socialists from all other member states (Progressive Alliance of Socialists and Democrats).

The Commission functions as the EU's executive arm and enjoys substantial independent decision-making authority. The Commission consists of the political "College of Commissioners," with one commissioner hailing from each member state. Each Commissioner is assigned responsibility over a certain policy department known as a Directorate-General (DG). Each DG focuses on a specific policy area, such as health and food safety or competition policy. Even though commissioners come from all twenty-eight member states, the commissioners advance the common EU interest as opposed to that of their own member state. In addition to the politically selected commissioners, the Commission has a large bureaucratic staff of approximately thirty thousand career civil servants.

The Commission has significant agenda-setting power through its right to propose legislation. It remains influential throughout the legislative process, acting in close cooperation with the Council and the EP, and is also in charge of the implementation and enforcement of EU legislation. As the "guardian of the treaties," the Commission oversees the enforcement of EU law. If an individual member state fails to implement certain regulations, the Commission has the authority to challenge the noncomplying member state before the European Court of Justice (ECJ or CJEU). It also negotiates treaties on behalf of the EU after receiving a mandate from the Council. In many policy areas, the Commission is a semi-autonomous actor, with extensive powers to engage in the legislative process and independent regulatory activity. The Council has delegated to the Commission significant regulatory powers in several policy areas, including competition law, allowing the Commission to pursue its regulatory agenda largely unconstrained by other EU institutions.

Finally, European courts play a significant role in interpreting and enforcing EU laws and regulations. The European courts consist of the ECJ and the General Court, both of which are composed of judges nominated by each of the member states. The main task of the European courts is to ensure the uniform application of EU law across member states. This uniformity is facilitated by the ECJ's authority to give preliminary rulings that guide national courts in EU member states in their interpretation and application of EU law. Many key elements of EU law, such as the concept of the primacy of EU law or "direct effect," did not originate in EU treaties but were later pronounced by the ECJ in its rulings.[2] In addition, the European courts are the key to ensuring that member states and EU institutions abide by EU law, and that the rights of individuals under EU treaties are upheld.

Promoting European Integration via Regulation

The desire to build a single market has always been a primary driver behind EU regulation. Developing harmonized EU regulations is critical for the operation of the single market as inconsistent product standards can hinder cross-border trade. If each of the twenty-eight individual member states adopted a different national standard to protect the environment or to safeguard personal data, the single market could not function efficiently, as companies would face a different regulatory environment in each country. This would force companies to modify their production and business practices from each member state to another, or even to produce different product varieties for different member states. For this reason, harmonized standards became a key goal for European integration early on, serving both the specific substantive goal (such as environmental protection) and the broader economic and political goal of achieving greater market integration. Thus, every directive and regulation—be it on chemical safety, environmental protection, or data privacy—typically has a dual purpose: it serves not only to advance consumer or environmental protection but also advances a single market where divergent national regulations are aligned so as to ensure free movement of goods and services across the EU.[3]

The pursuit of EU-level harmonization need not entail complete uniformity in national standards. Acknowledging the legal and cultural heterogeneity across member states and respecting their distinct regulatory preferences, the EU has often opted for "minimum harmonization" and mutual recognition of national standards. This is especially true after ECJ issued an influential judgement in *Cassis de Dijon*, where the Court established the principle of mutual recognition of national regulations.[4] According to this principle, member states must recognize each other's regulations as sufficient, as long as they equally protect the public interest in question. Minimum harmonization calls for a common EU standard only to the extent that is necessary to ensure the functioning of the single market, while preserving the flexibility for member states to enact more stringent standards domestically. This flexibility is also inherent in the directives, which are an often-used legislative instrument in the EU. Directives are legislative acts that set out the goals that all member states must achieve. Yet they preserve the freedom of member states to decide how to best achieve those goals. These flexible instruments have been essential in securing broad support for the EU's regulatory agenda.

Although EU-level regulations are the key drivers of the Brussels Effect globally, often those regulations have their origins in individual member states.[5] EU member states tend to be policy innovators in areas where the EU has not acted, and in areas where they retain authority to regulate under the EU treaties. For instance, Germany, the Netherlands, and the Nordic countries were the forebearers of the EU's environmental regulations.[6] Germany regulated automotive emissions before the EU by strengthening its emission standards. Sweden and Denmark restricted antibiotics in animal feed before the EU followed suit. Denmark and the United Kingdom had a national emissions trading scheme before the EU decided to adopt one at the EU level. Similarly, EU regulation on GMOs was preceded by similar regulations in Germany and Sweden. Further, France and Denmark were frontrunners in banning BPAs in products for infants, paving the way for the EU to do so later.[7] Similarly, regulators in France and Germany were some of the key member states that exported their privacy regulation upward within the EU.[8] Because these national regulations risk fragmenting the single market, the EU is prompted to harmonize standards at the EU level in an effort to preserve the integrity of the common market. Notably, the EU has tended not to pursue "downward harmonization," which would entail letting the member states with low levels of regulation set the common standard for everyone. Instead, as in the examples just mentioned, it has typically pursued "upward harmonization" and regulated toward more stringent standards of its members states—something which, as discussed later in this chapter, has been a key factor in extending the Brussels Effect.

There is always a risk that efforts to harmonize regulatory standards will lead to the lowest common denominator prevailing across all states. Too often in multilateral negotiations, the least ambitious state gets to set the standard. Especially where the consent of all states is needed, provisions get watered down as the threat of a veto held by each state hangs over each negotiation and vote. It is also often easier to harmonize to the least burdensome standard rather than forcing reluctant states to adopt rules that are costly to enact and enforce. Indeed, for the EU, there have been many incentives and pressures that could have caused it to pursue downward harmonization. For example, there have been obvious losers from high regulatory standards. These include individual consumers who would have preferred lesser protections in return for lower prices. Similarly, some of the less-wealthy member states would arguably have benefited from less-stringent regulations to facilitate much needed economic growth. Finally, corporate interests would typically advocate for a less-burdensome regulatory environment, citing costs on innovation and their international competitiveness.

Yet there are several reasons why "harmonizing up" as opposed to "harmonizing down" took place. First, stringent standards were often adopted to reassure the European public that economic integration would not be pursued at the expense of consumer health and safety or environmental quality. As economic integration deepened, Europeans began to resist the liberalization agenda that was seen as a threat to these non-economic values.[9] To defend continued economic integration and to vest themselves with greater legitimacy, EU institutions thus set out to expand the integration agenda to these other values, adopting stringent standards—in areas such as environmental protection, food safety, or data privacy—to ensure that economic gains from integration are not pursued without protecting quality of life.[10] Thus, upward harmonization of regulatory standards was seen as necessary to ensure continuing political support for economic liberalization.

Upward harmonization has also been politically more palatable among the states that already had the highest standards in certain regulatory areas. The Commission has thus found it easier to convince the regulatory laggards to respond to their citizens' demands for greater protections rather than trying to persuade the first movers to back down and repeal their domestic protections. The EU's efforts to harmonize regulations on the health and safety of workers illustrates this dynamic.[11] In the early 1990s, the EU member states with high standards—including Belgium, Denmark, France, and Germany—advocated for greater EU harmonization of labor protections to protect their industries that faced competition from other member states—including Greece, Ireland, Portugal, and Spain—whose domestic laws contained lower labor standards. In the end, all members (with the exception of the United Kingdom, which negotiated an opt-out) agreed to sign a Social Protocol, which was annexed to the 1992 Maastricht Treaty.[12] The Protocol contains provisions, for instance, on working conditions and equal treatment in the workplace. To persuade even the low-regulation member states to join the Protocol, the Commission agreed to provide them compensation in the form of structural funds that allowed them to offset some of the costs resulting from the adoption of higher labor standards.[13]

When considering the views of the various key interest groups, harmonizing up as opposed to down also provides a fertile ground for compromise. Marrying each standard's economic purpose to its broader societal purpose helps build coalitions among different stakeholders. During these harmonization efforts, for example, non-governmental organizations (NGOs) who advocate for environmental protection have at times been able to find common ground with businesses that desire a harmonized regulatory environment. While these businesses would often prefer laxer rules, upward harmonization remains preferable to discordant national standards, which inevitably increase costs and complexity. This rare alignment of interests paves the way for a distinctly powerful pro-regulation coalition, making the two interest groups—firms and consumers—unlikely allies in a quest for harmonized rules for the European and, ultimately, through the Brussels Effect, the global market. The EU also has a particularly strong incentive to act externally when the moral and economic imperatives of the Community coincide: that is, when it enjoys political rents from the EU industry and the consumer and environmental advocates at the same time.[14]

One example of such an alliance that resulted in foreign regulatory changes was a coalition between EU corporations and environmental groups regarding the EU's Eco-Management and Auditing Scheme (EMAS), which was first introduced in 1993.[15] EMAS regulates public disclosure of corporations' environmental improvement records. Already subject to the disclosure obligations, the EU corporations teamed up with environmental NGOs to lobby for the adoption of the same standards by US and Asian corporations. In the end, the campaign was successful and the International Organization for Standardization (ISO) adopted the European standard as a global standard in 1996.[16] Similarly, in the fight against GMOs in the mid-1990s, Greenpeace and other environmental and consumer NGOs mobilized overwhelming popular support from diverse sectors. NGOs found surprising allies for their cause, including European farmers, represented by Copa-Cocega, and the European retail industry, represented by Eurocoop and EuroCommerce.[17] The conventional farming industry in the EU was opposed to GMOs and shielded away from cultivating them. The retail industry similarly resisted the GMOs, largely in response to the public opposition. Through the lobbying by these key stakeholders, in 2003 the EU adopted two regulations—one establishing a system to trace and label GMOs and one regulating food derived from GMOs.[18] Since 2003, these partnerships have persisted, maintaining joint pressure on the Commission to ban all non-authorized GMOs in food.[19]

Similarly, this dual purpose behind regulations has often helped political parties from the left and the right find common ground. Harmonized environmental or product safety standards across the EU allow political parties on the left to protect consumers while also allowing parties on the right to prioritize trade across the common market. Of course, political tensions may still remain and interests are not always easy to align. However, this dual purpose broadens coalitions and increases the likelihood that the key interest groups—which in other political and regulatory contexts might have agendas firmly in opposition—have something to gain from a regulation, paving the way for a compromise that allows stricter standards to emerge.

The EU's tendency to harmonize standards upward has also been facilitated by changes to treaties that enabled regulations and directives to be adopted with a qualified majority of the Council—requiring the support of 55% of member states representing a minimum of 65% of the EU's population—as opposed to unanimity. This move toward qualified majority voting can be traced to the adoption of the 1987 Single European Act (SEA)—a major treaty revision that paved the way for the completion of the single market—and has continued with each treaty revision since.[20] The ability to proceed with legislation even in the absence of consensus established the foundation for significant rule-making in the aftermath of the SEA. Had the member states insisted on unanimity as the default decision-making rule, it is doubtful that its ambitious regulatory agenda would have emerged. The reliance on legislative techniques, such as minimum harmonization, further fostered an extensive regulatory agenda by relaxing the EU's insistence on complete uniformity in favor of greater flexibility in national implementation.

A qualified majority makes it easier to adopt regulations as it often silences the laggards; the more ambitious states prevail because they do not need to convince everyone to support a legislation.[21] However, wealth, expertise, and issue salience also matter. The member states eager to elevate regulatory standards in many policy areas are often wealthier countries from Northern Europe, vested with greater political leverage associated with their economic success. For example, high growth rates and competitive economies in Northern Europe enhance these countries' ability to advocate for environmental regulations that do not compromise economic goals. These countries are also often vested with greater persuasive authority stemming from their experience in already regulating that area domestically. These high-regulation states also have a strong incentive to Europeanize their standards so as to ensure that their domestic firms are not disadvantaged when competing in the European market. Indeed, research on Council voting suggests that the salience of issues often explains outcomes even more than raw voting power.[22] Small states are likely to intervene more selectively, advocating for their positions on issues particularly salient to them, making their positions more credible and influential.[23]

Pro-regulation member states have also found ways to influence EU decision-making through their greater expertise. The Commission relies heavily on expert groups in developing its regulatory policies, and recruits approximately half of these experts from national governments.[24] Considering that the pro-regulatory member states already regulate certain policy areas domestically, they often have a higher number of technical experts at their disposal, giving them a greater resource advantage as a result. These experts can be deployed to influence the Commission at the early stages of policy development.

For example, Germany and the Netherlands—both known for their progressive stance on environmental regulation—have exerted significant influence over the EU's environmental policy making by supplying staff power and expertise. The German Ministry of the Environment has 900 employees, and the Federal Environmental Agency in Germany has a further 850 experts. The Dutch environmental administration employs approximately 1,500 people.[25] Not surprisingly, German and Dutch experts are omnipresent in the environmental committees and hearings of the various European institutions including the Commission, the Council, the EP, the Economic and Social Committee, and the Committee of the Regions. These resources have allowed German and Dutch experts to assume an influential role in the committee work of the various European institutions involved in environmental policy making.

Finally, package deals (also known as issue linkages) offer another technique to facilitate regulatory rule-making in the midst of disagreements among member states or political groups. Package deals refer to the practice of deciding on multiple legislative proposals together in order to harness support for them from a wide variety of interest groups. Such bargains are often feasible in the EU given the breadth of the EU policies subject to negotiation. Some member states objecting to a given regulation may still be persuaded to support it in return for enhanced regional subsidies or additional transfers under the Common Agricultural Policy.[26] A study by Raya Kardasheva examined package deals between the EP and the Council that use issue linkages across multiple legislative proposals.[27] Kardasheva found that approximately 25% of all EU legislation completed between May 1999 and April 2007 was decided with the help of a package deal.[28] Issue linkages were most common in the budgetary sphere but were also used in environmental legislation as well as health care and consumer protection.[29] The addition of new member states to the EU through multiple rounds of EU enlargement has further enhanced the reliance on package deals as EU institutions have managed increasingly diverse policy preferences.[30] This way, the regulatory density in the EU has had the effect of enabling more ambitious rule-making as the reluctant member states have been brought onboard though concessions on other policy areas.

The Commission's Pro-regulation Agenda

The previous discussion has shown how the impetus for the EU's ambitious regulatory agenda has often come from the pro-regulation member states that have advocated upward harmonization at the EU level, yet emphasized the Commission's central role in promoting integration through ambitious regulation. While the Commission is at times able to exercise independent regulatory authority, the Council and the EP's approval is needed for legislative acts. This grants these institutions an important role in building and extending the European regulatory state. Yet it is within the Commission where regulations are initiated and drafted. Consequently, the Commission's agenda-setting role calls for a closer look at its powers and preferences in particular.

The Commission's overarching task is to advance the common interest of the EU, making it often the leading promoter of closer European integration. It is therefore only natural that the Commission has always played a critical role in ratcheting up regulatory standards at the EU level. It is quick to advocate for a harmonized European solution whenever a handful of member states proceed to regulate on their own by adopting stringent national standards. The Commission is spurred into action whenever it detects a risk that the single market is becoming more fragmented. For example, the Commission has been responsive to the demands of frontrunners in environmental regulation for the fear that their stringent national standards could distort trade between member states, thereby hindering the functioning of the single market.[31]

The Commission has a strong ideological commitment and institutional preference for European integration.[32] As more regulation typically amounts to more integration, the growing regulatory agenda has clearly served the Commission's fundamental goal of furthering European integration. The Brussels Effect itself has been important to this goal—for one, the Brussels Effect helps the Commission level the international playing field, thus mitigating concerns from EU firms of their global competitiveness. This helps win broader support for further EU regulation. For another, due to the Brussels Effect, the EU increasingly becomes a global standard setter, which enhances the legitimacy and influence of its standards, both at home and abroad.

The Brussels Effect also strengthens the Commission's bureaucratic interests by enhancing the impact of its regulatory activities. Regulators generally have the incentive to generate more regulation rather than less because their success is measured by how much of their agenda is accomplished.[33] Among the EU institutions, the Commission, in particular, is widely portrayed as a "competence-maximizer," constantly looking to expand its powers and increase its influence over policy making. And when the Commission seeks to expand its competencies, it tends to do so via regulation.[34]

To a large extent, the Commission's tendency to govern through regulation is a result of the EU's small budget. The EU's budget amounts to only around 1% of its GDP, which comes primarily as transfers from member states.[35] To put this figure in perspective, US federal government spending regularly exceeds 20% of its GDP.[36] These tight budgetary constraints restrict the Commission's ability to pursue direct-expenditure programs, such as large-scale industrial policy, innovation policy, or job creation programs at the EU level. In contrast, there is no "regulatory budget" to limit the amount of regulations and directives the Commission can promulgate.[37] The Commission does not even need significant funds to enforce its regulations—it can leverage member state funds by delegating the actual implementation and enforcement to them. Thus, the only way for the Commission to expand its influence without extensive financial resources is to engage in regulatory activity, as regulations do not depend on the tax revenues available to the Community institutions.

As Giandomenico Majone has noted, "since the [Commission] lacks an independent power to tax and spend, it could increase its competencies only by developing as an almost pure type of regulatory state."[38] In Majone's demand-and-supply model of EU regulation, the Commission is the primary actor on the supply side due to its right of legislative initiative.[39] Historically, vesting the Commission with so much regulatory power might have been unintentional: the member states wanted to restrict the powers of the Commission through tight budgetary discipline. Yet in the absence of traditional powers of states to tax and spend (not to mention wage a war), the Commission has built an empire of laws and regulations, maximizing its own influence in the process.[40]

Regulatory policies, including their extension though the Brussels Effect, are nearly costless for the Commission to pursue because the actual costs of complying with regulations fall on the firms and individuals that the regulations target. In addition, enforcement costs are borne by member state governments whose task is to implement the regulations.[41] Take, for example, the new data protection regulation GDPR (which is discussed in more detail in chapter 5). With that extensive regulation, the Commission can mandate firms to re-redesign their products and rewrite their privacy policies. These mandates are costless for EU institutions. Similarly, the GDPR is not enforced by the Commission but by each individual member state's data protection agencies, whose staff and enforcement budgets are funded by national governments, making the actual enforcement also a matter of member state budgets as opposed to that of the EU.

The Brussels Effect also offers an important foreign policy instrument, compensating the Commission for the lack of power it otherwise has in external affairs. The Commission's legal competence to act on its member states' behalf in foreign policy or security-related matters outside common commercial policy is limited.[42] For instance, imposing economic sanctions requires a unanimous decision in the European Council, making such decisions vulnerable to a veto exercised by any member state.[43] Nevertheless, the Commission is delegated with substantial powers to implement measures necessary to create and maintain the single market.[44] In Brussels Effect, the Commission has a powerful tool to shape global markets and the international regulatory environment, without the need to secure unanimity in the Council.

Although the Commission has been a key institution for extending the European regulatory state outside the EU, the other EU institutions—particularly the EP and the European Courts—have also been critical, and their role has grown in importance over time. These institutions also benefit from the externalization of the EU's regulatory agenda through the Brussels Effect. Mark Pollack, for instance, argues that the Commission's pro-integration agenda is shared by other institutions. Pollack analyzed six case studies involving conflicts with member states regarding the use of discretion by the Commission and the ECJ. The cases represented a mix of market liberalization and social policy issues.[45] He found that almost invariably, the Commission, the Court, and the EP behave as competence maximizers. These institutions tend to advocate for a broad interpretation of the objectives and powers the treaties vest on EU institutions, including the regulation of the single market. This, according to Pollack, is due to their "shared organizational preference for greater European integration" vis-à-vis the member states.[46]

This suggests that the Brussels Effect serves the interests of the EP and the Courts similarly to those of the Commission. For example, if the Parliament cares about the protection of personal data or privacy—as its strong support for the GDPR indicates—its gains are only magnified when the GDPR penetrates global markets, making the EU privacy norm a global norm. Indeed, in a brochure published in October 2017, *Future of Europe: European Parliament*

Sets Out Its Vision, the Parliament highlights its goal to "Export European Standards." The document refers to the Parliament's 2017 resolution on the impact on international trade, which details a variety of mechanisms by which the EU may export, monitor, and enforce the extension of European policies abroad.[47]

Similarly, the European Courts' pro-integration tendencies are likely to be reinforced by the Brussels Effect. The Brussels Effect creates market-based incentives for compliance with EU rules, including with court rulings aimed at enforcing them. This enhanced compliance further helps to preserve the authority and legitimacy of the European Courts. In some recent decisions, including a case still pending querying whether the right to be forgotten should extend to global domain names, the ECJ is clearly invited to consider the external effects of its rulings.[48] The 2009 Lisbon Treaty provided the court with a constitutional foundation for external policy considerations, authorizing the court to look beyond the single market.[49] These changes in treaty framework have made the ECJ even more conscious of the external effects of its rulings and empowered it to issue rulings that have an effect outside of the EU's frontiers. Regardless of how far the ECJ will push the EU's external powers, most commentators agree that all EU institutions have obtained significant gains from entrenching their regulatory priorities across the world.

The Emerging External Regulatory Agenda

Originally, the EU's supranational regulatory apparatus was created to establish and oversee an integrated, liberalized, and competitive market in Europe. The European regulatory state was hence a response to internal challenges driven by a political agenda that was largely inward looking. In its early decades— beginning in the 1960s but continuing well into the 2000s—the EU's external influence can thus best be viewed as an incidental by-product of its internal motivations. However, more recently, a conscious external agenda has emerged to complement the EU's internal regulatory agenda. This shift is associated with a broader global development in the early 1990s, where the external effects of countries' regulatory policies began to occupy the global trade agenda. Increased efforts to engage in "global governance" in various forms led to increased regulatory cooperation and multilateral standard setting. Various domestic regulations were increasingly seen as non-tariff barriers, prompting multilateral efforts to abolish them. These negotiations culminated in the establishment of the WTO in 1995. Partly for this reason, the external effects of the EU's regulatory policies became a more salient issue, both within and outside the EU.

Internal Motives: Single Market

The EU has traditionally externalized its regulations without any active effort to shape markets other than its own. It has been sufficient to simply generate regulations to strengthen its single market, with external influences emerging as incidental by-products of this internal goal. As noted earlier, inconsistent regulations among member states are seen to threaten the single market, prompting the need to enact EU-level regulations that harmonize laws across the member states. For instance, many regulations in the environmental domain were enacted to serve the dual purpose of protecting the environment and facilitating the single market through harmonized environmental standards.[50] Rather than aiming to provide global environmental standards, the EU was thus concerned with the efficient functioning and the legitimacy of the single market program.[51] Advancement of the single market also provided a solid legal basis for EU institutions to act, providing a rationale that regulation at the EU level, as opposed to the national level, was necessary.

The internal market rationale was central, for example, in enacting the chemical safety regulation "REACH," discussed in detail in chapter 6.[52] In its 2001 white paper, the Commission stated that one of the key objectives of the EU's new chemical policy was to "[p]revent fragmentation of the internal market."[53] In its first recital, the 2003 legislative proposal for REACH notes that "(1) The free movement of substances, on their own, in preparations and in articles, is an essential aspect of the internal market and contributes significantly to the health and wellbeing of consumers and workers, and to their social and economic interests, as well as to the competitiveness of the chemical industry; (2) The efficient functioning of the internal market for substances within the Community can be achieved only if requirements for substances do not differ significantly from Member State to Member State." Similarly, the 2005 Council's Political Agreement for a Common Position discusses REACH's aim and scope stating that "The purpose of this Regulation is to ensure a high level of protection of health and the environment as well as the free circulation of substances on the internal market while enhancing competitiveness and innovation."[54]

The EU's regulation of data protection similarly has its origins in the goal of establishing a single market for the transfer of data across the common market. Earlier statements by EU institutions make no references to the external aspects of data protection but rather cite disparate national measures as adversely impacting the single market.[55] For example, the 1981 Commission Recommendation regarding the automatic processing of personal data notes:[56]

> Divergent data-protection law in the EC Member States creates disparate conditions for data processing. The establishment and functioning

of the common market in data processing calls for extensive standardization of the conditions obtaining in relation to data processing and,
therefore, to data-protection at European level. Approximation of data-
protection is desirable so that there can be free movement of data and
information across frontiers and in order to prevent unequal conditions
of competition and the consequent distortion of competition in the
common market.

Several other preparatory works confirm that a key goal of the EU's data
protection regulation has always been the desire to "unleash the potential of the
Single Market."[57] The 1994 Commission white paper on "Europe and the Global
Information Society" emphasizes the risks associated with "[d]isparities in the
level of protection of such privacy rules [which] create the risk that national
authorities might restrict free circulation of a wide range of new services between
Member States in order to protect personal data."[58]

The 2010 Commission Communication on personal data protection similarly
warns of the "divergences between the national laws implementing the Directive,
which run counter to one of its main objectives, i.e. ensuring the free flow of
personal data within the internal market," acknowledging that private stakeholders have complained about administrative costs stemming from the lack of harmonization.[59] The legislative history of the GDPR continues to stress the single
market, emphasizing the need to remove a "considerable divergence in the rules
across Member States" and to remove "the uncertainty and uneven protection
for individuals" associated with the "fragmented legal environment" in the EU's
single market.[60]

These statements call into question critics' views arguing that the EU is a
"regulatory imperialist" that is consciously seeking to externalize the single
market.[61] Instead of having a deliberate external agenda, these communications illustrate how much of the EU's rule-making stems from the internal goal
to protect the integrity of the single market. Especially early on, the external
effects of the single market were, at best, an afterthought for the EU institutions that were preoccupied with the market integration goal. This internally
driven, passive externalization of EU rules has been particularly effective in
that the EU institutions have only had to generate the consensus to pursue
a goal that lies at the heart of the EU project: European integration and the
establishment of the single market. Often, EU standards have been externalized as a by-product of that mission, not by EU institutions but by market
participants who need to comply with EU rules and who often decide to apply
the EU standard globally.

External Motives: Global Norm Setting

While the primary objective of European regulatory activity has clearly been to establish the single market, this activity has had the ancillary effect of establishing the EU as a global regulatory hegemon. This external dimension of the single market was only fully realized when the EU's trading partners, including the United States, expressed concerns that the single market might impose costs on third countries.[62] Of course, the EU benefits from such "incidental externalities" associated with the single market, and the EU's internal motives are not inconsistent with the EU's external motive to shape the global regulatory environment and pursue global influence.[63] The Commission, for example, likely welcomes the EU's newfound external regulatory power, however unintended its origin. In addition, it appears that the EU's internal goals have been gradually giving way to a more multifaceted set of goals—both internal and external—that the EU is pursuing in setting its regulatory policy.

While the Commission has, in its communications, demonstrated a traditional focus on strengthening the internal market, a review of these communications reveals a trend toward increased attention on the external dimension of the single market over time. In its documents discussing the single market generally, references to its external effects begin to emerge around 2007, with multiple publications devoted solely to this topic since. This demonstrates a significant change compared to the 1985 white paper and a 1996 Commission communication on the single market, both of which reflect an almost purely internal perspective.[64] This indicates that the Commission is becoming more self-conscious of the need to externalize EU rules as well as its increased ability to do so.

In its 2007 working paper "The External Dimension of the Single Market Review," the Commission acknowledges that "[T]he EU is emerging as a global rule maker, with the single market framework and the wider EU economic and social model increasingly serving as a reference point in third countries as well as in global and regional fora."[65] The Commission also recognizes that "[t]here is a window of opportunity to push global solutions forward. The EU is in a good position to take a lead, promoting its modern regulatory framework internationally."[66] In another communication, the Commission emphasizes how the "EU [is] being looked upon as the global standard setter in many areas such as product safety, food safety, environmental protection, public procurement, financial regulation, and accounting."[67] These statements point to the EU's growing awareness of its ability to shape the global regulatory environment beyond the single market.

At the same time as the awareness of this opportunity grew, the Commission began to emphasize its potential for global impact. For example, in its 2007 policy

paper, "A Single Market for Citizens," the European Commission envisions the
EU and its internal market to be standard setters at the international level:[68]

> [The EU] has spurred the development of rules and standards in areas
> such as product safety, the environment, securities and corporate govern-
> ance which inspire global standard setting. It gives the EU the potential
> to shape global norms and to ensure that fair rules are applied to world-
> wide trade and investment. The single market of the future should be the
> launch pad of an ambitious global agenda.

Around this same time, in a notable change from its earlier communications
on data protection regulation, the Commission also began to emphasize the
importance of promoting EU data privacy laws as a benchmark for global standards. In its 2009 communication, for example, the Commission noted that the
"Union must be a driving force behind the development and promotion of international standards for personal data protection and in the conclusion of appropriate bilateral or multilateral instruments."[69] These comments are in contrast to
earlier statements when the Commission simply emphasized the need to harmonize standards to ensure a smoother flow of data across the common market. In a
2010 communication, the Commission defended its stringent standards, noting
that "[a] high and uniform level of data protection within the EU will be the best
way of endorsing and promoting EU data protection standards globally."[70] The
Commission also called for universal principles based on EU norms:

> Data processing is globalised and calls for the development of universal
> principles for the protection of individuals with regard to the processing
> of personal data. The EU legal framework for data protection has often
> served as a benchmark for third countries when regulating data protec-
> tion. Its effect and impact, within and outside the Union, have been of the
> utmost importance. The European Union must therefore remain a driving
> force behind the development and promotion of international legal and
> technical standards for the protection of personal data, based on relevant
> EU and other European instruments on data protection.[71]

This vision of the EU as providing a benchmark for the world affected the
drafting of the GDPR. In 2017, the year before the GDPR came into force, Vera
Jourova—the Commissioner for justice in charge of data protection—announced
unambiguously that "we want to set the global standard."[72]
Over time, the EU has also become more explicit in stating its goal to
promote its regulatory preferences through trade agreements.[73] Today, the

Council's website discussing the EU's trade policy denotes that "[o]ne of the most important aspect of EU's trade policy is that—alongside protecting European businesses and consumers—it is promoting the EU's principles and values," citing human rights and environmental regulation as examples.[74] Recent EU treaty revisions also reflect a change in the mindset toward a more externally focused Europe. For instance, the 2007 Lisbon Treaty vests the EU with an explicit mandate to project its internal norms and values externally, emphasizing the importance of those values in the EU's relations with the wider world.[75]

Overall, these statements point to a growing awareness of the external effects of the single market, and the realization that this dimension presents the EU with opportunities. The internal goals have not faded and the external motivations seem to supplement, rather than substitute, the internal agenda of EU institutions, which remains paramount. While the fundamental rationale underlying the internal goal to strengthen the single market is well understood, it is less obvious as to why the EU would care about being a global standard setter. What does the EU gain from being a global leader in regulatory reforms, setting benchmarks for rules and standards worldwide?[76]

The economic goal of ensuring a level playing field for, and protecting the competitiveness of, European industry likely goes a long way in explaining the EU's willingness to externalize its regulatory agenda. A failure to export its standards to other countries would put European firms at a competitive disadvantage.[77] Yet by acting as a global regulator, the EU can defend its social preferences without compromising the competitiveness of its domestic industries. If foreign companies adhere to EU norms on the European market, the import-competing industries are assured a level playing field. If the EU's norms further spread to third countries, the EU can ensure that its export-oriented firms are not disadvantaged either. Being able to influence global standards minimizes the adjustment costs for European companies, which are then able to operate in foreign markets based on their home market rules.

Beyond the concern over the competitiveness of the European industry, the EU may have additional incentives to project its regulatory power abroad. For one, the EU may be motivated by a desire to obtain greater legitimacy for its rules through globalizing them. If foreign companies and governments endorse EU standards, those standards are seen as having a wider appeal and thus greater legitimacy.[78] One concrete benefit from this is that the EU's trade partners are less likely to challenge the legality of EU standards before forums like the WTO if those standards are already replicated globally. Less tangibly, being the global standard setter has the benefit of expanding the EU's soft power and validating its regulatory agenda, both at home and abroad.

The EU may also be motivated by a desire to replicate its own governance model and regulatory experience abroad. The EU's own successful experience in creating a common market has encouraged it to pursue a global order based on those same rules. More regulation in EU has meant more predictability and stability. This has fostered a belief that an extensive regulatory system is similarly needed to preserve global public goods. The EU subscribes to a view that trade liberalization fails to achieve economic goals without a simultaneous harmonization of policies. For the EU, this offers the most efficient and universally valid model of economic and political integration,[79] and potentially a compelling reason to replicate its experience abroad.

In recent years, the broader geopolitical context may have provided an additional incentive for the EU to assume the role of a global standard setter. The WTO has become increasingly dysfunctional since the closing of the Uruguay Round in 1995. Its inability today to effectively address regulatory barriers to trade has left a vacuum that the EU has been uniquely positioned to fill. Also, the US government has increasingly retreated from domestic regulation and international institutions. The absence of US leadership in this area gives the EU a further impetus to act. Scandals such as the Snowden revelations that exposed extensive US government surveillance activities worldwide may have further increased the EU's resolve to act as the global guardian of personal data and the right to privacy. Finally, the awareness that the EU's role in the world economy is declining while Asia's is rising may have similarly contributed to the EU's desire to cement its rules globally at the time when the EU still has the power to do so.

Finally, being able to set norms globally allows the EU to prove to its critics that it remains relevant as a global economic power. Embracing the role of a regulatory hegemon reinforces the EU's identity and enhances the EU's global standing even in the times of crises where its effectiveness and relevance are constantly being questioned. If the EU wants to exert influence, it must do so with the means available to it. Lacking traditional means of power, the EU's greatest global influence is accomplished through the norms that it has the competence to promulgate. In the absence of military power or unconstrained economic power, the EU can exercise genuine unilateral power most effectively by fixing the standards of behavior for the rest of the world.[80] In the world where the United States projects hard power through its military and engagement in trade wars, and China economic power through its loans and investments, the EU exerts power through the most potent tool for global influence it has—regulation.

2

The Brussels Effect

ONLY LARGE ECONOMIES can become sources of global standards. However, market size alone does not vest a jurisdiction with global regulatory power—or else the "Washington Effect" or the "Beijing Effect" would likely exist alongside the Brussels Effect. Instead, unilateral regulatory power requires distinct political choices made by a large economy. The EU has become a global regulator not only because of the size of its internal market, but also because it has built an institutional architecture that has converted its market size into a tangible regulatory influence. The key stakeholders in the EU have further embraced stringent regulation as a key toward a better society, giving the critical political backing for an ambitious regulatory agenda. However, the EU does not exert global regulatory power over any policy area it desires—market forces successfully globalize some EU regulations but not others, setting limits on the Brussels Effect.

This chapter lays the theoretical foundation for the Brussels Effect. It identifies the conditions for, and the mechanism through which, the externalization of one jurisdiction's standards unfolds. A careful examination of unilateral regulatory authority suggests that there are five elements underlying the Brussels Effect—*market size, regulatory capacity, stringent standards, inelastic targets*, and *non-divisibility*. Existing literature focuses on market size as a proxy for the jurisdiction's ability to exercise regulatory authority over foreign entities.[1] Large market size is, indeed, a precondition for unilateral regulatory globalization. Yet the jurisdiction must also possess sufficient regulatory capacity to exercise global regulatory authority. This entails having in place institutional structures that are capable of adopting and enforcing regulations effectively. In addition, these regulatory institutions must promulgate stringent regulatory standards, reflecting the preferences of key stakeholders in the jurisdiction. A global regulatory authority is also tied to a choice of regulating inelastic targets such as consumer markets as opposed to more elastic targets such as capital. Only stringent standards aimed at targets that cannot flee the jurisdiction ensure that a country's regulations will

The Brussels Effect. Anu Bradford, Oxford University Press (2020). © Oxford University Press.
DOI: 10.1093/oso/9780190088583.001.0001

not be constrained by market forces or other jurisdictions' regulatory responses. Finally, unilateral standards become global standards only when the benefits of adhering to a single global standard are greater than the benefits of taking advantage of laxer standards in lenient jurisdictions—in other words, when a target's conduct or production is non-divisible across global markets.

All of these five elements are needed for the Brussels Effect to occur. Some of these conditions, such as market size, are rooted in jurisdictions' historical endowments and less dependent on decisions made by either political institutions or market participants. Regulatory capacity and the willingness to promulgate stringent rules typically reflect the political economy in the regulating jurisdictions and are therefore a function of the affirmative choices made by political institutions. Further, inelasticity of regulatory targets or non-divisibility of regulations are conditions embedded in the nature of the global economy. They are driven by the business considerations of private companies, leaving them largely outside the influence of regulators themselves. This suggests that the Brussels Effect emanates as a result of a combination of bestowed market size, political decision-making, and market forces that drive corporate behavior.

These five elements underlying the Brussels Effect are generic conditions for unilateral regulatory power, capable of explaining any jurisdiction's ability (or inability) to regulate global markets alone. Yet this chapter shows how the EU is currently the predominant regulatory regime where these conditions exist, explaining why the EU—and not, for example, the United States—wields unilateral influence across a number of policy areas.

Market Size

In the global economy, power is correlated with the relative size of any given country's internal market.[2] Existing scholarship on global regulatory influence emphasizes the significance of market size as the proxy for economic power. Daniel Drezner argues that global regulatory outcomes are a function of state power, which states derive from the size and diversity of their internal market. Large markets have a gravitational effect on producers, pulling them toward the regulatory standards prevailing in these countries.[3] Chad Damro agrees, conceiving the EU as a "Market Power Europe," and arguing that the EU's identity "is crucially linked to its experience with market integration."[4] The single market provides the foundation for the EU and is key to its ability to externalize its regulatory measures outside of Europe.[5]

Market size is a relative concept. The extent of any state's market power depends on the attractiveness of its consumer market compared to the alternative markets available. In the case of consumer goods, the number and affluence of potential consumers determine the benefits of market access. The opportunity costs of forgoing those consumers are equally relevant; these costs are particularly high when demand in the corporation's home market or in alternative third markets is limited. Thus, the larger the market of the importing country relative to the market of the exporting country, the more likely that companies will adjust to the standards of the importing jurisdiction.[6] Put differently, the greater the ratio of exports to the jurisdiction relative to sales in the home and third-country markets, the more likely the Brussels Effect will occur. At the same time, the better the exporter's ability to divert trade to third-country markets or increase demand in its home market, the less likely the Brussels Effect will occur.

A jurisdiction's market power is enhanced when companies perceive a high value in their access to that market. When assessing this value, foreign corporations compare the attractiveness of the consumer market to the adjustment costs associated with market entry. The adjustment costs can consist of initial setup costs (such as switching key components used in products), and recurring compliance costs (such as incurring higher production costs to comply with more stringent environmental standards). A foreign producer will have an incentive to comply with the importing jurisdiction's stringent standard whenever the benefits of market access outweigh the adjustment costs. The lower the adjustment costs relative to the benefits of market access, the more likely the producer will adjust to the importing country's standard and enter the market.[7]

Focusing on market size alone, several states could qualify as potential global standard setters. The EU is the second largest economy in the world with a gross domestic product (GDP) of over $17 trillion.[8] The EU's share of the global combined gross national income (GNI) is over 20%.[9] It is also the second largest importer of goods and the largest importer of services.[10] Of course, the United States, China, and Japan also possess domestic markets large enough to use as leverage. On some metrics, they have even larger economies than the EU. The United States has an economy of over $19 trillion, making it the largest economy in the world. China is the world's third largest economy with a GDP of $12 trillion, while Japan has an economy of nearly $5 trillion.[11]

The EU is also arguably the world's most significant consumer market. With a high proportion of affluent consumers, a large number of producers depend on their ability to supply products and services to those consumers. The EU's population is 516 million, and its GDP per capita is $40,900. The United States is relatively more affluent (GDP per capita of $59,500), but its consumer market is smaller (population of 327 million). China, on the other hand, has a larger consumer market (population of 1.4 billion), but its consumers are relatively less affluent (GDP per capita of $16,700). India is almost as populous as China (population of 1.2 billion), but it has a considerably lower GDP per capita ($7,200).[12]

As the importance of markets such as China and India continues to grow, producers may, over time, have the option to divert part of their exports there. Yet given the relatively small purchasing power of consumers in those markets today, few international firms are in a position to abandon the EU market and recoup the forgone revenue elsewhere. The distinctly high value of market access to the EU therefore explains why many producers are prepared to incur even significant adjustment costs to retain their ability to sell goods and services into the EU.

The value of access to the EU's internal market has also been growing notably over the past several decades as new countries have joined the EU. As a result of its 1995 enlargement, the EU grew by twenty-two million people, adding $383 billion to its GDP. With its 2004 enlargement, the EU grew by seventy-five million people, and added $685 billion to its GDP. Its 2007 enlargement added thirty million people and $267 billion in GDP, and its 2013 enlargement added four million people and $81 billion.[13] The EU's various association agreements, which extend its regulations to neighboring countries such as Georgia, Morocco, and Turkey, have further grown the Union's de facto market size.[14] These countries largely align their regulations with those of the EU, adding to the total GDP and consumer base covered by EU regulatory standards. This further increases the benefits of conforming to European standards.

Though it may seem that the enlargement process inevitably enhances the EU's market power, there are important limits to how much the EU can grow its market size through accession of new members without compromising the influence tied to its market size. In their study on the optimal size of a nation, Alberto Alesina and Enrico Spolaore highlight the trade-off between nation size and preference heterogeneity among the citizens.[15] The larger the market, the cheaper the provision of public goods. For example, when additional countries join the EU, the opportunities to trade across the single market grow, enhancing the value of the common market. At the same time, with each new member, the preference heterogeneity among EU member states increases as well. This complicates decision-making over optimal regulations and limits the policies the EU can pursue. Thus, while a larger union would seem to enhance the EU's market power, there is actually an equilibrium point after which the EU's market power begins to erode as policy making becomes stymied by member states that oppose further integration and additional regulations. Thus, there can be such a thing as a "suboptimally large market" where the market's ability to influence regulation actually fails to increase with market size. In this sense, the growing internal divisions within the EU suggest that the EU's influence tied to its market size may, indeed, already be at (or past) its peak.

Regardless, even a more static view on the EU's current market size suggests that the EU is an important destination for a large segment of foreign producers today.

Of course, specific countries, industries, and companies vary in their dependence on serving the EU market. For example, the EU is an important market for exporters in Russia, South Africa, China, the United States, India, and Brazil, comprising 43%, 31%, 22%, 21%, 19%, and 18% of their total exports, respectively. Conversely, the EU is a less important destination for countries like Canada and Australia, where only 9% and 7% of their total exports, respectively, are destined for the EU.[16] The EU is the number one export market for Russia, South Africa, India, and the United States; the second largest export market for China, Canada, and Brazil; and the third largest export market for Japan and South Korea.

Importance also varies by specific industries within each country. For example, 87% of US pharmaceutical exports and 36% of US organic chemicals are destined for the EU. The EU is also an important export destination for India's textiles (45% of country's textile exports), Chinese toys (40%), Korean pharmaceuticals (78%), Russian mineral fuels (65%), Canadian aircrafts (24%), Brazilian coffee (51%), South African fruit and nuts (74%), Japanese toys (50%), and various seeds and fruits from Australia (64%).[17] For these and many other similarly situated producers, the EU's market access is distinctly valuable, and so the EU's market size poses a powerful constraint on their business activity.

In particular, the European market is important for many American corporate giants. This is especially true in the electronics industry, which is "highly dependent on the EU market and is crucial to the U.S. economy. . . . It is the U.S.'s third biggest export sector to the EU."[18] The EU is also the most important export market for many US high-tech companies. With 277 million active daily users in the EU, Facebook has more customers in the EU than in the United States. European advertising also makes up 24% of Facebook's global advertising revenue. In 2017, this revenue also grew by 41% in Europe, reflecting the highest growth rate of any region for the company.[19] To provide further examples, Google's share of the search market in the EU is over 90% whereas most estimates suggest that Google's market share is around 67–75% in the United States.[20] Google also reports that its advertising revenue from EMEA (Europe, Middle East, and Africa) amounts to 33% of its 2017 revenue, while Germany and the United Kingdom alone contribute over $28 billion (16%) to Amazon's total net sales.[21] All of these figures illustrate the significance of the EU's market size as a foundation for the Brussels Effect.

While the EU is able to leverage its market size to regulate many aspects of economic life for such companies and industries, in cases where the EU is not an inevitable destination market for goods, its market power is more limited. In such instances, the Brussels Effect fails to take place. For example, a Japanese pharmaceutical company, Takeda, decided to discontinue its development of an insomnia drug Ramelteon for the European market after it struggled to obtain a marketing authorization in the EU.[22] Instead of seeking to generate additional clinical data to meet the European regulatory requirements, the company withdrew in 2008 its marketing authorization application submitted to the European Medicines Agency the previous year. At the same time, Takeda continues to sell the same insomnia drug—under the different name of Rozerem—in the United States and Japan where it obtained the necessary regulatory approvals in 2005 and 2010, respectively.[23] Thus, at times, the high costs of complying with the stringent EU standard lead companies to abandon the EU market altogether, instead of adjusting their global production to the EU standard.

Another example comes from the management of hazardous waste where the EU has also failed to export its standards to other countries.[24] Illegal transfers of hazardous waste remain common as producers have considerable incentive to evade costly regulations by finding jurisdictions that do not enforce waste management standards. Waste is movable, and so producers have the ability and incentive to dump it outside of Europe. This illustrates how regulatory power is much harder to project externally in instances where the goal is to limit exports to certain third countries versus preventing imports to one's own market.[25]

In some areas, the EU's market size is altogether irrelevant, and so the Brussels Effect fails to occur. First, the EU has little leverage over targets of regulation that are not subject to market access. Consider human rights, an area in which the EU has both regulatory capacity and a strong preference to pursue high levels of protection. However, the EU has not been particularly successful in exporting its human rights norms or democratic values to countries in North Africa or the Middle East, which lie outside of its direct sphere of influence.[26] For example, signing a human rights treaty can be a condition for a trade agreement with the EU.[27] Enforcing the treaty is another matter. It is much easier for the EU to deny market access to a product that does not meet EU standards than it is to police international practices that involve individuals who never enter the European market. In the end, the EU derives its power from its ability to offer conditional access to its large and valuable market. Thus, the jurisdiction's ability to leverage its large market size remains the foundational condition that sustains the Brussels Effect.

Regulatory Capacity

Large market size alone does not explain a state's ability to project its regulatory preferences onto others; not all states with large markets become sources of global standards. Being a regulatory power is a conscious choice pursued by a state rather than something inherent to its market size. The state must commit to building institutions and vesting them with regulatory capacity to translate its market power into tangible regulatory influence.[28] Regulatory capacity refers to a jurisdiction's ability to promulgate and enforce regulations. This requires both regulatory expertise and resources. Without this capacity, a country cannot effectively exert authority over market participants—within or outside its jurisdiction. An important element of regulatory capacity is the authority to impose sanctions in cases of noncompliance. Only those jurisdictions with the ability to inflict significant costs by excluding noncomplying firms from their markets are able to force regulatory adjustments and incentivize compliance.[29]

Regulatory capacity is often closely associated with another condition—the propensity to promulgate stringent rules—as jurisdictions that have the political will to adopt stringent regulations also often deploy that same political will to build strong regulatory institutions. However, there are also instances where a jurisdiction might want to impose regulation in a certain policy area but where it simply lacks the technical expertise or the financial resources to build the requisite regulatory capacity—hence the preference for stringent regulation should be considered an independent condition needed for the Brussels Effect to occur.[30]

The degree of regulatory capacity sets important limits on a country's ability to exert global regulatory authority. For instance, many Asian economies are growing at a staggering rate, but it will take time for their GDP growth to translate into regulatory experience and the institutional capacity necessary to enforce norms, in particular against foreign parties.[31] This is evident in the case of China, where the country's impact on global financial regulation has been limited, despite its vast capital reserves and extensive holdings of US treasuries. China's limited influence can be traced, in part, to its lack of effective and independent bureaucratic institutions overseeing national market rules in this area.[32] Thus, acknowledging that sophisticated regulatory institutions are required to activate the power of sizable domestic markets means that few jurisdictions aside from the United States or the EU today have the capacity to be regulators with global reach.[33] In the United States, administrative agencies' capacity to promulgate and enforce rules is well established. Similarly, the EU has seen a rise in the role of the regulatory state, as the institutional developments that accompanied the creation of the single market have bestowed the EU with substantial regulatory capacity.[34]

The EU has built extensive regulatory capacity, particularly since the 1986 adoption of the Single European Act (SEA), which launched the ambitious agenda to complete the single market by 1992. To implement this goal, member states vested the EU institutions with vast powers to formulate and enforce market regulations, as discussed in chapter 1. This capacity to promulgate rules and ensure compliance rests on EU institutions' significant regulatory expertise, coherence of policy making, and expansive sanctioning authority.[35] The EU's conscious efforts to build its extensive regulatory machine was motivated by the need to further the integration process and complete the single market, which was largely done through regulation.

The internal regulatory capacity of the EU has only continued to grow since. All key EU institutions—the Commission, the Council, and the European Parliament (EP)—have experienced significant bureaucratic growth over time. In 2016, EU institutions employed 39,715 staff members. These numbers have grown on average by 5.2% a year since the establishment of these institutions.[36] This has been continuous across all EU institutions from 1959 until 2011, at which point EU institutions deliberately cut staff in response to the 2008 financial and budgetary crisis under pressure to streamline. However, aside from the crisis response, the number of EU civil servants has been steadily growing. In 1959— the early years of the European Economic Community—the total staff of the EU consisted of 2,591 staff members, with Commission staff at 1,930, EP staff at 315, and Council staff at 264. In 2016, the Commission had the largest number of staff (24,044), followed by the EP (6,762), and finally the Council (3,040).[37] Further, the average annual growth rates for all three institutions were similar: 5.0% for the Commission, 6.0% for the EP, and 4.7% for the Council.

While the EU bureaucracy has exhibited steady growth over the years, it is still relatively low in staff when compared with the breadth of the EU's mandate and the EU population, which has expanded to over 500 million people. The relative size of the EU bureaucracy seems even more modest when compared to the US federal bureaucracy. The US federal government employs over 4 million people across the executive, legislative and judicial branches.[38] According to the Office of Personnel Management report, the federal executive branch consisted of 1.87 million employees in fiscal year 2017, a figure that reflects full time civilian employees (excluding postal service employees and uniformed military personnel).[39] For example, the Department of Agriculture and Department of Transportation alone had over 73,000 and 53,000 employees, respectively.[40] On a per capita basis, the relative size of the US federal government is even larger compared to the more populous EU.

Of course, a direct comparison of staff numbers between the US federal bureaucracy and that of the EU is somewhat misleading given that EU member states themselves are vested with significant responsibilities to implement and enforce EU law, indirectly but substantially adding to the EU's bureaucratic capacity. The EU has delegated the enforcement of many key EU regulations— including the General Data Protection Regulation (GDPR)—to its member states. The Commission is further vested with the power to bring infringement proceedings against individual member states that fail to fully implement or enforce EU law. This way, the Commission can ensure that the member states have the incentive to obey their mandate and thus effectively contribute to the EU's regulatory capacity.

Further, regardless of the metric used, the quantity of EU staff alone fails to capture the extent of regulatory capacity vested in EU institutions. The quality of the EU bureaucracy matters, as well. For example, the Commission has been able to carry out its competences with the help of a bureaucracy that is distinctly skilled and mission driven. It consists of highly educated bureaucrats that share a mission for European integration. No fewer than 70% of Commission officials hold a postgraduate degree, and 58% have studied in more than one country, partially explaining why the Commission is often viewed as being composed of a cosmopolitan, educated elite.[41] Commission officials also possess significant technical expertise, which gives their rule-making an additional layer of legitimacy and contributes to an aura of objectivity and neutrality that enhances their authority.[42]

The shared mission of Commission staff further amplifies its rule-making capacity. A recent survey of Commission officials carried out by Lisbet Hooghe reported that 72% of respondents claimed "commitment to Europe" as a motivation for joining the Commission, with supranationalists outnumbering state-centrists by more than two to one.[43] An earlier survey found that "top Commission officials appeared significantly more pro-European than either national elites or public opinion."[44] Rather strikingly, Hooghe's survey revealed that while over 40% of Europeans viewed themselves as maintaining national identity only, no member of the European Commission staff surveyed responded as such, with over 80% identifying themselves as European to some degree.[45] The Commission's culture "revolve[s] around a teleological vision of the EU, one that sees deeper integration as the means of achieving broader political goals."[46] This distinct homogeneity in its mission allows the Commission to substitute political infighting with a relatively clear and coherent vision of how to deploy its competences, paving the way for more extensive rule-making.

The Commission has also skillfully enhanced its expertise and resources through the establishment of European regulatory agencies (ERAs) over the past two decades, particularly in domains where it has had limited discretion or power. In this way, the Commission can leverage the ERAs to expand, rather than rival, its role in regulating the single market.[47] Furthermore, by not traditionally vesting the agencies with any general rule-making powers, the Commission has guarded its own rule-setting prerogatives instead. Thus, most ERAs provide the Commission with additional expertise, personnel, information, or financing when needed, adding to the regulatory capacity the Commission possesses without undermining its powers and control over policy making.[48]

A key feature of the EU's regulatory capacity is its extensive sanctioning authority, which creates an effective deterrent and induces compliance with EU regulations.[49] As the ultimate form of sanction, the Commission may deny access to the EU market by banning a certain product or service from being offered in its territory unless it meets the EU's regulatory requirements. The EU further has the authority to impose significant fines on companies that fail to obey its regulations. For example, what makes the EU's data protection regulation GDPR so potent is the ability of European data protection authorities in member states to impose a fine amounting to 4% of the company's global turnover (revenue) in cases of noncompliance.[50] Competition violations carry an even higher penalty: the Commission can impose a fine of up to 10% of overall annual turnover. The Commission has also repeatedly shown its willingness to exercise this sanctioning authority, as the recent $5 billion, $2.7 billion, and $1.7 billion fines imposed on Google illustrate.[51]

The history of the EU has further been marked by a constantly expanding regulatory agenda as the competences of EU institutions have grown significantly over the years.[52] The EU started off as an institution with a narrow focus on integrating Western European steel and coal industries in an effort to eliminate states' capacities to wage war against one another. However, the establishment of a customs union and removal of internal trade barriers soon ensued. The EU's competences have since grown to embrace a number of issues ranging from environmental and consumer protections to social policy, transport, public health, privacy, and criminal justice, to name a few.

Several reasons explain the substantial growth in the EU's regulatory competences over time. When the economic liberalization agenda grew in the aftermath of the 1986 SEA, skeptical member states' buy-in was obtained largely by balancing the liberal economic agenda with extensive social protections to offset any adverse effects of rapid economic integration.[53] Therefore, the broad regulatory mandate of today's EU originates from EU member states' disagreements on how to balance various domestic consumer or environmental protection measures with the need to guarantee economic freedoms within the common market. The easiest way to resolve such political disagreements was not to force a choice between an economic and social Europe—catering to some but not other member states—but to expand the EU's competences to cover both.[54]

The various amendments of the EU Treaties as well as the European Court of Justice's (ECJ) interpretation of those treaties have similarly paved the way for more expansive EU competences and hence a broader regulatory agenda. For example, the EU Treaties' "harmonization article"—Article 114 of the TFEU—which grants the EU the competence to harmonize member states laws to further the establishment and functioning of the single market—has often provided the legal basis for regulatory action, vesting the EU institutions with a relatively broad mandate to act. For example, the ECJ found in 2006 that this harmonization article allowed the EU to extend its capacity to regulate tobacco advertising even though the regulation of public health was outside the competences of the EU— as long as discordant national regulations on tobacco advertising obstructed the functioning of the internal market.[55] Relatedly, the EU institutions have been adamant in deploying the competences granted to them in a wide variety of ways. For instance, while the EU Treaties do not vest the Commission with the capacity to act in the corporate tax domain, the Commission has been pursuing the tax arrangements of companies such as Apple and Starbucks by relying on its wide powers under the Treaties' state aid provisions.[56] These provisions prohibit member states from giving selective financial advantage to certain companies[57]—as discussed further in chapter 4.

Changes to the EU institutions' voting rules have also been critical in extending the EU's regulatory capacity. The Council's ability to promulgate regulations has expanded over the years, in particular as a larger set of regulations have become subject to a qualified majority as opposed to unanimous voting.[58] For example, environmental policy has only required qualified majority voting since the 1992 Maastricht Treaty.[59] This has made it easier to pass legislation, further broadening the EU's regulatory reach. EU institutions have acquired these increased powers as a result of the need to further integrate the common market and maximize gains from deeper integration. Several rounds of enlargement have increased the heterogeneity of EU membership, making unanimous decision-making all the more challenging. The trend toward qualified majority voting has therefore been essential in allowing for continued regulatory action.

Another institutional change that has contributed to the EU's enhanced regulatory capacity is the gradual empowerment of the EP. Ever since the 1986 SEA and the 1992 Maastricht Treaty, the EP has gained influence in the EU's legislative process.[60] The Maastricht Treaty was particularly notable in that it introduced a co-decision procedure that vested the EP with the power to adopt legislation jointly with the Council. The Lisbon Treaty made this co-decision procedure the default mode of legislation.[61] Driven by concerns of democratic deficit in the EU, the strengthening of the EP has sought to address the need to further legitimize EU decision-making by granting a greater role to an institution directly elected by European citizens. The EP is known for its pro-regulation stance, typically supporting enhanced environmental regulation and consumer protection as part of its desire to demonstrate that it fulfills its mandate to serve the interests of European citizens. Greater European integration also tends to reinforce the role of supranational EU institutions, including that of the EP, further explaining the EP's pro-integration tendencies.[62]

The European courts have also been instrumental in expanding EU institutions' competences, adding to their regulatory capacity in the process.[63] The ECJ is often portrayed as an "activist" court that has pursued "judicial integration" with rulings that have bestowed the EU with powers not foreseen in treaties.[64] Many central concepts of EU law—including the supremacy of EU law[65] and its direct effect[66]—stem from ECJ rulings. The ECJ's pro-integration bias has often protected the Commission's prerogatives and extended the scope and depth of the EU's powers. This has been the case even when—or perhaps especially when—the political process has been deadlocked, and the consensus toward deeper integration among the member states has been lacking. Euroskeptic voices have accused the ECJ of overreaching and thereby threatening the delicate balance between supranationalism and member-state sovereignty.[67] Perhaps partially in response to existing (or anticipated) backlash, there are some signs that the ECJ is retreating from its activist stance in areas such as social policy.[68] Yet both critics and supporters of the Court would agree that the ECJ's expansionist jurisprudence has in many instances and over several decades strengthened the powers of EU institutions and upheld regulations that have paved the way for greater European integration.

This gradual, yet decisive, transfer of regulatory powers from the member states to the EU has been central to the rise of the regulatory state in Europe. Had member states been left to their own devices, the same level of regulatory capacity would not exist in Europe today. According to Giandomenico Majone, this "Europeanisation of policy making" has been crucial, leading to "the almost exponential growth [...] of the number of directives and regulations produced by the Brussels authorities each year."[69] The EU has legitimized its extensive regulatory powers in several ways, including by insisting on clear statutory objectives, transparency, public participation, and due-process provisions in regulatory decisions. This has mitigated concerns of a pro-regulation bias in the EU, allowing EU institutions to maximize their powers without compromising their legitimacy.[70]

Still, the EU's regulatory capacity varies across different policy areas. Ultimately, the EU can only have regulatory competence in a given area if the member states have granted it such competence.[71] The EU, over the years, has acquired extensive regulatory capacity in all areas relating to the single market, and these are the very regulations that carry the attributes that lend themselves to externalization. The EU's regulatory capacity is the greatest in areas where it enjoys exclusive—as opposed to merely shared or supportive—regulatory competence, such as in competition law.[72] In these areas of exclusive EU competence, member states are not permitted to make their own laws. However, there remain important policy areas where EU member states have not transferred powers to the EU—including corporate taxation, culture, or education. Naturally, the EU's global regulatory power is limited to policy areas in which the member states have ceded either exclusive or shared regulatory competence to the EU. In those instances, the EU enjoys the requisite regulatory capacity that can unleash the power of the single market and convert it into concrete regulatory influence.

Stringent Regulations

The institutional competence and expertise vested in the EU's key institutions—the European Commission in particular—form the foundation of the regulatory state in Europe. However, even significant regulatory capacity by a large market does not guarantee regulatory influence unless such regulatory capacity is supplemented with the political will to deploy it. Thus, the Brussels Effect requires that the jurisdiction also has the propensity to promulgate stringent regulatory standards.

The domestic preference for stringent regulation is more likely to be found in countries with high levels of income.[73] Wealthier countries can better afford pursuing environmental and consumer protection, even at the expense of the profitability of their firms, whereas less-wealthy countries remain more sensitive to the costs of regulation that constrain business activity and hence limit economic growth. This lower tolerance for the costs of stringent rules, together with their lack of regulatory capacity, explains why emerging markets are unlikely to exercise rule-making power that would match their growing market size anytime soon.

But even wealthy countries differ in their predisposition to regulatory intervention. Until the end of the 1980s, the United States set global norms in consumer and environmental regulation, leading European firms to adjust to the higher standards that originated from the United States.[74] At that time, American regulations also often served as benchmarks for European activists who criticized the EU for lagging behind, for instance, in the regulation of automotive emissions, the lead content of fuel, or chemicals harmful to the ozone layer.[75] Since the 1990s, the roles have been reversed as the EU has increasingly adopted more stringent consumer and environmental protection standards, while the United States has failed to follow the EU's lead.[76] The only way for the United States to supersede EU standards today would be to adopt even higher standards itself—something that it does not consider to be welfare enhancing and thus in its interest.

David Vogel explains the shift in the 1990s as a result of the changes in citizens' risk perception and decision-makers' increased willingness to respond to mounting demands for more regulation.[77] Europeans have perceived health, safety, and environmental risks caused by businesses as credible and politically unacceptable. This increased breadth and salience of public risk perception can partially be traced to "triggers" that have elevated the public's consciousness about the risks they face. While Americans experienced a cascade of alarming news about various such risks from the 1960s until the 1990s—ranging from contaminated cranberries, thalidomide, mercury-contaminated fish, or large oil spills—some widely published disagreements about those alarm bells had eroded their salience, tempering the demand for further regulations by the 1990s. In contrast, in Europe, alarm bells continued to ring ever more loudly—be it with regard to concerns of dead seals in the North Sea, "mad-cow" disease in the United Kingdom, HIV-contaminated blood in France, radioactive waste following the Chernobyl nuclear disaster, or a large-scale chemical spill turning the Rhine River red with toxins.[78] This nurtured a "precautionary risk culture" and elevated the need for regulation in the eyes of the public.

This shift in the citizens' perceptions is important, but likely not the only reason that caused the EU to eclipse the United States as the predominant global regulator. An alternative explanation emphasizes the EU's conscious decision to accelerate its integration process and embark on a determined policy to complete the single market by the early 1990s—through regulation. With the adoption of the EU's SEA in 1986, the EU reinvigorated the integration project with the objective of establishing a single market by the end of 1992. The SEA became a key catalyst for regulatory reforms and further integration.[79] The substantive scope of the EU expanded to new policy areas such as the environment and social policy. To help implement the SEA, the EU also vested its institutions with greater ability to pass regulations through qualified majority voting. Even the more Euroskeptic countries, including the United Kingdom, agreed to limit their sovereignty in favor of qualified majority voting given the benefits associated with the single market program.[80] These changes adopted in the early 1990s paved the way for an ambitious agenda to pursue stringent regulations that would serve the broader integration agenda.

In addition to leveraging the stringent regulatory agenda as a tool for promoting the broader goals of European integration, two additional factors are critical in explaining the EU's pursuit of distinctly stringent rules: Europeans' greater faith in government as opposed to markets to generate fair and efficient outcomes (*ideology*); and the relative importance of public regulation over private litigation and lower threshold for intervention by regulators in cases of uncertainty (*process*). These will be discussed in turn. For any given regulatory policy, the salience of these factors may vary, and their relative importance may change over time or across key decision-makers. Additionally, policy-specific drivers for high standards also exist. These will be addressed in Part II. The discussion of these two key factors—ideology and process—will, therefore, only seek to capture the more generic background norms that explain the EU's overall predisposition to promulgate stringent standards across many different policy areas. After reviewing these two factors, the discussion then provides some counterexamples where the missing regulatory propensity limits the Brussels Effect.

Ideology: Markets vs. Government

Europeans are generally less trusting of markets and more comfortable with government intervention. The state enjoys greater public trust in the EU, and can therefore assume a more prominent role in regulating markets.[81] In contrast, Americans tend to embrace a pro-business, free-market-oriented version of capitalism. It is difficult to garner public support for extensive federal regulation in the United States given the political will, in particular among conservative voters, to protect the rights of individual states from the encroachment of the federal government. Of course, exceptions exist in both directions, but in general, the United States is typically more sensitive to the costs of regulatory action while the EU emphasizes the costs of regulatory inaction to a greater degree. These differences often lead to more stringent regulations emanating from the EU.[82]

EU policy makers' preference for stringent regulation reflects their commitment to a social market economy and sustainable development. Article 3 of the Lisbon Treaty, which lists the objectives of the European Union, declares the following:

> The Union shall establish an internal market. It shall work for the sustainable development of Europe based on balanced economic growth and price stability, a highly competitive social market economy, aiming at full employment and social progress, and a high level of protection and improvement of the quality of the environment. It shall promote scientific and technological advance.

The references to "sustainable development," "balanced economic growth," "social market economy," "full employment and social progress," together with a "high level of protection and improvement of the quality of the environment" are illustrative of European values, which envision a prominent role for the government as a steward of regulated market outcomes. These goals require sustained government intervention, as they cannot be generated by market forces alone. They capture the regulatory philosophy that underlies the single market, providing a constitutional foundation for the high levels of regulatory activity that is now characteristic of policy making in Europe.

This pro-regulation ideology is rooted in economic policies embraced by most individual EU member states. Influential member states such as France and Germany have a long history of favoring government intervention in the economy.[83] France has historically been associated with a dirigiste economic policy with heavy state intervention in economic governance. Germany is the country where the social market economy model originated in the 1950s and where the state has retained its commitment to redistribute the gains of a market economy ever since.[84] Nordic countries—Denmark, Finland, and Sweden—as well as the Netherlands similarly embrace strong government as part of their commitment to the welfare state.[85] These countries, together with Germany, have incorporated environmental protection into their policies since the 1970s.[86] The prominent role of the government also comes naturally to many member states in Eastern Europe that lived under communism and have continued to allow state-owned enterprises to influence economic life even after joining the EU.[87] Even the United Kingdom, which features a notably more market-oriented political atmosphere than the rest of the EU, has often supported regulation that removes obstacles from trading across the single market. The United Kingdom has also been one of the most prominent supporters of the EU's fight against climate change, spearheading the emissions trading system in the EU. Yet still, the United Kingdom is arguably closer to the United States in its fear of regulatory overreach. The United Kingdom's discontent with the EU's "red tape" is, after all, one of the primary reasons the country voted in 2016 to leave the union.

Thus, most EU member states support government intervention as a way to ensure a more equitable distribution of wealth among their citizens, even if such sentiments arise for varying historic reasons. Thinking in terms of the influential literature on "varieties of capitalism," most European countries tend to exhibit features of a "coordinated market economy" as opposed to a "liberal market economy."[88] In general, coordinated market economies reserve a greater role for government regulation and non-market institutions.[89] With the exception of common law jurisdictions, such as the United Kingdom and Ireland, which are better characterized as liberal market economies, the majority of EU member states have structured their economies so as to allocate more rights to the state as opposed to the individual.[90]

Europeans' lesser faith in markets may stem largely from ideology, but in some areas of regulation, it is also a function of how markets operate in practice. For instance, EU competition laws reflect a belief that markets, left to their own devices, are likely to fail and that government intervention can improve outcomes. Conversely, US antitrust laws reflect a much greater trust in markets' ability to self-correct. Partially this is because capital markets are less well developed in the EU than in the United States, making market entry more difficult.[91] The contrary is often true in US capital markets where it is generally easier to raise capital and facilitate market entry, thus enabling new entrants to act as a more effective check on existing actors' anticompetitive behavior. This partially explains the EU's relative reliance on competition regulation versus the US' reliance on markets as a primary means of maintaining market competition.

The political environment in the EU has similarly been conducive to extensive rule-making. European political elites have been ideologically less divided than their US counterparts, and consequently are more responsive to the demands of the general public to provide more stringent regulations.[92] Parties across the ideological spectrum may differ in the extent of their support for regulation but share a fundamental commitment to a regulated market economy, including social protections.[93] It is illustrative that the Commission President Jean-Claude Juncker—who represents the conservative EPP Party—vowed during his candidacy speech to the European Parliament: "I will not sacrifice Europe's safety, health, social and data protection standards or our cultural diversity on the altar of free trade."[94] Thus, even the most pro-market, center-right parties endorse the EU's regulatory agenda that balances free trade with extensive protections for its citizens.

Process: The Preference for Administrative Rule-Making and Tendency for Precaution

The process of rule-making has also contributed to a regulatory environment that has led to the adoption of stringent regulations in the EU. There are two dimensions for this argument. First, the EU does not share the US' reliance on private litigation and tort liability rules to deter firms from placing unsafe or otherwise harmful products on the market. Instead, the EU relies on the government to promulgate, and then enforce, ex ante regulations. Second, the EU's administrative rule-making relies on a more precautionary approach to environmental and consumer protection. This can be contrasted with the US' administrative process, which places a greater reliance on cost-benefit analysis, leaving lesser ability for promulgating regulations based on a precautionary approach.

The EU's tendency to respond to various regulatory risks with stringent standards partially stems from its reliance on ex ante government regulation as opposed to ex post enforcement by private litigants. In the United States, a vigorous tort law that exposes manufacturers to potentially significant liability deters producers from placing harmful products on the market. Tort law can therefore act as a substitute for a regulatory system, reducing the need for agency rule-making and public enforcement.[95] In the absence of similar incentives for private parties to litigate in Europe, the EU has developed an administrative system that relies comparatively more on stringent regulatory standards to generate the necessary deterrence against harmful behavior.

In relying on the Commission and various national agencies to promulgate regulatory rules and enforce them, the EU has opted to rely on technocratic agency expertise over adjudication before generalized courts. Courts often lack specific knowledge of health and safety matters that require evaluation of scientific facts.[96] The Commission has a relatively large staff divided across specialized Directorate Generals, all of which focus on specific policy areas. This allows officials to develop considerable expertise in their area of regulation. For example, private individuals may not even be aware that some adverse health effects that they are experiencing are due to exposure to carcinogenic agents or materials. Without such knowledge, they would not even know to bring a liability suit against the manufacturer of the product containing such ingredients.[97] By leaving the regulation to the Commission, the EU mitigates some of the informational constraints that private litigants face in activating tort liability through litigation. Considerable scale economies also allow the EU to efficiently acquire the knowledge to prepare, promulgate, and enforce regulations across the common market that protect the rights of over five hundred million consumers.[98]

Whether countries rely more on private tort law or public regulation to organize their regulatory systems depends on broader features that characterize their legal and administrative systems. For example, the US-style tort system requires extensive rules of discovery, the availability of class actions, and substantial monetary awards to function effectively. In the EU, discovery and collective redress have both been historically limited. Monetary awards when fault is found are similarly modest compared to remedies such as treble damages that US litigants can obtain. These features reduce incentives to sue in the EU, making tort law a less-viable alternative for public action.

Addtionally, the EU is more ideologically comfortable than the United States with administrative regulation resting on "social command" exercised by public institutions.[99] Relying on the vigilance of private individuals is foreign to most European countries where the state has always played a key role in regulating markets. The United States takes the opposite view. It is accustomed to limiting the government's ability to exert social control in favor of reserving a larger role for private litigants. Private enforcement fits better with the US' individualistic tradition and culture of litigation. The United States also recognizes that government regulation can burden even harmless activity, making the tort system more appealing as it limits the liability to instances where actual harm has occurred.[100]

Finally, ex ante regulation also resonates more with Europeans who have a low tolerance for many health and environmental risks and often opt for precautionary regulation to eliminate even more distant or uncertain risks. A tort system has the inherent characteristic of allowing the harm to materialize before any action can be taken.[101] This feature is in tension with the more precautionary attitudes prevailing in Europe, leading the EU to embrace preventive control where regulators act before harm occurs. While the EU's regulatory process can obviously be slow at the outset, regulatory intervention is still designed to take place preventatively before risks have materialized.

The reasons just mentioned illustrate why the EU primarily relies on bureaucratic rule-making rather than judges to generate deterrence through tort litigation. Of course, administrative rule-making plays an important role in many areas of US law, and courts are not irrelevant in the EU. Many important ECJ rulings have emanated as preliminary references from national courts and are hence initiated by private litigants.[102] Also, private litigation may become more important in the EU going forward. In 2018, the Commission proposed legislation that seeks to introduce an EU-wide class action system in consumer protection cases.[103] The new Directive would extend class actions to several areas of EU regulation, including consumer protection, product liability, environment, financial regulation, health, tourism, passenger rights, and data protection. Even with these reforms, many proposed features such as the requirement that consumers must "opt in" as opposed to "opt out" of redress orders, more limited discovery rights, and the unwillingness to implement contingency fees will make it unlikely that the US-style mass-tort litigation culture would emerge in the EU anytime soon. There is also little to suggest that the class action reform would lead the Commission to rein in its rule-making and promulgate less-stringent regulations going forward.

The EU's emphasis of administrative rule-making over tort liability is not the only process-driven reason that has contributed toward the EU's stringent regulations. The EU's regulatory stringency is also explained by the different role that cost-benefit analysis (CBA) and precaution play in the regulatory process. Today, the EU and the United States both share the administrative culture of analyzing the costs and benefits of regulatory action before enacting a new regulation. However, the adoption of CBA—known as "impact assessment" in the EU—is more recent and hence less entrenched in the EU. When regulatory risks are uncertain and hard to accurately quantify, the EU is more comfortable intervening, even based on precaution. These reasons explain why, on balance, the EU remains more concerned with false negatives—instances when it erroneously fails to intervene, allowing a harm to materialize—than false positives—instances when it erroneously intervenes, limiting beneficial economic activity in an effort to protect its citizens from a potential risk that may or may not materialize.

In the United States, CBA dates back to President Reagan's 1981 executive order requiring all new rules to meet the cost-benefit test before being issued.[104] Every subsequent president since, whether Democrat or Republican, has endorsed a variant of CBA. CBA forces all US regulatory agencies to substantiate that the benefits of intervention outweigh its costs.[105] This obligation applies to all regulations that impose compliance costs exceeding $100 million or that raise significant novel policy questions.[106] As a result, in all these instances, any risk must first be quantified and found to be unreasonable before regulatory intervention can be justified.[107]

Impact assessment is more recent in the EU, being formally introduced in 2002.[108] The EU requires an impact assessment for all Commission initiatives that are likely to have "significant economic, environmental or social impacts."[109] The method underlying the impact assessment in the EU differs from the method employed in the United States.[110] While the CBA requires US agencies to provide a primarily quantitative assessment of the anticipated costs and benefits of a regulation and its alternatives, the Commission has adopted a more holistic approach. It integrates various types of ex ante policy evaluations, such as CBA, cost-effectiveness analysis, and multi-criteria analysis. It also conducts a more qualitative assessment of policy elements—including both aggregate and distributional impacts—which cannot easily be quantified. The Commission is further obliged to assess the impact of any legislative proposals on the fundamental rights in the EU.[111] The EU's impact assessment is subject to a review by the Regulatory Scrutiny Board. While the Regulatory Scrutiny Board's review focuses on whether the impact assessment reflects high quality analysis, its US-counterpart—the Office of Information and Regulatory Affairs (OIRA)—additionally reviews whether a regulation is consistent with the president's agenda, adding a layer of political control to the review process.[112]

The EU's impact assessment and the functioning of the Regulatory Scrutiny Board have over time evolved closer to their US counterparts.[113] For example, while the Regulatory Scrutiny Board initially could not veto proposals that did not pass the CBA, it gained such power in 2010. It would therefore be mistaken to exaggerate the US–EU differences and attribute the relative stringency of EU standards to differences in the CBA. That said, on balance, it is fair to say that the EU subscribes to a more flexible CBA that leaves more space for regulators to intervene with stringent standards.

The EU and the United States also differ in their relationship to scientific evidence and precautionary regulation in the face of uncertainty.[114] As of the 1990s, influential scholars, business elite, think tanks, and media in the United States began to increasingly question what they perceived as excessive precaution that dominated rule-making and that, in their view, had led to the enactment of overly burdensome health and safety regulations.[115] This also resulted in a change in the public perception, which became more skeptical of the need for regulation.[116] Partially due to this change, US agencies began to conduct a rigorous scientific assessment in their regulatory decision-making as of the 1990s.[117] The strict requirement to carry out a CBA and amass convincing scientific data—or else fail a possible judicial challenge to rule-making—elevated the administrative hurdle for all regulations promulgated by US agencies.

In contrast, while scientific evidence remains central to regulating risk in the EU,[118] it is tempered by the EU-wide adoption of the "precautionary principle." This principle dictates that precautionary regulatory action is proper even in the absence of an absolute, quantifiable certainty of the risk, as long as there are reasonable grounds for concern that the potentially dangerous effects may be inconsistent with the chosen level of protection.[119] The precautionary principle emanates from Swedish and German environmental law dating back to the 1960s,[120] and the Maastricht Treaty, which officially embraced the principle at the EU level in 1992,[121] largely reflecting Germany's effort to "Germanize" European environmental policy.[122] The additional impetus for the precautionary principle came from various food safety and environmental scandals that made the general public eager to preempt regulatory risks with precautionary regulation. As the public support for the precautionary principle grew, all institutions were eager to capitalize on it and endorse precaution to earn greater legitimacy in the eyes of the public.[123]

The Commission has sought to curtail the excessive reliance on the precautionary principle by member states as a pretext for limiting trade from other member states by emphasizing the importance of science as a foundation for risk regulation.[124] At the same time, the Commission is clear in its willingness to retain the ability to defend EU-level risk regulations vis-à-vis the EU's trade partners in instances where regulation was enacted in response to "potential risk" or based on "inconclusive" or "imprecise" evidence. For instance, in its 2000 communication, the Commission reserves for the EU the ability to act when faced with a "level of risk that the public considers appropriate,"[125] acknowledging citizens' fears as a legitimate basis for regulatory intervention.

In practice, the precautionary principle has become a central component of the EU's regulatory decision-making. It has been systematically incorporated into key policy documents,[126] providing a foundation for many regulations, such as REACH, the regulation of beef hormones, and GMOs.[127] The European courts have also been consistent in endorsing the principle[128] by granting the Commission wide discretion to act based on precaution.[129] The ECJ even elevated the precautionary principle to the status of a "general principle" of EU law in its *Artegodan* judgment,[130] further demonstrating the Court's strong approval of precautionary standards. This stands in stark contrast to US courts, which have exercised relatively strict scrutiny when reviewing agencies' regulatory measures.

PART II DESCRIBES in detail many selected policy areas where the Brussels Effect has already emerged. One common feature in all those areas is that the EU has exhibited a manifest preference for stringent regulation. These include competition policy and data protection, as well as the desire to limit hate speech online. They also include policies to protect the health and safety of consumers and citizens as well as the protection of the environment. These areas reflect the prevalent view in Europe that markets fail to deliver optimal outcomes, necessitating the government to step in. They also reflect the precautionary view according to which the EU is prepared to err on the side of intervention to prevent the harm from occurring. What they further have in common is the degree to which the European citizens and policy makers agree on the benefits of intervention and hence the necessity of stringent rule-making.

Yet it is important to note that there are policy areas where the EU fails to become the source of global standards because its regulatory propensity—the preference for high standards—is absent or where other economic powers prefer even higher standards. In some instances, all or most EU member states share a preference for low as opposed to high regulation. Often the EU's missing regulatory propensity, however, reflects a preference heterogeneity across the member states. Online gambling is an example of an area where harmonization within the EU has failed,[131] with the United Kingdom favoring legalization of online gambling, while countries such as Germany and France resisting legalization in an attempt to protect their state monopolies or licensing regimes on gambling.[132] The lack of a sufficient consensus within the EU itself means the EU has no common regulatory position to export.[133]

The EU is also divided on the question of corporate tax harmonization with countries such as Ireland (with its 12.5% corporate tax rate) opposing any step toward tax harmonization, and countries such as France (with its 33% corporate tax rate) endorsing common rules.[134] Given the requirement for unanimity in this area, it very unlikely that the EU could successfully harmonize tax rates or set some minimum levels for corporate taxation. Recognizing the difficulty of harmonizing tax rates, the EU is actively considering a proposal relating to a Common Consolidated Corporate Tax Base proposition (CCCTB).[135] The purpose of the CCCTB would be to standardize how large companies calculate their taxable profits and how they should allocate those profits to different parts of their business.[136] This could curtail companies' abilities to engage in aggressive tax planning by shifting their profits to low-tax jurisdictions.[137] Even though the proposal would leave actual corporate tax rates for each member state to decide, the CCCTB faces obstacles from countries such as Ireland. Ireland fears that profits currently taxed there could in the future be apportioned to other EU countries, shifting tax revenue away from the country and compromising Ireland's attractiveness as a low-tax jurisdiction.[138]

The EU's global regulatory clout is also limited in instances where other states prefer higher standards. For example, while the EU is generally more stringent on the regulation of food safety, the United State mandates pasteurization for all milk and milk products, whereas the EU allows for the sale, marketing, and distribution of raw milk.[139] The United States has also acted before the EU in regulating trans fats in food, banning partially hydrogenated oils since 2018,[140] while the EU is only in the process of carrying out impact assessments and consultations in preparation for a regulation of this area.[141]

Similarly, the United States' Sarbanes–Oxley Act of 2002 (Sarbanes–Oxley), which sought to improve corporate responsibility in the post-Enron environment, is widely perceived as establishing the highest global standard for corporate governance.[142] Another manifestation of the United States' preference for stringent financial regulation is the Dodd–Frank Wall Street Reform and Consumer Protection Act of 2010.[143] Where the United States opts for stringent standards, it can become the source of global standards, assuming the conditions for unilateral regulatory globalization are met. As the United States' recent regulatory pursuits have predominantly targeted the financial sector, it is unlikely that these rules will become global standards because of the elasticity of capital. For instance, it has been debated whether the effect of Sarbanes–Oxley was to heighten financial regulation standards worldwide, or to cause US stock exchanges to lose listings of foreign corporations.[144] In any event, it is evident that the EU's ability to set global rules alone is always contingent on it preferring the highest rule.

There may also be situations where one jurisdiction is most stringent on one dimension of a regulation but another country most stringent on another dimension. When that is the case, the EU standard does not incorporate all other standards, ensuring compliance worldwide. In instances where the corporations are unable to segment the markets, corporations may thus end up adhering to even more stringent standards than any single regulator would have required. The regulation of conflict minerals offers an example of an area where the EU and United States have both responded with stringent, yet somewhat different, standards. Conflict minerals refer to minerals extracted in conflict zones and traded to benefit the armed groups engaged in fighting. The US regulation is more stringent in the sense that it extends liability to downstream operators in addition to direct importers. In contrast, the EU regulation only covers direct importers.[145] At the same time, the geographical scope of the EU regulation is expected to be ultimately wider,[146] covering conflict minerals extracted in all "conflict affected and high-risk areas" in the world.[147] The EU regulation also imposes broader due diligence requirements.[148] Thus here, a multinational corporation engaged in this field typically has to comply with at least two different regulatory regimes—both stringent on different dimensions—to ensure its global compliance.

Another example comes from data protection. India's new proposed data protection regulation emulates many of the provisions embedded in the EU's data protection regulation (GDPR) but, in some ways, goes beyond the GDPR. For example, the Indian law, if adopted, would impose a general duty to process personal data in a fair and reasonable manner that respects the privacy of the individual.[149] This is in line with designating the data controller as a "data fiduciary" under an Indian draft bill,[150] which comes with more onerous obligations regarding the processing of personal data than data controllers have under the GDPR. The Indian draft bill also contains a generalized data localization requirement,[151] under which "a data fiduciary shall ensure the storage, on a server or data centre located in India, of at least one serving copy of personal data." Additionally, for certain categories of personal data that are determined by the Indian government, these categories of data can only be processed in India.[152]

These examples illustrate scenarios under which corporations may face multiple cumulative regulatory standards, potentially forcing them to conform to the combination of the most stringent regulations provided by different jurisdictions. Consequently, this could lead to an even more forceful version of unilateral regulatory globalization, where the global rule is racheted up by an interplay of regulations provided by different jurisdictions, as opposed to by the EU regulation alone. This amplified version of the Brussels Effect further highlights the central role that the relative stringency of regulations plays in explaining which jurisdiction(s) ultimately set the rules for the global marketplace.

Inelastic Targets

Stringent domestic regulations can operate as global standards only when aimed at inelastic—as opposed to elastic—targets.[153] "Inelastic targets" refer to products or producers that are non-responsive to regulatory change and hence tied to a certain regulatory regime. For example, when the EU regulates consumer health and safety, the targets of these regulations are products sold to consumers in the EU market. The location of the consumer within the EU, as opposed to the location of the manufacturer, determines the application of EU regulation to the targeted product. The inelastic nature of consumer markets does not leave producers with a choice regarding the jurisdiction; they cannot "shop" for favorable regulations without losing access to the regulated market. This makes the target producer inelastic or, using another word, immobile. The EU primarily regulates inelastic consumer markets, such as food safety or data privacy.

To illustrate the distinction between elastic and inelastic targets, consider the capital and consumer markets. Elastic regulatory targets, such as capital, are more mobile and thus can easily be moved to a different jurisdiction. In contrast, consumers of food, or data subjects bestowed with privacy rights, are typically immobile. Food manufacturers or data controllers cannot choose which sets of rules they apply to those consumers or data subjects, making it impossible to circumvent EU standards. Whenever a firm wants to sell products to the EU's over five hundred million consumers, it needs to comply with the EU's consumer protection regulations; these consumers cannot simply be transferred to a jurisdiction where lesser protections govern what products can be sold to them.

The examples of the Brussels Effect discussed in this book all involve inelastic targets that are difficult to detach from the EU's regulatory domain. For example, the REACH regulation on chemical safety is indifferent as to which company produces a restricted chemical or where the chemical is produced: as long as a chemical product is sold on the European market, REACH applies.[154] Many of the EU's environmental regulations follow the same logic: for example, the Restriction of Hazardous Substances (RoHS) Directive restricts the use of hazardous substances in electronics whenever such electronics are sold on the European market.[155] The manufacturer's location is irrelevant—moving to a new location will not allow the manufacturer to circumvent RoHS without losing access to the EU market. EU competition law is similarly indifferent with respect to the nationality of the companies regulated or the place where the anticompetitive conduct occurs. As long as a firm's conduct has an effect on the EU market, EU competition law applies. The EU's data protection regime, the GDPR, likewise applies to all companies processing personal data of data subjects residing in the EU, regardless of where the data processing takes place or where the company processing the data is located.[156] The company therefore cannot evade EU rules by relocating its data controllers or processors outside the EU. In each of these instances, the EU can effectively assert regulatory authority over market participants without fear of its regulatory targets evading regulation by moving to another jurisdiction.

This reality contrasts sharply with, for example, corporate law—where a global corporation has wide freedom in deciding what nationality to incorporate in without limiting its access to global markets. Another example is maritime law, where a shipping company can choose what flag its ships sail under without losing access to international ports. In such cases where the regulatory regime is determined by the location of the company's headquarters or place of incorporation, companies have a choice over what regulations will apply to them. In those instances, elastic regulatory targets—here, the incorporating company—have the ability, and in fact the incentive, to incorporate in the jurisdiction that offers the most favorable regulatory framework. The place of incorporation is relevant, for example, in determining the tax regime that applies to a corporation. Similarly, a company gearing up for an initial public offering (IPO) can choose from over a hundred stock exchanges for its listing. The regulatory burden of the jurisdiction is one relevant consideration in making that choice, given that the IPO destination determines the rules and requirements that apply to the listing and subsequent trading of the company's securities.

The challenge of regulating stock markets illustrates how difficult it is to assert jurisdiction over elastic targets such as capital. For example, Nikhil Kalyanpur and Abraham Newman examined the number of delistings from the US stock market following the adoption of the Sarbanes–Oxley Act of 2002, which introduced more stringent standards on public company accounting and investor protection.[157] While many foreign companies exhibited "inelastic behavior" in response to the new stringent rules—retaining their US stock market listing because the cost of exiting, relative to the regulatory burden, was too high—a notable number of EU-based companies responded with "elastic behavior" and switched their listing to the EU. The delisting was facilitated not only by the size of the EU market but also by the EU's credible institutional structure governing that market, including the introduction of a common set of accounting rules and the ability to issue Euro-denominated bonds. This suggests that capital is, indeed, often elastic and can move as long as a credible exit opportunity exists.

The regulation of over-the-counter derivatives (known as "swaps" in the United States) presents another example of financial regulation that deals with a highly elastic target. In the aftermath of the financial crises, both the EU and United States proceeded to regulate the derivatives market by requiring their central clearing. Such reliance on central counterparties (CCPs), as opposed to private bilateral contracts for clearing, concentrates the market risk with clearing houses. These specialized firms, reformers argued, are easier to regulate than disperse market participants.[158] Derivatives clearing relies on a jurisdictionally detached financial infrastructure in that it can take place in any jurisdiction in which parties to the contract reside or in any jurisdiction whose law the parties choose to govern the contract. According to a study by Yesha Yadov and Dermot Turing, traders of credit derivative contracts (credit default swaps) conduct business four times more often with counterparties outside their own jurisdiction than they do with counterparties in their home jurisdiction.[159] The authors illustrate this flexibility with the following example:

> [A] Swiss bank [...] enters into a fixed-floating interest rate swap on a notional principal amount expressed in British Pounds, where its counterparty is the New York branch of a Japanese bank. Such a transaction may be documented under New York law and supported by collateral that includes German Government bonds held in Euroclear (which is located in Belgium and operates under Belgian law).[160]

The absence of a requisite geographical link between a particular clearing-house and the parties to the transaction means that the parties have a choice as to where to conduct their clearing activities.[161] This high degree of elasticity suggests that regulators like the EU's ESMA—the European Securities and Markets Authority—face a serious threat of regulatory arbitrage. The CCPs can migrate to less-burdensome jurisdictions without difficulty if the EU regulation hinders their ability to offer services to their clients on a competitive basis.[162] Because there is nothing irreplaceable about the EU clearing markets that the CCPs lose by migrating to avoid the regulation, it is unlikely the EU would be able to promulgate overly stringent regulations and maintain an active market.

The examples mentioned reinforce the argument that capital, while not perfectly elastic, is significantly more elastic than consumer markets.[163] If the EU, for instance, tried to harmonize corporate taxation at excessively high rates, a number of corporations could flee its jurisdiction and incorporate elsewhere. Of course, this migration would not come without costs. However, the EU could only regulate to the point where the regulatory burden was less than the relatively low cost of relocating. In contrast, an inelastic consumer market allows the EU to regulate up to the point where the regulatory burden is less than the significantly higher cost of exiting the European consumer market entirely.

Similarly, if the EU were to impose a tax on financial transactions, as the Commission proposed in the wake of the Euro crises, trading activity could move to financial centers outside the EU.[164] The proposed tax would cover a broad range of financial transactions between banks and other financial institutions, including securities, bonds, currency transactions, and derivatives.[165] It is unclear if the proposal is politically viable,[166] particularly given the EU's recognition that the introduction of this tax could cause EU-based financial institutions to relocate to non-EU countries.[167] This reality constrains the EU's ability to successfully exert similar regulatory influence in taxing the trading of stocks, bonds, or derivatives, as it can over more inelastic targets.[168]

Elasticity of targets may pose similar limits to the EU's ability to regulate other aspects of corporate governance, including bankers' "bonus caps," which the EU has introduced.[169] Of course, corporate activity may not immediately respond to the introduction of caps in executive compensation by relocating outside the EU. Yet the EU's regulatory power remains constrained by the fact that, at some level, regulation may become onerous enough to create incentives for firms to relocate to less regulated jurisdictions.

Interestingly, the Commission has recently advocated some regulatory measures that would constrain the elasticity of capital and make it more inelastic in practice. For example, the Commission has proposed a major corporate tax reform that would standardize the way large corporations allocate their profits to different parts of their business.[170] While leaving the actual level of corporate taxation unregulated, this reform would restrict companies' ability to shift their profits to low-tax jurisdictions, limiting the de facto mobility of capital as a result. The EU is also considering a "digital tax," which would tax digital companies based on where they generate advertising revenue as opposed to where they claim their profits.[171] This would similarly eliminate these firms' ability to book profits in low-tax jurisdictions, forcing them to pay taxes in countries where actual value is created or business generated. If adopted, this tax would restrain the elasticity of corporate profits by attaching tax liability to the jurisdiction where the value is created, revenue earned, and customers located.

While most elastic regulatory targets pertain to the regulation of capital markets, other examples can be found elsewhere. For instance, the ECJ's recent denial of the patentability of embryonic stem cells is unlikely to lead to a global standard.[172] Critics claim that the EU's regulatory stringency only drives stem cell research and business out of the EU, highlighting the elasticity of patent protection and the mobility of the industry relying on patents.[173] Stem cell research remains patentable in many parts of the world, including the United States, where critical research activity could easily relocate in response to the EU's strict regulatory stance.[174] Another example comes from the EU's approach to regulating waste management. High standards for waste disposal are costly for domestic producers, and so producers gain little by disposing or recycling their waste in the EU.[175] Waste is movable, and illegal transfers of hazardous waste remain common as producers have an incentive to evade stringent regulations by finding jurisdictions that do not enforce waste management standards.[176]

The discussion of the elastic versus inelastic nature of regulatory targets is closely related to the literature on regulatory races and jurisdictional competition.[177] The early literature argued that globalization produces a "race to the bottom," which leads states to lower their regulatory standards in order to attract firms and capital. According to this view, mobile capital exploits regulatory arbitrage and locates to a jurisdiction where it can earn the highest rate of return. These returns are higher when firms are not burdened by high corporate tax rates or stringent labor or environmental protection standards. Other states then respond by lowering their respective regulatory standards to avoid capital flight.[178] The result of this race is, theoretically, regulatory convergence at the bottom. However, subsequent empirical studies have questioned the extent to which a race to the bottom occurs in practice.[179] Influential literature has further emerged to argue that economic globalization has instead produced a "race to the top," where countries are elevating their regulatory standards in response to first mover regulators' introduction of stringent regulatory standards.[180]

While empirical support for a global race to the bottom is limited, most would agree that corporate relocation is more likely in instances where the firm can freely select its regulatory jurisdictions (such as stock listing) without any need to physically move its operations to another jurisdiction.[181] In such instances, recent research demonstrates an occurrence of "Tiebout sorting" where no race to the top or bottom can be observed, but where firms instead sort themselves across jurisdictions depending on their differential cost structures, heterogeneous preferences, and market segments.[182] Some firms are likely to prefer lower regulatory standards, while others, in fact, prefer higher regulatory standards. Under this assumption, (some) elastic targets are likely to move to less-burdensome jurisdictions while others stay in more stringent jurisdictions and simply absorb higher costs. To the extent this sorting happens, certain regulatory targets are able to constrain the Brussels Effect by exiting to less-burdensome markets, or by threatening to do so.

Focusing on inelasticity of regulatory targets helps further illustrate why we observe the "Brussels Effect" more commonly than the "Washington Effect." The United States' regulatory efforts have predominantly targeted the more elastic financial sector in recent decades, making the United States a less likely source of global standards. In contrast, the EU's focus of regulating consumer markets and the environment has reinforced its role as a global standard setter whose regulations cannot be undermined by the elasticity of its targets. In this sense, governments are not typically able to influence the elasticity or inelasticity of their regulatory targets as such; elasticity is an inherent feature of the target itself, such as capital—which is typically elastic—or consumer goods—which are typically inelastic. However, the governments do retain influence over the choice of the types of targets they choose to regulate. Unlike the EU, the United States has chosen to regulate elastic targets, with an unintended side effect that it can rarely rely on markets to externalize its regulations outside its domestic jurisdiction.

Non-divisibility

The conditions just described only ensure that the stringent jurisdiction is able to regulate extraterritorially. The EU meeting these conditions does not, by itself, mean that the stringent standard will actually be globalized. The Brussels Effect is only triggered when the multinational corporation, after having converted its products or business practices to comply with the EU standard, decides to apply this new standard to its products or conduct worldwide. In other words, global standards emerge only when corporations voluntarily opt to extend the regulatory requirements of the most stringent regulator to their global operations.

A company has the greatest incentive to adopt a global standard whenever its production or conduct is non-divisible across different markets. Non-divisibility refers to the practice of standardizing—as opposed to customizing—production or business practices across jurisdictions and hence applying a uniform standard to govern the corporation's global conduct. Often this will occur when the benefits of a uniform standard due to scale economies exceed the costs of forgoing lower costs in less regulated markets. For example, complying with just one regulatory standard allows a corporation to maintain a single production process, which is less costly than tailoring its production to meet divergent regulatory standards.[183] When opting for standardization, a corporation further prefers to conform to the "leading standard,"[184] which typically is the most demanding standard imposed by a major jurisdiction that represents an important market for the corporation. This leading standard is particularly attractive in that it typically incorporates other standards as well, ensuring compliance across all markets in which the corporation operates.

For a simple illustration of non-divisibility, imagine someone hosting a dinner party and inviting eight guests. Two of them do not eat red meat. One other guest prefers red meat but happily eats everything—as long as it is gluten-free. The host could prepare a tailored meal for everyone, offering options with and without red meat and with and without gluten. However, the host is more likely to opt for fish and keep all dishes gluten-free to limit the time, hassle, and expense associated with customizing the dinner party experience to everyone's distinct dietary preferences. In the end, when faced with a variety of dietary restrictions, the most restrictive diet wins: a gluten-free and meat-free dish is served. For the same reason, schools often tailor their policies with a similar eye toward non-divisibility. While the school may only have a handful of students with a peanut allergy, the entire school adopts a nut-free policy to accommodate the more-restrictive needs of the minority.

The same principle applies for global producers serving many different markets, particularly when they cannot economically or practically tailor their production for every market. As the Brussels Effect encourages firms to standardize production, it also unavoidably limits the product variety that is available on the market. In the process, it produces a variation of the "tyranny of the market" originally described by Joel Waldfogel.[185] Waldfogel argues that markets do not produce efficient outcomes when fixed costs limit the number of product varieties that firms can economically produce. In these instances, only the majority's preferences will be satisfied. Waldfogel compares this market-driven outcome to the outcome produced by a political process where the "tyranny of the majority" dictates electoral outcomes, challenging the pro-market belief that markets always deliver more efficient outcomes. Markets thus entail shortcomings akin to the shortcomings associated with voting. Furthermore, with the growth in international trade, we may increasingly witness "the tyranny of alien majorities," as domestic producers operating on a global marketplace adjust their production patterns to cater to the majorities who may consist of predominantly foreign consumers.

The Brussels Effect partially validates and partially challenges this theory. The Brussels Effect differs from the tyranny of the market in that instead of simply the market dictating global standards, it is the duality of both the market *and* the government that gives rise to uniform production. Instead of focusing on market actors and fixed costs as a limitation to product variety, the Brussels Effect emphasizes government regulation and multiple factors—law, technology, and economics—as drivers of non-divisibility and hence lower product variety. This distinction points to the tyranny of the government as much as to that of the market.

Whenever producers offer only the EU-variant of the product globally, the market does not, indeed, seem to produce optimal outcomes for all consumers. For example, for many Americans, the Brussels Effect may represent an example of "the tyranny of alien majorities" where the EU can dictate the products available to them. However, globally, the Brussels Effect may also be seen as a manifestation of the "tyranny of the regulated alien *minority*" more than that of the global majority, further departing from the argument underlying the tyranny of the market. The product varieties that are offered can be interpreted as reflecting the stringency of government regulation as opposed to solely consumer choice. This is so even if market forces are critical in entrenching those choices globally. Regardless of the outcome, the Brussels Effect offers an alternative explanation for why firms forgo product variety and cater predominantly to customers in the most regulated jurisdictions.

Leaving aside the normative question on whether the Brussels Effect should even be viewed as a "tyranny" of any kind, the next discussion will focus on illustrating different types of non-divisibility. Non-divisibility of a corporation's production or conduct comes in three primary varieties: legal non-divisibility, technical non-divisibility, and economic non-divisibility—the last one being the most common variant driving the Brussels Effect. The discussion reviews the logic underpinning each type of non-divisibility and provides examples to illustrate how this feature leads businesses to standardize their production across the global marketplace.

Legal Non-divisibility

"Legal non-divisibility" refers to legal requirements and remedies as drivers of uniform standards. It typically manifests itself as a spillover effect that follows from the corporation's compliance with the laws of the most stringent jurisdiction. Global mergers provide an illustrative example in that they cannot be consummated on a jurisdiction-by-jurisdiction basis. Instead, the most stringent competition jurisdiction gets to determine the worldwide fate of the transaction.[186] For example, when the EU requires the company to spin off an asset as a condition for approving a merger—like ordering a divestiture of a production plant—such a divestiture cannot be consummated in the EU only. For the same reason, whenever the EU prohibits an anticompetitive merger, the transaction is banned worldwide. Facing the EU prohibition, the only way to proceed with the merger would require the parties to carve out enough assets from the transaction to strip the EU of jurisdiction over the merger. Given the importance of the EU market, such restructuring of the deal would often require a complete withdrawal from the EU market, removing the business rationale for the merger. This makes it all but impossible to circumvent the EU jurisdiction in practice.

Cartel remedies often have a similarly global effect. Leniency programs designed to destabilize cartels by incentivizing cartel participants to act as whistle-blowers often dissolve the cartel across all jurisdictions.[187] Thus, even if the European Commission implemented a leniency program aimed at seizing collusion that affects prices in Europe, cooperation with the Commission is likely to also unravel the collusion in other markets. This is because the trust sustaining the cartel among participating firms dissipates with such a defection. Similarly, if the Commission detects and pursues a cartel following its own investigation (as opposed to following a leniency application), the cartel participants likely abandon collusion worldwide. The cartel participants know that the Commission investigation will likely alert foreign authorities to the possibility of collusion in their markets as well, making the operation of the cartel in practice non-divisible whenever a major jurisdiction such as the EU proceeds to dismantle it.

While not manifesting a pure form of legal non-divisibility, legal risks associated with compliance errors induce companies to adopt internal policies that govern the company's global operations. These company-wide policies typically reflect the legal standards prevailing in the most demanding jurisdiction. For example, even if price fixing remains unregulated and hence potentially beneficial in some markets, most companies refrain from colluding even in those markets. Multinational corporations typically maintain a global compliance manual that prohibits discussion of prices with competitors regardless of the jurisdiction involved. This ensures that noncompliance does not accidentally spill into company practices in markets that maintain stringent regulation on price fixing, exposing the company to legal liability. When the management can monitor internally consistent company policies across all the markets in which the company operates, the risk-adjusted compliance costs are lower. This need to minimize compliance errors is even greater for listed companies because the stock price is not affected only by the legal risks materializing in the listing jurisdiction. Instead, the prospect of legal liability in any jurisdiction can destabilize a company's operations worldwide, adversely affecting its stock price.

The tendency to deploy standardized contracts manifest forces of both legal and economic non-divisibility.[188] When the company uses standardized clauses in its distribution contracts across multiple markets, internal monitoring processes are streamlined, resulting in fewer compliance failures and greater efficiencies. For example, a global company is unlikely to negotiate its licensing agreements or distribution agreements with numerous licensees or distributors anew in each market. Instead, those agreements are likely to be highly standardized.

Legal non-divisibility can further stem from the company's choice on the place of incorporation, which can expand the set of business operations that fall under the legal requirements of the chosen jurisdiction. Data protection regulation in the EU provides an example of this scenario. Since Facebook has its headquarters in Ireland, the GDPR applies to all Facebook entities that are part of the Irish corporate structure.[189] Until recently, most non-EU users outside the United States have been governed by the Irish corporate entity. By choosing to incorporate in Dublin, Facebook has therefore assumed a legal obligation to offer EU's privacy protections to data subjects outside the EU as well, making the rights enjoyed by Facebook users outside the EU legally non-divisible from those enjoyed by Facebook users in the EU. Interestingly, as will be discussed in chapter 5, in response to the entry into force of the GDPR, Facebook has revised its terms and conditions, moving users in Asia, Africa, Australia, and the Middle East away from the EU and placing them under its US legal structure. This allows Facebook to introduce divisibility, limiting the rights of non-EU users to complain about any foreign data protection violations to the data protection officers in Ireland.[190]

Technical Non-divisibility

The principle of "technical non-divisibility" refers to the difficulty of separating the firm's production or services across multiple markets for technological reasons. It often applies to the regulation of data privacy. For example, to operate in the EU, Google has to amend its data storage and other business practices to conform to European data protection standards. Given the difficulty of determining with certainty whether a particular user is a "European data subject," Google cannot easily isolate its data collection for the EU. As a result, Google adopts a strategy whereby the company adjusts its global operations to the most demanding EU standard.[191]

With the entry into force of the GDPR, companies are obliged to design their products with EU's regulatory requirements in mind. As will be discussed in chapter 5, companies including Microsoft and Apple follow this principle by incorporating the GDPR requirements into the initial technical design of their products, making privacy-consistent technological solutions on behalf of the consumer at the outset. It is, obviously, much harder to make such technically embedded data protections divisible across jurisdictions. Whether the consumer, as the "data subject," operates the devices in the EU or in a third country, the consumer is likely to adhere to the default settings incorporated in the device at the development stage. Thus, the GDPR's "privacy by design" principle, incorporated in Article 25 of the regulation, increasingly ensures that products are designed to a single standard, with the EU determining the default settings as the most stringent regulator of data protection.

A very different example of technical non-divisibility is the EU's general regulation of food safety and GMOs in particular.[192] This regulation has led to standardized production in farming industries where cross-contamination between crops can take place. For example, some farmers are deterred from using GMOs if they also want to produce non-GMO varieties for Europe due to the risks associated with cross-pollination and the resulting "adventitious presence" of GMOs in non-GMOs grown in neighboring fields. This type of contamination can occur in the growing, storage, or transportation stage of production if one fails to separate, however inadvertently, the GMO varieties from non-GMO varieties.[193] The same logic applies to pesticides and other chemicals used by the farming industry. It is often difficult to ensure that pesticides used in one field do not affect crops in adjoining fields due to the technical impossibility of preventing cross-pollination. Similarly, while farmers may sell different cuts of meat derived from the same animal to multiple geographical markets, the EU's meat safety and hygiene standards affect all markets due to the obvious impossibility to limiting the use of growth hormones or certain sterilization methods to only one part of the animal.

Economic Non-divisibility

Often companies are able to identify a technological solution that allows them to produce different product varieties for different markets. However, the underlying economics—in particular, the importance of scale economies associated with uniform production—can make such division untenable in practice. This type of "economic non-divisibility" is perhaps the most common reason why manufacturers opt for a global standard, and is most typically exemplified in corporations' responses to the EU's health, environmental, and product standards. An illustrative example is European chemical regulation, which applies to all companies seeking to enter the EU market.[194] Numerous US manufacturers, in the cases where they would find it too costly to develop different products for different consumer markets, choose to conform their entire global chemical production to the EU standard.[195] The scale economies associated with a single global production process therefore often allow the EU to effectively dictate global product standards. Other important drivers for economic non-divisibility are related to brand and reputation.

The benefits associated with scale economies often explain the observed preference for uniform production. When a company produces a greater quantity of a standardized product variety for its home and (potentially multiple) export markets, it saves costs in numerous ways.[196] Standardization allows it to buy production inputs in bulk, leading to a lower procurement cost per unit purchased. Production costs further decline when the firm forgoes the need to adjust the manufacturing processes and equipment used for different product varieties. Scale economies are particularly important in the presence of high fixed costs, as such costs often lead to a higher optimal scale, which incentives standardization in an effort to recover those costs. For example, large firms can carry out sophisticated research and development (R&D) more easily. The pharmaceutical industry is the prime example of an industry where R&D is crucial, giving companies the incentive to merge in an effort to spread their R&D expenditures across a greater volume of sales. This leads to a higher incentive for production of largely standardized pharmaceutical products for the global marketplace.[197]

We also expect to see uniform production in capital-intensive industries, or in industries relying on highly integrated global supply chains or inward foreign direct investment (FDI) in technology. For example, the majority of FDI in developing countries' automotive sectors originates from multinational corporations that also operate in developed countries' highly regulated markets. These multinationals are unlikely to change their production processes that were engineered to comply with the more stringent standards prevailing in the markets of major developed countries. This allows them to take advantage of scale economies in production and deploy similar technologies across their global or regional manufacturing networks.[198] This helps to explain why many automobiles sold in less regulated developing markets often meet the safety and environmental standards that prevail in leading markets characterized by stringent regulatory standards.

The automotive sector also tends to utilize a transnational assembly line where the different components that constitute a finished automobile are produced in multiple countries before their final assembly. Harmonized standards across different markets allow the manufacturers to achieve greater economies of scale as the same components and technologies can be used for cars sold in multiple markets.[199] This is an example that was first used to demonstrate the

"California Effect," which refers to California's emissions standards' emergence as the de facto US national standard for all US automobile manufacturing in 1990s. The California Effect occurred precisely because it was cheaper for automobile manufacturers to produce all cars to a single standard, distributing the costs of complying with California standards throughout all states, including those that placed no value on the environmental benefits of those standards.[200] A similar example comes from Europe and its stringent safety rules. Those regulations required General Motors to retool its Corvette factory in Kentucky because the cost of having to design and produce special parts just for the European market would have been hard to justify.[201]

Economic non-divisibility is also associated with simplification in manufacturing or service provision, leading to additional cost savings and safer products.[202] Adhering to a single global standard improves product quality as the company can concentrate its resources on producing a single product (or a smaller range of products) and focus on refining all aspects of that product. This reduces the complexity of operations and minimizes error costs. Be it product design, R&D, testing, inventory management, storage, marketing, or distribution, the uniform product standard streamlines those processes and reduces costs associated with all these stages.[203] The importance of scale economies associated with quality control has driven global production patterns and company size in industries as different as global trade in bananas or manufacturing of new pharmaceutical products.[204]

The agricultural sector offers additional examples why companies choose a uniform standard for economic reasons. For example, when the EU banned hormone-treated beef from its market, it became uneconomical for US meat producers to produce both hormone and hormone-free beef because the cost of distributing hormone-free beef in the existing distribution system would have been prohibitively high and led to losses.[205] Similarly, several US food processors selling their products internationally refused to buy genetically modified corn or soybeans in response to the EU's strict regulation of GMOs.[206] Doing so would have required them to make special non-GMO batches just for Europe, which was uneconomical. Given the importance of continued access to the European market, food processors could not ignore the EU standard and only serve countries that accepted GMOs. For this reason, the Illinois Department of Agriculture, for instance, asked farmers not to plant a type of corn from Monsanto that did not have EU approval.[207]

There are other scale advantages for corporations to prefer harmonization of global product offerings and incentivize them to retain that harmonization, once established. For example, a single product allows the company to easily divert exports to other markets whenever demand fluctuates across different markets.

Offering a standardized product across markets therefore reduces the need to accurately predict demand for each market. If the demand stagnates in one country due to economic malaise, change in consumer preferences, problems in the distribution chain, economic sanctions, or any other reason, the company may divert some of its products to an alternative market as long as it sells the same product in that market. For example, if General Motors had a different product range for each of its markets, then its decision to withdraw from India, Russia, and South Africa would have rendered the investments it had already made in those markets a sunk cost.[208] Instead, offering the same vehicles in multiple markets allows the company to divert the production originally aimed for those markets to its home or other export markets. Thus, producing to a single global standard provides the company the important ability to adjust to changing market conditions.

Beyond the advantages due to scale, a single standard also facilitates the preservation of a global brand and reputation.[209] Standardization allows for a uniform branding and advertising strategy, reducing costs from having to engage in mass advertising across different markets. For example, companies like Pepsi save millions of dollars each year by having common global branding.[210] A uniform brand name can also lead to cost savings in distribution, inventory, and packaging.[211] Trust in a brand and its uniform quality allows the consumer to forgo uncertainty and reduce search costs associated with product choices in a new market. For example, a frequent business traveler may stay loyal to the same hotel chain across the world due to familiarity with the brand. This is one of the reasons Hilton rooms look similar irrespective of the destination, and the services offered are largely standardized across markets.[212] This cultivates a sense of home for travelers as the room and amenities remain consistent across destinations. This feature sustains consumer loyalty, leading the consumer to choose the same product across jurisdictions.

Many global firms choose to comply with EU regulations outside the EU to protect their global brands and reputation even in the absence of a legal obligation to do so.[213] Extending the EU's privacy protections to US customers gives Google the opportunity to enhance the value of its global brand by conveying that it takes the privacy of its US users as seriously as it takes that of its European users. An opposite strategy would likely lead to a dissatisfaction by US consumers, who would be aware that the company was consciously leaving its US customers with lesser protections even though it had the ability and willingness to offer these protections elsewhere. Similarly, a company's brand could be tarnished globally if the company took advantage of lax standards on child labor or environmental practices in some foreign jurisdictions, risking that their customers abandon the product even if these practices did not take place in their home jurisdiction. For example, confectioner giant Nestlé has been plagued by reports in Western media that it employed child labor in its supply chain in Africa and South America.[214]

Activist pressures have given further impetus for companies to obey the most demanding standards across all markets in which they operate. Industries that produce consumer products, such as household goods or cosmetics, are common targets of such pressures. Consumer awareness is often further increased in the case of high-profile regulatory failures, or whenever a brand name is involved, as the public can relate to those products. In these instances, consumers and activists can easily call out the company for its efforts to exploit regulatory arbitrage and take advantage of less-burdensome obligations in some markets rather than others. Public campaigns by non-governmental organizations (NGOs) and other activists can effectively expose the double standards of multinational companies, if they, for example, continue to use or produce chemicals in the rest of the world that they no longer use in the EU.[215] As a result, many cosmetics firms protect the reputation of their highly visible and valuable brands by conforming to European standards worldwide.[216]

WHILE MULTIPLE PRESSURES for standardization exist, many products or types of conduct remain divisible, limiting the Brussels Effect. When products do not call for a uniform standard, the EU can at best achieve compliance with its standard, but not globalization of those standards. Consider the attempts to regulate labor standards. Labor markets are divisible as long as scale economies do not require the producer to concentrate production into a single production location. Adhering to one global minimum wage across jurisdictions, for instance, entails few scale economies. A corporation can therefore maintain different standards in different jurisdictions without difficulty—ranging from working hours and vacation policies to retirement plans and collective labor strategies.[217]

Several other products are also divisible across markets, and so evade global regulation through the Brussels Effect. DVDs have different region codes allowing film distributors to segregate release dates, content restrictions, and price across regions. Books and magazines are published in different languages in different jurisdictions. Patent protection, discussed earlier, is also divisible: the EU's ability to impose its rules on the patentability of human cells is constrained not only by the mobility of research firms but also by the ability of these firms to continue filing patents in other jurisdictions. Another example comes from competition law. In 2007, the EU launched an antitrust investigation into whether Microsoft's practice of offering its Windows software with only one internet browser, the Microsoft-owned Internet Explorer, presented antitrust concerns. In response, Microsoft presented Windows 7 E, a Europe-only version of Windows that came with no internet browser.[218] Similarly, in response to the EU's competition ruling banning Google from giving more prominent placement to its own comparison-shopping service (as opposed to its rivals') in its search results, Google spun off its comparison-shopping service in Europe into a stand-alone unit, thus limiting the adopted remedy to the European market only.[219] Finally, Google decided to avoid complying with new domestic copyright legislation in Spain that would have required Google to make payments to Spanish media outlets. Instead, Google decided to remove certain Spanish sources from its broader News service, by simply shutting down its Google News service in Spain[220]—something the company was able to do without also shutting down Google News in other jurisdictions.

At times, variance in consumer preferences limits the benefits of standardization. In the food industry, for example, consumer preferences remain balkanized by jurisdiction across numerous products.[221] For example, Coca-Cola has different levels of sugar for the same product in different markets.[222] Similarly, McDonalds has a highly uniform brand but continues to customize its products and menus across different markets.[223] This stands in stark contrast with the production of drugs designed to treat illnesses, given that consumer preferences rarely vary across the types of drugs, allowing the same drug to serve all markets.[224] In addition, while the automotive industry often benefits from standardized mass production, as discussed earlier, counterexamples exist showing that the industry must also sustain some level of local preference customization.[225]

The examples just discussed suggest that the globalization of EU standards is unlikely to happen whenever the costs of product diversification in some industry or product category remain trivial and where the benefits of customized production are significant. In such instances, firms are expected to make their production divisible and take advantage of the lower standards prevailing in markets outside the EU.[226] However, even in instances where differences in consumer preferences induce companies to produce several varieties, companies often benefit from standardizing the "product platform." They may introduce variety on some aspect of production while continuing to share standardized components and processes across these varieties. This strategy reduces complexity, risks, and the need for inventory, and hence lowers the costs associated with production.[227]

THE PREVIOUS DISCUSSION has argued that a single regulatory jurisdiction is able to supply global standards wherever five conditions hold—a *large domestic market*, sufficient *regulatory capacity*, preference for *stringent standards*, tendency to regulate *inelastic targets*, and *non-divisibility* of production. All of these conditions must be present for unilateral regulatory globalization to occur. For example, without a large market size, corporations may abandon the market of the stringent regulator and divert their trade elsewhere. In such a case, the presence of extensive regulatory capacity or the other remaining conditions are irrelevant. Similarly, if the jurisdiction lacks the regulatory capacity or fails to promulgate the most stringent standard, other jurisdictions may supersede its standards with those of their own, regardless of the presence of other conditions. Finally, if regulatory targets are elastic or corporate conduct divisible, multinational corporations may elect to move to less-burdensome jurisdictions or forgo a global standard in favor of customization across different markets, undercutting the Brussels Effect regardless of the strength of other conditions.

While all necessary, these conditions may vary in their relative significance across policy areas. For example, some policy areas are more complex to regulate—including the monitoring of the competitive conduct or data processing practices of technology companies—accentuating the importance of regulatory capacity in the theory. Some conditions may also be more invariant across policy areas—such as market size or regulatory capacity—while others are likely to be more variant—including non-divisibility that depends on a range of industry- and firm-specific considerations. Finally, the first three conditions are typically relevant as opposed to absolute. What matters is the relative market size, relative regulatory capacity, and the relative regulatory stringency, as compared to other larger economies. For example, there is no absolute market size that triggers the Brussels Effect. Instead, what matters is whether businesses can afford to forgo a large market, which depends not merely on the size of that particular market but also on the size of the other consumer markets that may offer an alternative destination for their products and services.

While developed to explain the Brussels Effect and the EU's role as a global regulatory hegemon, the conditions discussed in this chapter are generic as opposed to EU-specific, and hence designed to explain any jurisdiction's ability to unilaterally supply rules for the global marketplace. In this sense, they should outlive the EU's regulatory hegemony and also help us explain if and when such a hegemony might come to an end or be displaced by another unilateral global regulator. These conditions could therefore explain the already mentioned "Washington Effect" or the "Beijing Effect" alike—as long as the United States or China had the combination of the market power, the regulatory capacity, and the political will to generate stringent regulations, together with the desire to pursue inelastic targets that are non-divisible across jurisdictions.

As will be explained in chapter 9, which discusses the future of the Brussels Effect, each condition is also sustained or challenged by somewhat different external forces, influencing their durability over time. For example, the EU's market power will be constrained in the coming decades by the rise of China and other emerging economic powers. Consensus needed to promulgate stringent regulations can be harder in the future if divisions within the EU grow. At the same time, stringent rules may become easier to generate with the departure of the United Kingdom from the EU, which has often opposed the EU's extensive rule-making. Finally, a possible move toward greater divisibility of production is likely to be caused by advances in technology. This further suggests that each element has an independent role in explaining the emergence, or the persistence, of the Brussels Effect.

3

The Brussels Effect in Context

THE BRUSSELS EFFECT is certainly not the only way the EU exercises global regulatory influence. In fact, the EU wields norm-setting power through a number of different channels, including via trade agreements and participation in international institutions and transnational governmental networks. Many countries and regional organizations also adopt EU regulations in other ways, whether by engaging in legislative borrowing, replicating EU institutions, citing legal concepts and principles developed by European courts, or engaging in "copycat" litigation in cases where the EU has acted first. EU norms can similarly act as influential focal points for regulatory convergence, absent any market effects or effort on the EU's part, because of the EU's perceived role as a "normative power."

This chapter first reviews these various other channels of the EU's global regulatory influence in an attempt to provide context for the de facto Brussels Effect discussed in chapter 2. It also examines why EU law offers such an attractive template for emulation, facilitating the de jure Brussels Effect in all its forms. It then assesses the relative advantages and disadvantages of *market-driven harmonization* compared to *treaty-driven harmonization*, and considers when these other channels of influence are likely to complement, amplify, or substitute the Brussels Effect.

The EU's Mechanisms for Global Regulatory Influence

The de facto Brussels Effect refers to the unilateral regulatory power the EU derives from its market. However, the Brussels Effect is not the only manifestation of the EU's unilateral influence. The EU also exerts unilateral influence over foreign actors through legislative techniques such as extraterritoriality or territorial extension. Through these instruments, the EU seeks to directly apply its own regulations to foreign actors. These techniques are distinct from the

The Brussels Effect. Anu Bradford, Oxford University Press (2020). © Oxford University Press.
DOI: 10.1093/oso/9780190088583.001.0001

market-driven harmonization associated with the Brussels Effect or the EU's efforts to project its regulations via treaty-driven harmonization, as will be discussed in this chapter.

As a threshold matter, the Brussels Effect should be distinguished from these other unilateral mechanisms of influence. Some EU regulations are extraterritorial in that they impose obligations on persons who do not have a territorial connection to the EU.[1] For example, EU competition law applies to foreign parties even if their conduct originates abroad. As long as EU consumers are affected, the EU can enforce its laws against these foreign parties to restore competition in the EU. The EU's Derivatives Regulation provides another example of this kind of extraterritoriality. It contains an anti-evasion clause that "imposes obligations on contracts concluded between two entities established in one or more third (non-EU) countries, where the imposition of the obligation is necessary or appropriate to prevent the evasion of the provisions contained in the Regulation."[2]

The EU, however, does not solely rely on such explicit extraterritoriality or effects-based jurisdiction.[3] Rather, the EU also uses a legislative technique that Joanne Scott calls "territorial extension," whereby certain conduct or circumstances abroad establish a territorial connection to the EU.[4] Territorial extension allows the EU to regulate "activities that take place abroad but that also impact negatively upon the EU or upon globally shared resources."[5] The aviation regulations in the EU Emissions Trading Scheme, for example, can be considered an exercise of territorial extension under this characterization because the regulations consider the amount of emissions a flight produces outside of the EU as well as the third-country measures regulating aviation emissions.[6]

These mechanisms just mentioned, while reflecting different dynamics, offer pathways other than the Brussels Effect for the EU to shape the global regulatory environment unilaterally. In addition, the EU can also entrench its norms globally through cooperative mechanisms, such as via bilateral or multilateral treaties. The EU has negotiated an extensive array of economic and political agreements that, in their strongest form, set out the type of regulations that the EU's trade partners must adopt in order to secure access to the single market. These treaty obligations, at times, lead to a direct transposition of EU laws abroad. The EU can also shape global norms though participation in international institutions, standard-setting bodies, and transgovernmental networks. Finally, European courts contribute toward externalizing EU regulations by issuing judgments that serve as templates for foreign courts. All these mechanisms offer complementary and, when taken together, notable avenues for the EU's norms and regulations to shape the global regulatory environment.[7]

Treaties and Institutions

The EU systematically exports its standards through bilateral economic and political agreements—this occurs most clearly in accession agreements and partnership treaties,[8] but can also be seen in various preferential trade agreements (PTAs). The tendency to condition market access on the adoption of EU regulatory standards has led Sophie Meunier and Kalypso Nicolaidis to describe the EU not only as a power *in* trade but also as a power *through* trade.[9] Essentially, the EU trades its market access for trade partners' commitment to adopt specific standards embedded in bilateral or regional trade agreements. Using trade relations as the instrument, the EU is able to promote economic openness "the EU way"—be it through promoting democratization, rule of law, or some specific regulatory standards that govern the trade partners' internal market.

The EU's bargaining power through such conditional market access is strongest when foreign countries are seeking to join the EU. To date, the EU has expanded from its original six member states to the current union of twenty-eight countries, and is currently conducting accession negotiations with six candidate countries.[10] As a condition for joining the EU, prospective member states must demonstrate compliance with all EU regulations, effectively implementing the *acquis communitaire* in its entirety. Doing so requires detailed negotiations across thirty-five wide-ranging policy fields (also called "chapters"), including, for example: competition, development, energy, environment, fundamental rights, and transportation. Throughout all these policy-specific negotiations, the EU has nearly all of the bargaining power because it controls the ultimate prize of EU membership, allowing it to extract almost any conditions it wishes from the accession countries.

The EU itself considers enlargement "the Union's most successful foreign policy instrument."[11] Some scholars have described EU enlargement as "the most successful democracy-promotion programme ever implemented by an international actor," capable of "engineering permanent change" in "every aspect of state action" in the accession countries, driven by EU norms.[12] At the same time, it is unclear how long lasting the commitments that the EU can extract in the accession process are. The EU loses its highly asymmetrical bargaining power immediately after accession takes place. While there are many successful examples of enlargement, recent incidents of rule-of-law backsliding in countries such as Hungary, Poland, and Romania demonstrate the difficulty the EU faces in enforcing negotiated commitments once a member state has been admitted and becomes part of the institutional structure of the EU. These examples illustrate the limits to what the EU can accomplish through the accession process.

In addition to using the accession process to impose regulations on prospective members, the EU negotiates extensive economic partnership and association

agreements with third countries aimed at closer economic and political cooperation. With these agreements, the EU seeks to build a more stable, peaceful,
and prosperous world. To date, it has negotiated forty-nine economic partnership agreements, twenty-three association agreements, and eighteen other similar agreements such as global agreements, customs unions, and others.[13] The EU
has been particularly active in its engagement with its Southern and Eastern
neighbors, pursuing legislative approximation through the exporting of its *acquis
communitaire*.[14] At first, this was done through soft obligations embedded in
Europe Agreements and Partnership and Cooperation Agreements. Later, for
the countries that were not candidates for EU accession but sought otherwise
closer economic and political ties with the EU, the EU instituted a "European
Neighborhood Policy" (ENP) in 2004.[15] The ENP currently covers 16 countries
ranging from Morocco to Azerbaijan.

EU treaties consistently acknowledge that projecting the EU's norms and values is central to the EU's relations with the wider world.[16] The Lisbon Treaty
further gives EU institutions a "transformative mandate" in their relations to the
EU's neighboring countries.[17] The ENP, in particular, rests on the idea that the
EU either exports stability to, or imports instability from, its neighboring countries.[18] This need to ensure a stable political environment in its broader region
calls for the EU's deep engagement with these countries' economic and political
systems. In practice, this entails offering a closer economic and political relationship to ENP countries in return for "concrete progress demonstrating shared
values and effective implementation of political, economic and institutional
reforms, including aligning legislation with the EU's *acquis*."[19] Thus, while falling short of extending the promise of an actual EU membership, the bargaining
process remains highly asymmetrical, leaving the EU's neighbors few options but
to comply with the EU's existing members' demands.

However, in practice, many of the ENP's goals remain unfulfilled. The EU's
record in promoting democracy, rule of law, respect for human rights, and social
cohesion has been at least a disappointment and at worst, according to some,
an "outright failure."[20] The ENP's envisioned political, social, and institutional
reforms have largely failed to take place. Some ENP countries—including Libya,
Syria, and Ukraine—have been torn apart in violent conflicts and civil wars while
others—such as Egypt—have experienced military coups. Corruption remains
widespread across many countries in the region and rule-of-law reforms have
been modest or inexistent. Given the deep internal and external challenges these
countries continue to face, some commentators conclude that the EU has largely
failed to spread its values or protect its interests through the ENP.[21]

The EU's attempts to export its regulatory model via treaties beyond its
immediate region take place primarily through bilateral trade agreements. The

EU has negotiated an extensive array of PTAs that influence the type of regulations that trade partners must have in place in order to secure access to the EU's single market. To date, the EU has signed more than 50 PTAs of various forms,[22] in addition to various other economic and political partnership treaties. Its treaty partners comprise both large and small economies, ranging from economic powerhouses such as Japan and Canada to smaller economies such as Lesotho and the Faroe Islands; from other European countries such as Albania and Macedonia to countries halfway across the globe, such as Chile and Madagascar. Its network of PTAs is considerably larger compared to that of other big trade powers such as Japan and the United States, which have signed 18 and 14 PTAs, respectively.[23]

The EU's negotiated treaty obligations lead to a greater or lesser degree of externalization of EU regulations depending on the treaty partner. In particular vis-à-vis less-powerful trading partners, the EU can use its vast market size as an asymmetric bargaining chip that allows it to demand significant changes in treaty partners' domestic regulatory regimes—whether on environmental policy, development goals, competition laws, or human rights.[24] The PTAs that the EU has negotiated over the last decade in particular reflect such a trade agenda by incorporating extensive commitments to regulatory standards.[25] Furthermore, as most of the EU's PTAs follow the same template, they also serve as a model for other agreements,[26] further extending the EU's influence.

The types of regulatory standards that the EU exports through PTAs are substantively varied. For example, the EU's failure to institute a multilateral treaty framework on global forest governance led to a reliance on bilateral trade agreements in order to export EU norms on forest management strategies.[27] Other typical PTA provisions include obligations to adopt or maintain certain human rights and labor standards. Provisions requiring the adoption of domestic competition laws are also embedded in the EU's PTAs as a matter of course today. However, the EU does not always require its trade partners to adopt portions of the EU's *acquis* as a condition for market access.[28] Often, the EU uses PTAs to transmit general regulatory principles or international regulatory standards as opposed to EU-specific regulations.[29] The EU's demands for regulatory reforms addressed at weaker trading partners typically come with an offer of technical expertise or financial support given the difficulty of implementing many such reforms. However, it remains unclear if even those general provisions have led to lasting changes in trading partners' actual regulatory practices. At best, the EU's record in fostering change in recipient countries' regulations is mixed, as discussed further along in this chapter.

In addition to these general trade agreements that cover a substantial part of the economy, the EU has entered into various sectoral agreements with countries near and far. For example, the EU has concluded several Sustainable Fishing

Partnership Agreements (SFPAs) with primarily African countries.[30] Under the
SFPAs, the EU gains surplus fishing rights in these countries' waters in exchange
for financial and technical support geared toward enhanced resource conservation and sustainability of fishing in those waters. The EU's sectoral agreements
with its close neighbors typically aim at even deeper integration. A number
of such sectoral agreements between the EU member states and Balkan states
explicitly call for the implementation of relevant portions of the *acquis*. For
example, the External Aviation Policy "implies the adoption by [EU] neighbour-
ing partners of the part of the *Acquis* containing the European aviation rules."[31]
Similarly, the Energy Community Treaty "involves the implementation of a part
of community legislation, or *acquis communautaire*, in all the States parties to the
Treaty."[32] The Treaty Establishing the Transport Community likewise is based
on the progressive integration of transport markets on the basis of the relevant
acquis.[33] These treaties, often as an explicit goal, seek to integrate the third states
into the common market with respect to the regulated sector.

The EU also carries notable weight in many international institutions, though
its relative clout varies, and sometimes it can only wield power through member states or the European Central Bank (ECB).[34] EU members, for example,
have a sizable voting presence in the International Monetary Fund (IMF) and
the World Bank (WB), and the EU has traditionally chosen the head of the IMF.
In the WTO, the EU has historically been able to advance its preferred position
together with other trade powers such as the United States and Japan. However,
as the WTO's membership has grown and relative power has become diffuse
across the broader membership, it has become significantly harder for the EU to
influence outcomes and advance its positions.

The EU's influence is also tied to whether the EU as a representative body
or its member states individually exercise power in any given institution. In the
WTO, the EU acts on behalf of its member states, as trade policy falls within the
EU's exclusive competence. In contrast, in the United Nations (UN), the EU
is merely an observer, and it is formally represented only through its member
states whose actions the EU can seek to coordinate to form a common position;
however, this coordination is not always successful. In some organizations, the
EU and its member states share the stage. For example, in the informal Group of
Twenty (G-20)—a forum of the world's advanced economies that seek to coordinate policies to further financial stability and sustainable growth—the EU has
a seat alongside the leaders of France, Germany, Italy, and the United Kingdom.
In the 35-member Organisation for Economic Co-operation and Development
(OECD), 21 EU member states are official members, but the EU also enjoys
full participant status, giving it the ability to directly engage with and influence the work of the OECD in the absence of member state consensus.[35] In

the Basel Committee on Banking Supervision (BCBS), the ECB and the EU's Single Supervisory Board have full membership alongside nine EU member states, while the Commission and the European Banking Authority (EBA) have observer status as well.

The EU also exerts influence in international institutions focused on standard setting across different areas of market regulation. For example, the Food and Agriculture Organization (FAO) and World Health Organization (WHO) formed the Codex Alimentarius Commission to implement global food standards.[36] Historically, the EU—which petitioned for, and attained, membership alongside its member states—has successfully defended a number of controversial policy positions, such as the role of the precautionary principle in Codex decision-making.[37] The EU's extensive influence at Codex can be at least partially attributed to the EU's long experience in regulating food safety.[38] Food safety is a policy area where the EU successfully established the single market already in the 1960s. This has allowed the EU to accumulate valuable expertise, which it has often leveraged to shape standard setting at Codex. Today, the EU and Codex have some specific overlap in their standards, suggesting that two-way regulatory harmonization often takes place. For example, Codex adopted the 1999 EU standards for the detection of irradiated foods,[39] while a 2008 EU regulation on food additives utilized an almost identical definition for additives as that employed by Codex.[40] Such harmonization facilitates international trade and is one of the primary purposes of Codex as a standard-setting body.[41]

There are many examples of where the EU has successfully transmitted its rules to foreign jurisdictions via international organizations. The EU was able to export its motor vehicle emission control standards via UNECE—the UN's Economic Commission for Europe—not only to the broader European neighborhood, but also to countries as remote as Argentina, Brazil, China, India, Peru, and Thailand.[42] The relevant "Euro" standards were widely adopted over equivalent United States' "Tiers" standards, even though many viewed US standards to be more effective, and many of the adopting countries did not even export cars to the EU. The lack of a market-access motive for foreign producers to emulate the EU standard in this case is what differentiates this type of influence from the Brussels Effect. The EU's success in exporting its standard can thus be partially explained by its more universally appealing policy design, which may be more amenable to different market settings as compared with the US standard, which was designed with US-market idiosyncrasies in mind. In addition, given that UNECE is mainly composed of European countries, there was a strong inclination to adopt European standards. Yet UNECE also engages actively with other international organizations that have a geographically broader membership, and utilizes this network to promote its standards—in this case, EU standards— beyond Europe.

The International Maritime Organization's (IMO's) ban on single-hull oil tankers provides a somewhat different, yet distinctly intriguing, example.[43] Compared to safer double-hull designs, single-hull oil tankers are more likely to lead to oil spills in the event of collision. Following the catastrophic Exxon Valdez oil spill of 1989 off the coast of Alaska, the United States moved in 1990 to ban single-hull tankers unilaterally. Yet, the United States did little to globalize the norm. Instead, it was the EU that successfully globalized the double-hull safety standard that originally emanated from the United States. The EU emulated the US standard in 2000, and subsequently set out to internationalize the standard via the IMO, which agreed to phase out single-hull tankers in 2001 as part of its broader agenda to advance maritime safety. In many ways, this international standard grew out of US unilateralism, as dangerous ships were redirected to EU waters following the US ban. Thus, the EU had the impetus to regulate against this externality and disseminate the double-hull standard more broadly. As a result, this example demonstrates the importance of international organizations in providing a vehicle for EU influence, even where the EU is not the first mover in pursuing such standards or regulations.

Sandra Lavenex has emphasized how the EU's projection of its rules abroad often takes place through its regulators' technocratic and sector-specific outreach, rather than traditional diplomacy.[44] This channel of policy diffusion emphasizes the role of government networks and complements the Brussels Effect.[45] The EU's promotion of rules through transgovernmental networks often amounts to co-optive as opposed to coercive influence. This co-opting typically takes place in the context of the Commission's (and European Regulatory Agencies') active engagement in technical assistance and capacity-building activities. In this process, EU representatives not only lend their expertise but also often promote, intentionally or unintentionally, the EU's regulatory approaches as "best practice."[46] However, transgovernmental networks rarely provide a path for unilateral policy export, but instead aim for closer regulatory alignment through cooperation and dialogue.

These networks offer important channels of influence that complement the Brussels Effect. For example, EU competition laws, discussed in chapter 4, have diffused not only through the Brussels Effect, but also through the Commission's active role in transgovernmental networks such as the ICN and bilateral cooperative agreements between regulators.[47] Similarly, the strong Brussels Effect associated with the EU chemical regulation REACH, discussed in chapter 6, has been amplified by the EU's chemical agency ECHA's scientific and technical cooperation with its foreign counterparts.[48] The EU has also used other formal international organizations to promote REACH's regulatory approach, including the OECD, the UN's Environmental program UNEP, the WHO, and the FAO, in addition to informal networks such as the International Uniform Chemical Information database and the Global Portal to Information on Chemical Substances.[49]

European Courts and Foreign Litigants

European courts have also played a role in exporting EU norms, amplifying the Brussels Effect with their "pro-integration" rulings. At times, the courts have given extraterritorial expression to EU legislation in their interpretations of regulations emanating from the EU's legislative or administrative process. For instance, before the famous "right to be forgotten" principle was incorporated into the EU's General Data Protection Regulation (GDPR), the European Court of Justice (ECJ) pronounced the principle in its decision in *Google Spain v. Mario Costeja*, C-131/12 (*Google Spain*). Since then, the principle has been cited by plaintiffs before courts outside Europe and affirmed by courts in several jurisdictions. The ECJ's declared right has appeared in legal proceedings in at least Argentina, Brazil, Chile, Colombia, Israel, Mexico, Nicaragua, Japan, South Korea, and Hong Kong.[50] Russia even went so far as to codify the right to be forgotten in 2015.[51]

Beyond this interpretative role, which helps diffuse EU regulations, the European courts have provided an institutional template for regional courts. According to Karen Alter, there are currently 11 copies of the ECJ around the world.[52] These courts combined have issued over 2,000 binding rulings, making them active courts as opposed to institutions that only exist in name in their founding agreements.[53] The institutional emulation is particularly visible in Latin America and the Andean Community, a regional organization established among Bolivia, Colombia, Ecuador, and Peru. The 1969 Cartagena Agreement modeled the Andean Community after the Treaty of Rome and designed a governance structure that closely resembles the EU institutions. The initial community institutions were complemented by the Andean Tribunal of Justice (ATJ) in 1984.[54] The ATJ was closely modeled after the ECJ, both in its design features and legal doctrines.[55] It is the third-most active international court today in terms of the number of rulings it issues, behind the ECJ and the European Court of Human Rights.[56]

The ATJ copied many of the institutional features of the ECJ, including the preliminary reference procedure, which allows for national courts in member states to ask the ATJ's opinion in cases that require interpretation of the community law. The ATJ also established the doctrine of supremacy of Andean

Community law over national law, citing the ECJ's landmark case *Costa/Enel*, which established the doctrine of supremacy in the EU.[57] The ATJ has similarly cited the ECJ in numerous other landmark cases,[58] including *Van Gend & Loos* on the direct effect of community law,[59] as well as key cases regarding the operation of the internal market.[60] However, despite the extensive emulation of the ECJ, the ATJ does not resort to "blind mimicry" of the EU.[61] Instead, it engages in selective emulation to better serve the particular needs of the region.[62]

The close emulation of the ECJ by the ATJ is perhaps not surprising given the similarities in the founding treaties and institutions. In addition, experts from the Institute for the Integration of Latin America and the Caribbean (INTAL), who were tasked with evaluating the best judicial model for the Andean Community, recommended the ECJ as a template. Many of these experts had deep connections with, and knowledge of, the EU and the ECJ, having attended European universities, worked with major EU scholars, and participated in various pro-integration academic events in Europe.[63] Members of the Andean Community also consulted European experts such as ECJ Judge Pierre Pescatore and Professor Gerard Olivier, the assistant director general of the European Commission Legal Service,[64] further adding to the near inevitability that the ECJ model would serve as a template to follow.

In addition, some foreign courts have turned to European courts and other institutions, citing them in support of their judicial decisions as an example of a more established judiciary. The Colombian Constitutional Court (CCC), for example, in a case concerning the use of the herbicide glyphosate to eradicate certain illicit crops, turned to EU law and institutions in two ways. First, it requested the official opinion of the European Food Safety Authority about the risks involved in the use of glyphosate. Second, it cited the EU's General Court when analyzing the precautionary principle in the matter.[65] In another case concerning a controversy on GMOs, the CCC stated that "[t]he European Union has taken a clear position and has become an international reference in the fight against [GMOs], in accordance with its Resolution 1829 of 2003, which also establishes the labeling for this type of product."[66] Further, in a case concerning another health and safety matter, the CCC showed deference to the EU's view when ruling whether the HPV vaccine caused certain diseases in a minor. In deciding the matter, the CCC cited the EU and took into consideration the fact that the European Commission approved the vaccine's commercialization based on the European Medicines Agency's prior approval.[67]

Other foreign agencies and courts regularly cite EU competition law as well, often in support of their interpretations of domestic competition rules. For example, the Indian Supreme Court has referred to EU law in deciding whether certain entities fall within the scope of their domestic competition law's provisions on anticompetitive agreements,[68] while the Madras High Court in India has cited the EU's cartel settlement procedure in its decision regarding the permissibility of certain settlements.[69] Furthermore, the Indian competition agency, the CCI, has referred to EU treaties, courts, and Commission white papers in its decisions,[70] citing the "maturity" of the EU's competition regime as justification for the use of such models.

However, it is difficult to measure the actual influence of the ECJ based on institutional replication or citations alone. First, it is unclear how much influence these rulings have on the ground, including whether they are actually implemented by governments or enforced against private parties. Second, evaluating the relative influence of the ECJ would also require an understanding of the extent to which these same courts may cite other foreign courts, including, for instance, the US Supreme Court. Regardless, it is worth acknowledging that EU courts may play a role in disseminating key EU regulations to foreign jurisdictions, further entrenching the de jure Brussels Effect as a result.

Another manifestation of the EU's external influence is the tendency of some jurisdictions to follow the EU's lead and engage in "copycat" litigation in cases where the effects of some conduct—such as anticompetitive practice—extend across multiple markets. Some examples of this are discussed in chapter 4 with regard to competition laws, including the South Korean investigation of Microsoft, which closely followed the European Commission and General Court rulings in a very similar case pursued under EU competition law. Several reasons likely explain this phenomenon. First, an EU investigation has informational value, alerting governments and private plaintiffs in other jurisdictions of the conduct that calls for enforcement action. Second, relying on an EU investigation may lower the costs of enforcement for jurisdictions with fewer resources by allowing other agencies to rely on the evidence that the EU has gathered. This may allow those agencies to extract a fine and bolster their own enforcement record without incurring significant enforcement costs. Finally, copycat litigation may be spurred by the EU's request for assistance in its own investigation. This may happen, for instance, if some key evidence is located in a foreign jurisdiction. Once the relevant evidence is gathered for the EU, the foreign agency may then decide to use that same evidence in its own independent proceeding.

It is not always empirically possible to show that a simultaneous or subsequent investigation or litigation in another jurisdiction constitutes emulation of the EU. It is plausible that a foreign jurisdiction would have acted even in the absence of an EU enforcement action. However, often parties make explicit references to the EU in their complaints and submissions to an agency or court, indicating that the EU enforcement has been at least considered in the foreign matter. Similarities in arguments or the ultimate remedies may also indicate that

EU decisions have been used as an inspiration for complainants, litigants, agencies, or courts.

Foreign governments or courts are not the only ones to emulate the EU in enforcement of their own legal rules and regulations. Many foreign firms also strategically resort to the European Commission or European Courts as their preferred forum for disputes and litigation. EU competition law has been a particularly attractive area of EU regulation for foreign plaintiffs, as discussed in chapter 4. Foreign companies have frequently complained about the conduct of their domestic competitors to EU institutions, knowing that they have a better chance of obtaining a favorable decision under the EU's strict standards as compared with their domestic competition law. For example, Microsoft was a key complainant in the EU's competition investigations against Google. Similarly, the EU's competition ruling against Intel stemmed from a complaint by Intel's US rival, AMD.

The examples just mentioned illustrate how the EU judicial process can externalize EU regulations either by interpreting EU regulations and giving them a particular meaning that becomes entrenched in foreign laws; providing an institutional template that is replicated abroad; issuing rulings that get cited or even copied by foreign courts; or providing a forum for litigation for foreign parties that opt into EU jurisdiction. However, as already noted, while this influence can be very concrete and real in some instances—including the cases of copycat litigation or rulings that EU institutions hand down against foreign parties—it can be more uncertain in others, including in instances of court citations where there is less clarity that the EU's influence is actually entrenched or implemented.

Why the EU Law Appeals as a Template

Several reasons explain foreign countries' tendency to emulate EU law. First, the EU's market size and its ability to leverage its market access as a tool to extract regulatory adjustment remains a crucial structural factor in explaining the de jure Brussels Effect that follows the de facto Brussels Effect. As explained earlier, the de facto Brussels Effect paves the way for the de jure Brussels Effect by changing the political economy in foreign jurisdictions where multinational companies become advocates for the local adoption of EU norms. Similarly, the EU's ability to leverage its market power to force a regulatory change explains the regulatory influence the EU wields through trade treaties and economic partnerships. Here, the underlying dynamics—incentives stemming from the attractiveness of market access—are not different from the Brussels Effect, but the regulatory adjustment is driven by treaty-based bilateralism instead of market-driven unilateralism.

Further, the EU's ability to influence global norms through international organizations and transgovernmental networks rests on the EU's overall political influence and bargaining power coupled with its experience, expertise, and willingness to extend technical assistance and engage in capacity building. At the same time, it can be less clear why foreign courts would cite EU rulings, or why legislative borrowing would take place, outside the context of the Brussels Effect. With this in mind, the following discussion offers two additional reasons for voluntarily emulation of EU rules by foreign legislators, government agencies, and courts: one driven by pragmatism and the other by normative ideas.

A pragmatic reason for emulation of EU rules is simply the ease with which EU regulations can be copied. The civil law tradition of the EU typically promulgates more precise and detailed rules than the common law tradition of jurisdictions such as the United States. Such well-defined rules serve European integration by enhancing legal certainty and predictability. EU member states are generally less comfortable with the less predictable case-by-case approach to law that is deeply embedded in the legal tradition of the United States.[71] Competition law is a good example, with the TFEU Articles 101 and 102 offering considerably more precision than their United States counterparts, Articles 1 and 2 of the Sherman Act. This detailed treaty template, enhanced by supporting Commission regulations, notices, and guidelines, makes the EU competition rules easier to copy and hence more prone to diffusion.[72] Similarly, the ease of emulating the EU's data protection regulation, the GDPR, partially explains its global diffusion. The GDPR is comprehensive, covering all sectors of the economy and applying to private and government entities alike, making it easier for foreign jurisdictions to emulate when contrasted with the sector-specific and more fragmented US regulations on data privacy.[73] In particular, the well-specified nature of EU law is easier to emulate in developing countries that may have less-skilled administrative agencies and judiciaries. In these low-income countries, detailed and codified legal norms can act as substitutes for human capital, and are thus preferred to more flexible standards.[74] Such detailed rules diminish the need for discretion and allow for more mechanical rule-making and enforcement by agencies that lack the technical experience and training that more complex, case-by-case decision-making requires.

EU regulations are not only more precise and hence more accessible templates, but they also have the additional advantage of being promulgated in several languages, including French, Portuguese, and Spanish. This facilitates the copying of EU laws, particularly in Latin America and Francophone Africa. In addition, third countries with close cultural and historic—or, as often is the case, colonial—ties tend to look to individual EU member state laws for guidance. For example, environmental regulations in Latin America resemble those of the EU largely because of the strong cultural and linguistic bonds between Latin America and Europe—coupled with the EU's active outreach and technical assistance.[75] The African courts' tendency to copy the ECJ is similarly at least partly explained by the close linguistic and educational ties of both anglophone and francophone countries to the United Kingdom and France, respectively[76]—the same way that close ties of former colonies in Latin America to Spain and Portugal have facilitated the emulation of ECJ rulings there. Ecuador, which copied Spain's competition laws almost word for word, provides a specific example of this copy-cat legislation, as discussed in chapter 4.[77] In doing so, Ecuador indirectly emulated EU competition law given that Spanish competition law is, in turn, largely derived from EU law. This indirect leverage through the layered structure of EU law and institutions broadens the EU's sphere of regulatory influence. Another indirect form of influence takes place via regional organizations in Africa and Latin America, including the Andean Community, Economic Community of West African States (WAEMU), and Common Market for Eastern and Southern Africa (COMESA).[78] These organizations model their institutions directly on EU institutions, indirectly embedding EU rules into the legal systems of their member states in the process.[79]

Finally, the EU has combined statutory precision with flexible drafting. EU regulations are designed to work across many different legal systems. Their goal is to create a cohesive single market across individual countries with diverse legal traditions and political institutions. The regulations are drafted through a process that thus reflects member states' heterogeneous interests and accounts for a wide range of legal traditions. This balancing requires legislative techniques that achieve uniformity while preserving some degree of sovereignty. For example, many EU regulations are drafted as directives, which lay out clear objectives but allow for variation in implementation nationally. This flexibility embedded in EU regulation makes for better templates for export to foreign jurisdictions with different characteristics than those found in the EU.

These pragmatic reasons and the ease of copying may lead to greater emulation—at least when it comes to enacting laws on the books. However, whether this emulation is ultimately effective and leads to actual change in the conduct of market actors is a different question. If a foreign country adopts EU style rules because they were drafted in an accessible language, it is not certain the country has fully committed to actual implementation of such rules. Adoption following a deep domestic debate or a change of actual preferences better indicates genuine motivation to adopt similar rules. For this reason, the change in the preferences of the domestic business interests due to the de facto Brussels Effect may give a more lasting foundation for a regulatory reform.

Yet, EU rules do not serve as global templates merely because they are detailed and available in multiple languages. Several commentators also emphasize the "normative appeal" of EU rules, which increases their attractiveness as a model for emulation. If this appeal exists, the EU's influence also rests on the quality of its ideas and its normative power of persuasion. Ian Manners developed the concept of "Normative Power Europe" to capture the EU's ability to exert influence through persuasion.[80] Manners argues that the EU is best conceived as a normative power, which vests the EU with "ideational power" and the ability to shape what is normal in international relations.[81] This power can be traced to the goals and values that gave rise to EU integration, and to the EU's commitment to democracy, rule of law, human rights, and fundamental freedoms. The appeal of these principles means the EU sets a "virtuous example," leading to a diffusion of its norms across the world.

The normative appeal of EU rules may explain the willingness of foreign courts to cite and emulate EU laws and ECJ judgments, even in instances where no Brussels Effect takes places. In analyzing the reasons for the EU institutions' influence on other regional organizations, including their courts, Michel Levi Coral emphasizes the perceived success and visibility of EU integration, lending the EU experience notable credibility.[82] Amadeo Arena reaches the same conclusion, observing that EU principles are seen as having worked well for Europe and therefore can serve as an example for other regions pursuing deeper integration.[83]

In addition to the EU model's normative appeal, several commentators note how the EU actively promotes the replication of its institutional structures.[84] The EU provides legal and technical expertise and financial support to many third states implementing their rules.[85] Notably, studies of the EU's influence over foreign courts reveal no coercion, but rather persuasion. These studies suggest that norm recipients have embraced the EU model willingly, viewing the emulation of the ECJ as a way to enhance compliance with law and deploy the courts as a means of advancing integration in their own region.[86] According to Alan Tatham, references to ECJ rulings allow foreign courts to mitigate criticism of their own judicial activism, lending legitimacy to local pro-integration rulings by referencing the "regional court par excellence in integration."[87]

However, alternatively some have argued that there may be resentment associated with the idea that the EU would be portrayed as a "normatively superior" model for "lesser jurisdictions" to follow. Chapter 8 will address such criticisms, which are often associated with the perception of the EU as a regulatory imperialist whose norm exports, purportedly as a "benevolent hegemon," are really a new form of colonialism. The EU's recent struggles, ranging from financial crises to rule-of-law backsliding, also call into question whether the EU can still claim its integration project is a "virtuous example" fit for replication abroad.

Comparing the Brussels Effect
to Other Forms of Influence

As the discussion has just shown, there are a number of different paths to regulatory convergence. These paths include the Brussels Effect and other mechanisms of influence, and each one can prove optimal under different political–economy conditions. They may also operate in parallel or in sequence, amplifying or paving the way for one another. For example, the influence of European courts often complements the Brussels Effect by extending the regulatory capacity of EU institutions into new policy areas. Courts may also interpret the content of EU regulations in ways that make them more amenable to diffusion. The diffusion of EU regulatory influence through treaties and international institutions is made easier where preceded by the de facto Brussels Effect, as consensus is often easier to reach when some degree of regulatory alignment has already occurred. However, at times the EU deploys these treaty-driven mechanisms as substitutes for the de facto Brussels Effect, especially when the Brussels Effect is unavailable or undesirable.

This section discusses the relative advantages and disadvantages of *market-driven harmonization* compared to *treaty-driven harmonization*. It also explains how these two forms of influence interact. Here, the term "market-driven harmonization" refers to the more passive, market-driven harmonization of regulatory standards generated by the de facto Brussels Effect. The term "treaty-driven harmonization" refers to the more active, consensus-driven harmonization of regulatory standards achieved through negotiations or international institutions.

Advantages of the Brussels Effect's
Market-Driven Harmonization

As a market-driven harmonization, the Brussels Effect has a distinct advantage for the EU over treaty-driven harmonization: it entails lower contracting costs and limited enforcement costs. In relying on markets to transmit its regulations, the EU is not forced to seek the consent of other states. This avoids collective action problems, expensive transfer payments, or costly coercive measures toward countries reluctant to join a treaty or an institution. The EU can also forgo the uncertainties associated with the treaty ratification processes. The EU's unsuccessful efforts to revive deadlocked WTO negotiations or spearhead UN-led processes to negotiate a global forest convention reveal the difficulties associated with multilateral cooperation.[88] These processes require extensive political capital and diplomatic efforts, yet sometimes yield no results.

Treaty-driven harmonization is particularly difficult if states do not agree on the benefits of global standards. Moreover, multilateral standard setting is difficult even where most states agree in principle on the desirability of achieving uniform standards. States often have different views on the particular standard that would be optimal. Different points of convergence often entail different distributional consequences, making some states prefer one standard over another.[89] Market-driven harmonization solves such coordination problems: the most stringent rule becomes the point of convergence. A mutual understanding that the EU can retain its standards at no cost—and so, absent changing circumstances, will not change the standard—provides a predictable and stable equilibrium.

The existing divisions that make multilateral cooperation challenging appear to only be growing. International law scholars increasingly lament this "stagnation of international law" or "decay of consent."[90] By these terms, the commentators denote the growing inability of the traditional treaty structures to provide effective solutions for the modern challenges to the international order, with such mechanisms increasingly giving way to unilateral action and informal international lawmaking.[91] Joost Pauwelyn and his coauthors—relying on the results of a two-year research project involving over forty scholars and thirty case studies—argue that formal international law is stagnating both in terms of quantity and quality. This stagnation, they argue, is evidenced by the dramatic drop in negotiation of new multilateral treaties and the increasingly thin consent underlying those treaties that are concluded.[92] Most recently, the United States' disengagement from global institutions has further deepened their malaise and, in some cases, has compromised these institutions' ability to function.

Treaties are not only hard to conclude but are also difficult and expensive to enforce. When a stringent global standard is the expected product of an international treaty, there is no guarantee that the treaty will be implemented or enforced. The treaty on the world's marine fisheries is one of the many examples of negotiated global standards that fails to accomplish its goals: the treaty has not been successful in addressing the problem of overfishing and propelling sustainable management of fishing stocks.[93] Labor standards have also been difficult to enforce in practice despite the many negotiated ILO conventions.[94] Such examples are not anomalies in the world of global standards embedded in difficult-to-enforce treaties. Indeed, some commentators have noted that treaties producing "effectively enforced international standards are the exception rather than the rule."[95]

In contrast, market-driven harmonization often provides the most efficient form of regulatory globalization because it relies on firms' self-interest to enforce EU regulations globally. The EU's unilateral regulatory agenda requires the cooperation of foreign corporations willing to trade in its market rather than the cooperation of foreign sovereigns. Instead of engaging in slow and often uncertain diplomacy to endorse its standards, market-driven harmonization allows the EU to outsource lobbying to foreign firms who become advocates for higher standards in their own home markets after having incurred EU compliance costs. This way, with no active effort to externalize its rules, the EU will often witness not only a de facto Brussels Effect but eventually a de jure Brussels Effect as well without spending any political capital to persuade foreign governments to adopt its regulations.

The SEC's and US State Department's efforts to enforce US rules on insider trading provides a useful contrast. The efforts of these institutions to impose US rules have been complicated by the reluctance of foreign countries, particularly Switzerland, to cooperate with the United States due to their domestic bank secrecy laws. The United States has had to spend extensive political capital to persuade Swiss authorities to cooperate with them. This has been considered worth the effort given that Swiss banks hold approximately half of the world's private assets.[96] The United States' ability to curtail domestic insider trading would have been compromised had it not secured a change in the domestic rules of a foreign country. Merely incentivizing foreign corporations operating in the United States to cooperate with the US regulations would not have been sufficient to meet this goal.

Even when the EU is effective in incorporating its standards and regulations into international trade treaties, it is unclear whether those provisions lead to lasting change in trading partners' actual regulatory practices, as already noted. At best, the EU's record in fostering change in recipient countries' regulations has been mixed. One reason for this may be that the treaty provisions are at times written in a vague manner, holding countries to a "best efforts" standard as opposed to demanding actual results. For example, Nicolas A. J. Croquet claims that the vagueness characterizing environmental provisions in the EU-Korea trade agreement contributed to the ineffectiveness of such provisions in practice.[97]

However, often the enforcement problems go beyond vague treaty drafting and reflect inadequate follow-through, ineffective monitoring, and non-enforcement altogether. Axel Marx and Jadir Soares's empirical study on labor rights provisions in trade agreements casts deep doubt on the effectiveness of trade agreements as a tool for exporting norms and standards.[98] The authors examine two specific labor rights—freedom of association and the right to collective bargaining—in 13 countries with which the EU has concluded a PTA with strong labor provisions. Their analysis suggests that there is a steady decline in the protection of these rights over time, notwithstanding treaty obligations. While the authors are cautious not to advance a strong causal claim, their study leaves them skeptical that trade agreements can effectively be utilized to ratchet up labor protections in foreign jurisdictions.[99]

Even the monitoring and enforcement of unilateral trade instruments, such as the Generalized System of Preferences (GSP) programs, can be difficult. GSP programs are designed to provide preferential market access to developing countries' goods in order to facilitate their growth through trade. Both the United States and EU deploy GSP programs, attaching various domestic reforms as conditions for extending such preferences, where the breach of these conditions can lead to their unilateral withdrawal. Yet a review of the EU's GSP programs reveals that it rarely enforces commitments attached to the preferences it provides. Even though the EU holds considerable economic power over the GSP recipients—all of which are developing countries—it rarely suspends GSP preferences despite reported violations of GSP conditions.

Laura Beke and Nicolas Hachez's case study on Myanmar illustrates this dynamic, showing that the threat of withdrawal of GSP preferences fails to induce effective implementation of GSP standards.[100] Indeed, the EU has suspended preferences on only a handful of occasions: against Myanmar in 1997, Belarus in 2007, Sri Lanka in 2010, and Cambodia in 2019. This has led critics to conclude that "GSP withdrawals have the worst record of success of all EU sanctions"[101] and "have not recorded a single case of compliance yet."[102] There are several explanations for the ineffectiveness of GSP provisions in fostering regulatory change, including that until recently the Commission did not have the exclusive competence to make decisions regarding the withdrawal of benefits but needed to subject the contested decisions to the (often disagreeing) Council.[103] It remains unclear whether the recent 2014 GSP+ program reforms, which emphasize reporting and monitoring, will increase the effectiveness of this instrument.[104]

All of this suggests that the limits of exporting standards through trade agreements mainly relate to the difficulty of enforcement rather than the conclusion of agreements in the first place. However, every trade agreement also carries substantial contracting costs due to the often-protracted negotiations. It is also considerably harder to impose standards in cases where the EU is negotiating with strong trade partners. In addition, contracting costs are high not only because of the disagreements between the EU and its trading partners but also because of fragmentation within the EU itself. The modern trade agreements often contain provisions that convert them into "mixed agreements," indicating that the competence to negotiate the instrument does not rest exclusively with the EU but rather requires member states ratification as well.[105] For example, the recent EU-Canada Comprehensive Economic and Trade Agreement (CETA) almost failed due to the multiple internal veto points within the EU, including the need for ratification in Belgium alone by seven different federal, regional, and community bodies.[106] Another example comes from the failed Anti-Counterfeiting Trade Agreement (ACTA), which did not come into effect because the EU Parliament rejected its consent to the agreement.[107]

The difficulties associated with the negotiation and enforcement of treaty-driven obligations suggest a rather provocative conclusion: market-driven harmonization leads companies to change their behavior without foreign governments necessarily changing the law, while treaty-driven harmonization may lead governments to change the law without companies necessarily changing their behavior as a result. Of course, in reality the Brussels Effect is often incomplete, and treaty-driven mechanisms are not always doomed to fail. If treaty-driven cooperation yielded no results, the EU would likely have abandoned multilateralism and treaty-driven cooperation long ago. Yet, the EU's commitment to multilateralism and international institutions remains strong.

Reasons That Multilateralism and Treaty-Driven Cooperation Persist

To be sure, the EU has not and likely never will abandon international cooperation and consensus-based instruments altogether in favor of unilateralism. The EU's persisting, if selective, reliance on bilateral treaties and multilateral institutions may be surprising given the many benefits embedded in market-driven harmonization. Yet there are certain instances where unilateralism is unavailable or undesirable, prompting the EU to seek affirmative adoption of regulations by foreign governments. Naturally, when the critical conditions for unilateral harmonization are not present, no Brussels Effect takes place—whether de facto or de jure. In these situations, international cooperation is often the only path to regulatory globalization.

Multilateralism can be the product of affirmative choice in addition to necessity. Being itself a construct of multilateralism, the EU can be portrayed as having an existential interest in preserving multilateralism as a foundation for governing international relations. Multilateralism comes with certain advantages, and the EU has at times been very skillful in harnessing these advantages to its benefit. The EU has experienced many successes in international fora, notwithstanding the high contracting and enforcement costs discussed earlier. The EU and its key member states remain some of the main architects of the liberal international order and key supporters of the institutions that form the foundation for this order. As such, the EU has a substantial vested interest in the resilience and continuation of this order.

Of course, sometimes the EU's preference for treaty-driven harmonization reflects its attempts to pursue its own broader economic and political goals. This is readily apparent, for instance, in the EU's desire to stabilize its broader region, which it has sought to accomplish through accession negotiations and the European Neighbourhood Policy. The EU has a deeper political agenda when it comes to the countries in its region, and this agenda requires much closer economic alignment and political association than the Brussels Effect can by itself bring about. Even PTAs can be a tool for closer political engagement and an opening for a diplomatic process that paves the way for a broader cooperative agenda—eventually reaching issues such as national security, which have remained deeply political and outside the reach of any market-driven mechanism.

But even in instances where the EU's goals relate to regulatory alignment alone, multilateralism can provide both a feasible and attractive venue for cooperative standard setting. The EU has been at times very successful in incorporating its standards into international organizations, making the benefits of unilateralism over multilateralism less stark. The EU, itself a construction of intergovernmental cooperation, has extensive experience in promulgating rules that lend themselves to adoption by heterogeneous states. The EU is also skillful in using its institutional structure—a hybrid of states and a federation—to its advantage. In international negotiations, it can leverage the negotiating power of twenty-eight countries, or can use the same number as a constraint by portraying itself as an agent who can only sign onto a certain set of policies due to the existence of numerous domestic veto points.[108] Thus, depending on the political dynamics surrounding a particular issue, the EU may prefer to pursue treaty-driven harmonization rather than letting the Brussels Effect do the work.

The theory underlying the Brussels Effect offers predictions of when the EU is likely to pursue treaty-driven harmonization as opposed to rely on markets to transmit its standards. For instance, the theory suggests that the EU is expected to rely on cooperative instruments in situations where the Brussels Effect fails to reach EU corporations' important export markets. In the absence of a level playing field, the EU's export-oriented firms face difficulties penetrating these markets. Thus, when the EU is a net exporter as opposed to a net importer of a certain product, the EU is expected to care more about the standard of the export market than that of its home market. Further, it is precisely then that the Brussels Effect is least likely to automatically ratchet up the standard, because net importer countries have a smaller presence in the EU. The EU is therefore more likely to expend diplomatic efforts to negotiate multilateral standards in areas where it is a net exporter and rely on markets in areas where it is a net importer.

Similarly, the theory would suggest that the EU is more likely to pursue treaty-driven harmonization in areas where the EU has limited regulatory capacity and hence a diminished ability to generate regulations. In practice, the EU has had limited success in regulating harmful tax competition and tax avoidance due to its need for internal unanimity. As a result, it has actively sought international cooperation on corporate tax evasion, for example, by developing legally binding rules based on OECD recommendations and working with international partners to track non-cooperative tax jurisdictions.[109]

The EU is similarly incentivized to negotiate international standards in areas where other major jurisdictions prefer higher standards than it does. In those instances, the Brussels Effect is unavailable to support the externalization of EU preferences as it is not the most stringent standard. Then the EU's best option is to persuade such other jurisdictions to offer "mutual recognition" to the EU's own standards so that it may continue to adhere to its preferred standard yet trade internationally. For example, the EU and the United States have different regulations regarding trading venues for the mandatory clearing of derivatives. In 2017, after extended negotiations, the US Commodity Futures Trading Commission (CFTC) issued exemptions to certain EU-authorized trading facilities based on a determination that new EU-wide legal requirements satisfied the Commodity Exchange Act (CEA) standards.[110]

Financial regulation, in particular, is a field where the Brussels Effect is constrained due to the elasticity of capital, making international standard setting typically the only feasible path toward regulatory globalization. The EU has sought stronger international financial regulation to limit regulatory arbitrage and instability in the financial markets, especially in the aftermath of the 2008 financial crisis.[111] For example, the International Organization for Securities Commissions (IOSCO)—which develops international standards to govern capital markets globally—has provided the EU a platform to exert influence over international standards on securities regulation.[112] In the IOSCO, the EU is represented through the financial supervisory authorities of its member states, the European Securities and Markets Authority (ESMA), and the European Commission.[113] Similarly, through its member states and the ECB, the EU has wielded notable influence over global banking regulations instituted by the BCBS.[114] Given the interconnectedness as well as the elasticity of the global financial markets, unilateral influence would never accomplish the objectives achieved through multilateral standard setting.

The EU is also incentivized to seek treaty-driven harmonization to reinforce the effect of its own standards. For example, when standards are characterized by network effects—thus where the benefits associated with the standard increase with each additional country adopting the same standard—the EU has a greater incentive to engage in treaty making to take advantage of network externalities. [115] This is demonstrated by the push for global implementation of 5G, or "fifth generation" telecommunication systems, which the Commission considers critical for the digital economy and society in the next decade.[116] As such, the Commission "strongly supports international cooperation towards global interoperability" and has signed joint declarations of 5G with Brazil, China, Japan, and South Korea as of early 2019.[117]

The EU may also seek to encourage third countries to adopt its standards in cases where it is acting out of a moral imperative. If the EU is motivated by a moral quest to change behaviors globally—for example, to promote human rights—unilateral globalization is rarely sufficient. This is particularly likely when the issue is salient to influential domestic political groups that seek to export an ideology or moral conviction and when they care about establishing standards for universal conduct.[118] In these policy areas, the EU often cannot capitalize on its market access.[119] The EU cannot abolish torture, free political prisoners, solve migration crises, achieve nuclear disarmament, or control global energy supplies by leveraging its market access. In these non-market issues, treaty-driven harmonization—although often incomplete or ineffective—remains the only path.

Another reason to pursue treaty-driven harmonization is to obtain greater legitimacy for EU regulations through globalization. If foreign companies and governments endorse EU standards, those standards may be seen as having wider appeal and thus greater legitimacy.[120] A significant benefit of this legitimacy is that EU trade partners will be less likely to challenge the legality of EU standards before a forum like the WTO if those standards have been replicated globally. Less tangibly, being the global standard setter has the benefit of expanding the EU's soft power and validating its regulatory agenda, both at home and abroad. Unilateral globalization—even that driven by markets as opposed to active government measures—can be viewed as coercive given that the EU is not forced to seek consent from foreign governments when exporting its rules. This can lead to resentment abroad and even to accusations of "regulatory imperialism," as acknowledged earlier and discussed further in chapter 8. Complementing the Brussels Effect with treaty-driven harmonization may thus mitigate the criticisms often associated with the EU's unilateralism.

Treaty-driven harmonization is not necessarily an alternative for the Brussels Effect. Instead, it may offer an important complementary mechanism even in instances where the Brussels Effect might already exist. For example, the EU is likely to encourage foreign countries to adopt certain standards in situations where the actions (or inactions) of other countries produce negative externalities that adversely impact the EU's interests. This motivation may partially explain the EU's efforts to pursue bilateral treaties, regulatory cooperation agreements, and cooperation though international institutions and government networks to encourage diffusion of competition laws.[121] The deterrent effect of the EU's competition laws has the potential to be compromised if anticompetitive practices remain profitable elsewhere. This could be the case, for example, if members of a cartel have the ability to offset any EU fines by reaping supra-competitive profits in markets that fail to control for their collusive practices. Climate change offers another example, such as when China's failure to limit its greenhouse gas (GHG) emissions directly compromises the EU's efforts to halt climate change.[122] Even though the Brussels Effect could, under some conditions, constrain Chinese GHG emissions with respect to production of products that are imported into the EU, the Brussels Effect does nothing to constrain emissions that stay in China yet contribute to the global problem.

Furthermore, in some instances the EU may pursue treaty-driven harmonization in order to "lock-in" certain market-driven EU standards by institutionalizing them. This can be an astute way of preempting a future state of the world where market access becomes a less-effective tool for exerting influence. The EU knows that its relative economic clout will inevitably diminish in the future as the size and wealth of consumer markets in Asia and elsewhere continue to grow. The de jure Brussels Effect is less vulnerable to these economic shifts than the de facto Brussels Effect, providing a rationale for the EU to seek to embed its regulations in treaties as opposed to relying on markets to sustain them indefinitely.

Finally, market-driven and treaty-driven harmonization can also take place in sequence. The EU may be able to more successfully institutionalize its standard where a limited Brussels Effect has already taken place. In instances where a number of foreign companies or governments already follow EU regulations—whether as a result of a de facto or de jure Brussels Effect—the EU is better able to reach the critical mass necessary to tip the balance in the EU's favor in international negotiations. Thus, the Brussels Effect can facilitate the EU's efforts to reach an agreement on international standards that, while modeled after EU rules, will be embedded in treaties and viewed as reflecting an international consensus. The Brussels Effect may also pave the way for multilateral cooperation by changing the underlying bargaining dynamics. For example, the threat of the EU's unilateralism was an important factor in harnessing international consensus on regulating GHG emissions in aviation through the Carbon Offsetting and Reduction Scheme for International Aviation (CORSIA),[123] discussed in chapter 7. The participating countries were incentivized to agree on the CORSIA to a large extent because of the prospect that, absent international agreement, the EU was going to regulate the industry unilaterally. This example illustrates how the EU, at times, is able to leverage unilateralism to promote multilateralism.

THE BRUSSELS EFFECT is one of many mechanisms through which the EU's regulations transform corporate practices and regulatory regimes around the world. As a passive yet powerful market-driven mechanism, the Brussels Effect often prevails over other, more active, mechanisms through which the EU exerts regulatory influence. However, the Brussels Effect has its limits; it may variously be absent, incomplete, or sometimes an ineffective way to exert influence. Ultimately, the precise mechanism of regulatory influence chosen is likely to vary across policy areas or even over time—such as when market-driven harmonization gives way to more active promotion of regulations through treaties and institutions. What sets the EU apart is that, unlike in many other jurisdictions, both market-driven and treaty-driven mechanisms can coexist, or even amplify one another, maximizing the influence EU regulations have over market outcomes worldwide.

PREFACE TO PART TWO

Case Studies

Part II forms the empirical heart of the Brussels Effect by applying the theoretical frameworks of the previous section to its observed operation across four distinct policy areas. Chapter 4 focuses on market competition, discussing the EU's global influence through its competition regulation—both de facto and de jure. Chapter 5 focuses on the digital economy, demonstrating how the EU has exerted influence over digital companies' global data-protection practices as well as their policies regarding hate speech on their platforms, and prompted regulatory reforms abroad. Chapter 6 turns to risk regulation, showing how the EU's efforts to regulate consumer health and safety—in particular pertaining to food safety and chemical safety—have penetrated the global marketplace. Finally, Chapter 7 examines the global impact of the EU's environmental regulation through examples on the control of hazardous substances and electronic waste, protection of animal welfare, and mitigation of climate change. At times, the policy issues included in the chapters can be overlapping, and many of the issues could easily be examined in another chapter with alternative policy areas. For example, while the regulation of chemical safety and regulation of GMOs are both addressed in chapter 6 discussing consumer health, they could equally be handled as part of the chapter 7 discussion on environmental regulation.

These policy areas—market competition, digital economy, consumer health and safety, and the environment—were selected because they are important EU policy areas that illustrate the operation of the Brussels Effect in practice. While they share many features—including their origin in a strong EU-level regulatory mandate—they also exhibit important differences. Some of them represent well-established areas of traditional EU regulation (such as food safety), while others are more recent regulatory innovations (such as online hate speech). Some were driven by largely internal motives (such as hazardous substances in electronics), while others were promulgated from the outset with both internal and external motives in mind (such as emissions trading). In many areas, the EU regulation consists of mandatory rules (such as chemical safety) whereas others rely on voluntary regulatory instruments (such as hate speech online). Some policy areas feature extensive

Commission involvement in enforcement (such as competition policy) whereas in others, enforcement is delegated to member states (such as data protection). All these areas of regulation have been shaped by the Brussels Effect, even if to a different extent. They demonstrate both the strength of the Brussels Effect as well as occasionally its limits, offering an opportunity to illustrate the particular features of the theory that in most instances determine whether the Brussels Effect takes place or not.

The four case studies that will be presented follow a standard format for clarity in an effort to unpack occasionally dense regulatory material. Each case study first introduces the major EU legislation in the field, followed by a brief discussion of the political economy that underlies the legislation. Then, the discussion reviews examples of the Brussels Effect—both de facto and de jure—highlighting particular companies, industries, and countries that have been shaped by the EU's global regulatory reach. The discussion of the de facto Brussels Effect in each case study illustrates the conditions discussed in chapter 2 in the context of actual companies that have adjusted their global conduct or production to EU regulations—or offers reasons for why they have failed to do so. The discussion of the de jure Brussels Effect in each case study provides examples of the formal adoption of EU-style regulations by foreign governments. Empirically, it is seldom possible to disaggregate the various motivations that lead to the de jure Brussels Effect. For this reason, the case studies follow the less-strict definition of the de jure Brussels Effect and discuss empirical examples, whether they stem from the de facto Brussels Effect, various alternate mechanisms discussed in chapter 3, or a combination of them.

The case studies do not systematically test the conditions underlying the de facto Brussels Effect that were outlined in chapter 2. Nor do they claim that other mechanisms of influence, such as consumer pressure, would not influence companies' behavior alongside with the Brussels Effect. However, these case studies will empirically illustrate how the Brussels Effect has shaped various business practices in the presence of the conditions identified as drivers of the Brussels Effect: market size, regulatory capacity, stringent standards, inelastic targets, and non-divisibility. Some of the case studies will further help refine conditions themselves, such as by elucidating their relative importance in explaining whether the Brussels Effect occurs or not.

For example, the case studies all demonstrate the relevance of the EU's market size as a foundation for the theory. Examples of the Brussels Effect are always easiest to find among companies and countries that are most reliant on the EU as their primary export market—hence the multiple examples of the Brussels Effect affecting African farmers' food safety practices, Japanese and Korean electronics manufacturers' product designs, or Silicon Valley IT companies' privacy policies. While examples of the Brussels Effect influencing, for example, Australian companies surely exist, those are not as prevalent given that the EU rarely represents a major export destination for them.

Further, these case studies reveal little variance in three additional conditions underlying the Brussels Effect—strong regulatory capacity, preference for stringent rules, and the inelastic nature of regulation. While the EU acquired its regulatory capacity at different times and as a result of distinct political processes in various policy areas, these case studies suggest that the Brussels Effect occurs in policy domains where the EU has either exclusive competence or competence it shares with member states over the regulatory policy in question. The Brussels Effect is further amplified if the Commission enjoys substantial autonomy (such as in competition regulation), is supported by the expertise of the European Regulatory Agencies (such as in chemical safety or food safety), or where other regulatory powers such as the United States are particularly weak regulators, enhancing the EU's relative regulatory capacity (such as in digital economy).

The Brussels Effect in all case studies stems from the EU's preference for stringent rules—typically not just within the Commission that predictably favors regulation but also among European consumers, citizens, activists, some critical actors representing the industry, as well as among a group of influential member states that had been regulatory pioneers in the field. Obviously, there are examples of policy areas—including financial regulation—where other jurisdictions often harbor a preference for even more stringent rules. In these instances, no Brussels Effect takes place. These case studies identify one exception: in the regulation of online hate speech, some other major jurisdictions, including China, are even more restrictive regulators of online speech, yet global companies still converge to the EU's ("most stringent politically acceptable") rules.

Typically, the EU's stringent regulations encompass other jurisdictions' less-stringent standards. Regulatory standards are rarely mutually incompatible. No country orders companies to generate electronic waste, include harmful chemicals in toys, cultivate GMOs, fix prices with competitors, or infringe data privacy. Thus, by adhering to EU's protective regulations, multinational companies can typically ensure compliance worldwide. However, the case studies show that in a limited set of policy areas, other jurisdictions' standards may, indeed, be incompatible with those of the EU. In such instances—such as the case study discussing the EU's ban and China's requirement to conduct animal testing of cosmetics—compliance with the EU's stringent standard does not ensure compliance with all other markets. Here, a more limited or partial Brussels Effect takes place as companies likely apply the EU standard in most foreign markets but retain a separate production line for China to meet its conflicting standard. Case studies also reveal some (rare) examples where "the Brussels Effect plus" may occur (such as in the regulation of the digital economy). The EU may be more stringent on one dimension of a regulation, but some other jurisdiction may be more stringent on another dimension. In such a setting, an even stronger version of the Brussels Effect is likely to take place as companies can operate globally only by adhering to the combination of these (two or more) most stringent standards.

All these case studies further compound the importance of inelasticity as a core driver of the Brussels Effect—the discussed policy areas are all forms of consumer market regulation, which make it inherently more difficult to circumvent EU regulations through relocation or other corporate strategies as the location of the consumer in the EU determines the applicability of EU regulation. Inelasticity is therefore a fundamental yet simple condition in the case studies: one that shows little variance across regulatory policies that are targeted at consumer markets. In contrast, the Brussels Effect condition that shows the greatest variance both across and within the individual case studies is that of non-divisibility. Non-divisibility is often the single most salient factor explaining the variance in the occurrence of the Brussels Effect. This is demonstrated particularly in the case studies on competition regulation, digital economy, and food safety, which reveal many examples of product or service divisibility that have been sufficient to prevent the Brussels Effect from taking place—even when all of the other conditions underlying the theory were present. Another useful case study on the limits of the Brussels Effect is the EU's emissions trading scheme (ETS) and the EU's largely unsuccessful attempts to extend the ETS into the international aviation industry. It also provides one of the rare counter-examples where foreign governments have successfully reined in the Brussels Effect.

Aggregating the numerous examples from across Africa, Asia, Latin America, Middle East, Russia, and the United States, these case studies reveal a story of the vastly underestimated global reach of the de jure Brussels Effect, which complements the extensive de facto Brussels Effect. They demonstrate how many countries show a particularly strong willingness to emulate the EU with some countries explicitly acknowledging the use of the EU as a model for their own legislation (such as Korea), while other countries emulating the EU more selectively (such as Japan). The case studies also suggest that the Brussels Effect is not binary, but a greater or lesser force depending on the type of regulation and the particular jurisdiction emulating EU regulations. For example, the case study on the RoHS regulation demonstrates how the de jure Brussels Effect may exist in strong form in one market (Korea) while at the same time in a weaker form in another market (Japan). Some countries rarely want to be seen as copying the EU, presumably as they do not want to be seen as rule takers that are overly influenced by other powers—in particular if they are large powers themselves. The United States, for example, seldom features in case studies on the de jure Brussels Effect despite the extensive de facto Brussels Effect on American companies. At the same time, the de jure Brussels

Effect is more common among individual states in the United States. Finally, case studies reveal examples of the de jure Brussels Effect that exists on paper but may be limited in practice (such as China copying EU's data protection regulation). This serves as a reminder that the actual effectiveness of the de jure Brussels Effect is difficult to measure in precise terms.

While there is no separate case study dedicated to areas that do not lend themselves to the Brussels Effect of any kind—those would be short case studies—it is important to keep in mind that the Brussels Effect is inherently limited when its underlying conditions are weak or nonexistent. This is the case in instances where the EU is not a significant export market for foreign companies; where it does not have regulatory capacity to act; where it does not promulgate most stringent standards; where regulation is elastic; or where the corporate conduct or production is divisible. The case studies included in Part II are therefore not representative of the entire universe of economic regulation—while the Brussels Effect has penetrated many sectors of the economy, there remain many areas of regulation that do not emanate from Brussels and where the EU is not setting the global standards. Also, the case studies discussed do not represent the entire universe of regulatory policies that are characterized by the Brussels Effect. There are additional policy areas that lend themselves to the Brussels Effect even though there is no case study dedicated to them. For these reasons, Part II may be viewed as alternatively overstating or understating the prevalence of the Brussels Effect. Yet even with these limitations, the selected case studies that follow should provide a diverse set of examples that illuminate the theoretical claims made in Part I, and demonstrate the vast and varied areas where the Brussels Effect is driving the global regulatory agenda today.

4

Market Competition

COMPETITION LAW OFFERS one of the most prominent examples of the EU's global regulatory hegemony. In 2018, the European Commission fined Google $5 billion in a competition law case involving the company's operating system, Android.[1] This fine came on the heels of a $2.3 billion fine in 2017, which the Commission imposed after concluding that the company manipulated its search results to favor its own comparison-shopping service to the detriment of its rivals.[2] The Commission's third case against Google, focusing on the company's AdSense online advertising program, resulted in a $1.7 billion fine in 2019.[3] The EU's other enforcement targets over the last several years include two other US-based tech giants: Qualcomm[4] and Apple.[5] These prominent cases against US companies are not a new phenomenon. They build on a series of high-profile decisions against leading US corporations—including Intel,[6] Microsoft,[7] and General Electric[8]—over the past two decades. In all these instances, the companies' practices were also investigated by US agencies. However, in contrast with the EU, US regulators either responded with more modest penalties or chose not to levy any punishment at all. However, no matter what the US response, the United States has been powerless in constraining the EU's decisions, and the remedies imposed by the EU have led to notable changes in the companies' practices in the EU and at times also abroad, including in the United States.

In addition to shaping the global marketplace through the extraterritorial enforcement of its own competition law, the EU has been remarkably successful in exporting its regulatory regime abroad. Today, over 130 jurisdictions have a domestic competition law, making competition law one of the most widespread forms of economic regulation around the world.[9] A closer look at these laws reveals that a great majority of them have been drafted to closely resemble EU competition law.[10] This notable de jure Brussels Effect has led to a situation where

The Brussels Effect. Anu Bradford, Oxford University Press (2020). © Oxford University Press.
DOI: 10.1093/oso/9780190088583.001.0001

the majority of the global markets are covered, in practice, by a variant of EU competition law.

The following discussion first introduces the key aspects of EU competition law. It then explains why the EU has chosen to build an extensive regulatory capacity in this area, illustrating how competition law forms a critical dimension of the EU's broader single market program. Following that, it offers examples of the de facto and de jure Brussels Effects pertaining to competition regulation.

Major Legislation

EU competition law was enacted in 1957 as part of the EU's founding treaties. Article 101 of the Treaty of the Functioning of the European Union (TFEU) expressly prohibits anticompetitive agreements between firms.[11] Such prohibited agreements include, for example, price-fixing cartels between competing firms or distribution agreements where suppliers dictate the prices for their distributors. Article 102 of the TFEU prohibits the abuse of a dominant position.[12] This provision is targeted at companies that hold significant market power and engage in practices that reduce competition on the market. Examples of such abusive practices would be the dominant company's refusal to supply products to certain competitors or predatory pricing behavior in an effort to oust competitors from the market. The European Merger Control Regulation (EMCR) was first promulgated 30 years later, in 1990, and revised in 2004.[13] The EMCR introduced a pre-notification obligation for all mergers and acquisitions above a certain revenue threshold and vested the Commission with the power to attach conditions or prohibit a transaction when it harms competition in the common market.

EU competition law is considerably more recent than its US counterpart. Key US competition laws include the 1890 Sherman Act,[14] which regulates anticompetitive agreements and monopolies; and the 1914 Clayton Act, which regulates mergers.[15] The EU and US competition laws share many similarities but also important differences. Both jurisdictions recognize similar types of behavior as potentially anticompetitive and structure their laws around the following categories: 1) anticompetitive agreements, 2) monopolization, and 3) control of mergers. In addition, EU competition law regulates illegal state aid, which refers to selective advantage given by national authorities to certain but not all firms.[16] The EU and the United States differ in terms of the degree to which they tolerate market power and therefore intervene in the conduct of a dominant company. The EU is more likely to conclude that a company has a "dominant position" on the market and, once dominance is established, more likely to find that the company is abusing its dominance.[17] The EU is also generally viewed as more stringent when it comes to vertical agreements with suppliers or distributors. Merger control is an area of historical divergence—the EU adopted its merger control regulation significantly later than the United States. However, today, while substantive rules on mergers are largely aligned, the EU is more prone to challenge in particular vertical or conglomerate mergers.

In addition to these substantive differences, the institutional features and remedies underlying each system present an even greater divergence. For example, whereas the US agencies have to involve courts when seeking an injunction or another remedy, the Commission has vast administrative powers to carry out enforcement without needing to resort to courts.[18] However, the EU can be seen as trailing the United States in terms of the remedies at its disposal when competition infringement is established. Unlike the United States, the EU does not levy criminal penalties but instead relies exclusively on administrative fines and other civil remedies.[19] The United States also provides for sizable damages (including treble damages), which are common, given the prevalence of private right of action. Private enforcement is widespread in the United States, but much more limited in Europe. Only recently has the EU promulgated a directive to pave the way for greater private enforcement before member states courts.[20]

Despite its inability to deploy criminal remedies, few would dispute the characterization of the EU as the most stringent competition enforcer in the world. This is particularly consequential, given how jurisdiction works in this area of law. Competition law has a peculiar feature among areas of economic regulation, which allows several jurisdictions to intervene in the same transaction or against the same companies, as long as their market is "affected." As a result, the same conduct is often investigated simultaneously by multiple countries. In such instances, the most aggressive regulator typically prevails over more lenient ones. In other words, where conflict exists among different sets of laws and regulators, it is the most stringent competition law that often wins. For example, if the US government approves a global merger but the EU bans the very same transaction, the merger is prohibited worldwide. Facing a prohibition in one jurisdiction, companies seeking to merge have two options: abandon the merger or abandon their business in the jurisdiction challenging the merger. If the market of the most aggressive regulator is relatively insignificant, the company might choose the latter. However, if this market is large, abandoning it is not often a realistic option.[21] At the international level, the EU competition laws are, indeed, often the most stringent.[22] The EU also consists of a consumer market that is too large and important to abandon. For this reason, EU competition laws have often become the de facto global competition standards to which the more permissive US antitrust laws often must yield.[23]

Political Economy

Reasons for the differences between US and EU competition regulation are manifold, reflecting the different political economy conditions prevailing in the two jurisdictions. At the most fundamental or philosophical level, EU competition authorities are inherently suspicious of the markets' ability to deliver efficient outcomes and are therefore more inclined to intervene through a regulatory process.[24] While the EU is more fearful of the harmful effects of nonintervention (so-called false negatives, anticompetitive practices that the EU might fail to regulate), the US authorities are often more mindful of the detrimental effects of inefficient intervention (so-called false positives, pro-competitive practices that the United States might erroneously restrict).[25] This difference partly explains why the EU has generally been prepared to intervene more frequently and more aggressively.

This distinction between EU and US regulatory responses reflects, to some extent, a different ideology embraced by Europeans and Americans. Europeans place greater trust in the government whereas Americans trust the markets more. Yet it is also a reflection of past experiences with how markets work. Europeans remain more skeptical of the market's ability to self-regulate, partly due to the fact that many European economies were for a long time characterized by a large number of state-owned companies. Once these companies were privatized, they continued to enjoy market power as incumbents, which necessitated competition regulation to ensure that those incumbent privileges did not distort market competition.[26] In addition, capital markets are less well developed in the EU than in the United States, making it harder to raise the necessary funds to enter the market in Europe. Consequently, the threat of new entrants alone does not always provide a sufficient check on existing market players, making government intervention necessary.

EU competition law is driven by two primary objectives: the protection of consumer welfare and the furthering of the single market. Competition law is thus aimed at maximizing the welfare of European consumers and ensuring that the common market remains open and competitive. This long-standing tendency to link competition law to the EU's broader market integration agenda is perhaps the most distinctive feature of EU competition law.[27] As described by a European parliament document: "The fundamental objective of EU competition rules is to prevent distortion of competition. This is not however an end in itself. It is rather a condition for achieving a free and dynamic internal market."[28] Seen this way, competition law is an essential complement to trade liberalization, enacted to ensure that private anticompetitive practices do not frustrate the economic gains accomplished through the removal of public barriers, such as tariffs and quotas, between member states.

Surely, competition law has always been a mechanism to advance consumer welfare as such—and not only through its contribution toward market integration.[29] More competition pushes companies toward efficient allocation of their resources, which results in lower prices and better quality products for consumers.[30] While the EU has, over the decades, increasingly come to embrace consumer welfare as the primary goal of competition law, it has always been more open to considering a wider range of additional policy goals, even if at the margin.[31] For example, through its competition policy, the EU has advanced values such as fairness,[32] the protection of small- and medium-sized companies,[33] and the protection of the structure of the market and hence competition as such.[34] These multiple goals set the EU apart from the United States that has traditionally focused very narrowly on economic goals—whether determined by consumer welfare or efficiency.[35] Presumably, these broader goals behind EU competition law also allow for more bases of intervention, expanding the scope of competition enforcement compared to the scope of the law in the United States, which only allows for an intervention on a narrow basis of consumer harm.[36]

Beyond these well-established goals of EU competition law, a more skeptical view portrays EU competition policy as a political instrument that is leveraged not just for the benefit of consumers but deployed as a tool for protectionism.[37] Protectionist competition policy can manifest itself, for example, in the form of a biased enforcement strategy, with agencies applying more stringent standards to acquisitions by foreign-owned firms than companies that are locally owned. Similarly, agencies may turn a blind eye to domestic cartels or abusive behavior by domestic dominant companies, while pursuing the same conduct engaged in by foreign companies.

The Commission's 2001 decision to block the $42 billion acquisition of Honeywell by General Electric—a merger approved by the US Department of Justice—is perhaps the most well-known of these cases of the EU's alleged protectionism.[38] In the wake of *GE/Honeywell* decision, for example, US Treasury Secretary Paul O'Neill called the Commission's decision "off the wall," describing the Commission as "autocratic," and the Department of Justice's chief antitrust enforcement official noted the Commission's "divergence" from the principle that "the antitrust laws protect competition, not competitors."[39] Members of the US Congress expressly accused the Commission of "using its merger-review process as a tool to protect and promote European industry at the expense of U.S. competitors."[40]

But *GE/Honeywell* does not stand alone, and similar concerns have resurfaced repeatedly since. In the name of competition law, the Commission has repeatedly blocked or forced significant restructuring of mergers involving a wide range of well-known American firms, including Boeing, MCI WorldCom, Time Warner, and UPS.[41] These high-profile interventions have raised concerns that

the Commission is using its merger-review power to advance protectionist industrial policy rather than competition. The concern was expressed, for example, by
C. Boyden Gray, the former US ambassador to the EU, who stated more than
ten years ago that "there is now recognition [in the US] that the EU is being
aggressive about exporting their approach—which tends to favour their own
native companies."[42]

Today, the primary concern for the US business community is the European
Commission's mounting competition investigations of US high-tech companies, including Apple, Google, and Qualcomm, which critics say reflect the EU's
attempt to offset the US' technological edge and tilt the market in favor of their
weaker European rivals.[43] A lead lawyer by Apple accused the Commission of
choosing Apple as a "convenient target for an EU antitrust chief driven by headlines."[44] In 2015, President Obama described the EU's competition investigations
into Google and Facebook as reflecting European service providers' inability
to compete with their US counterparts, suggesting that the investigations were
motivated by the EU's need to "carve out some of their commercial interests."[45]
In 2018, President Trump reacted to the $5 billion competition fine on Google by
complaining how "American businesses were at a disadvantage in Europe"[46] and
how "[Europeans] truly have taken advantage of the U.S., but not for long!"[47] The
tweet by Senator Orrin Hatch, a Republican from Utah, further captured the
sentiment shared by many in the United States: "The EU has a history of engaging in regulatory, tax & competition actions & proposals that disproportionately
hit U.S. tech companies. This decision calls into question whether these actions
are anything more than a series of discriminatory revenue grabs."[48]

However, as detailed in chapter 8, accusations of EU's protectionism may be
misplaced, and there are several reasons to doubt that protectionism is driving
the EU's competition policy agenda. First, European companies are rarely the
main beneficiaries of the Commission's enforcement actions. In most instances,
it is other US companies (as opposed to European firms) that benefit from the
EU restricting the conduct of their US competitors. For instance, Google has no
direct European rival that would be able to gain any advantage when Google is
forced to change its business model. Further, numerous examples show that the
EU competition law also targets EU companies with a heavy hand. For example,
in a 2016 acquisition involving the world's largest and second largest brewers, the
Commission required the Belgian acquirer Anheuser-Busch InBev to sell practically the entire UK-based beer business as a condition for approving AB InBev's
over $100 billion acquisition of SABMiller.[49]

Of course, protectionism is often difficult to detect, let alone systematically measure, and much of the discussion until today has relied on anecdotes
on both sides. The most substantial effort to move beyond these anecdotes and

empirically study protectionist motives underlying EU merger control comes from an analysis conducted at Columbia University.[50] This study relies on original data that include all mergers notified to the Commission as of 1990—the year when EU merger control was established—until 2014, amounting to more than 5,000 proposed transactions in total. The analysis reveals no evidence that the Commission has systematically used its authority for protectionist ends. If anything, the analysis indicates that the Commission is *less* likely to challenge transactions involving foreign acquirers. Obviously, it cannot be excluded that protectionism might play an occasional role in European merger-review cases. However, this study suggests that there is no bias that systematically affects the Commission's merger-enforcement outcomes.

A different study by other authors comparing cartel enforcement in the EU and the United States similarly failed to detect any bias against US companies by the Commission.[51] The authors compared the tendency of the US and EU regulators to leverage cartel fines against the EU, US, and "ROW" firms—ROW referring to "the rest of the world," that is, non-US and non-EU firms. The authors found that the EU is more likely to fine domestic (EU) firms and ROW firms than US firms, and that the size of the fine does not differ according to the nationality. The United States, by contrast, appears to target ROW firms in particular and levies significantly higher fines on foreign firms—whether ROW or EU—than domestic firms. This finding further challenges the prior assumptions that protectionist motives are driving EU competition policy.

The narrative that emerges from these studies is that the EU is a tough competition regulator—but it is tough on everyone: US firms, EU firms, and the firms from the rest of the world. European firms can take no comfort that their nationality alone would give them an advantage in Commission investigations. Most recently, the Commission resisted the persistent calls by the two most powerful member states—Germany and France—to approve a rail merger between the German company, Siemens, and the French company, Alstom. This merger would have created a European champion[52] with the ability to compete against foreign—including formidable Chinese—rivals.[53] This suggests that, if anything, EU competition law is used as a tool to rein in EU member states' protectionist tendencies. At the same time, it will be interesting to see if this policy objective will change in the near future. As a result of the *Siemens/Alstrom* ruling,[54] politicians from France and Germany are calling for the reassessment of EU competition policy, given today's geopolitical realities.[55] This would, according to them, consist of recognizing the creation of "European champions" as a legitimate goal of EU competition law. Thus far, this effort has not resonated with the Commission. Brushing off the demands to promote "European giants" to better compete with China, Competition Commissioner Margarethe Vestager recently suggested that the EU should "[l]et the Chinese be Chinese. We would be lousy Chinese. They are much better at it."[56]

De Facto Brussels Effect

Most of the conditions underlying the Brussels Effect—market size, regulatory capacity, stringent standards, inelastic targets, and non-divisibility—are clearly present in the case of competition law. The EU is an important market for many multinational companies, and they cannot afford to forgo selling their products and services to the large number of relatively wealthy European consumers. Companies like Google, which have a heavy user base in the EU, will not be able to divert that amount of trade elsewhere because of the EU's market size. Any allegedly anticompetitive conduct or transaction pursued by these companies is likely to affect the EU market and thus invite scrutiny by the Commission.

Of course, there are still numerous business practices and corporate transactions taking place around the world that do not involve European markets and hence do not fall within the purview of EU competition law. For those instances, the EU's market size is irrelevant. A cartel fixing prices exclusively in Latin America would not involve the EU market and hence would not lead the EU to act. Similarly, a purely local or regional merger between two companies in Africa with trivial revenue in Europe would not trigger an EU merger review. A distribution agreement between a European supplier and a Japanese distributor would also fall outside the scope of EU competition law, as long as the distributor was only supplying products to Japanese customers. Yet, generally speaking, any company over a certain size and wishing to serve the EU market typically concludes that the costs of compliance with EU competition law are worth it in exchange for gaining access to over 500 million consumers. In these instances, the first condition of the Brussels Effect—market size—is met.

Several other conditions of the Brussels Effect are typically present as well. As already acknowledged, the EU has built tremendous regulatory capacity in this area. Competition law is one of the most well-established fields of EU-level competence, and the Commission has gained extensive experience enforcing competition rules since 1957. The Commission enjoys an unusually high degree of delegation in the enforcement of competition law, allowing it to often act without the need to involve other institutions.[57] This makes competition law an area where the EU's regulatory capacity is vast and least constrained by political checks— whether by the Council, European Parliament, or the individual member states. If anything, the EU has harnessed the regulatory capacity of the member states to further the goals of EU competition law. EU competition law coexists with 28 national competition regimes in its member states. These individual EU members have the power to enforce not only their national law but also EU competition rules, further adding to the regulatory capacity of the EU.[58]

The European Court of Justice (ECJ) exercises judicial review over the Commission decisions, yet these judicial checks are much more limited than those in the United States. For instance, unlike the DOJ antitrust division, which needs to go to a federal court to enjoin a merger, the Commission is authorized to impose remedies without pursuing litigation before European courts. In this sense, the Commission has a lower threshold at which it will dispatch its regulatory capacity than its US counterparts. Many critics have suggested that this procedure essentially renders the Commission the prosecutor, judge, and jury of merger review throughout Europe.[59] The parties do have the right to appeal the decision to the EU's General Court and, ultimately, the ECJ. Yet strikingly few Commission decisions in this area are appealed: 99% of mergers reviewed by the Commission are not challenged before the courts, making the Commission the single most important player in worldwide merger enforcement.[60]

The EU's regulatory capacity in competition law is also broad in the sense that it comprises control of state aid. This extends the EU's regulatory reach to instances where EU member states provide selective advantages (subsidies) to certain companies. For example, the EU's state aid rules formed the basis for the recent, controversial ruling involving the Irish government and Apple. In 2016, the Commission ordered Ireland to reclaim €13 billion ($15 billion) in unpaid tax revenue from Apple. According to the Commission, Apple took advantage of a parent-branch profit attribution scheme that attributed 90% of the profits the company derived from its non-US sales to Apple's Irish subsidiaries. This resulted in Apple paying a conspicuously low tax rate of 4% on nearly $200 billion in profits it earned outside the United States over the past decade. But to do so, Apple had relied on a tax ruling issued by Irish tax authorities back in 1991; a ruling that the Commission found to be contrary to EU state aid rules in this case. Consequently, the Commission ordered Ireland to claw back the unpaid taxes from Apple on grounds that it gave Apple an undue tax advantage, which distorted competition and hence violated EU's state aid rules. This is an interesting case as it sits between competition law and tax law. The EU has no regulatory authority over tax policy, which remains the prerogative of member states. Yet it found a basis to act based on its powers within EU competition law.

Market size and regulatory capacity alone do not explain the EU's global dominance in competition law. Both the US and EU agencies are vested with extraterritorial regulatory capacity and exert jurisdiction over a large domestic market.[61] It is thus not the regulatory capacity as such that has made the EU the world's de facto competition enforcer. Instead, it is the EU's sustained preference to more stringent competition law than the United States that sets it apart. The EU harbors a broad notion of what is prohibited under competition law. For example, as noted in the earlier discussion comparing EU to US competition law, the EU is generally more prone to find that a company enjoys a dominant position or engages in anticompetitive conduct. This relative stringency of EU competition law explains why companies that adjust their conduct to the most stringent competition rules in an effort to ensure global compliance typically look to the EU.

One manifestation of the well-known stringency of EU competition law relates to the EU often being a "forum of choice" for foreign companies that seek to leverage stringent EU competition regulations against their own competitors. This often results from these companies' belief that the EU is more likely to intervene in a competition matter, or to impose more invasive remedies if a violation is found. In particular, US producers have frequently turned to the Commission to challenge their competitors' practices, making Brussels the primary legal battleground for their competition disputes. For example, US-based United Technologies was the principal complainant in the *GE/Honeywell* merger investigation after having lost its acquisition bid to GE—the merger that the Commission ultimately prohibited in 2001. Two US companies, Novell and Sun Microsystems, similarly brought charges against Microsoft in the EU in 1998,[62] knowing that they were more likely to obtain remedies in the EU, which harbors a broader notion of what constitutes anticompetitive conduct. Interestingly, as the tables turned, it was Microsoft that lodged a competition complaint before the European Commission against Google in 2011.[63] Even though Microsoft ultimately dropped out after reaching a settlement with Google in 2016, other US companies, including Oracle, Kayak, Expedia, and Trip Advisor[64] continued to press the Commission to issue a decision against Google—which it did with heavy fines of $2.3 billion; $5 billion; and, in the most recent case, $1.7 billion.[65] Similarly, the EU's 2009 competition ruling against Intel stemmed from a complaint by Intel's US rival, AMD. Indeed, most of the high-profile EU competition battles today involve US companies on both sides of the dispute, each drawn to Brussels because of the perceived stringency of EU competition rules.

Competition law is also highly inelastic. EU competition law applies as long as allegedly anticompetitive conduct has an effect on the EU market. The nationality of the company is irrelevant. It is therefore impossible to circumvent EU competition rules by establishing or relocating a company outside the EU. As long as EU consumers are affected, the EU has the basis to act. In merger control, the EU's regulatory authority is triggered as long as the merging parties generate a specified amount of turnover (revenue) in the EU.[66] Again, it is irrelevant where the parties' headquarters are or even where the "gravity of the merger" is. As the companies cannot evade EU authority by relocating, the only way to escape the EU's regulatory review would be to carve out enough assets out of the merger (by, for example, spinning off EU subsidiaries) so that the parties to the transaction would not generate notable revenue in Europe. However, such restructuring of the transaction would typically remove the business rationale underlying the transaction.

With other conditions fulfilled, whether or not the Brussels Effect takes place typically turns on the question of divisibility. Here, notable differences exist across different types of competition matters: merger review, cartel behavior, and abuse of dominance. A prohibition by the EU of a transnational merger represents the purest example of the Brussels Effect due to the legal non-divisibility of such a merger. Yet in many cases against dominant companies, no de facto Brussels Effect takes place, as companies are able to divide their conduct across jurisdictions and limit their remedies to the EU only. The next discussion looks at these various examples in turn.

In terms of merger control, there are several examples where the de facto Brussels Effect has taken place. However, there are also many instances where it has not. As discussed in chapter 2, global mergers cannot be consummated on a jurisdiction-by-jurisdiction basis. In this sense, mergers are legally non-divisible. In practice this entails that the most stringent merger-review jurisdiction gets to determine the worldwide fate of the transaction.[67] The proposed *GE/Honeywell* merger, discussed earlier in this chapter, is arguably the most famous example of the Brussels Effect affecting large cross-border mergers.[68] When the Commission blocked the merger, it was irrelevant that the US antitrust authorities had previously cleared the transaction: the acquisition was banned worldwide because the merger was legally non-divisible—as a matter of law, it was impossible to let the merger proceed in one market and prohibit it in another.

Although the *GE/Honeywell* deal is the most prominent, there are several other examples of the Brussels Effect globalizing EU merger control decisions. In 1991, the EU blocked the acquisition of the Canadian company De Havilland by the French-Italian company Avions de Transport Régional, which had been approved by the Canadian authorities.[69] Soon thereafter, in 1996, the EU prohibited a merger between the South African company Gencor and the UK-based Lonrho,[70] even though the most significant effect on competition was felt in South Africa. More recently in 2013, the Commission blocked the attempted acquisition of the Dutch logistics company TNT Express by its US-based rival UPS.[71] While its primary market was Europe, TNT Express was active in over 60 countries. The EU decision had an impact on all those markets due to the Brussels Effect. This case is also particularly interesting for how it has evolved—because UPS had the merger decision overturned by the EU's General Court in 2017, it is now seeking $2.14 billion in damages from the EU based on that ruling. Yet regardless of the UPS's court victory, the *UPS/TNT* Express merger cannot be revived. Another US company, FedEx, acquired TNT Express in 2015 after receiving the Commission's approval.[72] This example, where one rejected acquisition is quickly replaced by a different one, shows how mergers typically cannot be reinvigorated after the Commission's prohibition. This makes the Commission the final arbiter of these global deals—and the Brussels Effect immune to a court reversal.

When the EU falls short of banning a merger but requests certain commitments from the merging parties as a condition for approving a merger—such as ordering a divestiture of a production plant—such a divestiture cannot typically be consummated in the EU only. That divestiture usually affects the entire global structure of the company through the Brussels Effect. For example, in 2009, the Commission imposed an obligation to divest one of the parties' factories in Japan as a condition for a merger between Panasonic and Sanyo.[73] The divestiture was legally non-divisible and hence had an obvious global effect. Many behavioral remedies similarly have an effect outside the EU. For instance, in 1997, the EU threatened to block a merger between two US companies, Boeing and McDonnell Douglas, even though the deal was already cleared by the US authorities without conditions.[74] In the end, the EU let the merger proceed subject to extensive commitments.[75] These included abandoning Boeing's exclusive dealing contracts with various US carriers.[76] As a result, those exclusive contracts became illegal globally. In 2011, the Commission required Intel to unbundle software and security solutions worldwide as a condition for the merger.[77] It also required Intel to release interoperability information relevant for its chipsets and central processing units to independent security software vendors on a royalty-free basis.[78] These examples further illustrate the significance of the Brussels Effect in the merger-review context.

However, sometimes the practical effect of seemingly global merger remedies can be limited to the EU. For example, when the EU approved a merger between AOL and Time Warner in 2000, it required AOL to first sever all structural links with German media group Bertelsmann AG.[79] Previously, AOL had conducted all its operations in Europe through two joint ventures in which Bertelsmann was a partner. The divestiture was globally effective—in other words, even if no other competition agencies required such divestment, the merged entity had to sever its links with respect to the company's global operations. At the same time, it is not clear the divestiture affected the merged entity's business strategy in other markets such as the United Sates as the divested entity was relevant for carrying out operations only in Europe.

Cartel investigations may also have a global effect and be thereby subject to the Brussels Effect. Whenever the EU uncovers a cartel—whether as a result of the Commission's leniency program that encourages whistle-blowing or following its own investigation—the cartel is likely to unravel worldwide. If one of the participating firms acts as a whistle-blower and chooses to collaborate with the Commission, there is likely no trust left among the colluding firms to sustain the cartel in other markets. In this sense, it is the trust that is non-divisible even if it continued to be legally, technically, or economically feasible to continue to operate the cartel in other jurisdictions. Similarly, if the Commission detects the cartel on its own initiative, other foreign agencies quickly learn about the cartel's existence and likely follow with their own investigations. These dynamics often render cartel investigations globally non-divisible in practice.

However, cartel enforcement rarely relies on the Brussels Effect alone. In most of the high-profile cartel cases, including the Air Cargo, LIBOR/interest rate derivatives, and Cathode Ray Tubes cases, several jurisdictions conducted joint raids to uncover evidence of the cartel or otherwise cooperated in investigations.[80] For example, in the Cathode Ray Tubes case, the EU, United States, and Japan began near simultaneous investigations and Korea joined the EU investigation two years later.[81] Further, the EU and the United States acted jointly in dismantling one of the most extensive and long lasting cartels in the world—the international vitamins cartel. This cartel, which lasted over ten years, entailed at least thirteen companies fixing prices in approximately twelve product markets.[82] It is estimated that the cartel affected $5 billion of commerce.[83] The EU and US' enforcement efforts, while focused on their respective markets, were ultimately successful in ending the cartel worldwide.[84]

There are several reasons for why the Brussels Effect is often incomplete (or even entirely inexistent) in cartel enforcement. First, many cartels are detected today through leniency programs, which give the parties an incentive to report their cartel in multiple jurisdictions at the same time to ensure that their cooperation with authorities in one jurisdiction will not lead to a liability being imposed elsewhere once the cartel's existence is revealed. This led, for example, Lufthansa to simultaneously disclose information about its participation in an air cargo cartel to the United States, EU, and 15–20 other key competition authorities.[85] Second, the detection of a cartel often requires uncovering evidence in multiple jurisdictions. The EU cannot alone conduct dawn raids in markets other than its own, giving it the reason to engage in enforcement cooperation as opposed to rely on unilateralism. In this sense, the EU's regulatory capacity in cartel matters is also more incomplete in comparison to its capacity in other competition matters. Third, in imposing the remedy, the EU only calculates the harm to its own market, and its fines fail to recover the overcharge in other markets. To effectively deter a cartel, these other jurisdictions need to follow with their own investigations, or else affected firms could recoup their EU-imposed fines through overcharges in other markets. Initiating their own investigations also allows foreign agencies to extract a fine—even if they are largely free riding on the investigative efforts of the EU.

While international cooperation in cartel investigations may be common, sometimes the remedies imposed in cartel cases by a single jurisdiction, such as the EU, have a global character. These are the instances where the Brussels Effect is likely to occur. For example, international maritime container shipping has been a frequent target of cartel investigations by various national competition authorities, often involving multiple jurisdictions and overlapping players and practices. The remedies that result from these investigations appear to be non-divisible insomuch as international maritime shipping pricing represents a single transaction across borders as any given shipment travels between continents; thus, regulating one side of the transaction inherently regulates both. For example, in 2017 the EU settled a cartel investigation with a number of Asian, European, and Middle Eastern shipping companies in order to change their pricing practices.[86] These pricing practices extended to various shipping routes, affecting also the many non-EU source jurisdictions from which the carriers depart for the EU. Here, the Brussels Effect was triggered by the technical non-divisibility of pricing linking the two jurisdictions—the origin and the destination.

In addition to its merger control and cartel investigations, the EU's enforcement of its rules against dominant companies offers a particularly intriguing area of competition law for examining the operation of the Brussels Effect. The EU's dominance investigations have garnered substantial attention recently. The Commission has imposed record-high fines and behavioral remedies against dominant US companies, including Google; Qualcomm; Intel; and, over a decade earlier, Microsoft.[87] These cases suggest that—while the EU is at times able to influence the conduct of dominant companies worldwide—in many instances, no Brussels Effect takes place. In these latter instances, the targets of the EU's dominance investigations are able to deploy divisibility and limit their compliance with the EU to the European market.

Whenever the remedies are non-divisible, the Brussels Effect is likely to occur. For example, in 2006, the Commission required a South African diamond company, De Beers, to stop buying rough diamonds from a Russian company, Alrosa.[88] Even if South African or Russian authorities would not have required such a commitment, the EU's decision impacted their markets as well, making it impossible to source from Alrosa worldwide.[89] Yet in other instances, the Brussels Effect fails to take place because of the existence of divisibility. For example, in 2005, Coca-Cola committed to substantial behavioral constraints to settle an EU competition investigation into exclusivity requirements in its distributorship agreements, as well as certain rebates and tying programs.[90] At the same time, because PepsiCo failed to prove Coca-Cola's market power in the United States, and different distributorship agreements could be made with non-European distributors, those restrictions were irrelevant to Coca-Cola's US activities.[91] Yet, in other cases involving similar conduct in smaller countries such as Israel where Coca-Cola had greater market share, the company "agreed to restrain its conduct . . . in the same fashion that was required by a consent decree in the EU."[92]

Recent Commission's investigations against Google offer further illustration of the divisibility of remedies. In the Commission's 2018 Google Shopping investigation, Google was found to violate EU competition rules by giving preference to Google's own shopping service over other similar online comparison-shopping platforms.[93] The Commission fined Google and ordered it to comply with the principle of equal treatment by removing any bias that favored its own platform. Google responded with a divisible remedy.[94] The company established a separate business unit to operate Google Shopping in the EU. This separate unit would oversee an auction system where Google Shopping would compete against other online shopping platforms in an auction for preferred advertisement placement on Google Search—in the EU only. As a result of this scheme, no change was made to Google Search or Google Shopping operations in the United States.[95] With the help of geolocation techniques, Google managed to ring-fence its European shopping business and ensure that the users who access Google sites using a non-European IP address will continue to be governed by its previous business model for Google Shopping.[96]

Sometimes, however, it is possible to see the Brussels Effect occur with respect to one element of a specific case, while in another part of the same case, the Brussels Effect is absent. The 2004 Microsoft case provides an illustrative example.[97] After finding that Microsoft had abused its dominance position by illegally withholding the interoperability information—information necessary to exchange and mutually use information related to software products for a workgroup server operating system—from its rivals, the Commission ordered the company to disclose that information. Microsoft implemented the disclosure on a worldwide basis in order to maintain a single worldwide license agreement.[98] This is a classic illustration of the Brussels Effect. In another aspect of the same case, however, the Brussels Effect failed to materialize. The Commission also found that Microsoft had been illegally tying its Windows Media Player to its Windows operating system, foreclosing the market from other providers of media players. The Commission ordered the company to unbundle the Windows Media Player from its operating system and offer a version of its OS without the company's own media player preinstalled. This was a remedy that Microsoft only implemented in Europe, continuing to offer a bundled version of its products in other markets such as the United States.[99] It is an equally classic illustration of, this time, the limits of the Brussels Effect due to the absence of non-divisibility.

Together, these examples show the critical role of non-divisibility in determining whether or not the Brussels Effect takes place in the end.

Beyond these major categories of competition law—mergers, cartels, and dominance cases—where the EU actively pursues certain conduct or reviews a transaction for its anticompetitive effects, corporate compliance programs can also be affected by the Brussels Effect. Many companies are likely to draft these (often global) programs in light of EU law as they seek to minimize compliance errors and associated legal risks. Global compliance with the most stringent regulatory regime—typically that of the EU—minimizes these errors as well as complexity that would arise if the company maintained different compliance policies in different markets. For example, a review of Siemens's Business Compliance Guidelines reveals that its competition provisions are drafted to closely resemble EU competition law.[100] Similarly, ExxonMobil's Legal Compliance Guide reflects several EU competition law provisions, in particular its guidance on the company's interactions with customers.[101]

Similarly, for reasons relating to the efficiency and simplicity of corporate operations, firms tend to deploy standardized contract clauses across their global network of distribution or licensing agreements. Few global companies are likely to find it efficient to negotiate different types of agreements with multiple licensees or distributors for each market in which they operate. Instead of introducing and managing such complexity, they are likely to resort to highly standardized contract terms. Here, the EU competition law often provides a template as compliance with EU rules typically ensures compliance in other markets as well, even if that template was at times adjusted to account for the variation in legal rules or different distribution models across different markets. For example, companies such as Microsoft base their agreements with distributors and licensees largely on EU competition law, thus extending the reach of EU regulations to their worldwide operations.[102] Thus, the efficiency benefits associated with standardization of compliance programs and corporate contracting alike often drive economic non-divisibility and, with that, the Brussels Effect.

De Jure Brussels Effect

The de jure Brussels Effect—the adoption of EU regulations by foreign legislators—in competition law is pervasive, and has had a significant impact on global market competition. There has been a remarkable proliferation of competition laws around the world over the past three decades. Most of these new laws closely resemble EU competition law. In addition to this type of "legislative borrowing," several jurisdictions look to the EU's actions to inform their own enforcement activities. In particular, the EU's competition investigations have on several occasions triggered so-called copycat litigations, where foreign jurisdictions follow the EU's lead and launch their own investigations vis-à-vis the same companies that the EU has pursued. At times, however, these foreign jurisdictions choose not to act. Instead, they willingly "free ride" on the EU's investigations. This way, they let the EU take the lead and spend the significant initial resources to restrict certain anticompetitive behavior, yet enjoy the benefit when an anticompetitive transaction is prohibited or some other anticompetitive conduct is modified—assuming, of course, that the EU's remedy has a global effect. All these examples contribute toward a greater Europeanization of the rules according to which companies compete in the global marketplace.

Legislative Borrowing

Today, over 130 jurisdictions have a domestic competition law, making competition law one of the most widespread forms of economic regulation around the world.[103] Anecdotally, competition scholars and practitioners have suggested that several countries look to the EU when drafting their competition laws.[104] They typically emulate both the substantive EU competition rules as well as the administrative model to enforce those rules. A deeper analytic look at many jurisdictions supports this conclusion, even as the specific reasons for emulating the EU may vary across them. The following discussion reviews several examples of countries—both big and small, and developed and developing—showing that the de jure Brussels Effect has reached countries in Africa, Asia, and Latin America alike.

To begin with the jurisdiction that most actively regulates competition law in Africa—South Africa—the EU has had a palpable influence in the country's modern competition law, which was enacted in 1998 as part of a broader set of reforms that brought an end to the country's apartheid regime.[105] Several areas of South Africa's competition law were modeled almost verbatim from EU legislation. In addition, the ECJ jurisprudence has been influential in legislative drafting: notably, the controversial excessive pricing provision in the South African Competition Act was taken directly from the ECJ's decision in the *United Brands* case.[106] According to the provision, a dominant firm is prohibited from charging an "excessive price to the detriment of consumers."[107] An "excessive price" is one that bears no reasonable relation to, and is higher than, the economic value of the good or service in question.[108] In addition, the ECJ's case law is routinely cited by South African courts on matters such as abuses of dominance[109] and price-fixing allegations.[110]

There are likely several reasons why South Africa chose to follow the EU's example in enacting its competition law. Among these, the frequent interactions with the Commission's Competition Directorate during the drafting process are cited as instrumental.[111] Some of the main architects of the new competition legislation in South Africa had also studied EU competition law, making the EU template a familiar one to turn to for direction.[112] In addition, the drafters of South African competition legislation sought to depart from an orthodox application of competition law principles in order to redress the vast economic and social inequalities wrought by apartheid.[113] In doing so, it is possible that they viewed the EU as an appropriate model in light of the EU's receptiveness to embrace goals beyond a narrow focus on efficiency—even if the goals that South African legislators came to embrace stemmed from a different set of public policy concerns.

Several Asian economies have been similarly receptive to the EU's influence. Singapore's Competition Law of 2005 provides an illustrative example. According to the parliamentary debates, it is closely modeled after UK competition law,[114] which itself is heavily influenced by EU competition law. Furthermore, the Competition and Consumer Commission of Singapore (CCCS) Guidelines, which outline how the CCCS will administer and enforce the provisions under the Competition Act, were largely based on the relevant EU Guidelines.[115] The decision to follow the UK Competition Act in "style, approach and substance" was made after extensively studying the competition legislation of Australia, Canada, Ireland, the United Kingdom, and the United States.[116] Even though the European influence was palpable, Singapore did not emulate all aspects of the UK/EU regime. Most notably, Singapore carved out vertical agreements from the scope of the law, which is an important departure from the UK/EU laws.[117] This decision at least partially reflects Singapore's small market size and limited resources, which explains the country's focus on more egregious anticompetitive practices.[118]

Singapore's decision to emulate the text of the UK/EU competition law has also made UK/EU case law an obvious template for the CCCS's enforcement decisions.[119] For instance, in one of its major infringement decisions against Singapore's largest ticketing service provider "Sistic," the CCCS relied heavily on UK and EU case law in its reasoning. The CCCS explicitly recognized that since Singapore's abuse of dominance provision is modeled after the UK Act—which in turn was modeled after EU law—cases from the EU and United Kingdom would be "persuasive or useful" in assisting CCCS in reaching its decision.[120] The Competition Appeals Board agreed with this approach, emphasizing the "highly persuasive" authority of the competition decisions of EU and UK courts.[121]

There are several reasons why Singapore chose to emulate the UK/EU model in the drafting of its competition law. For one, Singapore's colonial history and strong jurisprudential ties with the United Kingdom created a natural tendency to emulate the United Kingdom.[122] Second, the UK/EU model was seen as easier for both businesses and consumers to understand compared to the US model, which was built over time and which requires consultation of numerous different sources.[123] The EU had also amassed significant experience in interpreting its abuse of dominance positions given the frequent adjudication of such cases before the ECJ.[124] This experience lent credibility to using the EU as a model for enforcement in this particular area, and the clarity of EU competition law allowed for businesses to have more certain expectations of how the new domestic law would be enforced.

Another example of the de jure Brussels Effect on competition law in Asia can be found in India, where the Indian Competition Act of 2002 draws inspiration from the EU competition law. According to the 93rd Report on the Competition Bill from 2001, Indian law was revised with an eye on EU competition law, stating that "The new Act is more closely in tune with the Competition Law of the European Commission. Nearly all laws deal with horizontal/vertical agreement, monopoly, abuse of dominance and regulated by Competition Authority."[125] India's regulation of abuse of dominance provides an illustrative example in its similarity with Article 102 of the TFEU.[126] The Indian Act defines "dominant position" as "a position of strength, enjoyed by an enterprise, in the relevant market, i.e. India, which enables it to operate independently of competitive forces prevailing in the relevant market; or affect its competitors or consumers or the relevant market in its favour."[127] This definition is similar in terms to the one provided by the ECJ in its famous decision *United Brands*.[128] In *United Brands*, the Court references the (now) Article 102 of the TFEU and clarified that dominant position means "a position of economic strength enjoyed by an undertaking which enables it to prevent effective competition being maintained on the relevant market by giving it the power to behave to an appreciable extent independently of its competitors, customers and ultimately of its consumers."[129] The Competition Commission of India further relied on the *United Brands* in its decision in *HT Media Ltd. v. Super Cassettes*,[130] using its three-pronged test for excessive pricing. These examples of the de jure Brussels Effect—together with examples from South Africa and Singapore—illustrate not just the external influence of EU competition law on other states' domestic laws as they are drafted, but also the external influence that the EU is able to exert through the deference given to the ECJ's interpretation of competition law.

China's 2008 Anti-Monopoly Law similarly draws inspiration mainly from EU competition law, even though several other foreign models were also influential in the legislative process.[131] For example, China closely followed the wording of EU's key provisions—the TFEU's Article 101 on anticompetitive agreements and Article 102 on the abuse of dominance—while also emulating the European

Merger Control Review.[132] Interestingly, China also replicated the EU model in exempting agriculture from the scope of its competition law, showing how even such sector-specific carveouts can diffuse to foreign jurisdictions.[133] The EU seems to have retained its influence beyond the initial law adoption in China: China's recently released draft amendments for merger rules are also heavily influenced by the equivalent EU rules.[134]

Wan Jiang, an officer of China's National Development and Reform Committee (NDRC), noted that "In the view of legislative borrowing, it was a more reasonable choice for China to borrow European Competition Law for the Antimonopoly Law. When comparing relevant regulations of China Antimonopoly Law and European Competition Law, you may find that the two are very similar, and certain provisions therein are highly consistent with respect to the words being used."[135] China's former Vice Minister of Commerce, Ma Xiuhong, referred to EU competition law as "one of the most influential competition laws in the world," and confirmed that "China has borrowed many experiences of European Competition Law in various aspects for the enactment of Antimonopoly Law."[136] Professor Li Jian similarly acknowledges that China's law was "deeply influenced" by EU competition law, which he attributes to the shared civil law tradition in the EU and in China.[137] That said, China has not blindly emulated the EU. It has introduced some provisions that reflect the different role of the state in the economy, and declared the promotion of "socialist market economy" as one of the goals of its anti-monopoly law.[138]

These China-specific provisions notwithstanding, the de jure Brussels Effect in China has been extensive. It likely reflects not only China's willingness to pro-actively emulate the EU but also the EU's active efforts to promote its regulatory model to Chinese officials. For instance, the Commission has engaged in an active dialogue with the Chinese competition authorities, providing technical assistance and helping Chinese authorities build regulatory capacity. The EU has worked closely with the drafters from all of the key institutions in charge of competition policy—including MOFCOM, NDRC, and SAIC[139]—as well as the State Council's Legislative Affairs Office and, to some extent, some of the Chinese courts.[140] In 2004, the Ministry of Commerce of China and the Commission's Directorate General for Competition reached an agreement on a structured dialogue on competition called "EU-China Competition Policy Dialogue." The primary objective of this Dialogue was "to establish a permanent forum of consultation and transparency between China and the EU in this area and to enhance the EU's technical and capacity-building assistance to China in the area of competition policy."[141] This dialogue provides a venue for the EU to remain engaged in future regulatory developments in China, possibly further entrenching the de jure Brussels Effect in the country.

Latin America similarly offers numerous examples of the de jure Brussels Effect. Ecuador is among the several Latin American countries that have closely followed the EU in the drafting of their domestic competition laws. Ecuador adopted a competition law—The Organic Act for the Regulation and Control of Market Power—only recently, in 2011.[142] The provisions of the law track closely those of the competition law of Spain, which is modeled after EU law. These include, for example, articles on the abuse of dominance, cartels, and remedies.[143] In addition, Ecuador has copied some of the soft law instruments promulgated by the Commission, including the EU Guidelines on the definition of the relevant market.[144] One possible reason that the EU competition law provided an attractive model for Ecuador was the EU's tendency to embrace a broader set of public policy goals in its competition law beyond a narrow focus on efficiency. This provided a better fit given Ecuador's constitutional commitment to "promoting equitable and mutually supportive development."[145] The EU also may have been seen as a better model for Ecuador to follow given the civil law origins of Ecuador's legal system.

These countries just discussed offer some illustrations of the EU's de jure global influence. There are many other examples around the world. According to Evgeny Khokhlov, EU and German competition laws significantly influenced the 2006 Russian law on the protection of competition and subsequent amendments.[146] Hailegabriel Feyissa argues that the Ethiopian competition law regime is modeled after the EU, with the EU law offering the "primary material" in the drafting of the 2003 Trade Practice Proclamation that regulates competition.[147] Ana Julia Jatar similarly notes that many Latin American countries, including Colombia and Venezuela, drew heavily on Articles 101 and 102 of the EU Treaty when drafting their competition statutes.[148] All these examples support the conclusion that the adoption of EU competition law principles has been widespread.

As mentioned before, no single reason explains why these countries have primarily, even if not exclusively, turned to the EU in their search of a regulatory template to follow. The de facto Brussels Effect likely explains some governments' decisions to follow the EU's model. The more that firms around the world already adjust their conduct to comply with EU competition rules, the more likely it is that they support similar reforms at home. These firms prefer uniform rules and face fewer adjustment costs if their home governments adopt a law that already, de facto, governs their business conduct.

Competition law is also a field where other jurisdictions often have little to gain by adopting less-stringent competition rules compared to the EU, at least for firms that operate internationally. Any local, more lenient rules would often only be superseded by the EU rules, making their regulators obsolete when it comes time to enforce them. As explained before, if the EU prohibits an international merger, the merger is banned worldwide; it is irrelevant if the merger is deemed acceptable by other jurisdictions. This illustrates why deviating from the EU (as the most stringent jurisdiction) brings few gains for other jurisdictions. With respect to such international transactions where jurisdictions overlap, no de jure Brussels Effect is needed for the EU's preferred rules to prevail. However, absent the de jure Brussels Effect, domestic competition law continues to govern the market competition of a purely local nature. For the EU law to influence such practices, the EU has no choice but to rely on the de jure Brussels Effect to change the rules in foreign jurisdictions. This likely partially explains the EU's eagerness to export its rules to other jurisdictions through various means.

Additional reasons have further entrenched the EU's influence in diffusing its competition laws abroad—some more generic and others more competition policy specific.[149] As briefly noted in the case of Ecuador and South Africa, the EU's tendency to articulate a broader range of goals—instead of strictly limiting the objective of competition law to furthering consumer welfare—has made EU competition law an appealing template to numerous countries.[150] Developing countries, in particular, find the EU model more accommodating of the myriad concerns they have about the operation of the markets and the distributional effects of competition law. Relatedly, EU competition law is perceived as a compromise between the operation of free markets and the government's legitimate authority to intervene in those markets. US competition law, in contrast, is seen to reflect a more robust reliance on markets' ability to self-correct, lessening the need for government intervention.[151] Many countries are ideologically closer to the EU in this regard.

It is not only the content of EU competition law that makes it an appealing template for many jurisdictions, but also its form. EU competition law offers a template that is more precise and predictable than other prominent templates such as the United States, giving more detailed guidance for new competition regimes that are looking for clear ex ante rules that can guide their less-experienced agencies and courts in their decision-making.[152] This was noted as one of the reasons why the UK/EU model appealed to Singapore.[153] This feature is likely to make EU competition law an even more attractive template for low-income countries that have less-skilled administrative agencies and judiciary.[154] These countries, in particular, benefit from emulating precise rules that allow for more mechanical rule making by agencies that lack the technical experience required for engaging in more flexible case-by-case decision-making. The EU is also often eager to extend technical assistance to these jurisdictions, exporting EU's rules and interpretative approaches in the process.[155]

Linguistic and historical connections with the EU member states further explain why several countries have turned to the EU in their search for a legislative template to follow. EU competition statutes are published in several languages, which considerably, if unintentionally, facilitate the copying of EU laws globally, particularly in the Spanish- and Portuguese-speaking Latin America and in the Francophone parts of Africa. In addition, the EU can frequently exercise indirect leverage in these regions through its member states' close cultural ties across the world, given their colonial history. This additionally helps explain why Ecuador copied the Spanish competition laws (and thereby indirectly EU law) almost verbatim. Similarly, Hong Kong and Singapore, former British colonies, copied extensively from UK competition law, indirectly exporting many of the EU's competition provisions into their regimes.

Yet another reason why the EU template has come to prevail over that of the United States is the EU's tendency to leverage its preferential trade agreements (PTAs) and other economic and political cooperation agreements as vehicles for spreading its regulatory norms.[156] By offering preferential access to its vast consumer market, EU has significant bargaining power over its trade partners and is therefore in a position to set conditions for signing a PTA, as discussed in chapter 3. One of those conditions is typically the adoption of competition law. The EC-Turkey Customs Union agreement from 1995 provides an illustrative example.[157] In its Article 39, the agreement provides that "Turkey shall ensure that its legislation in the field of competition rules is made compatible with that of the European Community." Examples of competition law being exported through association agreements include countries such as Algeria, Egypt, and Georgia. For example, Georgia undertook the obligation to approximate its future competition laws with those of the EU when it signed the Partnership and Cooperation Agreement in 1996.[158]

This discussion has focused on anecdotes of the EU's influence and the reasons behind such influence. However, it is possible, and even likely, that most of these jurisdictions were influenced by some other jurisdictions as well. A recent research paper by scholars from Columbia University, UC Berkeley, and the University of Chicago moves beyond these anecdotes and measures the EU's relative influence more systematically using a novel dataset of competition statutes.[159] Specifically, it examines the relative influence of EU and US competition regimes in shaping the global regulatory landscape. Using data on dozens of competition law provisions from 125 countries, it traces the evolution of competition regimes from the year 1957, when the EU enacted its competition law, joining the United States as another major competition regulator in the world, to 2010. Specifically, the study compares the linguistic similarity of key competition provisions with the EU and US competition laws, respectively. It further measured the substantive similarity of those foreign laws with both the EU and the United States across all major categories of competition law, such as anticompetitive agreements, abuse of dominance, merger control, and remedies.

This study reveals that a vast majority of jurisdictions with competition law regimes have laws that more closely resemble the EU competition laws than the US antitrust laws—both in linguistic similarity and actual substance. More specifically, it shows that the emulation of the European model of competition law by third countries surpassed that of the United States in the 1990s, and the EU's "sphere of influence" in the domain of competition regulation has continued to increase ever since. Thus, a more systematic analysis lends support to the above anecdotes that the EU competition law has, indeed, provided the most commonly copied template for the world competition laws.

Among the countries whose substantive competition regulations more closely resemble US laws are countries with strong cultural and legal ties to America, including Australia, Canada, and New Zealand but also an important jurisdiction like Japan. However, in every region of the world, there are many more countries that have laws exhibiting greater substantive resemblance with the EU than the United States, including most of the major emerging markets, such as Brazil, China, India, Mexico, Russia, South Africa, and South Korea. The measurement of linguistic similarity reveals similar, if not identical, patterns. For instance, EU competition law language is used in China, India, and Mexico while few (primarily common law) countries resemble the United States.

In addition to copying the language and the broader substantive content of EU competition law, most foreign jurisdictions have emulated the EU's institutional model to enforce competition law. In doing so, their enforcement relies primarily on administrative actions brought by public authorities as opposed to private litigants. Indeed, private enforcement of competition law is rare outside the United States. This public enforcement regime reflects the greater involvement of government in the organization of economic life generally in most countries as compared to the United States. The notion of "private attorneys general"—and the large, active, plaintiff's bar associated therewith—is a tradition not found in much of the world outside the United States.[160] China's Anti-Monopoly Law, for instance, while allowing for private actions, relies largely on a purely administrative enforcement model.[161]

Copycat Litigation

There is an additional reason for why a foreign jurisdiction may find it beneficial to align its domestic competition rules with those of the EU. After emulating EU law, this jurisdiction can free ride on the EU's investigations and follow the

EU's lead in evaluating anticompetitive practices in individual cases. This way, it is able to leverage fines or impose other remedies domestically without the need to develop its own theories of harm, market definition, and competitive assessment. All of this takes time, technical expertise, and often substantial resources. This strategy—known as "copycat litigation"—is particularly appealing for less-experienced agencies, which lack the resources and the expertise to build the case on their own. Replicating the EU's reasoning and remedies will allow them to capture regulatory gains and pursue enforcement, their limited regulatory capacity notwithstanding. Yet even the more established competition agencies have been known to await the EU's—or, in the case of countries like Canada, the US'—decision before acting on their own. Seen this way, the de jure Brussels Effect facilitates free riding: different substantive rules would make free riding harder because an independent investigation based on a different legal framework might lead to a different regulatory outcome. However, replicating the EU's competition regime paves the way for replicating its enforcement decisions as well.

Copycat litigation is, in most instances, likely a reflection of a sheer informational benefit that the EU investigation generates. The EU's actions alert the foreign agencies of a possible anticompetitive conduct, giving them an impetus to act. It typically further articulates theories of harm or may even provide these agencies with critical evidence that competition agencies need to effectively build their case. This way, the main benefit of copycat litigation is that it lowers the enforcement costs for foreign agencies and allows even less well-resourced agencies to engage in enforcement actions. However, a more sinister view suggests that sometimes a copycat litigation may take a path that differs from the motives that led the EU to act. Non-EU jurisdictions may, conceivably, use an existing EU investigation as a pretext or cover for their own vexatious, protectionist, or otherwise ill-advised investigations against a certain company. Such an investigation could then be legitimized by pointing to an earlier EU investigation, even if that earlier investigation proceeded on different, more legitimate grounds.

Of course, engaging in a copycat litigation is only one plausible strategy for foreign governments. Some foreign jurisdictions may choose to forgo enforcement altogether and "outsource" their enforcement entirely to the EU. This constitutes a more comprehensive freeriding strategy whereby a foreign jurisdiction benefits from the EU's enforcement outcomes that are consistent with their own regulatory framework without engaging in any enforcement efforts on their own. For example, if the EU prohibits an international merger, smaller jurisdictions gain little by seeking to accomplish the same outcome through a copycat litigation. One prohibition is enough to ban the merger worldwide. The same applies for cartels that the EU alone can detect and deter. If the EU can unravel a global cartel, other foreign agencies see little advantage in spending their limited enforcement resources for replicating the same (and, here, redundant) outcome.

However, in reality, cartel enforcement often requires several jurisdictions to act, making it difficult to outsource enforcement entirely to the EU. For example, as discussed earlier, the EU excludes foreign harm from its calculation of a cartel fine, making it often necessary for other jurisdictions to impose a fine of their own, or else cartels are not sufficiently deterred. Bringing their own case also allows these jurisdictions to capture a monetary benefit by collecting a separate fine. In the abuse of dominance cases, free riding may work as long as the authorities across jurisdictions share the same competitive concerns and as long as the EU issues a global remedy that alleviates those concerns. However, whenever the EU's remedy is limited to the EU, foreign jurisdictions are likely to follow the EU's lead and engage in copycat litigation.

There are several examples of this type of copycat litigation, even though arguably it is difficult to always know whether another jurisdiction acts because the EU has acted first or whether its reasons are independent, and the timing simply happens to coincide or closely track the EU's investigation. For example, in 2005, South Korea followed closely the EU's 2004 ruling condemning Microsoft for an abuse of a dominant position in tying (or "bundling") the Windows Media Player with its operating system. This case was widely thought to have been inspired by a similar tying case brought by the EU a few years prior. The EU case began in 1998 with a complaint to the EU from Microsoft's competitor, Sun Microsystems. In 2004, the Commission held that Microsoft violated (now) Article 102 of the EC Treaty through its bundling behavior.[162] As a remedy, the Commission required Microsoft to produce a version of its Windows operating system without the Windows Media Player in addition to the bundled version that Microsoft offered on the market. Shortly thereafter, the Korean competition authorities went after Microsoft, investigating similar bundling claims. Following complaints by Microsoft's competitors such as Daum Communications in 2001[163] and RealNetworks in 2004,[164] the Korea Fair Trade Commission (KFTC) fined Microsoft 33 billion Won (approximately $32 million) in 2005 for abuse of its dominant position. It ruled that Microsoft had engaged in anticompetitive behavior by bundling the Windows Media Player and Windows Messenger with Windows operating system.[165] Like the Commission, the KFTC ordered Microsoft to market two versions of Windows, one with and the other without Windows Media Player and Windows Messenger.[166] Given the close approximation of the Korean remedy with that imposed by the EU, it seems highly likely that the KFTC used the EU's decision as a template. Daum, the complainant in the case, had also explicitly noted before the Korean decision that "[it] hopes that the case of European Union affects the decision of the Fair Trade Commission."[167]

Microsoft itself further drew a comparison between the EU and KFTC decision, yet described in its 2006 press release the KFTC decision as even "harsher" than the remedy ordered by the EU.[168]

The EU's multiple investigations into Google since 2010, which have received prominent attention worldwide, have also led to several instances of apparent copycat litigation. Several agencies in other jurisdictions have challenged Google's conduct following the EU's investigations. However, many of these jurisdictions do not explicitly refer to the EU's investigations, making it difficult to label them unambiguously as "copycat litigation." At the same time, it is unlikely that these agencies are building their cases in disregard of what the EU has done.

For example, Russia opened a formal investigation into Google's practices regarding Android concomitant with, or even slightly before, the Commission initiated its formal proceedings. In February 2015, the Russian Competition Authority—the Federal Antimonopoly Service of the Russian Federation or FAS—launched an investigation into Google's business practices regarding Android upon a complaint of Google's biggest local competitor, Yandex NV, a search engine. Yandex was also one of the complainants in the EU's investigation against Google. The opening of the investigation by the FAS in February 2015 precedes the formal initiation of proceedings by the Commission by a couple of months. However, it was public knowledge at the time that the Commission was already assessing Google's practices regarding Android ahead of issuing its formal initiation of proceedings.[169] In September 2015, the FAS issued a decision in which it found that Google had violated Russian competition laws through its illegal practices relating to Android. It also issued a cease-and-decease order and imposed a fine of approximately 440 million rubles (approximately $7.8 million).[170] With this, FAS became the "world's first competition authority to issue a negative assessment of Google's practices with respect to the Android operating system."[171] Yet a more skeptical view might note that the reason that Russia was able to complete its investigation before the EU was the lesser due process that was afforded to Google in the process. Regardless of the reason behind the Russia's early decision, it seems likely that the Russian investigation into Google's practices was at least partially triggered by a similar investigation simultaneously underway in the EU.

Another example of likely copycat litigation can be found in a Brazilian investigation of Google's business practices. In October 2013, Microsoft and local search engines, Buscapé and Bondfaro, lodged complaints against Google with the Brazilian Competition Authority (Administrative Council for Economic Defense or CADE). CADE stated that "it is looking into accusations that Google has unfairly used rivals' content, discouraged their advertisers and favored its own product listings in search results."[172] Even after Microsoft dropped its complaint against Google before CADE in 2015—replicating its similar decision in the EU—CADE continued its investigation.[173] While CADE's initial investigation against Google did not cover Google's business practices with regard to Android, this changed after the EU fined Google over abuse of dominance regarding its Android mobile operating system in the summer of 2018. At that time, CADE's president, Alexandre Barreto, indicated that "what we are doing now is analyzing the decision of the European Union to determine if we have grounds to act here."[174] This statement suggests that CADE may mirror the investigation launched and completed by the European Commission regarding Google Android.

In addition to these Brazilian and Russian cases, another instance of possible copycat litigation can be seen in a recent Turkish investigation of Google. In July 2015, the Turkish Competition Authority (Rekabet Kurumu or TCA) opened an investigation into Google's business practices regarding Android following a complaint lodged by Yandex. Yandex stated that Google violated Turkish competition rules by abusing its dominant position as it was imposing an obligation on mobile device manufacturers to preinstall certain Google apps in their smartphones. In September 2018, the TCA imposed a fine of TRY 93 million (approximately $15 million) against Google for abusing its dominant position with regard to its agreements with mobile device manufacturers for Android. This decision came shortly after the European Commission fined Google over $5 billion for similar practices. Commentators indicated that "the TCA's decision shows once again that the TCA is still following the European Commission's footsteps to a significant extent in evaluating anti-competitiveness of a behavior, especially in complex matters."[175]

Finally, South Korea's competition agency KFTC's competition investigation into Google provides further evidence of the broad influence of the EU's enforcement decisions in this area. This case provides a particularly interesting example because of the way the KFTC first cleared Google of any wrongdoing but, following the EU's decision, reconsidered its approach. In 2011, NHN Corp. (the owner of South Korea's biggest internet search engine, Naver) and Daum Communications Corp. urged the KFTC to investigate Google's anticompetitive practices. Specifically, these companies alleged that Google was restricting the preloading of certain mobile search window applications on smartphones.[176] The KFTC dismissed their allegations in its 2013 ruling, concluding that Google's share of the Korean search engine market was too small to threaten competition.[177] However, after the KFTC learned that the EU had issued a "statement of objections" regarding Google's business practices related to Android—an indication that the EU was suspecting anticompetitive conduct—it decided to take another look at Google. This led the KFTC to investigate whether the company unfairly used Android's dominance to restrict competition in Korean mobile search markets.[178] In 2016, a KFTC official acknowledged that "KFTC is re-monitoring Google, in light of the finding of antitrust violations under the EU investigation, as well as the changed market environment for OS/searches," and noted that "based on the results of the monitoring and EU's final ruling, KFTC will decide whether to open a formal investigation."[179]

While the mounting competition investigations against Google around the world have captured most attention, copycat litigation is not limited to Google, the high-tech sector, or abuse of dominance cases. Merger control offers another area of competition law that is amenable for copycat litigation, in particular when it comes to replicating remedies first imposed by a lead jurisdiction such as the EU.

A recent example comes from Ecuador, where the Ecuadorian Market Power Control Superintendence followed closely the EU's conditional merger approval of the AB InBev and SABMiller's transaction in 2015.[180] In order to obtain an approval from the European Commission, AB InBev offered to divest all of SABMiller's business in France, Italy, the Netherlands, and the United Kingdom to a third party. However, the Commission extracted an additional commitment from the parties, requiring AB InBev to divest SABMiller's business in Eastern Europe (Czech Republic, Hungary, Poland, Romania, and Slovakia) as well. This merger between AB InBev and SABMiller represented the most significant transaction the Ecuadorian Market Power Control Superintendence had to analyze to date. The merging parties' post-merger market share in Ecuador exceeded 97%, making intervention inevitable. Given the lack of experience of the Ecuadorian authority, which has only been reviewing mergers since 2011, it closely copied the types of commitments ordered by the Commission, including the request of the divestiture of part of AB InBev's business in Ecuador. Specifically, the Ecuadorian authority relied on certain concepts and words throughout its Resolution, which are identical with those used by the European Commission, suggesting that the EU decision was used as a model. For example, there is a strong emphasis in having to divest certain assets or businesses as a "package," in order to make the sale more attractive to potential buyers and to ensure that the buyers have sufficient assets to enter the market and operate there efficiently. Additionally, the Ecuadorian authorities included certain concepts that they had not used before and closely resembled the implementation of the commitments that parties agreed to with the Commission. For example, to carry out the divestiture, the Ecuadorian agency asked the parties to implement a Hold Separate commitment, together with a Hold Separate Manager and a Monitoring Trustee. The Hold Separate commitment requested by the Ecuadorian authorities was not even translated to Spanish, but simply listed as "commitment #7," which textually mentions a "Hold Separate."[181] This choice of wording leaves little doubt that the EU decision, indeed, was employed as a direct model by the Ecuadorian agency.

These examples illustrate some reasons for why copycat litigation—often emulating the EU—can be attractive for foreign governments. At the same time, there has been a parallel tendency for foreign companies to increasingly direct their competition complaints to the EU, making the EU the global arbiter of most prominent competition disputes of the day. By bringing their competition battles to the EU as opposed fighting them on their home turf, these firms engage in so-called forum shopping in order to take advantage of the EU's more stringent rules that are viewed as favoring intervention. This has made the Commission a "hub" for global competition enforcement even without actively seeking such a role or without the resources to pursue all complaints it receives. A few examples of this practice—including Microsoft complaining to the Commission about Google's anticompetitive behavior in 2011 after having been the object of a similar EU complaint by two US companies, Novell and Sun Microsystems, over a decade earlier—were briefly discussed earlier in this chapter.[182] Both forum shopping and copycat litigation, while driven by different actors and motivations, have the same effect of increasing the EU's influence through a variant of the de jure Brussels Effect and further entrenching the EU competition rules as the global norm.

A CLOSE EXAMINATION of the EU's influence in competition law reveals some of the most manifest examples of the Brussels Effect but also clearly exposes its limits. The first four conditions underlying the Brussels Effect— market size, regulatory capacity, stringent standards, and inelastic targets— typically permeate all competition policy matters. Their presence alone entails that EU competition law has a vast extraterritorial reach, and thus reaches foreign companies as long as their conduct affects the EU market. However, these four conditions alone do not trigger the Brussels Effect. The condition that ultimately dictates whether the Brussels Effect occurs is that of non-divisibility.

The chapter's discussion has shown how the question of non-divisibility explains nearly all variance in the manifestation of the Brussels Effect in competition matters. Non-divisibility acts as the trigger that leads companies to voluntarily extend the EU regulation to govern their global operations. A closer look into various areas of competition policy also reveals that non-divisibility is more common in some competition matters than others. For example, merger prohibitions offer a showcase of non-divisibility: a prohibition of a transaction cannot be implemented on a jurisdiction-by-jurisdiction basis, thus triggering the Brussels Effect. At the same time, mergers that are not prohibited but approved subject to conditions may or may not exhibit non-divisibility, depending on whether the conditions can be globally or locally implemented. Cartel investigations may be non-divisible, especially when the EU investigation is sufficient to dismantle the cartel worldwide. At the same time, foreign agencies do not always rely on the Brussels Effect alone. Even though the EU decision may bring the cartel to end globally, these agencies may have the incentive to extract fines, which they are only able to do if they follow the EU's investigation with one of their own. Abuse of dominance cases offer a particularly fascinating test of the Brussels Effect. In these investigations where the EU's role as the global enforcer has been prominent recently, the Brussels Effect is, perhaps surprisingly, least common. In many individual instances, the parties have been able to circumscribe their remedies to the EU market alone, continuing to offer different variants of their products in other markets. This has been the norm, for example, in various remedies the Commission has imposed on Google in the past few years.

While the occurrence of the de facto Brussels Effect has been inconsistent across the types of competition matters and industries, the de jure Brussels Effect has been persistent. Countries with different levels of economic development, varying legal and economic systems, and political alignments have turned to the EU when enacting their competition statutes. This influence can only partially be traced to market forces and results from a combination of factors that have made the EU an attractive model to follow. The EU has actively exported its competition laws to jurisdictions that have often shown notable willingness to receive the EU's export. Foreign jurisdictions' eagerness to copy the EU's enforcement decisions has further entrenched the EU's global influence over competition policy, as manifested by copycat litigation taking place in several jurisdictions.

Until recently, the United States has defended its restrained approach toward competition enforcement, even when the rest of the world has emulated the EU's competition statutes and copied its enforcement practices. However, even the United States may be in the process of re-evaluating its antitrust policy soon, as evidenced by the recent announcement of the US government about a broad antitrust investigation into leading online platforms. The US agencies are believed to be targeting Amazon, Google, and Facebook given the investigation's focus on "search, social media, and some retail services online."[183] Thus, even the United States may not be able to insulate itself from the de jure Brussels Effect for much longer, in particular if the political momentum shifts decisively toward more regulatory intervention. Such a development has the potential to either extend the de jure Brussels Effect or, alternatively, over time, balance it with an emerging "Washington Effect."

5

Digital Economy

THE POWER OF EU regulations to influence global markets has grown significantly over the last two decades, particularly in the area of digital economy. Few regulations have impacted global digital companies or their users more than the EU's 2016 General Data Protection Regulation (GDPR).[1] Prompted by the entry into force of the GDPR, consumers were flooded with e-mails from numerous companies, asking for their consent on the use of their personal data. Businesses around the world were forced to quickly adjust their data collection, storage, and usage practices in response to the EU's regulation. In addition to the GDPR, another impactful regulation for these companies and their users comes from the EU's ongoing efforts to regulate online hate speech. As a result of the establishment of the Commission's voluntary Code of Conduct on Countering Illegal Hate Speech Online with four US IT companies—Facebook, Twitter, YouTube, and Microsoft[2]—these and other digital companies have taken extensive measures to police the speech that appears on their platforms. Both of these regulations have had enormous impact across foreign jurisdictions, and demonstrate the global reach of the Brussels Effect.

The Commission's drive to regulate the digital economy arises from a growing recognition of the power that these companies are amassing through their possession of personal data and their control over conversations in social media. This power vests these companies with extraordinary commercial advantage, concentrating wealth in a handful of companies in ways, and to an extent, that has rarely been seen before. But even more disturbingly, these companies—due to the prominence of their platforms and the accumulation of vast data on individuals— have been found to influence political elections or incite crimes and abuses,[3] however inadvertently. For example, in 2013, news broke on the so-called Snowden revelations, which showed how the US National Security Agency had engaged in a mass surveillance campaign by harvesting Facebook data. And, in 2018, the world learned about a "Cambridge Analytica scandal," where a British political

The Brussels Effect. Anu Bradford, Oxford University Press (2020). © Oxford University Press.
DOI: 10.1093/oso/9780190088583.001.0001

consulting firm, Cambridge Analytica, was found to have acquired Facebook users' private data and used it in political campaigns, influencing the election of President Trump and the Brexit referendum alike. Most recently in 2019, a perpetrator who carried out a hate-motivated massacre of fifty people in a mosque in Christchurch, New Zealand, livestreamed his killings on Facebook. This led to millions of views on Facebook and various other online platforms where the footage was replayed all while these companies struggled to take down the various copies of the video appearing online. These scandals have drawn global attention to these companies' practices as well as the EU's relatively stringent efforts to regulate them.

This chapter builds from these examples and focuses on two areas of regulation that have been central to the EU's efforts to regulate the digital economy: data protection and the regulation of hate speech online. The discussion first reviews the EU legislation governing data protection and explains the economic and political drivers behind it. It then discusses some examples of both the de facto and de jure Brussels Effect on data protection. Then, the focus turns to online hate speech, again reviewing the regulation, the underlying economic and political motivations, as well as examples of how the EU has drawn the line between acceptable and unacceptable speech in the internet era—not just in Europe but around the world.

Digital Economy I: Data Protection

The EU sets the tone globally for privacy and data protection regulation. It has enacted comprehensive data protection legislation that covers all sectors of the economy and establishes privacy principles for both public and private entities. Privacy rights are given the status of a fundamental right in the EU, further elevating their significance in the EU's treaty structures. They are enforced across the EU member states by independent regulatory agencies, which can impose substantial remedies for violations of those protections. EU privacy protection rules have also had notable global impact through both the de facto and de jure Brussels Effect, making data protection a powerful manifestation of the Europeanization of the global regulatory environment.

Major Legislation

In the EU, privacy is considered a fundamental right that cannot be contracted away.[4] Building on the 1950 European Convention of Human Rights, which recognizes the right to privacy, the 2009 Lisbon Treaty elevated data protection as a fundamental right guaranteed by the EU institutions.[5] Specifically, the Lisbon

Treaty gave legal force to the EU Charter of Fundamental Rights, which had been proclaimed almost a decade earlier. The Charter affords individuals the right to privacy, including the right to the protection of their personal data.[6] The philosophy behind the EU's fundamental rights approach to privacy is to foster self-determination of individuals by granting them enhanced control over their personal data.[7]

In addition to these constitutional protections, the EU sets out detailed privacy protections in its 2016 GDPR that entered into force in May 2018.[8] The GDPR replaces the 1995 Data Protection Directive,[9] further solidifying the privacy rights that European citizens enjoy by making those rights directly applicable across all member states. The GDPR calls for lawfulness, fairness, and transparency in processing the data.[10] It also limits the quantity and purpose for which data can be collected, and requires that all the entities—whether private companies or government agencies—collecting and processing the data ensure the integrity, security, and accuracy of the data.[11] Data can further be stored only for a limited period.[12] The GDPR also adds new obligations, such as the "right to be forgotten" that gives the data subject the right to ask for erasure of certain data,[13] and "privacy by design," which requires manufacturers to design their products and services with GDPR obligations in mind.[14] It requires member states to establish independent data protection authorities to guarantee the enforcement of the protections embedded in the GDPR, together with establishing a European Data Protection Board.[15] The GDPR further provides for heavy sanctions, increasing the expected deterrence effect of the regulation: noncompliance with GDPR may result in administrative fines of up to €20 million or up to 4% of the company's total worldwide annual turnover of the preceding financial year, whichever is higher.[16]

The GDPR has a broad territorial reach.[17] It applies to all companies processing personal data of "data subjects"—that is, persons residing in the EU whose personal data is being collected, held, or processed—regardless of the company's location or where the data processing takes place. The GDPR thus also applies to controllers or processors not established in the EU, as long as these actors offer goods or services to EU residents or monitor behavior that takes place within the EU. Non-EU businesses processing the data of EU citizens will also have to appoint a representative in the EU. The EU believes that its high privacy standards are compromised if the protected data is made available in other jurisdictions. For this reason, the EU bans the transfer of data from the EU to third countries that fail to ensure "an adequate level of protection" of data privacy rights.[18] What constitutes "adequate" is defined case by case by the EU.

To complement the GDPR, the EU is also in the process of adopting a new ePrivacy Regulation,[19] with the goal of modernizing the existing 1995 ePrivacy Directive and ensuring its compatibility with the GDPR.[20] The ePrivacy Regulation imposes additional obligations on companies to safeguard European citizens' privacy with respect to their electronic communications, including data transmitted via text messages and e-mails. It will also limit the companies' ability to use cookies to track internet users' online activity or send out targeted advertising without an explicit user consent.[21] The legislative process surrounding the ePrivacy Regulation has been contentious, with intense lobbying coming from both civil society groups and industry trade associations.[22] On the one hand, critics of the new ePrivacy Regulation describe the law as redundant and possibly conflicting with the obligations stemming from the GDPR. On the other hand, supporters of the law emphasize the need to extend privacy protections to cover modern forms of online communication such as Skype or WhatsApp.[23] The new legislation has been adopted by the European Parliament and is currently being discussed in the Council.[24]

The European courts have further expanded the scope of European citizens' privacy rights. Already prior to the entry into force of the GDPR, the ECJ issued several rulings that extended the 1995 Data Protection Directive's territorial scope. One of its landmark privacy rulings is the *Google Spain*—better known as the "right to be forgotten" case—involving Google searches in Spain.[25] The "right to be forgotten" refers to the internet user's right to demand all data on him or her to be permanently deleted upon request. In this case, a user in Spain requested Google to remove from its search engine results that linked him to old newspaper articles detailing his financial troubles. According to the complainant, the information, while accurate, was no longer relevant since all debts were resolved. Google refused to delink the information. Through a preliminary reference, the ECJ was asked to rule on the scope of the privacy right and the applicability of the then-applicable 1995 Data Protection Directive on data processors or controllers such as Google.

The ECJ reaffirmed the broad scope of the right to be forgotten stemming from Article 12 of the 1995 Data Protection Directive. According to the ECJ, EU law requires search engines, including Google, to honor requests to make certain content, which is not adequate, relevant, or up to date, delinked and no longer searchable. This obligation is also not conditional on demonstrating actual harm to the data subject.[26] The Court further rejected Google's argument that the Article 12 should not apply to a search engine, which merely compiles information that was already in the public domain, and therefore should not have the obligations of a data controller. The Court also found the location of the search engine's headquarters or the location where the relevant processing or indexing of the data takes place irrelevant to the search engine's obligations as a data controller. Google's data processing activities outside the EU were "inextricably linked"[27] to the advertising and other activities of Google's subsidiary in Spain. The Court therefore held that Google's data processing activities were subject to Spanish data protection law, enacted on the basis of the EU Directive.[28] Notably, the GDPR goes even further in establishing jurisdiction over foreign data controllers. GDPR reaches data controllers even when they do not have any presence in the EU, as long as they serve EU residents or providers that process EU data.[29]

Google implemented the ruling by delinking the search not only from Google.sp but also from other European sites (such as Google.fr). However, Google insisted at first that the court ruling was limited to the EU's jurisdiction and did not require it to amend the search results globally. This meant that the delinked data remained accessible from the United States and even from Spain if the user conducts the search on Google's global "google.com" domain. However, European regulators insisted that the removal of the search result from country-specific domains such as Google.sp was not enough. Following the order by the French data protection authority (CNIL), Google agreed to block search results also from the Google.com platform whenever the search was conducted using an IP address located in the country where the ruling was in force. In other words, the data would be delinked on both Google.sp and Google.com when the query originated from Spain but would still be available when the query was made on Google.com in the United States or even on Google.com in France.[30]

Following these developments, in 2017, the CNIL requested for an even broader "right to be forgotten," which would entail mandating search engines to delete the search results in all domains, including those accessible only outside of the EU.[31] This decision is currently pending before the ECJ, and will be discussed further in this chapter. Regardless of how the ECJ eventually rules in the matter, the EU's right to be forgotten is likely to lead to significant delisting because of the asymmetrical incentives that the regulation imposes on search engines. While individual companies such as Google retain the authority to make decisions in individual cases as to whether to erase information, any borderline case is likely to result in the removal of the information from search results. Failure to erase the information can lead to heavy fines whereas excessive delinking carries no penalty, incentivizing erasure.[32] As evidence of its responsiveness to the delinking requests, Google has agreed to remove about 44% of the 2.8 million requests it has received since the May 2014 ruling, according to its latest transparency report.[33]

EU legislation and ECJ rulings are further reinforced by extensive privacy regulation and active enforcement at the EU member state level. The regulatory capacity of the national data protection authorities (DPAs) is central to the effectiveness of the GDPR as the DPAs are vested with the task of enforcing the GDPR in addition to their national data protection laws. The DPAs have further shown notable willingness to deploy their enforcement powers. For instance, the Hamburg data protection authority in Germany fined subsidiaries of Unilever, PepsiCo, and Adobe for "failing to properly ensure the privacy for employee and customer data transferred to the United States."[34] France has fined Facebook for collecting information on users with the aim of using the data in advertising "without having a legal basis" and "unfair" tracking of people on the internet without offering sufficient warning.[35] Other examples abound, ranging from Sweden suing American Airlines after the company transferred data from Sweden to a US electronic reservation system without prior customer consent,[36] to the Czech Republic banning Google's efforts to expand its mapping software program,[37] to Italy fining WhatsApp for sharing data with its parent company Facebook. Facebook also stopped showing targeted advertisements tailored to users' expressed sexual preferences, after the Dutch authorities challenged the practice.[38] These cases suggest that member states remain willing to actively enforce the privacy rights of their citizens, relying on the powers vested in them under both EU and national laws.

Political Economy

The foundation of stringent data protection in the EU can be traced back to World War II and the atrocities by the Nazi regime.[39] Nazis systematically abused private data to identify Jews and other minority groups they oppressed. The state surveillance and the infringement of individual rights continued under the post-war socialist dictatorship in East Germany when the Ministry for State Security, known as Stasi, continued the surveillance of its citizens.[40] These experiences have left Germans—and Europeans more broadly—suspicious of state surveillance and government data collection practices that are capable of infringing on individual rights. These suspicions, combined with a mistrust that corporations would act in the public interest in this regard, paved the way for a robust privacy rights regime in Germany, and later in Europe more broadly.

In addition to these historical reasons, EU data protection regulation emerged in response to the need to integrate the European market. By adopting common European data protection standards, the EU was able to harmonize conflicting national laws that were emerging as a trade barrier, inhibiting commerce in Europe. For this reason, GDPR and its predecessor 1995 Data Protection Directive were viewed as internal market instruments, facilitating the creation of a digital, single market by allowing an unhindered flow of data within the entire common market. This internal market rationale was also critical in offering a legal basis for the EU's capacity to regulate in this domain.[41] When the Data Protection Directive was enacted in 1995, the EU had no competence to enact fundamental privacy rights legislation, yet it had the competence to enact measures to safeguard the proper functioning of the single market. Of course, the market integration objective could also have been accomplished by adopting common standards that provided a low (yet harmonized) level of data protection. Yet, as explained in chapter 2, it was politically more feasible for the EU to harmonize upward than downward, elevating the data protection standards in low-regulation member states rather than forcing high-regulation member states to weaken the data protection laws already governing their domestic markets.

While these internal motivations to integrate the European market provided the initial impetus for regulating data privacy, the EU's current regulatory pursuits are also shaped by external motivations. Given the global nature of data processing and the importance of cross-border transfer of data—not just within the EU but across global markets—the EU has recognized the importance of promoting international standards for the protection of personal data.[42] With the GDPR, the EU is thus also seeking to contribute to set the global standard on data privacy with other like-minded countries, cognizant that "if we do not shape standards now, others do,"[43] emphasizing also that those alternative global standards that may emerge may be less desirable in requiring data localization, or leveraging data protection for censorship and state surveillance.[44]

These various motivations have provided a foundation for the EU's stringent data protection regulation. Yet those regulations have emerged through a distinctly contested political process. Some member states, including Germany, France, and Sweden, have been the most active promoters of European privacy protections. The first data protection legislation was introduced in the state of Hesse, Germany, in 1970.[45] The German Constitutional Court also played a significant role in the history of European data protection laws. In its landmark 1983 *Census* judgment (Volkszählungsurteil),[46] the Court found a proposed census of German population involving data transfers unconstitutional. In doing so, the Court pronounced a "fundamental right to informational self-determination," which later became a cornerstone of European data protection laws.[47] The right to informational self-determination refers to the right of individuals to determine the principles governing the disclosure and use of their personal data. Any limitation of this right must be proportionate and grounded on public interest, for which there must be a constitutional legal basis. The ruling also set limits regarding the purpose, accuracy, and retention of the data collected, together with promulgating the right for the data subject to access and revise information collected. Finally, the ruling broke new ground in requiring independence of DPAs. These principles provided the foundation of the later-enacted EU Data Protection Directive and the subsequent GDPR.

The pro-regulation member states further benefited from political support by green parties and other liberal groups in the European Parliament, which used data privacy issues as a means to distinguish themselves from other political parties.[48] The members of European Parliament (MEPs) from these groups were steadfast advocates of tough data protection rules, initially ushering in the adoption of the 1995 Data Protection Directive and subsequently providing critical backing for the GDPR. In addition, the DPAs in individual member states were instrumental in advocating for EU-level regulation on data protection.[49] As data protection regulators, they felt strongly that all European citizens should benefit from enhanced privacy protections. Yet, they may have also been at least partially motivated by a desire to protect their own regulatory autonomy.[50] Absent EU harmonization, there was a risk that companies could locate their data processing in member states without adequate data protection rules, thereby escaping the DPAs' regulatory review. This fear gave the DPAs the impetus to form transgovernmental networks and lobby for the inclusion of the data privacy into the EU's regulatory agenda.

Lobbying for and against the adoption of the GDPR was particularly fierce, making the legislative process highly contentious. It is telling that over three thousand amendments were introduced in the European Parliament's legislative process alone.[51] Companies—in particular those whose business models rely on data collection—advocated for self-regulation, including voluntary industry codes or certification mechanisms, and tried to minimize burdens for data controllers. At the same time, consumer and data protection advocates pushed for enhanced privacy protections, increasing responsibility for data controllers, and instituting robust penalties for violations.[52] Both sides agreed on one aspect: disparate enforcement of data protection across the member states was problematic, which supported the shift from a data protection directive (which grants more leeway for member states) to data protection regulation (which achieves greater uniformity across the member states).[53]

Foreign governments, companies, and business groups engaged in active lobbying to mitigate the costs of GDPR on their businesses. The US government was particularly active, opposing the regulation on the grounds that it would kill innovation and research, in addition to hindering national security cooperation. Leading US companies such as Cisco, Intel, Microsoft, and NBC Universal, as well as organizations such as TechAmerica Europe, American Chamber of Commerce, and Japan Business Council in Europe submitted comments at the consultation stage.[54] On the civil society side, several European NGOs such as European Digital Rights were active but also received support from foreign NGOs such as the Australian Cyberspace Law and Policy Center and the American Center for Democracy & Technology.[55] While the NGOs may not be able to declare a complete victory—for example, they lost the battle to keep the proposed fines for data protection violations at up to 5% of global turnover or €100 million, whichever was higher[56]—it is fair to say that what emerged from the legislative process was an unprecedentedly stringent data protection law, with extensive obligations imposed on data controllers, backed by severe penalties.

In addition to the member states with strong privacy protections and dedicated NGOs, individual citizens have given the impetus for stringent privacy rules in the EU. The most notorious example is an Austrian lawyer and data protection activist, Max Schrems, who launched a case against Facebook as a 23-year-old law student, requesting Facebook to hand over his personal data.[57] After learning that Facebook had amassed 1,200 pages of data on him, Schrems filed multiple complaints to the Irish Data Protection Commission (DPC), which had jurisdiction over Facebook. Schrems's complaints gained momentum with the Snowden revelations that the US National Security Agency (NSA) was harvesting Facebook data as part of a mass surveillance campaign. These revelations called into question the adequacy of a 2000 EU-US Safe Harbor Agreement,[58] which was meant to guarantee the protection of personal data transferred between the EU and the United States. After the Irish DPC declined to investigate the complaint made by Schrems (due to the validity of the Safe Harbor decision at the time), Schrems filed a lawsuit before Irish courts for judicial review of the DPC's refusal to investigate his complaint on its merits.[59] Through a preliminary reference from the Irish High Court, this lawsuit ultimately led to a ruling by the ECJ, which declared the Commission's Safe Harbor decision governing data transfers between the EU and United States invalid.[60]

While Max Schrems's activism may be unusual, his views regarding privacy resonate broadly among Europeans. The most recent Eurobarometer survey on European citizens' attitudes toward privacy was carried out in 2016.[61] While the survey was conducted in the context of measuring support for the new ePrivacy Regulation currently being debated by the EU, as opposed to GDPR, its results are illustrative of the public attitudes toward privacy more generally. The results clearly confirm the importance that Europeans place on online privacy. For example, over 80% of respondents say it is "important" that cookies and other tools for monitoring their activities can only be used with their permission, with 56% saying that this is "very important." Similarly, 90% of the respondents say that they should be able to encrypt their messages and calls to ensure that only the intended recipient reads them. Almost as many—89% of respondents—take the view that the default settings of their browser should prevent the sharing of their information. Most respondents remain against information sharing even if it helps companies provide new services they might like, with 71% of respondents finding this "unacceptable." The same survey also

confirms that Europeans take an active role in guarding their privacy by changing privacy settings on their computer and installing software to protect their
privacy. A total of 60% of the respondents have changed the privacy settings on
their internet browser by deleting the browsing history or cookies, while 40%
of the respondents avoid certain websites due to a concern that their online
activities are monitored. Additionally, 37% of the respondents have installed
software that protects them from seeing online advertisements while 27%
of respondents have installed software that prevents the monitoring of their
online activities. Unsurprisingly, active measures to enhance one's privacy are
particularly common among young, educated, and frequent users of e-mail,
internet, and social networks.

In contrast to their deep support among the European public, the EU data
protection rules have faced significant criticism abroad. The United States,
in particular, has been skeptical about the EU's approach, raising a concern
that data protection legislation is disguised protectionism.[62] US companies
have strongly criticized the EU's regulatory efforts, referring to "unreasonable restraints" on their business practices.[63] These companies also criticize the
compliance costs involved, with Google recently stating that it has spent "hundreds of years of human time" to achieve GDPR compliance.[64] US Fortune
500 companies had spent approximately $7.8 billion on GDPR compliance by
May 2018, averaging $16 million per company. Regardless of the costs involved,
many US companies are adjusting their global business practices to reflect
European norms, making data privacy one of the most powerful examples of
the Brussels Effect.

The US criticism is not surprising considering the depth of regulatory divergence between the EU and the United States in this domain. The US data privacy laws are considerably weaker and their scope restricted to the public sector
and some sensitive sectors, including health care and banking.[65] The data privacy issues of the private sector are largely relegated to self-enforcement by the
industry.[66] Individual companies are allowed to create their own privacy policies, and consumers are expected to contract with those companies for the level
of privacy they want.[67] Also the substance of any privacy right is more restrained.
For instance, the US courts have, to date, flatly rejected the right to be forgotten, and favored free speech considerations over individual privacy.[68] There is
also no independent regulatory authority with a power vested to enforce privacy
rights. Instead, it is part of a broader mandate of the Federal Trade Commission
(FTC) to protect consumers and police "unfair" or "deceptive" practices affecting commerce.[69]

This EU-US regulatory divergence can partially be traced to the different
preexisting views that Europeans and Americans have about markets versus

government intervention, as discussed in chapter 2. For example, Paul Schwartz and Karl-Nikolaus Peifer have contrasted the US and EU privacy regimes, emphasizing how the EU has created a privacy culture around rights discourse (or, as they call it, "rights talk") where the protection of individuals as "data subjects" is central. In the United States, in contrast, privacy rights are part of the "marketplace discourse" where the rights of "privacy consumers" are seen in a commercial context.[70] Marketplace discourse is amenable to the idea that an individual consumer can trade his or her commodity—personal data—without strict oversight by public institutions. In contrast, EU institutions assume a strong role in the rights discourse where they have a central role in safeguarding the fundamental rights of its citizens. Alex Turk has described the distinctions between the United States and EU in a similar vein, noting how personal data is viewed as "tradable commodity" in the United States while considered "attributes of our personalities" in the EU.[71]

The weak regulation of data privacy in the United States might also be explained by the economic strength and accompanying political influence of the digital companies in the US regulatory process. The tremendous importance of these companies to the US economic growth and innovation culture may make US legislators and regulators less willing to challenge the business models that are behind their economic success. In contrast, the EU does not share the same inclination for restraint, which may partially explain why the regulatory response in the EU has been so much more vigorous than that in the United States. The EU's proclivity to regulate the conduct of these companies may also reflect some degree of resentment toward the US' success in dominating the commercial internet.[72] By exerting control over data practices of these multinational companies, the EU is staking a clear position against the US' unregulated approach toward digital companies, thereby countering this dominance—even if only at the margin.[73]

The politics underlying the international privacy debates have recently shifted in the EU's favor. As mentioned earlier, a particularly important development was the 2013 Edward Snowden revelations regarding unauthorized NSA surveillance programs. In 2018, another high-profile scandal broke, further entrenching citizens' concerns about their privacy. That year, a British political consulting firm, Cambridge Analytica, was found to have acquired private data obtained from Facebook users. These unauthorized data were used in political campaigns, including in the 2016 US presidential election and the 2016 Brexit referendum in the United Kingdom. These scandals have fueled distrust and resentment toward data collectors among citizens, enhancing the EU's standing in the privacy discourse and bolstering its authority to advocate for stronger data protection laws abroad.[74]

De Facto Brussels Effect

The de facto Brussels Effect is particularly strong in the domain of data privacy. Indeed, given its extraterritorial reach, some commentators describe the GDPR as "unashamedly global."[75] The EU is an important market for many data-driven businesses, including Facebook and Google. Facebook has 250 million users in Europe,[76] contributing 25% of Facebook's global revenue.[77] Google's share of the search market is over 90% in most EU member states, which exceeds its 67–75% market share in the United States.[78] Abandoning the EU market is not even remotely a commercially viable option for them. It will further be difficult for these digital companies to circumvent the GDPR by moving their data processing activities outside the EU. The GDPR's protection of European data subjects regardless of where the data processing takes place makes the regulation both extraterritorial and highly inelastic.

The EU's regulatory capacity and stringency in data privacy are also considerable, further contributing to the Brussels Effect. This has been the case, especially after the GDPR bolstered the EU's data protection regime with demanding standards and robust sanctions that are calculated based on the global turnover of the data processors. However, while the GDPR conveys extensive regulatory capacity in principle, a different question is whether the DPAs across the member states will have the resources to deploy this capacity in practice. They would need both substantial technical expertise and monetary resources to take on powerful multinationals whose resources vastly outweigh the modest budgets of the DPAs. For example, the Irish DPA is responsible for enforcing GDPR against digital companies such as Airbnb, Apple, Facebook, Google, Twitter, and Microsoft, as these companies have their European headquarters in Dublin, Ireland.[79] At the same time, the annual budget of the Irish DPA is approximately $9 million—which is equivalent to the revenue that the digital companies based in Dublin generate roughly every 10 minutes.[80] Thus, the strength of the Brussels Effect may ultimately hinge on whether the member state governments will vest their DPAs with adequate resources to ensure the existence of the required regulatory capacity. Thus far, the vast number of investigations concluded and underway in various member states—some of which were mentioned earlier[81]—indicates that the DPAs are not forgoing enforcement while waiting for their governments to shore up their budgets. The following discussion also suggests that the digital companies are taking extensive measures in anticipation that the GDPR will, indeed, be vigorously enforced against them.

Whether the Brussels Effect occurs therefore often comes down to the question of non-divisibility of the products and services across global users. Various examples suggest that, for today's global digital companies, maintaining different data practices across global markets is often both difficult (due to technical non-divisibility) and costly (due to economic non-divisibility). It is imperative that these companies are able to move data seamlessly across borders, in particular, as they often store their data in servers that are located in markets different from those where they operate.[82] While privacy regulations may differ from jurisdiction to jurisdiction, these digital companies streamline their global data management systems to reduce their compliance costs with multiple regulatory regimes.[83] Instead of creating different programs for different markets, they tend to apply the most stringent standards across the board.[84] At times, it is technologically difficult, even impossible, to separate data involving European and non-European citizens.[85] Other times it may be feasible, but too costly, to create special websites or data processing practices just for the EU.[86] As a result, the technical or the economic non-divisibility of the EU rules has prompted several US companies ranging from Google to Netflix to amend their global privacy practices.[87] When opting for a single global policy, these companies typically choose to adopt the most stringent regulation so as to retain the ability to conduct business everywhere.[88] Indeed, today many multinational companies have only one company-wide privacy policy—and it is that of the EU.[89]

A review of global companies' privacy policies reveals the extent to which they are choosing to adopt EU privacy policy as their company standard. Apple recently adopted the EU's rights discourse on privacy, alerting its customers in the United States about their privacy protections with a notice popping up on the screen of the iPhone, led by the following sentence: "Apple believes privacy is a fundamental human right." Apple also subscribes to a single global privacy policy, which reflects the GDPR.[90] Importantly, it also implements the GDPR's Article 25 principle of "privacy by design," which entails that they design their products and services to comply with GDPR-consistent privacy rules by default, minimizing the data collection through privacy-conscious design choices at the outset.[91] The company further carries out privacy impact assessments, as required by the GDPR, across all its products, and rolls out updates required by the GDPR on its mobile operating systems (iOS) to Apple users worldwide.[92]

In preparation for the entry into force of the GDPR, Facebook COO Sheryl Sandberg announced that the company was going to "[roll] out a new privacy center globally that will put the core privacy settings for Facebook in one place and make it much easier for people to manage their data." This means that European privacy protections will de facto be extended to the company's 2.2 billion users worldwide. The GDPR also led Facebook to assemble "the largest cross functional team" in its history to prepare for its compliance with new EU rules.[93] Facebook has clarified that while its user content language or the format for settings and controls may vary across jurisdictions, "we'll make all controls and settings the same everywhere, not just in Europe."[94] Google similarly updated its privacy policy in anticipation of the GDPR, sending its users a notice saying that

"We're making these updates as new data protection regulations come into effect in the European Union, and we're taking the opportunity to make improvements for Google users around the world."

Airbnb also announced that its revised, GDPR-consistent privacy policy came into effect for all its existing users on May 25, 2018—the day the GDPR entered into force.[95] Uber similarly follows a single privacy policy worldwide, including its riders and drivers in all jurisdictions.[96] Other companies are similarly undertaking considerable investments to ensure compliance with GDPR. A recent PWC survey shows that GDPR readiness is a high priority for US multinationals.[97] Of the 200 respondents, 54% reported that GDPR readiness is the highest priority on their data privacy and security agenda. Another 38% said GDPR is one of several top priorities, while only 7% said it is not a top priority.

The GDPR's Article 25 further pushes companies toward global compliance by calling them to engage in "privacy by design" and "privacy by default." These concepts are designed to incorporate privacy considerations into the product development through privacy-conscious product design. They encourage companies to develop products with built-in features that conform to strictest privacy settings by default. Incorporating GDPR compliance into the product design is a powerful way to globalize the EU norms. Microsoft, for instance, is developing its products with features that help their clients maintain GDPR compliance.[98] The decision to incorporate EU data protection standards into products at the manufacturing stage is perhaps the most powerful manifestation of technical nondivisibility, affecting everyday products such as smartphones and more peculiar products such as domestic robots alike.[99]

The Brussels Effect typically occurs because of economic and technological considerations. However, it can also occur when global businesses choose a standardized, global policy to streamline their internal corporate processes. A desire to ensure even-handedness in recruiting is but one example. In 2017, the Article 29 working group consisting of the European data protection regulators issued guidelines, limiting the ability of employers to screen the social media profiles of their potential employees unless the information on those sites would be "relevant to the performance of the job."[100] This calls for a significant adjustment of hiring practices of companies, given that a recent survey suggests that 70% of employers review social media sites of their potential candidates before making a hiring decision.[101] A global firm hiring a multinational workforce is likely to be discouraged from selectively reviewing some, but not other, social media profiles, depending on the nationality of the candidate under consideration.

Global privacy policies can also be facilitated by enhanced consumer demand to obtain matching protection that a company makes available in other jurisdictions. For reputational and brand-related reasons, the companies may find it hard to deny privacy protections for some consumers while allowing them for others in another jurisdiction. For instance, Sonos, a wireless speaker company in California, extended the GDPR protections to its customers worldwide, citing their belief that "all Sonos owners should have the right to these protections, [hence] we are implementing these updates globally."[102]

At times, businesses have managed to limit their response to any new regulations to the jurisdiction where those regulations have been instituted. At other times, however, a broader corporate response has led to a global adjustment of policies. For instance, Yahoo! was prosecuted before French courts for the material that it made available on its US website because that material was accessible to French citizens.[103] While Yahoo! initially argued that it could not for technical reasons limit the remedy to France by blocking only French residents' access to the site, independent experts concluded that this could be done with approximately 90% accuracy.[104] Regardless of its technological ability to filter the material across jurisdictions, in the end Yahoo! opted to forgo geographic filtering and banned the material that was prohibited in France worldwide.[105]

While these examples illustrate the prevalence of the de facto Brussels Effect, there are also numerous instances where the Brussels Effect has failed to materialize. At times companies are able to, and find it in their interest to, introduce divisibility and limit their policy changes to a jurisdiction imposing the demand. For example, while the European Commission and the European privacy regulators have ordered Facebook to stop collecting WhatsApp data (after Facebook acquired WhatsApp) citing both privacy and antitrust concerns, Facebook continues to combine the data acquired through both platforms in the United States.[106] Some companies also responded to the entry into force of the GDPR by taking down their websites in Europe as they were exploring ways to comply with the new rules. Immediately after the GDPR took effect, the *LA Times* redirected European users to a website featuring the following statement: "Unfortunately, our website is currently unavailable in most European countries. We are engaged on the issue and committed to looking at options that support our full range of digital offerings to the EU market. We continue to identify technical compliance solutions that will provide all readers with our award-winning journalism."[107]

Facebook's response to the entry into force of the GDPR offers an example of legal divisibility. While the company has chosen to extend the EU protections to all its users worldwide, as discussed, it proceeded to limit its legal liability in the EU by introducing divisibility through changes in its corporate structure. Specifically, Facebook moved its users in Asia, Africa, Australia, and the Middle East away from the company's Irish corporate structure and placed them under its US legal structure.[108] Presumably, this type of legal divisibility was designed to limit the rights of users in these non-EU countries to report any data protection violations to the Irish DPA and thus reduce the company's exposure to the GDPR's tough remedies with respect to those users.

Some jurisdictions' requirements for data localization can also form an impediment to a single global privacy policy. Data localization requirement forces companies to store or process personal data in a particular jurisdiction. This may compel the company to create a distinct compliance process for that jurisdiction.[109] Currently, for example, Russia and China require data localization.[110] The proposed new privacy bill in India similarly contains such a requirement.[111] Data localization forces companies to make a choice on whether to create separate operations for a certain market or cease operating there. For example, Russia blocked the professional networking site LinkedIn's Russian operations due to the company's refusal to locate the data there.[112] At the same time, LinkedIn has given into China's demands for data localization and continues to operate there.[113]

Another example that may lead to jurisdictionally tailored privacy policies comes from the 2018 California Consumer Privacy Act, which grants the Californians the right to prevent the sale of their personal information.[114] To guarantee this right, businesses must "[p]rovide a clear and conspicuous link on the business' internet homepage, titled "Do Not Sell My Personal Information."[115] However, the same provision of the law offers the option to provide a California-specific website that provides this "opt out" right, allowing the businesses to confine their obligation vis-à-vis Californians.[116] However, it is unclear how many companies choose to host a special website only for California in practice.

Perhaps the most important development regarding the divisibility of privacy policies is currently pending before the ECJ. In 2019, the Court is expected to rule on whether the EU courts have the authority to order that search engines such as Google and Bing must apply the "right to be forgotten" decision to their search domains outside of the EU. This would potentially include delinking requested information on Google's global "google.com" site when accessed using a non-European IP address.[117] In July 2017, France's Conseil d'État, the country's highest administrative court, raised this question in a preliminary reference procedure to the ECJ following an appeal by Google. Google had appealed the decision by France's privacy watchdog, the Commission Nationale de l'Informatique et des Libertés (CNIL), which had fined Google €100,000 for failing to apply the privacy ruling across all of its global domains, including google.com. The CNIL called for even greater extraterritorial effect for the right to be forgotten—the case discussed earlier in this section.[118]

In January 2019, the ECJ's Advocate General Szpunar's Opinion was released in the case. In that Opinion, AG Szpunar proposed that search engines should not have to apply a delisting request made within the EU to all global domains.[119]

The opinion draws a distinction between searches executed from within the EU versus those executed from outside the EU.[120] While the Opinion acknowledges that there are other areas of regulation in which EU law does have extraterritorial effects—such as in competition and trademark law—and leaves open the possibility that global delisting might be required in some instances, it takes the view that the global nature of the internet makes extraterritorial effects less certain and less well-defined.[121] AG Szpunar also emphasizes the difficulty of balancing the fundamental right to be forgotten against the legitimate interest of the public in accessing information, especially if the applicability of EU law is global, while the balancing exercise focuses on interests within the EU.[122] The Opinion also recognizes the political sensitivity associated with any decision that would mandate global delisting; it could lead non-EU countries to retaliate and prevent EU citizens from accessing information.[123]

While the outcome of the pending lawsuit is uncertain, the digital companies are bracing themselves for a potentially adverse decision. For example, Google reported the possibility of being forced to delist content worldwide due to a court order among "Risk Factors" in its annual report to the US Securities and Exchange Commission (SEC) as part of its obligation to give a comprehensive summary of the financial state of the company, including the risks that it faces.[124] In the end, the ECJ may or may not follow the AG Opinion. It could side with the CNIL, and endorse the CNIL's view that the right to be forgotten becomes "meaningless" unless it applies universally, and hence includes the searches from outside the EU. Otherwise, the past actions and statements regarding the privacy subject could remain easily visible to American colleagues, or even to a "geeky curious neighbor" who could use a non-EU country IP address to access information.[125] Alternatively, it may accept Google's counterargument that such an extension of this right would create a serious risk that countries with "more egregious limitations on freedom of speech" would in their turn be able to universalize their restrictions.[126] If so, this would lead to a situation where the internet is strictly governed by whichever jurisdiction has the most restrictive speech regime in the world—something which would be a pure manifestation of the de facto Brussels Effect, indeed.

De Jure Brussels Effect

The EU's data protection regime has also led to a significant de jure Brussels Effect. According to Paul Schwartz and Karl-Nikolaus Peifer, "EU data protection has been stunningly influential: most of the rest of the world follows it."[127] Another privacy expert, Graham Greenleaf, notes that "[s]omething reasonably described as 'European standard' data privacy laws are becoming the norm in most parts of the world with data privacy laws."[128] To date, nearly 120 countries have adopted privacy laws, most of them resembling the EU data protection regime.[129] These countries range from large economies and regional leaders such as Brazil, Japan, South Africa, and South Korea to midsize economies such as Colombia and Thailand; and even to small economies and tiny island nations such as Bermuda.[130]

That countries choose to emulate EU data protection laws is not surprising. First, many countries look up to the GDPR as the "gold standard," providing the highest and most widely accepted standard to follow.[131] Second, given that all large firms handling EU citizens' data have already in practice adopted EU privacy standards, governments face little resistance in entrenching these laws within their domestic legal frameworks. Foreign corporations affected by EU laws face no additional compliance costs from the de jure Brussels Effect, giving them the incentive to lobby for the EU standard at their home market as well. This way, they can level the playing field vis-à-vis their domestically oriented companies that currently do not need to comply with the GDPR.

The US market illustrates this dynamic: In October 2018, Apple's CEO Tim Cook called the US government to adopt a comprehensive federal EU-style privacy law, saying that it was "time for the rest of the world" to follow the EU's lead and adopt a strict legal framework to protect users' personal data. Cook described the amount of data that companies collect of individuals "unsettling," referring to it as "surveillance" that can lead to an abuse of the data collected.[132] Even more strikingly, Facebook's privacy chief, Erin Egan, joined Cook in announcing Facebook's support for a GDPR-equivalent federal privacy law in the United States.[133] Six months later, Mark Zuckerberg, the company's founder and chief executive, called for the adoption of GDPR-style laws worldwide in an op-ed published in the *Washington Post* in the following terms:[134]

> [E]ffective privacy and data protection needs a globally harmonized framework. People around the world have called for comprehensive privacy regulation in line with the European Union's General Data Protection Regulation, and I agree. I believe it would be good for the Internet if more countries adopted regulation such as GDPR as a common framework. New privacy regulation in the United States and around the world should build on the protections GDPR provides.

Facebook's business model relies on data collection more than that of Apple's, making the stakes even higher for Facebook and Zuckerberg's statement all the more revealing of the new reality that these companies are facing, leading them to embrace, rather than disparage, the GDPR. In the absence of a federal law, companies fear the emergence of a complex patchwork of potentially conflicting state privacy laws, further complicating their compliance efforts. This is one of the primary reasons that these companies opposed California's Consumer Privacy Act.[135] When lobbying for a federal law, the GDPR presents an attractive template given that it already governs much of the corporate conduct by US-based global companies such as Apple and Facebook.

Another powerful reason for the proliferation of EU-style privacy regimes around the world is the countries' desire to obtain an "adequacy decision" from the EU.[136] An adequacy decision refers to a formal determination by the EU that a country's data protection standards provide sufficient protections so as to safely allow data transfers from the EU to that country. The finding of adequacy opens the data flows between the EU and the country whose laws are deemed adequate. European companies are also more likely to open new subsidiaries, branches, or call or data centers in a country whose laws are considered adequate.[137] To date, the EU has recognized the following non-EU countries as having adequate data protection laws: Andorra, Argentina, Canada (for commercial organizations only), Faroe Islands, Guernsey, Israel, Isle of Man, Japan, Jersey, New Zealand, Switzerland, and Uruguay.[138]

The ECJ applies a strict standard in exercising judicial review over "adequacy" of third countries' data protection regimes. In its *Schrems* judgment, the ECJ defined "adequate" as "essentially equivalent," which is expected to lead to an even closer replication of EU rules as third countries seek an adequacy decision that withstands judicial review.[139] With this, the ECJ has "effectively dictated the rest of the world's data protection legislation," at least for the countries that depend on the adequacy decision for their data transfers.[140] And while the essential equivalence is only required for data transfers involving the third country and the EU, it is difficult to imagine a country adopting a domestic privacy law that calls for different data protection standards that would depend on whether or not European data is involved.[141] In this sense, the requirement for adequacy renders data protection laws legally non-divisible, with the effect that the EU data protection standard likely becomes the foundation for any domestic privacy regulation.

If a country in which a company operates has not been deemed to have an adequate level of data protection, companies that still want to transfer data to that country must seek approval from a competent supervisory authority for Binding Corporate Rules (BCR). These rules set out the data protection obligations for all the entities in that corporate group.[142] If these BCRs are approved, they function as an EU-approved data protection law for that particular company.[143] Alternatively, these companies can use "standard contractual clauses" approved by the EU.[144] These clauses allow companies to enter into a contract with EU entities and pledge to meet the EU's privacy rules, offering a "workaround" for companies in instances where the country does not have adequate data protection laws. However, the future of these standard contractual clauses as a basis of data transfers is in doubt after the privacy activist Max Schrems challenged these clauses before the Irish DPC.[145] The preliminary decision of the DPC expressed its concerns that standard contractual clauses provided inadequate privacy guarantees. The case has proceeded to the ECJ via the Irish courts.[146] If the ECJ invalidates these clauses, foreign governments are likely to expend even greater efforts to adopt EU-style privacy laws in order to retain open data flows between their country and the EU.

The difficulties associated with cross-border data transfers absent adequacy recognition has given several countries a strong incentive to align their laws with the GDPR. For example, Argentina and Uruguay are the two Latin American countries that have obtained the EU's adequacy decision. Argentina adopted its data protection law in 2000,[147] closely resembling Spain's 1992 data privacy law and EU data protection standards. Three years later, the country obtained EU's adequacy recognition. In 2016, Argentina established a working group to study the legislative reforms that may be necessary in order for the country to retain its adequacy status in the post-GDPR legal environment, showing the country's willingness to keep updating their laws to retain conformity with the EU.[148] Uruguay similarly modeled its 2008 and 2009 data protection laws on the EU's data protection framework.[149] The prospect of EU's adequacy recognition, which the country secured in 2012,[150] was a key motivation behind the law.[151] Uruguay saw the EU's adequacy decision as important for attracting investment in the technology sector. For example, the Uruguayan Investment and Export Promotion Institute highlighted how "[t]he EU recognition will open the possibility for major European investments, in particular it will help Uruguay boost its outsourcing industry [. . .] and attract more EU-based companies looking for providers of administrative, financial and other data processing services in Latin America.[152]

Japan recently concluded its talks on reciprocal adequacy with the EU, which led both parties to agree in 2018 to recognize the other's data protection systems as equivalent.[153] Japan had amended its Act on the Protection of Personal Information (APPI) in 2015,[154] in part to bring it in line with the GDPR. The Japanese business community played a large role in supporting the new law because their international trading operations with European companies were already subject to significant data protection regulation, making it dramatically less costly to comply with similar domestic rules.[155] Obtaining the EU's adequacy decision was also seen as a boon to Japanese companies, including Toyota Motor Corp. and Sumitomo Mitsui Banking Corp., as such a decision allows them to transfer personal data from the EU.[156]

South Korea is currently negotiating an adequacy decision with the EU.[157] The country's data privacy law, Personal Information Protection Act (PIPA),[158] closely resembles that of the EU.[159] According to Park Jong-hyun, the director of the Personal Information Protection Cooperation Division in South Korea's Interior Ministry, there is "90 percent or more" similarity between the EU and South Korean privacy frameworks. However, the main objection to adequacy is the lack of independent agency oversight under the South Korean law, which is currently enforced by the country's Interior Ministry, rather than an independent agency.[160] To alleviate the EU's concerns, South Korea is considering designating the independent Korea Communications Commission (KCC) as the oversight authority for the EU-Korea data transfers, and vesting it with proper sanctioning authority.[161]

In contrast to these jurisdictions, the US data protection laws as such do not meet the EU standards for adequacy. At the same time, obtaining the EU's adequacy decision has been particularly important for the United States given the extent of EU-US data flows. According to the US Department of Commerce, the value of annual digital services trade between the United States and the EU is $260 billion.[162] The ECIPE, a think tank, has estimated that the end to transatlantic data transfers would reduce EU's GDP by 0.4% a year.[163] To resolve the issue and create a legal basis for transatlantic data transfers, the United States and the EU entered into a Safe Harbor agreement in 2000.[164] The EU-US Safe Harbor Agreement consisted of a set of negotiated principles, which the EU considered to meet the European "adequacy" standards. The US companies that voluntarily subscribed to these standards were allowed to receive data transfers concerning European data subjects. Over 5,000 US companies entered the Safe Harbor agreement.[165] However, following the Edward Snowden revelations about mass surveillance by NSA in the United States,[166] the ECJ struck down the Safe Harbor agreement in October 2015 in its *Schrems* decision, as previously discussed.[167] According to the Court, an adequacy standard required that the non-EU country guaranteed "a level of protection of fundamental rights and freedoms that were *essentially equivalent* to that guaranteed within the EU"[168]— and the Safe Harbor data-transfer agreement that governed EU data flows across the Atlantic for fifteen years did not meet that standard.[169]

This setback led the United States and the EU to negotiate a new agreement to govern transatlantic data transfers: The EU-US Privacy Shield.[170] This new agreement, which entered into force in August 2016, had 4,685 US companies as signatories in May 2019, including major players such as Facebook, Google, and Microsoft.[171] The US Department of Commerce will monitor these companies' compliance with the Privacy Shield, effectively ensuring that the data protection standards are equivalent to those found in EU. The Privacy Shield contains significantly stronger privacy protections, enhanced enforcement mechanisms,[172] and new safeguards related to US government access to personal data. For example, it calls for an appointment of a US ombudsman, who remains independent of US intelligence services and who can respond to individuals' complaints regarding misuse of personal data by US national security agencies.[173]

However, even the fate of the Privacy Shield is uncertain. The national privacy regulators in EU member states were critical of the agreement as soon as it was adopted, alleging that it does not go far enough to protect the internet users in Europe.[174] Legal challenges are also pending before European courts. Thus far, the Privacy Shield was unsuccessfully challenged by a NGO called Digital Rights Ireland, as the ECJ held that Digital Rights Ireland lacked standing to sue.[175] La Quadrature du Net, one of the parties that applied to intervene in support of Digital Rights Ireland, also launched its own challenge of the Privacy Shield, which is still pending before the ECJ.[176]

The Privacy Shield may also falter if the United States fails in its implementation. The Privacy Shield is subject to periodic review and assessment by the European Commission. The inaugural review in 2017 raised concerns in Europe as the Trump administration had delayed the appointment of the independent ombudsman as envisioned by the agreement.[177] The European Parliament further adopted a resolution in the aftermath of the Cambridge Analytica saga in 2018,[178] stating that the Privacy Shield arrangement does not provide an adequate level of data protection.[179] While the United States has since remedied some of the concerns raised—including the appointment of a permanent ombudsman for the Privacy Shield[180]—additional challenges remain. In its second review in 2019, the European Data Protection Board (EDPB) expressed concerns, for example, about the use of personal data transferred to the United States for national security purposes without yielding new privacy guarantees for EU citizens.[181]

In addition to countries that have benefited from the EU's adequacy decision, a great number of countries across Africa, Asia, and Latin America have followed EU data protection standards. For example, South Africa's 2013 data privacy law emulates the EU's 1995 Data Protection Directive.[182] While the law was drafted before the GDPR took effect, the South African drafters were mindful of the GDPR, and included many of the definitions that were ultimately part of the GDPR.[183] In 2008, Senegal similarly enacted a law on the protection of personal data, which similarly closely resembles the EU and French regulation on personal data.[184] The preamble of the law makes a reference to "the European requirements for the transfer of personal data to third countries." The law also establishes a Senegalese Personal Data Protection Commission (CDP) as an independent authority to oversee the implementation of the law, which is a key requirement under the EU regulatory framework.

Many Latin American countries have transplanted the concepts from Spanish data protection law, which is based on EU law.[185] Among the Latin American countries that have been "highly inspired by the European model"[186] are Columbia, Costa Rica, Mexico, Peru, and, most recently, Brazil[187]—in addition to Argentina and Uruguay which, as discussed earlier, benefit from the adequacy decision. An institution that has been influential in contributing in the expansion of the European model of data privacy in Latin America is the Ibero-American Data Protection Network (abbreviated as RIPD for its Spanish name [Red Iberoamericana de Protección de Data]).[188] Its members include Argentina, Chile, Colombia, Costa Rica, Mexico, Peru, and Uruguay.[189] The purpose of the RIPD standards is to establish common principles for the protection of personal data, which could serve as a basis for national legislation in the region.[190] RIPD has produced model standards in 2017 that emulate EU data privacy rules.[191] Some commentators describe the standards as "a carbon copy of the EU General Data Protection Regulation."[192] The RIPD's 2015–2018 agenda expressly included the promotion of the European data privacy model in Ibero-American countries, noting "the benefits that such adoption would bring to Spanish companies that desire to transfer an increasing volume of personal data with such countries."[193]

China is among the most important jurisdictions that have emulated the EU's data protection laws—at least on its face. It recently enacted a comprehensive data protection law—Cyber Security Law—in 2017.[194] The law builds upon earlier non-binding promulgations from the Chinese government, such as the "Guidelines for the Protection of Personal Information in Public and Commercial Service Information Systems" (GB/Z28812-2012), which came into effect on February 1, 2013.[195] The Cyber Security Law incorporates several GDPR concepts into Chinese domestic law. For example, "data must be adequate, relevant and not excessive in relation to the purposes for which they are processed," and "the data subject must give his explicit consent" which mirror purpose limitation and consent requirements from the GDPR.[196] The EU influence may also be seen in the "China-EU Information Society Project," a cooperation initiative between China and the EU that took place in 2005 to 2009.[197] The EU provided funding and technical advice to the Ministry of Commerce in China as part of the cooperation with a specific objective "to design a regulatory framework by introducing best practices from the EU."[198] Chinese scholars also supported EU-style legislation in China, noting that its reliance on EU-style government regulation as opposed to US-style self-regulation by the industry provided a better fit with the Chinese system.[199]

At the same time, it is unclear how much influence the EU has had on China's data protection regime in practice. China is well known for limiting its citizens' internet freedoms. The country's engagement in "digital authoritarianism" represents a stark departure from the internet governance and privacy principles in the EU.[200] For example, China continues to block and filter online content on a large scale. It has prohibited several companies from operating in the country. Many companies, including Google, have also withdrawn from China because of the extensive censorship rules and hacking attacks.[201] China's commitment to EU-style data privacy is all the more questionable after reports surfaced of China's large-scale deployment of the facial recognition technique that China uses for law enforcement purposes.[202] China has further implemented a social credit scheme that rates citizens for their trustworthiness on issues such as paying taxes or committing a crime.[203] An untrustworthy rating has negative consequences for the individual, including banning him or her from buying train or airplane tickets. Thus, China's practice of deploying data as a tool for social control is, in practice, a stark reminder that any de jure Brussels Effect on paper does not necessarily mean that the EU's regulations and principles are deployed in any meaningful way.

Finally, India presents an interesting example of a jurisdiction that is in the process of adopting a GDPR-style law, and which, in some respects, is expected to be even more stringent than the GDPR. To date, India has not enacted a comprehensive data privacy law even though many Indian IT consulting companies, such as Wipro[204] and Infosys,[205] have adopted many of the EU data protection norms to govern their conduct. However, in 2017, an expert committee was established to prepare a draft data protection bill. The draft Indian bill replicates many of the key provisions embedded in the GDPR, including the right to access and to correct data, right to data portability, and right to be forgotten.[206] It also incorporates the privacy-by-design principle and requires that organizations carry out Data Protection Impact Assessments and designate a Data Protection Officer. The draft bill further envisions sanctions similar to those the GDPR provides. Yet the bill also goes beyond the GDPR. Most notably, it contains a generalized data localization requirement, under which "a data fiduciary shall ensure the storage, on a server or data centre located in India, of at least one serving copy of personal data." Additionally, certain categories of data can only be processed in India. Data localization constitutes a significant departure from the EU data protection regime, and has met significant criticism and resistance given that it risks disrupting the efficient flow of internet traffic and data transfers.[207]

These examples illustrate the extent of the de jure Brussels Effect but also serve as a reminder of the dwindling influence of the US privacy regime. The United States has clearly been an exception, resisting the EU's lead in privacy protection—at least until very recently. The Safe Harbor agreement and the subsequent Privacy Shield have introduced changes in the US domestic legal framework that clearly bring the US laws closer to the EU privacy standards.[208] Yet no comprehensive legislative reform has taken place at the federal level. In February

2012, the Obama administration published a report, Consumer Data Privacy in a Networked World, which urges Congress to adopt a consumer privacy "bill of rights."[209] However, the bill wilted in Congress with no legislation emerging as a result.

In the absence of comprehensive federal privacy law, individual states have stepped in and regulated this area. As noted earlier, California passed a Consumer Privacy Act in June 2018.[210] The bill was initially prompted by a citizen ballot initiative, which collected over six hundred thousand signatories, thus triggering a statewide vote.[211] The group behind the ballot initiative—Californians for Consumer Privacy—agreed to withdraw the ballot initiative once the Consumer Privacy Act was adopted by the state senate. Several of the Privacy Act provisions bear resemblance to the GDPR, including mandating data collectors to provide notice of the categories of personal information collected and limiting the purpose for such data collection;[212] providing a right for citizens to know all data that business collects of the individuals;[213] and the right for citizens to request data pertaining to them to be deleted ("right to be forgotten").[214]

Notwithstanding the failed efforts to pass federal US legislation to date, the political moment for tougher privacy laws may, however, have arrived in the United States as well. Recent scandals, like the one involving Cambridge Analytica, have also changed the tone in privacy discussion in the United States, and even led to a recent landmark settlement between the FTC and Facebook, requiring the company to to pay a $5 billion fine.[215] These scandals have reduced the public trust in IT companies' self-regulation, potentially catalyzing greater demands to pursue more stringent regulation in the United States as well, whether at the federal level or, as we are already witnessing, at the level of individual states.[216] Now that even the most influential data-driven US companies are calling for a federal privacy law, the momentum may be sufficient for a legislative change. This suggests that the United States may not be able to hold out in perpetuity but may need to concede that time for a robust federal data protection law has come. This could mean that the de jure Brussels Effect will reach even its last frontier: the United States.

Digital Economy II: Hate Speech Online

One of the most recent areas of the EU's influence over global standards relates to its regulation of hate speech online. Freedom of expression is a fundamental right recognized by the EU and a core value that the EU institutions defend. However, in the EU, the right to free speech has never been as broadly conceived as in the United States. For reasons both historical and ideological, the EU is quick to condemn speech that incites hatred toward certain groups of individuals, irrespective of whether this type of speech is prone to lead to violence. While hate speech is an old phenomenon, its incidents have been on the rise recently. Hate speech is also increasingly moving online, which has created the need for new regulation.

The following discussion briefly reviews the origins of the EU's stringent approach toward regulating hate speech and its willingness to limit the freedoms of information technology (IT) companies, contrasting it with the United States' relative reluctance to make internet operators liable for speech that their platforms host. The comparison between the EU and the United States is particularly interesting in this domain given the stark regulatory differences between the two jurisdictions, and the reality that US companies are the ones most affected by EU regulations. It then examines the recent voluntary Code of Conduct that the EU has signed with leading IT companies and demonstrates how even this type of voluntary approach toward regulation has allowed the EU to shape the hate speech norms across the world through the Brussels Effect.

Major Legislation

The EU conceives illegal hate speech broadly, certainly compared with the approach taken by the United States. Not only is speech that incites violence banned in the EU, but also speech that incites hatred as such.[217] In contrast, the US Constitution only prohibits speech when that speech threatens and is likely to provoke an imminent violent response.[218] The United States is willing to extend protection to hateful ideas the same way it protects other types of ideas under its broader notion of free speech.[219] The EU also condemns speech that denigrates the dignity of a group, which the US jurisprudence does not do.[220]

These distinct approaches reflect differing philosophies that underlie the free speech doctrines of the United States and the EU. The US Constitutional tradition treats hate speech as an expression of racist or sexist *ideas*. Regardless of how repellent some of those ideas might be to many, they are perceived as having public utility and hence deserving of constitutional protection.[221] This reflects the United States' steadfast commitment to free speech and its reluctance to have the government decide which type of speech is valuable and which ideas should be silenced. As a further manifestation of this, the United States remains the only signatory to the International Covenant of Civil and Political Rights that objects to the Covenant's Article 20(2) prohibition of "any advocacy of national, racial or religious hatred that constitutes incitement to discrimination, hostility or violence."[222] For the United States, Article 20(2) remains unacceptable as it infringes on the United States' concept of the freedom of expression.

The EU's regulation of free speech is embedded in the Charter for Fundamental Rights, its primary treaties, and in the secondary legislation. Article 11 of the EU's

Charter for Fundamental Rights recognizes that "everyone has the right to freedom of expression." Yet, the case law by the European courts has made it clear that this freedom is far from absolute, and can be curtailed when non-discrimination norms prevail over free speech norms.[223] In its judgment *Feryn* in 2007,[224] the ECJ ruled that mere speech could constitute an act of discrimination that violated the principle of non-discrimination enshrined in EU Treaties.[225] This stringent stance toward speech is encapsulated in the opening line of the Advocate General Maduro's Opinion in *Feryn*—"contrary to conventional wisdom, words can hurt."[226]

The ECJ often cites the European Convention and the rulings of the European Court of Human Rights (ECtHR) in its own decisions, making the ECtHR's jurisprudence a part of the EU's fundamental rights fabric. The ECtHR shares the ECJ's view that the right of free expression must be balanced against the need to curtail speech that incites hatred and undermines the "equal dignity of all human beings."[227] In its 2006 decision *Erbakan v Turkey*, the ECtHR ruled that it may be necessary "in certain democratic societies to sanction or even prevent all forms of expression which spread, incite, promote or justify hatred based on intolerance . . . , provided that any 'formalities', 'conditions', 'restrictions' or 'penalties' imposed are proportionate to the legitimate aim pursued."[228] The ECtHR has also clarified its views on the role of IT companies in disseminating hate speech, noting that by "provid[ing] a platform for user-generated comments [these companies] assume the 'duties and responsibilities' associated with freedom of expression in accordance with Article 10 § 2 of the Convention where users disseminate hate speech or comments amounting to direct incitement to violence."[229]

EU law also requires member states to penalize the most severe forms of hate speech,[230] and the EU has passed directives to control racist and xenophobic behaviors in the media and online.[231] Even though the member states have responded with varying national norms on hate speech, it is telling that even the Netherlands—the bastion of free speech in the EU—prohibits the making of "public intentional insults" in its criminal code. The Dutch code also prohibits "engaging in verbal, written, or illustrated incitement to hatred, on account of one's race, religion, sexual orientation, or personal convictions."[232] Most prominently, the Netherlands has applied its rules on hate speech in the case involving its right-wing politician, Geert Wilders, who has targeted Muslims and Islam in much of his political rhetoric.[233] This shows that even among the European nations most sympathetic to defending free speech, hate speech is relatively broadly defined and strictly enforced.

Not only is the EU more willing to curtail hate speech as a phenomenon, it is also more willing to generally regulate digital companies.[234] It is therefore not surprising that the EU has evolved into a prominent regulator of hate speech taking place online, holding the IT companies responsible for the speech that takes place on their platforms. In contrast, the United States is not only a strong proponent of free speech; it also views the commercialization of the internet as a testament to the United States' commitment to entrepreneurship, innovation, and free markets, all of which have been the drivers of economic success and technological progress.[235] This has led to a light-handed approach toward regulating the online activities of the tech industry—including online hate speech.

While maintaining a strict legal framework on hate speech in general, the EU has chosen a participatory and voluntary approach in its efforts to police hate speech online. In 2016, the European Commission signed a voluntary Code of Conduct (Code) on Countering Illegal Hate Speech Online with four US IT companies: Facebook, Twitter, YouTube, and Microsoft.[236] The Code requires these signatories to adopt and maintain "Rules or Community Guidelines" (Community Guidelines) that reflect the European standard of hate speech. By signing up to the Code, these IT companies agree to "prohibit the promotion of incitement to violence and hateful conduct on their platforms." In addition, they agree to assess any request to remove any such content from their platform within 24 hours after receiving a request to do so, and proceed to remove the content when necessary. The EU complements this voluntary code with a set of non-binding recommendations that it released in 2017, and another set of non-binding operational recommendations released in March 2018.[237] These recommendations contain guidelines on how IT companies can effectively prevent, detect, and remove illegal content and how EU authorities can ensure efficient communication with these companies regarding the content that needs to be removed.

The EU's voluntary approach to regulation also operates in the shadow of binding law, which would consist of a potentially more drastic regulatory response in the future. The EU has made it clear that it can always implement binding legislative measures if the Code proves to be insufficient. When releasing its recommendations in 2017, the Commission announced that it would monitor the IT companies' activities closely to "assess whether additional measures are needed in order to ensure the swift and proactive detection and removal of illegal content online, including possible legislative measures to complement the existing regulatory framework."[238] The Commission confirmed the possibility of more coercive legislation once again in April 2018 as a response to Facebook's involvement in the Cambridge Analytica scandal.[239] The prospect of binding rules, backed by sanctions, gives firms an enhanced incentive to carry out their self-monitoring in ways that satisfy European regulators. Because of this threat of a more severe regulatory response, some commentators have described the EU's existing regulatory approach as neither voluntary nor a product of public-private partnership but instead "government coercion."[240]

Furthermore, the IT companies' incentives to comply with EU rules are heightened by stringent regulations emerging from individual EU member states. For example, Germany passed the Network Enforcement Act in July 2017.[241] This Act gives German regulators the authority to impose fines of up to €50 million for social media operators that fail to promptly remove illegal hate speech. France is also contemplating new laws imposing greater responsibility on social media companies to regulate racist and anti-Semitic content,[242] while the United Kingdom has announced new government measures specifically tackling hate speech online.[243]

Political Economy

The EU shares the United States' commitment to the freedom of expression but is significantly more prepared to curtail that freedom in the case of hate speech. Unlike the United States, the EU does not view the right to hate speech as a valuable part of public discourse. Instead, the EU views hate speech as a harmful manifestation of discrimination. Curtailing hate speech is seen as the opportunity to promote democracy, equality, and citizens' participation in society.[244] The EU's stand against hate speech is best understood in light of its history of racist and xenophobic violence, including most prominently the incitement of hatred by the Nazis against the Jews leading up to World War II. The burden of its history continues to define the European approach to hate speech, heightening its sense of the "duty of remembrance, vigilance and combat" against racist and xenophobic sentiments.[245]

Many individuals and activists in the EU welcome the recent regulatory push to make internet operators responsible for the speech their platforms host. The rise of populist parties with anti-migrant views has contributed to the rise in the incidents of hate speech, particularly on social media.[246] To counter this trend, several government institutions and NGOs in Europe maintain an active role in advocating policies and practices against hate speech. Among those organizations that have spoken forcefully against hate speech and that have called for increased responsibility for online platforms in censoring such speech are the following: The Council of Europe's European Commission against Racism and Intolerance (ECRI);[247] the Council of Europe's Youth Department, which has organized the "No Hate Speech Movement" across Europe;[248] and Galop UK.[249] Also, journalists in Europe—whose profession rests on the freedom of expression—have advocated restrictions on that freedom in order to curtail hate speech. The European Federation of Journalists (EFJ), supported by a coalition of civil society organizations, have launched a European wide #MediaAgainstHate campaign.[250] The purpose of the campaign is to counter discrimination and hate speech in both traditional and online media.

Beyond these organized advocacy groups, the European people share the sentiment that hate speech stifles respectful and healthy debates in society. A 2016 Eurobarometer survey on media pluralism and democracy inquired into European citizens' opinions about the diversity of views available in the media.[251] The survey was conducted among twenty-eight thousand EU citizens across the twenty-eight member states. The results were striking—three in four European social media users reported having experienced abuse, hate speech, or threats while engaging in debates online. Almost half of these citizens reported feeling discouraged from engaging in social media debates as a result.[252] This suggests that the Commission's efforts to pursue binding regulation in this area would also likely receive a strong mandate from European citizens.

The Brussels Effect

The EU's efforts to regulate hate speech online provides an interesting example of the de facto Brussels Effect as it represents a situation in which the EU is not, at least yet, externalizing a binding set of EU rules. Rather, this externalization involves voluntary commitments adopted by the companies in cooperation with the European Commission. Online hate speech is also an intriguing example of EU's unilateral regulatory influence because the EU is not the most stringent regulator of online speech globally, trailing behind other large markets such as China and Russia.

The EU's notable market power in this area is determinative, forming the foundation for the Brussels Effect. European consumers and revenue generated in Europe is key to the world's leading IT companies. The EU's large consumer base of 500 million potential customers makes it one of the IT companies' "most important overseas markets."[253] For example, the EU as a whole represents one of the largest markets for Facebook, with 250 million users.[254] Europe accounts for around 25% of Facebook's revenue, making Europe Facebook's second largest revenue source (behind the United States).[255] The European small and medium-sized enterprises (SMEs) market in particular is a significant source of advertising revenue for Facebook, with more than 60% year-over-year revenue growth.[256] For YouTube, five member states alone account for 14% of the company's global users.[257] In most EU member states, Google's share of the search market is over 90% whereas most estimates suggest that Google's market share is around 67–75% in the United States.[258] This likely explains, at least partially, why Google—after years of aligning its universal hate speech rule with the US First

Amendment—recently made a strategic choice to switch to a more restrictive European style of hate speech regulation.

Considering the great business opportunities that the European market provides, it comes as no surprise that these IT companies are committed to remaining in the European market even if they felt squeezed by the EU regulations. Google CEO Sundar Pichai communicated to investors that Google is "very committed to the region" and that Europe is an "important market for us."[259] This commitment is evidenced by the company's plans to expand new offices in Europe, to build an AI center on the continent, and to expand hiring of staff.[260] The most recent signatory to the Code, Snapchat, also regards Europe as one of its "core markets."[261]

Regardless of its notable market power, the EU has chosen not to leverage that power through binding rules but pursue voluntary standards instead. The main sanction for noncompliance with the Code of Conduct is reputational. The Commission, together with member state officials and civil society organizations, monitors signatories' compliance periodically and publishes the rates at which these companies are reviewing and taking down speech that violates the Code.[262] And as the discussion further along in this chapter reveals, the companies' compliance rates have been high. This suggests that even voluntary standards can reflect sufficient regulatory capacity and hence sustain the Brussels Effect.

A review of the IT companies' Terms of Service and Community Guidelines shows that these companies are, indeed, complying with the Code and converging to the European standard in practice regardless of its voluntary nature. The terms prohibit hateful speech without the need to prove violence and often use language that closely resembles the relevant European Framework Decision.[263] For example, YouTube's definition of hate speech refers to "content promoting violence or hatred against individuals or groups based on any of the following attributes: Age, Disability, Ethnicity, Gender, Nationality, Race, Immigration Status, Religion, Sex, Sexual Orientation, Veteran Status."[264] Thus, the firms not only ban speech that incites violence but also prohibit speech that incites hatred as such. Interestingly, the Code seems to be influencing the global standards for online hate speech even beyond its signatories. For example, Tumblr, which has not signed up to the Code, has adopted a European-style hate speech policy, urging its users not to encourage "hatred" as a separate category from encouraging violence.[265] This leads to the prohibition of a much broader set of content than what would be proscribed under the First Amendment rules in the United States.

This voluntary approach has several advantages. Perhaps most importantly, it allows the EU to pursue a near-costless approach to enforcement, as the companies themselves must dedicate the resources to police their own conduct. Second, the costly monitoring obligation creates incentives for these companies to develop technologies aimed at automatically detecting and eliminating harmful speech that appears on their platforms.[266] Ultimately, this could make the policing of online hate speech more comprehensive and efficient in the future. The EU institutions would hardly have the innovative capacity to automate their enforcement efforts this way.

However, outsourcing the monitoring of the compliance to the targets of the regulation themselves has certain downsides, including uncertainty over how the Code is implemented in practice. Even when the official Terms of Service of the IT companies mirror European standards, the lawyers within these companies ultimately use their own judgment on what constitutes illegal hate speech. The outcome is therefore less likely to perfectly align with the Commission's regulatory approach, compared to situations where the Commission carries out the enforcement. For example, if the Commission reaches a decision on the compatibility of a proposed merger with EU competition law, the outcome is clear. Parties are left with little discretion if the Commission decides that the merger cannot proceed or that a certain division needs to be divested. When it comes to removing hate speech, however, each content removal decision likely reflects the decision-maker's own views on freedom of expression, as well as the broader corporate culture.[267]

Marvin Ammori has argued that content removal decisions in these companies inevitably take place against the backdrop of American norms regarding free speech, given that the lawyers reviewing the content are likely to be educated in US law schools and hence are more familiar with the principles underlying the US free speech doctrine.[268] These decision-makers also report to executives who are equally steeped in the American free speech tradition, and who thus foster a corporate culture with a distinctive cultural emphasis on freedom of expression.[269] Jeffrey Rosen has advanced a similar view, describing online hate speech policies as having "European-style definitions," enforced sometimes "in an American way."[270] A recent leak of Facebook's internal policies provides an example of this, showing that Facebook's algorithms permit certain postings that deny the Holocaust, which is strictly prohibited under European standards.[271]

However, even if the IT companies were currently not perfectly aligned with European standards in their enforcement practice, they are clearly moving toward a more expansive hate speech standard as evidenced by a more extensive review and removal of reportedly illegal speech. The results of the periodic assessments under the Code confirm this. The results of the latest evaluation round conducted from November to December 2018[272] reveal that IT companies were removing, on average, 72% of all the illegal hate speech notified to them. The removal rate has gone up significantly in each evaluation period, increasing from 28% in the first monitoring round in 2016, from 59% in the second round in 2017, and even slightly from an already high removal rate of 70% in the third monitoring round in 2018. While the Code only calls for these companies to review "the majority" of the notifications within 24 hours, on average the companies are reviewing 89% of notifications within that time frame, which is over double the number compared to the first monitoring round.[273] The IT companies are also building up their capacity to comply by hiring more staff to review illegal content. Facebook alone announced in 2017 that it would hire an additional 3,000 moderators to identify hateful material on its platform, adding to the existing team of 4,500.[274] Finally, new companies are joining the Code, some of the latest signatories being Instagram, Google+,[275] and Snapchat in 2018.[276]

Despite the (relative) success of the voluntary regulation to date, the EU is considering abandoning the voluntary approach and introducing binding regulation in the near future. A comprehensive "Digital Services Act" is currently being drafted by the Commission, and may possibly be introduced by the end of 2020.[277] This new Act would vest the EU with "sweeping legal powers" to regulate hate speech as well as other illegal content and political advertising online. As a result, the removal of illegal content would become mandatory for social media platforms, and their failure to do so would result in fines. The reasons for the hardening regulatory approach are likely two-fold. First, the severity and frequency of controversies relating to illegal online content has reduced the public confidence in IT companies' self-regulation. Second, the decision by some large member states—including France, Germany and the United Kingdom—to introduce national legislation targeting online hate speech has given the Commission a strong internal market rationale to act, as it wants to prevent inconsistent national legislations from emerging across different member states.

Regardless of whether the proposed Digital Services Act will be adopted in the end, the case of online hate speech remains particularly interesting as an example of the Brussels Effect because of the way the EU's regulatory capacity has thus far been channeled to global markets through voluntary norms, leading to notable de facto Brussels Effect. Moreover, it is also an interesting case because the EU is not the most stringent regulator of speech online—a condition that is typically needed for the Brussels Effect to occur. When it comes to content that is allowed or censored online, the EU is considerably less stringent in comparison to countries such as China, Iran, or Russia, which maintain significantly higher restrictions on the freedom of expression—even if the focus of these governments' censorship was politically unacceptable speech more than hate speech as such. Yet IT companies do not choose to follow, for example, the more stringent Chinese standard and minimize the content that they allow online, even though this would guarantee their access to every market.

Instead, they are increasingly converging to the high—yet not excessively high—European standard, even if this means that they could be blocked from some significant markets, including China. These companies' decisions on what speech to tolerate is viewed as a reflection of their values. Being blocked from China is costly yet something that companies choose to tolerate—not least because they want to ensure that the free speech standard they embrace remains consistent with their values, brand, and corporate identity. In particular, they do not want to be viewed as "complicit"[278] in state censorship in the most speech-restricting nations.

In contrast, being shunned from the EU market is not a commercially viable option, which leads these companies to tolerate the relatively stringent, yet from a policy standpoint still acceptable, European standard. This way, regulation of hate speech online provides an interesting example of the Brussels Effect where the EU norms become globalized even when the EU is not the most stringent regulator but instead can generate global norms by providing a "middle ground" between freedom of expression and government censorship. A more nuanced argument would hence suggest that the Brussels Effect takes place when the EU is the most stringent regulator *that the companies respond to.*

The remaining conditions underlying the Brussels Effect—inelasticity and non-divisibility—are also present in this area, which is critical for the EU's unilateral regulatory influence. The platforms for speech are inelastic in the sense that IT companies cannot amend the IP address of Europeans that engage in online speech—they remain European consumers entitled to protections guaranteed by EU laws and institutions. In other words, the IT companies cannot evade EU rules by incorporating themselves elsewhere as EU law applies to them as long as European citizens access the speech that violates EU law.

Unlike the regulation of conventional hate speech, regulation of online hate speech tends to be technically or economically non-divisible. A review of IT companies' Terms of Service reveal that they tend to adopt the same definition globally after signing the Code with the EU. Typically, the European-style prohibitions are reflected in these companies' *global* Terms of Service, thereby applying to their operations worldwide. This is despite the European Commission explicitly clarifying that the Code only regulates the companies' conduct in Europe and that "(n)either the Framework decision nor the code contain any obligations on companies to make such content inaccessible in places where the relevant law(s) on illegal hate speech don't apply (for example in countries outside the EU or the specific countr(y/ies) in question)."[279]

In practice, IT companies' international user base presents them with a choice: companies can either adopt universal rules that apply across all their platforms, or they can choose country-specific rules to tailor to the nation where they operate.[280] A universal rule could further reflect either the most stringent standard, suppressing speech permitted in many markets yet allowing the company to operate in even the most speech-restrictive nations; or, alternatively, the universal rule could reflect the least stringent standard, which would maximize free speech but lead to the company being excluded from several markets, making the platforms unavailable to millions. If the companies instead forwent a single global rule and tailored their free speech rules to each nation in which they operate, they could push the outer limits of protection in each nation, retaining their freedom to operate across the world markets. From among these options, it appears that IT companies are predominantly choosing a universal rule. Facebook and Google adopted universal rules from early on. Twitter used to be the only internet company to adopt purely country-specific rules, but six months after signing the Code, it too moved toward adopting a universal standard, prohibiting "hateful conduct" in its global Terms of Service. The reasons for the globally uniform rules are technical, economic, and even social and cultural.

In principle, IT companies could try to pursue country-specific rules by resorting to "geo-blocking," which would allow them to ban selected content by geography.[281] Geo-blocking has emerged as a primary way to separate internet users according to their geography. This is done through the use of geolocation technology, which allows the service provider to determine where the user is located based on the location of the user's "Internet Protocol" (IP) address.[282] Geo-blocking can also be implemented through country-specific domain names. For example, because Germany and France have made it illegal to deny the Holocaust, the user cannot find Holocaust-denial sites on Google.de and Google.fr (the German and French Google default search engines) even when those sites would be available on Google.com.[283]

However, in practice it is often difficult to isolate European-only data, making geo-blocking an inadequate tool to make the online speech "divisible" across jurisdictions while ensuring compliance with EU standards. Rachel Whetstone, Google's former director of Global Communications and Public Affairs in the EMEA region, acknowledged that legal differences between how governments regulate freedom of expression "create real technical challenges, for example, about how you restrict one type of content in one country but not another."[284] For instance, geo-blocking is easy to circumvent as a user simply has to change its account's location settings.[285] Encryption technology also allows users to hide their locations online, meaning that it might be technically impossible to comply with jurisdiction-specific rules without removing content worldwide. Indeed, the difficulty of isolating European-only data has led to court orders that require IT companies to remove illegal content in both the specific country and globally.[286]

Beyond the technical challenges to non-divisibility, economic and other practical compliance considerations often limit the companies' ability to tailor their rules to each individual market. In operationalizing their Terms of Service and Community Guidelines to police hate speech, the IT companies have to translate their broader Terms of Service into detailed internal policy guidelines. For consistency and the ease of monitoring and compliance, companies often prefer to have a single internal policy in place.[287] These internal policy guidelines contain highly specific definitions, which hundreds of employees and contractors around the world must adhere to when reviewing the posts in a strict 24-hour timeline. It would hence be complicated and costly to create country-specific guidelines, which must be accompanied by multiple review processes.

In addition, there are social or cultural brand-related reasons to maintain uniform standards. These platforms view themselves as global operators that connect people and foster global conversations that take place across jurisdictional boundaries. A significant advantage of platforms like Facebook is one's ability to maintain friendships around the world, shrinking the "distance" between conversations that take place. This is an important reason why Facebook has expressed its reluctance to use geo-blocking as it undermines its "social network model."[288] Geo-blocking interferes with international conversations since portions of the exchange are hidden from some participants, and the posts would only appear in the news feeds of friends who live in countries where the geo-blocking prohibition does not apply. Hence, excessive geo-blocking would be contrary to Facebook's goal of creating global rules to ensure that "people are able to communicate in a borderless way."[289] Furthermore, Facebook asserts that there is "one Facebook,"[290] and thus it is less willing to remove speech in one region and not another.

The ECJ will also have the opportunity rule on the question of divisibility as a legal matter.[291] The Austrian Supreme Court has referred to the ECJ for a preliminary ruling a legal challenge regarding Facebook's responsibility to remove hate speech postings on its platform. The Austrian appeals court took the view that blocking the hate speech posts in Austria alone was not enough—they must be deleted across the entire global platform. The Austrian Supreme Court declined to rule either way, and instead referred the legal questions to the ECJ. The ECJ is asked to rule on how extensive Facebook's responsibility is, including whether it must remove access to the content not just locally, but globally and whether it has a duty to remove similar (but not identical) hate speech postings against the same person as part of its obligations under EU law.[292] In June 2019, Advocate General Szpunar issued an Opinion in the case, suggesting that Facebook can be ordered to identify all postings that are identical to a defamatory comment that has been found illegal. This obligation can be extended to similar (yet not identical) comments by the same user who posted the illegal information in the first place.[293] Significantly, the Opinion further suggests that because the relevant EU directive does not regulate the territorial scope of such an obligation, "it does not preclude a host provider from being ordered to remove such information *worldwide*." This case presents a similar issue to the other case also currently pending before the ECJ (and discussed earlier), querying whether the "right to be forgotten" imposes on the internet platforms such as Google the obligation to delist certain information worldwide. Together, these cases offer a novel—and highly consequential—opportunity for the ECJ to determine how far-reaching, indeed, the Brussels Effect should be.

AS THIS CHAPTER has shown, the EU has become a significant global regulator of digital companies. Through the GDPR, the EU is shaping transnational corporate conduct and foreign government legislative activity alike, enhancing the privacy protections enjoyed by individuals far beyond the EU. Through its regulation of online hate speech, the EU is redrawing boundaries of acceptable discourse similarly across jurisdictions around the world.

Data protection provides a strong example of the Brussels Effect, both de facto and de jure. The EU represents an important market for multinational companies, ensuring that the fundamental precondition of the Brussels Effect—market size—is met. The GDPR is also inelastic in that it protects the European data subjects even if the data processing takes place outside the EU. The GDPR has further strengthened the Brussels Effect by laying out even more stringent data protection standards than what existed in the EU before. It has also enhanced the EU's regulatory capacity although—unlike in the domain of competition law where the Commission remains a key enforcer—the enforcement of the GDPR rests almost entirely on member state DPAs. The long-term salience of the Brussels Effect will hence depend on the effectiveness of those national regulators in deploying the regulatory capacity that the EU institutions have bestowed upon them.

While the above conditions underlying the Brussels Effect are typically present, the occurrence of the Brussels Effect in data privacy often comes down to the existence of non-divisibility. This chapter has shown how most multinational companies today maintain a global privacy policy that closely conforms to the GDPR, likely for reasons of both technical and economic non-divisibility as well as to minimize complexity and compliance errors. Non-divisibility is also driven by these companies' need to preserve a global brand and offer equal protections to all their users, in particular today when data protection issues have grown in salience and drawn global attention to the corporate practices in this regard. While these dynamics have contributed toward non-divisibility, this chapter has also examined several examples where the companies have been both able and willing to divide their conduct across various markets. Thus—as was the case with competition law—data protection also highlights the importance of non-divisibility in explaining the variance in the manifestation of the Brussels Effect.

The de jure Brussels Effect has also been prevalent in the case of data protection, as illustrated by the number of jurisdictions across Asia, Africa, and Latin America adopting domestic data protection laws that closely emulate the GDPR. This extensive de jure Brussels Effect is likely driven by several forces, including the de facto Brussels Effect, which has made multinational companies keen advocates of the GDPR-type laws in their home markets—including recently in the United States. The EU's requirement for "adequacy" as a condition for international data transfers has given an additional impetus for foreign governments to emulate the GDPR. The recent scandals, such as Cambridge Analytica data breach, have exposed data privacy violations and further fueled demand for tougher data protection laws abroad. In all those instances, the foreign governments often turn to the GDPR in their legislative drafting, given both its comprehensiveness as well as reputation as the "gold standard" worldwide.

In addition to imposing extensive obligations on digital companies to maintain users' data privacy, the EU has put pressure on online platforms to police content that can be viewed as hateful. It embraces a broad notion of what constitutes hateful speech and does not share the US' liberal approach toward regulating the internet. It is notable how the targets of its regulation—some of the most powerful companies in the world—are adhering to the EU's rules even in the absence of binding rules and sanctions. This example thus illustrates that the Brussels Effect can occur even when the EU leverages its regulatory capacity through voluntary regulation. In addition to being a form of voluntary regulation, online hate speech offers an interesting variant of the Brussels Effect in that the EU's regulation does not present the most stringent regulatory standard—jurisdictions such as China and Russia are even more restrictive of online conversations. Indeed, China is among the few jurisdictions that have blocked, for instance, Facebook altogether.

There are signs that some other jurisdictions are also surpassing the EU in regulatory stringency, further testing the boundaries of the Brussels Effect. In the wake of the recent Facebook livestreaming of a massacre that took place in two mosques in New Zealand, Australia passed domestic legislation that orders social media companies to "expeditiously" remove "abhorrent violent material" from their platforms.[294] Failure to do so will lead to large fines or even jail time for the company executives. The law, hastily passed, is considerably more far-reaching than the online hate speech regulation in the EU, and has led to strong criticism by IT companies.[295] It remains to be seen how the Australian law will affect IT companies' global conduct. While not an insignificant market, Australia dwarfs the EU in its market size and hence the economic significance for IT companies. This has led to speculation that the legal risks associated with the new law may cause some IT companies to move their offices out of Australia.[296] It is alternatively possible that the Australian law might lead to a "Brussels Effect plus" type of phenomenon where corporate conduct follows the combination of the most stringent regulations around the world. In this case—and especially if other jurisdictions follow Australia's example—the EU might find further space to intensify its own regulations, amplifying the global political momentum and enhancing the perception of greater legitimacy associated with the regulation of online hate speech, or the digital economy more broadly.

6

Consumer Health and Safety

PROTECTION OF CONSUMER health and safety has been a long-standing concern for the EU regulators. Since the early days of the single market, the EU has sought to harmonize many regulations that minimize risks that consumers face from the exposure to unsafe food, dangerous substances, or defective products. When regulating these types of risks, the EU has always had dual goals: to advance consumer health and safety while furthering trade within the single market through harmonized rules. This chapter focuses on two specific areas of regulation that have been central to the EU's efforts to protect its citizens: food safety and chemical safety. Both areas reflect the EU's heightened concern for harm that consumers may experience if the market is left unregulated, giving the EU the impetus to intervene even on a precautionary basis to preempt such risks from emerging in the first place.

The first part of this chapter examines the Brussels Effect through the global impact of the EU's food safety regulation, while the second part of the chapter examines the Brussels Effect through the lens of chemical safety. The discussion first introduces the EU's key food safety regulations, and examines the underlying interest group dynamics that explain the emergence of such stringent regulations from the EU's legislative process. It then offers some examples of both the de facto and de jure Brussels Effect on food safety. Next, the chapter turns to chemical safety, again reviewing the relevant regulation, together with the politics behind that regulation. It then illustrates the pervasiveness of the Brussels Effect—both de facto and de jure—demonstrating the EU's entrenched regulatory influence across the global marketplace.

Consumer Health and Safety I: Food Safety

The food industry is the largest manufacturing and employment sector in Europe, and food affects the everyday lives of all Europeans. The EU is the world's biggest

The Brussels Effect. Anu Bradford, Oxford University Press (2020). © Oxford University Press.
DOI: 10.1093/oso/9780190088583.001.0001

importer and exporter of foodstuffs—a term that refers to both processed food as well as livestock and other raw material used for food.[1] According to Phil Hogan, the EU's commissioner for Agriculture and Rural Development, the EU's success as the biggest exporter of agri-food products in the world rests on various regulatory reforms that have made the EU producers competitive in global markets but is also explained by the "worldwide reputation of EU products as being safe, sustainably produced, nutritious and of high quality."[2] Preserving this high-quality reputation of the European food industry is therefore of enormous economic significance for the EU.

But beyond its economic importance, food is also often an emotional issue among Europeans, and food production and cuisine form an important part of cultural and regional identity in many parts of Europe. For instance, the Europeans' resistance to genetically modified organisms (GMOs) does not merely reflect safety concerns; it also stems from a desire to restrict intensive farming and limit the power of monocultures while maintaining the vitality and diversity of the European countryside and protecting the traditional farming culture. Because of these broader cultural and emotional attachments to food, along with the sector's economic importance, food safety has become a salient policy issue—both for European producers and consumers—and hence an important target of EU regulations.

In the last several decades, numerous food scandals have weakened consumer confidence in the food supply chain and prompted broad public support for regulatory intervention.[3] Perhaps the most notorious food scandal was the BSE—"mad cow disease"—crisis that originated in 1986 from the United Kingdom, where animal meat and bone meal had been used as feed for livestock. Once it was discovered that BSE might be transmitted to humans and cause the fatal Creutzfeldt-Jakob disease, the EU ordered an embargo of all British beef.[4] However, BSE had already spread to livestock in other parts of Europe, further aggravating the crisis and leading to mass slaughtering of infected cows. In the United Kingdom alone, the crisis led to 156 people dying of Creutzfeldt-Jakob disease in late 1990s after eating infected beef.[5] This scandal sparked widespread criticism about existing food safety regulations and highlighted the need for more concerted action at the EU level.[6] Other notable food crises that have motivated public support for strong EU-wide regulatory action include the detection of tainted Spanish colza oil (1981), Benzene-contaminated Perrier in the United Kingdom (1990), carcinogenic dioxin in feed for poultry and livestock in Belgium (1999), E. coli deaths in Germany following imports of Egyptian seeds and beans (2011), and the revelation that horse meat was being served as beef in burgers in several European countries (2013).

In addition to calling for new regulations after each of these individual food safety incidents, Europeans have also expressed concerns about food safety relating to broader technological and environmental changes in food production. For example, Europeans have expressed support for regulating the cultivation and marketing of GMOs, concerned about their potentially adverse health effects. Due to these concerns, the EU requires that all foods containing GMOs that are sold in the EU be labeled as such. GMOs also have to go through a lengthy approval process, including an evaluation of the risk they pose to human health and the environment, before they can be cultivated or used in food products, agricultural products, or feeds anywhere within the EU market.

The next discussion reviews key aspects of EU regulation pertaining to food safety in general and GMOs in particular. It also unpacks the political dynamics that explain the EU's stringent regulation in this area. Additionally, it offers several examples of the de facto and de jure Brussels Effect relating to food safety regulations. The EU has been very successful in externalizing its food safety regulations to some industries and countries. However, there are also several instances where the Brussels Effect has not taken place. Food remains a subject where consumer preferences and traditions vary significantly across the countries, limiting food producers' ability to take advantage of economic non-divisibility in all instances. These differences among national traditions relating to food consumption and production have also limited foreign governments' willingness to always emulate the EU. Given these variances, food safety provides a particularly interesting area to examine the relative importance of the various conditions that are required for the Brussels Effect.

Major Legislation

Since its founding, and particularly in recent decades in response to various food safety crises like those already discussed, the EU has enacted a broad range of food-related legislation. According to the Commission, "[e]very European citizen has the right to know how the food he eats is produced, processed, packaged, labeled and sold."[7] Notable regulations address the safety of food and animal feed, production hygiene, health and welfare of animals used as food, use of food additives such as preservatives and food colorings, food packaging, and labeling of food.[8] For example, the EU bans certain contaminants that may expose consumers to foodborne illness and restricts certain food additives due to their harmful health effects. The EU also imposes strict limits on the maximum pesticide residue permitted in food after it is harvested and enforces high standards of hygiene to be maintained in slaughterhouses. Producers must comply with robust certification processes that provide reliable information on compliance with food safety rules or, for example, verify that the criteria for organic production have been met. In addition to protecting public health, EU food regulations are aimed at providing accurate information to the consumer. Labeling requirements include clearly stating the country of origin and providing health, nutrition, and allergy information about the food product.[9] The EU's food safety regulations apply to domestic and imported food alike. To better control the safety of food imports, the EU has therefore adopted regulations that provide a legal framework for engaging with, and monitoring of, foreign countries' regulatory regimes, including carrying out pre-export inspections abroad.[10]

Cultivation and marketing of GMOs as well as GM food and feed have also been subject to extensive EU regulation.[11] Before GMOs can be cultivated and marketed in the EU, the European Food Safety Authority (EFSA),[12] in cooperation with scientific bodies of the EU member states, must evaluate their safety.[13] As part of this process, the importer has the burden to show that the GMO in question will not have adverse effects on human or animal health or harm the environment.[14] After a favorable risk assessment, the Commission submits a draft authorization decision for a committee composed of representatives of EU member states for a vote.[15] However, given the contested nature of GMOs, member state representatives have consistently failed to vote on authorizations, which under EU rules leads to the proposal being automatically adopted by the Commission.[16] This has entrenched the Commission's role as the decision-maker but also allowed the member states to blame the Commission for unpopular GMO authorizations.

Because of this onerous regulatory process and a high threshold for GMO authorization, the only GMO cultivated in the EU today is Monsanto's maize MON810,[17] which is grown primarily in Spain. Sale and marketing of GMO food and feed is also limited. Today, a small number of GMOs are authorized for use in food and feed in the EU.[18] At the same time, the EU imports substantial quantities of GM feed, including GM soybean to feed livestock, but imports hardly any GM food due to strong public opposition.[19]

As of 2015, the EU has granted more authority to its member states to regulate cultivation of GMOs in their territories. Today, member states have the freedom to individually restrict the cultivation of GMOs within their jurisdiction even if cultivation is authorized at the EU level.[20] Specifically, member states may request to opt out of the Commission decision authorizing the cultivation of a GMO, or may ban the sale of GM feed and food in their national market. It is telling of the strong public concern about GMOs among EU member states that shortly after gaining this authority, nineteen states banned the cultivation of the only EU-approved GMO—Monsanto's maize MON810—in their territory.[21]

The EU has also drafted major food safety legislation to regulate the traceability and labeling of GMOs to ensure that consumers and food chain operators can track GMOs and make informed choices about food.[22] The EU regulation calls for the labeling of most authorized foods, ingredients, and animal feeds containing over 0.9% GMOs.[23] All foods marketed in the EU that are prepackaged GMO food or GMO feed products must have a label indicating "genetically modified" or "produced from genetically modified [name of the organism]."[24] The EU's labeling threshold is the strictest in the world. By comparison, in many countries such as the United States and Japan, products may contain up to 5% GMO material before they trigger the labeling requirement.[25]

Political Economy

Food has long been a salient issue in Europe, and Europeans take risks associated with food seriously. A 2010 Eurobarometer survey suggests that Europeans remain particularly fearful of risks associated with animal infections, chemical contamination, and new technologies such as GMOs.[26] For instance, 70% of Europeans worry about pesticide residues, antibiotics or hormones in meat, mercury in fish, and dioxins in pork. Cloning of animals for food products invokes similar levels of concern. The same survey finds that Europeans also have a relatively high degree of confidence in public authorities in managing such risks, further explaining the public support for regulatory intervention in this area.

Europeans are also particularly supportive of stringent food safety regulations relating to food origins and traceability. In today's market, food is increasingly sourced from around the world, involving many producers from various jurisdictions before it reaches the final consumer. But these long supply chains can also lead to uncertainties and problems with traceability. For example, in 2013, the EU discovered that horsemeat was being served as beef in burgers in several countries. The horsemeat in question came from a Romanian slaughterhouse, and was sold by a Cypriot trader to a French supplier, which then passed it onto a French food processing company, which further sold the product to British and French supermarkets.[27] A few years earlier in 2011, tainted bean sprouts originating from Egypt killed twenty-two and further sickened two thousand people. Yet, before the chain of liability was discovered, Spanish farmers were falsely blamed and a trade ban was imposed on Russia, leading to substantial economic losses for both Spanish and Russian farmers.[28] Scandals like this helped catalyze European support of stringent traceability rules that can help identify the origin of a food crises and thus facilitate a regulatory response.

The EU's pro-regulation view is not always shared by other countries, particularly the United States, especially when the EU has acted on "precaution" in instances where the risks associated with food safety are harder to ascertain. This has made food safety a frequent subject of international trade disputes. For example, the EU has banned the importation of US beef treated with growth hormones and maintained the ban even when faced with an adverse WTO ruling regarding the legality of the ban.[29] The EU has also banned US poultry that has been rinsed with chlorine for sanitation purposes, similarly leading to a WTO complaint.[30] However, these high-level trade disputes between the EU and the United States have not restrained the EU's tendency to regulate food safety through stringent standards, something that has been critical for the broader global impact of the Brussels Effect.

Another major area in food safety regulation where the EU has consistently sought more rules and oversight than several other jurisdictions relates to the cultivation and sale of GMOs.[31] GMOs are regulated in widely divergent ways across the globe. But in the EU, there is strong political support for the heavy regulation of their use. Survey data from 2001 and 2006 shows that 62% of Europeans are worried about the food safety risks posed by GMOs, and 71% of Europeans do not want GMOs in their food.[32] A more recent survey from 2010 suggests that attitudes toward GMOs have not softened, confirming that a high proportion of Europeans (70%) agrees that GM food is fundamentally unnatural, and 61% of Europeans agree that GM food makes them feel uneasy. In addition, 61% of Europeans disagree that the development of GM food should be encouraged.[33]

This strong overall support for GMO regulation in the EU masks underlying variation across the member states. While less than half of the population in countries such as Ireland (46%), Sweden (48%), and the United Kingdom (48%) worry about GMOs, over 80% of the population in Greece and Lithuania harbor safety concerns. In Austria, GMOs are ranked as the most serious food safety concern (67%), together with pesticides.[34] Member states' regulatory policies are also divided on GMOs and often reflect the composition of their domestic agricultural sector and the influence of the country's strongest agricultural organizations. For example, Spain—the largest GMO producer in the EU—together with the Czech Republic, Portugal, Romania, and Slovakia favor GMO development, while Austria, France, Germany, Greece, Hungary, and Luxembourg remain against their cultivation and use. The member states that are reluctant to embrace GMOs refer to socioeconomic, ethical, or political reasons for their resistance.[35]

Despite some EU member states being in favor of more GMO cultivation, the anti-GMO movement in the EU is formidable, and it has generally shaped the legislative agenda on GMOs. This anti-GMO coalition includes major NGOs, whose advocacy against GMOs has been more successful in influencing EU legislation than that of the industry promoting the GMOs.[36] Importantly, these NGOs have also been able to harness the support of interest groups representing European farmers (Copa-Cocega) and the European retail industry (Eurocoop and EuroCommerce). This traditional "big farm" industry has not embraced

GMOs, preferring to focus on conventional farming while the food retailers are opposed to GMOs because of the intensity of public resistance among their customers. In the face of the ardent support for stringent regulation by this large anti-GMO coalition, the pro-GMO coalition, which includes the large agro- and food-industry groups such as Monsanto/BASF, Syngenta, Bayer, and DuPont— have not been successful in changing the consumer perception and influencing EU policy.[37] For example, after the BASF's genetically modified Amflora potato was authorized for cultivation in the EU, the online activist network Avaaz and Greenpeace collected one million signatures on a petition calling for a new moratorium on GMO cultivation,[38] forcing BASF to withdraw from the market.[39] Monsanto also withdrew all of its pending applications to cultivate GMO crops in the EU in 2013, conceding that the deep-seated resistance in the EU toward GMOs showed no signs of being alleviated in the foreseeable future.[40]

The EU's stringent regulations of GMOs and biotechnology, more broadly, also highlight the starkly opposing views between the EU and the United States. The EU's general position is against the production, use, and spreading of GMOs, unless they are proven safe with scientific certainty.[41] The EU's regulatory regime is based on pre-market approval, the precautionary principle, and post-market control. In contrast, the United States regards GMO products as substantially similar to products made using traditional production methods and allows them unless they are proven unsafe. GMO products can therefore be cultivated and marketed in the United States without extensive pre-market safety studies.[42] These differences replicate similar EU–US divisions in many other areas of regulation, where the EU tends to err on the side of caution whereas the United States is quick to embrace new technologies and remains skeptical of government intervention, in particular if any harm is uncertain or not fully substantiated.

There may, however, be additional motivations that explain the US–EU regulatory divergence on GMOs. The United States is the world's leading GMO producer, while at the same time GMOs are hardly cultivated in the EU.[43] In 2015, the United States had 70.9 million hectares devoted to farming genetically modified crops; but the EU member state with the highest acreage of genetically modified crops, Spain, devoted only .11 million hectares.[44] Biotechnology-enhanced production is seen as essential for the United States to remain competitive in export markets, while the EU places cultural importance on small-scale farming and remains skeptical of mass production technologies. Consequently, US farmers and the biotechnology industry are influential in the US political process regarding GMO regulation, whereas farmers producing non-GMO crops wield influence in the EU.

Consumer preferences are also reflected in the regulatory divergence. While Europeans are worried about the food safety risks posed by GMOs, US consumers have shown less concern for the issue. For example, according to an Environics poll, 78% of Americans support agricultural biotechnology, whereas the comparable figure in Germany was 54%, 52% in France, 36% in Britain, and 29% in Spain.[45] US consumers are also relatively uninformed about GMOs in general.[46] However, some recent surveys indicate that attitudes toward GMOs in the United States may be hardening. For example, recent US polls suggest that consumers favor mandatory GM food labeling.[47] Additionally, a 2014 study found that 72% of US consumers take the view that "avoiding genetically engineered or modified ingredients" was a "very important" or "important" objective when purchasing food.[48] These studies suggest that US consumers' skepticism toward GMOs is growing, which may pave way for a regulatory change going forward.

In the past 20 years, GMOs have been the subject of a prolonged trade dispute between the EU and the United States.[49] From 1998 to 2004, there was a de facto moratorium on GMO approval in place in the EU, where member states refused to support the approval of any GMOs until the EU regulatory framework changed.[50] This moratorium made it practically impossible for GMO producers to import unapproved varieties to the EU. In response, Argentina, Australia, Canada, Chile, Colombia, Egypt, El Salvador, Honduras, Mexico, New Zealand, Peru, the United States, and Uruguay filed a complaint before the WTO alleging that the EU's regulatory process was too slow, and its standards were unreasonable given the scientific evidence supporting the safety of GMOs. The WTO Dispute Settlement Body found in 2006 that the EU's de facto moratorium violated international trade rules. Despite this finding against the EU, the EU's trade partners allege that the EU's compliance with the WTO ruling has been tepid,[51] and that the EU continues to be extremely slow in granting authorizations for GMOs.[52] Further, even if the EU were to grant authorizations faster, GMOs would still have only limited access to EU markets.[53] The EU's strict requirements on traceability and labeling of GMO products remain intact, considerably limiting producers' ability to penetrate the European market given EU consumers' distrust of GMO foods. The EU has also tightened its regulation of GMO feed. In 2011 the EU passed a new regulation setting a 0.1% limit of non-authorized GMO material in feed imported from non-EU countries,[54] basically introducing a zero-tolerance policy for such feed. This has exacerbated trade tensions by effectively preventing animal feed imports from countries like the United States.[55]

There are competing arguments about the benefit or harm of the EU's GMO regulations for developing countries where GMOs are a significant issue given the importance of agriculture for their economies. GMOs could increase crop productivity and help developing nations feed their growing populations. Yet these countries have fewer resources to manage risks associated with GMOs. Traditional farming also retains an important cultural role in many societies, making many developing countries hesitant to embrace the GMOs.[56] Many African countries also rely on Europe as their main export destination, restricting their ability to use GMOs. Critics assert that the EU's certification, labeling, and traceability requirements are overly burdensome for producers in these less-resourced countries, and effectively exclude many small-scale farmers from global value chains.[57] At the same time, recent research demonstrates beneficial effects of EU's high food safety standards on African producers who earn a much higher return from trading in the EU once standards are achieved and certification obtained.[58] For instance, using farm-level data of 386 Ghanaian pineapple farmers who adopted either GlobalGAP or organic certification, Kleemann et al. found that certifications increased the farmers' return on investment, offsetting the costs of certification. Compliance with EU standards can hence have positive effect for producers in Africa, allowing farmers to access high-value export markets, improve their farming knowledge, and increase sales revenues.[59]

Overall, European citizens have retained their skeptical attitudes toward agricultural biotechnology and remain supportive of stringent food safety regulations. This has given the EU a strong mandate to continue to lead the way by setting the most ambitious safety standards shaping the food industry. Because of the deep interconnectedness of today's global food production through long supply chains, EU regulations of GMOs and other food safety issues frequently lead multinational companies and foreign jurisdictions to adopt those regulations in order to maintain access to the EU market. The next two sections in this chapter shine a light on how this influence is manifest both through the de facto and de jure Brussels Effect.

De Facto Brussels Effect

The de facto Brussels Effect in the case of food safety has been pervasive in some industries, yet largely absent in others. Three of the conditions underlying the Brussels Effect—regulatory capacity, regulatory stringency, and inelasticity of food safety regulation—are typically met in this area. With few exceptions—such as allowing for unpasteurized cheese—the EU regulates food safety with the most stringent regulatory standards in the world. Over time, the EU has also built the institutional capacity to exercise significant regulatory authority in this domain. Food is one of the first policy areas that fell under EU competence. The single market on food was established in the early 1960s, a longevity that has allowed the EU to accumulate considerable expertise in the domain. The 2002 establishment of the European Food Safety Authority, as well as national food safety authorities, further enhances EU's regulatory capacity.[60] Food safety regulation also clearly falls under inelastic consumer protection regulation, which ensures that the EU's regulatory clout cannot be circumvented by moving the regulatory targets to another jurisdiction.

There is some doubt as to whether the EU's 2015 regulatory reform relating to GMO cultivation enhanced or reduced the EU's regulatory capacity and stringency, and hence the pervasiveness of the Brussels Effect. That reform partially decentralized the EU's regulatory policy by granting the member states the right to make their own decisions on whether to permit the cultivation of GMOs in their territories. This new regulatory framework could be viewed as further tightening the regulatory environment for GMOs in the EU, as any applicant willing to cultivate GMOs in the EU now faces an additional hurdle in seeking for an authorization to do so. Accordingly, the Brussels Effect could be even stronger following this reform. However, the existence of a common EU-wide policy has often provided the incentive for companies to adjust globally to the EU rule. With the introduction of potentially significant variance across the members state regulations, the 2015 decentralization reform may remove that incentive, weakening the Brussels Effect. Regardless of how this particular reform affects the Brussels Effect, the effect is only limited to GMO cultivation, leaving the regulation of GMO sales and marketing untouched.

Further, while the EU's regulatory capacity, as well as the stringency and inelasticity of food safety regulation are generally well established, it is less clear that the other two conditions for the Brussels Effect are present. For example, the EU does not represent a significant market for all major exporters, suggesting that it may not have the requisite market size that would trigger the Brussels Effect. For instance, for US farmers, the EU is the fifth largest export market and accounts for only around 8% of total agricultural exports.[61] Many US producers can thus afford to forgo the EU market and divert their trade elsewhere if they consider regulatory compliance to be too onerous.[62] Indeed, trade statistics show that US producers are increasingly turning to other markets. While US agricultural exports to the world grew by 181% between 2000 and 2013, US exports to the EU only grew by 1%. This has been at least partially attributed to the EU's stringent regulations.[63] However, US farmers' scope for trade diversion may be narrowing as several key economies are increasingly emulating EU's food safety laws. For instance, Australia, Brazil, China, and Japan are following the EU's lead and adopting mandatory labeling schemes for GMO products.[64] This enhances the likelihood that the US farmers may, after all, experience the Brussels Effect.[65] In addition, for many African and some Latin American countries, the EU remains the most important export destination, suggesting that the Brussels Effect is likely to impact many of those markets.

The question of divisibility of production is a particularly convoluted one in the case of food safety, often explaining whether or not the Brussels Effect takes place. In many instances, producers respond to high variance in consumer preferences by producing different varieties for different markets. For example, artificial dyes used to enhance the appearance of food—such as rainbow candies and red-tinted salmon—are permitted in the United States, but restricted in the EU following the publication of studies that show these dyes trigger hyperactivity in kids.[66] As a result, companies like Kraft, Coca-Cola, Walmart, and Mars voluntarily removed artificial dyes from their products distributed in Europe,[67] but continue to use them in the United States. Similarly, M&Ms sold in the EU contain natural coloring, but M&Ms sold to American consumers contain artificial dyes. Nestlé's chocolate "Smarties" contain radish, lemon, and red cabbage extracts for coloring in the EU while the equivalent (yet brighter) color is derived from "Yellow No. 6" or "Red No. 40" in the United States.[68] In each instance, companies can conform with the two sets of standards cheaply enough to make it economically viable to serve both markets without adopting the higher standard (or, alternatively, without abandoning the high regulation market). These examples illustrate that the Brussels Effect is not inevitable, and will fail to emerge as long as the gains from catering to divergent customer preferences exceed the costs of doing so.

However, in many other contexts, companies opt for adopting the EU standard as a single global standard, eliciting the Brussels Effect as a result. For instance, in 2015, Kraft removed its Yellow No. 5 and Yellow No. 6 dyes from its iconic orange Mac & Cheese dinner in favor of natural coloring agents such as paprika and annatto, even though those dyes remain legal in the United States.[69] Pepsi and Coca-Cola also vowed to remove BVO—a chemical that keeps citrus flavoring from separating in beverages—from their drinks and switch to natural ingredients. BVO is banned in the EU because it has been linked to memory loss and nerve disorders, yet it is considered safe by the FDA.[70] Similarly, the sandwich chain Subway phased the bleaching chemical azodicarbonamide (ADA) out of its bread, even though the FDA has approved its use in food, because the EU bans it due to its carcinogenic properties.[71] Wendy's and McDonald's have followed Subway's lead and also removed the chemical from their products.[72] Of course, in these instances, corporations are likely also responding to domestic pressures to change their business practices, and not merely to economic benefits associated with non-divisibility. However, their willingness to do so is greatly enhanced by their existing need to adjust their production in order to trade into the EU market.

Whether global companies customize or standardize production across global markets likely depends on a few key considerations, particularly relating to costs and consumer preferences. For one, companies will likely decide it is worth making products divisible when consumer preferences are sufficiently different in major markets and where producers can hence obtain real gains from customization. For example, there are enough Americans who prefer the bright-colored Smarties for Nestlé to justify producing a different color variety for the US market. Presumably, in the case of Smarties, the costs of customization are also small, or at least offset by gains available from greater sales resulting from the ability to cater to the specific needs of US customers. In contrast, companies are likely to globalize the EU standard when customization is expensive or where gains from customization are trivial. Production to a global standard is also more likely to emerge whenever companies sense a growing customer demand for a more stringent standard emerging worldwide.[73]

Another important factor influencing how a company will respond to EU regulations is operational feasibility. In some cases, if it is too expensive to convert global production to meet EU standards, but not feasible to divide production within existing production facilities, a company may be prompted to search for alternative business strategies. For example, due to the EU's stringent food hygiene and safety standard,[74] a Japanese company, The Makurazaki Marine Products Processing Industries Cooperative, decided not to export bonito flakes (dried tuna flakes) to France. Instead, the company decided to open a factory in the EU to avoid having to make a Japanese factory comply with the EU regulation.[75]

When considering the feasibility of divisibility within food and agricultural production, GMOs present a complex issue, presenting a particularly valuable area to examine the operation of the Brussels Effect. Presumably, US farmers could, at least in principle, separate their production and cultivate both GMO and non-GMO varieties destined for domestic and EU markets, respectively. Yet such division can be difficult in practice for technical and economic reasons.[76] GMO crops must be segregated from the time they are planted throughout the processing and marketing chain. This entails separating growing areas and preventing pollen drift from GMO fields to non-GMO fields.[77] Producers and distributors must also use separate equipment, storage areas, and shipping containers, and establish trait identification systems that allow for the tracking of produce from the farm to the consumer.[78] These risks associated with cross-contamination can be substantial, especially when considering that if the economic operator makes an error anywhere in the process, the whole line is destroyed, leading to lost sales and the need to discard the entire production as unfit for market.[79] It is therefore not surprising that some farmers choose to forgo the risks and costs of separation and converge to the most stringent standard by either avoiding GMOs, or only cultivating EU-approved GMO crops—irrespective of where these crops are sold.[80]

Numerous factors can contribute to commingling of GMO and non-GMO varieties, including "pollen flow, volunteerism, mixing during harvesting, transport, storage and processing, human error and accidents."[81] If commingling occurs from any of these factors, the "adventitious presence" of GMOs—a term the food safety industry uses for the GMO content threshold that is accidental and hence unavoidable[82]—can easily cause the food product to exceed allowable levels. Strict thresholds, including EU's 0.9% threshold, make it harder to produce both GMO and non-GMO crops, as such cross-contamination can rarely be eliminated entirely. The difficulty of creating fully divisible production in the GMO context was also reinforced by a recent ECJ ruling. The ECJ found that honey containing traces of GMOs due to accidental contamination from GMO test fields 500 meters away was nonetheless considered food produced from a GMO under EU law.[83] The ruling underscores the technical difficulties and legal risks that farmers and food processors face when attempting to divide the production and cater to both GMO and non-GMO markets.

Indeed, a number of recent studies have confirmed the difficulty of avoiding the adventitious presence of GM traces in conventional planting seeds.[84] For example, a recent study examined whether bees transfer the pollen from genetically modified soy crops to the honey produced in the Yucatan Peninsula in Mexico given the proximity of the two farming areas.[85] A key concern among farmers and exporters was that GMO transfer could "provoke rejection from European marketers and consumers."[86] While the study found that Yucatan Peninsula's honey had "relatively low" amounts of GMO soy pollen, it still recommended measures to prevent such contamination.[87] These technical difficulties—and subsequently legal risks—associated with any attempts to divide the production and separate GMO seeds from non-GMO seeds are important factors in explaining the reach of the Brussels Effect in this area.

The influence and business practices of multinational food processors also amplify the non-divisibility of production, further entrenching the de facto Brussels Effect. For instance, Unilever and Nestlé have pledged not to use GMOs in any of their products, irrespective of the export destination. Gerber and Heinz similarly exclude GMOs from all of their baby food, including baby food sold in the US market.[88] They are often reluctant to make separate batches for the EU and United States and frequently refuse to, for example, buy corn that could lead to marketing problems in the EU.[89] Similarly, by refusing to purchase even conventional grain from farmers who also plant GMO varieties, these food processors have steered some US farmers away from GMO products altogether.[90] For instance, CHS Inc., the largest farm cooperative in the United States, does not sell seeds or buy grain that contain traits that lack approvals for export.[91] Archer Daniels Midland Co, a large Chicago-based global food processing and commodities trading corporation, refuses GMO crops that lack global approval. The reason is that it is "hard to segregate crops containing unapproved traits from the billions of identical-looking bushels exported every year." Stine Seed and Bayer similarly have a policy against selling seed traits that have not been approved by major export markets.[92]

The reasons for divisibility for these multinational food processors can be at the same time economic, legal, and technical. Running separate production lines is costly for the companies. These companies also want to avoid legal risks associated with accidental commingling of GMO and non-GMO varieties, especially considering the EU's stringent rule that tolerates only small traces (0.9%) of unauthorized GMOs. Further, these multinationals cannot guarantee that all their suppliers have been able to carry out the separation of authorized and unauthorized varieties for technical reasons, exposing the entire supply chain to potential liability.

Beyond GMOs, there are several examples of the de facto Brussels Effect affecting food safety policies of companies in Africa, Asia, and Latin America. The EU represents an important export market for the farmers in these jurisdictions, making it rarely possible for them to abandon the EU market and divert their trade elsewhere. As a result, they have typically no option but to comply with EU food safety regulations, however onerous and expensive it may be. Given the high compliance costs as well as the importance of the agricultural sector to these economies, the businesses in these countries have at times benefited from their governments' help in adjusting to meet the EU regulations. And once these producers have invested in compliance with EU regulations, they have typically extended their enhanced production methods and facilities across their entire production line, as predicted by the de facto Brussels Effect.

The EU is the most important destination for agricultural products from Africa, making producers highly sensitive to the EU's food safety regulation and thereby allowing the EU to transform agricultural practices in the region. The African cocoa industry provides an example of this. The EU is the world's biggest consumer of chocolate and the largest importer of cocoa beans. It also has a large-scale cocoa processing industry, making cocoa butter and powder out of cocoa beans.[93] The EU sets maximum levels for certain contaminants in foodstuffs, including for polycyclic aromatic hydrocarbons (PAH) in cocoa and cocoa products.[94] The rationale behind regulating contaminants in food is the concern over high toxicological levels in food and hence adverse effect on public health.[95] Some of the main health concerns are the use of pesticides, improper fermentation, unsanitary processing methods—like drying cocoa beans on roads or in smoky ovens—and the presence of cadmium, a cancer-causing metallic substance, in cocoa exports.[96] In addition to consumer health, the EU regulation of the industry has been motivated by its desire to ensure sustainable and ethical production of cocoa across West and Central Africa.[97]

As a result of EU regulations targeting these issues, the EU's regulatory influence in these regions via the de facto Brussels Effect has been significant. Cameroon, for example, is the world's fifth largest cocoa grower. [98] Cocoa beans, butter, and paste accounted for over 15% of the nation's exports, second only to petroleum as a proportion of exports. [99] To preserve the country's export opportunities, Cameroonian officials have undertaken several measures to help their companies comply with EU's regulatory demands, including carrying out tests, inspections, and education campaigns to ensure the industry's compliance with EU rules. [100] Regardless of these efforts, in 2013 the EU rejected a 2,000-ton consignment of cocoa beans from Cameroon due to the presence of high levels of harmful chemicals. [101] This led Cameroonian authorities to crack down on substandard cocoa processing practices and provide assistance to help the industry meet EU standards. [102] The government distributed tarpaulins free of charge, provided new or refurbished ovens for drying cocoa, and confiscated poorly dried beans. According to Omer Gatien Maledy, the executive secretary of Cameroon's Cocoa and Coffee Interprofessional Board (CCIB), "[t]his is part of the campaign to promote good practices in cocoa drying, to meet standards set by the European Union." [103] Yet, while implemented to meet EU standards, these "good practices" in cocoa drying have affected the entire production, and not just the cocoa destined for the EU. These examples illustrate how domestic governments can help amplify the de facto Brussels Effect—not by enacting domestic law to emulate EU rules but by offering financial and other support for their companies so that these companies can adjust their business practices to EU regulations.

The Brussels Effect has also had a significant impact on business practices of Kenyan companies. The Kenyan agricultural sector has adjusted to stringent EU food safety standards by undertaking substantial investments to improve their production standards. [104] For example, throughout the early 2000s, twelve large Kenyan agricultural companies undertook extensive modernization efforts to protect their substantial exports to the EU. The reforms consist of major upgrades to their existing warehouses—including improving air-conditioning and ventilation systems, water purification systems, cooler systems, and other equipment—to meet strict standards of hygiene. Some companies even invested in their own on-site laboratories for product and staff health tests and hired food technologists and scientists to carry out product testing, and provide food safety and hygiene training and health counseling for the staff. However, as with the example of cocoa drying in Cameroon, these refurbished facilities have presumably benefited these companies' entire production; it is doubtful that Kenyan farmers would divide their production and retain their old warehouses and inferior equipment for agricultural products destined for non-EU markets once the investment in new facilities is made.

African agricultural producers have also adjusted their business practices in response to the EU's regulation of information that food products need to convey to consumers to enable them make informed choices. Usually this is done through nutritional labeling. In addition to providing useful information to consumers, harmonized rules on labeling contribute to the smooth functioning of the internal market.[105] For example, the EU has standardized the informational requirements regarding wine labels, which affect wine producers abroad, including in South Africa—a country with extensive wine production and exports. The EU regulation specifies that 85% of the wine must be of grape variety stated in the label,[106] while in South Africa the similar requirement is only 75%.[107] However, South African regulation is rendered moot in practice given the producers' incentives to adhere to the EU's labeling requirement considering that the EU is the primary export market for South African wine, with the United Kingdom being the number one export market, followed by Germany and the Netherlands.[108]

While the EU remains a relatively more important export destination for farmers in Africa given the region's proximity to the EU, the EU is also a notable importer of food and agricultural products from countries in South America. As a result, South American producers have also at times changed their growing and distribution practices that impact their business in numerous markets. Brazil, for example, is one of the largest agricultural producers in the world, making many of its companies sensitive to EU's food regulations. The Brazilian company Citrosuco—the largest producer of orange juice in the world—provides an illustrative example of the Brussels Effect in Brazil. Citrosuco exports approximately 95% of its production to over 100 countries, with the EU being its biggest export market.[109] All three of the company's Brazilian plants, located at Matão, Catanduva, and Araras, were certified for complying with European standards of production and authenticity. All of these plants supply orange juice for global markets[110] and regardless of the destination, the products are subject to the same processes and regulations, conforming to the most restrictive (EU) standard.[111] Another Brazilian company, JBS, is one of the global leaders of the food industry, reaching 190 countries.[112] Every JBS unit in Brazil is certified to meet European standards, and even the products sold in Brazil follow the European food safety regulations.[113]

The de facto Brussels Effect is also amplified globally, even if more indirectly, through numerous industry-wide standardization mechanisms. One of these is GlobalGAP, a prominent independent verification system for good agricultural practices (GAP), that certifies compliance with a number of sustainability and food safety requirements that closely track the EU's food safety requirements.[114] Because EU retailers require producers to meet GlobalGAP certification, it has become a de facto requirement for exporting any agri-food products—crops, livestock, and aquaculture—into the EU market.[115] Global GAP is based on an EU standard. It began in 1997 as EurepGAP, which was initiated by several European supermarket chains to streamline various codes of conduct that individual retailers required of their suppliers. It has now become an important vehicle for the exportation and influence of EU's regulations around the world.

Agricultural producers in several markets produce their products in accordance with the GlobalGAP standards to ensure access to EU markets, including Agricola Famosa—a major Brazilian producer of fruit and vegetables—which exports over 150,000 tons of fruit a year.[116] In Japan, an apple producer, Katayama Ringo, was the first Japanese producer to obtain a GlobalGAP certification to sell their products in large UK supermarkets.[117] Some Japanese retailers have also introduced their own GAP system based on EurepGAP, including Aeon—a major retailer in Japan. Similarly, the Japanese Consumers' Co-operative Union introduced its own "JGAP" standard based on EurepGAP, covering fruits and vegetables, cereal, rice, and tea. While at first only Japanese farms that exported produce to the EU obtained GlobalGAP certification, GlobalGAP has since spread to other countries, such as Indonesia. This has incentivized Japanese farms to obtain the certification even if they export to non-EU countries. For example, a melon farm in Shizuoka prefecture obtained GlobalGAP certification in order to export melons to Indonesia, showing how a standard that originates from the EU ultimately comes to govern trade between two non-EU countries.

The food industry is globally interconnected and often relies on long supply chains that cross multiple regulatory jurisdictions. The EU's stringent food safety standards have transformed multinational companies' worldwide business practices in many instances, often because these companies want to avoid the legal risks and economic costs associated with mistakes somewhere along these supply chains. In many instances, the Brussels Effect occurs because of the technical difficulties or the economic costs of dividing the production destined at different export markets. This applies to large multinational food processors and developing country farmers alike. When Kenyan vegetable farmers respond to EU regulation by refurbishing their facilities, providing training, or improving hygiene standards, those improvements benefit their entire production, whether destined for the EU or not. Similarly, if the government refurbishes ovens for drying cocoa in Cameroon, those same new ovens are used to dry cocoa that is destined for Latin America, Russia, or the United States. Further, if global food processors reject GMO varieties not approved by the EU, consumers around the world consume food that is free of those GMO varieties. These examples highlight the EU's ability to shape foreign agricultural markets simply by regulating the safety of food that is sold in the EU, elevating the global food safety standards in the process.

De Jure Brussels Effect

There is also evidence of the de jure Brussels Effect around the world as governments are emulating EU's food safety standards. However, the diffusion of EU's food safety regulations is less extensive than the de jure Brussels Effect in many other areas, such as competition law and data protection. It is also difficult to find concrete evidence suggesting that foreign multinational companies would lobby for regulatory change at home after first having adjusted to EU regulations through the de facto Brussels Effect. Instead, often the EU's global influence is channeled through multinational standard-setting organizations such as Codex Alimentarius Commission, where the EU is an influential member, as discussed in chapter 3. Through its participation in Codex Alimentarius, the EU has multilateralized some of its food safety standards while also adjusting its own standards to reflect various jointly agreed Codex standards.[118] The EU has an additional incentive to align its food safety standards with the Codex framework given that the WTO requires its members to base their regulations on existing international standards, or else provide scientific evidence to justify departing from those standards.[119]

In addition to its engagement in multilateral standard setting, the EU's proactive bilateral engagement with regulatory authorities in foreign countries forms an important part of the EU's food safety regimes, as well as an opportunity to export EU regulations abroad. The EU has limited capacity to inspect every product that enters into the EU on the border. In addition to the official controls at the border, the EU seeks to ensure that the countries that export food products to the EU have robust domestic food safety regulations and control mechanisms in place. To facilitate this, the Commission engages in extensive capacity building and offers technical assistance to foreign regulators. The EU's Veterinary and Food Office ("FVO") also carries out inspections and audits in foreign countries as part of its mission to ensure the safety of food imports.[120] This often leads to the diffusion of EU regulations and administrative practices abroad. Foreign governments typically welcome the EU's assistance and inspections: the verified compliance with EU food safety regulations not only opens their producers' access to the EU market, but the EU's "seal of approval" also enhances export opportunities in other foreign markets due to the perception of high standards of the country's food production.[121]

Consequently, the de jure Brussels Effect in the food safety domain generally results from a combination of these unilateral, bilateral, and multilateral diffusion mechanisms. While this is the case with respect to any area of EU regulation, these alternative channels of influence are more prevalent in the food safety domain—partly because of the existence of robust multilateral cooperation mechanisms in this area but also because of the EU's more limited ability to rely on market-driven mechanisms to export its rules. As the discussion on the de facto Brussels Effect showed, multinational corporations do not always opt for a global standard or choose to advocate for EU standards domestically. While acknowledging the multiple channels of the EU's influence in this industry, the discussion next turns to examining some examples of how the de jure Brussels Effect arises with respect to food safety in general, followed by examples relating to the regulation of GMOs in particular.

One example where the de jure Brussels Effect is leading to changes in legislation is in Brazil, one of the world's largest developing economies and major agricultural producers. For example, EU law has affected the regulation of the beef industry in Brazil, including the adoption of a law, which prohibits the injection of growth hormones to promote cattle's growth.[122] The purpose of this law was to comply with international markets, such as the EU.[123] Interestingly, the EU's influence has been strong even though the EU does not represent the most important export market for Brazil, with approximately 13% of Brazilian beef exports destined for the EU, lagging behind, for example, China and Hong Kong, which capture 25% of Brazilian beef exports.[124]

Brazil also offers an example of a situation where the EU's suspension of foreign imports can initiate a broader regulatory reform abroad. In 2006, the EU suspended Brazilian honey imports because harmful residues and contaminants were detected in honey. Because of the potential loss of revenue from this suspension, the EU embargo sparked a regulatory reform in Brazil,[125] including the creation of a new institution—The Brazilian Chamber of the Productive Chain of Honey and Bee Products—which became known as "the Honey Chamber." The Honey Chamber went on to facilitate the revision of regulatory standards and implementation of rigorous monitoring of residues in honey. In addition to acting as a consultative forum bringing together public and private actors, it facilitated the adoption of the National Plan for the Control of Residues and Contaminants in Honey in 2007.[126] This National Plan provides general guidelines and residue-monitoring procedures tailored to the specific needs of the honey-producing sector. In response to this measure, the EU lifted its import ban on Brazilian honey in 2008.

Other examples relating to issues such as food labeling, tracking, and warning systems can be found from Asia as well as the Arab world. In Taiwan, for example, when amending the Act Governing Food Safety and Sanitation in 2013, Taiwanese Legislative Yuan referred to the EU's General Food Law Regulation.[127] Invoking Article 7 of the EU regulation, the Taiwanese legislator called for authorities at various levels to establish food safety monitoring and investigation mechanisms, together with warning and control measures for risky food. Furthermore, referring to Article 18 of the EU Regulation, the Taiwanese law requires enterprises to establish a tracking system for the sources of raw materials, semifinished products and finished products.[128] Examples of the de jure Brussels Effect can also be seen in the Middle East and North Africa. In 2013, the Cooperation Council for the Arab States of the Gulf published a new food labeling standard. Many major amendments to that standard, such as the introduction of mandatory nutrition labeling and allergen labeling, are similar to those in EU law. In the same year, Morocco and Algeria published a new labeling regulation comparable to the EU's Food Information for Consumers Regulation (FICR), following the EU standard in establishing minimum-type sizes for labels.[129]

One area of EU food regulation that is likely to lead to the de jure Brussels Effect in several countries in the near future relates to organic food production. The EU has, until today, relied on the "principle of equivalence" and granted mutual recognition for products coming from countries such as the United States, assuming those products have been certified as organic in their home markets.[130] However, this has led to highly varied standards for organic products, depending on the country of origin. For example, US standards fall below those of the EU. To illustrate, electric goads used for driving cattle are banned under EU organic standards while permitted under US standards. Similarly, ducks on US organic farms do not have to be given access to a pool or lake to swim in, which would lead to a denial of the label "organic" in the EU. Given these discrepancies, the EU is now revising its organic regulation, which extends EU rules to non-EU farmers who export their organic products to the EU market.[131] The new regulation, expected to take effect in 2021, will forgo the principle of equivalence in favor of the principle of conformity, requiring foreign producers to comply with standards identical to those in force in the EU if they want to serve EU's organic food market. This is likely to compel reforms in many of the countries currently exporting into the EU under equivalency rules.

The de jure Brussels Effect is also contributing to the global enactment of new regulations relating to GMOs, with several examples from around the world demonstrating the reach of the EU's influence. The Brazilian honey industry, discussed earlier in the context of other food safety issues, provides another example in the context of GMO regulation. Following the 2011 ruling by the ECJ requiring that honey containing traces of pollen from GM plants must be labeled as a GM product, the Brazilian Ministry of Agriculture, Livestock and Supply (MAPA), Brazilian Association of Honey Exporters, and other members of the Honey Chamber started to explore how traces of pollen from GM plants can best be detected. The Brazilian Beekeeping Confederation complemented these efforts by starting to identify areas free of GM crops where honey production could be shifted. The Brazilian Beekeeping Confederation (CBA) also called on the government to establish GMO-free regions where honey could be produced without a risk of cross-contamination of traces of pollen from GM plants.[132] Ultimately, Brazil adopted even more stringent standards than those imposed by the EU in this regard.[133] Brazil's willingness to pursue stringent domestic regulation on GMOs is significant, especially considering that Brazil is the second-largest GM crop producer in the world.[134]

Similar to its impact in Brazil, EU regulation of GMOs has had notable effects on other countries' legislation, with several foreign governments clearly following the EU's lead and restricting the cultivation and marketing of GMOs. Currently, over sixty countries require labeling of genetically modified foods.[135] These include many large economies such as Australia, China, Indonesia, Japan, Russia, South Africa, and South Korea. Many are also in the process of adopting other GMO regulations reminiscent of those of the EU. For example, South Korea has plans to "adopt rigorous 'EU-style' food testing standards in an effort to protect 'national health security' from genetically modified crops."[136] Various Latin American countries have acted to limit the import and use of GMOs.[137] These include Peru, which imposed a ten-year moratorium.[138] Bolivia and Ecuador have also banned the use of GMOs.[139] However, it is difficult to ascertain concretely the full extent to which EU law has influenced the law compared to other factors. Nevertheless, several Latin American countries that require labeling of GMOs, including Brazil[140] and Uruguay,[141] emulate the EU's 0.9% standard as a threshold for a GMO label.[142] This suggests that the EU law has been used at least partially as a template to follow.

Some foreign courts have also cited EU regulations in their rulings on GMOs. For example, Colombia's Constitutional Court held that a legislative gap in regulating GMOs poses a serious and unacceptable risk to the consumer's constitutional rights to relevant product information and the right to choose his or her food.[143] The Court then called on the Congress to issue regulations on the labeling of the GMO food item or GMO content.[144] In its reasoning, the Court examined the EU's treatment of GMOs and explained that the "European Union has taken a clear position and has become an international reference in the fight against [GMOs], in accordance with its Resolution 1829 of 2003, which also establishes the labeling for these type of products."

Although the broad global regulation of GMOs points to the existence of a de jure Brussels Effect in numerous jurisdictions around the world, the EU has not been alone in exerting global regulatory influence in this domain. The United States has also actively, and in some places successfully, exported its regulatory approach on GMOs. The United States has been particularly influential with countries that are major producers of GM crops, such as Argentina, Brazil, and Canada.[145] For example, Canada has followed the American approach to GMO regulation, and consumers in the two countries seem to have a similar attitude toward GMOs. In Africa, in particular, however, there has been a notable competition for influence between EU and US regulatory approaches. South Africa and Egypt, for example, have followed the US approach, and both have authorized commercial plantings of GM crops. Similarly, food shortages have led some other African countries opposed to GMOs, including Malawi and Kenya, to loosen their regulation. However, in other countries, such as Zambia, where economic, environmental, public health, and protection for traditional agriculture still constitute strong reasons for opposition to GMOs, EU influence is prevalent.[146] Thus, the global regulation of GMOs is best described in terms of a competition for influence, where the EU and the United States are both attempting to persuade countries to adopt their respective regulatory stance.[147]

Given its economic might and high tolerance of GMOs, the United States seems like an unlikely frontier for a de jure Brussels Effect. However, public opinion in the United States has been moving toward more skepticism of GMOs in recent years. A 2011 survey reported that 92% of Americans wanted the government to require mandatory labeling of GMOs, and 55% said they would avoid such products.[148] In 2011, following California's lead, the US Congress passed legislation prohibiting the FDA from approving GM salmon and required labeling in case of approval of a GM fish. In 2016, the United States also enacted the National Bioengineered Food Disclosure Standard,[149] which charged the US Department of Agriculture (USDA) Agricultural Marketing Service with developing a national mandatory system for disclosing GMOs in foods by July 2018.[150] As of 2014, three US states had already passed legislation requiring GMO food labeling.[151] They emulate aspects of EU's GMO labeling, such the 0.9% standard as a threshold for requiring a GMO label.[152] A 2015 poll for the labeling advocacy group "Just Label It!" indicated strong support among US citizens—up to 88%—for label requirements on GMO foods.[153] In its advocacy, Just Label It! has emphasized how the rest of the world has followed the EU's leadership in GMO labeling and how a "logical thought" would be that the "U.S. would begin to mirror" the EU as well.[154] Given these legislative developments and the shifts in US public opinion, it is no longer inconceivable to imagine EU-inspired regulation emerging in the United States as well.

Thus far, this chapter has examined the EU's global influence in shaping food safety standards around the world. Yet food safety represents only one of many areas of regulation where the EU has pursued stringent regulation in an attempt to protect the health and safety of European consumers—elevating global standards in the process through the Brussels Effect. Next, the discussion moves to examine one of these other areas of risk regulation where the Brussels Effect has been strongly felt in many parts of the world: chemical safety.

Consumer Health and Safety II: Chemical Safety

One notable aspect of the EU's consumer health regime is the regulation of the chemicals industry. Stringent chemical regulation in the EU reflects European citizens' elevated concern about the potential adverse effects that unsafe chemicals could have on humans and on the environment. These concerns, together with the desire to harmonize regulations to facilitate trade across the single market, drove the adoption of a broad EU regulation concerning the Registration, Evaluation, Authorisation, and Restriction of Chemicals (commonly known as REACH) in 2007.[155] REACH has had a substantial impact on the chemicals industry and chemicals regulation globally. The chemicals industry is multinational, and the EU is an important destination market for the vast array of chemicals and goods containing chemicals that fall within the scope of REACH. This has given multinational companies a strong incentive to align their global conduct with the EU's strict regulatory framework to maintain access to the European market[156] and spurred regulatory reforms around the world. The EU's influence in this area is particularly vast given that its regulation encompasses not just chemicals themselves but the large number of diverse goods containing chemicals including clothes, toys, cosmetics, cleaning products, paints, and plastic bottles. The fact that the EU reaches so many products through its chemical safety regime makes it a particularly important area of regulation to examine the mechanism through which the Brussels Effect arises.

Major Legislation

EU chemical safety regulations date back to the 1970s,[157] but the enactment of REACH in 2007 constituted a watershed moment in introducing the world's most robust regulatory framework for chemical safety. REACH is remarkable in that it places the burden of establishing the safety of chemicals intended for the EU market squarely on manufacturers and importers as opposed to regulators.[158] This differs notably, for example, from the US regulatory approach. This obligation entails that manufacturers and importers are required to gather information on the effects that their substances have on human health and the environment and to provide this information to EU authorities by registering their substances in a database.[159] Substances of "very high concern" must also be replaced by suitable alternatives where economically and technically feasible.[160] The EU further has the authority to restrict the use of substances that pose an "unacceptable" risk to human health or the environment.[161] REACH is also guided by the "precautionary principle," which justifies regulatory intervention in the case of scientific uncertainty, making the regulation applicable to an even wider range of chemicals.[162]

Further contributing to REACH's stringency is the feature that REACH not only regulates new chemicals, but also applies to the tens of thousands of substances already on the EU market at the time of its enactment.[163] According to the European Commission, the already existing chemicals represent 99% of the total substances on the EU market.[164] Their inclusion within REACH dramatically expanded the scope of the regulation, applying it to over twenty-two thousand chemicals in total.[165] This represents another departure from the US' approach. Unlike REACH, the Toxic Substances Control Act (TSCA)—the US' primary chemical regulation—grandfathered in 95% of existing chemicals and thus forwent any testing with respect to the vast majority of the chemicals on the market.[166] This has naturally led to a much wider set of chemicals being restricted under REACH than under TSCA.

The differences between EU and US chemical safety regimes are vast and extend beyond the TSCA's decision to shield existing chemicals from a safety review. The TSCA, enacted in 1976, has remained highly ineffective.[167] The US Environmental Protection Agency (EPA) rarely used its regulatory authority to block new substances, approving 90% of 24,000 applications submitted between 1976 and 1994 without restriction or additional testing.[168] TSCA's inefficacy meant that the United States largely relied on voluntary industry programs instead of decisive oversight by regulators.[169] For example, the Chemical Manufacturers Association founded a significant unilateral and preemptive self-regulatory program called "Responsible Care" in 1988.[170] Responsible Care was based on self-assessment and was deliberately designed to preempt more forceful regulation.[171] Even though there have been several attempts to reform the TSCA—partly prompted by REACH—the US chemical legislation continues to trail that of the EU in terms of its scope and overall stringency.

Political Economy

The EU's stringent chemical regulation reflects the high concern among European citizens regarding adverse impacts that chemicals can have on health and the environment. A 2017 Eurobarometer survey reported that 74% of Europeans worry about the health impacts of ordinary plastic products and 87% worry about plastic's environmental impacts.[172] Similarly, 84% worry about the health impacts of chemicals in ordinary products, and 90% worry about these chemicals' environmental impacts.[173] These citizens' concerns, together with significant benefits available from harmonized regulation to the single market,[174] gave the EU a strong impetus to act.

REACH, in part, responded to increasing public anxiety about the long-term effects of chemical exposure.[175] This public concern about chemical safety had become strong in the years before REACH was enacted in 2007, elevating the political salience of the issue. In advocating for more stringent regulation, consumers concerned about chemical safety found support from key member states, the European Parliament, and a handful of prominent NGOs. This coalition successfully elevated the issue on the EU's political agenda during the early 2000s. Sweden spearheaded a push for new chemicals regulation, supported by Austria, Denmark, Finland, and the Netherlands.[176] A number of environmental, health, and consumer advocacy NGOs voiced support for the precautionary principle.[177] NGOs also called for full risk identification, public information sharing, and a phaseout process for harmful chemicals.[178] The NGOs launched a "Chemical Awareness" campaign to generate public interest.[179] These advocacy groups received support from some parts of the business community as well. In particular, large retailers, who sought to bolster consumer confidence and avoid chemical scandals, supported REACH.[180] Regulators also received critical backing from the Commission's Directorate General for the Environment and the Parliament's Environment Committee.

Despite the strong support for REACH, the political process surrounding its adoption in 2007 was highly contentious. While the supporters of REACH emphasized its benefits to public health, consumer safety, and the environment, REACH's critics claimed that the regulation would impose significant costs on manufacturers and importers—costs that would be passed on along their long supply chains and, ultimately, to consumers.[181] At worst, the critics claimed, the regulation was going to impede the development of new, innovative substances due to fears that they would not meet stringent EU requirements.[182]

The opposition to REACH was unsurprising given the size and scope of the chemical industry. The European chemical industry is Europe's third-largest manufacturing industry, and it employed 1.7 million people in 2006 when REACH was enacted.[183] The industry lobby was predictably active throughout the development of REACH. Commentators have argued that this regulation "attracted more hostility from industry than any other item of EU environmental legislation in 30 years."[184] Major chemical companies including Bayer, BASF, and Shell Chemicals initially rejected outright the inclusion of existing chemicals within the purview of the regulation.[185] The industry lobby also argued for self-regulation or more voluntary measures and took a firm stand against the precautionary principle, citing high costs and negative impacts on competition and employment.[186] However, as it became evident that some kind of regulatory scheme would be adopted, the industry gradually started focusing on reducing the burden of REACH rather than opposing the legislation outright.[187]

Given the global reach of European regulations, REACH also prompted intense lobbying from the US chemical industry. With the full support of the Bush administration, US firms engaged in "eight years of vigorous opposition," arguing that REACH would burden manufacturers for little gain for health and the environment.[188] In 2002, then-Secretary of State Colin L. Powell directed American embassy staffs across Europe to oppose REACH, citing talking points developed in consultation with a manufacturers' trade group.[189] The US government filed formal comments with the Commission, opposing REACH, and EPA officials worked to lobby EU government and business representatives against the regulation.[190] Again with close cooperation of the industry, the US government further engaged in efforts to "educate" other countries so that they could join the United States in raising concerns about REACH.[191] In 2006, the US Diplomatic Mission to the EU organized a joint statement from the missions of Australia, Brazil, Chile, India, Israel, Japan, Malaysia, Mexico, Singapore, South Africa, South Korea, and Thailand, asking the European Parliament to reconsider the regulation.[192]

High-level politicians from countries with large chemical industries, such as France, Germany, Italy, the United Kingdom, and Ireland were sympathetic to the views of the industry.[193] Other important allies were business-friendly conservative or socialist Members of the European Parliament (MEPs) and the Commission's Directorate General for Enterprise. Their criticism of REACH echoed that of the industry, emphasizing the regulatory costs and adverse effects on the competitiveness of the European industry.[194] Yet a relatively smaller coalition of national environmental ministers, Commission officials, MEPs, and NGO representatives worked to pass the legislation against this stern resistance.[195]

Ultimately, the final version of REACH reflected a compromise between the two sides. Responding to the industry's concern regarding regulatory costs, the Commission reduced the costs of the regulation by estimated €10 billion by lessening certain reporting and informational requirements.[196] Some of the dilution of REACH may be attributed to US lobbying efforts, given that the revised 2003 proposal reflected many of the specific changes sought by the United States, including the exclusion of polymers.[197] Yet even with these compromises, REACH stands as the world's most stringent chemical regulation regime.

De Facto Brussels Effect

REACH has led to a significant de facto Brussels Effect, driving behavioral changes in a multitude of industries worldwide.[198] Many foreign chemical manufacturers that export a substantial amount of chemicals to the EU are switching to REACH standards globally to avoid being excluded from the EU market.

Because manufacturers often find it cheaper to create a single product for various markets, as opposed to numerous market-specific versions, they have an incentive to produce their products in accordance with the most stringent global standard, which is REACH.[199] In this context, this non-divisibility is primarily driven by scale economies in production rather than a legal or technical inability to produce different products: in principle, it would be possible for companies to run two production lines involving different chemicals. This would not be legally problematic or necessarily technically difficult. Yet this would often simply be uneconomical for companies that would face costs by separating their production. Another driver for global conformity to REACH is that many downstream users of chemicals refuse to include substances in their products if the EU has identified any such chemical as a "substance of very high concern."[200] Given chemicals' long and complex supply chains, even one noncompliant substance in the supply chain may foreclose the final product from the EU market, steering export-oriented manufacturers toward strictly EU-compliant production globally.

An additional reason for applying the higher EU standard uniformly is the information-generating feature of REACH and the sensitivity of consumers around the world for "unsafe" products. For example, Linda Fisher, vice president and chief sustainability officer for DuPont, was quoted as saying that her firm was "not looking at this as a European program—we're buying and selling all over the globe," adding that "once a chemical is included on the E.U. list, manufacturers are likely to feel pressure to abandon production . . . Linking the word 'concern' to a chemical is enough to trigger a market reaction."[201] Similarly, Johnson & Johnson makes a reference to both US and EU regulations[202] and claims that it phased out certain ingredients due to consumer confidence, without citing any health concerns.[203] This effect is likely to be even greater when concern is associated with items such as childrens' toys or baby bottles.[204] Thus, the reputational concerns linked to market information are further magnifying the Brussels Effect.

Several examples illustrate how multinational companies have increasingly adjusted their global production to meet REACH's requirements. Dow Chemical, a leader in the chemicals industry, announced all of its production to be REACH consistent, for products sold in the EU and elsewhere.[205] Hoffman-La Roche, a Swiss health care multinational, aims to phase out Substances of a Very High Concern (SVHCs) from its products within 10 years of the substance's addition to the REACH Candidate List.[206] To do so, the company is identifying and removing SVHCs used in their products on a global basis, regardless of whether the target market is subject to REACH or not. Large cosmetics producers such as Revlon, Unilever, and L'Oréal have similarly reformulated all their products to be REACH compatible.[207] L'Oréal, for example, acknowledges that it no longer uses methylisothiazolinone (MI) as a preservative in certain products, citing the European Scientific Committee on Consumer Safety recommendation concerning the chemical.[208] L'Oréal also asserts that "[t]he few nanomaterials used in certain of our products have undergone a specific safety assessment in compliance with European standards."[209] The company also describes the EU standards as a benchmark, saying that its "hair coloration products contain colorants that have obtained regulatory approval and para-phenylenediamine (PPD) concentrations that are at least 2 times less than the maximum concentration authorized in Europe."[210]

REACH's effects have not been limited to closely impacted fields such as chemicals manufacturing, pharmaceutical, or cosmetics industries. REACH has also had a significant impact on textile and retail industries. When certain phthalates—substances added to plastics to increase their flexibility and durability—were added to the authorization requirements under REACH, Adidas, Nike, and Zara committed to substituting the phthalates in their products with less hazardous alternatives.[211] Brazilian manufacturing giant Alpargatas S.A. likewise eliminated phthalates from its popular Havaianas sandals in response to REACH.[212] Although the EU represents less than 30% of the company's exports, Alpargatas imposed this costly adjustment on all the products in the Havaianas line, regardless of their export destination. H&M, a Swedish fashion retailer with operations in many non-EU countries,[213] ensures compliance with REACH and other regulations by "apply[ing] the precautionary principle" and developing its chemical restrictions "based on the highest legal standard in any of [its] sales countries."[214] The company's sustainability commitment, which any of its suppliers or business partners must sign, encourages those partners to avoid any substances that could be "persistent, bioaccumulative or toxic" even where there is no legal obligation to do so.[215] The large furniture retailer Ikea and toy manufacturing companies Lego and Mattel have similarly all declared their global production to be PVC free.[216]

As these various examples indicate, companies rarely find it in their interest to take advantage of lower standards in foreign markets if they seek to market their products in the EU. However, there are also examples where the Brussels Effect fails to reach some product lines. For instance, Estée Lauder has stated that it uses a single safety standard for 95% of its production, suggesting that a small portion of its production remains divisible.[217] Yet counter-examples such as this notwithstanding, the general trend in the chemical industry continues to favor non-divisible production, thus explaining the prevalence of the de facto Brussels Effect.

In the United States, REACH's impact on the $800 billion US chemical industry has been particularly profound.[218] Typically, the US industry has had no option but to comply with REACH in order to retain access to the EU market. In 2008, the *Washington Post* reported that "American manufacturers [we]re already searching for safer alternatives to chemicals used to make thousands of consumer goods, from bike helmets to shower curtains."[219] The article also cites Mike Walls, the American Chemistry Council's managing director of government and regulatory affairs, who noted that "90 percent of [the Council's] members are affected by the E.U. laws and [...] some cannot afford the cost of compliance. . . . The E.U. standards will force many manufacturers to reformulate their products for sale there as well as in the United States." Given that the examples mentioned contain numerous US-based corporations, it is clear these predications were borne out.

An interesting question remains whether the de facto Brussels Effect will off-set any of the Trump administration's ongoing efforts to repeal or limit US environmental regulations, particularly those on harmful chemicals.[220] For example, the EPA is pursuing "faster reviews" and a "less dogmatic approach to determining risk" associated with chemicals.[221] The EPA is also reviewing the limits on production of ten toxic chemicals, including the well-known chemical asbestos or hexabromocyclododecane (HBCD) that is commonly used in adhesives, paint strippers, solvents, cleaning products, and automobiles.[222] However, if past examples are any indication, the Brussels Effect suggests that as long as US manufacturers continue to export their chemical products to the EU, they are not likely to make any adjustments to their production processes to take advantage of laxer US regulations.

De Jure Brussels Effect

REACH has also triggered a significant de jure Brussels Effect, prompting the adoption of REACH-style laws in several markets. Jurisdictions that have implemented or planned REACH-like regulations include, for example, China, Japan, Malaysia, Serbia, South Korea, Switzerland, and Turkey.[223] Other nations such as India have also proposed REACH-like regulations.[224] The EU has welcomed such foreign emulation of REACH, declaring that the landmark legislation has the potential to inspire new standards worldwide,[225] and promising to offer technical assistance when needed. For example, following requests from Argentina, Chile, China, and Taiwan, the EU pledged compliance support.[226] In addition to providing technical assistance, the European Chemical Agency (ECHA) has engaged in frequent regulatory dialogues with its foreign counterparts, including with those from Australia, Canada, Japan, and the United States. This collaboration has led to the development of a pair of software tools—the International Uniform Chemical Information Database and the QSAR toolbox—available globally to help both regulators and manufacturers organize, assess, store, and exchange data on chemical safety.[227] The EU has further been a driving force behind a set of multilateral chemical conventions, at times successfully elevating global standards in the process.[228] However, in these settings, the EU's influence has been constrained by other powerful countries, such as the United States.[229] These multilateral conventions also address a more narrow set of specific chemical groups as opposed to providing an overarching regulatory regime across a range of chemicals.[230] The absence of any comprehensive global chemicals policy therefore makes the globalization of REACH even more significant.

There are many reasons for foreign governments to emulate REACH. For example, export-oriented producers have the incentive to pressure their home governments to adopt a REACH-equivalent legislation domestically. Because export producers already meet REACH standards due to the de facto Brussels Effect, these companies face no additional costs in producing similar products for their home market.[231] The de jure Brussels Effect levels their playing field against domestic competitors that are not active in the EU market and do not, therefore, need to conform to REACH's stringent rules. Another reason for emulation is foreign consumer health and environmental activists, empowered by the implementation of REACH, who have embraced the EU regulation as a benchmark in their efforts to push for legislative reform.[232]

The de jure Brussels Effect has been effective in varying degrees across different jurisdictions. The United States, on the one hand, has amended its federal chemicals regulations with some influence from REACH but still maintains a different regulatory posture. On the other hand, South Korea implemented legislation, K-REACH, closely modeled on REACH. In the middle ground, countries such as Japan and China have borrowed certain aspects of REACH to include in their broad chemical regulation strategy.

In the United States, REACH has prompted state-level regulatory reforms.[233] These efforts acknowledge the global nature of the chemicals industry and the existing need for US companies to comply with REACH, including collecting the safety information relevant for their production.[234] In California, for instance, the existing informational burden imposed by REACH was seen as a compelling reason to utilize the same data in-state. As a result, the California Department of Toxic Substances Control is now required to use "to the maximum extent feasible" the safety information generated in other nations in its regulation of chemical products, including, most importantly, the EU.[235]

The efforts by various advocacy groups to amend the TSCA—the US federal chemicals regulation legislation—were for a long time considerably less successful, largely due to powerful industry opposition. However, TSCA was finally amended in 2016, largely due to waning resistance from industry as state chemical laws were becoming increasingly fragmented and international regulation was expanding.[236] REACH, in part, provided a catalyst for the eventual amendment of TSCA.[237] Given that many of the large US chemical manufacturers were already complying with REACH, it was in the interest of those large manufacturers to support a similar regulation domestically as well. An additional impetus to amend the TSCA was also the realization that the United States had largely ceded the industry to the EU to regulate. Katja Biedenkopf's research shows how the adoption of REACH shifted the US chemicals industry's position from the opposition to endorsement of TSCA reform.[238] In a 2011 congressional hearing, the president of the American Chemistry Council argued that "[w]e must learn from what's working and not working in Canada and the EU. . . . the U.S. always has been and must remain the global leader. . . ."[239] DuPont's vice president and chief sustainability officer similarly argued that it was not "wise to cede to the EU or China the responsibility to set the policies that will guide commerce in chemicals."[240]

The TSCA Amendments introduced a regulatory approach more similar to that of REACH, although TSCA still requires less information about chemicals upfront. Richard Denison, a biochemist who tracks chemical safety for the Environmental Defense Fund, argued that the two regulatory schemes could be expected to have similar results, explaining that the EPA "now has to make an affirmative finding that a chemical is safe in order for that chemical to go on the market."[241] Industry commentators concluded that the TSCA Amendments moved the United States toward a system more similar to REACH, but also had some important differences.[242] For example, while the TSCA does force the EPA to make an affirmative determination on a new chemical before it is marketed, it also mandates the EPA to demonstrate "unreasonable risk" in order to regulate a chemical.[243] This stands in contrast with REACH's approach, which forces manufacturers and importers to demonstrate that chemical risk is adequately controlled.[244]

Some commentators have argued that it is difficult to distinguish the influence of REACH from other economic and political factors contributing to TSCA reform. Ondrej Filipec notes that it is "hard to determine the extent to which [changes in US regulations] are influenced directly by the attractiveness of REACH and to which they could be seen as a functional and gradual development within a single regulatory system without any foreign influence."[245] However, according to other commentators, the data produced by REACH has proven useful and influential in many jurisdictions, including in the United States. According to Katja Biendenkopf, the EU data generated under REACH was part of the legislative debate on amending the TSCA.[246] It was also used by the Environmental Defense Fund to illustrate the discrepancies between the two regulatory systems.[247] Following the trend set by REACH of greater data trans-parency, the EPA released information on more than 7,600 chemicals and made public information on more than 100 cases of formerly confidential chemical identities.[248] Further, as discussed earlier, California uses EU data in its online database, the Toxic Clearinghouse.[249]

Another potential pathway for REACH data to influence market behavior in other jurisdictions is through private toxic tort litigation.[250] For example, a coali-tion of European agencies and research institutions created an online tool—the Advanced REACH tool (ART)—to model and assess benzene exposure given inputs such as ventilation rate and room size. While at least one US federal court found that an expert opinion based on ART could be reliable in quantifying a plaintiff's benezene exposure,[251] there is no evidence yet that such testimony is common, or that REACH data is widely or often used in private litigation. This suggests that foreign governments, as opposed to private litigants, more often use the data generated under REACH. An interesting question is whether this will change as the current administration in the United States takes steps to roll back the regulations on chemical safety, as discussed earlier, and safety advocates increasingly turn to the courts as a defense.

The EU's influence on South Korean chemical safety regulation provides per-haps the best illustration of the de jure Brussels Effect. In 2013, South Korea passed the Act on Registration and Evaluation , etc. of Chemical Substances, also known as "K-REACH."[252] During the drafting process, South Korea consulted closely with EU institutions and agencies such as ECHA.[253] As a result, K-REACH closely resembles the EU's regulatory framework, replicating most of its registra-tion and reporting provisions.[254] While very similar in substance and language, K-REACH is not identical with EU's REACH.[255] For example, REACH does not require disclosure for substances produced or imported at a rate below one ton per year, while K-REACH was amended to require registration for new sub-stances imported or produced at a rate of > 100 kg annually, making K-REACH more stringent in this regard.[256] On the other hand, K-REACH originally did not require the registration of existing chemicals, only new chemicals, and was only expected to cover 2,000 substances.[257] This made the K-REACH much nar-rower in scope than REACH, which requires registration for all existing chemi-cals, and covers over 22,000 registered substances.[258] Under recent amendments to K-REACH, however, all existing substances will have to be pre-notified and registration will be phased in through 2030, with timing depending on tonnage manufactured or imported.[259]

The adoption of such similar legislation in South Korea is perhaps less sur-prising given the significant exposure of Korean companies to REACH. A 2007 report by the Korea Trade-Investment Promotion Agency emphasized that while chemicals do not take up a large proportion of Korean exports to the EU, most of Korea's key export products to the EU—such as cars, wireless communication equipment, semiconductors, and ships—contain chemicals, bringing them into the purview of REACH.[260] In 2008, the South Korean Minister of Environment characterized REACH as posing a "significant trade barrier" to South Korean companies with significant economic impact, given that the EU is the country's second-largest export market after China.[261] In the same speech, the Minister also stated that the EU appears to have the strategic intent to use REACH as a weapon to increase the competitiveness of EU products in the global market and to exert industry-wide influence.[262]

Legislative comments for K-REACH discuss the reasons for its adoption, including the need to respond to the EU's adoption of REACH and the increasing regulation of chemical substances in other major trade partners such as Japan.[263] The Korean Ministry of Environment similarly emphasized that K-REACH was a "necessity" given the EU regulation—together with Japan's and China's decisions to follow with similar regulations of their own. In addition to these external reasons, K-REACH was also seen as key to protecting citizens' health and the country's ecosystem.[264]

Japan offers another example of the de jure Brussels Effect—albeit of a less exact kind. Japan has replicated some elements of REACH, but has also drawn other elements from Canada's chemical legislation, such as prioritization and risk assessment.[265] For example, it partly followed REACH in amending its Chemical Substances Control Act in 2009[266] to designate endocrine disruptors as high-risk chemicals.[267] Furthermore, Japan follows REACH in how it defines the scope of chemicals of high concern and provision of expedited review for substances already on the market.[268] However, Japanese law imposes a lesser informational burden on the industry compared to REACH. Japan does not, for instance, extend the need to disclose information regarding the entire supply chain. Importantly, the government conducts risk assessment in Japan, whereas under REACH, industries that manufacture or import chemicals in quantities exceeding ten tons bear that responsibility.[269] According to Yoshiko Naiki, the introduction of the principle of industry responsibility was probably not necessary in Japan because the safety and toxicity information was already supplied under REACH and hence likely already publicly available for regulators outside the EU.[270]

REACH has also influenced regulatory reforms in China. Katja Biedenkopf and Dae Young Park argue that the similarities between China's 2010 "Measures on the Environmental Management of New Chemical Substances" and REACH is evidence that China has borrowed from EU policy.[271] For example, China's tonnage-based notification system (that is, a system requiring different disclosures for quantities of 1 ton, 10 tons, etc.) is similar to REACH's structure. Thus, both systems apply the principle of "higher volume, more data."[272] Also, the Chinese reform, like REACH, subjects both producers and importers to annual reporting and record-keeping requirements.[273] Finally, Article 2 of China's 2010 regulation uses similar wording as REACH in applying the regulation to products that release new chemical substances in their normal use—although the Chinese regulation is slightly narrower in scope.[274]

China's regulation of various consumer products and children's toys and rugs also stem from the Chinese companies' exposure to EU regulations as their key export destination. For example, a year after the EU restricted the use of phthalate plasticizers in toys, China similarly updated its own toy safety standard in 2014.[275] The new Chinese safety standard presented a significant change, and it was made with reference to the prevailing EU standards.[276] China has also released a Draft Outline for the Industry Standard of Safety Requirement of Children's Rugs, which restricts the use of a substance called formamaide.[277] Such material is listed by REACH as requiring "priority attention," and categorized by the ECHA as a harmful substance that could damage fertility or unborn children. The new Chinese regulation further restricts the use of soluble metals in elements in children's' rugs, again referring to the relevant EU standard.[278]

These examples show how REACH has not only shaped the business practices of private companies but how legislators around the world have enacted laws that have entrenched the EU's chemical safety standards into their regulatory frameworks. As expected, REACH has been particularly closely emulated by governments for whom the EU remains a major export market. At the same time, the United States has steadfastly retained its own approach, unwilling to embrace the EU's more precautionary regulatory model. However, given the extent to which the de facto Brussels Effect has influenced the conduct of large US companies, the absence of the de jure Brussels Effect in the United States is perhaps less relevant, especially as the wide adoption of REACH across the world makes it increasingly hard to find alternative export destinations for products that are not REACH compliant. As a result, only purely domestic operators in the United States are likely to take advantage of the lax regulations prevailing in their home market.

THIS CHAPTER HAS examined two important areas of EU consumer health and safety regulation: food safety and chemical safety. Food safety provides an interesting case study to examine the prevalence and the limits of the Brussels Effect alike. The discussion has illustrated how in some areas of food safety, including GMO regulation, the Brussels Effect has been prevalent. This is largely due to the technical non-divisibility of GMO cultivation, as any accidental cross-contamination of GMOs could make non-GMO products containing even small traces of GMOs unfit for the EU market. The Brussels Effect is enhanced by legal non-divisibility, especially as multinational food processors prefer to avoid the legal risks associated with accidental cross-contamination of GMOs and often avoid sourcing products from farmers that cultivate both varieties.

However, in some other cases, divisibility has not been a constraint and companies have customized their food products to varying consumer preferences. In general, divisibility is more common in products where consumer preferences are both diverse and salient and where divisibility is both technically feasible and economically manageable. In addition, from the limited set of examples examined in this chapter, it seems that divisibility is more likely—and hence the Brussels Effect less common—with respect to processed food (such as M&Ms) where manufacturers can better control the production processes and keep different production lines separate. In contrast, non-divisibility is more likely—and hence the Brussels Effect more common—in the case of cultivation of crops on open fields where the risks of commingling of EU-compliant and non-EU-compliant varieties, such as certain GMOs or pesticides, would be higher. In addition, the Brussels Effect is more likely to occur in case of long supply chains, where even one mistake by one actor at one stage of the supply chain may cause the entire supply chain lose access to EU market.

Chemical industry manifests somewhat different dynamics in this regard. In contrast to food, where manufacturers can reap significant gains from customizing their production to varying consumer preferences, there are fewer gains available from tailoring the production of chemicals in the same way. Consumers around the world are likely to want their chemicals to be safe—even if their willingness to pay for enhanced safety may vary. Some consumers also likely care about sustainability of chemicals while others likely place more importance on the retail price they pay. Yet, beyond those consideration, end consumers rarely have as deeply held preferences on the precise composition of chemicals in the products they buy versus the food they consume. For this reason, economic considerations, such as the benefits of scale economies, have been more important drivers behind the Brussels Effect in the chemical industry. What these two areas of regulation have in common is the salient role of multinational production processes, globally connected industries, and long supply chains as factors that have facilitated the de facto Brussels Effect.

In addition to influencing global business conduct, the EU has been successful in exporting many of its food and chemical regulations abroad, both unilaterally and multilaterally. The de jure Brussels Effect has relied less on the EU's unilateralism in the area of food safety regulation—where multilateral and bilateral channels of diffusion have been more established—compared to the area of chemical safety regulation where the de jure Brussels Effect has taken place even when these other channels have been weaker.

Despite the varying dynamics underneath each area of regulation, the EU's food safety and chemical safety regimes both illustrate how the Brussels Effect can lead to higher regulatory standards around the world—whether as a result of companies independently adjusting their standards globally to EU rules or alternatively through foreign governments emulating more stringent EU regulations. In both of these areas, multinational businesses as well as consumers far outside the EU have felt the effects of EU regulations, both by producing and consuming safer and more sustainable food or manufacturing and buying products containing safer chemicals.

7

Environment

ENVIRONMENTAL PROTECTION IS one of the policy areas where the EU's dedication to protect the global commons and willingness to promulgate stringent regulatory standards in this regard is well known. However, in the public discourse the EU is often best known for its commitment to multilateralism and active backing of global environmental treaties. This chapter's discussion acknowledges the important role that the EU plays in multilateral environmental cooperation yet argues that its environmental goals are often most effectively accomplished through the Brussels Effect.

After reviewing selected examples of the EU's environmental regulation, the discussion describes the origins of the EU's pro-environmental attitudes. It then examines a few notable policy areas where the EU has successfully influenced global environmental standards through the Brussels Effect. These include the regulation of hazardous substances and electronic waste, the protection of animal welfare, and the mitigation of climate change through an emissions trading system. Although each of these provides a strong example of the Brussels Effect in environmental regulation, in fact, these areas comprise only a fraction of the EU's environmental policy. According to The Institute for European Environmental Policy, the entire body of EU environmental law amounts to over 1,100 directives, regulations, and decisions.[1] This illustrates the salience of environmental law in the EU's regulatory architecture and its significance for the operation of the single market. Further, given the global nature of many of the environmental problems, it is not surprising that environmental law offers some of the most prominent examples of the Brussels Effect.

Major Legislation

The EU's regulatory capacity in environmental matters was built in parallel with the rising environmental consciousness among the European public. Before

The Brussels Effect. Anu Bradford, Oxford University Press (2020). © Oxford University Press.
DOI: 10.1093/oso/9780190088583.001.0001

acquiring any formal competence on environmental matters, the European Council emphasized the importance of a harmonized EU environmental policy and called for a concrete action plan in a 1972 Paris declaration.[2] The 1987 Single European Act formally implanted environmental protection in the EU treaties, making it a primary treaty objective and vesting the EU institutions with the competence to undertake measures to protect the environment.[3] Following this treaty change, the locus of legislative action began to shift from member states to the EU level.[4] The EU's regulatory capacity was further enhanced in the 1992 Maastricht Treaty, which recognized the importance of "sustainable growth" and added the "precautionary principle" to guide decision-making in environmental matters. The Maastricht Treaty also acknowledged for the first time the EU's role in promoting measures multilaterally outside the EU.[5] In the 1999 Amsterdam Treaty, the EU institutions acquired the duty to promote sustainable development by integrating environmental protection into all EU policy areas.[6] Later, the 2009 Lisbon Treaty made "combating climate change" a specific goal of EU Treaties, giving EU's climate action a strong constitutional foundation,[7] together with the recognition that sustainable development must guide the EU's foreign relations.[8] As a result of these developments, the EU became an international leader in environmental regulation, eclipsing the United States in the process.

To effectively carry out its new mandate, in 1990s the Commission began to build substantial technical expertise that allowed its civil servants to engage in complex decision-making in environmental policy. Throughout, however, it benefited, and continues to benefit, from outside expertise. For example, the European Environment Agency supports the Commission's regulatory agenda by gathering and disseminating information about the state of the environment in the EU.[9] The European Courts have further expanded the competences of the EU institutions in environmental policy over the years with their pro-environment rulings. Notably, in the landmark 2005 decision of *Council v. Commission*, the Court authorized the Commission to extend criminal sanctions to environmental offenses.[10] Similarly, in 2018 the Court approved unprecedented action to immediately halt the illegal deforestation of the primeval Białowieza forest district in Poland. After Poland refused to comply with earlier injunctive actions, the court expanded its interim powers to issue a €100,000 per day penalty against Poland until a final judgment could be issued.[11]

The EU has exercised global environmental leadership in many areas of environmental regulation. One of these areas is the management of hazardous substances and electronic waste. The EU's regulatory efforts in this area culminated in the adoption of the Restriction of Hazardous Substances Directive (RoHS Directive or RoHS 1) in 2002.[12] The RoHS Directive bans the use of hazardous substances in electrical and electronic equipment, with the goal of preventing these substances from leaking into the environment when many common products such as household appliances and computers reach the end of their useful life.[13] The Directive applies to all products placed on the market in the EU regardless of whether they are produced in the EU or in non-EU countries. In 2011, the Directive was extended to cover all electrical and electronic equipment, including medical devices and monitoring and control instruments (RoHS 2).[14] The EU's Waste Electrical and Electronic Equipment Directive (WEEE),[15] first adopted in 2002, complements the RoHS in that it is aimed at removing e-waste from landfills and redirecting it to recycling.[16] Both sets of directives impose upon the manufacturer the responsibility for product management throughout the life cycle of the product.[17] These directives have therefore had a dramatic impact on the entire electronics industry.

The EU has also taken decisive regulatory measures to advance animal welfare. The first such provision in 1974 focused on governing slaughterhouses.[18] Regulation in this area was expanded in a 1998 Council Directive that lays down general rules on the protection of animals kept for farming purposes, incorporating the "five freedoms" for animals as declared in the European Convention for the Protection of Animals kept for Farming.[19] The 1999 Amsterdam Treaty contains a Protocol on animal welfare, declaring that animals are sentient beings, a position confirmed by the 2009 Lisbon Treaty.[20] From the Lisbon Treaty's affirmation that animals feel pain and pleasure grew the EU Strategy for the Protection and Welfare of Animals 2012–2015. This Strategy implemented new welfare standards around housing, feeding, transportation, and slaughter while also targeting the competitiveness of European producers.[21] Another prominent example is the EU's decision to ban animal testing for cosmetics. Since 2013, no cosmetics tested on animals can be marketed in the EU.[22]

The final example discussed in this chapter concerns climate change—in particular the EU's emissions trading scheme (ETS). Known as a "cap-and-trade" system, ETS imposes a limit on overall emissions and, within this limit, allows companies covered by the scheme to buy and sell emission allowances as needed. The ETS comprises 11,000 power stations and manufacturing plants in the EEA area, reaching a total of 45% of EU greenhouse gas (GHG) emissions.[23] Initially, climate change emerged as a policy concern at the member-state level, including in Germany, the Netherlands, and the United Kingom.[24] The EU had first opposed flexible market mechanisms such as the ETS during the 1997 Kyoto climate negotiations. However, after realizing the significance of the issue for the European integration, the Commission changed its course and argued that an EU-wide ETS was necessary to avoid market distortions after the United Kingdom and Denmark had introduced national ETSs.[25] Further, once the EU undertook to fulfill its own Kyoto commitments regarding the reduction of GHG emissions by 2008, it became a priority to convince other countries outside the EU to do likewise, both to protect the global commons and to retain the competitiveness of the European industry. [26]

These examples ranging from electronic waste to animal welfare and climate change are illustrative of the EU's stringent environmental policy. They have also provided a foundation for the EU's global influence as they have subsequently been externalized through the Brussels Effect. Before examining the de facto and de jure Brussels Effect in this area, the discussion will briefly review the key political dynamics that lie behind the EU's environmental leadership.

Political Economy

The EU's pro-environmental stance, which is typically the strongest of any major markets in the world, can be traced to a number of factors. These include public opinion favoring stringent environmental regulation, active environmental NGOs (ENGOs), and a wide-reaching political consensus in favor of high levels of environmental protection. Environmental regulation has also offered an important tool for market integration, while also providing an avenue for the EU to exert soft power by promoting norms associated with a benevolent and value-driven world power.

The European public has migrated strongly in favor of environmental regulation over the past fifty years. The modern environmental movement in the EU dates back to the 1960s, when an increasing awareness was emerging regarding the deteriorating state of the environment and the threats posed by pollution and human activities to the planet.[27] The publication of a pathbreaking study, the "Limits to Growth," produced in 1972 by a group of prominent researchers, further magnified concerns about the earth's resources and the ability to sustain economic and population growth.[28] This increased awareness set the EU on a course toward common environmental policy in the subsequent decades.

A series of specific events also catalyzed public awareness regarding environmental damage and paved the way for stronger environmental regulation. Particularly salient was the 1986 Chernobyl nuclear disaster in Ukraine, which released extensive amounts of radioactive material over Russia, Belarus, Ukraine, and parts of Europe.[29] This had major adverse effects on human health and the environment, impacting agricultural and ecosystems in Europe and exposing millions of Europeans to severe health risks. Another catalyst was the detection of acid rain in many parts of Europe in the 1970s and 1980s. Acid rain is frequently a trans-boundary problem whereby acid pollutants—including substances such as sulfur dioxide and nitrogen oxides—emitted in one country get carried through winds and are ultimately deposited as acid rain in another country. This became a notable problem in Europe as it was rapidly industrializing and building power plants across the continent, leading to significant environmental damage in countries such as Austria, Norway, Sweden, and Switzerland.[30]

Public opinion polls over the last three decades demonstrate the widespread support for environmental protection among Europeans. By the late 1980s, the Eurobarometer surveys found environmental problems to rank among the primary concerns among citizens in all member states.[31] Today, public concern for the environment is unquestionable: according to a 2017 Eurobarometer survey, 94% of Europeans felt that protecting the environment was important to them personally.[32] Europeans further associate environmental policies with economic benefits and job creation.[33] They also rank climate change as the "third most serious global problem, after poverty (28%) and international terrorism (24%)."[34] The same surveys reveal that while Europeans place the blame for environmental damage on industry, they also recognize individual responsibility.[35] They also want to attribute a significant role to EU institutions and EU laws in protecting the environment. [36] Accordingly, Europeans support an expansive role for the government in regulating the environment: 89% agreed that the government should set renewable energy targets, and 88% agreed that it should support efforts to improve energy efficiency.[37] Moreover, recent global opinion surveys have suggested that Europeans' pro-environment attitudes are among the strongest in the world. For example, in a global 2015 survey, the Pew Research Center found that Europeans, at 87% approval, are the most supportive of their government limiting GHG emissions. By contrast, in the United States, only 69% of Americans support emission limitations, well below the global median of 78%.[38]

Politicians have internalized this shift in public attitudes in Europe and come to embrace environmental goals across the political spectrum. The presence and influence of Green parties in European and national parliaments have further elevated the salience of environmental matters on the legislative agenda.[39] The 1989 European Parliament elections became known as "green tide" elections as the green parties in the European Parliament increased their share of votes from 2.7% to 7.7%,[40] lifting them from a marginal player to a credible political force. This was significant, as the European Parliament has always played a critical role in supporting stronger environmental protection, calling for a common climate change policy as early as 1986.[41] By the end of the 1990s, Green parties were represented in almost 75% of national parliaments in the EU, further bolstering the EU's green legislative agenda.

The ENGOs have also played an active role in advocating more comprehensive environmental regulations in Europe.[42] A number of these NGOs have come together to create and promote initiatives to influence legislation. Two notable initiatives are the "Greening the Treaty" initiative and the "Greening the EU Budget" initiative.[43] The Greening the Treaty initiative refers to efforts by the NGOs to propose environmentally friendly treaty amendments whenever EU treaties are being revisited, while the Greening the Budget initiative refers to efforts to convince EU legislators to direct funds away from environmentally harmful measures. The most significant civil society actor is a coalition of the largest ENGOs called the "Green 10." The group includes many of the key environmental advocacy groups, including Friends of the Earth Europe, Greenpeace European Unit, and WWF European Policy Office.[44] Acting as a coalition has allowed these NGOs to pool their resources and better counter the lobbying power by business interests.[45] Climate Action Network Europe has also been a critical actor in EU climate policy since the 1980s. In an effort to gain more influence, it has formed alliances with business lobbies such as the European Association for the Conservation of Energy and European Wind Energy Association.[46]

Despite the ardent NGOs' advocacy, many commentators argue that the industry has more influence over policy outcomes in the EU.[47] Numerous individual companies and industry associations engage in lobbying for less burdensome environmental measures. Indeed, some of the most active industry lobbying in the EU targets the Commission's Directorate-General for the Environment. Yet even the industry lobbying can lead to more, as opposed to less, EU-level legislation. When the industry knows that some regulation is inevitably forthcoming, it typically supports EU-level measures, as opposed to divergent and potentially conflicting national regulations that would increase their compliance costs.[48] This was evident, for instance, in the EU legislation on electronic waste where the industry organizations supported EU-level harmonization to correct the market distortion caused by regulatory differences across the member states.[49] For the same reason, the EU's pro-environmental policy is bolstered by the EU institutions' efforts to use environmental regulation as a tool for market integration.[50] Common standards on environmental measures facilitate intra-EU trade as firms can operate in a single European market without facing different regulatory regimes that impede cross-border trade.

The EU's environmental leadership and high domestic standards have also served the EU's aim of presenting itself as a global "soft power," providing a contrast to the more traditional statecraft associated with the US' leadership.[51] For example, the Commission President Jean-Claude Juncker recently articulated the EU's commitment to mitigating climate change in his State of the European Union address 2017 in the following terms:

> I want Europe to be the leader when it comes to the fight against climate change. . . . Set against the collapse of ambition in the United States, Europe must ensure we make our planet great again. . . . The EU must seize this opportunity and become a global leader . . .[52]

This vision portrays the EU as a "normative power," wielding influence through promoting norms that are based on values such as human rights and sustainable development. It emphasizes the EU's self-identification as a righteous power that acts in normatively justified and principled ways in the international arena.

There are numerous examples of the EU's environmental leadership in the international fora. Early manifestations of the EU's efforts to facilitate international environmental treaties can be found at the 1992 Rio Summit, where the EU was a key actor in the UN Conference on Environment and Development (UNCED). The EU's leadership role was significant also in the negotiations leading up to the 1997 Kyoto Protocol on Climate Change,[53] and more recently in concluding the framework agreement on climate change in Paris.[54] The EU's active engagement in international environmental cooperation reflects its ideological commitment to sustainable growth and understanding that global commons cannot be protected by the EU alone. However, its global leadership also likely reflects strategic considerations, including the desire to ensure that the competitiveness of EU companies is not undermined by making them alone bear the costs of environmental regulation.[55] Beyond these multilateral efforts to promote environmental norms, the EU has exercised extensive unilateral influence, as will be discussed next.

De Facto Brussels Effect

The de facto Brussels Effect has been common in many areas of environmental regulation. This section reviews its occurrence with respect to hazardous substances and electronic waste, animal welfare, and climate change regulation. These various examples show how the Brussels Effect manifests itself with respect to both traditional, direct product regulation—as in the cases of hazardous substance and animal welfare—as well as with respect to regulation relying on market mechanisms—including climate change mitigation through emissions trading.

In each of these areas, the Brussels Effect has often been amplified by the EU's large market size and strong regulatory mandate, and further strengthened by the recognition of environmental protection as a constitutional obligation for the EU institutions. In addition, the "precautionary principle"—which allows for regulatory intervention even in the presence of uncertainty regarding the harm—features prominently in the EU's environmental policy making, further contributing to the EU's regulatory capacity and regulatory stringency across all the examples that will be examined. As well, the EU's willingness to protect the environment with high standards is well established, with consumers and parties across the political spectrum typically endorsing stringent environmental regulation. Also, environmental regulation is typically inelastic as EU regulations apply to all products that end up on the European market no matter where they are produced. Thus, a multinational company is not able to circumvent EU's stringent standards by relocating production to jurisdictions with fewer environmental protections as long as they want to retain the option of exporting into the European market. Further, environmental regulation is often non-divisible. After an investment in compliance with the EU's stringent environmental rules is made, the company typically extends those same sustainability practices across its global conduct or production.

Hazardous Substances and Electronic Waste

The 2002 enactment of both RoHS—the Directive banning hazardous substances in electronics—and WEEE—the Directive regulating electronic waste and recycling—led to a global change in the design of electronic products, as multinational companies who sell into the EU's market often opted to use the EU's stringent standards across their global production to save production costs.[56] As a result, these two Directives have led to a number of examples of the de facto Brussels Effect. Both Oracle and Fujitsu, two major multinational electronics companies exporting products to the EU, have made public statements affirming that foreign manufacturers like them rarely split their production lines. Instead, they typically prefer to comply with one set of standards and thus make their entire production line RoHS compliant.[57] According to Katja Biedenkopf's research—which included extensive industry interviews—"the electronics industry is highly globalised . . . [and] maintaining two or more separate product lines is often undesirable and difficult."[58] As a result, most manufacturers apply the EU's requirements globally, making the RoHS a "de facto standard for global material policy within the electronics industry."[59]

The de facto Brussels Effect takes place notwithstanding the costs of complying with EU standards and even in instances where the EU is not a company's largest target market. Indeed, as *The Boston Globe* reported in 2006, American companies were spending "billions of dollars to redesign their products" in response to the RoHS Directive.[60] George Wilkish, a senior quality engineer at M/A-Com, Inc., a business unit of Tyco Electronics Corp., describes RoHS 1 as "probably the biggest change in electronics in 50 years."[61] Many companies like M/A-Com, which only exports 20% of its products to Europe, planned to implement the changes required by the RoHS in all their products, no matter where they were sold.[62]

Surprisingly, the Brussels Effect has even reached industries to which the RoHS does not directly apply. For example, the automotive and aerospace sectors have eliminated some RoHS-regulated substances.[63] Similarly, the degree of compliance with RoHS for most products is so high that companies have reported difficulties in obtaining noncompliant products for sectors not covered by the RoHS.[64] Many companies also see compliance with the EU as a necessity in the competitive environment where the entire marketplace is shifting toward the EU standard. When electronics giants such as Dell and Apple advertise their RoHS-compliance,[65] and customers have easy access to sustainable products,[66] it is difficult for smaller players not to follow.

The de facto Brussels Effect has been particularly notable among Japanese, Taiwanese, and South Korean companies, given the prominence of these countries' information technology and electronics industries. For example, in response to the EU RoHS directive, Hitachi decided to phase out worldwide six chemical substances included in about 70 of its products that were subject to EU RoHS by March of 2005.[67] The company also decided to switch to lead-free solder for its products produced by factories in Japan, and subsequently for its products produced throughout the world.[68] Taiwan Semiconductor Manufacturing Company—the fourth largest semiconductor sales leader in the world[69]— similarly guarantees that all its products meet EU's directives, including RoHS, WEEE, and REACH.[70] According to the MediaTek's 2015 Corporate Social Responsibility Report, the company's environmental standards meet simultaneously European, Asian, and Taiwanese standards for environmental protection.[71] Finally, a June 2006 *Korean Science Times* article reported that Korean exporters such as Samsung complied with EU RoHS.[72] At that time, the EU market took up only one-fifth of all Korean electronics exports,[73] yet that was sufficient to steer the industry toward the European standards. Samsung further confirms on its website that "all [Samsung] products" are RoHS compliant as part of the company's global compliance strategy.[74]

Animal Welfare

Animal welfare offers another prominent set of examples of the de facto Brussels Effect. For example, the EU's ban on the sale of animal-tested cosmetics and chemicals used for such products in particular has had a wide-reaching impact on corporate behavior.[75] The EU is the world leader in the manufacturing of cosmetics: of the world's 50 leading cosmetic brands, 22 are domiciled in Europe.[76] In 2017, European cosmetics and personal care retail sales were valued at €77.6 billion,[77] and exports totaled €20.2 billion.[78] The EU has also built significant institutional expertise and capacity to regulate the industry, as manifested by the creation of the European Centre for the Validation of Alternative Methods (founded in 1991 to develop alternatives to animal testing) and the Scientific Committee on Consumer Products.[79] Thus, the EU—which regulates both the safety of the chemicals included in the cosmetics as well as the testing methods employed—has become an "undisputed regulatory hegemon" in this domain, setting the benchmark for the entire industry.[80]

Japanese cosmetics firms are among those that have adjusted their global manufacturing to conform to EU animal welfare regulations. Shiseido—Japan's largest cosmetics manufacturer—halted animal testing in 2013 to abide by the EU ban on the sale of animal-tested cosmetics.[81] Several other Japanese cosmetics companies, such as Kao Corp. and Kose Corp., followed suit.[82] These companies are now increasingly using cultured human cells to replace animal testing on products.[83] The manufacturers are under no legal obligation to do so in Japan, but they still refrain from animal testing as it would cost them revenue from abroad.[84] Some manufacturers are even demanding that their suppliers of ingredients promise not to conduct tests on animals.[85]

Interestingly, while Shiseido abolished animal testing at both its domestic and overseas laboratories, the company continues to test on animals for its products sold in China, as Chinese laws require such testing as a condition for market access by foreign companies.[86] More generally, while broadly adhering to the EU ban across the multiple markets, the cosmetics firms seem to be prepared to engage in animal testing when such testing is a formal requirement for serving a certain foreign market. According to e-mail correspondence with Shiseido's Customer Care Team in March and April 2018:

> Shiseido does not test its cosmetic products or ingredients on animals except when absolutely mandated by law, or where there are absolutely no alternative methods for guaranteeing product safety. Shiseido's mission is to provide safe and effective products to customers, and to comply with the cosmetics regulations in force, while understanding and respecting the principles behind animal protection.[87]

Shiseido's decision to carry out animal testing for products destined for China while refraining to do so for other markets shows a particularly interesting variant of the Brussels Effect. In such a setting, the company cannot achieve global compliance by adhering to EU rules alone. In other words, the EU standard fails to incorporate all other (weaker) standards as long as Chinese and EU standards are mutually incompatible. In these rare instances, companies are forced to divide their production to serve two (or more) markets that require opposite behaviors.

Because of the incompatibility between EU and Chinese regulatory standards on animal testing, some European cosmetics manufactures have also opted to produce two different varieties of their products. For the fear of legal risks in the EU, they refrained from incorporating in their cosmetics sold in the EU the ingredients they used in China because those ingredients had been tested on animals for the purpose of qualifying for the Chinese market.[88] In seeking legal clarity, the European Federation of Cosmetic Ingredients brought a case before the European Court of Justice (ECJ) in 2014,[89] asking the ECJ to determine whether the EU's Cosmetics Regulation prohibits the sale of cosmetics in the EU if an ingredient in those cosmetics has been tested on animals for the purpose of complying with a third-country regulatory requirement. The ECJ ruled that, in such an instance, a cosmetic product could not be marketed in the EU if the producer relied on those animal test results to prove the safety of the product also in the EU.[90] Thus, the ruling suggests that manufacturers had to maintain two different testing methods—one with and the other without using animals—yet they could produce a single product for both European and Chinese markets. Had the ECJ instead ruled otherwise and prohibited the use of such ingredients in the cosmetics sold in the EU, the manufacturers would in practice be required to produce two different products, or choose between selling their products in the EU or in China. However, this question of divisibility may be moot soon as the Brussels Effect on animal testing might be closing in on China as well: in 2014, China abolished its requirement for domestic companies to conduct animal testing on "ordinary" cosmetics.[91]

In many other areas of animal welfare, the EU's global regulatory influence is more difficult to trace and measure. It is not always clear if foreign producers are adjusting their global practices given their exposure to the EU as a key export market or whether they are changing their practices due to growing domestic pressures. The EU institutions themselves take the view that EU regulations have had a significant global impact. The Commission, in its report on the impact of animal welfare measures on the competitiveness of European livestock producers, notes that "The EU animal welfare standards have had a lighthouse effect and often represented a source of inspiration for voluntary industry initiatives on animal welfare."[92]

At times, the de facto Brussels Effect is quite evident, with producers explicitly citing the EU measures as reasons for the change in their production practices. For example, the Brazilian farming industry acknowledges how it is responding to the business opportunity presented by Europe's sustainable meat market. Leaders of the country's pork industry have argued that the country's producers must start investing in animal welfare because the EU's standards were essentially becoming a requirement of the international market.[93] Incorporating European welfare standards would also increase the value of Brazilian pork and improve its competitiveness on the international market.[94] This is significant given that Brazil is the world's third-largest pork producer and its fourth-largest exporter.

The EU regulations on slaughtering conditions have also triggered the Brussels Effect. In 1993, the EU passed a Council Directive on the protection of animals at the time of slaughter or killing.[95] It requires that all animals be stunned before slaughter.[96] The Directive permits only specific methods of slaughtering that prevent unnecessary suffering, and it applies to domestic and imported meat products alike.[97] Producers looking to export meat products to the EU must thus comply with the Slaughter Directive. Therefore, slaughter-houses in Brazil, Thailand, Namibia, Canada, and many other countries "uti-lise information from EFSA reports and methods of stunning that are effective and allowed by EU legislation."[98] Once these slaughterhouses have decided to adjust to EU regulations, it is unlikely that they would maintain multiple stun-ning methods in practice.

The 1997 EU Directive to protect the welfare of calves by banning the use of veal crates has also informed changes in corporate practices around the world.[99] Veal crates lead to "restriction of movement," "unsuitable flooring," "lack of exercise," "social deprivation," "inability to groom," "stress," and "disease."[100] The United States has no federal legislation on veal crates and as of 2012, the major-ity of calves were raised in crates.[101] However, since the EU ban came into effect, a growing number of states within the United States have banned or regulated their use.[102] In 2007, the American Veal Association approved a policy that the veal industry fully transition to group housing by 2017, citing consumer concerns about animal welfare.[103] That same year, major US producers Strauss Veal and Marcho Farms announced that they would convert their farms to group housing by 2010. Strauss Veal described its goal as "to be 100-percent converted to raising calves by the European-style, group-raised method within the next two to three years."[104] This quote suggests that the EU regulation has at least informed the change, whether it provided the primary impetus for it or not. The US domestic activist pressures have likely also been relevant, with the EU's more stringent ani-mal welfare regulations supplying an important argument for advocacy groups. For example, the Humane Society highlighted that the customary produc-tion practices used in the United States were "illegal throughout the European Union."[105]

The EU has similarly shaped the conditions for chicken farms around the world with its 2007 Directive laying down minimum rules for the protection of chickens kept for meat production (the "Broiler Directive").[106] The Broiler Directive sets maximum stocking densities for chickens, ensuring adequate hous-ing space. It also lays out certain requirements and inspection policies regarding feeding, drinkers, litter, ventilation, heating, lighting, and cleaning.[107] A 2005 study reported that meat exporters are adapting to the demands of European con-sumers, with the result that "increasing proportions of chicken meat production in Argentina and Thailand is now designed to comply with EU legislation and food company standards."[108]

The EU's 2005 animal transport regulation triggered one of the most apparent incidences of the Brussels Effect.[109] In 2015, the ECJ ruled on a seminal case, *Zuchtvieh-Export*, regarding the treatment of animals departing from an EU country into third countries.[110] Zuchtvieh-Export was attempting to transport cattle via truck from Germany to Uzbekistan. However, the German customs officials at the departure point denied clearance as the trip's final 29-hour leg from Kazakhstan to Uzbekistan was deemed to violate the EU's animal transport regulation. The ECJ determined that the Regulation applied to transport in third states, so long as that transport began in the EU.[111] This decision exemplifies a technique identified by Joanne Scott as territorial extension,[112] which enables the EU to extend its regulatory reach into activities outside the EU when there exists a relevant territorial connection—in this case, Kazakhstan.[113] At the same time, this case serves as an example of a de facto Brussels Effect.[114] Here, the Brussels Effect is driven by technical non-divisibility—the non-divisibility of geographic distance in animal transport—which obliges the transport company to obey EU animal welfare regulations even with respect to the part of the journey that takes place outside the EU.

Climate Change and Emissions Trading in Aviation

The EU's efforts to externalize its emissions trading scheme (ETS) to aviation offers a particularly fascinating case study on the extent—but also the clear limits—of the Brussels Effect. The ETS forms the cornerstone of the EU's climate change policy.[115] In a particularly controversial move, the EU tried to force international action by including aviation emissions in its ETS in 2008, and thus sought to apply this Aviation Directive extraterritorially.[116] Few countries outside the EU had adopted effective national legislation to combat greenhouse gases (GHG) at that time. And although the Kyoto Protocol provided that GHGs emitted by airlines were to be regulated by the International Civil Aviation Organization (ICAO), negotiations had come to a standstill. The EU's decision to seek to externalize its ETS was strengthened by the 2009 failure to reach consensus in the Copenhagen climate talks, after which the EU's international leadership in climate policy was severely damaged.[117] This arguably prompted the EU to resort to unilateralism and use its vast market size as leverage to force a change globally.[118]

Specifically, the Aviation Directive required all airlines, including foreign ones, to buy emission permits for all their flights departing from, or landing at, European airports. This way, airlines would not be able to limit their compliance to the part of the journey that takes place in the European airspace, making the scheme non-divisible. For instance, on a flight from San Francisco to London, only 9% of the emissions are calculated to occur in the EU airspace (29%, 37%, and 25% of the emissions occurring over the United States, Canada, and the high seas, respectively).[119] Yet, according to the Directive, the airline was expected to acquire emission permits for each ton of emissions emitted across the entire flight since the point of landing was in the EU.[120]

The Aviation Directive qualified the EU's unilateralism on two fronts: First, airlines were exempted from the ETS with respect to their flights landing in the EU (although not with respect to their flights taking off from the EU) if they were subject to "equivalent measures" in their home jurisdiction.[121] Whether domestic climate regulation in the United States or China, for instance, would qualify as an equivalent provision was, however, subject to the EU's unilateral decision.[122] Second, the Directive stated that the EU could forgo extraterritorial measures if a global agreement on reducing the GHG emissions from aviation was negotiated. The Commission further backed up the Directive with tough sanctions to ensure compliance: a foreign airline refusing to comply was subject to a fine[123] or, even more severely, could be banned from European airports.[124]

If fully enforced, the Aviation Directive would have provided one of the most dramatic examples of the operation of the Brussels Effect. However, foreign airlines, supported by their governments, launched a series of concerted measures to counter the EU's unilateralism. United Airlines, Continental, and American Airlines, supported by the US Air Transport Association, challenged their inclusion in the ETS before UK courts, alleging that the United Kingdom's decision to implement the EU Directive violated international law.[125] The UK Court referred the question to the European Court of Justice. In an important victory to the Commission, the ECJ backed the EU measure. It confirmed the validity of the Aviation Directive with various international agreements and customary international law.[126]

Yet the international resistance persisted.[127] China canceled Airbus aircraft orders and decried the alleged extrajudicial application of EU regulations, in particular against developing countries.[128] The Civil Aviation Administration of China also banned all Chinese airlines from participating in the EU ETS in 2012.[129] India similarly challenged the extraterritorial reach of the ETS. In 2011, the Indian Ministry of Civil Aviation hosted a meeting of 26 countries opposing the Aviation Directive. The participants signed the "Delhi Declaration," calling on the EU to reverse its decision.[130] China, India, and 21 other countries convened another meeting in Moscow and signed the "Declaration on Inclusion of International Civil Aviation in the EU-ETS," which "reject[ed] the EU's move as unilateral, and called on the EU to reverse its decision."[131] Ultimately, EU member states with deep commercial interests at stake given their connection to the Airbus persuaded the EU to change its position. The EU "froze" implementation of the Aviation Directive until the end of 2016, provided the ICAO came to a global agreement by then.[132]

Against this backdrop, multilateral negotiations were revived. On October 6, 2016, the ICAO announced it had reached an agreement, called the Carbon Offsetting and Reduction Scheme for International Aviation (CORSIA).[133] CORSIA's pilot phase will come into effect in 2021, but participation by ICAO states will not be mandatory until 2027. Unlike the ETS, CORSIA includes exceptions for Least Developed Countries, Small Island Developing States, Landlocked Developing Countries, and States with very low levels of international aviation activity.[134] In March 2017, the ICAO also adopted "the world's first global design certification standard governing CO_2 emissions for any industry sector." This certification standard will apply to new aircraft type designs as of 2020, and extends to aircraft type designs already in-production as of 2023.[135] As a result of these measures, the EU agreed to forgo extraterritoriality and limit the geographic scope of the ETS to intra-EEA flights from 2017 onward.[136]

The EU's decision to suspend the extraterritorial aspect of the ETS can be viewed through two different lenses. On one hand, it shows the limits of the Brussels Effect. When faced with salient and broad-based international pressure, the EU is prepared to give in. Imposition of concrete costs on EU member states—here the loss of Airbus sales—proved a viable method of reining in the Brussels Effect. On the other hand, the ETS and the aviation saga shows how the EU can use the Brussels Effect as a way to facilitate an international agreement. It is unclear if the political consensus for the ICAO would have ever emerged but for the Brussels Effect and the opportunity costs associated with enduring the costs of the EU's unilateralism. Granted, CORSIA and The Standard represent a "fundamental[ly] different" scheme for aviation than the EU ETS cap-and-trade system.[137] Yet still, it is geared at accomplishing the same policy outcome without the EU having to face criticism of its aggressive unilateralism.

De Jure Brussels Effect

In many instances, these same areas of environmental regulation—hazardous substances and electronic waste, animal welfare, and climate change regulation—have also triggered legislative change abroad, leading to the de jure Brussels Effect. The EU's influence in these policy areas manifests through multiple channels. Environmental policy has long been a subject of numerous multilateral, regional, and bilateral negotiations.[138] The EU has often played a key role in these negotiations, spearheading several multilateral and regional conventions and concluding bilateral trade agreements with strong environmental provisions. The EU institutions also often extend technical assistance to foreign regulators, at times exporting EU regulations in the process. The environmental movement is also influential in many parts of the world, and NGOs (both European and foreign) have in many instances played an active role in pushing for reforms abroad—often using existing EU regulations as a benchmark in their advocacy. Thus, the narrower de jure Brussels Effect—a legislative change following the de facto Brussels Effect—typically operates alongside these various other channels through which regulatory standards become elevated outside the EU.

Hazardous Substances and Electronic Waste

Environmental regulation offers several examples of the de jure Brussels Effect where countries around the world emulate the EU laws. RoHS and WEEE—the regulations geared at managing hazardous substances and electronic waste—have been particularly influential in this regard. Interestingly, the EU was not the first mover in regulating electronic waste. Major electronics manufacturing countries, Japan and Taiwan, had WEEE-style laws in place shortly before the EU. However, the EU's WEEE exceeded them in scope.[139] RoHS was particularly groundbreaking in restricting the use of six substances in a broad range of products.[140] This made the EU law the global standard toward which businesses have converged, both due to the de facto and de jure Brussels Effect. The Commission itself notes that both RoHS 1 and RoHS 2 Directives "have stimulated a reduction in hazardous materials all over the world: several countries, including China, Korea and the US, have developed RoHS-like legislation."[141]

The wide emulation of EU RoHS worldwide is not as much the result of the Commission's proactive efforts to globalize its regulation; rather, RoHS provides an example of an EU regulation where the internal goals associated with environmental protection and single market dominated, and the regulation's global reach was largely an incidental side effect of those internal goals. In this case, an extensive de facto Brussels Effect likely explains the emulation of RoHS by foreign governments to a considerable extent. Global companies already forced to comply with RoHS have had the incentive to advocate RoHS-type regulations in their home markets, paving the way for the de jure Brussels Effect.

In the United States, the de jure Brussels Effect on hazardous waste management has occurred at the state level as attempts to introduce binding federal legislation have been unsuccessful.[142] The EPA recognized e-waste as a problem in 2001, but its regulatory efforts failed in 2004, largely due to disagreement among the industry on how to allocate responsibility.[143] Another contributing factor is likely the delegation of the hazardous waste management to the states through the Resource Conservation and Recovery Act, relegating e-waste as a policy issue that states could regulate themselves compared to more salient issues such as climate change that were seen as more compelling to include on the federal agenda.[144]

At the same time, RoHS has inspired several US states to follow the EU's example.[145] California offers the most far-reaching illustration. Like the EU, California regulates electronic waste mainly through two related statutes: the California RoHS[146] and the California Electronic Waste Recycling Act.[147] California's RoHS was clearly modeled on the EU RoHS.[148] It also explicitly incorporates EU standards into its Electronic Waste Recycling Act of 2003.[149] This Act, referred to as the "Cal RoHS," bans or permits the sale of electronic devices in California depending on how those devices are regulated under EU RoHS Directive. For example, it does not allow the California Department of Toxic Substances Control to prevent the sale of products, which the EU RoHS Directive does not prohibit from sale in the EU. "Therefore, specific applications of lead, mercury, cadmium and hexavalent chromium that are exempt from the EU RoHS Directive are also exempt from California RoHS regulations."[150] Rather strikingly, the Cal RoHS also states that amendments to the EU directive will be incorporated into California law.[151] However, the California RoHS is narrower in scope than its EU counterpart,[152] covering only various video display devices and cathode ray tubes.[153] Interestingly, there was little industry opposition to Cal RoHS, most likely because manufacturers had already absorbed the costs of complying with the EU RoHS.[154] Some interest groups supporting the legislation even used the existence of the EU's laws in this area as evidence of the feasibility of California's plan.[155]

More recently, further evidence of the de jure Brussels Effect associated with RoHS can be seen in New Jersey's 2017 Electronic Waste Management Act, which tasked its administrative departments to adopt rules and regulations in line with EU's RoHS.[156] Also in 2017, Indiana added a similar requirement to its State Code regarding Electronic Waste.[157] Before those legislative enactments, Minnesota added a reference to RoHS disclosure requirements to its code in 2007.[158] Illinois' Electronic Products Recycling and Reuse Act, entering into force in April 2009, similarly invokes RoHS disclosure requirements for manufacturers.[159] The New York State Electronic Equipment Recycling and Reuse Act[160] added a similar disclosure requirement in May 2010.[161] Wisconsin and Rhode Island Recycling laws further contain similar provisions.[162]

Several countries or states outside the United States have either adopted or considered similar legislation.[163] These include Argentina, Brazil, China, India, Japan, Malaysia, Singapore, South Korea, Switzerland, Taiwan, Turkey, and Vietnam.[164] Notably, the list includes developed and developing countries alike, indicating that even countries that may be less well equipped to handle high compliance costs opt for EU standards given their industry's dependence on the EU market.[165]

South Korea offers perhaps the most striking example of the de jure Brussels Effect by closely emulating RoHS and WEEE, as well as a related EU regulation on End of Life Vehicles (ELV),[166] which sets targets for "reuse, recycling and recovery of the ELVs and their components" and encourages manufactures to produce new vehicles without hazardous substances.[167] South Korea passed the Act on the Resource Circulation [also translated as "Recycling"] of Electrical and Electronic Equipment and Vehicles in 2007.[168] The Act seeks to promote the recycling and reuse of electrical and electronic equipment as well as vehicles, and restricts the use of hazardous materials in those products. It also requires businesses to design and manufacture products to make recycling easier.[169] On the basis of this law, the Ministry of Environment and Korea Environment Corporation implemented an Eco-Assurance System for Electrical and Electronic Equipment and Vehicles (EcoAs).[170]

Several sources indicate that the EU was used as a model for South Korea's law. The Korean Ministry of Environment website notes that "Advanced countries enforce a variety of environmental regulations on electrical & electronic and automobile industry more strictly to serve the cause of sustainable development, and such regulations as WEEE, RoHS are expected to influence the export of domestic companies. Accordingly, on January 1, 2008, South Korea implemented an Act on the Resource Circulation of Electrical and Electronic Equipment and Vehicles for resource circulation and environmental conservation."[171] The EcoAs website, managed by the Ministry of Environment and Korea Environment Corporation, refers to stringent EU regulations when discussing Korea's implementation of its Act in this area.[172] It also notes that the Korean law encompasses features of EU RoHS, WEEE, and ELV.[173] Notably, in the section titled "Summary of EcoAs," it displays the following equation: "EU RoHS + WEEE + ELV, etc = Act on the Resource Circulation of Electrical and Electronic Equipment and Vehicles." Finally, in a 2014 symposium hosted by the Korean Ministry of Environment, the deputy director of the Resource Recycling Division of the Ministry characterized the Korean Act and the EU law as equally restrictive, and stated that "by 2018, the Ministry plans to reach recycling rate of 57% of production, which matches the EU level."[174]

Japan offers an example of more distant emulation of the EU. In 2005, the Japanese Industrial Standards Committee of the Ministry of Economy, Trade and Industry (METI) issued JIS C 0950:2005, also known as "J-MOSS." J-MOSS is the Japanese Industrial Standard for Marking the presence of the specific chemical substances for electrical and electronic equipment.[175] J-MOSS is similar to, but less stringent than, the EU RoHS. Like the EU's RoHS, J-MOSS regulates the same six substances and has the same concentration levels. However, while the EU's RoHS restricts the use of these substances, J-MOSS relies on mandatory labeling requirements.[176] When the products' content exceeds the values set in J-MOSS, the manufacturers must display the "content mark"—which is a two-hand clasping "R" symbol on the product and packaging—and the substance information must be disclosed in catalogs and instruction manuals, as well as on the internet.[177] According to Yoshiko Naiki, Japan did not simply mirror RoHS but was influenced by EU RoHS in introducing its own version of the regulation.[178]

China adopted a "RoHS 2" in 2016. On the one hand and in some dimensions, the China RoHS is weaker than EU RoHS 2, while in other dimensions it is even more stringent. The China RoHS regulates the same six hazardous substances as the EU's RoHS 2, except that the EU added four phthalates in 2015.[179] On the other hand, the China RoHS can be considered even more stringent than the EU RoHS in that it does not exempt several electronic and electrical products or components which qualify for EU RoHS exemptions.[180] China's decision to emulate the EU is not surprising given that all producers in the supply chain need to follow RoHS to guarantee the access of the final product to the EU market. In the case of electronic products, the component manufacturers at the beginning of the supply chain are often based in China.[181]

In Latin America, the efforts to follow the EU's lead in this area have been less successful. The Argentine Senate passed a RoHS-like bill in 2010,[182]citing the EU as an inspiration for its content. However, the bill did not gain final approval, and was only partially enacted in 2011. The categories and list of products covered under the bill "are nearly verbatim (with slight modifications) to those identified under Annex I of the European WEEE Directive."[183] According to a 2018 news report, "[t]he Brazilian government has announced plans to propose a regulation similar to the EU's Directive on the Restriction of Hazardous Substances (RoHS) in electrical and electronic equipment (EEE)."[184] While existing examples of legislative copying in Latin America of EU RoHS, WEEE, and similar regulations are limited, a momentum for legislative reform across Latin America is growing. These legislative efforts might gain force with the growing tendency for producers across global markets to meet EU regulatory standards, making it possible that Latin America will feature examples of the de jure Brussels Effect in the near future.

Animal Welfare

As with the de facto Brussels Effect on animal welfare standards, the EU's influence on legislative change is often hard to disentangle from the domestic advocacy pressures. The EU institutions, again, take the view that the EU's animal welfare legislation has been critical in informing regulatory reforms abroad. For example, the European Parliament has described the EU Directive prohibiting the use of barren battery cages for laying hens as:[185]

> [having] led to a great improvement in hen welfare and has had much influence around the world. Similar legislation and retail company standards are now in place in New Zealand, India, Taiwan, an Australian state, and several states of the U.S.A. Demand from consumers for high welfare egg products has increased in many other countries. The EU legislation, rather than solely EU consumer attitudes, has been a major factor in this world-wide change, which is accelerating.[186]

In some other areas, foreign governments also refer to EU laws in their government reports and other legislative documents, suggesting that they are at least partially emulating the EU in their own legislative endeavors. For example, the EU's regulation banning the confinement of sows during pregnancy has led to the de jure Brussels Effect in several jurisdictions. The EU regulates this area by a 2008 Council Directive laying down minimum standards for the protection of pigs.[187] The Directive prohibits the tethering of sows and sow stalls, except during the first four weeks of pregnancy.[188] Although the ban did not come into effect until 2013,[189] it was promulgated already in 2001, and since that time, a number of other countries have moved toward similar bans. In New Zealand, for example, sow stalls were phased out in 2015.[190] The government reported that "[t]he new code confirms New Zealand's position as a world leader on animal welfare and demonstrates the priority this Government places on it."[191] The New Zealand pork industry publicly supported the ban, noting how "[c]onsumers prefer gestation stalls are not used—we have listened and we are making a change and removing them."[192] New Zealand was likely also influenced by the EU's example: a government report on the amendment of the pig welfare legislation makes frequent mention of EU standards and legislation as a point of comparison.[193] Similarly, in Australia, sow stalls were phased out in 2017,[194] and in Canada, crates will be phased out by 2024. In the United States, many states began to ban sow stalls after the EU legislated the ban in 2001. For example, the first US state to ban sow stalls was Arizona in 2006. California, Colorado, Florida, Maine, Michigan, Ohio, Oregon, and Rhode Island followed suit by 2012.[195]

Climate Change and Emissions Trading

In the case of the ETS, the de jure Brussels Effect was always an explicitly stated goal of the EU. Given the inherently global nature of climate change, the de facto Brussels Effect alone was never going to be sufficient to address the challenge. In particular, the de facto Brussels Effect was not going to mitigate foreign GHG emissions that were completely local in nature. Conscious of this, the EU chose to adopt ETS over various other regulatory mechanisms, such as carbon tax, partly because it knew that the ETS was more likely to gain traction internationally.[196] In fact, around the same time, a limited carbon trading was also being implemented in the United States, where several states participate in a Regional Greenhouse Gas Initiative (RGGI), a regional emission trading scheme to reduce GHGs. The United States had also advocated carbon trading as a preferred regulatory mechanism in international negotiations. By adopting the ETS, the EU hoped to gain the support of the United States and thus also pave the way for subsequent multilateral cooperation—with the United States as its partner—in climate change mitigation. This strategy suggests that climate unilateralism never constituted a permanent or preferred regulatory response for the EU. Instead, it always hoped to inspire other jurisdictions to follow its example to ultimately forge a joint global action to mitigate climate change.

On many metrics, the EU has been successful in this regard. The EU's efforts to mitigate climate change through the ETS has similarly gained noteworthy traction abroad, inspiring other countries to develop their own ETSs. According to data compiled by the Grantham Institute of Imperial College London, 39 national and 23 sub-national jurisdictions have either implemented or are scheduled to implement carbon-pricing instruments similar to the ETS.[197] Many of these are individual EU member states but also comprise jurisdictions such as Australia, Switzerland, and regional schemes in Canada, China, Japan, the United States.[198]

This de jure Brussels Effect has occurred despite criticism leveled against the EU ETS. The EU has been criticized for grandfathering emission allowances, which distorts competition.[199] In addition, the number of allowances given undermined the effectiveness of the system, preventing prices from driving the expected reduction in emissions.[200] The price of EU emission allowances further dropped drastically during the financial crises—from approximately €30/tCO2 in mid-2008 to approximately €5/tCO2 in mid-2013[201]—casting further doubt on the effectiveness of the EU ETS and its suitability as a global model. Finally, the EU's efforts to extend the coverage of its ETS to international aviation emissions, and the subsequent retreat from this strategy, may be viewed as undermining the EU's soft power to exert leadership and provide a legislative model for foreign governments with its ETS.[202]

However, despite its flaws and limitations, the ETS remains unprecedented as a system that attempts to set a price for greenhouse gas emissions in a supranational context, providing the most innovative template for others to follow.[203] The diffusion of the ETS is further motivated by the possibility of "linking" another jurisdiction's ETSs with the EU's,[204] assuming these foreign schemes meet the EU ETS's minimum conditions for linking.[205] Some jurisdictions, such as Australia, California, and Quebec tailored their ETS programs to closely resemble that of the EU with an aim of linking those programs with the EU ETS market.[206]

Again, South Korea offers a prominent example of the de jure Brussels Effect. The country adopted K-ETS—Korean Emissions Trading Scheme ("Act on the Allocation and Trading of Greenhouse Gas Emission Permits") in 2012.[207] The implementation took place three years later.[208] The K-ETS covers approximately 599 of the country's largest emitters, which account for around 68% of national GHG emissions.[209] The Act reflects at least partially the realization that Korean companies are affected by EU's ETS and that the ETS can play a significant role in developing new technologies. For example, a 2012 Korean news article mentions the impact of EU-ETS on Korean airlines operating flights to and from Europe. It notes that Korean airlines might fall behind European airlines in the global competition because European airlines have had a head start to innovate in an effort to respond to the EU-ETS, such as developing environmentally friendly fuels.[210]

Several sources indicate that EU-ETS was used as a model for K-ETS. The 2012 notice of legislation, issued by the Ministry of Environment in relation to the enforcement decree for K-ETS, notes that "The enforcement decree designed the emissions trading scheme by *referencing foreign examples such as the EU's* and by reflecting both the global standard and the realities of the Korean economy."[211] The Q&A for K-ETS, posted by the Presidential Committee for Green Growth in May 2012, emphasizes the positive effects of the ETS by referring to the EU: "After the EU adopted ETS, greenhouse gas emissions decreased, whereas businesses did not flee abroad or lose their competitiveness."[212]

South Korea also provides an example of the EU's use of technical assistance programs to further facilitate the diffusion of its regulatory models abroad. In July 2016, the Korean Ministry of Strategy and Finance (MOSF) and the EU launched a €3.5 million, three-year cooperation project, through which the EU would provide technical assistance for the implementation of K-ETS and also support policy development regarding K-ETS. The EU will provide a consultation hotline, training workshops, and expert forums.[213] Korea welcomes the EU's advice as an opportunity to learn from an established and experienced regulator. According to a statement by vice minister of Korean MOSF: "I hope that sharing EU's ample experience in operating the EU ETS [for] more than 10 years would help K-ETS to become a successful policy instrument for reducing GHGs in Korea."[214] A statement by Minister Counsellor [*sic*] of Delegation of the European Union to the Republic of Korea expresses a similar sentiment, noting also how this offers a path for broader emulation of ETS in the region: "[The EU-Korea ETS Project] aims to share the best technical expertise and lessons learned over the past decade of the EU's ETS operation, the world's first and largest emissions trading system. By assisting Republic of Korea in the implementation and operation of its ETS, we aim to set a positive example for other countries in the region."[215]

Finally, China is a particularly remarkable example of the de jure Brussels Effect, given its role as the leading emitter of GHGs. Today, it has the second-largest carbon market trading scheme after the EU. China piloted a carbon trading program in different parts of the country, including in Beijing, Shanghai, and Guangdong,[216] and approved a national ETS in 2017.[217] China's willingness to emulate the EU's lead can be traced to different factors, including its increasing recognition of the limits to command-and-control regulation and its unsuccessful past experiences with emissions trading for sulfur dioxide.[218] The EU has also engaged in active dialogue with Chinese regulators, building regulatory capacity and assisting local regulators with tasks such as data gathering, monitoring, and inspections.[219] Despite these efforts and concrete signs that China is taking action, it is not yet clear that the EU ETS can be meaningfully transplanted in China, given its tradition of government intervention with markets and a political aversion to energy price increases.[220]

The ETS is not the sole example of the de jure Brussels Effect involving emissions control and the EU's efforts to mitigate climate change. The EU has also taken extensive measures to set emissions standards for the automotive industry, both to reduce local pollution and thereby improve air quality, and to mitigate harmful GHGs that contribute to climate change. The EU adopted the Euro-5 standard for passenger cars in 2009 and Euro-6 standard in 2014. Euro-5 primarily reduces fine particulate matter produced by diesel cars, while Euro-6's core objective is the reduction of nitrogen oxide (NOx) and carbon monoxide (CO).[221] Additionally, Euro-6 moves beyond direct human health concerns related to pollutant exposure and addresses broader climate change objectives by imposing limitations on carbon dioxide.[222]

In 2016, shortly after the EU adopted these standards, the Russian government made Euro-5 standard mandatory in Russia.[223] It was natural for Russia to emulate the EU standard—as opposed to, for example, the prevailing US standard—given that 69% of the total Russian car exports are destined to Europe.[224] This de jure Brussels Effect was also preceded by a significant de facto Brussels Effect, paving the way for the domestic legal change. Indeed, many domestic companies were already producing and selling cars compatible with the Euro-5 and even Euro-6 standards to ensure their access to the important EU market.[225] Russian oil refineries had similarly begun to adjust their production to EU standards. For example, a Russian energy company Lukoil completely switched its refineries to Euro-5 standard in 2012, while Gazprom Neft and Rosneft started producing some of their petrol and diesel under the EU standard in 2013.[226] At the same time, the Brussels Effect has not been complete in Russia. Some local companies continue to produce cars that fail to meet the EU standard for domestic use—especially to serve the more remote parts of the country, where access to high-quality fuel is limited.[227]

South Africa provides a curious illustration of an interplay between the corporate and government interests in the country's efforts to move toward the EU's fuel standards. The South African government has acknowledged how several foreign jurisdictions have tightened fuel specifications in line with those of the EU,[228] and have proposed to incorporate the EU's fuel standards into South African law as well. The country's current fuel regulations, "Clean Fuels I," are equivalent to the Euro III fuel specifications.[229] Updated "Clean Fuels II" regulations, which are equivalent to Euro V specifications, were intended to become effective in July 2017. However, the new draft regulations were rescinded as the government refused to pledge necessary assistance to refineries that would be forced to upgrade their facilities to make the transition to cleaner fuel production.[230]

South African oil refineries acknowledge that the market is shifting toward the European fuel standards and support the local adoption of EU standards to keep up with the growing demand of cleaner fuels. At the same time, they emphasize the necessity of government support to make the substantial capital investment to upgrade their facilities.[231] The industry claims that, absent such support, the imported supply of cleaner fuels would crowd out the domestic market whenever the new standards were adopted.[232] Sasol—a large chemicals and energy company in South Africa—is engaged in ongoing negotiations with the South African government to ensure that sufficient investment is in place to make the transition.[233] In addition, SAPIA, an industry association representing the collective interests of the South African liquid fuels industry, has established a joint task force with the Department of Energy to resolve the impasse.[234]

This dialogue between the government and the key corporate players shows how the path toward the de jure Brussels Effect can be long and complicated—even when commercial realities support the adoption of the EU standard, and when such emulation is backed by the government and the industry alike. Lobbying on the part of influential companies like Sasol and industry associations have played a crucial role in the development of fuel regulations that mirror those prevailing in the EU by the South African government.[235] Yet it is these same companies' inability to adjust to EU standards absent government support that has delayed the manifestation of the de jure Brussels effect in the country.

THE EU HAS exerted significant and growing global influence on environmental policy over the past two decades. Given the global nature of many environmental problems, it has been a policy issue in which the EU has had a keen and proactive interest in externalizing its regulations. This chapter has illustrated the global impact of the EU's environmental regulation—both de facto and de jure—through examples pertaining to management of hazardous substances in electronics, protection of animal welfare, and mitigation of climate change through the emissions trading system. The discussion showed that the de facto Brussels Effect has been particularly strong in the case of management of hazardous substances in electronics, revealing extensive de facto convergence among multinational electronics companies on EU rules across their worldwide production. This common de facto Brussels Effect has also paved the way for the de jure Brussels Effect in multiple countries. The de facto Brussels Effect was similarly shown to be prevalent in the area of animal welfare, manifested by examples ranging from the cosmetics industry abandoning animal testing to slaughterhouses amending the ways they stun animals before slaughter. Examples of the EU's influence on foreign legislative practices may be found in this area, but it often remains difficult to link the various domestic reforms to the de facto Brussels Effect given the various additional channels, such as consumer and NGO activism, which also drive domestic reforms in this area.

The EU's emissions-trading mechanism provided an alternate case study to examine the dynamics and the limits of the Brussels Effect in environmental regulation. While foreign governments have often had little success in curtailing the EU's regulatory ambitions in other areas, they were ultimately successful in restraining the EU's efforts to extend its ETS into international aviation unilaterally. This suggests that the Brussels Effect has its limits, in particular when the EU pursues aggressive unilateralism in an area that is simultaneously economically salient for foreign jurisdictions and politically controversial. However, the threat of the EU's unilateralism was sufficient to catalyze multilateral negotiations, which eventually led to an international agreement to regulate emissions in the aviation industry, an outcome that might not have happened without the EU's attempts to drive regulatory change. Further, despite the EU's inability to foster regulatory adjustment through the de facto Brussels Effect, it has achieved success through the de jure Brussels Effect as several countries have since emulated its ETS domestically. This illustrates a different relationship between the de facto and de jure Brussels Effect: while the de facto Brussels Effect often paves the way for the de jure Brussels Effect, the de jure Brussels Effect can also take place in the absence of any meaningful de facto Brussels Effect, though most effectively when the EU assumes a proactive role in its promotion.

PREFACE TO PART THREE

Assessment

This book has thus far focused on the theory behind the Brussels Effect as well as its manifestation through case studies into a number of policy areas. That discussion has been purely descriptive, seeking to explain why the EU is in a unique position to exert, both intentionally and unintentionally, global regulatory influence today. In this last part of the book, the discussion turns to the ongoing and future impact of the Brussels Effect—both by asking the normative question of whether the Brussels Effect is beneficial and to whom (chapter 8) and whether the Brussels Effect will persist or transform in the future (chapter 9). The discussion that follows will therefore be inherently more subjective than in the previous chapters, consisting of both value-driven assessments on the costs and benefits associated with the Brussels Effect as well as inevitably indeterminate predictions on its endurance.

Chapter 8 takes on the normative charge and examines the various costs and benefits associated with the Brussels Effect, considering whether the Brussels Effect, on balance, advances or reduces people's welfare—in the EU and outside of it. In assessing the EU's global regulatory power from a normative standpoint, the chapter engages with three primary strands of criticism that can be leveled against the Brussels Effect. First, it asks whether the EU's global regulatory reach is costly and detrimental to innovation, imposing a cost on the society as a result. Second, it engages with the criticism alleging that the Brussels Effect reflects the EU's protectionism and can hence be viewed as an industrial-policy driven attempt to impose costs on non-EU companies while tilting the market in favor of its own firms. Finally, it asks whether the Brussels Effect amounts to regulatory imperialism, compromising the foreign sovereign interests and undermining the political autonomy of their citizens.

Chapter 9 looks into the future, asking if the Brussels Effect will likely prevail as the balance of global economic power changes, technological innovation progresses, and the EU faces internal challenges ranging from Brexit to rising anti-EU sentiments cultivated by populist Euroskeptic political parties. Specifically, the chapter asks whether the distinct conditions underlying the Brussels Effect—*market size, regulatory capacity, stringent standards, inelastic targets*, and *non-divisibility*—are affected by the various external and internal challenges to the EU's regulatory hegemony. For example, will the Brussels Effect be undermined as the relative size of the EU's market diminishes as China's grows? Will the EU's regulatory capacity or ability to generate stringent regulations be compromised with the rise of anti-EU parties and their efforts to reinstate national sovereignty and repatriate powers delegated to EU institutions? Will the new technologies such as additive manufacturing bring an end to non-divisibility as companies are increasingly able to customize their production for different consumer markets, potentially allowing companies to forgo implementing EU regulations globally? These are among the questions that determine the staying power of the Brussels Effect. Ultimately, they also determine whether the Brussels Effect will give way to, for example, the "Beijing Effect" or gradually fade into history as new forces of economic regulation—whether driven by unilateralism, multilateralism, or overall fragmentation—sweep into the global marketplace in the decades to come.

Neither question—the normative desirability of the Brussels Effect or its endurance into the future—is simple to answer. The welfare effects associated with the Brussels Effect are not uniformly beneficial, and EU regulation does not make everyone better off. Yet the Brussels Effect generates substantial welfare gains in many areas, and can be a powerful force for change and good, not just in Europe but around the world—even when those welfare gains are achieved at the cost of foreign sovereignty and without respecting individual political autonomy. The future of the Brussels Effect is also difficult to predict, yet the Brussels Effect may turn out to be surprisingly resilient in the face of both external and internal threats to its existence. The more long lasting the Brussels Effect, the more urgent the normative conversation on its merits. And, the more consequential the welfare effects associated with the Brussels Effect, the more important the conversation of how long lasting the Brussels Effect will be.

8

Is the Brussels Effect Beneficial?

THIS BOOK HAS thus far demonstrated the existence and importance of the Brussels Effect in many areas of global regulatory policy, and revealed the powerful impact the EU has on global markets as a result. When considering this broad impact, an important question arises: Is the prevalence of the Brussels Effect desirable or undesirable? Of course, since the Brussels Effect creates both winners and losers, the answer to this question likely depends on whom one asks.

This chapter addresses the normative question of whether the Brussels Effect is beneficial, specifically by asking whether it advances, rather than reduces, people's welfare both in the EU and outside of it. Welfare in this context should be measured in terms of giving people access to better products and services—"better" being defined as cheaper, safer, or more sustainable, depending on what people value—while respecting people's political autonomy within the democratic structures of the societies they live in.

In comparing this welfare benefit to the costs incurred to achieve it, three broad strands of criticism can be leveled against the Brussels Effect. First, one critique that has been frequently made by businesses is that the proliferation of more restrictive EU regulations is costly and hinders innovation. Consequently, according to this argument, numerous consumers may become priced out of the market, leaving them worse off than if less restrictive regulations existed. Industrial progress would also be thwarted, levying a cost on society at large. Second, another frequent critique expressed by foreign governments and companies is that institutional and ideological motivations underlying the Brussels Effect reflect the EU's protectionism. According to this critique, as a manifestation of industrial policy, the EU's regulatory practices may distort the operation of the market and thereby deprive consumers of the gains that undistorted competition would produce. Third, a number of scholars have suggested that the Brussels Effect may reflect the EU's regulatory imperialism, compromising the democratic prerogatives of foreign sovereigns and the political autonomy of their citizens.

The Brussels Effect. Anu Bradford, Oxford University Press (2020). © Oxford University Press.
DOI: 10.1093/oso/9780190088583.001.0001

These criticisms cannot be dismissed, and should be considered in any calculus of net benefit. The Brussels Effect does impose real economic and political costs that are, for some segments of society, welfare reducing. The economic costs are both absolute and distributional, burdening less-wealthy consumers and smaller companies in particular. The sovereignty costs are felt in foreign jurisdictions, regardless of whether they stem from the EU's benevolent or sinister motives. Yet some of these criticisms, such as accusations of prevalent protectionism, are less well founded. And even the criticism that is more valid needs to be considered on balance with the benefits that the Brussels Effect generates, including the ability of the Brussels Effect to mitigate deficient regulatory capacities or offset sometimes excessive corporate influence abroad, thus enhancing rather than reducing the welfare of foreign consumers. This chapter looks at a number of important criticisms of the Brussels Effect, while also considering those criticisms within the context of the benefits that the Brussels Effect entails.

Does the Brussels Effect Increase Costs and Deter Innovation?

Undoubtedly, by raising the standards for a number of different products and services, the Brussels Effect imposes often involuntary costs on firms and consumers alike—both in the EU and abroad. Compliance with the EU's stringent regulations is often costly for companies, and these companies further typically pass these costs on to consumers, increasing the final price consumers pay. While some consumers are prepared to pay the higher price in return for products and services that they find safer or more environmentally sustainable, others would trade off the costs and these other considerations differently. Excessive regulation can also deter innovation, imposing a dynamic cost on the society at large.

Chapter 2 argued that the Brussels Effect is sustained by strong stakeholder demand for stringent regulations. The majority of European consumers and citizens support the imposition of high regulatory standards. However, this is not true with respect to every consumer. Some European citizens who would value access to cheaper consumer goods likely question whether enhanced product standards justify the higher costs often associated with them. This is also true with respect to foreign consumers, many of whom may be resentful when the preferences of EU consumers get foisted on them, increasing the costs of products and services.

In addition, some European businesses view the high regulatory standards as unsustainable for the European economy. They argue that excessive reliance on the precautionary principle may slow economic growth and innovation,[1] pricing EU firms out of critical export markets.[2] An illustrative example comes from the REACH regulation, discussed in chapter 6. European corporations continue to critique REACH's high cost of compliance more than twelve years after the regulation came into force. Tony Bastock, vice president of the chemical industry's lobby group, CEFIC, complains that compliance with REACH cripples the industry's ability to compete in the global market. Bastock describes a grim future, as further deadlines pass for registering even the smallest quantities of chemicals: "The burdens that are awaiting us are still there. And yet this monster continues to devour the innovation of Europe."[3]

The US chemical industry expresses similar concerns. Jim DeLisi, president of Fanwood Chemical Inc., claims REACH hampers innovation with little-known benefits: "[w]hether REACH will improve human health or the environment will not be known for years, if ever, but its ability to tie up regulators and commerce is already clear," calling REACH an "unproven, highly bureaucratic approach to chemical regulation."[4] According to the US International Trade Commission (USITC), regulatory compliance with REACH reportedly increased the costs on US chemical exporters by more than 20%.[5] The GDPR, the EU's data protection regulation discussed in chapter 5, was similarly seen as imposing a costly burden on companies. According to a recent PricewaterhouseCoopers survey of 200 top executives from US companies,[6] the costs of adjusting their business practices to GDPR were high: 68% of the respondents noted that they will invest between $1 million and $10 million to achieve GDPR compliance while another 9% expect to spend over $10 million and a further 24% under $1 million.[7] Few would expect companies to simply absorb these costs. Instead, some of them will inevitably be passed on to consumers.

Examining specifically the dynamic costs on innovation, the Brussels Effect can deter innovation in at least four different ways. First, by increasing the costs of compliance, firms may have fewer resources to spend on the development of new products. Second, by constraining certain types of business practices, some avenues for technological and business development are curtailed or foreclosed. Third, in policy areas where the Brussels Effect is particularly pervasive, we may see less experimentation as harmonization pushes all market participants toward certain conduct or production. In such a case, there is a risk that corporations and countries converge to a wrong or inefficient standard. All these costs might halt industrial progress and prevent or delay the development of new and potentially welfare-enhancing products. Finally, innovation can be hampered by entrenching a cultural norm that discourages risk-taking and ventures aimed at transformative as opposed to incremental innovation. A remark by an Uber executive is illustrative in this regard. Commenting on the differences between the United States' and the EU's regulatory philosophies with respect to the technology industry, this executive noted how "[i]n Europe, the goal when dealing with tech companies is for regulators to satisfy a consumer need. In the US, the goal is more broadly to change the world or, at least, allow it to change."[8] If the Brussels Effect pushes all firms and jurisdictions toward the goal of "satisfying a consumer need" as opposed to "changing the world," arguably some products may never be developed and some progress never be realized as a result.

In addition to absolute costs, the Brussels Effect introduces distributional costs. The costs of complying with EU regulations are often particularly, even prohibitively, high for small- and medium-sized enterprises, while the large multinationals arguably have the resources to meet almost any standard that the EU sets. Thus, if anything, high regulatory barriers in the EU have the potential to protect and further entrench the power of already large companies that can more easily afford to comply at the expense of small companies and entrants struggling to meet accumulating regulatory burdens. In the end, while big multinationals such as Facebook or Google make the headlines, the real hidden cost of the Brussels Effect is borne by the small entrants who do not have the same capacity to engineer their products and services to meet the EU's demands. For example, the EU's new copyright reform requires platform companies displaying copyrighted content to run filters that scan uploaded content for copyright violations.[9] These filtering systems cost $100 million to develop and run, which can be prohibitive for small entrants yet trivial for companies such as Google.[10] This distributive effect is one of the unintended consequences of EU regulations, tilting the relative regulatory burden in favor of the large incumbents and further cementing their dominance in the process.

These criticisms are all important, and they present genuine challenges for regulators, businesses, and voters to consider. However, it is also true that costs to businesses and high prices for consumers are not automatically an indication that people's welfare is being reduced. One way to view the high prices generated by stringent regulation is through the lens of regulatory paternalism, which justifies government intervention as a way to force or nudge individuals away from unwise decisions.[11] This lens suggests that while regulations may lead to higher prices, they also reduce other kinds of costs—both in the present, but also in the future. For example, in the absence of stringent regulation, consumers may make decisions that will lead to hidden costs they had not considered; they might choose cheaper products because they do not have the right information on the health costs of less safe products or a full appreciation of the long-term societal costs of lesser environmental protections. This might be because they do not spend the time to educate themselves on the harmfulness of certain chemicals or consider negative consequences associated with relinquishing control over their personal data. They may also inappropriately discount the welfare of future generations, opting for cheaper products today that will lead to environmental harm in the future. These kinds of consumer choices impose a burden on the next generation of consumers and citizens. In these instances, markets fail to produce optimal outcomes. For these reasons, government regulation, even when it deviates from individual preferences, should arguably at times override those preferences.

Benefits to businesses can also result, including when the Brussels Effect harmonizes discordant regulations—an outcome that often leads to a net benefit for economic operators. From this perspective, instead of burdening corporations and deterring innovation, the EU regulations reduce operating costs by enhancing predictability and legal certainty, allowing companies to produce products that increase consumer confidence and satisfaction. Furthermore, despite having to shoulder burdensome compliance costs, firms may stand to realize meaningful gains from the Brussels Effect: firms can trade across the entire EU based on a harmonized legal framework instead of facing conflicting national regulations. Common EU rules reduce uncertainty and facilitate planning and long-term investment.[12] For these reasons, the benefits generated by the Brussels Effect on business could actually outweigh the costs, reducing consumer prices.

Similarly, the effects on innovation can also be positive as EU regulations push companies to develop products that are not only more environmentally sustainable but at the same time more cost efficient. For instance, it is well documented that energy efficiency technologies often save consumers and businesses money, providing substantial risk-adjusted returns for those who adopt them. However, due to many informational and behavioral market failures, consumers regularly under-adopt them unless regulation is in place to compel them.[13] Compliance with high standards can therefore also be an important source of cost savings and competitiveness for firms.

In addition to considering compliance costs or incentives to innovate, firms care about their brand and consumer confidence. They are therefore also prepared to advocate regulation if it improves their reputation or enhances consumer confidence in their products and services. While companies may not welcome all EU rules, they understand the advantages that come with regulation. The vice president for Microsoft, John Frank, emphasized that a company like Microsoft is "not trying to remain unregulated."[14] Companies want customers to feel comfortable buying their products, and clear regulations can help accomplish that.[15] For the same reason, the president of Microsoft recently called for the regulation of facial recognition technology in the United States.[16] He stressed the importance of clear rules on this area of technology, which, if left unregulated, can unsettle consumers and be used "for ill as well as good." Amazon similarly called for the governments to "weigh in" after discovering an embarrassing mistake in its facial recognition technology.[17] Established rules therefore enhance consumer confidence and can boost demand for new products.

Reputational benefits and brand equity can also arise from compliance with higher standards. Firms can send the markets and consumers a valuable signal by associating themselves with high standards across many areas of regulation, be it by listing their company in a stock exchange that holds them to more stringent reporting requirements,[18] or by adhering to high environmental, human rights, or labor standards. In this way, firms can enhance their legitimacy, obtain reputational gains, and win over consumers whose values drive their customer behavior.[19] For example, observance of EU food standards engenders customer confidence in many parts of the world. Several domestic companies in China proclaim that they produce their dairy products in compliance with EU standards in an effort to send markets a signal of the safety of their products. A Chinese milk producer Jun Le Bao announced that it is using equipment imported from European countries, and that every technical aspect of the production line complies with EU standards.[20] Similarly, the Shengmu Group produces organic infant milk powder that complies with EU standards after having invested in a new specialized factory. The company emphasizes how EU-compliant milk powder will be available in China and worldwide.[21] The Chinese dairy industry has also actively advocated for the elevation of national standards to meet the EU standard in an effort to further enhance consumer confidence in the domestic dairy industry.[22] For instance, the Chinese industry association, China State Farms Production Dairy Association, embraces the EU standard, offering accreditation for domestic producers that join the association. Many Chinese companies have thus joined the association specifically to signal their compliance with EU standards.

Consequently, the criticism on the costliness of the Brussels Effect must be tempered with the realization of the many economic benefits engendered through more harmonized, predictable, and stable business environments. These benefits have created efficiencies that are often passed on to consumers through more reliable and sustainable products and services that may not inevitably be more expensive. This is not to say that the Brussels Effect would not reduce some consumers' welfare—it does. Subscribing to regulatory paternalism may in the end be the only way to argue that even these consumers, against their individual preferences, are still better off under the Brussels Effect—even though it remains debatable if the particular EU regulation (as opposed to some alternative regulation) is optimal for them. Of course, a question remains if the EU should be making this choice for foreign firms and consumers as well. This changes the argument to a political, as opposed to merely economic, dimension of the Brussels Effect. The argument over the potential for EU's "regulatory imperialism" and the erosion of foreign regulatory sovereignty will be examined in more detail later in this chapter.

Does the Brussels Effect Reflect the EU's Regulatory Protectionism?

Those skeptical of the EU's external regulatory influence often portray the EU as a protectionist actor, eager to impose costs on foreign firms in an effort to protect EU firms under the guise of concern for consumer and environmental health and safety.[23] There have been several recent attempts to portray the EU as a protectionist regulator—especially when US-based companies are the targets of EU regulation. The United States' dominance of the tech sector has been described as a "source of resentment in Europe,"[24] and critics attribute the EU's pursuit of US tech companies to envy-driven protectionism. There would certainly be grounds for envy: fifteen out of the world's most valuable tech firms are American while one is from Europe.[25] It is therefore no wonder that the EU's enforcement actions against US tech giants are often viewed in Washington, DC, as part of a "protectionist plot."[26] For example, as the Commission was getting ready to unveil its Digital Single Market Strategy, the *New York Times* wryly remarked that "Europe calls it consumer protection. Silicon Valley calls it protectionism."[27] In 2015, even President Barack Obama weighed in, suggesting that European regulatory actions against US tech companies reflected an attempt to give an edge to European firms lagging behind their more successful competitors in Silicon Valley:

> We have owned the Internet. Our companies have created it, expanded it, perfected it in ways that they can't compete. And oftentimes what is portrayed as high-minded positions on issues sometimes is just designed to carve out some of their commercial interests.[28]

Similar comments accusing the EU of "green protectionism" have been leveled against a range of environmental policies.[29] For example, the 2009 Renewable Energy Directive was heavily criticized for affording domestic biofuel producers favorable access to the EU market at the expense of more sustainable foreign producers. The European Centre for International Political Economy alleged, "[l]ike other forms of green protectionism, it is not environmental ambitions or policies that cause problems for international trade policy. It is the use of these policies for [the EU's] own industrial policy ambitions."[30] Similarly, the EU's regulation of GMOs has been labeled as "blatant trade protectionism."[31] Comparable sentiments have been expressed against recent environmental protections from the insistence on importing only beef that was free of growth hormones and the regulation of GMOs, to import restrictions reflecting EU forestry and land management standards.[32]

The EU firmly denies that it has a protectionist agenda. Its stated agenda aims to cultivate a regulatory environment that guarantees a level playing field where EU companies can compete with their foreign counterparts on equal terms.[33] The EU often emphasizes its commitment to the welfare state and the sustainability of its economic policies. By exporting its standards to other countries, the EU can pursue its ambitious social and environmental agenda without compromising the competitiveness of its industries.[34] However, the line between "concern for competitiveness"—that is, subjecting domestic and foreign companies to the same rules—and "regulatory protectionism"—that is, favoring domestic companies at the expense of foreign companies—is sometimes blurry. If the EU enforces its competition laws against a US firm, it can be difficult to determine whether the enforcement action is motivated by industrial policy and the desire to deliver an advantage to European firms, or whether it is driven by an objective application of EU law that would be similarly applied, regardless of the nationality of the target firm.

In perhaps no other domain have accusations of European protectionism been voiced more frequently than in competition policy, where the European Commission has issued many rulings against high-profile US companies. In response to these rulings, the Commission has been accused of using its competition powers to advance European industrial policy objectives over competition. These accusations go back as far as the 2001 *GE/Honeywell* merger[35]—a merger between two US companies that US authorities cleared but which the Commission blocked. The US Department of Justice's chief antitrust enforcement official responded to the EU decision by accusing the Commission of protecting competitors as opposed to competition.[36] This idea that the EU is protecting competitors and not competition became somewhat of a mantra in the years that followed.[37] Members of the US Congress similarly expressed concerns, accusing the Commission of "using its merger review process as a tool to protect and promote European industry at the expense of U.S. competitors."[38] In addition to *GE/Honeywell*, the Commission has blocked or forced significant restructuring to several mergers involving a wide range of well-known American firms, including MCI WorldCom, Time Warner, NYSE Euronext, and UPS.[39] These cases keep alive the critics' distrust in the motives that underlie EU's competition policy.

Most recently, the EU's competition enforcement has targeted dominant companies, which, according to the Commission, have abused their dominant market position. For example, in 2018, the EU imposed a $5 billion fine on Google, accusing the company of abusive behavior involving its Android operating system.[40] This record-high fine ensued an earlier $2.3 billion fine imposed on Google in 2017 for manipulating its search results to favor its own shopping comparison service to the detriment of its rivals.[41] A third fine of $1.7 billion followed in 2019, after the Commission found that Google abused its search systems to force third-party sites to use its AdSense network.[42] Other recent US corporate giants targeted by the EU's competition enforcement include Qualcomm[43] and Apple,[44] which build on earlier adverse decisions against Intel[45] and Microsoft.[46] In these high-profile cases, the EU was critiqued for advancing a protectionist regulatory agenda.

Yet a closer look at these cases suggests that European companies are hardly the main beneficiaries of the Commission's competition actions, calling into question protectionism as the EU's motive. In most instances, the winners are other US companies, including the ones who had filed complaints with the Commission as affected competitors in the first place. For example, Microsoft was the company that initially lodged a complaint against Google.[47] Similarly, the main beneficiary of the Commission's enforcement action against Intel was another US company, AMD, whereas Intel and Apple stood to benefit most from the Commission's decision against Qualcomm. While these competition actions might also benefit some European companies seeking to enter the market in the future, the direct and current beneficiaries are unambiguously other US companies.

Regulatory disputes in several other areas also involve US interests on both sides, further bringing into question the allegation that EU regulations are geared at advancing EU interests at the expense of US companies. For example, the US music industry has leveraged EU regulations against (mostly US-based) internet platforms in the industry's fight over liability rules concerning pirated audio content uploaded online.[48] The EU's new Copyright Directive has presented them with an important opportunity to seek to impose greater responsibility for online platforms to detect and remove copyright-infringing content posted on their sites.[49] A number of traditional US telecommunications firms have similarly lobbied the EU regulators to subject the (mostly US-based) internet-based messaging companies such as WhatsApp, Skype, and FaceTime to the same regulatory requirements as telecommunication companies are subject to. Facebook and Microsoft—the owners of these messaging companies—have opposed any such EU regulatory requirements proposed by their US-based competitors.[50] Given these multiple examples where US companies leverage EU laws against other US companies, it becomes questionable to portray the EU as a biased regulator that is targeting US companies in an effort to offer protectionist gains for their European competitors.

Even if the EU regulation has not been explicitly motivated by a desire to protect EU firms, it is possible that the EU is not balancing the costs and benefits of intervention in the tech sector correctly, in part because there are few European tech giants. Specifically, the Commission may not fully internalize the benefits generated by the industry, given its narrow focus to maximize the welfare of European consumers. The Commission may thus generally over-value the benefits of intervention to consumers and undervalue the costs of its regulations on companies. While this would not amount to direct protec-tionism, it may still disadvantage foreign interests at the expense of European interests.

The Commission's enforcement record further suggests that it would be mis-leading to portray the EU as a regulator that primarily has US companies in its sight. While the EU's prominent decisions against major US companies receive much press coverage, many Commission competition decisions target EU com-panies with the same fervor. For example, in a 2016 acquisition involving the world's largest and second largest brewer, the Commission required the Belgian acquirer Anheuser-Busch InBev to sell practically the entire UK-based beer busi-ness in Europe as a condition for approving the AB InBev's over $100 billion acquisition of SABMiller.[51] In addition, the year after the Commission prohib-ited a merger between Deutsche Börse and the American NYSE Euronext,[52] it prohibited a similar acquisition attempt by a European acquirer: the proposed merger between the London Stock Exchange (LSE) and Deutsche Börse.[53] In cases where the EU has investigated companies for receiving illegal state aid, the EU has not only ruled against Apple, Amazon, and Starbucks, but also against the Italian company Fiat.[54] The Commission is also currently investigating poten-tially illegal state aid granted to Alitalia and Ryanair.[55] These examples suggest that the Commission is likely just as eager to go after European companies in its quest to protect the welfare of European consumers.

Protectionism is, nevertheless, often difficult to detect, let alone measure sys-tematically. Any protectionist motive would hardly be cited in legislative goals or as grounds for an enforcement decision against foreign firms. Several arguments, however, suggest that protectionism is unlikely to be the driver of EU competition enforcement. For example, consider the Commission's governance structure as it investigates mergers. The Commission's case teams that review proposed mergers consist of lawyers and economists from across the EU, only a few of which come from the same nation as the target of the merger. Any final decision rests on the vote of the entire College of Commissioners, consisting of a Commissioner from each member state—only one hailing from the target nation. Any decision to challenge a welfare-enhancing merger to protect a target nation's economic inter-ests would hence require the majority of the twenty-eight Commissioners and a multinational case team to forgo benefits to consumers across Europe to hand a protectionist victory to a particular nation's industry. Such a collective decision in support of one member state's protectionist agenda is hard to imagine under any circumstances.[56]

A recent study conducted at Columbia University examined protectionist motives underlying EU merger control using the most comprehensive data to date.[57] The study, which was discussed in chapter 4, examined the entire universe of over 5,000 mergers notified to the Commission between 1990 and 2014. After controlling for all key elements of a transaction, including the deal value and the industry in which the merger takes place, the analysis reveals no evidence that the Commission has systematically used its authority to protectionist ends. If anything, the results suggest that the Commission is less likely to challenge transactions involving foreign acquirers, and equally or more likely to challenge acquisition attempts by European companies. This indicates that the Commission is not seeking to build European champions or protect EU firms from being acquired by foreign companies through its merger review powers. The analysis in the merger control area therefore calls into question the common notion of European antitrust protectionism.

The question remains as to whether protectionism still seeps into other areas of EU competition policy, including investigations into the behavior of dominant companies or the Commission state aid decisions. Those areas are harder to test empirically as the entire universe of unilateral conduct cases or instances of state aid (including those that the Commission does not pursue) are not known. However, it is the very same institution within the Commission—the Directorate General for Competition—which engages in investigations across mergers, abuse of dominance, cartels, and state aid cases alike. If protectionism were indeed permeating into other areas of EU competition policy, there would need to be some reason why the Commission would rein in its protectionist tendencies in the merger area while engaging in biased enforcement elsewhere. However, it is unclear what that reason would be and, to date, there is little evidence to support a claim that such biased enforcement might exist in one area, but not in another.

Outside the domain of competition law, there is similarly sparse hard evidence suggesting that the EU would be motivated by its desire to tilt the playing field in favor of Europeans. For example, the Commission's food safety decisions seem to reflect genuine consumer preferences rather than industrial policy. The EU's decision to ban hormone-treated beef hardly conveyed a protectionist benefit to EU producers, as the restriction of imports of hormone-treated beef led to an increase in imports of non-hormone-treated beef from abroad.[58] In addition, several European companies, as producers of hormones themselves, lost sales following the ban. A similar interest group dynamic characterizes the EU's ban on GMOs. After the EU banned GMO-produced soy and corn, European companies captured no tangible benefit as European farmers produce hardly any soy or corn that could have captured the market following the ban. Instead of bolstering production in Europe, GMO-soy and GMO-corn imports were simply substituted with permissible soy and corn from non-GMO producers abroad.[59]

The EU's environmental and health regulations seem to reflect a similar pattern that is hard to reconcile with any protectionist agenda. For example, while the EU's emissions trading scheme (ETS) was initially designed to regulate foreign aviation emissions as well, the ETS continued to operate in Europe even after the EU lost the battle to fold foreign carriers into its ETS. In other words, the EU kept the regulation in force even when its ability to enforce it against foreign companies was compromised. Similarly, in assessing the safety of chemicals under the REACH regulation, the nationality of the exporter of a chemical is typically not even known to the scientific expert evaluating the safety of the chemical.[60] The file containing the information used in the safety evaluation similarly does not generally allow a precise determination as to whether the chemical in question is predominantly produced by domestic or foreign parties, making it difficult to incorporate industrial policy considerations into the assessment. Instead, the experts evaluate the dossiers and substances purely from the perspective of their safety.

In the absence of compelling evidence of any systematic protectionism guiding the EU's regulatory agenda, a more plausible explanation might be that the EU is simply a tough regulator—whether against foreign or domestic firms. The EU's tough regulatory stance is also consistent with the views of the EU's citizens who have demanded more protective regulations, as discussed in chapter 2, providing an alternative motive for the EU to act. European citizens and NGOs have been vocal in demanding more stringent consumer, environmental, and health protections. They have similarly become increasingly distrustful of the conduct of dominant companies and more concerned about the integrity of their personal data, leading to greater regulatory scrutiny of companies' data protection and competition practices.

Citizen activism also explains the EU's efforts to externalize the single market. Many environmental risks, such as climate change, are global in their nature, and cannot be resolved by the EU alone. Instead, they require corporations to adjust their practices globally and foreign governments to respond with domestic regulation. Examples include a ban on importation of timber that has been illegally harvested in foreign countries, which is critical to EU's efforts to tackle deforestation and preserve rain forests.[61] Similarly, many health problems, such as deadly viruses, are known to transmit easily around the globe, harming European citizens if not contained at their source. Such concerns have given impetus for the EU to pursue renewed action to contain health risks such as anti-microbial resistance, irrespective of their origin.[62] Many Europeans have also called for the EU to address concerns that emanate primarily from foreign practices, with lesser, if any, territorial connections to the EU. The disregard of animal welfare in foreign countries offends the Europeans' sense of morality just as much as the neglect of, or cruelty toward, animals in Europe. The 2014 WTO trade dispute between the EU and Canada regarding an EU ban on seal products to combat what the EU perceived as inhumane seal hunting by the Canadian Inuit is illustrative. The WTO Appellate Body upheld the ban as "necessary to protect public morals," relying on the EU's assertion that "moral concern regarding the protection of animals is a value of high importance in the European Union."[63]

If the accusations of the protectionism were well founded, they would provide a powerful basis for criticizing the Brussels Effect. However, the lack of clear evidence of protection, together with the alternative explanation that focuses on entrenched citizen preferences, suggest that the concerns of the EU's regulatory protectionism are likely misplaced or, at best, misinterpretations of a broader regulatory scheme.

Does the Brussels Effect Amount to Regulatory Imperialism?

The Brussels Effect can also be criticized for its tendency to undermine the regulatory sovereignty of other jurisdictions. In particular, many consumers in developing country markets likely view the trade-off between product safety and cost differently than Europeans but are denied these preferences when the Brussels Effect steers companies toward more stringent regulation also in those markets. These consumers lose, the argument goes, when they are forced to pay more for various products only because they are required to adopt, however derivatively, the choices made by European consumers in this regard.[64] A pertinent example relates to the cultivation of GMO crops to alleviate hunger and poverty in Sub-Saharan Africa.[65] The use of GMOs could potentially increase crop yields in countries that desperately need access to cheap agricultural products. Qualitative research further indicates that GMOs bring particular benefits to women and children who value the decrease in labor associated with insect resistant and herbicide-tolerant GMO crops.[66] However, developing countries, including those in Africa, are reluctant to adopt GMO crops for the fear of losing trade relationships with the EU.[67] African farmers—who are reliant on farming for income and subsistence—might therefore be forced to pay the price for European ideological luxuries.[68]

Some commentators go as far as to allege that the externalization of the EU's single market reflects "imperialistic" motives. According to these critics, the EU is seeking to exert political and economic domination over other countries.[69] This critique has been particularly pertinent in the context of the EU's efforts to export its norms in its immediate neighborhood through accession and other partnership treaties. The EU has significant leverage over countries that seek closer cooperation with the Union, or eventual membership within it.[70] According to Jan Zielonka, the EU is an empire that seeks to assert control over its neighbors, with the help of "economic and bureaucratic imperial instruments."[71] The only way for Europeans to maintain their current standards of life without putting European firms at a comparative economic disadvantage, Zielonka holds, is for the EU to export its laws and administrative practices to other countries, even when the European model of governance imposes significant costs on them.[72]

Raffaella Del Satro argues in the same vein, asserting that the EU's practice of exporting its practices to the periphery and reproducing its normative identity abroad is done to ingrain the EU's imperial order in the region.[73] The EU seeks to expand its imperial order by cultivating EU-friendly elites, which share the interests of the core. This, she notes, is "a classical aspect of imperial relations."[74] In this endeavor, the EU may be a quasi-benevolent exporter of norms, including democracy and human rights, to its neighboring states. However, at the same time, the EU is exerting a formidable form of power over those states.[75]

But even outside of its immediate sphere of influence, critics maintain that the EU is engaged in a novel form of imperialism. Instead of pursuing its goals through military and political instruments, the EU has been accused of using economic and bureaucratic tools to dominate over countries that are dependent on access to its vast domestic market.[76] This critique has been levied against different manifestations of the Brussels Effect. For example, in discussing the global reach of the GDPR, Mark Scott and Laurens Cerulus describe how "Europe wants to conquer the world all over again," yet this time without military means but rather through its "legal juggernaut aimed at imposing ever tougher privacy rules on governments and companies from San Francisco to Seoul."[77] They point out that in countries like South Africa, which base their domestic data protection legislation on the GDPR, this European legislative export risks "being viewed as yet another diktat handed down by former colonial powers in a form of 'data imperialism.' "[78] Lawrence A. Kogan, criticizing the EU's extensive regulatory reach in environmental and food safety matters, puts it bluntly:

> [T]he EU has embarked upon an adventure in environmental cultural imperialism. This is a global practice reminiscent of an earlier European colonial era. And the fact that Europe is using "soft power" to enforce it will hardly make it more palatable to people who will be unable to feed themselves as a result.[79]

The EU counters these criticisms by arguing that it is not engaged in coercion—it is not using force or threats to persuade any company or government to do anything—in particular, when the EU is exporting its rules through the market-driven Brussels Effect. Instead, the EU is simply asking others to play by its rules when operating in its home market, and enforcing the norms of the single market equally on domestic and foreign players.[80] If the self-interest of multinational corporations leads them to voluntarily adopt the EU regulation across their global operations, the EU can hardly be accused of "imperialism." The EU is not compromising US sovereignty if Twitter adopts the EU's definition of hate speech to govern its global operations or Dow Chemical conforms to the EU's REACH regulation globally. Of course, these companies may be conforming to the EU rule sometimes reluctantly, following "involuntary incentives" that stem from the interplay of stringent EU regulation and their market-based incentives to globalize the EU rule. At most, some may describe the EU's unilateralism as "soft coercion," but even that characterization is subject to dispute given the EU's passive role in how the markets transmit its rules.

In addition, the EU often defends its regulatory reach by portraying itself as a benign global hegemon,[81] whose values and policies are both normatively desirable and universally applicable.[82] This way, the EU is a champion of norms that serve global welfare. The EU emphasizes its quest to create a rule-based world and offer an alternative to the more controversial and self-serving worldview advanced by the United States. For example, former Commission president Jose Manual Barroso noted that "the EU's comparative advantage lies in its normative power or the power of its values [...]. In the post-crisis world, when people are looking for new ways to ensure their well-being, peace, prosperity, the European experience has a great deal to offer the world."[83] An American economist and Nobel laureate, Joseph Stiglitz similarly emphasizes the global appeal of European values, calling for Europe to project its " 'soft power'—the power and influence of ideas and example," which should become "one of the central pillars of [the] world." According to Stiglitz, "Europe's success is due in part to its promotion of a set of values that, while quintessentially European, are at the same time global."[84]

The EU's active role in the fight against climate change serves as an example of a regulation that is presumably driven by largely benevolent as opposed to imperialistic motives. Climate change is a global problem that requires a global response. The EU has a limited capacity to mitigate climate change alone if other states continue to emit greenhouse gases into the atmosphere. As a result, the EU has led numerous efforts to conclude a new and more potent global climate change treaty.[85] Yet the difficulties associated with international treaty negotiations gave the EU the imperative to act unilaterally and to establish an emissions trading regime with extraterritorial effect.[86] The EU defended its unilateral regulation by arguing that it was acting in the collective interest to provide a global public good: mitigation of climate change.[87]

By emphasizing the universal benefits of its regulatory agenda, the EU often succeeds in obscuring the de facto unilateralism that drives its implementation. Even if the EU were able to portray itself as a benevolent, normative power that is advancing universal values,[88] skeptics point out that the notion of a normative power has neocolonial undertones as the EU is, in the end, effectively exporting its "standards of civilization."[89] For example, even if the EU's efforts to generate global action against climate change were driven by its benevolent motives, the EU may be accused of acting as a regulatory imperialist that is imposing unjustified costs on other nations, in particular developing countries. Critics are quick to point out that it was developed countries, such as those in the EU, which caused the climate change problem in the first place, which may justify having developed countries bear most of the costs of mitigating the problem as opposed to imposing similar regulatory obligations on developing countries[90]—doing otherwise may not be "benevolent" and hence normatively justifiable.

Even if critics fall short of accusing the EU of a new form of "imperialism," many raise concerns that the Brussels Effect undermines democratic accountability. The EU's ability to override domestic political processes and institutions abroad can amount to a form of "policy laundering"[91]—whereby the origins of regulations become disguised for ordinary citizens in those countries—or to a form of "collusive delegation"[92]—whereby regulations become insulated from the interest groups that typically influence domestic regulatory policy. This type of sovereignty criticism is not limited to the EU's economically weaker trade partners. The EU can also undermine the sovereignty of jurisdictions such as the United States. For instance, the idea that unelected European civil servants have the ability to block global transactions by US companies can be disconcerting to those involved. The US government therefore has a reasonable claim that the Brussels Effect constrains its regulatory freedom, thereby undermining US sovereignty. The US' regulatory agenda becomes compromised whenever the EU rules prevail over those promulgated by the US government, undercutting the US' ability to make decisions regarding its economy. American citizens cannot hold European politicians accountable for decisions they disagree with. This countermajoritarian element inherent in the Brussels Effect undermines the ability of foreign governments to serve their citizens in accordance with their democratically established preferences.

Yet even if one accepts that the Brussels Effect interferes with foreign sovereigns' regulatory space, a plausible argument still exists that it does not undermine foreign democratic interests, including the US democracy. While the EU's regulatory process is not flawless nor perfectly democratic,[93] it is arguably less susceptible to corporate influence compared to the United States. The Brussels Effect may thus have the effect of balancing the alleged overrepresentation of business interests in American public life by empowering consumers.[94] For instance, after the US Supreme Court's ruling in *Citizens United*[95]—which opened the door for unlimited corporate spending to influence elections after ruling that political spending constitutes a form of free speech—many in the United States worry that the extent of business lobbying has distorted the democratic process. While corporate lobbying also increasingly takes place in Brussels, business interests are considerably less influential there, and often constrained by the influence exerted by civil society groups.[96] Thus, if regulations in countries outside the EU are too permissive, too weakly enforced, or otherwise suboptimal, the Brussels Effect might be a desirable means of overriding them.

It is also important to realize that foreign (non-EU) actors do not monolithically view the Brussels Effect as sovereignty infringing: quite the contrary. Often, foreign advocacy groups welcome the externalization of the EU single market in particular because it allows them to raise awareness of a policy problem at home. EU regulation can serve as an important benchmark in their efforts to influence domestic debates on the issue.[97] By referring to the EU regulation as an example that some governments are, indeed, regulating in certain policy domains, they can more effectively point to deficiencies in those policy domains in their own legal systems. For example, US consumers who prefer higher levels of consumer protection and a civil society that advocates environmental protection often seize on EU policies and use them in their attempts to forge change in the United States.[98]

The REACH regulation provides a useful illustration. US-based NGOs, including the Environmental Defense Fund, have used REACH to advocate for domestic reform. For example, a Swedish-based NGO "ChemSec," which advocates for safe chemicals, published a report "Using Reach Outside Europe," demonstrating how the European REACH regulation can be used as a model when advocating for regulatory reform in other countries.[99] Relying on this advocacy work, the Environmental Defense Fund published a report in the United States entitled "Across the Pond: Assessing REACH's First Big Impact on US Chemicals and Companies," in which it identified particularly harmful chemicals that were in active commerce in the United States, and called for a regulatory reform.[100] In 2008, another US advocacy organization, "MomsRising," joined various experts and other activists in calling on the Obama administration to address "the urgent chemical exposure crises in the US." The cofounder of MomsRising contrasted the US standards to those prevailing in Europe, noting—with outrage—that parents today need to look for labels that say the product meets European regulatory standards because they cannot trust the American standards.[101]

Similar arguments have been leveled at both the Food and Drug Administration (FDA) and American companies regarding the use of synthetic dyes in food.

In 2007, UK researchers found that consuming artificial colors increased hyperactivity in children.[102] This research led to an EU warning label requirement. In the United States, awareness of the study caused the Center for Science in the Public Interest (CSPI) to petition the FDA to ban several artificial food colors.[103] While the FDA's Food Advisory Committee considered the UK study in its March 2011 meeting, CSPI's efforts were ultimately unsuccessful.[104] Undeterred, CSPI criticized the decision across multiple platforms including radio, web, and print media, publicly shaming American companies for "marketing safer, natural dyes in Europe, but not the United States."[105] Michael Jacobson, executive director of CSPI, lobbied US companies directly, saying, "Hey McDonald's, hey Mars, you're not using dyes in Europe, but you are using them in exactly the same products in the United States."[106] As a result, and despite the FDA's inaction, consumer support for regulation of synthetic dye has prompted many American companies, including Kraft[107] and Mars,[108] to voluntarily remove artificial dyes from their local products.

Even beyond the organized activists, individual consumers in weakly regulated markets may welcome the EU's unilateralism, hailing the EU as the benevolent provider of global public goods in situations where their own governments or multilateral cooperation mechanisms fail to provide them.[109] For example, some American consumers are content if web operators cannot place cookies—software files that track consumers' internet searches to gather marketing information—on personal computers.[110] Others likely welcome the Brussels Effect in the environmental domain, in particular at the time when the US government is engaged in "crude cull of environmental rules" that many believe will leave the United States "dirtier and less safe."[111] Similarly, if multinational companies producing plastic toys use safer chemicals across global markets because of the Brussels Effect, children in developing markets benefit even if their own governments left chemicals unregulated. Obviously, many foreign consumers are passive beneficiaries of EU regulations. If the EU pursues global cartels, foreign consumers benefit, as they no longer pay the overcharge for products on their home markets. Yet few of them would know to attribute that gain to the efforts of the Commission's Directorate General for Competition that detected collusion and unraveled the cartel. Similarly, foreign families exposing their teenagers to less hateful discourse online—thanks to the global reach of EU regulations—are unlikely to make a connection between the EU and the regulatory benefit they enjoy.

In addition, some progressive states within the United States endorse the EU's leadership, voluntarily choosing to incorporate EU regulations into their own state laws, as discussed in various examples in Part II of this book.[112] For example, the success of the EU's RoHS directive, prohibiting the use of toxic heavy metals in electronics, prompted a broad coalition of local governments, environmental NGOs, and electronics producers to support the inclusion of RoHS in California's 2004 E-Waste bill. California's bill began with NGO advocacy at the national level for a federal bill similar to RoHS.[113] After efforts to pass a federal regulation failed, the California state government decided to take independent action, culminating in California's adoption of the California RoHS Law.[114]

Some developing country governments similarly welcome the Brussels Effect. The Brussels Effect presents these countries with an opportunity to outsource their regulatory pursuits to a more resourceful and experienced agency. Developing country competition agencies, for example, often free ride on the EU's competition investigations, benefiting from the global effects of the EU's decision to ban anticompetitive mergers or force firms to amend their conduct and products globally. Similarly, governments with the desire, but limited resources, to provide safer products for their consumers hence benefit from the EU imposing stringent standards that affect production patterns globally.

Thus, while the sovereignty criticism associated with the Brussels Effect is not without merit, it is unlikely to offer a fatal normative critique to the Brussels Effect. It is true—and, for many, justifiably troubling—that when the Brussels Effect shapes the global regulatory environment, the European citizens' preferences count more than those of non-European citizens. Yet that criticism seems more valid under the assumption that foreign regulators have the requisite capacity and the right incentives to act—in other words, when their regulatory capacity or the willingness to exercise that capacity is not compromised by the lack of resources or excessive corporate influence. When those conditions do not hold, the Brussels Effect seems more benevolent in normative terms. A related argument could be made regarding international cooperation on regulation. One could argue that instead of through the EU's unilateralism, regulatory globalization should take place through cooperative, consensus-based mechanisms in the context of international organizations. However, as discussed in chapter 3, those treaty-based mechanisms have often failed in effectiveness, making the Brussels Effect a next-best alternative. This way, the theory of "the second best" may offer the best defense for the Brussels Effect:[115] ideally, all governments would regulate their own economies and coordinate, as needed, internationally. However, when these assumptions do not hold, the Brussels Effect becomes a less objectionable, and more necessary—second best—alternative.

Foreign Attempts to Constrain the Brussels Effect

As the earlier discussion suggests, the Brussels Effect produces both costs and benefits. While many of the costs that the Brussels Effect imposes are offset by its benefits, because those costs and benefits are distributed in uneven ways, it is certain the Brussels Effect will continue to be a target for criticism. However, for those who view the Brussels Effect as detrimental to their welfare, the opportunities for challenging EU regulations can be limited. This is particularly the case for foreign corporations and governments that cannot hold EU leaders accountable in democratic elections.

Foreign Firms' Response to the Brussels Effect

Given the global reach of EU regulations, foreign stakeholders have the incentive to invest considerable resources in trying to influence regulatory outcomes in the EU.[116] As a result, lobbying activity is particularly salient in Brussels. This is because the benefits available from the possible regulatory capture of the Commission or another EU institution are expected to exceed the benefits of successfully influencing any other regulatory agency with less global clout.

Therefore, foreign firms invest heavily in the EU regulatory process through lobbying, with the Commission and the Parliament as their primary targets. It is difficult to quantify the extent of lobbying taking place historically in the EU given that the EU's transparency register was only established in 2011.[117] But since 2011, a considerable number of entities—nearly 12,000 by March 2019—have registered, comprising corporations and civil society representatives alike.[118] Out of those registrations, over 1,000 have a head office outside the EU, most commonly in Switzerland and the United States.[119] American technology companies in particular are increasing their lobbying presence in the EU: Google and Microsoft's EU lobbying budget are among the five highest in the EU.[120] In addition, the Information Technology Industry Council—a US-based lobbying group representing technology companies such as Apple, Facebook, and Google—is increasing its staff in Brussels because they recognize that the EU is "driving and directing policy."

EU institutions welcome lobbying as part of their commitment to consulting stakeholders about the effect of regulations on them.[121] Rather than unduly influencing the regulatory process, the EU views this type of stakeholder engagement as providing valuable information and increasing the legitimacy of EU policy making.[122] Yet critics are quick to remind that exposure to corporate lobbying can lead to agency capture and result in welfare-reducing outcomes.[123] Foreign critics in particular emphasize how weaker lobbying regulations in Brussels—both regarding attorney-client privilege and lax ethical rules permitting government officials to utilize their influence immediately upon leaving office—allow international lobbying firms to sidestep more stringent foreign laws. This favorable environment for lobbyists attracts international lobbying firms and undercuts transparency in the EU regulatory process.[124]

The most lobbied pieces of EU legislation are REACH and the GDPR—two regulations with far-reaching, global regulatory consequences. Some commentators have referred to REACH as having "set in motion one of the most colossal lobbying campaigns in the history of EU law-making."[125] The consultations that the Commission held on REACH before the regulation was enacted in 2006 garnered over 6,300 contributions by industry and civil society alike.[126] Foreign parties were distinctly active in their efforts to influence REACH, including most notably the US corporations and government. As expected, US chemical manufacturers were actively involved. However, also the US civil society weighed in, submitting a proposal in favor of REACH, backed by sixty US organizations and over ten thousand citizens.[127] Interestingly, according to a report by California Congressman Henry A. Waxman, the official US government's position on REACH was closely coordinated with US corporations, though without any effort to also include the position advocated by US civil society interest groups.[128]

The global reach of EU regulations via the Brussels Effect in certain policy domains also encourages international business groups to coordinate their EU lobbying positions. For example, the US publishing and the music industries both cooperated with their European counterparts in seeking to impose greater obligations on the online platforms as part of EU's copyright reform.[129] Similarly, 1,160 health-care companies and hospitals across fifty-five countries have joined Global Green and Healthy Hospitals (GGHH) to coordinate global advocacy and innovative health-care initiatives.[130] The action items of the group include the replacement of all products including Substances of Very High Concern, as defined by the EU's REACH directive.[131] What further facilitates the formation of transnational interest groups and lobbying coalitions is the membership strategy of EU-based business associations, which welcome third-country actors as affiliated members.[132] For example, The European Chemical Industry Council (ECIC), a critical player in the legislative process resulting in REACH, is open to non-EU actors, representing several companies with headquarters outside the EU. Digital Europe—an industry association representing over thirty-five thousand technology companies around the world, with members ranging from Amazon to Sony and from Siemens to Cisco—similarly welcomes EU and non-EU members alike.[133] Digital Europe provided a coordinated voice for the IT industry in the preparation for the GDPR, which included a joint submission as part the Commission consultation.[134] These coordinated lobbying efforts have enhanced the foreign companies' voice—and, at times, their influence—in the EU's regulatory process.

Despite their concerted efforts, foreign companies are rarely able to mitigate the Brussels Effect extensively through lobbying. Many EU regulations emerge from the EU's regulatory process largely unscratched despite a fierce corporate opposition. And even when foreign companies manage to win some concessions or water down certain aspects of a regulation they oppose, their influence may be offset by that of other interest groups. Indeed, in a recent empirical study, Andreas Dür and his coauthors show that business interests are no more influential than other interests in shaping EU regulations.[135] They may be able to delay the enactment of regulations but not prevent their adoption given the strong influence of citizen groups and other non-business actors in the EU's legislative process.[136]

This relative lack of success through lobbying, at times, sends foreign firms to search for alternative strategies. As a result, "if you cannot beat them, join them" guides the response of many foreign firms after a failed attempt to stop Brussels from regulating. The de facto Brussels Effect may lead foreign firms to turn to their home governments to lobby for EU-equivalent regulation at home—akin to what Apple and Facebook recently did by urging the US federal government to adopt GDPR-style federal privacy law.[137] Given that these firms already have to bear the costs of complying with EU rules, they now have the incentive to advocate further externalization of the single market to their home markets: a strategy that allows them to level the playing field with respect to their domestic, non-export-oriented competitors which, absent domestic regulation, remain unaffected by EU regulations. Their advocacy at times converts the de facto Brussels Effect to the de jure Brussels Effect, as foreign governments enact legislation similar to the EU's—a dynamic discussed in earlier chapters.[138]

Another strategy available for foreign firms is to turn the EU's regulatory prowess to their advantage by leveraging those stringent regulations against their own competitors. As noted earlier in this chapter and discussed in chapter 3, the EU has increasingly become a "forum of choice" for litigation by foreign companies against other foreign companies. The Commission often provides a hospitable forum for US producers to challenge their competitors' practices. For example, the REACH regulation allows interested parties to collaborate with the European Chemicals Agency (ECHA) to restrict the use of certain chemicals. This allows any producer of chemicals, including a US company, to seek denial of its competitors' (including other US companies') substances in the EU.[139] In the competition law realm, US corporations have found the EU to offer a particularly valuable legal battleground whenever they seek to halt practices of their (often domestic) competitors, as discussed earlier in this chapter and in chapter 4. These examples illustrate how some foreign firms are occasionally able to turn the Brussels Effect to their advantage—even if only by shifting the harmful effects of EU regulations to their competitors.

These examples show that foreign companies adversely affected by the Brussels Effect have limited strategies at their disposal to rein in the EU's regulatory power over them. These companies can—and frequently do—engage in extensive lobbying of the EU institutions, and occasionally succeed on delaying or weakening some aspect of a regulation they oppose. They may also urge their own governments to try and convince the EU to amend or abandon its regulations, as will be discussed next. Yet, on many occasions these companies find their direct lobbying attempts frustrating and their governments unable to reverse the EU's regulatory agenda. This leaves these companies with few options but to adjust their global operations to EU regulations—however reluctantly. After any such adjustment, these companies' interest calculus often changes, and they can even become advocates of EU regulation as a way to further harmonize the global regulatory environment in which they and their competitors operate.

Foreign Governments' Response to the Brussels Effect

Foreign companies are not the only ones who try to push back against the Brussels Effect. Foreign governments, including the United States, are also often critical of the Brussels Effect—whether because they view EU regulations as costly, protectionist, or sovereignty infringing. Yet the US government, like any other foreign government, has few ways to rein in the EU's regulatory reach: the EU is regulating its own market, which it has the sovereign right to do. If US firms voluntarily change their global practices due to the de facto Brussels Effect, the US government can find it difficult to attribute blame to the EU for the impact on the US market that arises as a by-product of those decisions. As a result, the US government is often left to the role of a spectator, unable to influence the market forces that push the companies and governments toward EU regulations. This often leaves it resentful about the economic and political costs it faces as the Brussels Effect reaches the US shores.

As discussed earlier, the primary concern of the US government is that EU regulations impose adjustment costs on US corporations. Another related concern is that US consumers end up paying more for goods when producers are forced to accommodate concerns that US consumers do not necessarily share. Second, the US government often views EU regulations as protectionist and hence unfair. Third, the US also resents its loss of sovereignty as the EU regulation overrides those of its own. These interests have often led the US government to express its opposition to EU policies. For example, prompted by the American chemicals industry, the US government engaged in extensive efforts to curtail the REACH regulation.[140] The US government's reaction to the EU's interventionist competition laws has at times been equally hostile.[141] This was also true for the EU's initial plan to subject foreign airlines to its ETS, which was vehemently opposed by US airlines and the US government, as well as other foreign governments.[142] Finally, the GDPR triggered fierce opposition in the United States, resulting in unprecedented lobbying activity by US companies and the government alike. However, at times it is difficult for the US government to adopt a coherent government position for or against any given EU regulation. Anthony Gardner, the former US ambassador to the EU, remarked that he did not lobby the Commission in competition disputes, as there were typically US companies on both sides of the dispute, which made it difficult to distill an unambiguous US interest in any given case.[143]

Even in instances where the United States has a uniform lobbying interests and would actively want to resist the Brussels Effect, there is very little it can do to stop the EU from regulating its domestic market. In this sense, the Brussels Effect differs starkly from the California Effect. California cannot promulgate regulations that are inconsistent with US federal laws absent an explicit waiver from the federal government.[144] Furthermore, each new administration inherits the ability to reinterpret such waivers, as we are witnessing now that the Trump administration is challenging California's Clean Air Act waiver that has allowed California to maintain more stringent emission standards.[145] Federal preemption thus imposes a serious limitation on the scope of the California Effect; the effect is particularly circumscribed when the administration disagrees with California's regulatory choices and uses preemption to limit the state's regulatory freedom.[146] There is nothing akin to federal preemption that similarly constrains the EU's regulatory powers.

When US producers are forced to either comply with higher standards or be shut out of the EU market, the US government has four potential ways to respond: 1) try to compel the EU to change its rules by means of, for example: diplomacy, suing the EU in the WTO, or offering the EU some rewards or threatening the EU with sanctions; 2) seek a cooperative solution, such as by pursuing an international standard that reflects some combination of US and EU preferences; 3) converge to the EU standard by replicating the EU regulation domestically (the de jure Brussels Effect); or, finally, (4) do nothing and witness its businesses conform to the EU regulations through the de facto Brussels Effect.[147]

The most controversial strategy for the United States, or any other foreign government, would be to threaten the EU with sanctions. However, the prospect of a trade war is often too costly for the countries themselves to pursue as a strategy—even in the present political climate where trade conflicts are rapidly escalating. In many instances, trade sanctions would also be inconsistent with the countries' obligations under the WTO. In past US-EU competition enforcement conflicts, for instance, the United States threatened the EU with trade sanctions unless the EU ceased its opposition to the *Boeing/McDonnell Douglas* merger.[148]

Yet, notwithstanding the heightened rhetoric of retaliation, the competition controversies led the US government to concede that "[w]e have no power to change EU law."[149]

Although the EU regulations generally withstand threats of retaliation, there have been some limited instances, where a threat of sanctions has caused the EU to retreat, or at least modify its regulatory stance. For example, the EU's decision to include foreign airlines into its ETS provoked threats that foreign carriers may forgo European Airbus planes in favor of the competing US-based Boeing planes.[150] This particular threat led the EU to temporarily halt the implementation of the Aviation Directive vis-à-vis foreign carriers.[151] In this instance, the threat was effective given the extent of commercial interests at stake, the brazenly unilateralist and controversial nature of the EU's measure, and the sheer number of EU trade partners that protested the Directive. However, except in rare cases like this one, even threats of retaliation from powerful governments such as the United States are ineffective in compelling the EU to reverse its regulatory policies.[152]

Under some circumstances, international institutions could provide a venue for foreign governments to challenge the EU regulations. The WTO prevents countries from restricting imports from countries with less-stringent regulations unless the importing country can, for example, provide a scientific justification for the restriction, or if the restriction is necessary to protect public health or related to conservation of the environment.[153] Much of WTO litigation centers on parties' disagreement as to whether domestic regulations reflect a legitimate exercise of domestic regulatory authority or whether they instead advance merely protectionist goals.

The United States did resort to the WTO in challenging the EU's prohibition on hormone-treated beef in 1996 and GMO food in 2003, eventually winning its core claims in both trade disputes.[154] The United States claimed that the EU's alleged pursuit of food safety and concern for the health of its consumers in reality reflected its desire to protect its farmers from foreign competition.[155] The EU defended its measures on grounds of genuine consumer preferences, as Europeans harbor deep skepticism of GMOs and growth-promoting hormones,[156] and argued that scientific studies supported its health concerns.[157] The WTO ruled for the United States, requiring the EU to lift its import ban of hormone-treated beef and similarly approve GMO products without undue delay.[158] Most recently, the United States has challenged the EU's import ban of US poultry that is rinsed in chlorine—a process that, according to the United States, makes poultry safe for consumption.[159] These challenges suggest that the WTO might impose some limits on the EU's regulatory pursuits in instances where those regulations are protectionist or when they are not backed by sufficient scientific evidence.

However, turning to the WTO does not ultimately offer a strong tool to combat the impact of the Brussels Effect. Despite the occasional victories like the ones noted for the United States, the WTO offers, at best, imperfect remedies for foreign jurisdictions frustrated by the reach of EU regulations. The WTO dispute settlement mechanism is characterized by weaknesses such as non-retroactive damages.[160] In addition, the WTO system cannot compel a member state to lift restrictive measures. It can merely authorize sanctions against a noncompliant member state.[161]For instance, the EU has maintained its import ban on hormone-treated beef, preferring to endure US retaliation.[162] The EU has also repeatedly allowed the deadline for implementing the GMO ruling to lapse, while the United States has suspended its retaliatory measures in anticipation of a settlement or the EU's future compliance.[163] The difficulties that a leading world economy like the United States has faced in obtaining the EU's compliance suggest that the EU's weaker trading partners will find even less relief for their grievances by going to the WTO. Authorizing a small developing country—which typically has few tools for retaliation at its disposal—to punish its powerful trading partner thus hardly guarantees that this right will be used. Thus, the WTO's system of remedies, including the authorized retaliation, rarely offers an avenue for foreign governments to effectively constrain the EU.

The WTO's ability to constrain the Brussels Effect is further limited by its restricted mandate. The WTO bans discrimination between importers and domestic producers.[164] To successfully challenge EU regulations before the WTO, foreign governments would need to show that EU regulations are discriminatory. Yet many of the EU regulations, while perhaps costly to foreign producers, are not discriminatory in their nature: EU companies are subject to the same rules. If the EU regulations have no disparate impact on foreign producers, allegations of discrimination are difficult to maintain, and the WTO can do little to restrain them. Further, many areas—such as competition and privacy—do not fall within the purview of the WTO.[165] There have been several attempts to include competition law, among other new issue areas, under the WTO framework, but all those attempts have failed.[166] Expanding the scope of the WTO to new issue areas is even more unlikely today, as the consensus among over 160 member countries is increasingly beyond reach. The WTO therefore offers, at best, a limited avenue for foreign governments to mitigate the costs they incur because of the Brussels Effect.

Indeed, the WTO does not only fail to adequately constrain the Brussels Effect; at times, it may even help to facilitate it. Exported EU regulations, globalized through the Brussels Effect, can be viewed as contributing to the WTO's underlying goal of facilitating international trade by harmonizing standards.[167] The WTO rules also limit the ability of the EU's trade partners to respond to the EU's regulatory pursuits with unilateral retaliation.[168] Had the United States, for instance, imposed trade sanctions on the EU when faced with the EU's data transfer ban, it would have violated the WTO rules and subjected itself to a WTO complaint by the EU. In this sense, the WTO can also provide a shield for, and not only a limitation to, the Brussels Effect.[169]

In theory, the EU's increasing regulatory clout and its impact on US businesses may, or at least should, lead the United States to support greater market oversight by international institutions. Though often skeptical of international institutions' ability to regulate the markets, an enhanced understanding of the Brussels Effect should awaken the United States to the benefits of international cooperation. Such cooperation would offer the United States an opportunity to play a shared, rather than obsolete, role in the regulation of global commerce in many industries. This resembles the idea of "preemptive federalism," whereby the United States could seek international regulation as a means to preempt the Brussels Effect. Having some influence over regulatory standards would be better than ceding influence to the EU altogether.[170] The regulation of aviation emissions provides an illustrating example. Faced with the EU's unilateralism in the ETS, the United States was among the countries that supported the conclusion of an international agreement—the Carbon Offsetting and Reduction Scheme for International Aviation (CORSIA)[171]—to address the issue in a multilateral setting, which ultimately gave the United States considerably more say over how its aviation industry is regulated.

Given that international regulatory cooperation should typically serve US interests more than any unilateral regulatory measure by the EU, it is surprising that the United States has deliberately turned its back to international trade deals, including the Transatlantic Trade and Investment Partnership (TTIP).[172] Existing transatlantic disagreements about regulatory standards were always the greatest stumbling block for the negotiations.[173] At the same time, the possibility to overcome those disagreements presented the greatest opportunity for economic gains from the TTIP for both parties. The United States should have welcomed the chance to address divergent regulations jointly with the EU, in particular given the alternative of the EU setting those standards alone. The EU may also have been willing to forgo unilateralism in certain regulatory contexts in favor of a bilateral deal. The threat of the Brussels Effect certainly would have enhanced the EU's bargaining power in any such negotiations, allowing it to extract valuable gains from the United States in return for modifying its stance on some areas of regulatory policy. Regardless, it seems evident that making no bargain with the EU has undermined US interests in establishing advantageous global standards, further ceding ground to the EU in this regard.

Even a powerful country such as the United States typically gains nothing from defending its regulatory standard, even if that country's standard is viewed by many as being a more desirable one than the EU's. As a less-stringent regulator, the US position simply becomes irrelevant in the fields where the de facto Brussels Effect takes place.[174] Yet still, the United States is unlikely to adopt an EU standard domestically as a regular course of action. Regulatory change always entails costs. Firms need to reorganize their production processes or practices in order to comply with new and different standards.[175] Governments incur costs relating to legislating and retraining its regulators.[176] And most importantly, the United States must forgo the efficiencies that its preferred regulation would generate. When holding onto its own domestic standards, the United States can at least ensure that its standard governs the activity that is purely domestic in nature. And given how large the US market is, this often provides an adequate incentive to retain its preferred regulation domestically, absent overwhelming lobbying by domestic export-oriented industries to the contrary.

However, in some cases, even initially reluctant governments come to embrace EU regulations with time and adopt domestic rules that resemble those of the EU. Once they fail to prevent the EU from furthering its regulatory agenda, the domestic political economy may change as well, as explained earlier in the context of discussing the de jure Brussels Effect across the many products and services discussed herein. These governments may now face lobbying from their own export-oriented companies to follow the EU's lead, offering domestic political gains from emulating EU regulations. Sometimes EU rules also give them no choice but to adapt. For example, in the data protection domain, governments have the incentive to emulate EU rules to obtain adequacy decisions and hence a reassurance that data can flow freely between countries. The governments' economic interests, dictated by the needs of their companies, may thus push them toward EU rules—even if reluctantly.

THE BRUSSELS EFFECT produces both costs and benefits, and there is no unambiguous answer to the question of whether it is, overall, desirable. It imposes economic costs on individual consumers in the EU and abroad by, at times, raising prices and preventing access to products and services that some segment of the population would value. It may also impose political costs by constraining the regulatory space of foreign governments and hence their ability to respond to the demands of their citizens to whom they are politically accountable. Finally, the Brussels Effect may, at times, impose distributional costs by transferring wealth from new entrants to powerful incumbents that are in a better position to absorb the costs of burdensome regulations.

Acknowledging these various costs associated with the Brussels Effect might lead to renewed efforts to seek to mitigate them—some of those efforts might indeed already be underway. For example, an effective implementation of the Commission's "Better Regulation Agenda" has the potential to reduce some of the regulatory burdens that remain a critics' key concern.[177] In addition, the greater incorporation of foreign stakeholders' views as part of the impact assessment process—the EU's variant of the US government agencies' cost-benefit analysis—could mitigate some of the criticism associated with regulatory imperialism.[178] Enhanced efforts to pursue international regulatory cooperation through consensus-based mechanisms may similarly alleviate some of the political costs associated with unilateralism.[179] Finally, a realization that the Brussels Effect has the unintended consequence of empowering the powerful incumbents might lead the EU to increasingly differentiate the regulatory burdens across the companies' ability to comply—a policy stance that would be highly consistent with the EU's existing regulatory philosophy.[180]

At the same time, regardless of whether these various costs associated with the Brussels Effect can or will be mitigated, it is important to acknowledge that the Brussels Effect also generates many benefits that are felt both in the EU and abroad. Often those benefits are diffused across a large consumer base that experiences a cleaner environment and enhanced product safety, an enhanced control over their personal data, and less exposure to hateful discourse online, to name a few. Of course, everyone does not share the same preferences and would not trust the government—even that of their own, let alone a foreign government—to make the choices for them in this regard. In the end, whether the Brussels Effect is positive or negative depends on individual preferences that vary across policy areas, individuals' socioeconomic and cultural backgrounds, values, and ideologies. However, the discussion in this chapter supports a conclusion that, on balance, the Brussels Effect is more likely to generate net benefits that are valuable—even if not uniformly in all instances and for all the people.

However, the ultimate answer to the question of the desirability of the Brussels Effect might be that it may not even matter, given that little can be done to counter it, as the many examples discussed in this chapter have shown. Regardless of whether they like it or not, individuals, corporations and governments—particularly foreign ones—can do little to rein in the Brussels Effect as long as the fundamental criteria for its emergence exist. Whether the Brussels Effect should be viewed positively or negatively is hence secondary to the less disputed conclusion that the Brussels Effect simply exists and matters in today's global political economy—it is both penetrating and pervasive across a number of policy areas, and far more impactful than commonly appreciated. Instead, the more important question may therefore be whether the Brussels Effect will persist and how it might evolve going forward. This is precisely the question examined in the next chapter.

9

The Future of the Brussels Effect

THIS BOOK HAS described the origin and conditions that have led to the Brussels Effect, and shown how these conditions have established the EU as a global regulatory hegemon with extraordinary regulatory influence over the rest of the world. Given the significant impact that the Brussels Effect has on the global marketplace, one remaining and important question is whether the Brussels Effect will last, or whether it will be likely to change or diminish as the underlying conditions evolve over time.

Several external and internal challenges to the EU's regulatory hegemony loom on the horizon. Among the external challenges to the Brussels Effect include the continuing rise of China and other emerging powers, which will gradually diminish the relative size of the EU market, thus likely challenging the fundamental precondition for the de facto Brussels Effect. At the same time, the growing backlash to globalization and the accompanying decline in international cooperation has the potential to contribute toward the erosion of the de jure Brussels Effect. With that, the EU risks losing its ability to export regulations through multilateral treaties and institutions, further diminishing the EU's role as the global regulatory hegemon. Further, innovative new technologies, such as additive manufacturing, may revolutionize industrial processes, allowing for greater customization and localization of production. Should this happen, fewer industries would be characterized by the non-divisibility of production that is critical to the de facto Brussels Effect.

In parallel with these external developments, a set of internal challenges risk undermining the Brussels Effect from within. Among them is the impending departure of the United Kingdom from the EU—known as Brexit—which threatens to reduce the EU's regulatory influence. With the United Kingdom leaving, both the EU's market size and its regulatory capacity will diminish, weakening the first two conditions sustaining the de facto Brussels Effect. Internal challenges are compounded by the EU's growing political struggles with the rise

The Brussels Effect. Anu Bradford, Oxford University Press (2020). © Oxford University Press.
DOI: 10.1093/oso/9780190088583.001.0001

of anti-EU parties, conceivably compromising the EU's ability to engage in effective rule-making if and when any anti-EU sentiment grows. This would potentially weaken two other critical conditions driving the Brussels Effect—namely the EU's regulatory capacity as well as its preference for stringent regulations.

This final chapter looks at these possible trajectories and assesses the ability of these external and internal challenges to compromise any of the five conditions—*market size, regulatory capacity, stringent standards, inelastic targets,* and *non-divisibility*—sustaining the Brussels Effect. While the potential of these developments to undermine the Brussels Effect going forward is certainly there, there are also a number of reasons to conclude that the Brussels Effect will be, perhaps surprisingly, resilient in the face of these developments, despite the gravity of the threat they seem to pose.

External Challenges

Various external challenges have the potential to undermine the de facto and de jure Brussels Effect in the near future. In particular, the relative decline of the EU's market size, the rising antiglobalization sentiment, and the emergence of new technologies may each undercut the influence the EU exercises through the Brussels Effect. These developments will be discussed in turn.

Could the Beijing Effect Eventually Replace the Brussels Effect?

Chapter 8 explained how foreign governments today have a limited ability to constrain the Brussels Effect. However, this may be changing. The rise of new powers will, over time, increase the availability of alternative export markets, providing multinational companies with an option to shift more trade away from the EU. China in particular may increasingly be in a position to offer an alternate destination for various goods if European standards make it too costly for businesses to trade there. This development could constrain the EU's ability to leverage its market power and write regulations for global markets as one critical condition for the emergence of the Brussels Effect—market size—would have diminished in significance. It also raises the question whether, one day, the "Beijing Effect" might even replace the Brussels Effect.

While the EU maintains a large role in the world economy, its relative market size will inevitably wane as long as developing nations in Asia and elsewhere continue to grow at relatively higher rates. Today, corporations are rarely able to carve out the EU as a market for their products and services and divert trade elsewhere. Even in the near future, it is difficult to imagine that genuinely multinational companies—be it Coca-Cola, Facebook, or General Electric—would choose to forgo trade in Europe in order to avoid the need to comply with EU regulations. But as demand in places like China grows, businesses' dependence on their access to the EU market will inevitably diminish.[1]

Even the most optimistic economic forecasts acknowledge that the EU's relative share of the global GDP will significantly decline in the coming decades. As the EU's economic might is gradually waning, economic power is increasingly shifting to fast-growing Asia. The most significant economic growth will occur in highly populated developing nations, such as China and India, which have the ability to leverage their supply of lower-cost human capital. In the aftermath of the financial crises, the EU's GDP growth has been slow. In the period from 2010–2018, the EU's growth substantially trailed behind that of the United States.[2] When compared to large developing countries such as China, the difference in growth rates becomes even more apparent.[3] For example, while in 2017 the EU's economy grew by 2.4%, China's economy grew by 6.9%.

These trends will likely continue, gradually undermining the EU's global market position. For example, according to a 2010 estimate by a leading French research institute—The Centre d'Études Prospectives et d'Informations Internationales (CEPII)—the EU's share of the global nominal GDP will dwindle down from 30% in 2008 to 24% by 2025, and to 16% by 2050.[4] However, even those numbers may be too optimistic. According to the IMF, the EU's share of the global nominal GDP had already declined to 21.3% as of 2017,[5] surpassing CEPII's projection for 2025 by a substantial margin. The EU's relative economic decline is even more evident when measured in terms of PPP-adjusted GDP. Private accountancy firm PwC predicts that the EU's share of global PPP-adjusted GDP will fall to 9% by 2050, compared to China's 20% and India's 15%.[6] According to the CEPII projection, "the Chinese and Indian economies could grow 13-fold between 2008 and 2050 at constant relative prices. Over the same period, the US economy would double and Europe's economy would inflate by 60%."[7] Regardless of the measure used—nominal or PPP-adjusted GDP—or the particular institution projecting growth forecasts, it is clear that the EU will experience a substantial reduction in its market power.

EU institutions are well aware of the relative decline of Europe's economic power in the coming decades. The European Commission's "Global Europe 2050" report contemplates three potential futures for Europe: a Europe under threat, a Europe where "nobody cares," and a resurgent Europe experiencing a renaissance. The most optimistic "European renaissance" scenario envisions an EU that continues to enlarge and become stronger, consolidating its political, fiscal, and military integration.[8] Even under this positive scenario, the EU's share of the global GDP is projected to be almost halved between now and 2050. The European Parliament's predictions for 2030 portray a similar picture, projecting that the EU's market power will experience a steady decline, leaving it with a 17–18% share of global nominal GDP by 2030.[9]

Given that the possession of large relative market size is critical to exercising unilateral regulatory influence, most would agree that the EU's relative economic decline has the potential to significantly undermine the Brussels Effect. As opportunities to trade outside the EU grow, forgoing the EU market and diverting trade elsewhere may become more viable. This will, inevitably, constrain the EU's ability to set global standards. New economic powers can therefore curtail the EU's rule-setting power simply by growing, thereby offering an alternative destination for goods and services. However, while these countries may be able to rein in the Brussels Effect, it does not necessarily follow that they will become sources of global standards themselves.

There is some evidence that China has increased its willingness to regulate over the past two decades. During this time, there has been a sharp increase in the level of regulations in competition law, consumer protection, environmental protection, financial regulations, and food safety. In many of these areas, new comprehensive laws have been passed in the last decade, including the Anti-Monopoly Law (2007),[10] a revised food safety law (2015),[11] a comprehensive cybersecurity law (2016),[12] and new rules surrounding environmental disclosure (2014).[13] Academics have disagreed over the cause for such an increase in regulatory activity, with some pointing out that much of the increase in regulations has coincided with China's accession to the WTO.[14] Others have emphasized several domestic scandals that have prompted China to regulate, explaining for instance the emergence of stringent food safety standards. Greater citizen access to information has also been cited as a motivation for the increase in China's willingness to promulgate new regulations.[15] Some further question whether the laws are applied equally to foreign and Chinese enterprises,[16] raising questions of industrial policy and trade protectionism as a motive driving regulatory reforms.

Nevertheless, even though China will occupy a higher share of the global GDP in the coming decades and has moved to regulate some policy areas, the country is unlikely to replace the EU as a source of global standards anytime soon. China's regulatory capacity and the willingness to elevate the protection of consumers and the environment over the pursuit of economic growth are not increasing at the same rate as its GDP. While China has engaged in recent efforts to build regulatory capacity in areas such as competition law, it has by no means overtaken the European Commission as the most ardent guardian of competitive markets. Chinese institutions have a long way to go before they can generate and enforce the type of regulatory policies that the EU pursues. Also, in most policies outside competition law, the Chinese government's enforcement mechanisms for its regulatory measures remain underdeveloped.

In addition, while China may soon be the largest consumer market, GDP per capita—which is a better prediction of a country's regulatory propensity than is overall GDP[17]—suggests that EU member states continue to fare much better against the rising economic might of China. According to an HSBC report, in 2050, China's income per capita (in year 2000 USD) will be $17,372. This will remain well short of the figure for many, if not all, EU member states, including Germany ($52,683), France ($40,643), and Spain ($38,111).[18] Affluence and social regulation are often correlated, suggesting that domestic demand for high levels of regulation is likely to be weak in China for some time to come.[19] As long as Chinese consumers are not as wealthy on a per capita basis, they are likely to have a lower appetite for high levels of regulation that might compromise growth and economic development. This, however, is likely to change as China continues to grow and individual Chinese citizens become wealthier. Yet overall GDP growth in China will also inevitably continue to slow down, as it has done in the past several years. This may dampen China's enthusiasm for burdensome regulation. As a manifestation of this, Chinese authorities have already loosened their pollution regulations aimed at improving air quality in 2018 in an effort to reverse the economic slowdown.[20]

Pressures to deregulate are likely to build even more if China falls short of the lofty projections of China's future economic success. Capital Economics, an independent research firm, argues that China's past high-paced economic growth cannot be sustained.[21] Several fundamentals underlying the Chinese economy contribute toward the prediction that China's economic outperformance will come to an end.[22] These include excessive debt accumulation and an unsustainably high investment rate. These factors, together with the aging population, the increasingly autocratic political system, and hostility toward reforms, may pave the way for a sharp deceleration. Should that happen, few would expect China's appetite for introducing new regulations to outpace that of the EU if those regulations may further dampen economic growth in China.

Yet even if the robust Chinese economic growth continues, the "Beijing Effect" is unlikely to replace the Brussels Effect as long as Chinese growth relies primarily on exports. The key to the EU's regulatory influence is the dependence of foreign firms on access to the EU market and hence the importance of the EU as an import destination. To date, exports have fueled China's growth, leading to a significant trade surplus—exceeding $500 billion in 2016.[23] For this reason, relatively fewer foreign companies have had to tailor their products to Chinese standards, instead worrying whether Chinese imports meet their domestic standards. Of course, over time, China's importance as a large consumer market will also grow. But until a higher GDP per capita leads to the emergence of a mass-consumer market in China, the country is unlikely to become a significant source of global standards.

Finally, even if China were to (1) continue on a path of rapid economic growth; (2) balance its trade and become the most significant import destination; (3) build the necessary regulatory capacity to engage in notable regulatory rule-making; and (4) achieve the level of consumer wealth that generates a sustained demand for higher levels of regulation, it is not clear that Chinese regulatory state would be able to reverse the Brussels Effect. First, the EU has already entrenched its regulations in numerous other jurisdictions through the de jure Brussels Effect, changing the way business is conducted in a lasting way. Second, China is among the countries that have been most eager to emulate the EU regulations. As discussed in Part II, this is true with respect to data protection, food safety, competition policy, and environmental protection. Thus, if anything, any future "Beijing Effect" may simply entail China leveraging its market power to globalize the EU regulations that China itself initially imported from Brussels.

Will the Retreat of Globalization Undermine the De Jure Brussels Effect?

Today, most observers would agree that international institutions and multilateral cooperation are under threat. This narrative was reinforced after the election of President Trump in the United States, who was spurred to victory with a populist antiglobalization campaign. President Trump is not the only such world leader these days; his worldview resonates with many politicians who have embraced nativist policies and advocated international disengagement and economic protectionism. This populist turn in geopolitics poses a grave challenge to the liberal international order and the worldview that the EU has always championed. As a result, the EU's ability to shape the world through diplomacy, treaties, and institutions is increasingly vanishing, posing a challenge to any treaty-driven de jure Brussels Effect.

While the liberal international order might be on the verge of unraveling, the Brussels Effect challenges the view that globalization is necessarily in retreat. International cooperation may, indeed, be in crisis. However, the Brussels Effect shows that international norms may continue to emerge in many policy areas even in the absence of multilateral cooperation—those regulations may be just increasingly generated by the EU alone. If anything, the retreat of global institutions will leave a greater regulatory vacuum for the de facto Brussels Effect to fill. The method of norm production will thereby change from treaty-driven multilateral negotiations to the EU's market-driven unilateralism as the de facto Brussels Effect replaces the attempts to negotiate common standards.

To be clear, the Brussels Effect alone will not revive multilateralism and restore institutionalized cooperation. Yet it offers a way to potentially mitigate the demise of international cooperation and institutions in some policy areas. It is true that the United States under President Trump may withhold its cooperation under NATO, refuse to sign trade agreements, pull the United States out of the Paris climate accord, or walk away from the Iran nuclear deal. Yet the US antiglobalist stance will not undermine the global regulations that the EU produces and passively externalizes via the Brussels Effect. The crises posed by a lack of international cooperation are hence most acute in non-economic areas where there are few substitutes to multilateralism, such as the common defense and critical deterrence provided by NATO or the efforts of the international community to contain nuclear ambitions of countries such as Iran or North Korea. However, the EU's unilateralism can more easily fill the void when the United States withdraws its cooperation on international regulatory standards. In these areas, President Trump and other nativists are—effectively even if inadvertently—trading globalization for Europeanization.

Trade treaties offer an example of how globalization may be in retreat but where the Brussels Effect may still be able to sustain global standards. Trade agreements today deal primarily with regulatory barriers to trade, such as the amount of emissions that automobiles can generate before gaining market access, or whether chlorine-rinsed chicken or hormone-treated beef are safe for importing.[24] Thus, what is at the core in modern trade deals is precisely the rules and regulations that the EU can promulgate unilaterally.

For this reason alone, the United States' withdrawal from the Transpacific Partnership (TPP) seems surprising and contrary to the country's interests. The TPP is a proposed preferential trade agreement (PTA) among twelve Pacific countries—Australia, Brunei, Canada, Chile, Japan, Malaysia, Mexico, New Zealand, Peru, Singapore, Vietnam, and the United States. It was signed in February 2016 but never ratified. The agreement failed to take effect because of President Trump's decision to withdraw the US signature in January 2017,[25] leading the remaining TPP parties to go ahead with a now more modest free trade agreement of their own.[26] Yet by turning its back to the TPP, the United States removed one of the few plausible means that it had at its disposal to counter the unilateral globalization of many EU standards. By establishing a large enough trade area with the rest of the TPP signatories, the United States had the potential to influence global standards or, at the minimum, provide an alternative standard that the EU would be more likely to accept through mutual recognition. Instead, by ceding this opportunity to regain regulatory influence, the US regulators paved the way for an even deeper penetration of EU standards through the Brussels Effect.

One of the key goals behind the TPP was the desire to influence regulatory standards worldwide. The negotiators saw the opportunity to establish "gold standards," which could then form a blueprint for future negotiations at both multilateral and bilateral fora. Early on, the then-vice president of United States, Joe Biden, stated that the "goal is for high standards of Trans-Pacific Partnership to enter the blood stream of the global system and improve the rules and norms."[27] Stephen Harper, former prime minister of Canada, similarly hailed the TPP as a model for future 21st-century trade agreements,[28] while Mexico's foreign minister Luis Videgaray recently stated that the standards and rules negotiated in the TPP could be integrated into other regional trade agreements.[29]

Geographical Indications (GIs) provide an example of TPP's proposed regulatory standards that could have potentially mitigated the Brussels Effect, had those standards been widely accepted by countries around the world following the success of the TPP. GIs refer to signs attached on goods that indicate their geographic origin—such as Parma ham, champagne from Champagne, or Roquefort cheese—which convey important information on the quality of the product that is tied to certain local or regional conditions. Such protections are especially important for spirits and other alcohol, as the EU has ensured globally that terms such as "scotch," "ouzo," and "cognac" are restricted to products made in their appropriate home countries (Scotland, Greece, and France, respectively). The EU and United States hold starkly different views on GIs. The EU emphasizes the supremacy of GIs over trademarks by expressly providing that parties should refuse to register a trademark if the trademark is confusingly similar to a protected GI.[30] In contrast, the United States seeks to protect GIs through its trademark system.[31] To date, the EU has been successful in exporting its regulation of GIs outside its jurisdiction. For instance, the EU's recent trade agreement with Canada includes protections for Italian Asiago cheese, Greek Kalamata olive oil, and over 150 other food products from across the EU.[32] The EU's recent agreement with Vietnam extended GI protection to 169 products.[33]

The TPP offered a potential vehicle for the United States to counter the EU's influence by exporting its preferred regulatory model on GIs.[34] Although the TPP recognized that GIs could be protected through the trademark system (following the US approach) or the *sui generis* system (following the EU approach), the TPP reflected an emphatic shift in favor of trademarks over GIs. For example, the TPP allowed for cancellation or opposition of a GI in cases where the "geographical indication is likely to cause confusion with a trademark that is the subject of a pre-existing good faith pending application or registration."[35] This represented a departure from the EU's approach. Had the United States not withdrawn its participation from the TPP, this relegation of GIs in favor of trademarks could have gained broader international traction, offering a rival standard to the one favored by the EU.

In addition to forgoing the opportunity to counter the Brussels Effect indirectly by joining the TPP and providing an alternative global regulatory standard, the United States could have potentially reined in the EU's standard-setting directly by prioritizing the negotiations of the Trade and Investment Partnership (TTIP) with the EU. The TTIP is a proposed trade agreement between the EU and the United States, which the trade partners began to negotiate in 2013. However, upon taking office, President Trump halted the talks and initiated a trade conflict with the EU. It is unclear if the talks will resume and lead to the TTIP becoming effective one day.

A trade pact between the EU and the United States would be monumental. The two trade powers combined comprise half of the world's economic output and represent a third of the world's trade flows. However, the creation of such a pact is a substantial undertaking under the best of circumstances. In addition to the rising antitrade sentiments on both sides of the Atlantic, existing transatlantic disagreements about regulatory standards—ranging from beef hormones to GMOs and from geographic indicators to rules governing investment arbitration—have been viewed as stumbling blocks for the negotiations.[36] Yet, instead of seeing such differences as an obstacle, the dynamics of the Brussels Effect suggests that the United States should have enthusiastically embraced the opportunity to address competing regulations jointly with the EU. The alternative is that the EU sets these standards alone. The TTIP would therefore offer the best opportunity for the United States to have a say on global regulatory standards, calling into question the underlying rationale of the Trump administration's antitrade agenda.

Will Technological Revolution Bring an End to Non-divisibility?

A different potential challenge to the Brussels Effect is likely to come from technological developments that make it feasible for companies to make their products divisible.[37] Non-divisibility of production is a key element underlying the Brussels Effect. Yet in the future, companies may find it technologically feasible and economically viable to produce a greater range of product varieties to serve different markets. This may allow them to forgo a unitary global standard and exploit lower standards in various markets, possibly reining in the EU's de facto regulatory reach going forward. The acknowledgment of the Brussels Effect may further incentivize companies to develop technologies that allow for greater divisibility at lower costs. Such a development, to the extent that it applies to a significant number of product markets, may gradually erode the EU's ability to exert global regulatory clout in the future.

One of the most notable new technologies enabling greater customization and local production is additive manufacturing, such as 3D printing.[38] Using additive manufacturing, the same machines can produce goods with different features simply by changing the digital file that is used to provide the blueprint. Additive manufacturing relies less on economies of scale and thereby allows for mass customization. In practice, this may give manufacturers the ability to conform to a number of different production standards without substantial additional costs and rely on more dispersed production networks. When production is decentralized across different local markets, products can easily be tailored to local (or even individual) demand, as logistical costs such as long-distance transport are eliminated.[39] Additive manufacturing will have the potential to undermine the Brussels Effect in certain industries by disrupting traditional supply chains, lowering the per-unit costs of small production, and allowing for intricate customization. If this happens, there will be circumstances where it is no longer necessary, from a cost perspective, to conform all products to EU standards.

Additive manufacturing is growing quickly and is expected to continue to do so over the next several years. Industry analysts predict that by 2020, the direct market for additive manufacturing will grow to $20 billion, possibly reaching $100 billion–$250 billion by 2025.[40] Additive manufacturing will have a differential impact on different industries. While it has largely been used for prototyping to date, it is increasingly becoming a commercially viable technology for production in high-value industries such as the aerospace, medicine, and automotive sectors.[41] As the technology further improves and costs decline, its use may extend to sectors such as energy, robotics, and consumer and retail products.

However, the costs associated with additive manufacturing suggest that the technology may in the near future be limited to high-value industries. There are also several other technical and commercial limitations. Most notably, additive manufacturing is primarily geared toward low-volume production where there are few scale economies and where traditional manufacturing methods are therefore not available.[42] Currently, there are few applications that are suitable for mass production. As soon as production volume increases, the cost advantage associated with additive manufacturing will wane. Even with low-volume production, additive manufacturing often remains more expensive than traditional manufacturing methods because of factors such as high materials costs, slow buildup rates, and the long machining hours that result.[43] As long as these limitations persist, additive manufacturing will be unlikely to significantly curtail the Brussels Effect.

Another example of a technology aimed at a greater divisibility of production and service provision is geo-blocking. Geo-blocking refers to a technology that restricts the user's access to internet content based on his or her geographical location as determined by the IP address used. Geo-blocking would therefore seem to allow for a near-perfect divisibility of the internet, enabling service providers to tailor their internet sites separately for each geographical market. In theory, this technology should also offer a way to circumscribe the effects of the EU's regulation of the digital economy to European users. However, while geo-blocking is prevalent in certain areas, it has not been as widely adopted as early predictions suggested. As discussed in chapter 5, social media companies such as Facebook have chosen to forgo geo-blocking because their business model relies on "global conversations." A selective removal of online speech based on a geo-blocking technology would compromise this idea of a "One Facebook". Geo-blocking technology is also imperfect as users can hide their locations online, making it difficult for IT companies to isolate European-only data and avoid legal liability for their failure to do so. Pending court challenges, similarly discussed in chapter 5, also suggest that European Courts may restrict the use of geo-location as a way to limit compliance with the EU's regulation of the digital economy.

The most common use of geo-blocking is with regard to service providers of copyrighted material. The largest online content providers, including Netflix, Amazon Prime Video, YouTube, Hulu, and BBC iPlayer all use geo-blocking to deny access to content to users from specific countries. In most cases, such restrictions are necessary as the provider only has the license to the copyrighted material in certain jurisdictions. Use of geo-blocking of such services has become widespread and remains protected by law, including by the new EU regulation on geo-blocking.[44] Geo-blocking has also been used in the field of online sales of both products and services, often motivated by the opportunity to engage in price discrimination. For instance, a 2013 report by the Australian government concluded that techniques such as geo-blocking were being used to implement substantial price discrimination to the disadvantage of Australian consumers.[45] This included Australians paying 50% more on average for professional software. Geo-blocking could therefore, in theory, significantly limit the use of cross-border e-commerce. However, in practice, many of the world's largest online retailers such as eBay and Amazon do not geo-block prospective customers from foreign internet sites. For example, an American resident can choose to shop on Amazon.ca or Amazon.co.uk, in addition to Amazon.com. Overall, only 14% of online shopping sites have at least one country geo-blocked, while the rest allow access to all users irrespective of their geographic location.[46]

There are several reasons for the more limited utilization of geo-blocking than initially predicted. One of them is consumer backlash and public outrage following the public learning about the price effects of geo-blocking. Second is the risk associated with legal exposure. For instance, the EU bans geo-blocking in case of sales of electronic services, as well as the sale of physical products without physical delivery.[47] The EU also actively enforces its regulation in this area. In 2018, the European Commission fined the clothing retailer Guess €40 million for blocking retailers from advertising and selling across borders in other EU member states, maintaining artificially high retail prices.[48] Third, the existence of competition limits the utility derived from geo-blocking. Price discrimination is compromised in instances where alternative providers exist, ready to undercut the supra-competitive price charged in a geo-blocked market. Thus, companies are less likely to resort to geo-blocking when doing so would only hand over the blocked market to their competitors. Finally, it is unlikely that developing technologies to accomplish divisibility is the best use of company talents and resources. While many of the world's renowned high-tech companies would likely have the engineering capacity to make products divisible, these companies prefer to focus on innovating forward rather than using their talents to develop technologies that allow them to take advantage of lower regulations in some markets.[49]

A third example of an emerging technological development that has the potential to increase the divisibility of production and thereby undermine the Brussels Effect relates to the cultivation of GMOs. The development of "Genetic Use Restriction Technologies" (GURTs)—also known as "terminator seeds" or "suicide seeds"—is a technology that might be able to prevent adventitious presence of even the smallest amounts of GMOs.[50] As discussed in chapter 6, "adventitious presence" refers to GMO content that is accidental and hence unavoidable due to commingling of GMO and non-GMO varieties in various stages of cultivation and processing. The risk of adventitious presence has made it difficult to produce both GMO and non-GMO crops as cross-contamination can rarely be eliminated in its entirety. This non-divisibility of GMO production has prompted many farmers and food processors to adhere to EU's stringent GMO standards, as the Brussels Effect would predict.

However, GURTs seeds have specific genetic switch mechanisms that restrict the unauthorized use of genetic material by hampering reproduction or the expression of a trait in a genetically modified (GM) plant. The technology is geared precisely to avoid concerns related to commingling of different seed varieties.[51] Thus, GURTs may help farmers and food processors to produce to divisible standards and cater to both GMO- and non-GMO markets. Specifically, "GURTs could reduce or remove the need for buffer zones for gene containment and drastically limit the eventuality of volunteer plants by preventing volunteer seeds from germinating . . . or from expressing the GM-trait."[52] Sygenta—a global agribusiness that produces agrochemicals and seeds—has experimented with this technology.[53] However, to date, GURTs seeds are still in the experimental phase. and it is unclear when and to what extent they will transform the

GMO industry and hence contain the Brussels Effect's influence on agribusiness in the future.

The examples discussing additive manufacturing, geo-blocking, and GURTs seeds illustrate how modern technology can be harnessed to revolutionize industrial processes, the provision of services online, and farming technologies. If widely adopted, they have the potential to make products more divisible, thereby compromising the EU's ability to globalize its standards through the erosion of the "non-divisibility" condition that has been critical in sustaining the Brussels Effect. However, the discussion also shows the limits, risks, and uncertainties associated with these technologies, suggesting that their ability to counter the Brussels Effect will be deferred and likely limited to certain producers, markets, and industries.

Internal Challenges

In addition to the external challenges discussed, the Brussels Effect faces another set of challenges that are internal to the EU. Brexit presents the most visible challenge in this regard. Yet there are broader anti-EU sentiments that may contribute toward the erosion of the Brussels Effect due to the crises and challenges that, many would say, are the EU's own making. These include the rise of populist anti-EU parties and the general turn away from integration in an effort to restore national sovereignty and rein in the powers of the EU. Thus, as much as the emergence of the Brussels Effect was initially a product of the EU's internal regulatory ambitions, the greatest threat to the resilience of the Brussels Effect may, in the end, come from within the EU itself.

Brexit and the Illusion of a Regulatory Freedom

Brexit is an unprecedented challenge to the future of the EU. Never before has a member state chosen to leave the EU, making the Brexit process distinctly uncertain and unsettling. Among its many negative implications, the United Kingdom's departure would seem to undermine the EU's relative economic might and, with that, its global regulatory clout. The United Kingdom is the second largest economy in the EU by GDP, and the third largest in terms of population. The Brussels Effect is amplified when a jurisdiction represents a large market. Since the EU's market size will diminish by 15% after the United Kingdom's departure, Brexit will reduce the relative size of the remaining EU market versus foreign ones.[54] Beyond just its size and scale, the United Kingdom has also supplied notable regulatory capacity—which also enhances the Brussels Effect—to the EU institutions, including a distinctly competent bureaucracy and technical expertise across a range of policy areas. Despite this decline in the EU's market size and regulatory capacity following Brexit, however, Brexit will be unlikely to dampen the Brussels Effect. If anything, it may have the potential to make the Brussels Effect even more salient.

The anti-EU forces in the United Kingdom that campaigned for Brexit argued that the departure from the EU would finally liberate the United Kingdom from the EU's excessive regulations, reinstating the UK's regulatory sovereignty. Compared to other EU member states, the United Kingdom has always been more skeptical of regulation, emphasizing the virtues of markets and the need to preserve the competitiveness of European firms.[55] The United Kingdom has fiercely fought against many regulations in the Council only to be outvoted by other member states.[56] This has, understandably, nurtured resentment and contributed to the critics' narrative that the EU has overreached, encroaching on UK's sovereignty.

Yet the dynamics driving the Brussels Effect show that the promise of restoring the UK's regulatory sovereignty post-Brexit constitutes a false campaign promise that the government will not be able to deliver. Instead, EU regulations will continue to govern critical aspects of the UK's economy. Roughly half of the UK's exports are destined for the EU, with little expectation of change.[57] The United Kingdom will therefore continue to rely on access to the EU's large consumer market long after Brexit. The EU is the number one destination for its exports at least in the following key industries: pharmaceuticals (48% exports to EU), aircraft (51%), petroleum fuels (64%), and machinery (37%).[58] This high degree of dependence on the access to the EU market means that UK companies will continue to adhere to EU rules in the future, as the de facto Brussels Effect suggests. While British companies could, in principle, adopt one set of standards for the European market and multiple other sets of standards for the rest of the world post-Brexit, scale economies and other benefits of uniform production make this unlikely. Thus, the Brussels Effect shatters the illusion of the regulatory freedom that Brexit is meant to deliver to the United Kingdom.

In addition to this de facto Brussels Effect, the post-Brexit UK will also likely witness a significant de jure Brussels Effect. In areas such as financial regulation and data privacy, the UK government will have a substantial incentive to retain close regulatory alignment to ensure "equivalence" or "adequacy" of its regulatory regime, which remains a precondition for UK companies to do business in the EU.[59]

Several key policy areas illustrate the interconnectedness of the United Kingdom and EU economies and the incentives that this creates for UK companies and the UK government to follow the EU regulations even after the United Kingdom leaves the EU. The following discussion describes this dynamic with examples from data protection, financial regulation, and chemical regulation. These examples show the difficulty of dividing production across different markets, keeping the UK businesses tightly connected to the regulations emanating from Brussels long after leaving the EU.

To begin with data protection, the importance of the digital economy and the magnitude of the cross-border data flows between the EU and the United Kingdom cannot be overstated. Digital economy comprises 10% of the UK's GDP.[60] Further, services account for 44% of the UK's total global exports, and about half of all trade in services is enabled by digital technologies and the associated data flows.[61] The UK economy has the highest percentage of GDP attributed to digital economy in Europe and the highest percentage of individual internet users of any G7 economy.[62] Importantly, three quarters of the UK's cross-border data flows are with EU countries.[63] It is therefore not surprising that both the de facto and de jure Brussels Effect will ensure that "Brexit should not mean Brexit when it comes to standards of data protection," as the UK's information commissioner, Elizabeth Debham, stated in September 2016.

Beyond the revealing comments by Elizabeth Debham, several other representatives of the UK government have affirmed that the UK's data protection rules continue to follow those of the EU, both de facto and de jure. For instance, the UK's digital minister Matt Hancock indicated in February 2017 that UK data protection laws needed to mirror EU data protection laws even after Brexit because "the government wants to ensure unhindered data flows after Brexit."[64] The easiest way to ensure this, according to Hancock, was to "put [the EU's General Directive of Privacy Regulation] into UK law in full."[65]

The most compelling reason for the United Kingdom to emulate the GDPR post-Brexit stems from a provision of the GDPR that bans the transfer of data from the EU to third countries that fail to ensure "an adequate level of protection" of data privacy rights.[66] Thus, in the absence of the EU reaching a determination that the UK's data protection laws are "adequate" post-Brexit—which the ECJ has defined to mean "essentially equivalent" with the EU—data transfers from the EU to the United Kingdom will be forced to come to a halt.[67] This provides powerful incentives for continuing regulatory alignment. The UK government is aware of this. The House of Lords European Union Committee denoted in its July 2017 report that the United Kingdom is so heavily integrated with the EU that it would be difficult for the United Kingdom to get by without an adequacy arrangement. The Committee therefore recommends "that the Government should seek adequacy decisions to facilitate UK–EU data transfers after the UK has ceased to be a member of the EU."[68]

The pro-Brexit voices, which have emphasized that the cumbersome data protection rules are an impediment for competitiveness and innovation, will likely be left disappointed with the UK's inability to disentangle itself from the GDPR post-Brexit on purely economic grounds. However, the de jure Brussels Effect on data protection will likely have consequences that extend beyond economic considerations. A particular concern for many in the United Kingdom is that the EU's data protection rules may be in tension with the UK's national security interests. The UK's 2016 Investigatory Powers Act contains provisions on data retention and surveillance for national security purposes.[69] The UK Information Commissioner recently acknowledged this tension, noting that "it seems likely that the UK's surveillance and data retention regime would be a risk for a positive adequacy finding."[70]

While EU member states can invoke the GDPR's national security exceptions to justify some data collection and retention for national security purposes, the same article is not automatically available for non-member states that seek positive adequacy finding by the Commission.[71] To overcome this, some commentators have argued that the United Kingdom could potentially obtain a partial adequacy finding, whereby the UK rules would be found to be adequate with respect to commercial data but not with respect to data protection in law enforcement. Canada provides an example of a jurisdiction that has obtained an adequacy finding from the EU just for its commercial sector. Commenting on this option, the UK Information Commissioner noted that while "partial adequacy is better than no adequacy," the best way forward was to have a "unified, harmonized approach across all sectors."[72] This suggests that the United Kingdom may choose to seek full adequacy even if this potentially entails a need to change UK surveillance and security rules.

Another example of the Brussels Effect's constraining influence post-Brexit is the financial services industry. The United Kingdom is the world's second largest financial center.[73] The industry relies heavily on access to the EU's single market, with 44% of the UK's financial service exports currently going to the EU.[74] Unhindered access to the EU market has also made the United Kingdom an attractive base for operations for non-UK financial institutions. In 2017, 49% of bank assets in the United Kingdom were related to non-UK banks.[75] For these foreign banks, the United Kingdom serves as an access point from which they can serve the broader European market.

Financial institutions' access to the EU market rests on an existing regime known as "financial passporting."[76] Passporting refers to a mechanism that allows banks to operate across the entire EU and the broader European Economic Area (EEA) as long as they are regulated and supervised by one member state—such as the United Kingdom. This mutual recognition of individual member state regulations rests on all EU members' commitment to abide by a "single rulebook," which provides a unified regulatory framework for the EU financial sector.[77]

Thus, alignment with the EU's regulations is critical in sustaining the UK's financial services industry, providing a gateway for the large EU market and thereby allowing the United Kingdom to act as a financial capital of the world.

Upon exiting the EU, UK banks and the foreign banks registered in the United Kingdom will lose their passporting rights.[78] To retain those rights, they would need to establish a separate subsidiary in another EU member state and subject themselves to that member state's regulatory regime. Alternatively, these banks could continue to serve the EU market from the United Kingdom based on a legal concept knows as an "equivalence regime."[79] An equivalence regime entails the EU recognizing the UK's regulatory regime as comparable with that of the EU, achieving the same results as the corresponding EU rules.[80] An equivalence regime is, however, clearly an inferior regime compared to passporting, offering fewer rights and greater legal risks.[81] The Commission makes the decision on equivalence in consultation with other key EU institutions such as the European Banking Authority (EBA) and European Securities and Markets Authority (ESMA).[82] The United Kingdom would further need to keep adjusting its legal framework to the European one in subsequent years, or else the Commission could unilaterally revoke the equivalence decision. This entails that, post-Brexit, the UK financial industry would not be able to break free from the EU's financial regulations but would need to retain the "equivalence" with the EU's single rulebook going forward as well.

Another potential manifestation of UK-based financial institutions' proclivity to gravitate toward EU regulation is the prospect of them relocating to the EU altogether. Even in the absence of a mass exodus that some media reports predicted,[83] some banks and other financial institutions have relocated personnel to other financial centers in the EU, including to Frankfurt, due to the relative elasticity of capital.[84] A decision to relocate is partly motivated by the uncertainty associated with the entire Brexit, including the ambiguity underlying any equivalence regime that is subject to a threat of a sudden revocation. Regardless, it is evident that the financial industry in the United Kingdom is not able to escape the Brussels Effect. Instead, it is actively opting for the EU regime—whether through regulatory equivalence or relocation—showing once again the difficulty of implementing the promised post-Brexit regulatory freedom in practice.

Yet another example of the continuing regulatory influence that the EU will have over the United Kingdom post-Brexit comes from chemical regulation. The EU's Registration, Evaluation, Authorization, and Restriction of Chemicals (REACH) regulation governs not just the trade in chemicals but also the trade in downstream industries that use chemicals within their products.[85] As discussed in chapter 6, EU laws set the highest and hence the most burdensome regulatory standards on the safety of chemicals in the world, impacting the global business practices of multinational companies as a result. For example, REACH determines the chemicals that are permitted in a wide range of products, such as paints, detergents, textiles, furniture, toys, and electrical appliances.

The economic significance of the chemical industry to the UK economy is notable. The UK chemical industry is the second largest exporter to the EU after the country's automotive industry. It is also the country's second largest manufacturing industry overall.[86] When all the affected downstream industries are added to this, the continuing role that the REACH regulation will have in the UK economy will make the promises of the post-Brexit regulatory freedom even hollower in practice. It is illustrative that there are over 9,000 REACH registrations made by UK companies to date.[87]

The REACH regulation has long been derided by the United Kingdom as "symbolic of onerous EU regulation."[88] REACH was voted the most burdensome piece of legislation by UK's small- and medium-sized enterprises in 2013.[89] Echoing these concerns, Prime Minister David Cameron's "Cut EU Red Tape" campaign included making the implementation of REACH more business friendly.[90] Yet even Brexit will not free UK companies from the regulatory burdens of REACH. UK companies will continue to produce products that are REACH compliant in order to retain access to the EU market, given the importance of the UK–EU trading relationship in the industry. For example, the CEO of UK Chemical Business Association, Peter Newport, made this clear by saying that the UK chemicals industry prefers to "remain in EU's REACH regulation" to guarantee access to the single market.[91] The UK government acknowledges this as well. The House of Commons Environmental Audit Committee recently warned of the costs associated with any attempt to subject the chemical industry to two different sets of regulations, urging that the United Kingdom should negotiate to remain a participant in the REACH registration system, even paying for access if necessary.[92]

The examples just discussed—data protection, financial services, and chemical safety—suggest that UK companies will continue to be subject to many EU rules even after the United Kingdom leaves the EU. The Brussels Effect will similarly penetrate other areas of the UK economy, including the regulation of pharmaceuticals, medical devices, and approvals; the regulation of pesticides and agriculture; the regulation of vehicles, including environmental, safety, and security standards; and the regulation of environment and renewable energy. This lingering presence of EU regulations alone is likely to unsettle the proponents of Brexit who are forced to concede that the promises of regulatory sovereignty were unfounded.

However, what may be even more disconcerting for "Brexiteers" is the realization that the United Kingdom's departure may lead to an even stronger variant of the Brussels Effect. The departure of the United Kingdom will remove the biggest internal constraint on the EU's regulatory rule-making, opening the door for more interventionist standards as the UK's exit may allow Germany and France to gain more influence.[93] Typically, the United Kingdom has been the voice for moderation in the EU's regulatory pursuits, calling for restraint and the need to balance regulation with considerations of competitiveness. After Brexit, that important pro-market voice will be gone, shrinking the coalition of the pro-market member states and possibly opening a door for pro-regulation states to push through an increasingly ambitious European regulatory agenda.[94] This will have an effect not only on the United Kingdom itself but also on the world beyond.

In reality, the United Kingdom's departure from the EU will not liberate the country from the EU's regulatory leash, despite the belief and campaign rhetoric of Leave campaigners. Instead, the United Kingdom may soon find itself in the position of being bound by EU regulations without any ability to influence the content of those regulations. As a result, with Brexit, the United Kingdom will be ceding its role as a rule maker in return for becoming a voiceless rule taker in an even more tightly regulated Europe.

The Rise of Anti-EU Sentiments

Today, the EU faces a distinctive challenge as populist, anti-EU parties are gaining strength in several member states. The most relevant political divide in Europe today is not between the right and the left, but between those who are turned inward and those who embrace further integration. The former would scale back the powers transferred to the EU in the name of reinstating the sovereignty of European nations.[95] Fearful of these demands, even the integrationists are growing timid in their calls for expanding EU powers at the expense of national sovereignty.[96] More European regulation means less sovereignty. And less sovereignty means more unpredictability and loss of control, as has been seen with the crises surrounding the common European currency or unmanaged migration. This growing gap between these different visions within Europe for Europe in the end presents perhaps the greatest challenge to the EU's broader regulatory agenda.

There is a possibility that these internal struggles risk a gradual erosion of the Brussels Effect. As multiple crises continue to linger and anti-EU sentiments within the EU grow,[97] the EU's ability to transfer new powers to Brussels will likely slow down, or even come to an end. The EU's ability to exercise its regulatory capacity may become compromised, as decision-making in EU institutions becomes increasingly deadlocked. The growing anti-EU sentiment may also lead to general skepticism toward (any) rules emanating from Brussels. Should these developments penetrate mainstream politics across a sufficient number of member states, they have the potential to remove the two key conditions supporting the Brussels Effect—regulatory capacity and preference for stringent rules.

If this happens, the global regulatory influence of EU institutions would likely wane, as they would no longer enjoy the backing of the EU citizenry, the support of the European Parliament, and the sufficient votes by the member state governments in the Council. Even if the Commission and the Courts remained committed to European integration, they would not be able to pursue an ambitious regulatory agenda without the support of the other institutions. Although anti-EU parties may not embark on an agenda of repealing existing regulations, we still may see a drastic slowdown in new regulations that are geared at further integrating the single market.

In addition to battling general anti-EU sentiments, other economic and political pressures may lead the EU to regulate less going forward. For example, the EU may be forced to rethink the costs and benefits of regulation in the future, especially as its economic growth slows to the point where its welfare model becomes unsustainable, and its aging populations increase the financial burden on the member states.[98] This could lead the union to prioritize competitiveness and innovation, exercising more regulatory restraint. For instance, the Commission under Jean-Claude Juncker has already embarked on a "better regulation" agenda, with the goal of "doing less more efficiently."[99] As part of this agenda, the Commission has pledged to minimize regulatory burdens. This suggests that the EU may be willing to rein in its pro-regulation tendencies more often than in the past. At the same time, such a development is not inevitable. The EU has experienced relative lack of growth and competitiveness for a few decades yet it has not embraced deregulation as a solution to those problems. Thus, it may well be that the EU's proclivity to regulate remains intact even as the economic fundamentals across the EU are struggling to sustain the European welfare state and way of life.

In addition to Europe's economic trajectory, political developments may also lead the EU to re-evaluate some of its most stringent regulations. For example, if incidents of terrorism become more frequent, the EU may consider rebalancing the privacy protections embedded in the GDPR with greater surveillance and even allow for mass retention of personal data for national security purposes. France, for instance, has experienced multiple terrorist attacks in recent years, and is moving to expand government surveillance powers as a result.[100] Similarly, after the 2017 terrorist attacks in London, interior ministers called for enhanced access by law enforcement to encrypted online communications, such as WhatsApp.[101] This is an area that may pose a challenge to European Courts as they have jurisdiction over issues of privacy but not over national security and criminal justice.[102]

Yet it is unclear if the courts will have a final say if political pressures for legislative change build among the member states.

However, despite these risks, it is also plausible that the EU's regulatory agenda could remain largely unaffected by anti-EU sentiments and the ongoing crises. The broader anti-EU sentiment is not generally focused on the regulation of the single market. The populist parties reigning across the EU are most concerned about their budgetary sovereignty, their right to organize their judiciary, their right to control domestic media, or their ability to exert control over their intake of refugees.[103] The EU's pursuit of tough competition policy, data protection, or food safety remain well outside their populist agendas. Thus, even if the EU is otherwise forced to scale back on controversial issues such as Eurozone architecture, curtailment of rule-of-law backsliding in Hungary and Poland, or its role in the management of migration, the Brussels Effect may remain largely, or even entirely, unaffected, since these are not direct threats to the EU's regulatory agenda.

There is, however, a risk of collateral damage on the EU's regulatory agenda due to anti-EU sentiment, even in the absence of any direct attacks on the regulations underlying the Brussels Effect. This could happen if the anti-EU parties gain significant leverage over the European Parliament and Council decision-making, and adopt a general strategy to vote against anything that vests EU institutions with power at the expense of national sovereignty. Still, any such collateral damage is likely to be mitigated in areas where the Commission can govern through non-legislative acts—and those powers are both vast and well entrenched. The EU's regulatory activity may hence continue in all policy areas where the Commission is engaged in non-legislative rule-making through implementation acts or delegated rule-making. At the same time, it is possible that there will be a slowdown in legislative acts that require the support of the Council and the EP—in the event those institutions will increasingly be captured by parties with an anti-EU platform. However, given the relative prevalence of regulatory activity undertaken by the Commission alone, even this might not lead to a significant curtailment of the Brussels Effect.[104] In 2018, there were 423 legislative acts in total, consisting of regulations, directives, or decisions promulgated either by the Council or by the Council and the European Parliament jointly in a legislative process. That figure was dwarfed by the total of 1570 non-legislative acts adopted, of which 1417 were Commission regulations, directives, and decisions.[105]

The technocratic nature of EU rule-making may further contribute to the resilience of the Brussels Effect. The Commission bureaucracy consists of technocrats who remain focused on their assigned regulatory domain and are unlikely to become distracted by the broader crises. This tendency insulates many of the EU regulations from political crises raging around it. For example, the Commission met the day after the Brexit vote in 2016 to vote on a pesticide (glyphosates) regulation. Some news commentators attributed this vote to the Commission's desire to keep the appearance of "implacable calm" when confronted with the biggest crisis of its history.[106] This may be true but it also shows how the technocratic rule-making simply follows its own timetable and procedures regardless of the political realities that surround it. The need to decide on the extension of the glyphosate license was brought before the Commission as part of the comitology proceedings where the Commission has little control over the timing. Hence, the Commission soldiers on with its technocratic agenda even when a major political shock hits the core of its economic and political system.

More broadly, the regulation of the single market—including high-profile regulations such as the GDPR or large competition law fines against US tech giants—provides a welcome distraction and comfort to the public in the midst of the crises. The EU's ability to promulgate new regulations, at least, gives the public a sense of normalcy and shows that Brussels is, still, fully in business. It also gives the EU institutions the opportunity to show that they can still deliver tangible gains to European citizens.

Finally, the result of the current crises discussed may not only be that the Brussels Effect remains intact—the Brussels Effect may even become strengthened. Throughout its history, the EU's solution to many crises has typically been the pursuit of "more Europe," as shown by increasing the role of Frontex—the EU's Border and Coast Guard Agency—in managing migration or ambitious expansions of Eurozone governance in response to the Euro crises, instead of increasing the sovereign powers of member state governments.[107] Thus, the EU's expansive regulatory agenda may not only persist, but might even grow despite the growing anti-EU sentiment, as many of the EU's existing problems can be best resolved through further integration and additional regulations.

In the same vein, the relative significance of the Brussels Effect may also grow when compared to the EU's other tools of global influence. As governments with populist agendas gain prominence across the EU member states, the EU's global role as a "normative power" could increasingly be called into question. The EU has traditionally assumed a prominent role in promoting human rights and rule of law abroad. However, these efforts are now undermined by blatant violations of those same rights among EU member states themselves, in particular by the defiant governments in Hungary and Poland. This leaves the EU with an ever-greater need to rely on its regulatory power, which can more easily be insulated from its internal struggles and therefore be employed to project the EU's power and relevance, at home and abroad.

THERE ARE SEVERAL existing and emerging threats and challenges—both external and internal—that have the potential to undermine the conditions sustaining the Brussels Effect in the future. In particular, the EU's relative *market size* could diminish, whether due to the rise of China or the departure of the United Kingdom. The EU's relative *regulatory capacity* could weaken, whether as a result of Brexit, due to the threat posed by populist anti-EU parties or following China's relative increase in regulatory capacity. The EU's willingness to promulgate *stringent rules* could similarly be undermined, in particular if the populists' anti-EU agenda leads to attempts to repatriate powers back to the member states. The *non-divisibility* of production could become less common due to technological developments such as additive manufacturing or geo-blocking. Further, the weakening of the de facto Brussels Effect could be accompanied by the fading de jure Brussels Effect as the antiglobalization sentiment hinders treaty making and institutionalized cooperation.

However, it is unclear if any of these developments will challenge the Brussels Effect in the immediate future. EU regulations will continue to penetrate many critical aspects of the UK economy long after Brexit, illustrating how Brexit is easier to execute as a slogan than as a viable policy in practice. If anything, the UK's departure may open greater room for the EU's pro-regulatory coalitions to thrive. The retreat of the United States from global institutions and the general backlash against globalization might also do little to undermine the Brussels Effect. If anything, the withering multilateralism leaves a greater vacuum for the EU's unilateralism to fill. And the more futile the EU finds its attempts to revive multilateral rule-making, the more likely it will focus on simply regulating its own market and letting the Brussels Effect do the work of globalizing those rules. China is unlikely to replace the EU as a global standard setter anytime soon and, by the time it might be able to do so, many EU regulations will already have been entrenched in business practices and by jurisdictions around the world—China included. Similarly, while technological developments may transform some industries, technical challenges and the cost of the technology and materials make it unclear how fast and extensively technologies such as additive manufacturing can be deployed to undermine the Brussels Effect. Finally, while political challenges to the EU decision-making may slow down regulatory rule-making, it is less likely that the key regulations that propagate the Brussels Effect around the world will become the targets of repeal by anti-EU parties and Euroskeptic governments.

Of course, these forces and challenges combined may, over time, corrode the most potent version of the Brussels Effect, squeezing the EU's regulatory hegemony from the outside and as well as from within. If that were to happen, the EU may need to prepare for the world where the Brussels Effect may become less common, forcing the EU to abandon its reliance on markets and unilateralism in favor of regulatory cooperation and multilateralism. Even then, many EU regulations will likely survive, thanks to a combination of path dependency and the EU's past success to institutionalize its rules across legal regimes through treaty-driven mechanisms. It is also highly plausible that the EU's regulatory machinery simply hums along, largely unaware and unscathed, of the crises surrounding it. The Brussels Effect is therefore not only pervasive today, but there is a convincing argument that it will persist, extending the EU's regulatory hegemony into the foreseeable future.

Notes

PREFACE

1. The European Commission support for the production of this publication does not constitute an endorsement of the contents, which reflects the views only of the author, and the Commission cannot be held responsible for any use that may be made of the information contained therein.

INTRODUCTION

1. Walter Russell Mead, *Incredible Shrinking Europe: The Continent's Grand Unity Project is Failing, and its Global Influence is Fading,* WALL ST. J. (Feb. 12, 2019), https://www.wsj.com/articles/incredible-shrinking-europe-11549928481 (on file with author).

2. Ana Palacio, *The European Unraveling?* LA NACION (Feb. 16, 2017), https://www.nacion.com/opinion/internacional/the-european-unraveling/PY5GRBN4PVDRXOXYXJBTUVH6NY/story/ [https://perma.cc/2LUT-BAPX].

3. RICHARD YOUNGS, EUROPE'S DECLINE AND FALL: THE STRUGGLE AGAINST GLOBAL IRRELEVANCE 1 (2010).

4. Stephen Walt, *The Coming Erosion of the European Union,* FOREIGN POLICY (Aug. 18, 2011), https://foreignpolicy.com/2011/08/18/the-coming-erosion-of-the-european-union/ [https://perma.cc/TQ3Y-JPX3].

5. Richard Haas, *Why Europe No Longer Matters,* WASH. POST (June 17, 2011), https://www.washingtonpost.com/opinions/why-europe-no-longer-matters/2011/06/15/AG7eCCZH_story.html?utm_term=.9bc86c66d9b4 (on file with author).

6. Tony Barber, *The Decline of Europe is a Global Concern,* FIN. TIMES, Dec. 21, 2015, at 1 (on file with author).

7. Theodore R. Bromund, *Europe Paves the Way for Its Decline,* HERITAGE FOUNDATION (Oct. 9, 2018), https://www.heritage.org/europe/commentary/europe-paves-the-way-its-decline [https://perma.cc/5F49-75DN].

8. *See, e.g.,* Jed Rubenfeld, Commentary, *Unilateralism and Constitutionalism,* 79 N.Y.U. L. REV. 1971, 1975-76, 2005-06 (2004); *see also* Eva Pejsova, *Europe: A New Player in the Indo-Pacific,* DIPLOMAT (Jan. 19, 2019), https://thediplomat.com/2019/01/europe-a-new-player-in-the-indo-pacific/ [https://perma.cc/LNU2-942W].

9. *See* Anu Bradford & Eric A. Posner, *Universal Exceptionalism in International Law*, 52 HARV. INT'L L.J. 1, 53 (2011).

10. *See* Leslie H. Gelb, *GDP Now Matters More than Force: A U.S. Foreign Policy for the Age of Economic Power*, FOREIGN AFF., Nov./Dec. 2010, at 35, https://www.foreignaffairs.com/articles/united-states/2010-10-21/gdp-now-matters-more-force (on file with author).

PREFACE TO PART ONE

1. *See generally* DAVID VOGEL, TRADING UP: CONSUMER AND ENVIRONMENTAL REGULATION IN A GLOBAL ECONOMY (1995).

2. Robert Howse & Donald Regan, *The Product/Process Distinction—An Illusory Basis for Disciplining "Unilateralism" in Trade Policy*, 11 EUR. J. INT'L. L. 249 (2000); Douglas A. Kysar, *Preferences for Processes: The Process/Product Distinction and the Regulation of Consumer Choice*, 118 HARV. L. REV. 525 (2004).

3. *See, e.g.*, Daniel W. Drezner, *Globalization, Harmonization, and Competition: The Different Pathways to Policy Convergence*, 12 J. EUR. PUB. POL'Y 841, 841–59 (2005); Beth Simmons, *The International Politics of Harmonization: The Case of Capital Market Regulation*, *in* DYNAMICS OF REGULATORY CHANGE (David Vogel & Robert A. Kagan eds., 2004), at 42, 50–52; Bruce Carruthers & Naomi Lamoreaux, *Regulatory Races: The Effects of Jurisdictional Competition on Regulatory Standards*, 54 J. ECON. LIT. 52 (2016).

4. *See, e.g.*, Ralph Nader, *Preface* to LORI WALLACH & MICHELLE SFORZA, WHOSE TRADE ORGANIZATION?: CORPORATE GLOBALIZATION AND THE EROSION OF DEMOCRACY, at ix, xi (1999).

5. *See* ALAN TONELSON, THE RACE TO THE BOTTOM: WHY A WORLDWIDE WORKER SURPLUS AND UNCONTROLLED FREE TRADE ARE SINKING AMERICAN LIVING STANDARDS 14–15 (2002). For a general discussion of this dynamic, *see* DALE D. MURPHY, THE STRUCTURE OF REGULATORY COMPETITION: CORPORATIONS AND PUBLIC POLICIES IN A GLOBAL ECONOMY (2004), in particular Parts I, II, and V.

6. *See* David Vogel & Robert A. Kagan, *Introduction* to DYNAMICS OF REGULATORY CHANGE: HOW GLOBALIZATION AFFECTS NATIONAL REGULATORY POLICIES 4–5 (David Vogel & Robert A. Kagan eds., 2004).

7. *See* Debora L. Spar & David B. Yoffie, *A Race to the Bottom or Governance from the Top?*, *in* COPING WITH GLOBALIZATION 31, 31–51 (Aseem Prakash & Jeffrey A. Hart eds., 2000); David Vogel, *Trading Up and Governing Across: Transnational Governance and Environmental Protection*, 4 J. EUR. PUB. POL'Y 556, 563 (1997); Vogel & Kagan, *supra* note 6, at 2–8; *see also* ELIZABETH R. DESOMBRE, FLAGGING STANDARDS: GLOBALIZATION AND ENVIRONMENTAL, SAFETY, AND LABOR REGULATIONS AT SEA (2006).

8. *See* John C. Coffee, Jr., *The Future of Corporate Federalism: State Competition and the New Trend Toward De Facto Federal Minimum Standards*, 8 CARDOZO L. REV 759, 761–63 (1987).

9. VOGEL, *supra* note 1.

10. Vogel & Kagan, *supra* note 6, at 9.

11. Vogel, *supra* note 6, at 562 (1997).

12. *See* JOHN BRAITHWAITE & PETER DRAHOS, GLOBAL BUSINESS REGULATION 518–19 (2000); Beth Simmons, *supra* note 3, at 42, 50–52; Vogel & Kagan, *supra* note 6, at 14.

13. *See* Drezner, *supra* note 3, at 841.

14. *Id.* at 850.

CHAPTER 1

1. *See* MARGOT HORSPOOL & MATTHEW HUMPHREYS, EUROPEAN UNION LAW 39–70 (6th ed. 2010) (providing an overview of the various institutions of the European Union);

see also COUNCIL EUR. UNION, https://www.consilium.europa.eu/en/european-coun-cil/ (last visited August 10, 2019) [https://perma.cc/97RY-QDL5]; EUR. COMMISSION, https://ec.europa.eu/commission/index_en (last visitedAugust 10, 2019) [https://perma.cc/S8D3-K7T9]; EUR. PARLIAMENT, http://www.europarl.europa.eu/portal/en (last visitedAugust 10, 2019) [https://perma.cc/H9PG-W2MJ].

2. Case C-26/62, Onderneming van Gend & Loos v. Neth. Inland Revenue Admin., 1963 E.C.R. 3; Case C-6/64, Flaminio Costa v. E.N.E.L., 1964 E.C.R. 585.

3. Chad Damro, *Market Power Europe*, 19 J. EUR. PUB. POL'Y 682, 687 (2012).

4. Case C-120/78, Rewe-Zentral AG v. Bundesmonopolverwaltung für Branntwein, 1979 E.C.R. 00649; Stephen Weatherill, *"Pre-emption, Harmonisation and the Distribution of Competence to Regulate the Internal Market," in* THE LAW OF THE SINGLE EUROPEAN MARKET, UNPACKING THE PREMISES (Catherine Barnard & Joanne Scott eds., 2002).

5. DAVID VOGEL, THE POLITICS OF PRECAUTION: REGULATING HEALTH, SAFETY, AND ENVIRONMENTAL RISKS IN EUROPE AND THE UNITED STATES 244 (2012) [here-inafter VOGEL, POLITICS].

6. *See* Henrik Selin & Stacy D. VanDeveer, *Raising Global Standards: Hazardous Substances and E-Waste Management in the European Union*, ENVIRONMENT, Dec. 2006, at 6, 10–11.

7. VOGEL, POLITICS, *supra* note 5, at 244.

8. ABRAHAM L. NEWMAN, PROTECTORS OF PRIVACY: REGULATING PERSONAL DATA IN THE GLOBAL ECONOMY 11 (2008).

9. *See* Ian Manners, *Normative Power Europe: A Contradiction in Terms?*, 40 J. COMMON MARKET STUD. 235 (2002); *See* VOGEL, POLITICS, *supra* note 5, at 237–41.

10. *See, e.g.*, Christian Zacker, *Environmental Law of the European Economic Community: New Powers Under the Single European Act*, 14 B.C. INT'L & COMP. L. REV. 249, 264 (1991).

11. Daniel P. Gitterman, *European Integration and Labour Market Cooperation: A Comparative Regional Perspective*, 13 J. EUR. SOC. POL'Y 99, 106–09.

12. Treaty on European Union (Maastricht, Feb. 7, 1992), Protocol on Social Policy, 1992 O.J. (C 191) 196, https://europa.eu/european-union/sites/europaeu/files/docs/body/treaty_on_european_union_en.pdf [https://perma.cc/FD3P-GYLZ].

13. *Id.*

14. *See* DAVID VOGEL, TRADING UP: CONSUMER AND ENVIRONMENTAL REGULATION IN A GLOBAL ECONOMY 67 (1995).

15. *See* Regulation (EC) 1221/2009 of the European Parliament and of the Council of 25 November 2009 on the Voluntary Participation by Organisations in a Community Eco-Management and Audit Scheme (EMAS), art. 1, 2009 O.J. (L 342) 1 (replacing the original EMAS Regulation 1836/93); Walter Mattli & Ngaire Woods, *In Whose Benefit? Explaining Regulatory Change in Global Politics, in* THE POLITICS OF GLOBAL REGULATION 1, 35 (Walter Mattli & Ngaire Woods eds., 2009).

16. *See* Mattli & Woods, *supra* note 15; Magali A. Delmas, *The Diffusion of Environmental Standards in Europe and in the United States: An Institutional Perspective*, 35 POL'Y SCI. 91, 91 (2002).

17. Paulette Kurzer, *Biased or Not? Organized Interests and the Case of Food Information Labeling*, 20 J. EUR. PUB. POL'Y 722 (2013); Yves Tiberghien, THE BATTLE FOR THE GLOBAL GOVERNANCE OF GENETICALLY MODIFIED ORGANISMS: THE ROLES OF THE EUROPEAN UNION, JAPAN, KOREA, AND CHINA IN A COMPARATIVE CONTEXT 2016, https://www.sciencespo.fr/ceri/sites/sciencespo.fr.ceri/files/etude124.pdf [https://perma.cc/Y62H-JKJ3].

18. Regulation (EC) No. 1829/2003 of the European Parliament and of the Council of 22 September 2003 on Genetically Modified Food and Feed, 2003 O.J. (L 268) 1; Regulation (EC) No 1830/2003 of the European Parliament and of the Council of 22 September 2003 Concerning the Traceability and Labelling of Genetically Modified Organisms and the

Traceability of Food and Feed Products Produced from Genetically Modified Organisms and Amending Directive 2001/18/EC, 2003 O.J. (L 268) 24.

19. *See, e.g.*, Letter from Friends of the Earth Europe, ARGE, Coop Italy, EuroCoop, Greenpeace EU, VLOG, to Tonio Borg Commissioner Health and Consumer Policy, European Commission (July 8, 2013), https://gmwatch.org/en/news/archive/2013/14644-keep-zero-tolerance-of-unapproved-gmos [https://perma.cc/2P2C-6N47].

20. UK HOUSE OF COMMONS, THE EXTENSION OF QUALIFIED MAJORITY VOTING FROM THE TREATY OF ROME TO THE EUROPEAN CONSTITUTION, 2004, https://researchbriefings.parliament.uk/ResearchBriefing/Summary/RP04-54 [https://perma.cc/Y6HH-JBUN].

21. DANIEL KELEMEN, THE RULES OF FEDERALISM: INSTITUTIONS AND REGULATORY POLITICS IN THE EU AND BEYOND 29–30 (2009); *see* R. Daniel Kelemen et. al., *Wider and Deeper? Enlargement and Integration in the European Union*, 21 J. EUR. PUB. POL'Y 647, 657 (2014).

22. *See* Gerald Schneider et al., *Bargaining Power in the European Union: An Evaluation of Competing Game-Theoretic Models*, 58 POL. STUD. 85, 98–99 (2010).

23. *See* Andreas Warntjen, *Do Votes Matter? Voting Weights and the Success Probability of Member State Requests in the Council of the European Union*, 39 J. EUR. INTEGRATION 673, 676 (2017).

24. *See* Åse Gornitzka & Ulf Sverdrup, *Access of Experts: Information and EU Decision-making*, 34 WEST EUR. POL. 48, 64 (2011).

25. *The Ministry: Tasks and Structure*, GERMAN MINISTRY FOR THE ENVIRONMENT, NATURE CONSERVATION AND NUCLEAR SAFETY (last updated Mar. 25, 2019), https://www.bmu.de/en/ministry/tasks-and-structure/ [https://perma.cc/HVK6-9UC2]; *About Us*, Umwelt Bundesamt (last updated Mar. 7, 2018), https://www.umweltbundesamt.de/en/the-uba/about-us [https://perma.cc/TZU3-E4QP]; *About RIVM*, Dutch National Institute for Public Health and the Environment (last updated May 13, 2019), https://www.rivm.nl/en/about-rivm/rivm [https://perma.cc/83JF-6XE2].

26. *See, e.g.*, VOGEL, POLITICS, *supra* note 5, at 242. However, counter-examples of bargaining failures exist as well. *See, e.g.*, Paul Copeland, *The Negotiation of the Revision of the Working Time Directive*, *in* EU ENLARGEMENT, THE CLASH OF CAPITALISMS AND THE EUROPEAN SOCIAL DIMENSION 72, 87–93, (2014).

27. *See* Raya Kardasheva, *Package Deals in EU Politics*, 57 AM. J. POL. SCI. 858, 858 (2013).

28. *See id.* at 861.

29. *Id.*

30. *See* Manuele Citi & Mogens Justesen, *Measuring and Explaining Regulatory Reform in the EU: A Time-Series Analysis of Eight Sectors, 1984–2012*, 53 EUR. J. POL. RES. 709, 723 (2014).

31. Tanja Börzel, *Pace-Setting, Foot-Dragging, and Fence-Sitting: Member State Responses to Europeanization*, 40 J. COMMON MKT. STUD. 193, 200 (2002).

32. Simon Hix, *The European Union as a Polity*, *in* HANDBOOK OF EUROPEAN UNION POLITICS, 141 (Knud Erik Jørgensen et al. eds., 1st ed. 2006); MARK A. POLLACK, THE ENGINES OF EUROPEAN INTEGRATION: DELEGATION, AGENCY, AND AGENDA SETTING IN THE EU 384–85 (2003). *But see, e.g.*, Simon Hug, *Endogenous Preferences and Delegation in the European Union*, 36 COMP. POL. STUD. 41, 67 (2003).

33. Giandomenico Majone, *From the Positive to the Regulatory State: Causes and Consequences of Changes in the Mode of Governance*, 17 J. PUB. POL'Y 139, 157 (1997) [hereinafter Majone, *Causes and Consequences*].

34. Giandomenico Majone, *The European Commission as Regulator*, *in* REGULATING EUROPE 61, 64 (Giandomenico Majone ed., 1996) [hereinafter Majone, *Commission as*

Regulator]; James A. Caporaso et al., *Still a Regulatory State? The European Union and the Financial Crisis*, 22 J. EUR. PUB. POL'Y 889, 901 (2015).

35. *See Fact Check on the EU Budget*, EUROPA, https://ec.europa.eu/info/about-european-commission/eu-budget/how-it- works/fact-check_en (last visited May 15, 2019) [https://perma.cc/RA53-4EFR]; *EU Budget 2017: Strengthening the Economy and Responding to Migration Challenges*, EUROPA, http://ec.europa.eu/budget/library/biblio/documents/2016/factsheet-on-eu-%20budget-2017_en.pdf (last updated Dec. 10, 2016) [https://perma.cc/TCW5-Y8ZC].

36. *See Graphics*, Congressional Budget Office, https://www.cbo.gov/publication/most-recent/graphics (last visited Oct. 14, 2018) [https://perma.cc/5FSU-XN7T].

37. Majone, *Causes and Consequences, supra* note 33, at 150–51.

38. *Id.* at 150.

39. Majone, *Commission as Regulator, supra* note 34, at 64.

40. *See* Giandomenico Majone, *The Rise of the Regulatory State in Europe*, 17 W. EUR. POL. 77, 85, 98 (1994).

41. Majone, *Commission as Regulator, supra* note 34, at 63–64; Giandomenico Majone, *From Regulatory State to a Democratic Default*, 52 J. COMMON MKT. STUD. 1216, 1217 (2014).

42. Consolidated Version of the Treaty on the Functioning of the European Union arts. 23–25, Mar. 30, 2010, 2010 O.J. (C 83) 47, 58 [hereinafter TFEU].

43. *See id.*

44. *See id.* art. 3(3); Single European Act art. 6, Feb. 17, 1986, 1987 O.J. (L 169) 1.

45. POLLACK, *supra* note 32, at 14–15.

46. *Id.* at 384–85.

47. EUROPEAN UNION, EUROPEAN PARLIAMENT, FUTURE OF EUROPE: EUROPEAN PARLIAMENT SETS OUT ITS VISION (2017), https://www.europarl.europa.eu/resources/library/media/20171023RES86651/20171023RES86651.pdf [https://perma.cc/8XSG-YXP7].

48. Case C-507/17, Google v. CNIL, Request for a Preliminary Ruling from the Counseil d'État (France), 2017 O.J. (C 347) 22.

49. *See, e.g.*, Consolidated Version of the Treaty on European Union art. 3, ¶ 5, May 9, 2008, 2008 O.J. (C 115) 13 [hereinafter TEU].

50. *See, e.g.*, Case C-300/89, Comm'n v. Council (Titanium Dioxide Case), 1991 E.C.R. I-02867; Case C-155/91, Comm'n v. Council (Directive on Waste—Legal Basis), 1993 E.C.R. I-00939.

51. *See* VOGEL, POLITICS, *supra* note 5, at 237.

52. Council Regulation 1907/2006 of Dec. 18, 2006, Concerning the Registration, Evaluation, Authorisation, and Restriction of Chemicals (REACH), and Creating a Chemicals Agency, 2006 O.J. (L 396).

53. *Commission White Paper: Strategy for a Future Chemicals Policy*, 7, COM (2001) 88 final (Feb. 27, 2001).

54. Political Agreement for a Council Common Position (EC) No. 15921/2005 of Dec. 19, 2005, art. 1, 2005, http://ec.europa.eu/environment/chemicals/reach/pdf/background/political_agreement_council.pdf [https://perma.cc/QM2Q-H754].

55. GLORIA GONZÁLEZ FUSTER, THE EMERGENCE OF PERSONAL DATA PROTECTION AS A FUNDAMENTAL RIGHT OF THE EU 126 (2014).

56. Commission Recommendation 81/679 of July 29, 1981, Relating to the Council of Europe Convention for the Protection of Individuals with Regard to Automatic Processing of Personal Data, recital 3, 1981 O.J. (L 246/31).

57. *Communication from the Commission to the European Parliament and the Council: A European Data Protection Framework for the 21st Century*, at 8, COM (2012) 43 final (Jan. 25, 2012).

58. *Commission White Paper: Europe and the Global Information Society*, at 22 (June 24, 1994), http://aei.pitt.edu/1199/1/info_society_bangeman_report.pdf [https://perma.cc/B7RC-YL76].

59. *Proposal for A Comprehensive Approach on Personal Data Protection in the European Union*, at 3–4, 10, COM (2010) 609 final (Apr. 11, 2010), https://eur-lex.europa.eu/legal-content/GA/ALL/?uri=CELEX%3A52010DC0609 [https://perma.cc/K7NH-5SG8].

60. *Commission Staff Working Paper and Executive Summary of the Impact Assessment on the General Data Protection Regulation*, at 2, SEC (2012) 73 final (Jan. 25, 2012), https://eur-lex.europa.eu/legal-content/EN/TXT/PDF/?uri=CELEX:52012SC0073&from=EN [https://perma.cc/F3NB-UQLD].

61. See chapter 9 discussing regulatory imperialism and other criticism of the Brussels Effect.

62. *See* Sieglinde Gstöhl, *Political Dimensions of an Externalization of the EU's Internal Market* 4-5 (Dep't of EU Int'l Relations & Diplomacy Studies, EU Diplomacy Papers No. 3/2007, 2007), http://aei.pitt.edu/9593/1/EDP_3-2007_Gst%C3%B6hl.pdf [https://perma.cc/B2FX-ZJ7F].

63. According to polls, 70% of Europeans want Europe to assume this role. *See* Benita Ferrero-Waldner, European Comm'r for External Relations & European Neighbourhood Pol'y, Speech at George Bush Presidential Library Foundation and Texas A&M University EU Center of Excellence: The European Union: A Global Power? (Sept. 25, 2006), http://europa.eu/rapid/pressReleasesAction.do?reference=SPEECH/06/530&format=PDF&aged=1&language=EN&guiLanguage=en [https://perma.cc/JWT3-RMN6]; *see also* European Comm'n, Taking Europe to the World 59 (2004); Alasdair R. Young & John Peterson, *The EU and the New Trade Politics, in* The European Union and the New Trade Politics 1, 2 (John Peterson & Alasdair R. Young eds., 2007).

64. *See Commission White Paper: Completing the Internal Market*, at 22 COM (85) 310 final (June 28, 1985), https://eur-lex.europa.eu/legal-content/EN/ALL/?uri=CELEX%3A51985DC0310 [https://perma.cc/SXF6-GYS3]; *Commission on The Impact and Effectiveness of the Single Market*, COM (96) 520 final (Oct. 30, 1996), https://publications.europa.eu/en/publication-detail/-/publication/84e25462-8584-43db-bcca-da3aee83522f/language-en [https://perma.cc/P6YR-VB69].

65. *Commission Staff Working Document on The External Dimension of the Single Market Review*, at 5–6, SEC (2007) 1519 (Nov. 20, 2007).

66. *Id.* at 8.

67. *Communication on A Single Market for 21st Century Europe*, at 7, COM (2007) 725 final (Nov. 20, 2007) [hereinafter *A Single Market for 21st Century Europe*].

68. *Communication on A Single Market for Citizens*, at 7, COM (2007) 60 final (Feb. 21, 2007); *see also Reducing Emissions from the Aviation Sector*, Eur. Comm'n, http://ec.europa.eu/clima/policies/transport/aviation/index_en.htm (last updated Nov. 13, 2012) [https://perma.cc/X69S-F3GW].

69. *Communication on An Area of Freedom, Security and Justice Serving the Citizen*, at 9, COM (2009) 262 final (June 10, 2009).

70. *Communication on A Comprehensive Approach on Personal Data Protection in the EU*, at 19, COM (2010) 609 final (Nov. 4, 2010).

71. *Id.* at 16 (original emphasis removed).

72. Mark Scott and Laurens Cerulus, *Europe's New Data Protection Rules Export Privacy Standards Worldwide*, Politico (Jan. 31, 2018), https://www.politico.eu/article/europe-data-protection-privacy-standards-gdpr-general-protection-data-regulation/ [https://perma.cc/PKM3-BA3V].

73. European Commission, Trade for All—Towards a More Responsible Trade and Investment Policy, 14 October 2015, https://publications.europa.eu/en/publication-detail/-/publication/84e25462-8584-43db-bcca-da3aee83522f [https://perma.cc/48EY-35SX].

74. European Council, *Promoting EU Value Through Trade* (last updated Nov. 14, 2017), http://www.consilium.europa.eu/en/policies/trade-policy/promoting-eu-values/ [https://perma.cc/B6X3-XAW9].

75. See TEU art. 3 ¶5, art. 21 ¶1.

76. *A Single Market for 21st Century Europe, supra* note 67, at 3.

77. *See, e.g.,* Emma Tucker, *Plastic Toy Quandary that EU Cannot Duck,* FIN. TIMES, Dec. 9, 1998, at 3.

78. VOGEL, POLITICS, *supra* note 5, at 13.

79. *See* Jan Zielonka, *Europe as a Global Actor: Empire by Example?,* 84 INT'L AFF. 471, 475 (2008).

80. *See* Zaki Laïdi, *The Unintended Consequences of European Power* 5 (Les Cahiers Européens de Sciences Po. No. 5, 2007), http://www.cee.sciences-po.fr/erpa/docs/wp_2007_5.pdf [https://perma.cc/V5MK-SFNW].

CHAPTER 2

1. *See, e.g.,* Daniel W. Drezner, *Globalization, Harmonization, and Competition: The Different Pathways to Policy Convergence,* 12 J. EUR. PUB. POL'Y 841, 847 (2005) [hereinafter Drezner, *Different Pathways*]; *see also, e.g.,* David A. Wirth, *The EU's New Impact on U.S. Environmental Regulation,* 31 FLETCHER F. WORLD AFF. 91, 96 (2007).

2. *See* Drezner, *Different Pathways, supra* note 1, at 843.

3. DANIEL W. DREZNER, ALL POLITICS IS GLOBAL: EXPLAINING INTERNATIONAL REGULATORY REGIMES 33–62 (2008).

4. Chad Damro, *Market Power Europe,* 19 J. EUR. PUB. POL'Y 682, 683 (2012).

5. *Id.* at 687.

6. *See* DAVID VOGEL & ROBERT A. KAGAN, DYNAMICS OF REGULATORY CHANGE: HOW GLOBALIZATION AFFECTS NATIONAL REGULATORY POLICIES 13 (David Vogel & Robert A. Kagan eds., 2004).

7. *See* Alasdair R. Young, *Political Transfer and "Trading Up"? Transatlantic Trade in Genetically Modified Food and U.S. Politics,* 55 WORLD POL. 457, 459 (2003).

8. *European Union,* CIA WORLD FACTBOOK, https://www.cia.gov/library/publications/the-world-factbook/geos/ee.html (last visited Sept. 24, 2018) [https://perma.cc/23LD-7NEU]. The GDP figure is the nominal GDP.

9. *GNI, Atlas Method (Current US$),* THE WORLD BANK, https://data.worldbank.org/indicator/NY.GNP.ATLS.CD?locations=EU-1W (last visited Sept. 24, 2018) [https://perma.cc/GK32-68NU].

10. *Country Comparison: Imports,* CIA WORLD FACTBOOK, https://www.cia.gov/library/Publications/the-world-factbook/rankorder/2087rank.html (last visited Sept. 24, 2018) [https://perma.cc/4RZ9-RCQZ]. *See International Trade in Services,* EUROSTAT, https://ec.europa.eu/eurostat/statistics-explained/index.php?title=International_trade_in_services (last visited Sept. 24, 2018) [https://perma.cc/RAQ5-VR5R]; *U.S. Imports of Services by Major Category,* U.S. CENSUS BUREAU, https://www.census.gov/foreign-trade/Press-Release/current_press_release/exh4.pdf (last visited Sept. 24, 2018) [https://perma.cc/QC6K-WCRN].

11. *United States,* CIA WORLD FACTBOOK, https://www.cia.gov/library/publications/the-world-factbook/geos/us.html (last visited Sept. 24, 2018) [https://perma.cc/4CYP-SC63]; *China,* CIA WORLD FACTBOOK, https://www.cia.gov/library/publications/the-world-factbook/geos/ch.html (last visited Sept. 24, 2018) [https://perma.cc/B9YW-6X6E]; *Japan,* CIA WORLD FACTBOOK, https://www.cia.gov/library/publications/the-world-factbook/geos/ja.html (last visited Sept. 24, 2018) [https://perma.cc/E5SG-J8U8]. The GDP figures are the nominal GDP.

12. *European Union, supra* note 8; *United States, supra* note 11; *China, supra* note 11; *India*, CIA World Factbook, https://www.cia.gov/library/publications/the-world-factboo k/geos/in.html (last visited Sept. 24, 2018) [https://perma.cc/CAR8-PYX9].

13. *Statistics Relating to Enlargement of the European Union*, Wikipedia, https:// en.wikipedia.org/wiki/Statistics_relating_to_enlargement_of_the_European_Union (last visited Sept. 24, 2018) [https://perma.cc/XFT5-XY3W].

14. *See Negotiations and Agreements*, European Commission, http://ec.europa.eu/ trade/policy/countries-and-regions/negotiations-and-agreements/ (last visited Sept. 24, 2018) [https://perma.cc/F2Y9-YUGP].

15. *See generally* Alberto Alesina & Enrico Spolaore, The Size of Nations (2003).

16. *Bilateral trade between European Union (EU 28) and United States of America*, ITC, https://www.trademap.org/Bilateral_TS.aspx?nvpm=1||14719|842||TOTAL|||2|1|1|1 |2|1|1|1 (last visited Sept. 24, 2018) [https://perma.cc/N795-4LSR]; *Bilateral trade between European Union (EU 28) and Russian Federation*, ITC, https://www.trademap. org/Bilateral_TS.aspx?nvpm=1||14719|643||TOTAL|||2|1|1|1|2|1|1|1|1 (last visited Sept. 24, 2018) [https://perma.cc/P5F4-K7F]; *Bilateral trade between European Union (EU 28) and South Africa*, ITC, https://www.trademap.org/Bilateral_TS.aspx?nvpm=1||147 19|710||TOTAL|||2|1|1|1|2|1|1|1|1 (last visited Sept. 24, 2018) [https://perma.cc/AS76-E5GL]; *Bilateral trade between European Union (EU 28) and China*, ITC, https://www. trademap.org/Bilateral_TS.aspx?nvpm=1||14719|156||TOTAL|||2|1|1|1|2|1|1|1|1 (last vis-ited Sept. 24, 2018) [https://perma.cc/KJ9R-FAAU]; *Bilateral trade between European Union (EU 28) and Canada*, ITC, https://www.trademap.org/Bilateral_TS.aspx?nvpm =1||14719|124||TOTAL|||2|1|1|1|2|1|1|1|1 (last visited Sept. 24, 2018) [https://perma.cc/ P663-8XA6]; *Bilateral trade between European Union (EU 28) and Japan*, ITC, https:// www.trademap.org/Bilateral_TS.aspx?nvpm=1||14719|392||TOTAL|||2|1|1|1|2|1|1|1| 1 (last visited Sept. 24, 2018) [https://perma.cc/2SER-6HFN]; *Bilateral trade between European Union (EU 28) and India*, ITC, https://www.trademap.org/Bilateral_TS.asp x?nvpm=1||14719|699||TOTAL|||2|1|1|1|2|1|1|1|1 (last visited Sept. 24, 2018) [https:// perma.cc/5JJK-6CP7]; *Bilateral trade between European Union (EU 28) and Brazil*, ITC, https://www.trademap.org/Bilateral_TS.aspx?nvpm=1||14719|076||TOTAL|||2 |1|1|1|2|1|1|1|1 (last visited Sept. 24, 2018) [https://perma.cc/689M-BNEY]; *Bilateral trade between European Union (EU 28) and Australia*, ITC, https://www.trademap.org/ Bilateral_TS.aspx?nvpm=1||14719|036||TOTAL|||2|1|1|1|2|1|1|1|1 (last visited Sept. 24, 2018) [https://perma.cc/P9LS-QDCA]; *Bilateral trade between European Union (EU 28) and Korea, Republic of*, ITC, https://www.trademap.org/Bilateral_TS.aspx?nvpm= 1||14719|410||TOTAL|||2|1|1|1|2|1|1|1|1 (last visited Sept. 24, 2018) [https://perma.cc/ R6PD-D7EG].

17. *United States, supra* note 16; *Russia, supra* note 16; *China, supra* note 16; *India, supra* note 16; *Brazil, supra* note 16; *Canada, supra* note 16; *Australia, supra* note 16; *Korea, supra* note 16; *Japan, supra* note 16; *South Africa, supra* note 16.

18. Sorin Burnete & Pilasluck Choomta, *The Impact of European Union's Newly-Adopted Environmental Standards on Its Trading Partners*, 10 Stud. in Bus. & Econ. 5, 11 (2015) *quoting* Jan Ahlen, The "EU Effect" and the Export of Environmental Standards to the U.S., (2009) (unpublished MA thesis, University of North Carolina), https://cdr.lib.unc. edu/indexablecontent/uuid:5045f331-b321-4b5b-991b-596dcod74bo6 [https://perma. cc/HJ3H-5HAX].

19. Facebook, Inc., Annual Report (Form 10-K) 35–38 (Feb. 1, 2018).

20. Robinson Meyer, *Europeans Use Google Way, Way More Than Americans Do*, Atlantic (Apr. 15, 2015), https://www.theatlantic.com/technology/archive/2015/04/europeans-use-google-way-way-more-than-americans-do/390612/ [https://perma.cc/Y6RN-JSNG].

21. Alphabet, Inc., Annual Report (Form 10-K) 32 (Feb. 5, 2018); Amazon.com, Inc., Annual Report (Form 10-K) 70 (Feb. 1, 2018).

22. Kevin Grogan, *Takeda Gives Up on Getting European OK for Sleep Drug*, PHARMA TIMES (Oct. 7, 2011), http://www.pharmatimes.com/news/takeda_gives_up_on_getting_european_ok_for_sleep_drug_980275 [https://perma.cc/MTU2-CB5E].

23. *Id.*

24. Kate O'Neill, *The Changing Nature of Global Hazardous Waste Management: From Brown to Green?, in* DYNAMICS OF REGULATORY CHANGE, 156, 156–58 (David Vogel & Robert A. Kagan eds., 2004).

25. *See id.* at 156–58.

26. *See* Jan Zielonka, *Europe as a Global Actor: Empire by Example?*, 84 INT'L AFF. 471, 477–80 (2008).

27. *See* Emilie M. Hafner-Burton, *Trading Human Rights: How Preferential Trade Agreements Influence Government Repression*, 59 INT'L ORG. 593 (2005).

28. *See* David Bach & Abraham L. Newman, *The European Regulatory State and Global Public Policy: Micro-Institutions, Macro-Influence*, 14 J. EUR. PUB. POL'Y 827, 831 (2007).

29. *See id.* at 832.

30. *See* David Bach & Abraham L. Newman, *Domestic Drivers of Transgovernmental Regulatory Cooperation*, 8 REG. & GOVERNANCE 395 (2014).

31. *See* Colin Kirkpatrick & David Parker, *Infrastructure Regulation: Models for Developing Asia* 40–41 (Asian Dev. Bank Inst. Discussion Paper No. 6, 2004), https://www.adb.org/sites/default/files/publication/156701/adbi-dp6.pdf [https://perma.cc/9C9L-GSEF]; *see* Xiaoye Wang, *Highlights of China's New Anti-Monopoly Law*, 75 ANTITRUST L.J. 133, 145 (2008).

32. *See* Nikhil Kalyanpur & Abraham L. Newman, *Mobilizing Market Power: Jurisdictional Expansion as Economic Statecraft* 8 (International Organization 2018), https://www.cambridge.org/core/services/aop-cambridge-core/content/view/880511974FC84FF93C95403A11788147/S0020818318000334a.pdf/mobilizing_market_power_jurisdictional_expansion_as_economic_statecraft.pdf [https://perma.cc/8J8R-36VZ].

33. *See* Sophie Meunier & Kalypso Nicolaïdis, *The European Union as a Conflicted Trade Power*, 13 J. EUR. PUB. POL'Y 906, 907-08 (2006).

34. *See* Giandomenico Majone, *The Rise of the Regulatory State in Europe, in* A READER ON REGULATION 77, 83–101 (1998).

35. *See* Bach &. Newman, *supra* note 28, at 831.

36. *See* Andreja Pegan, *The Bureaucratic Growth of the European Union*, 13 J. CONTEMP. EUR. RES. 1208–34, 1210 (2017).

37. *See id.* at 1210.

38. OFFICE OF MGMT. & BUDGET, EXEC. OFFICE OF THE PRESIDENT, ANALYTICAL PERSPECTIVES: BUDGET OF THE U.S. GOVERNMENT FISCAL YEAR 2018 62 (2018), https://www.gpo.gov/fdsys/pkg/BUDGET-2018-PER/pdf/BUDGET-2018-PER.pdf [https://perma.cc/8BYG-9Q8M].

39. OFFICE OF PERSONNEL MGMT., EXEC. OFFICE OF THE PRESIDENT, SIZING UP THE EXECUTIVE BRANCH: FISCAL YEAR 2018 6 (2018), https://www.opm.gov/policy-data-oversight/data-analysis-documentation/federal-employment-reports/reports-publications/sizing-up-the-executive-branch-2016.pdf [https://perma.cc/426U-UB5T].

40. *See id.*

41. HUSSEIN KASSIM, JOHN PETERSON & MICHAEL W. BAUER, THE EUROPEAN COMMISSION OF THE TWENTY-FIRST CENTURY 39 (2013).

42. ANTONIS A. ELLINAS & EZRA SULEIMAN, THE EUROPEAN COMMISSION AND BUREAUCRATIC AUTONOMY 10–11 (2012).

43. *See* Liesbet Hooghe, *Images of Europe: How Commission Officials Conceive Their Institution's Role*, 50 J. COMMON MKT. STUD. 87, 101 (2012).

44. *See* Liesbet Hooghe, *Several Roads Lead to International Norms, but Few via International Socialization: A Case Study of the European Commission*, 59 INT'L ORG. 861, 874 (2005).

45. *Id.*

46. *See* Antonis Ellinas & Ezra S. Suleiman, *Supranationalism in a Transnational Bureaucracy: The Case of the European Commission*, 49 J. COMMON MKT. STUD. 924, 941 (2011); Jeremy Richardson, *The Onward March of Europeanization: Tectonic Movement and Seismic Events, in* CONSTRUCTING A POLICY-MAKING STATE? POLICY DYNAMICS IN THE EU 334, 340 (Jeremy Richardson ed., 2012).

47. *See* Berthold Rittberger & Arndt Wonka, *Introduction: Agency Governance in the European Union*, 18 J. EUR. PUB. POL'Y 780, 782 (2011); Mark Thatcher, *The Creation of European Regulatory Agencies and its Limits: a Comparative Analysis of European Delegation*, 18 J. EUR. PUB. POL'Y 790, 801–02 (2011); Daniel Kelemen, *The Politics of 'Eurocratic' Structure and the New European Agencies*, 25 W. EUR. POL. 93 (2002); David Levi-Faur, *Regulatory Networks and Regulatory Agencification: Towards a Single European Regulatory Space*, 18 J. EUR. PUB. POL'Y 810, 813 (2011).

48. John Peterson, *The Commission and the New Intergovernmentalism, in* THE NEW INTERGOVERNMENTALISM: STATES AND SUPRANATIONAL ACTORS IN THE POST-MAASTRICHT ERA 185, 197 (Bickerton et al. eds., 2015).

49. *See* Bach & Newman, *supra* note 28, at 832.

50. Regulation (EU) 679/16, art. 83, 2016 O.J. (L119) 1.

51. European Commission Press Release IP/17/1784, Antitrust: Commission Fines Google €2.42 Billion For Abusing Dominance as Search Engine by Giving Illegal Advantage to Own Comparison Shopping Service (June 27, 2017), https://europa.eu/rapid/press-release_IP-17-1784_en.htm [https://perma.cc/BEX2-FPRZ]; European Commission Press Release IP/18/4581, Antitrust: Commission Fines Google €4.34 Billion for Illegal Practices Regarding Android Mobile Devices to Strengthen Dominance of Google's Search Engine (July 18, 2018), https://europa.eu/rapid/press-release_IP-18-4581_en.htm [https://perma.cc/BEX2-FPRZ]; European Commission Press Release IP/19/1770, Antitrust: Commission Fines Google €1.49 Billion for Abusive Practices in Online Advertising (Mar. 20, 2019), http://europa.eu/rapid/press-release_IP-19-1770_en.htm [https://perma.cc/8L6C-PD2J].

52. LORNA WOODS & PHILIPPA WATSON, STEINER & WOODS EU LAW 51 (12th ed. 2014).

53. R. Daniel Kelemen, *Law, Fiscal Federalism, and Austerity*, 22 IND. J. GLOBAL LEGAL STUD. 379 (2015).

54. Case C-438/05, Int'l Transp. Workers' Fed'n v. Viking Line ABP, 2007 E.C.R. I-10779; *See* Darren G. Hawkins, David A. Lake, Daniel L. Nielson & Michael J. Tierney, *Delegation Under Anarchy: States, International Organizations, and Principal-Agent Theory, in* DELEGATION AND AGENCY IN INTERNATIONAL ORGANIZATIONS 3–38 (Darren G. Hawkins et. al. eds., 2006)

55. Case C-376/98 Germany v Parliament and the Council ("Tobacco Advertising I"), 2000 E.C.R. 8419 and Case C-380/03 Germany v Parliament and the Council ("Tobacco advertising II"), 2006 E.C.R. 11573.

56. See Philip Blenkinsop, *EU Takes Ireland to Court for Not Claiming Apple Tax Windfall*, REUTERS (Oct. 4, 2017), https://www.reuters.com/article/us-eu-apple-taxavoidance-court/eu-takes-ireland-to-court-for-not-claiming-apple-tax-windfall-idUSKCN1C913I [https://perma.cc/B27G-RUH3]; Simon Bowers, *Starbucks and Fiat Sweetheart Tax Deals with EU Nations Ruled Unlawful*, GUARDIAN (Oct. 21, 2015), https://www.theguardian.com/business/2015/oct/21/starbucks-and-fiat-tax-deals-with-eu-nations-ruled-unlawful [https://perma.cc/F8PT-KLMY].

57. Consolidated Version of the Treaty on the Functioning of the European Union, June 7, 2016, 2016 O.J. (C202) 59 [hereinafter TFEU], arts. 107,108, 109.

58. Stephen C. Sieberson, *Inching toward EU Supranationalism—Qualified Majority Voting and Unanimity under the Treaty of Lisbon*, 50 VA. J. INT'L L. 919 (2010).

59. Elisa Morgera, *Environmental Law, in* EUR. UNION LAW 657 (Barnard & Peers eds., 2014).

60. *See, e.g.*, Single European Act art. 6, Feb. 17, 1986, 1987 O.J. (L 169) 1; Treaty on European Union art. G, Feb. 7, 1992, 1992 O.J. (C 191) 1, 5-44; Treaty of Lisbon Amending the Treaty on European Union and the Treaty Establishing the European Community, Dec. 13, 2007, 2007 O.J. (C 306) 1 [hereinafter Treaty of Lisbon].

61. TFEU art. 294.

62. George Tsebelis & Geoffrey Garret, *Legislative Politics in the European Union*, 1 EUR. UNION. POL. 9 (2000); Oliver Costa & Nathalie Brack, *The Role of the European Parliament in Europe's Integration and Parlamentarization Process, in* PARLIAMENTARY DIMENSIONS OF REGIONALIZATION AND GLOBALIZATION 45, 45–69 (2013).

63. RENAUD DEHOUSSE, THE EUROPEAN COURT OF JUSTICE: THE POLITICS OF JUDICIAL INTEGRATION (1998).

64. R. Daniel Kelemen & Susan K. Schmidt, *Introduction—the European Court of Justice and Legal Integration: Perpetual Momentum?*, 19 J. EUR. PUB. POL'Y 1 (2012); JUDICIAL ACTIVISM AT THE EUROPEAN COURT OF JUSTICE (Mark Dawson et al., 2013).

65. Case C-6/64, Flaminio Costa v. E.N.E.L., 1964 E.C.R. 585.

66. Case C-26/62, Onderneming van Gend & Loos v. Neth. Inland Revenue Admin., 1963 E.C.R. 3.

67. Duncan Robinson & Alex Barker, *EU's top judge defends ECJ against charges of integration agenda*, FINANCIAL TIMES (Nov. 22, 2016), https://www.ft.com/content/0e132ef8-af0c-11e6-a37c-f4a01f1b0fa1 (on file with author); *see* Keleman & Schmidt, *supra* note 64.

68. *See, e.g.*, Case C-333/13, Dano v. Jobcenter Leipzig, 2014 E.C.R. 2358.

69. *See* Giandomenico Majone, *From the Positive to the Regulatory State: Causes and Consequences of Changes in the Mode of Governance,* 17 J. PUB. POL'Y 139, 144 (1997).

70. *See id.* at 163.

71. *Compare* TFEU, *supra* note 57, arts. 3–4, *with id.* art. 6.

72. *See* TFEU, 2016 O.J. (C202) 59, arts. 3, 4, and 6.

73. J. Luis Guasch & Robert W. Hahn, *The Costs and Benefits of Regulation: Implications for Developing Countries*, 14 WORLD BANK RES. OBSERVER 137, 138 (1999); *see also* Euel Elliott, James L. Regens & Barry J. Seldon, *Exploring Variation in Public Support for Environmental Protection*, 76 SOC. SCI. Q. 41 (1995).

74. *See, e.g.*, Ragnar E. Löfstedt & David Vogel, *The Changing Character of Regulation: A Comparison of Europe and the United States*, 21 RISK ANALYSIS 399, 400-01 (2001).

75. *See* DAVID VOGEL, THE POLITICS OF PRECAUTION: REGULATING HEALTH, SAFETY, AND ENVIRONMENTAL RISKS IN EUROPE AND THE UNITED STATES 10 (2012) [hereinafter VOGEL, POLITICS].

76. *See* R. Daniel Kelemen & David Vogel, *Trading Places: The US and the EU in International Environmental Politics*, 43:4 COMP. POL. STUD. 427.

77. *See supra* note 75 at 22–42.

78. *See supra* note 75 at 34–42, 235–36.

79. Single European Act, Feb. 17, 1986, 1987 O.J. (L169) [hereinafter SEA].

80. *See* IAN BACHE & STEPHEN GEORGE, POLITICS IN THE EUROPEAN UNION 160 (1st ed. 2006).

81. MITCHELL P. SMITH, ENVIRONMENTAL AND HEALTH REGULATION IN THE UNITED STATES AND THE EUROPEAN UNION: PROTECTING PUBLIC AND PLANET 2 (2012).

82. Paulette Kerzer, *Transatlantic Risk Perceptions, Public Health, and Environmental Concerns: Coming Together or Drifting Apart?, in* THE STATE OF THE EUROPEAN UNION VOL. 7: WITH US OR AGAINST US? EUROPEAN TRENDS IN AMERICAN PERSPECTIVE (2006).

83. Ben Clift, *Comparative Capitalism, Ideational Political Economy and French Post-Dirigiste Responses to the Global Financial Crisis,* 17 J. NEW POL. ECON. 565 (2012); Ulrich Witt, *Germany's "Social Market Economy": Between Social Ethos and Rent Seeking,* 6 INDEP. REV. 365 (2002).

84. *See* Clift, *supra* note 83, at 565; Witt, *supra* note 83, at 365.

85. Stein Kuhnle, *The Beginnings of the Nordic Welfare States: Similarities and Differences,* 21 ACTA SOCIOLOGICA 9 (1978).

86. VEIT KOESTER, NORDIC COUNTRIES' LEGISLATION ON THE ENVIRONMENT WITH SPECIAL EMPHASIS ON CONSERVATION—A SURVEY, (1979); KONRAD ADENAUER STIFTUNG, HISTORY OF ENERGY AND CLIMATE ENERGY POLICY IN GERMANY: CUD PERSPECTIVES 1958–2014 (2014).

87. *Commission Institutional Paper on State-Owned Enterprises in the EU: Lessons Learnt and Ways Forward in a Post-Crisis Context,* No. 031, COM (July 2016), https://ec.europa.eu/info/sites/info/files/file_import/ipo31_en_2.pdf [https://perma.cc/QSC8-83ZZ].

88. *See* PETER A. HALL & DAVID SOSKICE, VARIETIES OF CAPITALISM: THE INSTITUTIONAL FOUNDATIONS OF COMPARATIVE ADVANTAGE (2001).

89. Treaty of Lisbon, *supra* note 60, art. 1(4).

90. Katharina Pistor, *Legal Ground Rules in Coordinated and Liberal Market Economies,* ECGI—LAW WORKING PAPER No. 30/2005 (2005), https://ecgi.global/sites/default/files/working_papers/documents/SSRN-id695763.pdf [https://perma.cc/FW5U-Z98N].

91. Kira Brecht, *How US and EU Capital Markets are Different,* OPEN MARKET (Oct. 29, 2015), http://openmarkets.cmegroup.com/10431/how-u-s-and-eu-capital-markets-are-different [https://perma.cc/2K4Y-BUB7]; Ines Goncalves Raposo & Alexander Lehmann, *Equity Finance and Capital Market Integration in Europe,* EUROPEAN UNION (Jan. 2019), http://bruegel.org/wp-content/uploads/2019/01/PC-2019-03.pdf [https://perma.cc/B5XV-SMYJ].

92. *See* Jonathan B. Wiener & Michael D. Rogers, *Comparing Precaution in the United States and Europe,* 5:4 J. OF RISK RESEARCH 317, 336 (2002), https://scholarship.law.duke.edu/cgi/viewcontent.cgi?article=1985&context=faculty_scholarship [https://perma.cc/Z2HJ-DWJC].

93. Andreas Ladner, *The Polarization of the European Party System—New Data, New Approach, New Results* 7 (Sept. 5, 2014) (paper presented in panel P361—"The Methodological Challenges of Designing Cross-National Voting Advice Applications" at the ECPR General Conference), https://ecpr.eu/Filestore/PaperProposal/f989009a-d679-465d-aff7-f6573671fd16.pdf [https://perma.cc/W4UQ-PBQU].

94. Jean-Claude Juncker, Candidate for President, Eur. Comm'n, Opening Statement in the European Parliament Plenary Session, A New Start for Europe: My Agenda for Jobs, Growth, Fairness and Democratic Change §6 (July 15, 2014).

95. Susan Rose-Ackerman, *Regulation and the Law of Torts,* 81 AM. ECON. R. 54, 54 (1991).

96. *See* W. K. Viscusi, *Structuring an Effective Occupational Disease Policy: Victim Compensation and Risk Regulation,* 2 YALE J. REG. 53 (1984); Richard Posner, *Regulation (Agencies) versus Litigation (Courts): An Analytical Framework, in* REGULATION VS. LITIGATION: PERSPECTIVES FROM ECONOMICS AND LAW 11, 20 (2011).

97. *See* Steven Shavell, *Liability for Accidents, in* HANDBOOK FOR LAW AND ECONOMICS 142, 176 (Vol. 1, 2007).

98. *See* Steven Shavell, *Liability for Harm versus Regulation of Safety,* 13 J. L. STUD. 357, 369 (1984) [hereinafter Shavell, *Liability for Harm*].

99. *See id.* at 357.
100. *See* Posner, *supra* note 96, at 14.
101. *See* W. Kip Viscusi, *Toward a Diminished Role for Tort Liability: Social Insurance, Government Regulation, and Contemporary Risks to Health and Safety*, 6 YALE J. REG. 65, 71 (1989) [hereinafter Viscusi, *Tort Liability*].
102. *See* R. DANIEL KELEMEN, EUROLEGALISM: THE TRANSFORMATION OF LAW AND REGULATION IN THE EUROPEAN UNION 28 (2011).
103. European Commission Press Release IP/18/3041, A New Deal for Consumers: Commission Strengthens EU Consumer Rights and Enforcement (Apr. 11, 2018). This proposed legislation would replace the EU's 2009 Injunctions Directive, which allows for representative actions to obtain injunctive relief but does not recognize collective redress. *See* Directive 2009/22/EC of the European Parliament and of the Council of 23 April 2009 on Injunctions for the Protection of Consumers' Interests, 2009 O.J. (L 110) 30.
104. *See* VOGEL, POLITICS, *supra* note 75, at 257.
105. *See* 3 C.F.R. 215.
106. *See* Exec. Ord. No. 12,866, 3 C.F.R. 638 (1994); Unfunded Mandates Reform Act of 1995, Pub. L. No. 104-4, §§ 201-202 109 Stat. 48 (codified at 2 U.S.C. §§ 1503–32 (2014)).
107. *See, e.g.*, Indus. Union Dep't, AFL-CIO v. Am. Petroleum Inst. (*The Benzene Case*), 448 U.S. 607, 642–46 (1980); *see also* Exec. Order No. 13,563, 3 C.F.R. 215, 215 (2011). *See also* CASS R. SUNSTEIN, THE COST BENEFIT REVOLUTION 4 (2018).
108. *Communication from the Commission on Impact Assessment*, COM (2002) 276 final (June 5, 2002).
109. *Commission Staff Working Document, Better Regulation Guidelines*, at 15, SWD (2017) 350 (July 7, 2017), https://ec.europa.eu/info/sites/info/files/better-regulation-guide-lines.pdf [https://perma.cc/Q8TL-ENG2].
110. *See* Richard Parker & Alberto Alemanno, *Comparative Overview of EU and US Legislative and Regulatory Systems: Implications for Domestic Governance & the Transatlantic Trade and Investment Partnership*, 22 COLUM. J. EUR. L., 61, 85–89 (2016).
111. *Commission Staff Working Paper: Operational Guidance on Taking Account of Fundamental Rights in Commission Impact Assessments*, SEC (2011) 567 final (May 6, 2011), http://ec.europa.eu/smart-regulation/impact/key_docs/docs/sec_2011_0567_en.pdf [https://perma.cc/Y2PL-HA5D].
112. *See id.* at 87.
113. *See* Jonathan Wiener & Alberto Alemanno, *Comparing Regulatory Oversight Bodies Across the Atlantic: The Office of Information and Regulatory Affairs in the US and the Impact Assessment Board in the EU*, *in* COMPARATIVE ADMINISTRATIVE LAW (Susan Rose-Ackerman & Peter Lindseth eds., 2010).
114. *See* VOGEL, POLITICS, *supra* note 75, at 261–66. For an alternative view, *see* Swedlow et al., *A Quantitative Comparison of Relative Precaution in the United States and Europe, 1970–2004*, *in* THE REALITY OF PRECAUTION: COMPARING RISK REGULATION IN THE UNITED STATES AND EUROPE 377, 378–79 (Jonathan Wiener et al. eds., 2011).
115. *See* VOGEL, POLITICS, *supra* note 75, at 4.
116. *See* VOGEL, POLITICS, *supra* note 75, at 261–66.
117. *See id.* at 259.
118. *See, e.g.*, *Communication on the Precautionary Principle*, at ¶ 1, COM (2000) 1 final (Feb. 2, 2000).
119. *See, e.g., id.; see also* Sarah Harrell, *Beyond "REACH"?: An Analysis of the European Union's Chemical Regulation Program Under World Trade Organization Agreements*, 24 WIS. INT'L L.J. 471, 481-89 (2007). *See* Case T-13/99, Pfizer Animal Health SA v. Council, 2002 E.C.R. II-3318, ¶ 142.

120. Ragnar E. Löfstedt, *The Swing of the Regulatory Pendulum in Europe: From Precautionary Principle to (Regulatory) Impact Analysis*, 28 J. RISK & UNCERTAINTY 237, 243–44 (2004).

121. Maastricht Treaty: Treaty on European Union, art. 1, 7 February 1992, 1992 O.J. (C191) 1, 31 I.L.M. 253.

122. *See* Löfstedt, *supra* note 120, at 243–45.

123. *See* Yves Tiberghien, *Competitive Governance and the Quest for Legitimacy in the EU: The Battle over the Regulation of GMOs since the mid-1990s*, 31 J. EUR. INTEGRATION 389, 404–05 (2009); Giandomenico Majone, *Political Institutions and the Principle of Precaution, in* THE REALITY OF PRECAUTION: COMPARING RISK REGULATION IN THE UNITED STATES AND EUROPE 377, 414 (Jonathan Wiener et al. eds., 2011).

124. *Communication from the Commission on the Precautionary Principle*, COM (2000) 1 final (Feb. 2, 2000); THE PRECAUTIONARY PRINCIPLE IN THE 20TH CENTURY: LATE LESSONS FROM EARLY WARNINGS 5 (Harremoes et al. eds., 2013).

125. *See* VOGEL, POLITICS, *supra* note 75, at 268–69. *See also* Giandomenico Majone, DILEMMAS OF EUROPEAN INTEGRATION 125–26 (2005).

126. *See* David Vogel, *The Hare and the Tortoise Revisited: The New Politics of Consumer and Environmental Regulation in Europe*, 33 BRIT. J. POL. SCI. 557, 566 (2003).

127. *See* VOGEL, POLITICS, *supra* note 75, at 271.

128. *See* Kenisha Garnett & David Parsons, *Multi-Case Review of the Application of the Precautionary Principle in European Union Law and Case Law*, 37 RISK ANALYSIS 502, 511 (2017).

129. *See, e.g.*, Case T-70/99, Alpharma v. Council, 2002 E.C.R. II-3506; Joined Cases T-74, T-76, T-83, T-84, T-85, T-132, T-137, T-141/00, Artegodan GmbH v. Comm'n, 2002 E.C.R. II-4948; Case T-13/99, Pfizer Animal Health, 2002 E.C.R. II-3318.

130. Joined Cases T-74, T-76, T-83, T-84, T-85, T-132, T-137, T-141/00, Artegodan GmbH v. Comm'n, 2002 E.C.R. II-4948, ¶ 184.

131. For an overview of the different regimes applied across the EU (14 countries), *see European Online Gambling Outlook 2017*, GAMBLING COMPLIANCE (Jan. 17, 2017), https://gamblingcompliance.com/premium-content/research_report/european-online-gambling-outlook-2017 [https://perma.cc/TF5K-X65N].

132. Loi 2010-476 du 12 mai 2010 relative à l'ouverture à la concurrence et à la régulation du secteur des jeux d'argent et de hasard en ligne [Law 2010-476 of May 12, 2010 on the Opening Up to Competition and Regulation of the Online Gambling Industry], https://www.legifrance.gouv.fr/affichTexte.do?cidTexte=JORFTEXT000022204510 [https://perma.cc/MY8J-LNA4]; Taylor Wessing, *Gambling Law in Germany*, LEXOLOGY (June 7, 2017), https://www.lexology.com/library/detail.aspx?g=6111b061-3533-4573-97a9-70bfd7f46d2b [https://perma.cc/9B8G-UJLV].

133. A similar issue plays out when the EU must garner some level of external regulatory consensus before it can begin to export its preferred regulation. *See, e.g.*, AR Young, *Europe as a Global Regulator: The Limits of EU Influence in International Food Safety Standards*, 21 J. EUR. PUB. POL'Y 904 (2014).

134. *See* Stephen Castle, *Europeans Introduce Corporate Tax Plan*, N.Y. TIMES, Mar. 17, 2011, at B5; *EU Corporate Tax Plan Deals Blow to Irish*, EURACTIV.COM (Mar. 16, 2011), https://www.euractiv.com/section/euro-finance/news/eu-corporate-tax-plan-deals-blow-to-irish/ [https://perma.cc/M7SM-EKRM]; *see also Tax Wars: New Versus Old Europe*, ECONOMIST, July 24, 2004, at 61.

135. See *Common Consolidated Corporate Tax Base (CCCTB)* EUROPEAN COMM'N, https://ec.europa.eu/taxation_customs/business/company-tax/common-consolidated-corporate-tax-base-ccctb_en [https://perma.cc/GK4W-VQV6]; Press Release, European Comm'n, Commission Proposes Major Corporate Tax Reform for the EU

(Oct. 25, 2016), http://europa.eu/rapid/press-release_IP-16-3471_en.htm [hereinafter Tax Reform Press Release] [https://perma.cc/NW46-Q8TN].

136. Jim Brunsden, *Brussels Proposes Europe-Wide Corporate Tax System*, FT.COM (Oct. 25, 2016), https://www.ft.com/content/4bfe986c-9ac4-11e6-b8c6-568a43813464 (on file with author).

137. Tax Reform Press Release, *supra* note 135.

138. Pat Leahy, *Michael Noonan Attacks EU Body Over Corporate Tax Plans*, IRISH TIMES (Feb. 28, 2017), https://www.irishtimes.com/business/economy/michael-noonan-attacks-eu-body-over-corporate-tax-plans-1.2991443 [https://perma.cc/JHJ5-KWN9].

139. 21 C.F.R. § 1240.61 (2018); Corrigendum to Regulation 853/2004 Laying Down Specific Hygiene Rules for Food of Animal Origin, 2004 O.J. (L 226) 22.

140. Final Determination Regarding Partially Hydrogenated Oils, 80 Fed. Reg. 34650 (June 17, 2015).

141. European Comm'n, Report From the Commission to the European Parliament and the Council Regarding Trans Fats in Foods and in the Overall Diet of the Union Population, COM (2015) 619 final (Dec. 3, 2015), https://ec.europa.eu/food/sites/food/files/safety/docs/fs_labelling-nutrition_trans-fats-report_en.pdf [https://perma.cc/F965-VHGR]; European Comm'n, *Open Public Consultation on the Initiative to Limit Industrial Trans Fats Intakes in the EU*, https://ec.europa.eu/info/consultations/open-public-consultation-initiative-limit-industrial-trans-fats-intakes-eu_en [https://perma.cc/BDE4-WWFD].

142. Sarbanes–Oxley Act of 2002, Pub. L. No. 107-204, 116 Stat. 745 (codified at 15 U.S.C. §§ 7201-7266 (2006)). *See* ABRAHAM L. NEWMAN, PROTECTORS OF PRIVACY: REGULATING PERSONAL DATA IN THE GLOBAL ECONOMY, 146 (2008).

143. Dodd–Frank Wall Street Reform and Consumer Protection Act, Pub. L. No. 111-203, 124 Stat. 1376 (codified as amended in scattered sections of 12, 15, 22, and 26 U.S.C.).

144. *See, e.g.*, Bob Sherwood, *Long Arm of the US Regulator*, FT.COM (Mar. 9, 2005, 6:37 PM), https://www.ft.com/content/be157b6a-90c6-11d9-9980-00000e2511c8 (on file with author); *see also* John C. Coffee, Jr., *Racing Towards the Top?: The Impact of Cross-Listings and Stock Market Competition on International Corporate Governance*, 102 COLUM. L. REV. 1757 (2002).

145. Regulation 2017/821 of the European Parliament and of the Council Laying Down Supply Chain Due Diligence Obligations for Union Importers of Tin, Tantalum and Tungsten, Their Ores, and Gold Originating from Conflict-Affected and High-Risk Areas, 2017 O.J. (L 130), 1 [hereinafter "Regulation 2017/821]. The substance of the regulation will enter into force in 2021 per Regulation 2017/821, Art. 20(3).

146. *See* Sue Miller, Nate Lankford & Quinnie Lin, *3 Ways EU Conflict Minerals Rule Differs from US Approach*, LAW360 (Mar. 20, 2017, 5:26 PM), https://www.law360.com/articles/903845/3-ways-eu-conflict-minerals-rule-differs-from-us-approachl [https://perma.cc/G4B3-CRFZ]; Cydney S. Posner, *European Parliament Approves Conflict Mineral Rules for EU*, COOLEY PUBCO (Mar. 20, 2017), https://cooleypubco.com/2017/03/20/european-parliament-approves-conflict-minerals-rules-for-the-eu/ [https://perma.cc/VH3G-MUNF].

147. These areas must still be defined by the EU Commission. Regulation 2017/821, Art. 14(2).

148. The US regulation limits the due diligence duties of importers to an initial "reasonable country of inquiry" test whereby the company must perform due diligence only if it has knowledge or reason to believe that a conflict mineral they employ in production comes from a country covered by the regulation. In contrast, the EU regulation requires all importers covered by the EU regulation to conduct due diligence.

149. The Personal Data Protection Bill 2018 (Draft) (India), art. 4, https://meity.gov.in/writereaddata/files/Personal_Data_Protection_Bill%2C2018_0.pdf [https://perma.cc/8ZTN-6YAX].

150. *Id.* at art. 3(13).

151. *Id.* at art 40.

152. *Id.* at art 40.

153. Note that this book takes some liberties in its use of the concepts "elastic" and "inelastic" and departs somewhat from their traditional use in economics, such as the use of the concept of demand elasticity (which refers to how sensitive demand of a good is to changes in other economic variables such as price).

154. Regulation (EC) 1907/2006, of the European Parliament and of the Council of 18 December 2006 Concerning the Registration, Evaluation, Authorisation and Restriction of Chemicals (REACH), Establishing a European Chemicals Agency, 2007 O.J. (L 136) 3 [hereinafter REACH].

155. Directive 2002/95/EC, of the European Parliament and of the Council of 27 January 2003 on the Restriction of the Use of Certain Hazardous Substances in Electrical and Electronic Equipment, 2003 O.J. (L 37) 19 [hereinafter RoHS Directive].

156. Regulation 2016/679, of the European Parliament and of the Council of 27 April 2016 on the protection of natural persons with regard to the processing of personal data and on the free movement of such data, and repealing Directive 95/46/EC (General Data Protection Regulation) 2016 O.J. (L 119) 32, 33 [hereinafter GDPR].

157. Kalyanpur & Newman, *supra* note 32.

158. Paul L. Davies, *Financial Stability and the Global Influence of EU Law, in* EU LAW BEYOND EU BORDERS: THE EXTRATERRITORIAL REACH OF EU LAW (Marise Cremona & Joanne Scott eds.2019).

159. Yesha Yadav & Dermot Turing, *The Extraterritorial Regulation of Clearinghouses*, 2 J. FIN. REG. 21, 22 (2016).

160. *Id.* at 23.

161. *Id.*

162. *Id.* at 26.

163. International capital mobility is contingent on numerous factors and assumes limited exchange controls and the ability of foreign corporations and individuals to engage in foreign direct investment (FDI) and invest in foreign stock markets.

164. *Commission Proposal for a Council Directive on a Common System of Financial Transaction Tax and Amending Directive 2008/7/EC*, COM (2011) 594 final (Sept. 28, 2011).

165. *See* Joshua Chaffin et al., *Business Lashes Out at Trading Tax Plans*, FIN. TIMES (London), Sept. 29, 2011, at 1. Press Release, European Comm'n, Common Rules for a Financial Transaction Tax—Frequently Asked Questions (Sept. 28, 2011), http://europa.eu/rapid/pressReleasesAction.do?reference=MEMO/11/640 [https://perma.cc/9A4V-AG63].

166. Boris Groendahl & Alexander Weber, *Austria Says EU Financial Transaction Tax is on Wrong Track*, BLOOMBERG (Sept. 5, 2018), https://www.bloomberg.com/news/articles/2018-09-05/austria-says-europe-s-push-for-transaction-tax-is-on-wrong-track (on file with author).

167. *See* European Comm'n, *supra* note 165. The financial transaction tax is an example where the other conditions for the Brussels Effect are also missing: the EU currently lacks the regulatory competence (or capacity) to impose this tax; the required regulatory propensity is also missing, as some member states oppose the proposal. There are also alternative markets for trading activity, reducing the EU's leverage. Finally, the tax is also divisible in the sense that all jurisdictions do not have to apply the same tax, but instead retain their autonomy to regulate trade in their jurisdictions.

168. However, a narrower proposal made by Germany and France during 2018, based on a tax levy implemented in France, showed promise during an early 2019 meeting of the finance ministers involved. *See* Alexander Weber, *Germany, France Try to Jump-Start EU Financial-Transaction Tax*, BLOOMBERG (Dec. 3, 2018), https://www.bloomberg.com/news/articles/2018-12-03/germany-france-try-to-jump-start-eu-financial-transaction-tax (on file with author).

169. Parliament and Council Directive 2013/36/EU, On Access to the Activity of Credit Institutions and the Prudential Supervision of Credit Institutions and Investment Firms, 2013 O.J. (L 176) 338.

170. Jim Brunsden, *Brussels Proposes Europe-Wide Corporate Tax System*, FIN. TIMES (Oct. 25, 2016), https://www.ft.com/content/4bfe986c-9ac4-11e6-b8c6-568a43813464 (on file with author).

171. Mehreen Khan et. al., *Google, Facebook and Apple Face 'Digital Tax' on EU Turnover*, FIN. TIMES (Mar. 15, 2018), https://www.ft.com/content/e38b60ce-27d7-11e8-b27e-cc62a39d57a0 (on file with author); *Commission Proposal for a Council Directive on Laying Down Rules Relating to the Corporate Taxation of a Significant Digital Presence*, COM (2018) 147 final (Mar. 21, 2018).

172. Case C-34/10, Brüstle v. Greenpeace eV., EUR-Lex62010CJ0034 (Oct. 18, 2011).

173. *See Scientists Fear Stem Cell Ruling Deals Blow to EU Research*, EURACTIV.COM (Oct. 19, 2011), https://www.euractiv.com/section/health-consumers/news/scientists-fear-stem-cell-ruling-deals-blow-to-eu-research/ [https://perma.cc/275L-3M9Z].

174. Mary Beth Warner, *'German Reasoning Won Out' in Stem Cell Ruling*, SPIEGEL (Oct. 19, 2011) http://www.spiegel.de/international/the-world-from-berlin-german-reasoning-won-out-in-stem-cell-ruling-a-792721.html [https://perma.cc/E4UB-M2ZR].

175. Until recently, China received and repurposed approximately 14% of the EU's paper waste and 20% of the EU's plastic waste. *See* Paola Tamma, *China's Trash Ban Forces Europe to Confront its Waste Problem*, POLITICO (Feb. 21, 2018), https://www.politico.eu/article/europe-recycling-china-trash-ban-forces-europe-to-confront-its-waste-problem/ [https://perma.cc/ARB9-634U].

176. EUR. ENVTL. AGENCY REPORT, MOVEMENTS OF WASTE ACROSS THE EU'S INTERNAL AND EXTERNAL BORDERS (2012), *EU Exporting More Waste, Including Hazardous Waste*, EUR. ENV'T AGENCY (Nov. 6, 2012), https://www.eea.europa.eu/highlights/eu-exporting-more-waste-including [https://perma.cc/96PT-J9G8]; Sandra Laville, *UK Worst Offender in Europe for Electronic Waste Exports—Report*, GUARDIAN (Feb. 7, 2019), https://www.theguardian.com/environment/2019/feb/07/uk-worst-offender-in-europe-for-electronic-waste-exports-report [https://perma.cc/XAJ7-WAHJ].

177. For an overview of this literature, *see* Bruce Carruthers & Naomi Lamoreaux, *Regulatory Races: The Effects of Jurisdictional Competition on Regulatory Standards*, 54 J. ECON. LIT. 52 (2016); VOGEL & KAGAN, *supra* note 6.

178. Daniel Drezner, *Globalization and Policy Convergence*, 3 INT'L STUDIES REV. 53, 57–58 (2001) [hereinafter Drezner, *Globalization and Policy*].

179. *Id.* at 69, 75.

180. VOGEL & KAGAN, *supra* note 6.

181. Bruce Carruthers & Naomi Lamoreaux, *supra* note 177, at 89–90.

182. *Id.* at 54. *See also* Charles M. Tiebout, *A Pure Theory of Local Expenditures*, 64 J. POL. ECON. 416 (1956).

183. *See* Drezner, *Different Pathways supra* note 1, at 844–45; David Lazer, *Regulatory Interdependence and International Governance*, 8 J. EUR. PUB. POL'Y 474, 476–78 (2001).

184. *Oracle's Use of Potentially Harmful Substances,* Oracle, http://www.oracle.com/us/products/applications/green/harmful-substances-185039.html (last visited Oct. 21, 2018), [https://perma.cc/7UW7-S8QW].

185. *See* JOEL WALDFOGEL, THE TYRANNY OF THE MARKET: WHY YOU CAN'T ALWAYS GET WHAT YOU WANT (2007).

186. *See* Anu Bradford, *Antitrust Law in Global Markets, in* RESEARCH HANDBOOK ON THE ECONOMICS OF ANTITRUST LAW 283, 308-11 (Einer Elhauge ed., 2012).

187. *See* US DEP'T OF JUSTICE, CORPORATE LENIENCY POLICY (1993) https://www.justice.gov/atr/file/810281/download [https://perma.cc/3X5L-89NB]; *Leniency,* EUROPEAN COMMISSION, http://ec.europa.eu/competition/cartels/leniency/leniency.html (last visited Oct. 22, 2018) [https://perma.cc/N2CT-2DJS].

188. *See generally* on the benefits of standardized contracts in Marcel Kahan and Michael Klausner, *Standardization and Innovation in Corporate Contracting (Or "The Economics of Boilerplate"),*VIRGINIA L. REV., Vol, 83, May 1997 No 4.

189. GDPR, *supra* note 156, at 48.

190. David Ingram, *Exclusive: Facebook to Put 1.5 Billion Users Out of Reach of New EU Privacy Law,* REUTERS (Apr. 18, 2018), https://www.reuters.com/article/us-facebook-privacy-eu-exclusive/exclusive-facebook-to-change-user-terms-limiting-effect-of-eu-privacy-law-idUSKBN1HQ00P [https://perma.cc/BX7R-B998].

191. *See* Ryan Singel, *EU Tells Search Engines to Stop Creating Tracking Databases,* WIRED (Apr. 8, 2008), http://www.wired.com/threatlevel/2008/04/eu-tells-search/ [https://perma.cc/ZH4T-S3QW].

192. *See, e.g.,* Regulation (EC) 1829/2003 of the European Parliament and of the Council of 22 September 2003 on Genetically Modified Food and Feed, 2003 O.J. (L 268).

193. *See, e.g.,* Case C-442/09, Bablok v. Freistaat Bayern, EUR-Lex 62009CJ0442, at 8 (Sept. 6, 2011); CHARLES E. HANRAHAN, CONGR. RESEARCH SERV., RS21556, AGRICULTURAL BIOTECHNOLOGY: THE U.S.-EU DISPUTE 5 (2010).

194. *See* REACH, *supra* note 154, arts. 5-7, at 37-38.

195. Wirth, *supra* note 1, at 102–03; Joanne Scott, *From Brussels with Love: The Transatlantic Travels of European Law and the Chemistry of Regulatory Attraction,* 57 AM. J. COMP. L. 897, 908–20, 939–40 (2009); VOGEL, POLITICS, *supra* note 75, at 169, 204, 217; Henrik Selin & Stacy D. VanDeveer, *Raising Global Standards: Hazardous Substances and E-Waste Management in the European Union,* ENVIRONMENT, Dec. 2006, at 7, 14.

196. *See* Theodore Levitt, *The Globalization of Markets,* HARV. BUS. REV., May 1983, at 39–49 https://hbr.org/1983/05/the-globalization-of-markets [https://perma.cc/42XS-ENV7]; Simón Teitel, *Economies of Scale and Size of Plant: The Evidence and the Implications for the Developing Countries,* 13 J. COMMON MKT. STUD. 92, 94 (1974).

197. *Economies of Scale and Scope,* ECONOMIST (Oct. 20, 2008), https://www.economist.com/node/12446567 [https://perma.cc/UMC5-2ZFW].

198. Richard Perkins & Eric Neumayer, *Does the 'California Effect' Operate Across Borders? Trading- and Investing-Up in Automobile Emission Standards,* 19 J. EUR. PUB. POL'Y. 217, 232 (2012).

199. For a contrary view to Perkins & Neumayer's *California Effect Across Borders, see* KPMG INTERNATIONAL, THE TRANSFORMATION OF THE AUTOMOTIVE INDUSTRY: THE ENVIRONMENTAL REGULATION EFFECT (2010).

200. Lazer, *supra* note 183, at 490.

201. Brandon Mitchener, *Rules, Regulations of Global Economy are Being Set in Brussels,* WALL ST. J. (Apr. 23, 2001), https://www.wsj.com/articles/SB101952124026284536o (on file with author).

202. Alan Schwartz, *Statutory Interpretation, Capture and Tort Law: The Regulatory Compliance Defense,* 2 AM. L. & ECON. REV. 1, 17.

203. NAT'L RESEARCH COUNCIL, STATE AND FEDERAL STANDARDS FOR MOBILE-SOURCE EMISSIONS 140 (2006), https://www.nap.edu/read/11586/chapter/7#140; *see also* Fiona Miller, *The Advantages of Selling a Standardized Product* BIZFLUENT (Sept. 26, 2017), https://bizfluent.com/info-8788551-advantages-selling-standardized-product.html [https://perma.cc/FF9P-6BWX].

204. MARK CASSON, MULTINATIONALS AND WORLD TRADE 56–57 (2012).

205. Lazer, *supra* note 183, at 477.

206. Wirth, *supra* note 1, at 104.

207. *See* Mitchener, *supra* note 201.

208. *See* Mike Colias, *General Motors Will Stop Selling Cars in India*, WALL ST. J. (May 18, 2017), https://www.wsj.com/articles/general-motors-will-stop-selling-cars-in-india-1495092601 [https://perma.cc/QY5E-SGW8].

209. VOGEL, POLITICS, *supra* note 75, at 16.

210. Warren J. Keegan, *Multinational Product Planning: Strategic Alternatives*, 33 J. MARKETING 58, 59 (1969).

211. Aref A. Alashban et. al., *International Brand-Name Standardization/Adaptation: Antecedents and Consequences*, 10 J. INT'L MARKETING 22, 29 (2002).

212. *See* Marriott Set To Standardize On HSIA, HOTEL BUSINESS (Dec. 7, 2002), https://www.hotelbusiness.com/marriott-set-to-standardize-on-hsia/ [https://perma.cc/T6XM-3ZAR].

213. VOGEL, POLITICS, *supra* note 75, at 16

214. *See, e.g.*, Joe Sandler Clarke, *Child Labour on Nestle Farms: Chocolate Giant's Problems Continue*, GUARDIAN (Sept. 2, 2015), https://www.theguardian.com/global-development-professionals-network/2015/sep/02/child-labour-on-nestle-farms-chocolate-giants-problems-continue [https://perma.cc/NH69-6H6Z].

215. Scott, *supra* note 195, at 923.

216. VOGEL, POLITICS, *supra* note 75, at 217.

217. Of course, labor standards may be successfully exported to other jurisdictions through other means. The argument here is only that to the extent that they are divisible, labor standards are not amenable to the Brussels Effect. *See, e.g.*, Brian Greenhill et al., *Trade-Based Diffusion of Labor Rights: A Panel Study, 1986–2002*, 103 AM. POL. SCI. REV. 669, 678-80 (2009).

218. *See* Emil Protalinski, *Windows 7 to Be Shipped in Europe Without Internet Explorer*, ARSTECHNICA (June 11, 2009, 2:57 PM), http://arstechnica.com/microsoft/news/2009/06/windows-7-to-be-shipped-in-europe-sans-internet-explorer.ars [https://perma.cc/TY63-UTY5].

219. Aiofe White, *Google to Create Shopping Service Unit to Satisfy EU* (Sept. 26, 2017), https://www.bloomberg.com/news/articles/2017-09-26/google-said-to-split-off-shopping-service-to-meet-eu-demands (on file with author);

220. Vlad Savov, *Google News Quits Spain in Response to New Law*, THE VERGE (Dec.11, 2014), https://www.theverge.com/2014/12/11/7375733/google-news-spain-shutdown [https://perma.cc/FL2M-D9YF].

221. *European Commission Report on The Single Market Review: Impact on Competition and Scale Effects, Economies of Scale*, at 15 (1997) (on file with the author) [hereinafter *EU Single Market Review*].

222. *See* Daniel Schwartz, *Why Coke is Lowering its Sugar Levels in Canada*, CBC NEWS (Mar. 1, 2015), https://www.cbc.ca/news/health/why-coke-is-lowering-its-sugar-levels-in-canada-1.2961029 [https://perma.cc/7FGB-JFFN].

223. *EU Single Market Review, supra* note 221, at 15; Maria Doriza Loukakou & Nampungwe Beatrice Membe, Product Standardization and Adaptation in International Marketing: A Case of McDonalds (2012) (Master's thesis in Business Administration, University West), http://hv.diva-portal.org/smash/get/diva2:543563/FULLTEXT01.pdf [https://perma.cc/AWH4-PD8Y].

224. *EU Single Market Review, supra* note 221, at 15.

225. *See, e.g.,* KPMG INT'L, THE TRANSFORMATION OF THE AUTOMOTIVE INDUSTRY: THE ENVIRONMENTAL REGULATION EFFECT 16 (2010).

226. VOGEL, POLITICS, *supra* note 75, at 284.

227. KNOWLEDGE@WHARTON, WHY COMPANIES ARE INCREASINGLY MOVING TOWARDS STANDARDIZATION 4 (2013), http://d1c25a6gwz7q5e.cloudfront.net/papers/sponsor_collaborations/KW_Wipro_Future_of_Industry_Anand_Sankaran.pdf [https://perma.cc/N8B7-YCFP].

CHAPTER 3

1. Joanne Scott, *Extraterritoriality and Territorial Extension in E.U. Law*, 62 AM. J. COMP. L. 87, 88–90 (2014).

2. *Id.* at 94.

3. *Id.*

4. *Id.* at 90.

5. *Id.* at 124.

6. *Id.* at 98.

7. Surely, the three forms of influence discussed here are not the only ways in which EU rules become entrenched outside the EU. *See, e.g.,* Katerina Linos, *Diffusion Through Democracy*, 55 AM. J. POL. SCI. 678 (2011); *see also* Charles F. Sabel & Jonathan Zeitlin, *Learning from Different: The New Architecture of Experimentalist Governance in the European Union*, 14 EURO. L.J. 271 (2008); JONATHAN ZEITLIN, EXTENDING EXPERIMENTALIST GOVERNANCE?: THE EUROPEAN UNION AND TRANSNATIONAL REGULATION (2015).

8. *See Communication from the Commission to the Council and the European Parliament: Wider Europe—Neighbourhood: A New Framework for Relations with Our Eastern and Southern Neighbours*, at 5, COM (2003)104 final (Mar. 11, 2003).

9. Sophie Meunier & Kalypso Nicolaidis, *The European Union as a Trade Power, in* INTERNATIONAL RELATIONS AND THE EUROPEAN UNION 275, 279 (Christopher Hill & Michael Smith eds., 2011).

10. *See EU Enlargement Factsheet*, EUROPEAN COMMISSION, https://ec.europa.eu/neighbourhood-enlargement/sites/near/files/pdf/publication/factsheet_en.pdf [https://perma.cc/Q3CF-YCGD].

11. *See Communication from the Commission to the Council and the European Parliament: Wider Europe—Neighbourhood: A New Framework for Relations with Our Eastern and Southern Neighbours*, at 5, COM (2003)104 final (Mar. 11, 2003)

12. *See* Sophie Meunier & Kalypso Nicolaides, *The European Union as a Conflicted Trade Power*, 13:6 J. EU PUB. POL'Y 906, 913 (2006).

13. *Negotiations and Agreements*, EUROPEAN COMMISSION, *available at* http://ec.europa.eu/trade/policy/countries-and-regions/negotiations-and-agreements/ [https://perma.cc/BAS2-QNTA].

14. *See generally* LEGISLATIVE APPROXIMATION AND APPLICATION OF EU LAW IN THE EASTERN NEIGHBOURHOOD OF THE EUROPEAN UNION: TOWARDS A COMMON REGULATORY SPACE? (Peter van Elsuwge & Roman Petrov eds., 2014); NARINÉ GHAZARYAN, THE EUROPEAN NEIGHBOURHOOD POLICY AND THE DEMOCRATIC VALUES OF THE EU (2014).

15. "European Neighbourhood Policy (ENP)," EUROPEAN UNION EXTERNAL ACTION (21 Dec. 2016, 4:25 PM), https://eeas.europa.eu/diplomatic-network/

european-neighbourhood-policy-enp/330/european-neighbourhood-policy-enp_en [https://perma.cc/NZ6J-NFT2].

16. Consolidated Version of the Treaty on the Functioning of the European Union arts. 3(5) & 21(1), Mar. 30, 2010, 2010 O.J. (C 83) 47, 88–89 [hereinafter TFEU].

17. *See* Treaty of Lisbon Amending the Treaty on European Union and the Treaty Establishing the European Community, Dec. 13, 2007, 2007 O.J. (C 306) 1, art. 8 [hereinafter Treaty of Lisbon]; Christophe Hillion, *The EU Neighborhood Competence under Article 8 TEU, in* Thinking Strategically about EU's External Action 204 (Elvire Fabry ed., 2011).

18. Johannes Hahn, First Vice President of the European Commission (2010–2014), Address at Chatham House Conference: Beyond Berlin: What Does the Next Decade Hold for the Western Balkins? (July 10, 2018).

19. *Communication from the Commission to the Council and the European Parliament: Wider Europe—Neighbourhood: A New Framework for Relations with our Eastern and Southern Neighbours*, at 10, COM (2003) 104 final (Mar. 11, 2003).

20. Eduard Soler i Lecha & Elina Villup, *Reviewing the European Neighbourhood Policy: A Weak Response to Fast Changing Realities*, Barcelona Centre for Int'l Affairs (June 2011), https://www.cidob.org/en/publications/publication_series/notes_internacionals/n1_36/reviewing_the_european_neighbourhood_policy_a_weak_response_to_fast_changing_realities [https://perma.cc/U84X-79LT].

21. Judy Dempsey, *Judy Asks: Is the European Neighborhood Policy Doomed?*, Carnegie Europe (May 20, 2015), https://carnegieeurope.eu/strategiceurope/60138?lang=en [https://perma.cc/FLF3-QZ7M].

22. Euro Comm'n, Report on Implementation of EU Free Trade Agreements 7 (2018).

23. Raymond J. Ahearen, Europe's Preferential Trade Agreements: Status, Content, and Implications, Congressional Research Service 2 (2011), https://fas.org/sgp/crs/row/R41143.pdf [https://perma.cc/22UG-R8TW].

24. Emilie M. Hafner-Burton, *Trading Human Rights: How Preferential Trade Agreements Influence Government Repression*, 59 Int'l Org. 593 (2005); Sophie Meunier & Kalypso Nicolaidis, *supra* note 9.

25. Billy A. Melo Araujo, The EU Deep Trade Agenda: Law and Policy 2 (2016).

26. Todd Allee & Manfred Elsig, *Are the Contents of International Treaties Copied-and-Pasted? Evidence from Preferential Trade Agreements* 11–12 (NCCR Working Paper No. 8, 2016), https://www.wti.org/research/publications/998/are-the-contents-of-international-treaties-copied-and-pasted-unique-evidence-from-preferential-trade-agreements/ [https://perma.cc/2JB4-W9YR].

27. Annalisa Savaresi, *The EU External Action on Forests: FLEGT and the Development of International Law, in* External Environmental Policy of the European Union: EU and International Law Perspectives 149 (Elisa Morgera ed., 2012).

28. Billy A. Melo Araujo, The EU Deep Trade Agenda: Law and Policy 226 (2016).

29. *Id.*

30. *Fisheries: Bilaterial Agreements With Countries Outside the EU*, European Commission, https://ec.europa.eu/fisheries/cfp/international/agreements_en [https://perma.cc/2XRB-L939].

31. *External Aviation Policy—A Common Aviaion Area with the EU's neighbours*, European Commission, https://ec.europa.eu/transport/modes/air/international_aviation/external_aviation_policy/neighbourhood_en [https://perma.cc/5Y47-CCRS].

32. *The Energy Community Treaty,* EUR-LEX, https://eur-lex.europa.eu/legal-content/EN/LSU/?uri=CELEX:32006D0500 [https://perma.cc/NQ53-XFST]; Council Decision 2006/500, 2006 O.J. (L 198) 15 (EC).

33. Treaty establishing the Transport Community, art. 1, 2017 OJ (L 278) 3.

34. For example, the EU is not a member of the IMF, but it coordinates the positions of its member states. *See* Joachim A. Koops & Dr. Dominik Tolksdorf, *The European Union's Role in International Economic For a Paper 4: The IMF,* EUROPEAN PARLIAMENT 44 (2015), http://www.europarl.europa.eu/RegData/etudes/STUD/2015/542193/IPOL_STU(2015)542193_EN.pdf [https://perma.cc/94GN-Y8E9].

35. *The OECD and the EU,* EUROPEAN EXTERNAL ACTION SERVICE (Jun. 23, 2016, 1:52 AM), https://eeas.europa.eu/delegations/paris-oecd-and-un_en/12350/The%20OECD%20and%20the%20EU [https://perma.cc/ZJH3-SNVS].

36. FOOD AND AGRICULTURE ORG. OF THE UNITED NATIONS, UNDERSTANDING CODEX 15 (5th ed. 2018).

37. *See,* Sara Poli, *The European Community and the Adoption of International Food Standards within the Codex Alimentarius Commission,* 10 EURO. L.J. 613 (2004).

38. In-person Interview with Sabine Juelicher, Director of Directorate-General for Health and Food Safety, European Commission (July 18, 2018).

39. *Food: Legislation,* EUROPEAN COMMISSION, https://ec.europa.eu/food/safety/bio-safety/irradiation/legislation_en [https://perma.cc/4NTZ-WJHL].

40. Pasqualina Lagana et al., *The Codex Alimentarius and the European Legislation on Food Additives, in* CHEMISTRY AND HYGIENE OF FOOD ADDITIVES 27 (Maria Eufemia Gioffré, Salvatore Parisi & Santi Delia eds., 2017).

41. *Codex and the International Food Trade,* FOOD AND AGRICULTURE ORGANIZATION OF THE UNITED NATIONS, http://www.fao.org/3/w9114e/w9114e06.htm [https://perma.cc/N8J2-2YNV].

42. Bill Canis & Richard K. Lattanzio, *US and EU Motor Vehicle Standards: Issues for Transatlantic Trade Negotiations,* CONGRESSIONAL RESEARCH SERVICE (2014).

43. Mathieu Rousselin, *The EU as a Multilateral Rule Exporter,* (Kolleg-Forschergruppe (KFG) The Transformative Power of Europe, Working Paper No. 48, 2012), http://userpage.fu-berlin.de/kfgeu/kfgwp/wpseries/WorkingPaperKFG_48.pdf [https://perma.cc/H8TA-5MTK].

44. Sandra Lavenex, *The Power of Functionalist Extension: How EU Rules Travel,* 21 J. OF EU PUB. POL'Y 885 (2014).

45. ANNE-MARIE SLAUGHTER, A NEW WORLD ORDER (2004).

46. David Bach & Abraham L. Newman, *Governing Lipitor and Lipstick: Capacity, Sequencing, and Power in International Pharmaceutical and Cosmetics Regulation,* 17 REV. INT'L. POL. ECON. 665, 672 (2010).

47. *See* Anu Bradford, *Antitrust Law in Global Markets, in* RESEARCH HANDBOOK ON THE ECONOMICS OF ANTITRUST LAW 283, 314–16 (Einer Elhauge ed., 2012).

48. Sandra Lavenex, *supra* note 44, at 894.

49. *Id.*

50. Giancarlo F. Frosio, *The Right to Be Forgotten: Much Ado about Nothing,* 15. J. ON TELCOMM. & HIGH TECH. L. 307, 310 (2017); Arie Reich, *The Impact of the EU Court of Justice on the Israeli Legal System* (Bar Ilan University Faculty of Law Research Paper, No. 18-24, 2018).

51. *See* Frosio *supra* note 50, at 6.

52. Karen J. Alter, *The Global Spread of European Style International Courts,* 35 W. EUR. POL. 135, 139 (2012)

53. *Id.* at 140.

54. Agreement on Andean Subregional Integration, art. 29, May 26, 1969, 8 I.L.M. 910; KAREN J. ALTER & LAURENCE HELFER, TRANSPLANTING INTERNATIONAL COURTS: THE LAW AND POLITICS OF THE ANDEAN TRIBUNAL OF JUSTICE 10 (2017).

55. ALTER & HELFER, *supra* note 54.

56. Karen J. Alter et. al., *Transplanting the European Court of Justice: The Experience of the Andean Tribunal of Justice*, 60 AM. J. OF COMP. L., 629, 631 (2012).

57. *See* ATJ Case 2-IP-1988 point 2, at 2–3 (May 25, 1988).

58. *See, e.g.*, ATJ Case 2-IP-1988 (May 25, 1988); ATJ Case 3-AI-1996 (Mar. 24, 1997); ATJ Case 2-AI-1997 (Sept. 24, 1988); ATJ Case 3-AI-1997 (Dec. 8, 1997); ATJ Case 7-AI-1998 (Nov. 12, 1999); ATJ Case 16-AI-1999 (Mar. 22, 1999); ATJ Case 51-AI-2000 (Nov. 16, 2001); ATJ Case 53-AI-2000 (Apr. 24, 2002); ATJ Case 89-AI-2000 (Sept. 28, 1001); ATJ Case 93-AI-2000 (Jan. 22, 2002); ATJ Case 1-AN-1997 (Feb. 26, 1998); ATJ Case 3-AN-1997 (Mar. 9, 1998); ATJ Case 4-AN-1997 (Aug. 17, 1998); ATJ Case 24-AN-1999 (Feb. 2, 2000); ATJ Case 23-AN-2002 (Aug. 19, 2003); ATJ Case 214-AN-2005 (Nov. 17, 2006); ATJ Case 3-AN-2006 (Mar. 21, 1997).

59. *See* ATJ Case 3-AI-1996 (Mar. 24, 1997).

60. *See, e.g.*, ATJ Case 2-AI-1997 (Sept. 24, 1998) (citing Case 2-282/96 Commission v Fr. Republic, 1997 E.C.R. I-2929 (E.C.J.) and Case 293/96 Irish Farmers Ass'n and Others v Minister for Agric., Food and Forestry, Ir. and Attorney General, 1997 E.C.R. I-01809 (E.C.J.).

61. Alter, *supra* note 56, at 640.

62. *Id.* at 633.

63. *Id.* at 644.

64. *Id.* at 645.

65. Corte Constitucional [C.C.] [Constitutional Court], abril 21, 2017, Sentencia T-236/17 (Colom.), [http://www.corteconstitucional.gov.co/relatoria/2017/T-236-17.htm].

66. Corte Constitucional [C.C.] [Constitutional Court], septiembre 8, 2015, Sentencia C-583/15 (Colom.), [http://www.corteconstitucional.gov.co/relatoria/2015/c-583-15.htm].

67. Corte Constitucional [C.C.] [Constitutional Court], junio 2, 2017, Sentencia T-365/17 (Colom.), [http://www.corteconstitucional.gov.co/relatoria/2017/t-365-17.htm].

68. Competition Comm'n of In. v. Co-ordination Comm. of Artists and Technicians of W.B. Film and Television, C.A. 6691 of 2014, Supreme Court of India, 2014.

69. Tamil Nadu Film Exhibitors Ass'n v. Competition Comm'n of India, (2015) 2 LW (Mad.) 686, 695.

70. *See* In Re Surinder Singh Barmi and Board of Control for Cricket in India, C.A. 61 of 2014, Supreme Court of India, 2014.

71. *See, e.g.*, Roger Van den Bergh, *The Difficult Reception of Economic Analysis in European Competition Law*, *in* POST-CHICAGO DEVELOPMENTS IN ANTITRUST LAW, 34, 46–50 (Antonio Cucinotta et al. eds., 2002). *Compare with Antitrust Guidelines for the Licensing of Intellectual Property*, U.S. DEPARTMENT OF JUSTICE AND FEDERAL TRADE COMMISSION (Jan. 12, 2017), https://www.ftc.gov/system/files/documents/public_statements/1049793/ip_guidelines_2017.pdf [https://perma.cc/X42M-Z2AZ]; *and* Commission Regulation 772/2004, 2004 O.J. (L 123) 11. *Contra* DAMIEN GERADIN & EINER ELHAGUE, GLOBAL ANTITRUST LAW AND POLITICS, 208–32 (2007).

72. *See* Rafael la Porta et. al., *The Economic Consequences of Legal Origin*, 46 J. ECON. LITERATURE 285 (2008); *see also* Holger Spamann, *Contemporary Legal Transplants: Legal Families and the Diffusion of (Corporate) Law*, 6 BYU L. REV. 1813 (2009).

73. *See* Brazilian Internet Law (Law No. 13,709 of Aug. 14, 2018) (Braz.); *see also* Paul M. Schwartz, *Global Data Privacy: The EU Way*, 94 NYU L. Rev. (forthcoming 2019),

27–29, https://papers.ssrn.com/sol3/papers.cfm?abstract_id=3338954 [https://perma.cc/Z86X-P37E].

74. Hans-Bernand Schafer, *Rules versus Standards in Rich and Poor Countries: Precise Legal Norms as Substitutes for Human Capital in Low-Income Countries*, 14 SUP. CT. ECON. REV. 113 (2006).

75. Madeleine B. Kadas & Russel Fraker, *Chapter 20: Central and South American Overview: Emerging Trends in Latin America*, in INTERNATIONAL ENVIRONMENTAL LAW 366 (Roger R. Martella, Jr. & J. Brett Grosko eds., 2014).

76. Allan Tatham, "Judicial Variations on the Theme of Regional Integration": Diffusing the EU Model of Judicial Governance 10 (Sant'Anna Legal Stud. STALS Res. Paper 6/2015, 2015), http://www.stals.sssup.it/files/Tatham%20stals_rechecked.pdf [https://perma.cc/K7X6-HDL9].

77. *Compare, e.g.*, Article 27 of the Market Power Control and Regulation Act and Article 3 of the Spanish Competition Defense Act or the Art 11 of the Market Power Control and Regulation Act with Article 101 of the TFEU or the Art 1 of the Spanish Competition Defense Act.

78. *See, e.g,* Hailegabriel G. Feyissa, *European Influence on Ethiopian Antitrust Regime: A Comparative and Functional Analysis of Some Problems,* 3 MIZAN LAW REVIEW 271, 275 (2009); *see also* Gabriela Mancero-Bucheli, *Intellectual Property and Rules on Free Movement: A Contradiction in the Andean Community (ANCOM),* 4 L. & BUS. REV. AM. 125 (1998).

79. WAEMU has not only emulated the EU antitrust laws, but its Court of Justice has also held that the Treaty of Dakar (establishing WAEMU) should be interpreted with reference to the Treaty of Rome, which is the founding treaty of the European Community, and the jurisprudence of the Court of Justice of the EU. *See* Advisory Opinion 3/2000/CJ/UEMOA (June 27, 2000).

80. Ian Manners, *Normative Power Europe: A Contradiction in Terms?*, 40 J. OF COMMON MARKET STUD. 235, 236 (2002).

81. *Id.* at 239, 240–41, 244.

82. Michel Leví Coral, *La Unión Europea y la nueva integracion latino Americana parámetros de comparación aplicados en diferentes estudios sobre los procesos de integración* [The European Union and the New Latin American Integration: Comparison Parameters Applied in Different Studies About Integration Processes], 11 REVISTA DEL CENTRO ANDINO DE ESTUDIOS INTERNACIONALES 217, 223 (2011).

83. Amadeo Arena, *Primacy: Three (Not So) Unshakable Certainties About a Foundational Principle of EU Law*, Conference at Columbia University (Nov. 8, 2017).

84. Leví Coral, *supra* note 82, at 224. *See also* Samuel Fernandez Illanes, *El proceso de integración europeo: ¿Un ejemplo para otras regiones?* [The European Integration Process: An Example for Other Regions?], 5 Instituto de Ciencias Sociales y de la Comunicacion 36 (2009), http://www.ubo.cl/icsyc/wp-content/uploads/2011/09/2-Fern%C3%A1ndez.pdf [https://perma.cc/VV4F-C2DL].

85. ALTER & HELFER, *supra* note 54, at 5.

86. Alter, *supra* note 52, at 145.

87. Tatham, *supra* note 76, at 11.

88. Literature and commentary on the failure of these negotiations are legion. *See, e.g.*, Megan Dee, *Tackling the EU's Emerging Irrelevance in the Doha Round*, Commentary for the European Council on Foreign Relations 'EU Performance Scorecard 2012' (2012); JEREMY RAYNER, ALEXANDER BUCK & PIA KATILA (EDS.), EMBRACING COMPLEXITY: MEETING THE INTERNATIONAL FOREST GOVERNANCE CHALLENGE (2011); Editorial Board, *Global Trade After the Failure of the Doha Round*, N.Y. TIMES (Jan. 1, 2016), https://www.nytimes.com/2016/01/01/opinion/global-trade-after-the-failure-of-the-doha-round.html (on file with author).

89. *See* Anu Bradford, *International Antitrust Negotiations and the False Hope of the WTO*, 48 HARV. INT'L L.J. 383, 413-22 (2007).

90. *See* Nico Krisch, *The Decay of Consent: International Law in an Age of Global Public Goods*, 108 AM. J. INT'L L. 1 (2014); *see also* Joost Pauwelyn et al., *When Structures Become Shackles: Stagnation and Dynamics in International Lawmaking*, 25:3 EUR. J. INT'L L. 733 (2014).

91. Pauwelyn et al., *supra* note 90.

92. *Id.*

93. *See* Christopher J. Carr & Harry N. Scheiber, *Dealing With a Resource Crisis: Regulatory Regimes for Managing the World's Marine Fisheries*, 21 STAN. ENVTL. L.J. 45, 53, 62, 76–79 (2002).

94. Frank Hendrickx et al., *The Architecture of Global Labor Governance*, 155:3 INT'L LAB. REV. 339 (2016).

95. *See* David Vogel & Robert A. Kagan, *Introduction* to DYNAMICS OF REGULATORY CHANGE: HOW GLOBALIZATION AFFECTS NATIONAL REGULATORY POLICIES 23 (David Vogel & Robert A. Kagan eds., 2004).

96. *See* Jonathan R. Macey, *Regulatory Globalization as a Response to Regulatory Competition*, 52 EMORY L.J. 1353, 1367–69 (2003).

97. *See* Nicolas A.J. Croquet, *The Climate Change Norms under the EU-Korea Free Trade Agreement: Between Soft and Hard Law*, in GLOBAL GOVERNANCE THROUGH TRADE: EU POLICIES AND APPROACHES 124 (Jan Wouters et al., 2015).

98. *See* Axel Marx & Jadir Soares, *Does Integrating Labor Provisions in Free Trade Agreements Make a Difference? An Exploratory Analysis of Freedom of Association and Collective Bargaining Rights in 13 EU Trade Partners*, in GLOBAL GOVERNANCE THROUGH TRADE: EU POLICIES AND APPROACHES 158 (Jan Wouters et al. eds., 2015).

99. *See also* Billy Melo Araujo, *Labour Provisions in EU and US Mega-Regional Trade Agreements: Rhetoric And Reality*, 67:1 INT'L & COMP. L. QUART. 233 (2018).

100. Laura Beke & Nicolas Hachez, *The EU GSP: A Preference for Human Rights And Good Governance? The Case of Myanmar*, in GLOBAL GOVERNANCE THROUGH TRADE: EU POLICIES AND APPROACHES 185 (Jan Wouters et al. eds., 2015).

101. CLARA PORTELA, EUROPEAN UNION SANCTIONS AND FOREIGN POLICY: WHEN AND WHY DO THEY WORK?, 160 (Routledge 2010).

102. CLARA PORTELA, ENFORCING RESPECT FOR LABOUR STANDARDS WITH TARGETED SANCTIONS, 7 (2018).

103. Laura Beke & Nicolas Hachez, *supra* note 100, at 207.

104. Commission Report on GSP 2016-2017, 19 January 2018, COM (2018) 36 final.

105. Opinion Procedure 2/15, Request for an Opinion pursuant to Article 218(11) TFEU—Conclusion of the Free Trade Agreement between the European Union and the Republic of Singapore—Allocation of competences between the European Union and the Member States, 2017 E.C.R. I-376.

106. *Belgium Walloons Block Key EU CETA Trade Deal with Canada*, BBC NEWS (Oct. 25, 2016), https://www.bbc.com/news/world-europe-37749236 [https://perma.cc/8247-ESSQ]; Eric Maurice, *Belgium Green Lights Unchanged CETA*, EU OBSERVER (Oct. 28, 2016), https://euobserver.com/economic/135717 [https://perma.cc/3M9S-K6GL].

107. *ACTA: Controversial Anti-Piracy Agreement Rejected by EU*, BBC (July 4, 2012), https://www.bbc.com/news/technology-18704192 [https://perma.cc/5R37-4Q7Q].

108. *See* Sabrina Safrin, *The Un-Exceptionalism of U.S. Exceptionalism*, 41 VAND. J. TRANSNAT'L L. 1307, 1324–27 (2008).

109. Press Release, European Comm'n, New EU Rules to Eliminate the Main Loopholes Used in Corporate Tax Avoidance Come Into Force on 1 January (Dec. 30, 2018), https://europa.eu/rapid/press-release_IP-18-6853_en.htm [https://perma.cc/RE76-PAVE].

110. Press Release No. 7656-17, U.S. Commodity Futures Trading Comm'n, CFTC Approves Exemption from SEF Registration Requirement for Multilateral Trading Facilities and Organised Trading Facilities Authorized Within the EU (Dec. 8, 2017), https://www.cftc.gov/PressRoom/PressReleases/pr7656-17 [https://perma.cc/673X-DBNP]; *see also* Shanny Basar, *US and EU Equivalence Works Well*, MARKETSMEDIA (Sept. 26, 2018), https://www.marketsmedia.com/us-and-eu-equivalence-works-well/ [https://perma.cc/GL3Y-LJMD].

111. *A Global Financial Market*, EUROPEAN COMMISSION, https://ec.europa.eu/info/business-economy-euro/banking-and-finance/international-relations/international-cooperation-financial-regulation-and-capital-movements_en [https://perma.cc/RRU6-C2K8].

112. Pierre-Henri Conac, *The European Union's Role in International Economic Fora Paper 6: The IOSCO*, EUROPEAN PARLIAMENT: DIRECTORATE GENERAL FOR INTERNAL POLICIES 12, 37 (2015).

113. *Id.* at 24.

114. Stefan Ingves, Chairman, Basel Committee on Banking Supervision, Keynote Speech at the Institute for Law and Finance Conference: Basel III Are We Done Now? (Jan. 29, 2018).

115. *See* Vogel & Kagan, *supra* note 95, at 13.

116. *See Towards 5G*, EUROPEAN COMMISSION (last updated Mar. 14, 2019), https://ec.europa.eu/digital-single-market/en/towards-5g [https://perma.cc/36GS-CZNK]; *see also, e.g.*, David E. Sanger et al., *In 5G Race With China, U.S. Pushes Allies to Fight Huawei*, N.Y. TIMES, (Jan. 26, 2019) (on file with author).

117. *International Cooperation on 5G*, EUROPEAN COMMISSION (last updated Mar. 8. 2019), https://ec.europa.eu/digital-single-market/en/5G-international-cooperation [https://perma.cc/4JPJ-DF7X].

118. *See* Macey, *supra* note 96, at 1369.

119. Lavenex, *supra* note 48, at 895.

120. DAVID VOGEL, THE POLITICS OF PRECAUTION: REGULATING HEALTH, SAFETY, AND ENVIRONMENTAL RISKS IN EUROPE AND THE UNITED STATES, 13 (2015).

121. Bradford, *supra* note 89, at 408.

122. *See, e.g., A Large Black Cloud: Rapid Growth Is Exacting a Heavy Environmental Price*, ECONOMIST (Mar. 15, 2008), at 13, 17.

123. *Historic Agreement Reached to Mitigate International Aviation Emissions*, International Civil Aviation Organization (ICAO) (Oct. 6, 2016), https://www.icao.int/Newsroom/Pages/Historic-agreement-reached-to-mitigate-international-aviation-emissions.aspx [https://perma.cc/4VVC-6B8J].

CHAPTER 4

1. European Commission Press Release IP/18/4581 Antitrust: Commission Fines Google €4.34 Billion for Illegal Practices Regarding Android Mobile Devices to Strengthen Dominance of Google's Search Engine (July 18, 2018), http://europa.eu/rapid/press-release_IP-18-4581_en.htm [https://perma.cc/L8NT-8U9W]. Google has appealed the case before the European Courts. *See* Case T-604/18, Google & Alphabet v. Comm'n, 2018 O.J., (C 445) 21.

2. Commission Decision in Case No. AT.39740 (Google Search—Shopping), C(2017) 4444 final (June 27, 2017) *cited in* 2018 O.J. (C 9) 11, http://ec.europa.eu/competition/antitrust/cases/dec_docs/39740/39740_14996_3.pdf [https://perma.cc/6XA3-34ND]. Google has appealed the case before the European Courts. *See* Case T-612/17, Google & Alphabet v. Comm'n, 2017 O.J. (C 369) 37.

3. European Commission Press Release IP/19/1770, Antitrust: Commission Fines Google €1.49 Billion for Abusive Practices in Online Advertising (Mar. 20, 2019) http://europa. eu/rapid/press-release_IP-19-1770_en.htm [https://perma.cc/2XSR-6Q6V].

4. In 2018, the Commission fined Qualcomm $1.2 billion for its exclusive dealing contracts with Apple on the computer chips market. *See* Summary of Commission Decision in Case No. AT.40220 (Qualcomm—Exclusivity Payments), 2018 O.J. (C 295) 25 (No public version of the full Decision available as of Apr. 13, 2019).

5. The Commission ordered Ireland to recover $14.5 billion in illegal state aid from Apple. Commission Decision in Case No. SA.38373 (Ireland/Apple State Aid), 2017 O.J. (L 187) 1.

6. Commission Decision in Case No. COMP/C-3/37.990 (Intel), D(2009) 3726 final (May 13, 2009) *cited in* 2009 O.J. (C 227) 13. In September 2017, the European Court of Justice overturned the fine levied by the Commission in its decision. *See* Case C-413/14 P, Intel v. Comm'n, Judgment of September 6, 2017 (Grand Chamber), https://eur-lex. europa.eu/legal-content/EN/TXT/PDF/?uri=CELEX:62014CJo413 [https://perma. cc/4UTG-NLTC].

7. Commission Decision in Case No. COMP/C-3/37.792 (Microsoft), C(2004) 900 final, (Mar. 24, 2004) *cited in* 2007 O.J. (L 32) 23.

8. Commission Decision in Case No. COMP/M.2220 (General Electric/Honeywell), 2004 O.J. (L 48) 1.

9. Anu Bradford et al., *Competition Law Gone Global: Introducing the Comparative Competition Law and Enforcement Datasets*, 16 J. EMPIRICAL LEGAL STUD. 411 (2019).

10. Anu Bradford et al., *The Global Dominance of European Competition Law Over American Antitrust Law* (forthcoming in J. EMPIRICAL LEGAL STUD 2019) (on file with author).

11. Consolidated Version of the Treaty on the Functioning of the European Union, art. 101, 13 Dec. 2007, 2012 O.J. (C 326) 47 [hereinafter TFEU].

12. TFEU art. 102.

13. Council Regulation 139/2004 of Jan. 20, 2004, on the Control of Concentrations Between Undertakings, 2004 O.J. (L 24) 1 (EC).

14. Sherman Act, 15 U.S.C. §§ 1–7 (2018).

15. Clayton Act, 15 U.S.C. §§ 12–27 (2018). *See also* Federal Trade Commission Act, 15 U.S.C. §§ 41–58 (2018). While the Clayton Act was initially passed in 1914 along with the FTC Act, the modern US Merger Control regime began in 1976, when the Hart-Scott-Rodino Act introduced the pre-merger notification process. Hart-Scott-Rodino Antitrust Improvements Act of 1976, Pub. L. 94-435, 90 Stat. 1383.

16. TFEU arts.107–09.

17. Michael S. Gal, *Monopoly Pricing as an Antitrust Offences in the U.S. and the E.C.: Two Systems of Belief About Monopoly?*, 49 ANTITRUST BULL. 343, 345–6 (2004); Eleanor M. Fox, *EU and US Competition Law: A Comparison in* GLOBAL COMPETITION POLICY 339, 344 (Edward M. Graham & J. David Richardson eds., 1997).

18. *See* Council Regulation 139/2004 of Jan. 20, 2004 On the Control of Concentrations Between Undertakings, art. 8, 2004 O.J. (L 24) 1 (EC); *See* William E. Kovacic, *Transatlantic Turbulence: The Boeing-McDonnell Douglas Merger and International Competition Policy*, 68 ANTITRUST L.J. 805, 851 (2001).

19. However, some EU member states employ criminal penalties in their enforcement of their national and EU competition law.

20. Directive 2014/104/EU of the European Parliament and of the Council of 26 November 2014 on Certain Rules Governing Actions for Damages Under National Law for Infringements of the Competition Law Provisions of the Member States and of the European Union, 2014 O.J. (L 349) 1.

21. *See* Anu Bradford, *Antitrust Law in Global Markets, in* RESEARCH HANDBOOK ON THE ECONOMICS OF ANTITRUST LAW 283, 310 (Einer Elhauge ed., 2012).

22. *Id.*

23. *Id.* at 309.

24. *See* Gunnar Niels & Adriaan ten Kate, *Introduction: Antitrust in the U.S. and the EU—Converging or Diverging Paths?*, 49 ANTITRUST BULL. 1, 11-15 (2004).

25. *See, e.g.*, Deborah Platt Majoras, Deputy Assistant Attorney Gen., Antitrust Div., US Dep't of Justice, Remarks on GE-Honeywell: The U.S. Decision Before the Antitrust Law Section, State Bar of Georgia 16 (Nov. 29, 2001), http://www.justice.gov/atr/public/speeches/9893.pdf [https://perma.cc/7MXL-84YB].

26. Maureen K. Ohlhausen, Federal Trade Commissioner, U.S.-E.U. Convergence: Can we bridge the Atlantic?, Remarks at the 2016 Georgetown Global Antitrust Symposium Dinner 9 (Sept. 19, 2016), https://www.ftc.gov/system/files/documents/public_statements/985133/ohlhausen_dinner_speech_09192016.pdf [https://perma.cc/99DA-2LZK]; Roger D. Blair & D. Daniel Sokol, *Welfare Standards in U.S. and E.U. Antitrust Enforcement*, 81 FORDHAM L. REV. 2497, 2501-02 (2013).

27. Fox, *supra* note 17, at 340; *see also* Blair & Sokol, *supra* note 26, at 2502.

28. STEPHANIE HONNEFELDER, EUROPEAN PARLIAMENT FACT SHEET ON THE EUROPEAN UNION—COMPETITION POLICY (2018), http://www.europarl.europa.eu/ftu/pdf/en/FTU_2.6.12.pdf [https://perma.cc/UYT7-RTA4].

29. Commission Guidelines on the Application of Article 81(3) of the Treaty, ¶ 33, 2004 O.J. (C 101) 97, 102; Commission Guidance on the Commission's Enforcement Priorities in Applying Article 82 of the EC Treaty to Abusive Exclusionary Conduct by Dominant Undertakings, ¶ 19, 2009 O.J. (C 45) 7, 9; *see also* Case C-94/00, Roquette Frères SA v. Comm'n [2002] ECR I-09011, ¶ 42; Case C-52/09 Konkurrensverket v. TeliaSonera Sverige AB [2011] ECR I-527, ¶ 22.

30. Commission Guidelines on the Application of Article 81(3) of the Treaty, ¶ 13, 2004 O.J. (C 101) 97, 98; Commission Guidance on the Commission's Enforcement Priorities in Applying Article 82 of the EC Treaty to Abusive Exclusionary Conduct by Dominant Undertakings, ¶ 13, 2009 O.J. (C 45) 7, 8-9.

31. Fox, *supra* note 17, at 339-40; Alexander Italianer, European Commission Director-General for Competition, Fighting Cartels in Europe and the US: Different Systems, Common Goals, Address to the Annual Conference of the International Bar Association (Oct. 9, 2013), http://ec.europa.eu/competition/speeches/text/sp2013_09_en.pdf [https://perma.cc/EC8A-F3PV]; Nicholas Levy, *Mario Monti's Legacy in EC Merger Control*, 1 COMPETITION POL'Y INT'L 99 (2005); *see generally* Ariel Ezrachi, *EU Competition Law Goals and the Digital Economy* (Aug. 2018) (BEUC Discussion Paper), https://www.beuc.eu/publications/beuc-x-2018-071_goals_of_eu_competition_law_and_digital_economy.pdf? [https://perma.cc/GN4T-H3MF].

32. Article 102 prohibiting abuses of dominant position contains in its illustrative list of abuses a reference to "directly or indirectly imposing *unfair* purchase or selling prices or other unfair trading conditions" (emphasis added). TFEU art. 102. The reference to fairness is also found in relation to anticompetitive agreements: companies violating the prohibition of Article 101(1) TFEU can clear the violation by demonstrating that their conduct generates efficiencies, and that customers received a *fair* share of the benefits (emphasis added). TFEU art. 101(3).

33. Blair & Sokol, *supra* note 26, at 2504-05.

34. Council Regulation 1/2003 of Dec. 16, 2002 on the Implementation of the Rules on Competition Laid Down in Articles 81 and 82 of the Treaty, Recitals ¶ 9, 2003 O.J. (L 1) 1, 2 (EC); *Commission Green Paper on Vertical Restraints in EC Competition Policy*, ¶ 180, COM(96) 721 final (Jan. 22, 1997); Case C-8/08 T-Mobile Netherlands BV v. Raad

van bestuur van de Nederlandse Mededingingsautoriteit [2009] ECR I-4529, ¶ 38; Case C-501/06 P GlaxoSmithKline Services Unlimited v. Comm'n [2009] ECR I-9291, ¶ 63.

35. Fox *supra* note 17, at 340.

36. *See* D. Daniel Sokol, *Troubled Waters Between U.S. and European Antitrust*, 115 MICH L. REV 955, 958 (2017). *See also* William E. Kovacic, U.S. Fed. Trade Comm'n Chairman, Competition Policy in the European Union and the United States: Convergence or Divergence?, Remarks at Bates White Fifth Annual Antitrust Conference (June 2, 2008), https://www.ftc.gov/sites/default/files/documents/public_statements/competition-policy-european-union-and-united-states-convergence-or-divergence/080602bateswhite. pdf [https://perma.cc/NE9D-RTR5].

37. *See* Anu Bradford et al., *Is E.U. Merger Control Used for Protectionism? An Empirical Analysis*, 15 J. EMPIRICAL LEGAL STUD. 165 (2018); Anu Bradford, *International Antitrust Enforcement and the False Hope of the WTO*, 48 HARV. INT'L L.J. 383 (2007).

38. Commission Decision in Case No. COMP/M.2220 (General Electric/Honeywell), 2004 O.J. (L 48) 1.

39. John Wilke, *U.S. Antitrust Chief Chides EU for Rejecting Merger Proposal*, WALL ST. J. (July 5, 2001, 12:01 AM ET), https://www.wsj.com/articles/SB99428227597056929 (on file with author).

40. *Id.*

41. Commission Decision in Case No. IV/M.877 (Boeing/McDonnell Douglas), 1997 O.J. (L 336) 16; Commission Decision in Case No. COMP/M.1741 (MCI WorldCom/ Sprint) 2003 O.J. (L 300) 1; Commission Decision in Case No. COMP/M.1845 (AOL/Time Warner), 2001 O.J. (L 268) 28; Commission Decision in Case No. COMP/M.6570 (UPS/ TNT Express), C(2013) 431 final (Jan. 30, 2013) *cited in* 2014 O.J. (C 137) 8.

42. Tobias Buck, *How the European Union Exports Its Laws*, FIN. TIMES (July 9, 2007), https://www.ft.com/content/942b1ae2-2e32-11dc-821c-0000779fd2ac (on file with author).

43. Mark Scott, *E.U. Commission Opens Inquiry Into E-Commerce Sector*, N.Y. TIMES (May 6, 2015), https://www.nytimes.com/2015/05/07/business/international/european-commission-e-commerce-inquiry-american-tech-companies.html (on file with author).

44. Julia Fioretti, *Apple Appeals Against EU Tax Ruling, Brussels Says No Cause For Lower Tax Bill*, REUTERS (Dec. 18, 2016 7:12 PM) https://www.reuters.com/article/us-eu-apple-taxavoidance-idUSKBN148007 [https://perma.cc/B65D-KYPQ].

45. Interview by Kara Swisher with Barack Obama, President of the United States of America, in Standford, Cal. (Feb. 15, 2015), https://www.recode.net/2015/2/15/11559056/white-house-red-chair-obama-meets-swisher [https://perma.cc/Q6MQ-NYZ2].

46. Adam Satariano & Jack Nicas, *E.U. Fines Google $5.1 Billion in Android Antitrust Case*, N.Y. TIMES (July 18, 2018) https://www.nytimes.com/2018/07/18/technology/google-eu-android-fine.html (on file with author).

47. John Cassidy, *Why Did the European Commission Fine Google Five Billion Dollars?* NEW YORKER (July 20, 2018), https://www.newyorker.com/news/our-columnists/why-did-the-european-commission-fine-google-five-billion-dollars [https://perma. cc/9WFS-GBBM].

48. Senate Finance Committee (@SenFinance), TWITTER (Jul. 18, 2018, 8:33 AM), https:// twitter.com/SenFinance/status/1019605981968371712 [https://perma.cc/ZDN2-B2D7].

49. *See* Commission Decision in Case No. M.7881 (ABInBev/SABMiller) C (2016) 3212 final (May 24, 2016).

50. Bradford et al., *supra* note 37.

51. Pierre Cremieux & Edward A. Snyder, *Enforcement of Anticollusion Laws against Domestic and Foreign Firms*, 59 J.L. & ECON., 775 (2016).

52. *See* Press Release, Alstom, Siemens and Alstom Join Forces to Create a European Champion in Mobility (Sept. 26, 2017), https://www.alstom.com/press-releases-news/2017/9/siemens-and-alstom-join-forces-to-create-a-european-champion-in-mobility [https://perma.cc/SE7T-33UT].

53. *See* Commission Decision of 6 February 2019 in case M. 8677 Siemens/Alstom (not yet published since last verified on Apr. 14, 2019). *See also* European Commission Press Release IP/19/881, Merger: Commission Prohibits Siemens' Proposed Acquisition of Alstom (Feb. 6, 2019), http://europa.eu/rapid/press-release_IP-19-881_en.htm [https://perma.cc/5FQY-8TCD]; Rochelle Toplensky, *EU Blocks Planned Siemens-Alstom Rail Deal in Landmark Decision*, FIN. TIMES (Feb. 6, 2019), https://www.ft.com/content/6e344f6a-29fd-11e9-88a4-c32129756dd8 (on file with author).

54. Commission Decision of 6 February 2019 in case M. 8677 Siemens/Alstom (not yet published since last verified on Apr. 14, 2019).

55. Foo Yun Chee & John Revill, *EU Antitrust Policy Under Fire After Siemens-Alstom Deal Blocked*, REUTERS (Feb 6, 2019, 5:51 AM), https://www.reuters.com/article/us-alstom-m-a-siemens-eu/eu-antitrust-policy-under-fire-after-siemens-alstom-deal-blocked-idUSKCN1PV12L [https://perma.cc/7CL3-HZ8N].

56. Mehreen Khan, *A Clash of EU's Titans Over China*, FIN. TIMES (Apr. 2, 2019), https://www.ft.com/content/abd1ef0c-54ce-11e9-a3db-1fe89bedc16e (on file with author).

57. *See* Council Regulation 1/2003 of December 16, 2002, on the Implementation of the Rules on Competition Laid Down in Articles 81 and 82 of the Treaty, O.J. (2003) (L 1) 1 (EC); and Council Regulation 139/2004 of Jan. 20, 2004, on the Control of Concentrations Between Undertakings, 2004 O.J. (L 24) 1 (EC). *See also* Nicolas Petit & Norman Neyrinck, *A Review of the Competition Law Implications of the Treaty on the Functioning of the European Union*, COMPETITION POL'Y INT'L ANTITRUST J. (Jan. 2010), at 7, http://www.emulation-innovation.be/wp-content/uploads/2013/09/Petit-Neyrinck-102-2-Lisbon.pdf [https://perma.cc/8SZE-5MVU].

58. *See* Council Regulation 1/2003 of 16 December 2002 on the Implementation of the Rules on Competition Laid Down in Articles 81 and 82 of the Treaty, O.J. (2003) (L 1) 1 (EC).

59. *See, e.g., Competition Policy: Prosecutor, Judge and Jury*, ECONOMIST (Feb. 18, 2010), https://www.economist.com/leaders/2010/02/18/prosecutor-judge-and-jury [https://perma.cc/B5J5-A9AK];; Tom Fairless, *EU Displaces U.S. as Top Antitrust Cop*, WALL ST. J. (Sept. 3, 2015, 5:04 PM ET), https://www.wsj.com/articles/eu-displaces-u-s-as-top-antitrust-cop-1441314254 (on file with author).

60. Bradford et al., *supra* note 37, at 191.

61. *See, e.g.,* Foreign Trade Antitrust Improvements Act of 1982 (FTAIA), 15 U.S.C. § 6a (2018); United States v. Aluminum Co. of Am., 148 F.2d 416, 444 (2d Cir. 1945); Case T-102/96, Gencor Ltd v. Comm'n, 1999 E.C.R. II-759, ¶¶ 73, 92, 96; *see also* Eleanor M. Fox, *National Law, Global Markets, and Hartford: Eyes Wide Shut*, 68 ANTITRUST L.J. 73, 79-86 (2000); Damien Geradin et al., *Extraterritoriality, Comity, and Cooperation in EU Competition Law, in* COOPERATION, COMITY, AND COMPETITION POLICY 21, 24-29 (Andrew T. Guzman ed., 2011).

62. *See* Commission Decision of 24 May 2004, Case COMP/C-3/37.792 (Microsoft), 2007 O.J. (L 32) 23; Commission Decision of 24 March 2004, Case COMP/C-3/37.792 (Microsoft), 3-4, C (2004) 900 final (Apr. 21, 2004).

63. *See* Steve Lohr, *Antitrust Cry from Microsoft*, N.Y. TIMES, Mar. 31, 2011, at B1, https://www.nytimes.com/2011/03/31/technology/companies/31google.html?mtrref=www.google.com&gwh=A598C6EBBF881EE0FCBA67C3037A8078&gwt=pay&assetType=PAYWALL (on file with author); Brad Smith, *Adding Our Voice to Concerns About Search in Europe*, MICROSOFT ON THE ISSUES (Mar. 30, 2011, 9:00 PM); https://blogs.

microsoft.com/on-the-issues/2011/03/30/adding-our-voice-to-concerns-about-search-in-europe/ [https://perma.cc/X8L7-357W].

64. Vlad Savov, *What is Fair Search and Why Does It Hate Google So Much?*, THE VERGE (Apr. 12, 2013), https://www.theverge.com/2013/4/12/4216026/who-is-fairsearch [https://perma.cc/JE3A-W5KB].

65. European Commission Press Release IP/17/1784, Antitrust: Commission Fines Google €2.42 Billion For Abusing Dominance as Search Engine by Giving Illegal Advantage to Own Comparison Shopping Service (June 27, 2017), https://europa.eu/rapid/press-release_IP-17-1784_en.htm [https://perma.cc/BEX2-FPRZ]; European Commission Press Release IP/18/4581, Antitrust: Commission Fines Google €4.34 Billion for Illegal Practices Regarding Android Mobile Devices to Strengthen Dominance of Google's Search Engine (July 18, 2018), https://europa.eu/rapid/press-release_IP-18-4581_en.htm [https://perma.cc/BEX2-FPRZ]; European Commission Press Release IP/19/1770, Antitrust: Commission Fines Google €1.49 Billion for Abusive Practices in Online Advertising (Mar. 20, 2019), http://europa.eu/rapid/press-release_IP-19-1770_en.htm [https://perma.cc/8L6C-PD2J].

66. *See* Council Regulation 139/2004 of Jan. 20, 2004, on the Control of Concentrations Between Undertakings, art. 1(2), 2004 O.J. (L 24) 1 (EC).

67. *See* Bradford, *supra* note 21, at 308–11.

68. *See* Commission Decision in Case No. COMP/M.2220 (General Electric/Honeywell), 2004 O.J. (L 48) 1. In contrast, for the position of US regulatory authorities, see Press Release, US Dep't of Justice, Justice Department Requires Divestitures in Merger Between General Electric and Honeywell (May 2, 2001), http://www.justice.gov/atr/public/press_releases/2001/8140.pdf.[https://perma.cc/KF3G-PGPV].

69. Commission Decision in Case No. IV/M.053 (Aerospatiale-Alenia/de Havilland), 1991 O.J. (L 334) 42.

70. Commission Decision in Case No. IV/M.619 (Gencor/Lonrho), 1997 O.J. (L 11) 30.

71. Commission Decision in Case No. COMP/M.6570 (UPS/ TNT EXPRESS), C(2013) 431 final (Jan. 30, 2013) *cited in* 2014 O.J. (C 137) 8.

72. Commission Decision in Case No. M.7630 (FedEx/TNT Express), C(2015) 9826 final (Jan. 8, 2016) *cited in* 2016 O.J. (C 450) 12.

73. Commission Decision in Case No. COMP/M.5421 (Panasonic/Sanyo) C (209) 7572 (Sept. 29, 2009) *cited in* 2009 O.L. (C 322) 13.

74. Boeing Co. et al., Joint Statement Closing Investigation of the Proposed Merger, 5 Trade Reg. Rep. (CCH) ¶ 24,295 (July 1, 1997).

75. Commission Decision in Case No. IV/M.877 (Boeing/McDonnell Douglas), 1997 O.J. (L 336) 16,36-38.

76. *See* Kovacic, *supra* note 18, at 838-39.

77. Commission Decision in Case No. COMP/M.5984 (Intel/McAfee), C(2011) 529 Final (Jan. 26, 2011).

78. *Id.*

79. Commission Decision in Case No. COMP/M.1845 (AOL/Time Warner), 2001 O.J. (L 268) 28.

80. *See* Commission Decision in Case No. COMP/39258 (Airfreight), C(2010) 7694 final (Nov. 21, 2001) *re-adopted in* Summary Commission Decision in Case No. AT.39258 (Airfreight), 2017 O.J. (C 188) 14; Commission Decision in Case AT.39924 (Swiss Franc Interest Rate Derivatives/LIBOR), C(2014) 7605 final (Oct. 21, 2014) *cited in* 2015 O.J. (C 72) 9; Commission Decision in Case AT.39924 (Swiss Franc Interest Rate Derivatives/ Bid Ask Spread Infringement), C(2014) 7602 final (Oct. 21, 2014) *cited in* 2015 O.J. (C 72) 14; Commission Decision in Case No. AT.39861 (Yen Interest Rate Derivatives)

C(2015) 432 final (Feb. 4, 2015) *cited in* 2017 O.J. (C 305) 10; Commission Decision in Case No. AT.39437 (TV and Computer Monitor Tubes) C(2012) 8839 final (Dec. 5, 2012) *cited in* 2013 O.J. (C 303) 13.

81. *See* Commission Decision in Case No. AT.39437 (TV and Computer Monitor Tubes) C(2012) 8839 final (Dec. 5, 2012) *cited in* 2013 O.J. (C 303) 13; SOUTH KOREA, IMPROVING INTERNATIONAL COOPERATION IN CARTEL INVESTIGATIONS: CONTRIBUTION TO THE OECD GLOBAL FORUM ON COMPETITION (2011), http://www.oecd.org/officialdocuments/publicdisplaydocumentpdf/?cote=DAF/COMP/GF/WD(2012)13&docLanguage=En [https://perma.cc/6HPB-75TM]; *2008 Year-End Criminal Antitrust Update*, GIBSON DUNN (Jan. 7, 2009), https://www.gibsondunn.com/2008-year-end-criminal-antitrust-update/ [https://perma.cc/U3P3-G2RP].

82. *See* Commission Decision in Case No. COMP/E-1/37.512 (Vitamins), 2003 O.J. (L 6) 1. The Commission's decision cites the following undertakings as addressees of its decision: F. Hoffmann-La Roche AG; BASF AG; Aventis SA (formerly Rhône-Poulenc); Lonza AG; Solvay Pharmaceuticals BV; Merck KgaA; Daiichi Pharmaceutical Co. Ltd; Eisai Co. Ltd; Kongo Chemical Co. Ltd; Sumitomo Chemical Co. Ltd; Sumika Fine Chemicals Ltd; Takeda Chemical Industries Ltd; Tanabe Seiyaku Co. Ltd. *Id.* ¶ 1. The Decision further notes that "The products with which this decision is concerned are those bulk synthetic substances which belong to the following groups of vitamins and closely related products: A, E, B1, B2, B5, B6, C, D3, biotin (H), folic acid (M), beta-carotene and carotinoids." *Id.* ¶ 8.

83. Harry First, *The Vitamins Case: Cartel Prosecutions and the Coming of International Competition Law*, 68 ANTITRUST L.J. 711 (2001).

84. First, *supra* note 83, at 711–34.

85. Howard Bergman & D. Daniel Sokol, *The Air Cargo Cartel: Lessons for Compliance, in* ANTI-CARTEL ENFORCEMENT IN A CONTEMPORARY AGE: LENIENCY RELIGION 301, 308–11 (Caron Beaton-Wells & Christopher Tran eds., 2015).

86. Commission Decision in Case No. AT.39850 (Container Shipping) C (2016) 4215 final (July 7, 2016) *cited in* 2016 O.J. (C 327) 4.

87. *E.g.*, Commission Decision in Case No. COMP/C-3/37.990 (Intel), D(2009) 3726 final (May 13, 2009) *cited in* 2009 O.J. (C 227) 13; Commission Decision In Case No. COMP/C-3/37.792 (Microsoft) C(2004) 900 final (Mar. 24, 2004) *cited in* 2007 O.J. (L 32) 23; *see* Stephen Castle, *Microsoft Gets Record Fine and a Rebuke from Europe*, N.Y. TIMES, Feb. 28, 2008, at C3, https://www.nytimes.com/2008/02/28/technology/28soft.html (on file with author); Editorial, *Europe v. U.S. Business*, WALL ST. J., Jan. 17, 2008, at A16, https://www.wsj.com/articles/SB120053154686996085 (on file with author); European Commission Press Release IP/18/4581 Antitrust: Commission Fines Google €4.34 Billion for Illegal Practices Regarding Android Mobile Devices to Strengthen Dominance of Google's Search Engine (July 18, 2018), http://europa.eu/rapid/press-release_IP-18-4581_en.htm [https://perma.cc/BEX2-FPRZ]; Alex Barker & Mehreen Khan, *EU Fines Google Record €4.3bn Over Android*, FIN. TIMES (July 18, 2018), https://www.ft.com/content/56ae8282-89d7-11e8-b18d-018173120340 (on file with author); Summary of Commission Decision in Case No. AT.40220 (Qualcomm (Exclusivity Payments) 2018 O.J. (C 269) 25; *Qualcomm Fine Shows EU Antitrust Enforcers Aren't Daunted by Intel Ruling*, MLEX (Jan. 24, 2018), https://mlexmarketinsight.com/insights-center/editors-picks/antitrust/europe/qualcomm-fine-shows-eu-antitrust-enforcers-arent-daunted-by-intel-ruling [https://perma.cc/78G9-BM9Y].

88. *See, e.g.*, Commission Decision in Case No. COMP/B-2/38.381 (De Beers), C(2006) 521 final (Feb. 22, 2006) *cited in* 2006 O.J. (L 205) 24.

89. Andrew E. Kramer, *Russia Stockpiles Diamonds, Awaiting the Return of Demand*, N.Y. TIMES (May 11, 2009), https://www.nytimes.com/2009/05/12/business/global/12diamonds.html (on file with author).

90. Commission Decision in Case COMP/A.39.116/B2 (Coca-Cola), C(2005) 1829 final (June 22, 2005) *cited in* 2005 O.J. (L 253) 21.

91. PepsiCo, Inc. v. Coca-Cola Co., 315 F. 3d 101, 108 (2d Cir. 2002).

92. Michal S. Gal, *Antitrust in a Globalized Economy: The Unique Enforcement Challenges Faced by Small and Developing Jurisdictions*, 33 FORDHAM INT'L L.J. 1, 41 (2009).

93. European Commission Press Release IP/17/1784, Antitrust: Commission Fines Google €2.42 Billion for Abusing Dominance as Search Engine by Giving Illegal Advantage to Own Comparison Shopping Service (June 27, 2017), http://europa.eu/rapid/press-release_IP-17-1784_en.htm [https://perma.cc/ZN2D-4SS9].

94. Google Europe Twitter post, Sept. 27 2017, https://twitter.com/googleeurope/status/913071852146315264 [https://perma.cc/Z4RL-C6B3]; Oliver Heckmann, *Changes to Google Shopping in Europe*, GOOGLE BLOG (Sept. 27, 2017), https://adwords.googleblog.com/2017/09/changes-to-google-shopping-in-europe.html [https://perma.cc/QSH6-CEXC].

95. Aoife White, *Google to Create Shopping Service Unit to Satisfy EU*, BLOOMBERG (Sept. 26, 2017), https://www.bloomberg.com/news/articles/2017-09-26/google-said-to-split-off-shopping-service-to-meet-eu-demands (on file with author).

96. Jeff John Roberts, *Google's $2.7 Billion Fine: What it Means and What Happens Next*, FORTUNE http://fortune.com/2017/06/27/google-eu-fine-faq/ [https://perma.cc/29X8-3VUM]; Rochelle Toplensky & Richard Waters, *Google Changes Shopping Search to Sooth EU Antitrust Concerns*, FIN. TIMES (Sept. 28, 2017), https://www.ft.com/content/9c9d196a-a432-11e7-b797-b61809486fe2 (on file with author).

97. Commission Decision in Case No. COMP/C-3/37.792 (Microsoft), C(2004) 900 final, ¶ 2.1 (Mar. 24, 2004) *cited in* 2007 O.J. (L 32) 23.

98. *Id* ¶ 427.

99. Nicolas Economides & Ioannis Lianos, *The Elusive Antitrust Standard on Bundling in Europe and the United States in the Aftermath of the* Microsoft *Cases*, 76 ANTITRUST L.J. 483, 484 (2009).

100. SIEMENS, BUSINESS CONDUCT GUIDELINES (2009), https://new.siemens.com/global/en/company/sustainability/compliance.html (on file with author).

101. EXXONMOBIL, ANTITRUST AND COMPETITION LAW: LEGAL COMPLIANCE GUIDE 7–8 (2014), https://corporate.exxonmobil.com/-/media/Global/Files/policy/Antitrust-and-Competition-Law-Legal-Compliance-Guide.pdf [https://perma.cc/JAM5-8NLX].

102. Interview with John Frank, Vice President of Microsoft, in Brussels (July 16, 2018).

103. Anu Bradford et al., *supra* note 9.

104. Michal S. Gal, *The 'Cut and Paste' of Article 82 of the EC Treaty in Israel: Conditions for a Successful Transplant*, 9 EUR. J.L. REFORM 467 (2007); William E. Kovacic, *Merger Enforcement in Transition: Antitrust Controls on Acquisition in Emerging Economies*, 66 U. CIN. L. REV. 1071, 1086–89 (1998).

105. Competition Act 89 of 1998, Preamble (S. Afr.).

106. Case 27/76, United Brands Co. v. Comm'n 1978 E.C.R. 207 164.

107. Competition Act 89 of 1998, § 8(a) (S. Afr.).

108. Competition Act 89 of 1998, § 1(1)(ix) (S. Afr.).

109. See the seminal South African dominance case *Competition Commission and South African Airways (Pty) Ltd* (final) (18/CR/Mar01) [2005] ZACT 50 *citing, inter alia,* Commercial Solvents Case 6/73 etc [1974] ECR 223; *Sealink/b and Holyhead* [1992] 5 CMLR 255; *Virgin/British Airways OJ* [2000] L30/1, [2000] CMLR 999 21.

110. See, for example, the lengthy discussion of Article 101 and the characterization of horizontal and vertical agreements in *Competition Commission v South African Breweries Limited and Others* (129/CAC/Apr14) [2015].

111. David Lewis, Thieves at the Dinner Table: Enforcing Competition Rules in South Africa 247 (2012).

112. *Id.* at 24–26.

113. Competition Act 89 of 1998, Preamble (S. Afr.).

114. 2004 Parliamentary Debate, at 864; Other sources confirm this view. *See* Kala Andarajah & Dominique Lombardi, *Competition Law in Singapore*, Aug. 24, 2015, at 3, https://www.competitionpolicyinternational.com/competition-law-in-singapore/ [https://perma.cc/HV6G-6WPD]; Burton Ong, *The Origins, Objectives and Structure of Competition Law in Singapore*, 29 Kluwer L. Int'l 269, 280 (2006).

115. *Compare, e.g.,* Competition and Consumer Commission of Singapore, Guidelines on the Section 34 Prohibition 2016 (Dec. 1, 2016) *with* Commission Guidelines on the Applicability of Article 101 of the Treaty on the Functioning of the European Union to Horizontal Co-operation Agreements, 2011 O.J. (C 11).

116. Ong, *supra* note 114, at 280.

117. Competition Act, Third Schedule,¶ 8 (Cap. 50B, 2006 Rev. Ed.) (Sing.).

118. Robert Ian McEwin et al., Competition Law in Singapore: Principles Practice & Procedures 1–5 (2007).

119. Competition Commission of Singapore Infringement Decision in Case No. CCS/600/008/07 (SISTIC.com PTE Ltd.), ¶ 4.1.3 (June 4, 2010), https://www.cccs.gov.sg/~/media/custom/ccs/files/public%20register%20and%20consultation/public%20consultation%20items/abuse%20of%20dominant%20position%20by%20sisticcom%20pte%20ltd/sistic20infringement20decision20nonconfidential20version.ashx [https://perma.cc/8J63-QZG4].

120. *Id.* ¶ 4.1.3.

121. SISTIC.com PTE Ltd. v. Competition Commission of Singapore, App. No. 1 of 2010 ¶ 287(Competition App. Bd., May 28, 2012) (Sing.), https://www.cccs.gov.sg/~/media/custom/ccs/files/public%20register%20and%20consultation/public%20consultation%20items/abuse%20of%20dominant%20position%20by%20sisticcom%20pte%20ltd/sistic20appealcab20decision120june202012redacted.ashx [https://perma.cc/P5B8-2WPV].

122. Ong, *supra* note 114, at 270.

123. Competition Commission of Singapore, 10 Years of Championing Growth and Choice 56 (2015), https://www.cccs.gov.sg/-/media/custom/ccs/files/media-and-publications/publications/annual-reports/ccs-ar250811final.pdf [https://perma.cc/HS5K-2U72].

124. Nicholas Tan, *A Big Ticket Issue for Singapore's Biggest Ticketing Issuer*, 23 Sing. Academ. L.J. 538, 542 (2011).

125. Ninety-Third Report on the Competition Bill, 2001, Rajya Dabha Secretariat, AUGUST 2002/SRAVANA, 1924(SAKA), 14, http://www.prsindia.org/uploads/media/1167471748/bill73_2007050873_Standing_Committee_Report_on_Competition_Bill__2001.pdf [https://perma.cc/GE39-ZSPE].

126. *See* The Competition Act, No. 12 of 2003, § 4, India Code (2019), https://indiacode.nic.in/bitstream/123456789/2010/2/A2003-12.pdf [https://perma.cc/RY4A-HSPS]; *see also* Pratibha Jane & Simone Reis, *Competition Law in India—Jurisprudential Trends and the Way Forward*, Nishith Dsai Associates (Apr. 6, 2013), http://www.nishithde-sai.com/information/nda-in-the-media/audio/article/competition-law-in-india-juris-prudential-trends-and-the-way-forward-1.html?tx_ttnews%5Border%5D=title&tx_ttnews%5Bdir%5D=desc&cHash=d619c816715a4137798584d0af1cf9c9 [https://perma.cc/3ZQV-TWME].

127. The Competition Act, No. 12 of 2003, § 4(e), India Code (2019), https://indiacode.nic.in/bitstream/123456789/2010/2/A2003-12.pdf [https://perma.cc/RY4A-HSPS].

128. Case 27/26, United Brands v. Comm'n, 1978 E.C.R, 207

129. *Id.* 65–66.

130. HT Media Ltd. v. Super Cassettes (2014) CCI 109.

131. *See* Li Jian (李剑), *Zhong Guo Fan Long Duan Fa Shi Shi Zhong De Ti Xi Chong Tu Yu Hua Jie (*中国反垄断法实施中的体系冲突与化解*) [System Conflict and Resolution for the Enforcement of China Antimonopoly Law]*, CHINA LEGAL SCIENCE (*2014*), http://zgfxqk.org.cn/WKA3/WebPublication/wkDownLoad.aspx?fileID=29930f86-115c-4c84-9807-660efb90fbde&pid=ce18f75c-5bf9-4c87-b69e-800680816003 [https://perma.cc/V3ZY-6GG7].

132. *See* Wan Jiang (万江), *Zhong Guo Fan Long Duan Fa Yu Ou Meng Jing Zheng Fa Nei Rong Dui Bi Biao (*中国反垄断法与欧盟竞争法内容对比表*) [Comparison of Chinese Antimonopoly Law and EU Competition Law]*, LEXIS PRACTICAL GUIDE http://hk.lexiscn.com/asiapg/articles/29e3d1ef-5bbb-20ab-d13f-3a18e2a80385.html [https://perma.cc/2E67-ECVT].

133. *See* TFEU Article 42; Anti-Monopoly Law of the People's Republic of China, Art. 56 (promulgated by the Standing Comm. Nat'l People's Cong., Aug. 30, 2007, effective Aug. 1, 2008), 2007 STANDING COMM. NAT'L PEOPLE'S CONG. GAZ. 68.

134. *See* Qian Dali (钱大立), Huang Kai (黄凯), *Jian Xi Jing Ying Zhe Ji Zhong Shen Cha Ban Fa Xiu Ding Cao An Zheng Qiu Yi Jian Gao (*简析经营者集中审查办法修订草案征求意见稿*) [Brief Analysis of draft version of Amendment to the Measure for the Undertaking Concentration Examination]*, LAW REVIEW OF CORPORATE & ACQUISITIONS BY LLINKS LAW OFFICE (Sept. 2017), http://www.llinkslaw.com/uploadfile/publication/60_1515059367.pdf [https://perma.cc/N3LT-96X6].

135. *See* Wan Jiang (万江), *supra* note 132.

136. *See* Li Meiying (李梅影), *Fan Long Duan Fa You Wang Ming Nian Chu Tai Jiang Jie Jian Ou Meng Jing Zheng Fa Jing Yan (*反垄断法有望明年出台将借鉴欧盟竞争法经验*) [Antimonopoly Law is Expected to Be Released Next Year, Will Learn From EU Competition Law Experience]*, INT'L FIN. NEWS (Apr. 25, 2005), http://it.people.com.cn/GB/3346561.html [https://perma.cc/3NRJ-ABLH].

137. *See* Li Jian (李剑), *supra* note 131.

138. *See* Shang Ming (尚明), *Fa Zhan Zhong De Zhong Guo Jing Zheng Zheng Ce Yu Li Fa (*发展中的中国竞争政策与立法*) [Competition Policies and Legislation of the Developing China] (Apr. 27, 2005)*, http://tfs.mofcom.gov.cn/article/bc/200504/20050400081489.shtml [https://perma.cc/UG8W-76DL].

139. MOFCOM refers to China's Ministry of Commerce, NDRC refers to China's National Development and Reform Commission, and SAIC refers to China's State Administration for Industry and Commerce.

140. *See* Torben Toft, *Update on Competition Developments in China: EU-China Competition Law Cooperation* (Sept. 2016) (on file with Pritzker School of Law), http://www.law.northwestern.edu/research-faculty/searlecenter/workingpapers/documents/Torben_Toft_update_on_competition_developments_in_China.pdf [https://perma.cc/F86X-UEQ7].

141. *See Terms of Reference of the EU-China Competition Policy Dialogue*, entered on May 6, 2004 (last visited on Nov. 10, 2017). Item 2.7, downloaded via http://ec.europa.eu/competition/international/bilateral/china_tor_en.pdf [https://perma.cc/KP9P-4L33].

142. Organic Law for the Regulation and Control of Market Power (Ley Orgánica de Regulación y Control del Poder de Mercado), Registro Oficial Suplemento 555, Oficio No. T.364-SNJ-11-1287, 2011.

143. For example, *compare* Article 27 of the Market Power Control and Regulation Act and the Article 3 of the Spanish Competition Defense Act or the Art 11 of the Market Power

Control and Regulation Act with Article 101 of the TFEU or the Art 1 of the Spanish Competition Defense Act.

144. Los Metodos para la Definicion del Mercado Relevante – Junta de Regulacion de Poder de Mercado – Registro Oficial 885 del 18 de noviembre de 2016 (Methods for Relevant Market Definition – Market Power Board – Official Register No. 885 from November 18, 2016).

145. REPUBLIC OF ECUADOR, CONSTITUTION OF 2008, Art. 3 (unofficial English transla- tion http://pdba.georgetown.edu/Constitutions/Ecuador/english08.html) [https:// perma.cc/6XVU-4YYG]).

146. Evgeny Khokhlov, *The Current State of Russian Competition Law in the Context of Harmonization with EU Competition Law*, 5 J. EUR. L. & PRAC. 32, 32–38 (2014).

147. Hailegabriel G. Feyissa, *European Influence on Ethiopian Antitrust Regime: A Comparative and Functional Analysis of Some Problems*, 3 MIZAN L. REV. 271 (2009).

148. Ana Julia Jatar, Symposium, *Competition Policy in Latin America: Introduction*, 24 BROOKLYN J. INT'L L. 357 (1998).

149. Bradford, *supra* note 10.

150. David Gerber, *Constructing Competition Law in China: The Potential Value of European and U.S. Experience*, WASH. U. GLOBAL STUD. L. REV. 315 (2004); William E. Kovacic, *Merger Enforcement in Transition: Antitrust Controls on Acquisition in Emerging Economies*, U. CIN. L. REV. 66:1071–12 (1998).

151. Gal, *supra* note 17, at 345–46.

152. *See, e.g.*, Roger Van den Bergh, *The Difficult Reception of Economic Analysis in European Competition Law*, in POST-CHICAGO DEVELOPMENTS IN ANTITRUST LAW, 34, 46–50 (Antonio Cucinotta et al. eds., 2002).

153. *See* Burton Ong, *The Competition Act of 2004: A Legislative Landmark on Singapore's Legal Landscape*, J. SINGAPORE LEGAL STUD. 172, 174 n 8 (2006).

154. Hans-Bernd Schäfer, *Rules Versus Standards in Rich and Poor Countries: Precise Legal Norms as Substitutes for Human Capital in Low-Income Countries*, 14 SUP. CT. ECON. REV. 113, 113–34 (2006).

155. *See* Mr. Mario Monti, EU Commissioner for Antitrust, International Co-operation and Technical Assistance: A View from the EU, Geneva (July 4, 2001), http://www.europa. eu/rapid/press-release_SPEECH-01-328_en.pdf [https://perma.cc/M8LH-ADB5].

156. *See* discussion in Bradford et al., *supra* note 10.

157. *See* EC-Turkey Assoc. Council Decision No 1/95 of 22 December 1995 On Implementing The Final Phase of the Customs Union (96/142/EC), 1996 O.J. (L 35) 1, 9 art. 39.

158. Solomon Menabdishvili, *Recent Developments in the Competition Law of Georgia. Changes Resulting from the Association Agreement*, 8 Y.B. ANTITRUST & REG. STUD. 213 (2015).

159. Bradford et al., *supra* note 10.

160. *See* Hanna L. Buxbaum, *The Private Attorney General in a Global Age: Public Interests in Private International Antitrust Litigation*, 26 YALE L.J. 219, 251 (2001).

161. Anti-Monopoly Law of the People's Republic of China (promulgated by the Standing Comm. Nat'l People's Cong., Aug. 30, 2007, effective Aug. 1, 2008), 2007 STANDING COMM. NAT'L PEOPLE'S CONG. GAZ. 68.

162. Commission Decision in Case No. COMP/C-3/37.792 (Microsoft), C(2004) 900 final, ¶ 2.1 (Mar. 24, 2004) *cited in* 2007 O.J. (L 32) 23.

163. Jeremy Kirk, *Korea to Hear Microsoft Competition Case: Company Protests Windows XP-Messenger Tie-in*, INFOWORLD (Jul. 8, 2005), https://www.infoworld.com/ article/2670535/operating-systems/korea-to-hear-microsoft-competition-case.html [https://perma.cc/DC6X-3BH3].

164. *Id.* at 622.

165. David J. Silverthorn, *Microsoft Tying Consumers' Hands? The Windows Vista Problem and the South Korea Solution*, 13 Mich. Telecomm. & Tech. L. Rev. 617, 621–22 (2007).

166. *Id.* at 622.

167. Marius Meland, *Microsoft Battles South Korean Antitrust Decision*, Law360 (Mar. 27, 2006), https://www.law360.com/articles/5854 (on file with author).

168. Press Release, Microsoft Korea (한국마이크로소프트), Microsoft's Position on the Release of Decision by the Korean Fair Trade Commission (공정거래위원회 의결서 송부에 대한 '마이크로소프트의 입장') (Feb. 24, 2006) *reprinted in* Newswire. kr (Feb. 24, 2006 6:51 PM) http://www.newswire.co.kr/newsRead.php?no=127294 [https://perma.cc/226L-DSM4].

169. Maria Kiselyova, *Russian Competition Watchdog Opens Case Against Google*, Reuters (Feb. 20, 2015, 5:20 AM), https://www.reuters.com/article/us-russia-crisis-google-investigation/russian-competition-watchdog-opens-case-against-google-idUSKBN-0LO0RJ20150220 [https://perma.cc/7TXC-VCK8].

170. Press Release Russian Federal Antimonopoly Service, FAS Russia reached settlement with Google (Apr. 2017), https://en.fas.gov.ru/press-center/news/detail. html?id=49774 [https://perma.cc/9S3Z-VQBP]; E. Kroh, *Google Pays $7.7M Fine To End Russian Antitrust Probe*, Law360, (May 12, 2017, 5:06 PM EDT) ,https://www. law360.com/articles/923370/google-pays-7-7m-fine-to-end-russian-antitrust-probe (on file with author).

171. Evgeny Khokhlov, *The Russian Federal Antimonopoly Service's Case Against Google Related to Bundling and Other Anticompetitive Practices with Respect to Android*, 8 J. Eur. Competition L. & Prac. 468, 468 (2017). *See also* Decision of FAS of Russia in Case No. 1-14-21/00-11-15 (Oct. 15, 2015), https://br.fas.gov.ru/ca/upravlenie-regulirovaniya-svyazi-i-informatsionnyh-tehnologiy/ad-54066-15/ [https://perma.cc/NY9U-B4C3] (unofficial English translation http://www.benedelman.org/docs/yandex-vs-google-translation-18sep2015.pdf).

172. Brad Haynes, *Brazil Investigates Google Over Antitrust Charges*, Reuters (Oct. 11, 2013, 11:37 AM), https://www.reuters.com/article/us-google-brazil-idUSBRE99A0JM20131011 [https://perma.cc/VYM7-JHDK]; Press Release, Brazilian Administrative Council for Economic Defense, CADE Investigates Google's Possible Anticompetitive Practices in the Brazilian Online Search Market, (Oct. 11, 2013), http://en.cade.gov.br/ press-releases/cade-investigates-google2019s-possible-anticompetitive-practices-in-the-brazilian-online-search-market [https://perma.cc/W3X6-M5AG].

173. Jeff Zalesin, *Brazil Continues Google Antitrust Probe Without Microsoft*, Law360 (May 5, 2016), https://www.law360.com/articles/792935/brazil-continues-google-antitrust-probe-without-microsoft (on file with author).

174. *Brazil: CADE considers opening probe into Google*, Competition Pol'y Int'l (Aug. 20, 2018), https://www.competitionpolicyinternational.com/brazil-cade-considers-joining-investigations-against-google/ [https://perma.cc/3PNM-S6CJ].

175. B. Balki, *Google fined—this time by the Turkish Competition Watchdog*, Kluwer Competition Law Blog (Nov. 5, 2018), http://competitionlawblog.kluwercompe-titionlaw.com/2018/11/05/google-fined-this-time-by-the-turkish-competition-watch-dog/ [https://perma.cc/P5XD-7VN4].

176. Jung-Ah Lee, *South Korean Search Portals File Phone Complaint Against Google*, Wall St. J. (Apr. 18, 2011), https://www.wsj.com/articles/SB10001424052748703983104576264012635638314 (on file with author).

177. Youkyung Lee, *South Korea's fair trade commission clears Google after 2-year probe*, NBC News (July 18, 2013) ,https://www.nbcnews.com/business/south-koreas-fair-trade-commission-clears-google-after-2-year-6C10669675 [https://perma.cc/VR73-TWS3];

Samuel Gibbs and agencies, *Google's South Korean offices inspected in Android antitrust probe*, GUARDIAN (July 21, 2016), https://www.theguardian.com/technology/2016/jul/21/google-south-korean-offices-inspected-android-antitrust-probe [https://perma.cc/D7EC-YTKF]; *see also* Zach Miners, *South Korea Drops Antitrust Investigation Against Google*, PCWORLD (July 18, 2013, 4:35 PM PT), https://www.pcworld.com/article/2044695/s-korea-drops-antitrust-investigation-against-google.html [https://perma.cc/RW6C-9ACR].

178. Song Jung-a, *South Korea Confirms Google Antitrust Probe*, FIN. TIMES (Aug. 12, 2016, https://www.ft.com/content/59bd6b78-6044-11e6-b38c-7b39cbb1138a (on file with author).

179. Hyunsuk Cho & Sooryun Park, KFTC monitors Google regarding alleged violation of antitrust laws, JoongAng Ilbo (Apr. 21, 2016), http://news.joins.com/article/19921051 [https://perma.cc/CFU8-L4QY] (Translated from Korean to English).

180. Commission Decision in Case No. M.7881 (ABInBev/SABMiller) C (2016) 3212 final (May 24, 2016).

181. Superintendencia del Poder de Mercado. Expediente No. SCPM- CRPI- 2016- 017, http://www.scpm.gob.ec/images/RESOLUCIONES-CRPI/notificacion-obligatoria/2016/SCPM-CRPI-2016-017-06-05-2016.pdf [https://perma.cc/3PLG-5673]. *See* Commission Decision in Case No. M.7881 (ABInBev/SABMiller) C (2016) 3212 final (May 24, 2016). The Commission engaged Mazars LLP as Monitoring Trustee. Trustee Details, Case No., M.7881 (ABInBev/SABMiller) (June 24, 2016), http://ec.europa.eu/competition/mergers/cases/additional_data/m7881_2794_3.pdf [https://perma.cc/8WFM-9H7D].

182. *See supra* note 62 and accompanying text.

183. Richard Waters, *Department of Justice opens review into Big Tech's market power*, FIN. TIMES, July 24, 2019, *available at* https://www.ft.com/content/4f008ab0-ad8c-11e9-8030-530adfa879c2 (on file with author).

CHAPTER 5

1. Regulation 2016/679, of the European Parliament and of the Council on the Protection of Natural Persons with regard to the Processing of Personal Data and on the Free Movement of Such Data, and Repealing Directive 95/46/EC, 2016 O.J. (L 119) 1 [hereinafter GDPR].

2. *Code of Conduct on Countering Illegal Hate Speech Online*, EUROPEAN COMMISSION 2 (May 31, 2016), http://ec.europa.eu/justice/fundamental-rights/files/hate_speech_code_of_conduct_en.pdf [https://perma.cc/RD57-XXCF] [hereinafter The Code].

3. Kevin Granville, *Facebook and Cambridge Analytica: What You Need to Know as Fallout Widens*, N.Y. TIMES (Mar. 19, 2018), https://www.nytimes.com/2018/03/19/technology/facebook-cambridge-analytica-explained.html?register=google (on file with author); Paul Mozur, A Genocide Incited on Facebook, With Posts From Myanmar's Military, N.Y. TIMES (Oct. 15, 2018), https://www.nytimes.com/2018/10/15/technology/myanmar-facebook-genocide.html (on file with author).

4. The fundamental right to privacy can be traced back to The European Convention of Human Rights (ECHR), a treaty document drafted by the Council of Europe, which guarantees a fundamental right to privacy; *see* Council of Europe, European Convention for the Protection of Human Rights and Fundamental Freedoms, art. 8, *opened for signature* Nov. 4, 1950, ETS 5 [hereinafter ECHR]. The European Court of Human Rights, which is vested with the task of enforcing the ECHR, has extended the right to privacy to data protection; *see* Copland v. United Kingdom, 253 Eur.Ct.H.R. (2007). All EU

member states are among the 47 signatories of the ECHR, making all Europeans beneficiaries of its privacy rules.

5. *See* Treaty on the Functioning of the European Union art. 16, Oct. 26, 2012, 2012 O.J. (C
326) 1 [hereinafter TFEU].

6. Charter of Fundamental Rights of the European Union, arts. 7–8, Dec. 12, 2007, 2007
O.J. (C 303) 1 [hereinafter Charter of Fundamental Rights].

7. ORLA LYNSKEY, THE FOUNDATIONS OF EU DATA PROTECTION LAW 11 (2015).

8. Regulation 2016/679, of the European Parliament and of the Council on the Protection
of Natural Persons with regard to the Processing of Personal Data and on the Free
Movement of Such Data, and Repealing Directive 95/46/EC, 2016 O.J. (L 119) 1 [herein-
after GDPR].

9. Council Directive 95/46, On the Protection of Individuals with Regard to the Processing
of Personal Data, 1995 O.J. (L 281) 31 [hereinafter Data Protection Directive].

10. GDPR, *supra* note 1, at art. 5(1)(a).

11. *Id.* at arts. 5(1)(b)–1(c).

12. *Id.* at art. 5(1)(d), (5)(1)(f).

13. *Id.* at art. 17.

14. *Id.* at art. 25.

15. *Id.* at arts. 51, 68.

16. *Id.* at art. 83.

17. SLAUGHTER AND MAY, "NEW RULES, WIDER REACH: THE EXTRA-TERRITORIAL
SCOPE OF THE GDPR" (2016), https://www.slaughterandmay.com/media/2535540/
new-rules-wider-reach-the-extraterritorial-scope-of-the-gdpr.pdf [https://perma.cc/
C9RK-CHW7]; *see also* DELOITTE, "GDPR TOP TEN: #3 EXTRATERRITORIAL APPLI-
CABILITY OF THE GDPR" (Apr. 3, 2017), https://www2.deloitte.com/nl/nl/pages/risk/
articles/cyber-security-privacy-gdpr-top-ten-3-extraterritorial-applicability-of-the-gdpr.
html [https://perma.cc/2DTG-BHUJ].

18. *See* GDPR, *supra* note 1, at art. 45.

19. *Proposal for a Regulation of the European Parliament and of the Council concerning the
respect for private life and the protection of personal data in electronic communications and
repealing Directive 2002/58/EC (Regulation on Privacy and Electronic Communications)*,
COM (2017) 10 final (Jan. 10, 2017).

20. Directive 2002/58/EC of the European Parliament and of the Council of 12 July 2002
Concerning the Processing of Personal Data and the Protection of Privacy in the
Electronic Communications Sector, 2002 O.J. (L 201) 37.

21. Mehreen Khan, *EU States Urged to Agree Online Privacy 'Cookie Law,'* FIN. TIMES (Apr.
23, 2018), https://www.ft.com/content/1ebf5a9e-4707-11e8-8ee8-cae73aab7ccb (on file
with author).

22. Natasha Singer, *The Next Privacy Battle in Europe is Over this New Law*, N.Y. TIMES (May
27, 2018), https://www.nytimes.com/2018/05/27/technology/europe-eprivacy-regula-
tion-battle.html (on file with author).

23. Summary of the Opinion of the European Data Protection Supervisor on the Proposal for
a Regulation on Privacy and Electronic Communications (ePrivacy Regulation), 2017 O.J.
(C 234) 3.

24. *Proposal for a Regulation of the European Parliament and of the Council Concerning the
Respect for Private Life and the Protection of Personal Data in Electronic Communications and
Repealing Directive 2002/58/EC (Regulation on Privacy and Electronic Communications)—
Examination of the Presidency text*, (COD) 2017/0003 10975/18 (July 10, 2018), https://
eur-lex.europa.eu/legal-content/EN/TXT/PDF/?uri=CONSIL:ST_10975_2018_
INIT&from=EN [https://perma.cc/6XQZ-CQCE].

25. Case C-131/12, Google Spain SL v. Agencia Española de Protección de Datos, ECLI:EU:C:2014:317, http://curia.europa.eu/juris/document/document.jsf?docid= 152065&doclang=en [hereinafter Google Spain].

26. *Id.* at 91–99.

27. *Id.* at 56.

28. *Id.* at 51–60.

29. Jennifer Daskal, *Borders and Bits*, 71 VAND. L.R. 179, 212 (2018).

30. Mark Scott, *Google Will Further Block Some European Search Results*, N.Y. TIMES (Feb. 11, 2016), https://www.nytimes.com/2016/02/12/technology/google-will-further-block-some-european-search-results.html (on file with author).

31. Mark Scott, *French Court Refers Google Privacy Case to ECJ*, POLITICO (July 19, 2017), http://www.politico.eu/article/french-court-refers-google-privacy-case-to-ecj/ [https://perma.cc/8TDU-P2GK].

32. Daskal, *supra* note 29, at 214.

33. *See Transparency Report—Search Removals Under European Privacy Law*, GOOGLE (May 29, 2014), https://transparencyreport.google.com/eu-privacy/overview [https://perma.cc/ZF5L-KMEA] (these numbers are accurate of May 14, 2019. Google updates the figures periodically).

34. David F. Katz & Elizabeth K. Hinson, GERMANS FINE U.S. COMPANIES FOR UNLAWFUL DATA TRANSFERS TO STATES, LEXOLOGY (2016), https://www.lexology.com/library/detail.aspx?g=743c9b6f-fc67-4479-893c-3a4384f9296e [https://perma.cc/Q3R9-N2R9].

35. Duncan Robinson, *Facebook Fined by French Regulator Over Data Protection Rules*, FIN. TIMES (May 16, 2017), https://www.ft.com/content/10f558c6-3a26-11e7-821a-6027b8a20f23 (on file with author).

36. *See, e.g.*, Gregory Shaffer, *Globalization and Social Protection: The Impact of EU and International Rules in the Ratcheting Up of U.S. Privacy Standards*, 25 YALE J. INT'L L. 1, 43 (2000).

37. Cecilia Kang, *Promise by Google Ends FTC's Privacy-Breach Probe*, WASH. POST, Oct. 28, 2010, at A15.

38. Robinson, *supra* note 35.

39. Thomas Shaw, PRIVACY LAW AND HISTORY: WWII-FORWARD THE PRIVACY ADVISOR (Mar. 1, 2013), https://iapp.org/news/a/2013-03-01-privacy-law-and-history-wwii-forward/ [https://perma.cc/6XE2-8SWA].

40. Alvar C.H. Freude and Trixy Freude, *Echoes of History: Understanding German Data Protection*, NEWPOLITIK 2 (Oct. 1, 2016), https://www.bfna.org/wp-content/uploads/2017/04/Echoes_of_history_Understanding_German_Data_Protection_Freude.pdf [https://perma.cc/D6ZB-WQ7H].

41. LYNSKEY, *supra* note 7, at 46–47.

42. *Communication on A Comprehensive Approach on Personal Data Protection in the EU*, at 19 (COM) (2010) 609 final (Nov. 4, 2010).

43. Interview with Bruno Gencarelli, Head of the International Data Flows and Protection Unit, European Commission, Directorate General Justice and Consumers, in Brussels, Belgium (Jul. 17, 2018).

44. *Id.*

45. *Id.* at 47.

46. *Id.*

47. Shaw, *supra* note 39.

48. HENRY FARRELL & ABRAHAM L. NEWMAN, OF PRIVACY AND POWER: THE TRANSNATIONAL STRUGGLE OVER FREEDOM AND SECURITY 52 & 108 (2019).

49. ABRAHAM L. NEWMAN, PROTECTORS OF PRIVACY: REGULATING PERSONAL DATA IN THE GLOBAL ECONOMY 11 (2008).

50. *Id.*

51. LOBBYPLAG, https://lobbyplag.eu/lp (last visited May 20, 2019).

52. All 168 submissions to the European Commission can be found at EUROPEAN COMMISSION, *Consultation on the legal framework for the fundamental right to protection of personal data*, https://ec.europa.eu/home-affairs/what-is-new/public-consultation/2009/consulting_0003_en [https://perma.cc/A2GS-WNLW] (last visited Oct. 28, 2018) [hereinafter GDPR Public Consultation]; *compare* PRIVACY INTERNATIONAL, PRIVACY INTERNATIONAL'S RESPONSE TO THE EUROPEAN COMMISSION CONSULTATION 2–4 (2009), https://ec.europa.eu/home-affairs/sites/homeaffairs/files/what-is-new/public-consultation/2009/pdf/contributions/unregistered_organisations/privacy_international_en.pdf [https://perma.cc/NR85-KVJ8] *with* TECHAMERICA EUROPE, TECHAMERICA EUROPE'S RESPONSE TO EU COMMISSION CONSULTATION ON THE LEGAL FRAMEWORK FOR THE FUNDAMENTAL RIGHT TO PROTECTION OF PERSONAL DATA 3 (2009), https://ec.europa.eu/home-affairs/sites/homeaffairs/files/what-is-new/public-consultation/2009/pdf/contributions/registered_organisations/tech_america_europe_en.pdf [https://perma.cc/43PC-ZDKT].

53. *Compare* TechAmerica Europe, *Id.* at 3 *with* Privacy International, *Id.* at 3.

54. *See* GDPR Public Consultation, *supra* note 52.

55. *Id.*

56. European Parliament Legislative Resolution of 12 March 2014 on the Proposal for a Regulation of the European Parliament and of the Council on the Protection of Individuals with Regard to the Processing of Personal Data and on the Free Movement of such Data (General Data Protection Regulation) (COM(2012)0011 – C7-0025/2012 – 2012/0011(COD)) (Ordinary legislative procedure: first reading), EUR. PARL. DOC. (P7_TA(2014)0212) (2014).

57. Hannah Kuchler, *Max Schrems: the Man who Took on Facebook—and Won*, FIN. TIMES (Apr. 5, 2018), https://www.ft.com/content/86d1ce50-3799-11e8-8eee-e06bde01c544 (on file with author).

58. Commission Decision 2000/520/EC of 26 July 2000 pursuant to Directive 95/46/EC of the European Parliament and of the Council on the Adequacy of the Protection Provided by the Safe Harbour Privacy Principles and Related Frequently Asked Questions Issued by the U.S. Department of Commerce, 2000 O.J. (L 215) 7 [hereinafter Safe Harbor Decision].

59. Schrems v. Data Protection Commissioner, [2014] IEHC 310 (H.Ct.) (Ir.).

60. Case C-362/14, Maximillian Schrems v. Data Protection Commissioner, 2015 E.C.R. 650 [hereinafter Schrems I].

61. Commission Flash Eurobarometer 443 Report—ePrivacy (Dec. 2016), http://ec.europa.eu/commfrontoffice/publicopinion/index.cfm/Survey/getSurveyDetail/search/privacy/surveyKy/2124 [https://perma.cc/Y6CA-ZS5Z].

62. Henry Farrell & Abraham Newman, *The Transatlantic Data War*, FOREIGN AFF. (2015), https://www.foreignaffairs.com/articles/united-states/2015-12-14/transatlantic-data-war (on file with author).

63. *See* Shaffer, *supra* note 36, at 75; *cf.* Data Protection Directive, *supra* note 9, at arts. 17–20.

64. Ashley Rodriguez, *Google Says it Spent "Hundreds of Years of Human Time" Complying with Europe's Privacy Rules*, QUARTZ (Sept. 26, 2018), https://qz.com/1403080/google-spent-hundreds-of-years-of-human-time-complying-with-gdpr/ [https://perma.cc/SP4H-BKTK].

65. *See, e.g.,* Privacy Act of 1974, 5 U.S.C. § 552a(4) (2006); *see also* Shaffer, *supra* note 36, at 23-28.

66. *See* David Bach & Abraham L. Newman, *The European Regulatory State and Global Public Policy: Micro-Institutions, Macro-Influence*, 14 J. Eur. Pub. Pol'y 827, 833 (2007).

67. *Id.*

68. Samuel W. Royston, *The Right to be Forgotten: Comparing the US and European Approaches*, 48 St. Mary's L.J. 253 (2016).

69. 15 U.S.C. § 45 (a) (1) (2012).

70. Paul M Schwartz & Karl-Nikolaus Peifer, *Transatlantic Data Privacy Law*, 106 Geo. L. J. 115, 119 (2017).

71. Constance Chevallier-Govers, *Personal Data Protection: Confrontation Between the European Union and the United States*, *in* The European Union and the United States: Processes, Policies, and Projects 150 (Yann Echinard et al. eds., 2013) (quoting Alex Turk).

72. Jack Goldsmith, Emerging Threats, The Failure of Internet Freedom, Knight First Amendment Institute at Columbia (2018), https://knightcolumbia.org/sites/default/files/content/Emerging_Threats_Goldsmith.pdf [https://perma.cc/B6W4-JX3U].

73. *Id.*

74. Franz-Stefan Gady, *EU/U.S. Approaches to Data Privacy and the "Brussels Effect": A Comparative Analysis*, 4 Geo. J. Int'l Aff. 12–23 (2014).

75. Duncan Robinson, *EU Removes Carrot but Keeps Stick in Data Laws*, Fin. Times (Jan. 20, 2016), https://www.ft.com/content/9d774734-a4b1-11e5-a91e-162b86790c58 (on file with author).

76. There was a total of 252,070,00 users in the EU28 as of June 30, 2017; *see* Internet World Stats, http://www.internetworldstats.com/stats4.htm [https://perma.cc/H8SU-ZYXM].

77. Shona Ghosh, *Facebook in Europe is About to Get Massively Disrupted by New Laws Meant to Bring it to Heel*, Business Insider (Apr. 10, 2018), http://www.businessinsider.com/gdpr-privacy-law-eu-massive-timely-facebook-2018-4?utm_content=buffere825a&utm_medium=social&utm_source=facebook.com&utm_campaign=buffer-biuk [https://perma.cc/2GLA-TDUY.]

78. Robinson Meyer, *Europeans Use Google Way, Way More Than Americans Do*, Atlantic (Apr. 15, 2015), https://www.theatlantic.com/technology/archive/2015/04/europeans-use-google-way-way-more-than-americans-do/390612/ [https://perma.cc/9RV6-PUWJ].

79. Adam Satariano, *New Privacy rules could make this woman one of the tech's most important regulators*, N.Y. Times (May 16, 2018), https://www.nytimes.com/2018/05/16/technology/gdpr-helen-dixon.html (on file with author).

80. *Id.*

81. *See* discussion *supra* page 36.

82. *Legal Confusion on Internet Privacy: The Clash of Data Civilizations*, Economist, June 19, 2010, at 63.

83. *See* Bach & Newman, *supra* note 66, at 29; *see also* Dorothee Heisenberg, Negotiating Privacy: The European Union, the United States, and Personal Data Protection 119 (2005).

84. Daskal, *supra* note 29, at 23–34; Heisenberg, *Id.* at 119.

85. *See* Ryan Singel, *EU Tells Search Engines to Stop Creating Tracking Databases*, Wired (Apr. 8, 2008), http://www.wired.com/threatlevel/2008/04/eu-tells-search/ [https://perma.cc/5N5G-228K].

86. *See* Brandon Mitchener, *Standard Bearers: Increasingly, Rules of Global Economy are Set in Brussels*, Wall St. J., Apr. 23, 2002, at A1; Editorial, *Regulatory Imperialism*, Wall St. J. (Oct. 26, 2007), https://www.wsj.com/articles/SB119334720539572002 (on file with author).

87. *See, e.g., Legal Confusion on Internet Privacy*, *supra* note 82; Kevin J. O'Brien, *Anger in Europe over Google and Privacy*, N.Y. Times, May 17, 2010, at B5; David Scheer, *For Your*

Eyes Only—Europe's New High-Tech Role: Playing Privacy Cop to the World, WALL ST. J., Oct. 10, 2003, at A1; *see also* Mark Berniker, *EU: Microsoft Agrees to.NET Passport Changes*, DATAMATION (Jan. 30, 2003), https://www.datamation.com/entdev/article. php/1576901/EU-Microsoft-Agrees-to-NET-Passport-Changes.htm [https://perma.cc/ Z79U-3GZ2].

88. Daskal, *supra* note 29, at 232–34.

89. *See, e.g., Privacy Policy & Terms*, GOOGLE (Jan. 22, 2019), https://policies.google. com/privacy?hl=en&gl=ZZ [https://perma.cc/PHQ9-RBDJ]; *Privacy Statement*, NETFLIX (Apr. 24, 2019), https://help.netflix.com/legal/privacy [https://perma.cc/ TF7G-H774]; Mitchener, *supra* note 86.

90. *See Apple Customer Privacy Policy*, APPLE, https://www.apple.com/legal/privacy/ [https://perma.cc/TG8J-YD7N].

91. *Privacy Policy*, APPLE, https://www.apple.com/legal/privacy/en-ww/governance/ [https://perma.cc/42BC-X6MJ].

92. Alex Hern, *Apple Launches iOS 11.3 with Raft of Privacy Features*, GUARDIAN (Mar. 29, 2018), https://www.theguardian.com/technology/2018/mar/29/apple-launches-ios-113-privacy-features-gdpr-data-protection [https://perma.cc/5G9X-D9KX].

93. Natasha Lomas, *Facebook to Roll Out Global Privacy Settings Hub—Thanks to GDPR*, TECHCRUNCH (Jan. 24, 2018), http://social.techcrunch.com/2018/01/24/facebook-to-roll-out-global-privacy-settings-hub-thanks-to-gdpr/ [https://perma.cc/BK5K-A8AD]; Jim Brunsden, Tim Bradshaw & Hannah Kuchler, *Facebook's Sheryl Sandberg to Hold Talks with Top EU Data Official*, FIN. TIMES (Apr. 6, 2018), https://www.ft.com/ content/88a8682a-3996-11e8-8b98-2f31af407cc8 (on file with author).

94. Hard Questions Q&A with Mark Zuckerberg, FACEBOOK NEWSROOM (Apr. 4, 2018), https://newsroom.fb.com/news/2018/04/hard-questions-protecting-peoples-information/ [https://perma.cc/NEP5-9748].

95. *Updates to Terms*, AIRBNB, https://www.airbnb.com/home/terms-of-service-event?euid=76ed6f04-5530-5d81-7aaa-ce7e07e16be9 [https://perma.cc/X9BJ-WRYN].

96. *Privacy Policy*, UBER (May 25, 2018), https://privacy.uber.com/policy [https://perma. cc/43JZ-MP4N].

97. PRICEWATERHOUSECOOPERS, GDPR PREPAREDNESS PULSE SURVEY (2016), https://www.pwc.com/us/en/increasing-it-effectiveness/publications/assets/pwc-gdpr-series-pulse-survey.pdf [https://perma.cc/2BZB-FGWK].

98. *See* Preparing for a New Era in Privacy Regulation, MICROSOFT (Apr. 16, 2018), https://www.microsoft.com/en-us/microsoft-365/blog/2018/04/16/preparing-for-a-new-era-in-privacy-regulation-with-the-microsoft-cloud/ [https://perma.cc/7XMV-G3U6]; Brendon Lynch, *Get GDPR Compliant with the Microsoft Cloud*, MICROSOFT ON THE ISSUES (2017), https://blogs.microsoft.com/on-the-issues/2017/02/15/get-gdpr-compliant-with-the-microsoft-cloud/ [https://perma.cc/Y2Z5-F6WS]; Rich Sauer, *Earning Your Trust with Contractual Commitments to the General Data Protection Regulation*, MICROSOFT ON THE ISSUES (2017), https://blogs.microsoft.com/on-the-issues/2017/04/17/earning-trust-contractual-commitments-general-data-protection-regulation/ [https://perma.cc/UEQ8-SBCS].

99. Ugo Pagallo, *The Impact of Domestic Robots on Privacy and Data Protection, and the Troubles with Legal Regulation by Design*, DATA PROTECTION ON THE MOVE 403 (2016).

100. Opinion 2/2017 on Data Processing at Work WP 249, Article 29 Working Party (June 8, 2017), https://iapp.org/resources/article/wp29-opinion-on-data-processing-at-work/ [https://perma.cc/A5CT-MQ9X].

101. *Number of Employers Using Social Media to Screen Candidates at All-Time High, Finds Latest CareerBuilder Study*, CAREERBUILDER (June 15, 2017), http://press.careerbuilder.

com/2017-06-15-Number-of-Employers-Using-Social-Media-to-Screen-Candidates-at-All-Time-High-Finds-Latest-CareerBuilder-Study [https://perma.cc/7BRH-R4DB].

102. Daniel Michaels, *Hot U.S. Import: European Regulations*, WALL ST. J. (May 7, 2018), https://www.wsj.com/articles/techs-pickup-of-new-data-privacy-rules-reflects-eus-growing-influence-1525685400 (on file with author).

103. *The Internet: Vive La Liberté!*, ECONOMIST, Nov. 25, 2000, at 75.

104. Daskal, *supra* note 29, at 216.

105. Jeff Pelline, *Yahoo to Charge Auction Fees, Ban Hate Materials*, CNET (Mar. 29 2002), https://www.cnet.com/news/yahoo-to-charge-auction-fees-ban-hate-materials/ (on file with author).

106. Mark Scott, *E.U. Fines Facebook $122 Million Over Disclosures in WhatsApp Deal*, N.Y. TIMES (Jan. 20, 2018), https://www.nytimes.com/2017/05/18/technology/facebook-european-union-fine-whatsapp.html (on file with author).

107. Alex Hern & Martin Belam, *LA Times Among US-based News Sites Blocking EU Users due to GDPR*, GUARDIAN (May 25, 2018), https://www.theguardian.com/technology/2018/may/25/gdpr-us-based-news-websites-eu-internet-users-la-times [https://perma.cc/3WNB-53RS].

108. David Ingram, *Exclusive: Facebook to Put 1.5 Billion Users Out of Reach of New EU Privacy Law*, REUTERS (Apr. 18, 2018), https://www.reuters.com/article/us-facebook-privacy-eu-exclusive/exclusive-facebook-to-change-user-terms-limiting-effect-of-eu-privacy-law-idUSKBN1HQ00P [https://perma.cc/U6M8-7BVB].

109. *Are we Looking at the New Global Standard for Data Privacy?*, REUTERS (May. 7, 2018), https://blogs.thomsonreuters.com/answerson/new-global-standard-for-data-privacy/ [https://perma.cc/Q9D3-B7FV].

110. Matthew Newton & Julia Summers, *Russian Data Localization Laws: Enriching "Security" & the Economy*, HENRY M. JACKSON SCHOOL OF INTERNATIONAL STUDIES (2018), https://jsis.washington.edu/news/russian-data-localization-enriching-security-economy/ [https://perma.cc/82BY-5RAC]; Yuxi Wei, *Chinese Data Localization Law: Comprehensive but Ambiguous*, HENRY M. JACKSON SCHOOL OF INTERNATIONAL STUDIES (2018), https://jsis.washington.edu/news/chinese-data-localization-law-comprehensive-ambiguous/ [https://perma.cc/FWC9-MR7G].

111. *India's Misguided move Towards Data Localisation*, FIN. TIMES (Sept. 29 2018), https://www.ft.com/content/92bb34a8-b4e5-11e8-bbc3-ccd7de085ffe (on file with author).

112. Olga Razumovskaya & Laura Mills, *Russia to Block LinkedIn Over Data-Privacy Dispute*, WALL ST. J. (Nov. 11, 2016), https://www.wsj.com/articles/russia-may-block-linkedin-if-company-loses-court-case-on-personal-data-law-1478775414 (on file with author).

113. Paul Mozur & Vindu Goel, *To Reach China, LinkedIn Plays by Local Rules*, N.Y. TIMES (Oct. 5, 2014), https://www.nytimes.com/2014/10/06/technology/to-reach-china-linkedin-plays-by-local-rules.html (on file with author).

114. CAL. CIV. CODE § 1798.120(a) (West).

115. CAL. CIV. CODE § 1798.135(a)(1) (West).

116. CAL. CIV. CODE § 1798.135(b) (West).

117. Scott, *supra* note 30.

118. *Id.*

119. Court of Justice of the European Union, Advocate General's Opinion in Case C-507/17 Google v. CNIL (Jan. 10, 2019), http://curia.europa.eu/juris/document/document_print.jsf?docid=209688&text=&dir=&doclang=FR&part=1&occ=first&mode=req&pageIndex=0&cid=7572825 [https://perma.cc/RV9J-97TF].

120. *Id.*, at 46.

121. *Id.*, at 53.

122. *Id.*, at 59.

123. *Id.*, at 61.

124. Alphabet Inc., Annual Report (Form 10-K) (Feb. 5, 2018).

125. Alex Hern, *ECJ to Rule on Whether "Right to Be Forgotten" Can Stretch Beyond EU*, GUARDIAN (July 20, 2017), https://www.theguardian.com/technology/2017/jul/20/ecj-ruling-google-right-to-be-forgotten-beyond-eu-france-data-removed [https://perma.cc/5JNZ-W6DP].

126. *Id.*

127. Schwartz & Peifer, *supra* note 70, at 122.

128. GRAHAM GREENLEAF, ASIAN DATA PRIVACY LAWS: TRADE & HUMAN RIGHTS PERSPECTIVES 57 (2014).

129. Daniel Michaels, *Hot U.S. Import: European Regulations*, WALL ST. J. (May 7, 2018), https://www.wsj.com/articles/techs-pickup-of-new-data-privacy-rules-reflects-eus-growing-influence-1525685400 (on file with author).

130. Mark Scott & Laurens Cerulus, *Europe's New Data Protection rules Export Privacy Standards Worldwide*, POLITICO (Jan. 31, 2018), https://www.politico.eu/article/europe-data-protection-privacy-standards-gdpr-general-protection-data-regulation/ [https://perma.cc/WRW7-G6LN]; *see also* Angelica Mari, *Brazilian President Signs Data Protection Bill*, ZDNET (Aug. 16, 2018), https://www.zdnet.com/article/brazilian-president-signs-data-protection-bill/ [https://perma.cc/BB2D-JREC]; Asina Pornwasin, *Thai Data Protection Laws Must Quickly be Updated to EU Standards: Experts*, THE NATION (May 25, 2018), http://www.nationmultimedia.com/detail/national/30346209 [https://perma.cc/T729-LKBV].

131. Graham Greenleaf, *The Influence of European Data Privacy Standards Outside Europe: Implications for Globalization of Convention 108*, 2 INT'L DATA PRIVACY L. 68, 75 (2012); *see, e.g.*, María Paz Canales, *Protección de datos en América Latina, urgente y necesaria* [*Data Protection in Latin America, Urgent and Necessary*], DERECHODIGITALES (July 7, 2017), https://www.derechosdigitales.org/11282/proteccion-de-datos-en-america-latina-urgente-y-necesaria/ [https://perma.cc/5EBL-L7B4] (translation supplied).

132. Tim Cook Calls for US Federal Privacy Law to Tackle "Weaponized" Personal Data, GUARDIAN (Oct. 24, 2018), https://www.theguardian.com/technology/2018/oct/24/tim-cook-us-federal-privacy-law-weaponized-personal-data [https://perma.cc/TG55-FTMB].

133. Mehreen Khan & Tim Bradshaw, *Apple and Facebook Call for EU-style Privacy Laws in US*, FIN. TIMES (Oct. 24, 2018), https://www.ft.com/content/0ca8466c-d768-11e8-ab8e-6be0dcf18713 (on file with author).

134. Mark Zuckerberg, *The Internet needs new rules. Let's start in these four areas*, WASH. POST (Mar. 30, 2019), https://www.washingtonpost.com/opinions/mark-zuckerberg-the-internet-needs-new-rules-lets-start-in-these-four-areas/2019/03/29/9e6f0504-521a-11e9-a3f7-78b7525a8d5f_story.html?fbclid=IwAR2dyE8yvRAI2SIUUsAJEj6nwcZatkpOWaSok_cxHWsRkrpJI_qUZDpiDLw&utm_term=.bdb2c94b7c87 (on file with author).

135. Meghashyam Mali, *Tech Mobilizes Against California Privacy Law*, THEHILL (July 1, 2018), https://thehill.com/policy/technology/394928-tech-mobilizes-against-california-privacy-law [https://perma.cc/GWU6-ZGQB]; *see also* Daisuke Wakabayashi, *Silicon Valley Faces Regulatory Fight on Its Home Turf*, N.Y. TIMES (July 30, 2018), https://www.nytimes.com/2018/05/13/business/california-data-privacy-ballot-measure.html (on file with author).

136. *See* GDPR, *supra* note 1, at art. 45; *see also Communication from the Commission to the European Parliament and the Council Exchanging and Protecting Personal Data in a Globalised World* (COM) (2017) 7 final (Jan. 10, 2017).

137. Manuel Martínez-Herrera, *From Habeas Data Action to Omnibus Data Protection: The Latin American Privacy (R)Evolution*, WHITE & CASE LLP (Sept. 30, 2011), https://www.whitecase.com/publications/article/habeas-data-action-omnibus-data-protection-latin-american-privacy-revolution [https://perma.cc/N9J8-4PZQ].

138. EUROPEAN COMMISSION, Adequacy of the Protection of Personal Data in non-EU Countries (last visited May 19, 2019), https://ec.europa.eu/info/law/law-topic/data-protection/data-transfers-outside-eu/adequacy-protection-personal-data-non-eu-countries_en [https://perma.cc/BLS2-DVTK].

139. Schrems I, *supra* note 60.

140. Christina Lam, *Unsafe Harbor: The European Union's Demand for Heightened Data Privacy Standards in Schrems v. Irish Data Protection Commissioner*, 40 BOS. COL. INT'L COMP. L.R. 1, 8 (2017).

141. *Id.*

142. *See* GDPR, *supra* note 1, at art. 47.

143. *See, e.g., IBM Controller Binding Corporate Rules*, IBM (2018), https://www.ibm.com/privacy/details/us/en/bcr.html [https://perma.cc/8SMW-3KGF]; *Twilio Receives Approval for Binding Corporate Rules, Commits to Highest Standard of Data Protection*, TWILIO (June 8, 2018), https://investors.twilio.com/all-news/press-release-details/2018/Twilio-Receives-Approval-for-Binding-Corporate-Rules-Commits-to-Highest-Standard-of-Data-Protection/default.aspx[https://perma.cc/4T84-684X].

144. Stephen Gardner, *EU, South Korea Look to Data Transfer Privacy Deal in 2018*, BLOOMBERG (Nov. 20, 2017), https://www.bna.com/eu-south-korea-n73014472278/ [https://perma.cc/5SAW-659A].

145. Data Protection Commissioner v. Facebook Ireland Limited & anor [2017] IEHC 545 (H. Ct.) (Ir.)

146. Case C-311/18: Reference for a Preliminary Ruling from the High Court (Ireland) made on 9 May 2018—Data Protection Commissioner v. Facebook Ireland Limited, Maximillian Schrems, 2018 O.J. (C 249) 15 [hereinafter Schrems II].

147. PROTECCIÓN DE LOS ATOS PERSONALES [PERSONAL DATA PROTECTION ACT], Ley 25,326, Nov. 2, 2000, BOLETÍN OFICIAL [B.O.] 1 (Arg.), http://www.uba.ar/archivos_secyt/image/Ley%2025326.pdf [https://perma.cc/L5A4-EMCS].

148. CIVIL RIGHTS ASSOCIATION, *The Future of Personal Data Protection in Argentina: Reflections of a Working Group* at 3, 6–8 (June 2016), https://adcdigital.org.ar/wp-content/uploads/2016/07/Reflexiones-futuro-datos-personales-ADC.pdf [https://perma.cc/SAW3-UQWZ] (translation supplied).

149. *See* Ley No. 18.331, Aug.11, 2008; *see also* Regulation No. 414/009, Aug. 31, 2009 (the accompanying regulations to the actual data protection law).

150. Commission Implementing Decision of 21 August 2012 Pursuant to Directive 95/46/EC of the European Parliament and of the Council on the Adequate Protection of Personal data by the Eastern Republic of Uruguay with Regard to Automated Processing of Personal Data, 2012 O.J. (L227) 11.

151. Julio César Fernández, *Ley de Protección de Datos Personales* ("Law for Personal Data Protection") 7 (2009), https://www.ort.edu.uy/fi/pdf/florenciasarasolalicsistemasort.pdf [https://perma.cc/GP5X-RX4W] (translation supplied); *see also* Martínez-Herrera, *supra* note 137.

152. Martínez-Herrera, *supra* note 137.

153. European Commission Press Release IP/18/4501, The European Union and Japan agreed to create the world's largest area of safe data flows (July 17, 2018); *see also* Gardner, *supra* note 144.

154. Brian Yap, *Multinationals Struggle to Adapt to Japan's New Privacy Law*, BLOOMBERG BNA (Aug. 31, 2017), https://www.bna.com/multinationals-struggle-adapt-n73014464003/ [https://perma.cc/MGP5-2YUL].

155. Andrew A. Adams, Kiyoshi Murata & Yohko Orito, *The Japanese Sense of Information Privacy*, 24 AI & SOC. 327 (2009).

156. *See* Gardner, *supra* note 144.

157. European Commission Press Release IP/17/4739, Press Statement by Commissioner Věra Jourová, Mr. Lee Hyo-seong, Chairman of the Korea Communications Commission and Mr. Jeong Hyun-cheol, Vice President of the Korea Internet & Security Agency (Nov. 20, 2017); Alexandros Koronakis, *Europe's Privacy Culture*, NEW EUROPE (Apr. 16, 2018), https://www.neweurope.eu/article/europes-privacy-culture/ [https://perma.cc/7XDJ-UPAP].

158. Personal Information Protection Act, Act No. 11990, Sept. 30 2011, (S. Kor.), translated by Korean Legal Information Institute, http://www.law.go.kr/lsInfoP.do?lsiSeq=14256 3&chrClsCd=010203&urlMode=engLsInfoR&viewCls=engLsInfoR [https://perma.cc/R3V4-2BQN].

159. Scott Warren, *Security and Privacy: A View from Asia and the Middle East*, SQUIRE PATTON BOGGS (Jan. 24, 2018), https://www.securityprivacybytes.com/2018/01/security-and-privacy-a-view-from-asia-and-the-middle-east/ [https://perma.cc/FV2J-KJ2H].

160. *See* Gardner, *supra* note 144.

161. *Id.*

162. Penny Pritzker & Andrus Ansip, *Making a Difference to the World's Digital Economy*, U.S. DEP'T OF COM. (Mar. 11, 2016), https://www.commerce.gov/news/blog/2016/03/making-difference-worlds-%20digital-economy-transatlantic-partnership [https://perma.cc/QS9J-M3P3].

163. Duncan Robinson, *EU and US Reach Deal on Data Sharing*, FIN. TIMES (Feb. 2, 2016), https://www.ft.com/content/7a9954d2-c9c8-11e5-be0b-b7ece4e953a0 (on file with author).

164. Commission Decision 2000/520/EC of 26 July 2000 Pursuant to Directive 95/46/EC of the European Parliament and of the Council on the Adequacy of the Protection Provided by the Safe Harbour Privacy Principles and Related Frequently Asked Questions Issued by the U.S. Department of Commerce, 2000 O.J. (L 215) 7 [hereinafter Safe Harbor Decision].

165. *U.S.-EU Safe Harbor List*, U.S. DEP'T. OF COM., https://www.export.gov/safeharbor_eu [https://perma.cc/2RR3-SZ9U].

166. MARTIN A. WEISS & KRISTIN ARCHICK, U.S.-EU DATA PRIVACY: FROM SAFE HARBOR TO PRIVACY SHIELD, CONGRESSIONAL RESEARCH SERVICES (2016), https://fas.org/sgp/crs/misc/R44257.pdf [https://perma.cc/A4UJ-VG22].

167. *See* Schrems I, *supra* note 60.

168. Schwartz & Peifer, *supra* note 70, at 160 (citing Schrems I, *supra* note 60, at ¶73).

169. Natasha Lomas, *Europe's Top Court Strikes Down 'Safe Harbor' Data Transfer Agreement with U.S.*, TECHCRUNCH (Oct. 6, 2015), https://techcrunch.com/2015/10/06/europes-top-court-strikes-down-safe-harbor-data-transfer-agreement-with-u-s/ [https://perma.cc/KH2D-HM5Z].

170. Commission Implementing Decision (EU) 2016/1250 of 12 July 2016 Pursuant to Directive 95/46/EC of the European Parliament and of the Council on the Adequacy of the Protection Provided by the EU-U.S. Privacy Shield (notified under document C(2016) 4176), 2016 O.J. (L 207) 1.

171. See *Privacy Shield Framework List of Companies*, U.S. DEPT. OF COM. (last visited May 19, 2019), https://www.privacyshield.gov/list [https://perma.cc/4SAP-2Z3A].

172. *See* European Commission Press Release IP/16/2461, European Commission Launches EU-U.S. Privacy Shield: Stronger Protection for Transatlantic Data Flows (July 12, 2016).

173. Judicial Redress Act of 2015 § 2, PL 114-126, 130 Stat 282 (2016).

174. Mark Scott, *Europe's Privacy Watchdogs Call for Changes to U.S. Data-Transfer Deal*, N.Y. TIMES (Dec. 21, 2017), https://www.nytimes.com/2016/04/14/technology/europe-us-data-privacy.html (on file with author).

175. Case T-670/16, Digital Rights Ireland Ltd. v. Commission, ECLI:EU:T:2017:838.

176. Case T-738/16, La Quadrature du Net and Others v. Commission, ECLI:EU:T:2018:520.

177. European Data Protection Board, EU—U.S. Privacy Shield—Second Annual Joint Review (Jan. 22, 2019), https://edpb.europa.eu/sites/edpb/files/files/file1/20190122e dpb_2ndprivacyshieldreviewreport_final_en.pdf? [https://perma.cc/7NJX-Z7AA]; Barney Thompson & Mehreen Khan, *Brussels Losing Patience with US Over Data-Sharing Agreement*, FIN. TIMES, Sept. 18, 2017, https://www.ft.com/content/ed13ad0a-9bb8-11e7-8cd4-932067fbf946 (last visited Oct. 29, 2018) (on file with author).

178. Natasha Lomas, *Pressure Mounts on EU-US Privacy Shield After Facebook-Cambridge Analytica Data Scandal*, TECHCRUNCH (June 12, 2018), http://social.techcrunch.com/2018/06/12/pressure-mounts-on-eu-us-privacy-shield-after-facebook-cambridge-analytica-data-scandal/ [https://perma.cc/3MQ9-L3S8].

179. Natasha Lomas, *EU Parliament Calls for Privacy Shield to be Pulled until US Complies*, TECHCRUNCH (July 5 2018), http://social.techcrunch.com/2018/07/05/eu-par-liament-calls-for-privacy-shield-to-be-pulled-until-us-complies/ [https://perma.cc/C5D8-2Y7S]; *see also* European Parliament Resolution on the Adequacy of the Protection Afforded by the EU-US Privacy Shield, EUR. PARL. DOC. B8-0305 2645(RSP) (2018), http://www.europarl.europa.eu/sides/getDoc.do?type=MOTION&reference=B8-2018-0305&language=EN [https://perma.cc/RKR9-V6FB].

180. European Data Protection Board, *supra* note 177; Amanda Lee, US to Appoint Permanent Privacy Shield Ombudsmen, as EU Pressure Tells, EURACTIV.COM (Jan. 23, 2019), https://www.euractiv.com/section/data-protection/news/us-to-appoint-permanent-privacy-shield-ombudsperson-following-eu-pressure/ [https://perma.cc/4UF8-UBVN].

181. European Data Protection Board, *supra* note 177, at 6.

182. Era Gunning & Ridwaan Boda, *"Is Your Organisation Ready for POPI and the GDPR?"* ENSAFRICA, MONDAQ (Feb. 6, 2018), http://www.mondaq.com/southafrica/x/670728/Data+Protection+Privacy/Is+Your+Organisation+Ready+For+POPI+And+The+GDPR [https://perma.cc/265L-4SZU].

183. *Id.* at 29; *see also* Adrian Naude, Data Protection in South Africa: The Impact of the Protection of Personal Information Act and Recent International Developments (Dec. 2014) (unpublished LL.M thesis, University of Pretoria), https://repository.up.ac.za/handle/2263/46094 [https://perma.cc/4WHE-V55M].

184. Loi n° 2008-12 sur la Protection des données à caractère personnel [Law No. 2008-12 on the Protection of Personal Data] (Sen.).

185. Ann Brian Nougréres, *Data Protection and Enforcement in Latin America and in Uruguay, in* David Wright & Paul De Hert, ENFORCING PRIVACY: REGULATORY, LEGAL AND TECHNOLOGICAL APPROACHES, 145–80, 176 (2016), at 153; Maria de Lourdes Zamudio Salinas, *El marco normative latinoamericano y la ley de protección de datos personales del Perú* [The Latin American Regulatory Framework and the Personal Data Protection Law of Peru] 9, Revista Internacional de Protección de Datos Personales (2010), at 10.

186. Zamudio Salinas, *supra* note 185.

187. Lei No. 13.709, de 14 de Agosto de 2018, Diário Oficial da União [D.O.U.] de 15.8.2018 (Braz.); *see also* Paul M. Schwartz, *Global data privacy: The EU Way*, 94 N.Y.U. L. Rev. 1, 29 (2019).

188. *See, e.g.,* Nougréres, *supra* note 185, at 145; Greenleaf, *supra* note 128, at 75; Zamudio Salinas, *supra* note 185, at 10.

189. *See* Red Iberoamericana de proteccion de datos [Ibero-American Data Protection Network], Miembros [Members], http://www.redipd.es/la_red/Miembros/index-ides-idphp.php [https://perma.cc/F86L-LLMQ].

190. *Id.*

191. Red Iberoamericana de proteccion de datos [Ibero-American Data Protection Network], *Standards for Personal Data Protection for the Ibero-American States* (June 20, 2017), http://www.redipd.es/documentacion/common/Estandares_eng_Con_logo_RIPD.pdf [https://perma.cc/8HBH-5N6J]; *see also New Ibero-American Standards to Provide Consistency in the Protection of Personal Data*, Jones Day (Oct. 2017), http://www.jonesday.com/new-ibero-american-standards-to-provide-consistency-in-the-protection-of-personal-data-10-03-2017 (on file with author); *see also,* Nougréres, *supra* note 185, at 145.

192. Magnus Franklin, *Latin American Endorsement of EU Privacy Model Bolsters Brussels' Leadership Claim,* MLex Market Insight (Aug. 14, 2017), https://mlexmarketinsight.com/insights-center/editors-picks/Data-Protection-Privacy-and-Security/cross-jurisdiction/latin-american-endorsement-of-eu-privacy-model-bolsters-brussels-leadership-claim [https://perma.cc/SX2G-UFYR].

193. Programa de Acción de la Red Iberoamericana de Protecctón de Datos Periodo 2015–2017 [*2015–2017 Action Program of the Iberoamerican Network for Data Protection*] 2 (2015), http://www.redipd.es/documentacion/common/PROGRAMA_DE_ACCION_DE_LA_RIPD_2015-17.pdf#aqui [https://perma.cc/7QA8-HQDB].

194. (中华人民共和国网络安全法)[Cyber Security Law] (promulgated by the Standing Comm. Nat'l People's Cong., Nov. 7, 2016, effective June 1, 2017); 2016 Standing Comm. Nat'l People's Cong. Gaz. (China). For a US translation, *see* Creemers et al., *Translation: Cybersecurity Law of the People's Republic of China (Effective June 1, 2017)*, New America (June 29, 2018), https://www.newamerica.org/cybersecurity-initiative/digichina/blog/translation-cybersecurity-law-peoples-republic-china/ [https://perma.cc/L38D-2TKN]; *see also* Jack Wagner, *China's Cybersecurity Law: What You Need to Know,* The Diplomat (June 1, 2017), https://thediplomat.com/2017/06/chinas-cybersecurity-law-what-you-need-to-know/ [https://perma.cc/6SSN-SMX7].

195. *See* Scott Thiel & Arthur Cheuk, *China's Evolving Personal Data Privacy Landscape,* DLA Piper (Feb. 8, 2013), https://www.dlapiper.com/en/us/insights/publications/2013/02/chinas-evolving-personal-data-privacy-landscape/ [https://perma.cc/TN2L-DXMX]. The Reference List on p. 5 expressly sets out the EU Privacy and Electronic Communications Directive (2002/58/EC).

196. *Compare Data Protection Laws of the World—China,* DLA Piper, https://www.dlapiperdataprotection.com/system/modules/za.co.heliosdesign.dla.lotw.data_protection/functions/handbook.pdf?country-1=CN [https://perma.cc/65KC-7525] *with* GDPR, *supra* note 1, at art. 5(1)(b), 6(1)(b).

197. 张新宝 [Zhang Xinbao], 中国个人数据保护立法的现状与展 [The Status Quo and Prospect of China's Personal Data Protection Legislation], 香港中英文版《中国法律》杂志2007年第3期 [3 China Law (2007)], http://article.chinalawinfo.com:81/article_print.asp?articleid=37590 (on file with author) (translation supplied).

198. *Id.*

199. *See* 张新宝[Zhang Xinbao], 采取国家立法主导模式保护网络个人资料[*Adopting Nation Legislation Oriented Model for Internet Individual Data Protection]*, 检察日报

[People's Procuratorial Daily] (Oct. 27, 2003), http://www.china.com.cn/chinese/OP-c/429899.htm [https://perma.cc/NM7Y-PE37].

200. COUNTRY REPORT—CHINA, FREEDOM ON THE NET 2018 (2019), https://freedomhouse.org/report/freedom-net/2018/china [https://perma.cc/9977-5RZS].

201. https://www.technologyreview.com/s/612601/how-google-took-on-china-and-lost/ [https://perma.cc/RLT5-9LMW].

202. Paul Mozur, *Inside China's Dystopian Dreams: A.I., Shame and Lots of Cameras*, N.Y. Times (Oct. 15, 2018), https://www.nytimes.com/2018/07/08/business/china-surveillance-technology.html (on file with author).

203. Lily Kuo, *China Bans 23m From Buying Travel Tickets as part of "Social Credit" System*, Guardian (Mar. 1, 2019), https://www.theguardian.com/world/2019/mar/01/china-bans-23m-discredited-citizens-from-buying-travel-tickets-social-credit-system [https://perma.cc/5PB5-J6UD].

204. Policy in Action through the Information Security Management System, Wipro Sustainability Report 2016–17 (2017), http://wiprosustainabilityreport.com/16-17/policy_in_action_through_the_information_security_management_system [https://perma.cc/CNA3-ENFD].

205. Annual Report for 2015–16, Infosys (2016), https://www.infosys.com/investors/reports-filings/annual-report/annual/Documents/infosys-AR-16.pdf [https://perma.cc/XYQ8-WTDY].

206. Christopher Nilesh, *The India draft bill on data protection draws inspiration from GDPR, but has its limits*, Economic Times (July 28, 2018), https://economictimes.indiatimes.com/tech/internet/the-india-draft-bill-on-data-protection-draws-inspiration-from-gdpr-but-has-its-limits/articleshow/65173684.cms [https://perma.cc/M88H-NFJJ] (India).

207. Mozilla Foundation, Mozilla's Comments on the White Paper of the Committee of Experts on Data Protection Framework for India 13 (Jan. 31, 2018), https://blog.mozilla.org/netpolicy/files/2018/02/Mozilla-submission-to-Srikrishna-Committee.pdf [https://perma.cc/J2LN-ZVB3].

208. Daskal, *supra* note 29, at 233.

209. *See* White House, Consumer Data Privacy in a Networked World: A Framework for Protecting Privacy and Promoting Innovation in the Global Digital Economy 1-26 (2012), https://obamawhitehouse.archives.gov/sites/default/files/privacy-final.pdf [https://perma.cc/R47Z-LDMX].

210. *See, e.g.*, Daisuke Wakabayashi, *California Passes Sweeping Law to Protect Online Privacy*, N.Y. Times (July 30, 2018), https://www.nytimes.com/2018/06/28/technology/california-online-privacy-law.html (on file with author).

211. Issie Lapowsky, *California Unanimously Passes Historic Privacy Bill*, Wired (June 28, 2018), https://www.wired.com/story/california-unanimously-passes-historic-privacy-bill/ [https://perma.cc/AW6H-VWTW].

212. *Compare* Cal. Civ. Code § 1798.110(a) (West) *with* GDPR, *supra* note 1, at art. 5(1)(b), 12.

213. *Compare* Cal. Civ. Code § 1798.100(a) (West) *with* GDPR, *supra* note 1, at art. 15.

214. *Compare* Cal. Civ. Code § 1798.105(a) (West) *with* GDPR, *supra* note 1, at art. 17.

215. Cecilia Kang, *F.T.C Approves Facebook Fine of About $5 Billion*, N.Y. Times (July 12, 2019), https://www.nytimes.com/2019/07/12/technology/facebook-ftc-fine.html (on file with author)

216. Conor Dougherty, *Push for Internet Privacy Rules Moves to Statehouses*, N.Y. Times (Dec. 22, 2017), https://www.nytimes.com/2017/03/26/technology/internet-privacy-state-legislation-illinois.html (on file with author).

217. Council Framework Decision 2008/913/JHA, *Combating Certain Forms and Expressions of Racism and Xenophobia by Means of Criminal Law,* art. 1 2008 O.J. (L 328) 55, 56 [hereinafter Council Framework Decision].

218. *Brandenburg v. Ohio,* 395 U.S. 444, 447 (1969); *see also Chaplinsky v. New Hampshire,* 315 U.S. 568, 572 (1942).

219. Eugene Volokh, *No, There's No "Hate Speech" Exception to the First Amendment,* WASHINGTON POST (May 7, 2015), https://www.washingtonpost.com/news/volokh-conspiracy/wp/2015/05/07/no-theres-no-hate-speech-exception-to-the-first-amendment/?utm_term=.e96978325c4d (on file with author).

220. *Id.*

221. *See, e.g.,* Snyder v. Phelps, 562 U.S. 443, 458 (2011).

222. Ira Steven Nathenson, *Super-Intermediaries, Code, Human Rights,* St. Thomas University School of Law Legal Studies Research Paper No. 2014-09, 96–97; Senate Comm. on Foreign Relations, Report on the International Covenant on Civil and Political Rights, S. Exec. Rep. No. 23, 4-7 (102d Cong., 2d Sess. 1992), reprinted in 31 I.L.M. 645 (1992).

223. Case C-247/99, P Bernard Connolly v. Comm'n, 2001 E.C.R. I-1611

224. Case C-54/07, Centrum voor gelijkheid van kansen en voor racismebestrijding v. Firma Feryn NV, 2008 E.C.R. I-05187.

225. TFEU, *supra* note 5.

226. Advocate General's Opinion in Case Case C-54/07, Centrum voor Gelijkheid van Kansen en voor Racismebestrijding v. Firma Feryn NV (Mar. 12, 2018), http://curia.europa.eu/juris/document/document.jsf?text=&docid=70156&pageIndex=0&doclang=EN&mode=lst&dir=&occ=first&part=1&cid=96546 [https://perma.cc/DVQ7-UPPV]; *see also* Uladzislau Belavusau, Fighting Hate Speech through EU Law, 4 AMSTERDAM L. FORUM 20, 30 (2012).

227. *Erbakan v Turkey,* No. 59405/00, 56 (Eur. Ct. H.R. July 6, 2006).

228. *Id.*

229. EUROPEAN COURT OF HUMAN RIGHTS, FACT SHEET ON HATE SPEECH, 1 (Mar. 2019), https://www.echr.coe.int/Documents/FS_Hate_speech_ENG.pdf [https://perma.cc/FHY6-HDWV].

230. Council Framework Decision, *supra* note 217.

231. Directive 2010/13/EU of the European Parliament and of the Council of 10 March 2010 on the coordination of certain provisions laid down by law, regulation or administrative action in Member States concerning the provision of audiovisual media services (Audiovisual Media Services Directive), 2010 O.J. (L 95) 1.

232. Art. 137(c) & Art. 137(d), para. 1, SR.(Neth.).

233. *See, e.g.,* Sheena McKenzie, *Geert Wilders guilty of 'insulting a group' after hate speech trial,* CNN (Dec. 9, 2016), https://www.cnn.com/2016/12/09/europe/geert-wilders-hate-speech-trial-verdict/index.html [https://perma.cc/QXQ3-KUQA].

234. *See, e.g.,* European Commission, Code of Conduct on countering illegal hate speech online: First results on implementation (Dec. 2016), https://ec.europa.eu/information_society/newsroom/image/document/2016-50/factsheet-code-conduct-8_40573.pdf [https://perma.cc/CM67-8Z2H].

235. Jeffrey Eisenach, *Don't Make the Internet a Public Utility,* N.Y. TIMES (Oct. 28, 2016), https://www.nytimes.com/roomfordebate/2015/02/04/regulate-internet-providers/dont-make-the-internet-a-public-utility (on file with author).

236. The Code, *supra* note 2; *see also How the Code of Conduct helped countering illegal hate speech online,* EUROPEAN COMMISSION (Feb. 2019), https://ec.europa.eu/info/sites/info/files/hatespeech_infographic3_web.pdf [https://perma.cc/M2AW-CYFL].

237. European Commission Press Release IP/18/1169, A Europe that protects: Commission reinforces EU response to illegal content online (Mar. 1, 2018).

238. European Commission Press Release IP/17/3493, Security Union: Commission steps up efforts to tackle illegal content online (Sept. 28, 2017).

239. Daniel Boffey, *EU Threatens to Crack Down on Facebook over Hate Speech*, GUARDIAN (Apr. 11, 2018), https://www.theguardian.com/technology/2018/apr/11/eu-heavy-sanctions-online-hate-speech-facebook-scandal [https://perma.cc/K86F-AKRM].

240. Danielle Keats Citron, *Extremist Speech, Compelled Conformity, and Censorship Creep*, 93 NOTRE DAME L.R. 1035, 1070 (2018).

241. *Gesetz zur Verbesserung der Rechtsdurchsetzung in sozialen Netzwerken* [Netzwerkdurchsetzungsgesetz—NetzDG] [Network Enforcement Act], Sept. 1, 2017, ELEKTRONISCHER BUNDESANZEIGER [eBAnz] at 3352ff 2017 I (Ger.); *see also* Philip Oltermann, *Tough new German law puts free speech and tech in spotlight*, GUARDIAN (Jan. 5, 2018), https://www.theguardian.com/world/2018/jan/05/tough-new-german-law-puts-tech-firms-and-free-speech-in-spotlight [https://perma.cc/47LA-RXC5].

242. *France to Get Tougher on Social Media Hate Speech—PM,* REUTERS (Mar. 19, 2018), https://www.reuters.com/article/france-racism-socialmedia/france-to-get-tougher-on-social-media-hate-speech-pm-idUSL8N1R14G0 [https://perma.cc/HKS7-QQ26]; *see also* Jajer M'tiri, *France Reveals New Plan to Counter Online Hate Speech,* AA (Mar. 19, 2018), https://www.aa.com.tr/en/europe/france-reveals-new-plan-to-counter-online-hate-speech/1093371 [https://perma.cc/YWV6-3BYV].

243. Ginger Hervey, *Theresa May to Call for increased policing of online hate speech*, POLITICO (Feb. 6, 2018), https://www.politico.eu/article/theresa-may-to-call-for-increased-policing-of-online-hate-speech/ [https://perma.cc/LQ7U-QGZN].

244. Noah Feldman, *Free Speech In Europe Isn't What Americans Think*, BLOOMBERG (Mar. 19, 2017), https://www.bloomberg.com/view/articles/2017-03-19/free-speech-in-europe-isn-t-what-americans-think (on file with author); *see also* Jeffrey Rosen, *The Delete Squad, Google, Twitter, Facebook and the new global battle over the future of free speech*, NEW REPUBLIC (Apr. 29, 2013), https://newrepublic.com/article/113045/free-speech-internet-ssilicon-valley-%EF%BF%BCmaking-rules [https://perma.cc/G925-7396].

245. European Commission against Racism and Intolerance General Policy Recommendation No. 15 on Combating Hate Speech, ECRI (2016), 3 (Dec. 8, 2015), https://rm.coe.int/ecri-general-policy-recommendation-no-15-on-combating-hate-speech/16808b5b01 [https://perma.cc/CB9N-ZJMH].

246. *See* Ericha Panzen, *Xenophobic and Racist Hate Crimes Surge in European Union*, HUMAN RIGHTS BRIEF (Feb. 28, 2017), http://hrbrief.org/2017/02/xenophobic-racist-hate-crimes-surge-european-union/ [https://perma.cc/2CTV-Y387].

247. *Supra* note 245.

248. COUNCIL OF EUROPE, NO HATE SPEECH YOUTH CAMPAIGN (last visited Oct. 17, 2018), https://www.coe.int/en/web/no-hate-campaign [https://perma.cc/BN3H-F642].

249. MELANIE STRAY, GALOP UK ONLINE HATE CRIME REPORT 2017 (2017), http://www.galop.org.uk/wp-content/uploads/2017/08/Online-hate-report.pdf [https://perma.cc/BH2E-9G9J].

250. *See* EUROPEAN FEDERATION OF JOURNALISTS, ABOUT, MEDIA AGAINST HATE (last visited Oct. 17, 2018), http://europeanjournalists.org/mediaagainsthate/about/ [https://perma.cc/QF8D-8QUL].

251. *See* EUROPEAN COMMISSION, MEDIA PLURALISM AND DEMOCRACY: SEPCIAL EUROBAROMETER 452 REPORT (Nov. 2016), http://ec.europa.eu/commfrontoffice/publicopinion/index.cfm/ResultDoc/download/DocumentKy/75538 [https://perma.cc/RA7E-D8DB].

252. *Id.* at 45–48.

253. Mark Scott, *What U.S. Tech Giants Face in Europe in 2017*, N.Y. TIMES (Jan. 1, 2017), https://www.nytimes.com/2017/01/01/technology/tech-giants-europe-2017.html [https://perma.cc/7CV7-RDQB].

254. There was a total of 253,480,00 users in the EU28 as of Dec 31, 2017; *see* INTERNET WORLD STATS, Internet Usage in the European Union—March 2019 (Mar. 2019),

255. Shona Ghosh, *Facebook in Europe is About to get massively disrupted by new laws meant to bring it to heel*, BUSINESS INSIDER (Apr. 10, 2018), http://www.businessinsider.com/gdpr-privacy-law-eu-massive-timely-facebook-2018-4?utm_content=buffere825a&utm_medium=social&utm_source=facebook.com&utm_campaign=buffer-biuk [https://perma.cc/86GR-QXC2].

256. Facebook Inc. (FB) Third Quarter 2017 Results Conference Call (Nov. 1, 2017), https://s21.q4cdn.com/399680738/files/doc_financials/2017/Q3/Q3-'17-Earnings-call-transcript.pdf [https://perma.cc/9F77-CYQR] ("One of our strongest areas this quarter was SMBs in Europe, with revenue growing more than 60% year-over-year."); *see also* Press Release, Facebook Inc. (FB) Fourth Quarter and Full Year 2017 Results Conference Call (Jan. 31, 2018), https://investor.fb.com/investor-news/press-release-details/2018/facebook-reports-fourth-quarter-and-full-year-2017-results/default.aspx [https://perma.cc/GBX7-Y7TM].

257. There was a total of 141.2 million users in the United Kingdom, Germany, France, Poland, and Spain as of May 2016; *see* STATISTA, COUNTRIES WITH THE MOST YOUTUBE USERS AS OF MAY 2016 (2016), https://www.statista.com/statistics/280685/num-ber-of-monthly-unique-youtube-users/ [https://perma.cc/L4QC-Y8BK]. There are approximately 1 billion YouTube users worldwide; *see* SOCIAL BAKERS, ALL YOUTUBE STATISTICS IN ONE PLACE (last visited May 24, 2019), https://www.socialbakers.com/statistics/youtube/ [https://perma.cc/B86Y-WKUK].

258. Robinson Meyer, *Europeans Use Google Way, Way More Than Americans Do*, ATLANTIC (Apr. 15, 2015), https://www.theatlantic.com/technology/archive/2015/04/europeans-use-google-way-way-more-than-americans-do/390612/ [https://perma.cc/5J5C-7CVA].

259. Alphabet Q4 2017 Earnings Call (Feb. 1, 2018), https://abc.xyz/investor/pdf/2017_Q4_Earnings_Transcript.pdf [https://perma.cc/T532-EYHE].

260. *Id.*

261. Snap Inc., Quarterly Report (Form 10-Q, Aug. 11, 2017) ("We averaged 173 million DAUs across the quarter, as compared to 143 million in the second quarter of 2016, an increase of 21%. The majority of that growth continues to be driven by core markets like North America and Europe.").

262. *The EU code of conduct on countering illegal hate speech online*, EUROPEAN COMMISSION, COMBATTING DISCRIMINATION (last visited May 19, 2019), https://ec.europa.eu/info/policies/justice-and-fundamental-rights/combatting-discrimination/racism-and-xenophobia/countering-illegal-hate-speech-online_en#monitoringrounds [https://perma.cc/WQ4W-GFLF].

263. *How the Code of Conduct helped countering illegal hate speech online—Factsheet*, EUROPEAN COMMISSSION (Feb. 2009), https://ec.europa.eu/info/sites/info/files/hatespeech_infographic3_web.pdf [https://perma.cc/76C7-E7V3]; *see also Code of Conduct on countering illegal hate speech online, Fourth evaluation confirms self-regulation works*, EUROPEAN COMMISSION (Feb. 2009), https://ec.europa.eu/info/sites/info/files/code_of_conduct_factsheet_7_web.pdf [https://perma.cc/37BV-797D].

264. *See* YOUTUBE HELP, HATE SPEECH (last visited May. 19, 2019), https://support.google.com/youtube/answer/2801939?hl=en [https://perma.cc/GX28-ZJA4].

265. TUMBLR COMMUNITY GUIDELINES (Dec. 17, 2018), https://www.tumblr.com/policy/en/community [https://perma.cc/8CSP-CZQH].

266. European Commission, Press Release Security Union: Commission steps up efforts to tackle illegal content online (Sept. 28, 2017), http://europa.eu/rapid/press-release_IP-17-3493_en.htm [hereinafter September 28 Press Release].

267. Martin Ammori, *The "New" New York Times*, 127 Harv. L. Rev. 2259, 2260 (2014).

268. *Id.* at 2283.

269. *Id.*

270. Jeff Rosen, *Who Decides? Civility v. Hate Speech on the Internet*, ABA, 33 (Winter 2013), https://www.americanbar.org/content/dam/aba/administrative/public_education/insights/Insights13-2.pdf [https://perma.cc/Z6P8-CXCW].

271. Julia Angwin & Hannes Grassegger, *Facebook's Secret Censorship Rules Protect White Men from Hate Speech But Not Black Children*, ProPublica (June 28, 2017), https://www.propublica.org/article/facebook-hate-speech-censorship-internal-documents-algorithms [https://perma.cc/J6N6-Y5HZ].

272. The exact time period was November 5 to December 14 2018 (6 weeks); *see* European Commission, Code of Conduct Fourth evaluation, *supra* note 263.

273. European Commission Press Release IP/19/805, Countering illegal hate speech online—EU Code of Conduct ensures swift response (Feb. 4, 2019).

274. Hannan Kuchler, *Facebook defends guidelines for moderators*, Fin. Times (May 22, 2017), https://www.ft.com/content/3daf880e-3f45-11e7-82b6-896b95f30f58 [https://perma.cc/9J56-ZHSB].

275. European Commission Press Release IP/18/261, Countering illegal hate speech online—Commission initiative shows continued improvement, further platforms join (Jan. 19, 2018).

276. European Commission Daily News, *Snapchat joins the EU Code of Conduct to fight illegal hate speech online*, European Commission (May 7, 2018), http://europa.eu/rapid/press-release_MEX-18-3723_en.htm [https://perma.cc/PHT9-4T6L].

277. Mehreen Khan, EU draws up sweeping rules to curb illegal online content, Fin. Times, (July 23, 2019) https://www.ft.com/content/e9aa1ed4-ad35-11e9-8030-530adfa879c2 (on file with author).

278. Ammori, *supra* note 267, at 2279.

279. *Code of Conduct—Illegal Online Hate Speech, Questions and Answers*, European Commission Question 8 (June 2016), https://ec.europa.eu/info/sites/info/files/code_of_conduct_hate_speech_en.pdf [https://perma.cc/W6ZG-BQRF].

280. Ammori, *supra* note 267, at 2279.

281. Angwin & Grassegger, *supra* note 271.

282. Nathenson, *supra* note 222, at 127.

283. Jeffrey Rosen, *Google's Gatekeepers*, N.Y. Times (Nov. 28, 2008), http://www.nytimes.com/2008/11/30/magazine/30google-t.html (on file with author).

284. Rachel Whetstone, *Free Expression and Controversial Content on the Web,* Official Google Blog (Nov. 14, 2007), https://googleblog.blogspot.com/2007/11/free-expression-and-controversial.html [https://perma.cc/353H-HWZ4].

285. Eva Galperin, *Twitter Steps Down from the Free Speech Party,* Electronic Frontier Foundation (May 21, 2014), https://www.eff.org/deeplinks/2014/05/twitter-steps-down-free-speech-party [https://perma.cc/C2QK-H8K4].

286. In May 2017, an Austrian court ordered Facebook to remove posts not just within Austria, but globally, as merely blocking the messages in Austria, without removing them for users abroad was not sufficient; *see generally* BBC News, *Facebook Must Delete Hate Postings, Austria Court Rules*, BBC News (May 9, 2017), http://www.bbc.com/news/world-europe-39852623 [https://perma.cc/RD6A-8QBN]; *see also* Alphabet Inc., Annual Report (Form 10-K, Feb. 5, 2018).

287. Ammori, *supra* note 267, at 2276.

288. Angwin & Grassegger, *supra* note 271.

289. *Id.*

290. Ammori, *supra* note 267, at 2281 (citing interviews with Dave Willner & Monika Bickert).

291. In another case involving protection of privacy and the scope of the famous "right to be forgotten," the ECJ is also considering whether to extend the obligation to remove certain information from search results globally, and not just in Europe. *See supra* notes 117–26 and accompanying text.

292. Natasha Lomas, *ECJ to Rule on Whether Facebook Needs to Hunt for Hate Speech*, TECHCRUNCH (Jan. 11, 2018), https://techcrunch.com/2018/01/11/ecj-to-rule-on-whether-facebook-needs-to-hunt-for-hate-speech/ [https://perma.cc/MQH8-83ME].

293. Press Release No. 69/19, Court of Justice of the European Union, Eva Glaswischnig-Piesczek v. Facebook Ireland Limited (June 4, 2019), https://curia.europa.eu/jcms/upload/docs/application/pdf/2019-06/cp190069en.pdf [https://perma.cc/GJ8M-BHC6].

294. Criminal Code Amendment (Sharing of Abhorrent Violent Material) Bill 2019 (Cth) (Austl.).

295. Damian Cave, *Australia Passes Law to Punish Social Media Companies for Violent Posts*, N.Y. TIMES Apr. 3, 2019), https://www.nytimes.com/2019/04/03/world/australia/social-media-law.html?login=email&auth=login-email&login=email&auth=login-email (on file with author).

296. *Id.*

CHAPTER 6

1. *Import Conditions*, EUROPEAN COMM'N, https://ec.europa.eu/food/safety/international_affairs/trade_en [https://perma.cc/W2WB-P9AE] (last visited May 24, 2019).

2. George Smith, *EU Remains Biggest Importer and Exporter of Agri-Food Products*, NEW FOOD MAGAZINE (June 8, 2018), https://www.newfoodmagazine.com/news/67520/eu-biggest-importer-exporter/ [https://perma.cc/XTK8-5GAE].

3. *See, e.g. A Brief Look at Europe's Tainted Food Scandals*, DAILY SABAH EUROPE (Aug. 11, 2017, 8:53 PM), https://www.dailysabah.com/europe/2017/08/11/a-brief-look-at-europes-tainted-food-scandals [https://perma.cc/5LW2-35CW].

4. European Commission Press Release, "BSE: UK Beef Embargo to be Lifted" (Mar. 8, 2006) (http://europa.eu/rapid/press-release_IP-06-278_en.htm [https://perma.cc/YUN4-8T4Q]). It should be noted that there is no scientific certainty that infected beef did in fact transmit BSE to humans. *BSE: What is It and Where Does it Come From?* IRISH TIMES (Jun. 11, 2015, 1:12 PM), https://www.irishtimes.com/news/ireland/irish-news/bse-what-is-it-and-where-does-it-come-from-1.2245903 [https://perma.cc/DC33-KP3L].

5. Rose Troup Buchanan, *Mad Cow Disease in the UK: What is BSE and What Are the Symptoms?* THE INDEP. (Oct. 1, 2015, 2:45 PM), https://www.independent.co.uk/news/uk/home-news/mad-cow-disease-in-the-uk-what-is-bse-and-what-are-the-symptoms-a6675351.html [https://perma.cc/SC5D-X75J].

6. MARIA WEIMER, RISK REGULATION IN THE INTERNAL MARKET 59 (2019).

7. *Food Safety: Overview*, EUROPEAN COMM'N (last visited Apr. 23, 2019), https://ec.europa.eu/food/overview_en [https://perma.cc/TW82-DLNJ].

8. *See generally Food Safety in the EU*, EUROPEAN UNION (last visited Apr. 23, 2019), https://europa.eu/european-union/topics/food-safety_en [https://perma.cc/T3NY-6UQT].

9. Regulation (EU) No 1169/2011 of the European Parliament and of the Council of 25 October 2011 on the Provision of Food Information to Consumers, Amending

Regulations (EC) No 1924/2006 and (EC) No 1925/2006 of the European Parliament and of the Council, and Repealing Commission Directive 87/250/EEC, Council Directive 90/496/EEC, Commission Directive 1999/10/EC, Directive 2000/13/EC of the European Parliament and of the Council, Commission Directives 2002/67/EC and 2008/5/EC and Commission Regulation (EC) No 608/2004, 2011 O.J. (L 304).

10. *See, e.g.*, Regulation (EC) No 178/2002 of the European Parliament and of the Council of 28 January 2002 laying down the general principles and requirements of food law, establishing the European Food Safety Authority and laying down procedures in matters of food safety, 2002 O.J. (L 31); Regulation (EC) No 882/2004 of the European Parliament and of the Council of 29 April 2004 on official controls performed to ensure the verification of compliance with feed and food law, animal health, and animal welfare rules, 2004 O.J. (L 165).

11. *See, e.g.*, Directive 2001/18 on the Deliberate Release Into the Environment of Genetically Modified Organisms, 2001 O.J. (L 106), 1; Regulation (EC) No. 1829/2003 of the European Parliament and of the Council of 22 September 2003 on Genetically Modified Food and Feed, 2003 O.J. (L 268); Regulation (EC) No 1830/2003 of the European Parliament and of the Council of 22 September 2003 Concerning the Traceability and Labelling of Genetically Modified Organisms and the Traceability of Food and Feed Products Produced from Genetically Modified Organisms and Amending Directive 2001/18/EC. The term GMO refers to the use of biotechnology to modify the genetic make-up of living cells and organisms in an effort to improve their properties such as resistance to diseases or increased crop productivity. Such modified organisms are called GMOs. Food and feed produced using GMOs are called GM food or GM feed. The EU regulates both the cultivation and trading of GMOs as well as GM food and feed. *See* European Commission, Press Release MEMO/15/4778, "Fact Sheet: Questions and Answers on EU's Policies on GMOs" (Apr. 22, 2015), http://europa.eu/rapid/press-release_MEMO-15-4778_en.pdf.

12. *About EFSA*, European Food Safety Auth., https://www.efsa.europa.eu/en/aboutefsa [https://perma.cc/4KN5-RRG2] (last visited Apr. 23, 2019).

13. Regulation (EC) No. 178/2002 of the European Parliament and of the Council of 28 January 2002 Laying Down the General Principles and Requirements of Food Law, Establishing the European Food Safety Authority and Laying Down Procedures in Matters of Food Safety, 2002 O.J. (L 31), 13.

14. *See* Commission Implementing Regulation (EU) No 503/2013 of 3 April 2013 on Applications for Authorisation of Genetically Modified Food and Feed in Accordance with Regulation (EC) No 1829/2003 of the European Parliament and of the Council and Amending Commission Regulations (EC) No 641/2004 and (EC) No 1981/2006, 2013 O.J. (L 157), 6.

15. Regulation (EU) No 182/2011 of the European Parliament and of the Council of 16 February 2011 laying down the rules and general principles concerning mechanisms for control by Member States of the Commission's exercise of implementing powers, 2011 O.J. (L 55).

16. *Id.*

17. *EU Register of Authorised GMO*, European Comm'n, http://ec.europa.eu/food/dyna/gm_register/index_en_new.cfm (reviewing records for "Registered" products for "Authorized use" of "seeds for cultivation") (last visited Apr. 23, 2019).

18. *Id.*

19. European Comm'n, Press Release, *supra* note 11.

20. *See* Directive (EU) 2015/412 of the European Parliament and of the Council of 11 March 2015 amending Directive 2001/18/EC as regards the possibility for the Member States to restrict or prohibit the cultivation of genetically modified organisms (GMOs) in their

territory Text with EEA relevance, 2015 O.J. (L 68); *See also* European Commission, Press Release, *supra* note 11.

21. *Majority of EU Nations Seek Opt-Out from Growing GM Crops*, REUTERS (Oct. 4, 2015, 11:26 AM), https://www.reuters.com/article/us-eu-gmo-opt-out/majority-of-eu-nations-seek-opt-out-from-growing-gm-crops-idUSKCN0RY0M320151004 [https://perma.cc/AG7M-MPPT].

22. Regulation (EC) No 1830/2003 of the European Parliament and of the Council of 22 September 2003 Concerning the Traceability and Labelling of Genetically Modified Organisms and the Traceability of Food and Feed Products Produced from Genetically Modified Organisms and Amending Directive 2001/18/EC, 2003 O.J. (L 268); Regulation (EC) No 1829/2003 of the European Parliament and of the Council of 22 September 2003 on Genetically Modified Food and Feed (Text with EEA relevance), 2003 O.J. (L 268).

23. Regulation (EC) No 1830/2003 of the European Parliament and of the Council of 22 September 2003 Concerning the Traceability and Labelling of Genetically Modified Organisms and the Traceability of Food and Feed Products Produced From Genetically Modified Organisms and Amending Directive 2001/18/EC, 2003 O.J. (L 268), 24, 26-27.

24. *Traceability and Labelling*, EUROPEAN COMM'N, https://ec.europa.eu/food/plant/gmo/traceability_labelling_en [https://perma.cc/AH7B-7FXT] (last visited Apr. 29, 2019); Regulation (EC) No. 1830/2003 of the European Parliament and of the Council of 22 September 2003 Concerning the Traceability and Labelling of Genetically Modified Organisms, 2003 O.J. (L 268) 24, 26–27.

25. Koreen Ramessar, Teresa Capell, Richard M Twyman & Paul Christou, *Going to Ridiculous Lengths—European Coexistence Regulations for GM Crops*, 28 NATURE BIOTECH 133, 134 (2010).

26. *See* EUROPEAN COMM'N, SPECIAL EUROBAROMETER 354: FOOD-RELATED RISKS (2010), http://ec.europa.eu/commfrontoffice/publicopinion/archives/ebs/ebs_354_en.pdf [https://perma.cc/F282-G2KA].

27. Joshua Chaffin & Hugh Carnegy, *How Food Scares Galloped Across Europe*, FIN. TIMES (Feb. 11, 2013), https://www.ft.com/content/8b94164c-7452-11e2-80a7-00144feabdc0 (on file with author).

28. *Id.*

29. *DS 26: European Communities—Measures Concerning Meat and Meat Products (Hormones)*, WORLD TRADE ORG., https://www.wto.org/english/tratop_e/dispu_e/cases_e/ds26_e.htm [https://perma.cc/ES5P-KBBQ] (last updated Apr. 12, 2016).

30. *DS 389: European Communities—Certain Measures Affecting Poultry Meat and Poultry Meat Products from the United States*, WORLD TRADE ORG., https://www.wto.org/english/tratop_e/dispu_e/cases_e/ds389_e.htm [https://perma.cc/SU46-DLGN] (last updated Feb. 24, 2010).

31. TOM DELREUX & SANDRA HAPPAERTS, ENVIRONMENTAL POLICY AND POLITICS IN THE EUROPEAN UNION 186 (2016)

32. *See* EUROPEAN COMM'N, EUROBAROMETER 55.2: EUROPEANS, SCIENCE, AND TECHNOLOGY 40 (2001), http://ec.europa.eu/research/press/2001/pro612en-report.pdf [https://perma.cc/ND4A-J4V3]; EUROPEAN COMM'N, SPECIAL EUROBAROMETER 238: RISK ISSUES 53 (2006), http://ec.europa.eu/public_opinion/archives/ebs/ebs_238_en.pdf [https://perma.cc/9JJ8-HKT9].

33. See EUROPEAN COMM'N, SPECIAL EUROBAROMETER 341: BIOTECHNOLOGY 31 (2001), http://ec.europa.eu/commfrontoffice/publicopinion/archives/ebs/ebs_341_en.pdf [https://perma.cc/CH7G-SZQW].

34. EUROPEAN COMM'N, EUROBAROMETER 354: FOOD RELATED RISKS 30 (2010), http://ec.europa.eu/commfrontoffice/publicopinion/archives/ebs/ebs_354_en.pdf [https://perma.cc/NH2C-9Q8A].

35. Hans-Georg Dederer, *The Challenge of Regulating Genetically Modified Organisms in the European Union: Trends and Issues, in* CONTEMPORARY ISSUES IN ENVIRONMENTAL LAW JAPAN AND EU 152 (Yumiko Nakanishi, ed., 2016).

36. Tomasz Twardowski & Aleksandra Małyska, *Social and Legal Determinants for Marketing of GM Products in Poland*, 29 NEW BIOTECHNOLOGY 249 (2012).

37. TOM DELREUX & HAPPAERTS, *supra* note 31, at 183.

38. Andrew Willis, *EU Receives Anti-GMO Petition Amid Raging Legal Battle*, EU OBSERVER (Dec. 10 2010, 9:25 AM), https://euobserver.com/environment/31474 [https://perma.cc/MJD9-5KWU].

39. James Kanter, *BASF to Stop Selling Genetically Modified Products in Europe*, N.Y. TIMES (Jan. 16, 2012), https://www.nytimes.com/2012/01/17/business/global/17iht-gm017.html (on file with author).

40. Joshua Chaffin & Jim Pickard, *Monsanto to Drop Applications to Grow GM Crops in EU*, FIN. TIMES (July 17, 2013), https://www.ft.com/content/aed5e0a8-ef1e-11e2-9269-00144feabdc0 (on file with author).

41. TOM DELREUX & HAPPAERTS, *supra* note 31, at 183.

42. *See* Statement of Policy: Foods Derived from New Plant Varieties, 57 Fed. Reg. 22,984, 22,988, 22,991 (May 29, 1992).

43. Prakash & Kelly L. Kollman, *Biopolitics in the EU and the U.S.: A Race to the Bottom or Convergence to the Top?*, 47 INT'L STUD. Q. 617, 627, 629-34 (2003).

44. *What GM Crops are Currently Being Grown and Where?* ROYAL SOC'Y, https://royalsociety.org/topics-policy/projects/gm-plants/what-gm-crops-are-currently-being-grown-and-where/ [https://perma.cc/HB6L-CWPP] (last visited Apr. 22, 2019).

45. Thomas J. Hoban, *Public Attitudes Towards Agricultural Biotechnology*, Table 1 (The Food and Agriculture Organization of the United Nations, ESA Working Paper No. 04-09, 2004).

46. *Id.* citing *MSU Food Literacy and Engagement Poll: Wave I*, FOOD@MSU (Aug. 17, 2017), http://www.canr.msu.edu/news/msu-food-literacy-and-engagement-poll [https://perma.cc/YH8E-W285]; Brad Buck, *UF Study: Consumers see 'Organic' and 'non-GM' Food Labels as Synonymous*, UF IFAS BLOGS (Oct. 23, 2017), http://blogs.ifas.ufl.edu/news/2017/10/23/uf-study-consumers-see-organic-non-gm-food-labels-synonymous/ [https://perma.cc/D6DN-427Q].

47. *U.S. Polls on GE Food Labeling*, CTR. FOOD SAFETY, https://www.centerforfoodsafety.org/issues/976/ge-food-labeling/us-polls-on-ge-food-labeling [https://perma.cc/W2WV-GSKQ] (last visited Apr. 22, 2019).

48. CONSUMER REPORTS NAT'L RESEARCH CTR., CONSUMER SUPPORT FOR STANDARDIZATION AND LABELING OF GENETICALLY ENGINEERED FOOD 2 (2014), http://www.justlabelit.org/wp-content/uploads/2015/02/2014_GMO_survey_report.pdf [https://perma.cc/GJ8D-T5GF].

49. *DS 291: European Communities—Measures Affecting the Approval and Marketing of Biotech Products*, WORLD TRADE ORG., https://www.wto.org/english/tratop_e/dispu_e/cases_e/ds291_e.htm [https://perma.cc/76FT-DZ2X] (last updated Apr. 16, 2019); *See also* MARK A. POLLACK AND GREGORY C. SHAFFER, WHEN COOPERATION FAILS: THE INTERNATIONAL LAW AND POLITICS OF GENETICALLY MODIFIED FOODS (2009).

50. DAVID LANGLET & SAID MAHMOUDI, EU ENVIRONMENTAL LAW AND POLICY 339–40 (2016).

51. *See* CHARLES E. HANRAHAN, CONG. RESEARCH SERV., RS21556, AGRICULTURAL BIOTECHNOLOGY: THE U.S.-EU DISPUTE 6 (2010); *see also* Minutes of Meeting, WT/DSB/M/311, at 6–7 (Mar. 15, 2012); *DS 291: European Communities—Measures Affecting the Approval and Marketing of Biotech Products: Current Status*, WORLD

TRADE ORG., http://www.wto.org/english/tratop_e/dispu_e/cases_e/ds291_e.htm [https://perma.cc/76FT-DZ2X] (last updated Apr. 16, 2019).

52. Dederer, *supra* note 35, at 147–48.

53. *See* HANRAHAN, *supra* note 51.

54. Commission Regulation (EU) No 619/2011 of June 24, 2011, Laying Down the Methods of Sampling and Analysis for the Official Control of Feed as Regards Presence of Genetically Modified Material for Which an Authorisation Procedure is Pending or the Authorisation of Which has Expired, 2011 O.J. (L 166).

55. Commission Regulation (EU) No 619/2011 of 24 June 2011 Laying Down the Methods of Sampling and Analysis for the Official Control of Feed as Regards Presence of Genetically Modified Material for Which an Authorisation Procedure is Pending or the Authorisation of Which has Expired, 2011 O.J. (L 166).

56. Richard B. Stewart, *GMO Trade Regulation and Developing Countries* 6–7 (Pub. Law & Legal Theory Research Paper Series, Working Paper No. 09-70, 2009).

57. *See, e.g.*, Stewart, *supra* note 56, at 10; Linda Kleemann et. al., *Certification and Access to Export Markets: Adoption and Return on Investment of Organic-Certified Pineapple Farming in Ghana*, 64 WORLD DEV. 79 (2014); Spencer Henson, Oliver Masakure & John Cranfield, *Do Fresh Produce Exporters in Sub-Saharan Africa Benefit from GlobalGAP Certification?* 39 WORLD DEV. 375 (2011).

58. Kleemann, *supra* note 57 at 87.

59. *See, e.g.*, ANDREW GRAFFHAM, ESTHER KAREHU & JAMES MACGREGOR, FRESH INSIGHTS NUMBER 6: IMPACT OF EUREPGAP ON SMALL-SCALE VEGETABLE GROWERS IN KENYA (2007), https://assets.publishing.service.gov.uk/media/57a08be 6ed915d3cfd001018/60506fresh_insights_6_EurepGapKenya.pdf; Andrew Graffham & James MacGregor, FRESH INSIGHTS NUMBER 5: IMPACT OF EUREPGAP ON SMALL-SCALE VEGETABLE GROWERS IN ZAMBIA (2007), https://assets.publishing.service.gov. uk/media/57a08be840f0b64974000e70/60506FI5_EurepGAPZambia.pdf.

60. *EU Member States*, EUROPEAN FOOD SAFETY AUTH, https://www.efsa.europa.eu/en/ partnersnetworks/eumembers [https://perma.cc/PY8T-6BD6] (last visited Oct. 27, 2018).

61. U.S.D.A., Press Release, "U.S. Farm Exports Hit Third-Highest Level on Record," 16 Nov. 2017 (https://www.fas.usda.gov/newsroom/us-farm-exports-hit-third-highest-level-record) [https://perma.cc/HB5Q-YFE6].

62. However, trade diversion may entail the producers being able to sell their crop at a lower price in alternative export markets.

63. Katharine Gostek, *Genetically Modified Organisms: How The United States' and the European Union's Regulations Affect the Economy*, 24 MICH. ST. INT'L L.R. 761, 787–90 (2016).

64. *See* Prakash & Kollman, *supra* note 43, at 632.

65. Gostek, *supra* note 63, at 790–94.

66. *Why M&M's Are Made With Natural Coloring in the EU and not the U.S.*, WBUR (Mar. 28, 2014), http://www.wbur.org/hereandnow/2014/03/28/artificial-dyes-candy [https://perma.cc/GM93-6M3H]; Donna McCann et. al. *Food Additives and Hyperactive Behaviour in 3-Year-Old and 8/9-Year-Old Children in the Community: A Rendomised, Double-Blinded, Placebo-Controlled Trial*, 370 LANCET 1560 (2007).

67. Robyn O'Brien, *US Food Companies Have Removed Food Dyes in the UK—Why Not Here?*, ROBYN O'BRIEN (Apr. 9, 2015), https://robynobrien.com/us-food-companies-have-removed-food-dyes-in-the-uk-why-not-here/ [https://perma.cc/S7XJ-L4QM].

68. WBUR, *supra* note 66.

69. Melissa Kravitz, *6 Foods that are Legal in the US but Banned in Other Countries*, BUS. INSIDER (Mar. 1, 2017, 5:49 PM), https://www.businessinsider.com/foods-illegal-out-side-us-2017-3?IR=T [https://perma.cc/4R44-FRPF].

70. Kravitz, *supra* note 69.

71. *Id.*

72. The globalization of the EU standard in all these instances was facilitated by consumer pressure in the United States. For example, ADA is also known as the "yoga mat chemical"—given that the same chemical is used in yoga mats—making it a catchy reference in public campaigning against the use of ADA in food. Virginia Chamlee, *Subway Wasn't the Only Chain to Use the 'Yoga Mat Chemical' in Its Bread*, EATER (Aug. 8, 2016, 4:00 PM), https://www.eater.com/2016/8/8/12403338/subway-yoga-mat-chemical-mcdonalds-burger-king-wendys [https://perma.cc/7ZQJ-TQSN].

73. *See, e.g.*, SARAH KOBYLEWSKI & MICHAEL E. JACOBSON, FOOD DYES: A RAINBOW OF RISKS (2010), https://cspinet.org/sites/default/files/attachment/food-dyes-rainbow-of-risks.pdf [https://perma.cc/G2M8-FVCA; WBUR, *supra* note 66.

74. In France, food importers are required to acquire "EUHACCP" certification—the EU version of Hazard Analysis and Critical Control Point ("HACCP")—which is a stringent food hygiene and safety standard.

75. Tomohiro Machida, *Japanese Dried Fish Flake Group Hope to Find Agreeable French Palates*, NIKKEI ASIAN REV. (Sept. 27, 2014, 1:00 PM), https://asia.nikkei.com/Business/Trends/Japanese-dried-fish-flake-group-hopes-to-find-agreeable-French-palates [https://perma.cc/B952-NKN7].

76. *See The Costs of GMO Labeling*, FOODIE FARMER (Apr. 8, 2014), https://thefoodiefarmer.blogspot.com/2014/04/the-costs-of-gmo-labeling.html [https://perma.cc/3ZQ9-XJ9A].

77. *See* CHARLES E. HANRAHAN, CONG. RESEARCH SERV., RS21556, AGRICULTURAL BIOTECHNOLOGY: THE U.S.-EU DISPUTE 5 (2010).

78. *See* HANRAHAN, *supra* note 51, at 5.

79. *Id.* at 245.

80. *Id.* at 469; *see also* DAVID VOGEL, THE POLITICS OF PRECAUTION: REGULATION HEALTH, SAFETY, AND ENVIRONMENTAL RISKS IN EUROPE AND THE UNITED STATES 86 (2012).

81. CROPLIFE INT'L, FACT SHEET: ADVENTITIOUS PRESENCE (AP) OR LOW LEVEL PRESENCE (LLP), https://croplife.org/wp-content/uploads/pdf_files/Fact-Sheet-Adventitious-Presence-or-Low-Level-Presence.pdf.

82. Nicholas Kalaitzandonakes, *The Economics of Adventitious Presence Thresholds in the EU Seed Market*, FOOD POLICY 43 (2013) 237.

83. Case C-442/09, Bablok v. Freistaat Bayern, EUR-Lex 62009CJ0442, at 8 (Sept. 6, 2011).

84. Kalaitzandonakes, *supra* note 82, at 237.

85. Pamela Rosalía Narváez Torres, *Detección de polen convencional y geneticamente modificado de soya, glycine max l., en la miel de abeja, apis mellifera, de los estados Campeche y Yucatán* ("*Detection of Conventional Pollen and Genetically Modified Soy, Glycine Max L., in the Honey, Apis Mellifera, of the States of Campeche and Yucatán*"), UNIVERSIDAD AUTONOMA DE MEXICO (2013), https://www.conacyt.gob.mx/cibiogem/images/cibiogem/Fomento-investigacion/Tesis/Deteccion-polen-convencional-y-GM-soya.pdf [https://perma.cc/B67R-ZJH2].

86. *Id.* at 37.

87. *Id.* at 86.

88. *See* VOGEL, *supra* note 80, at 86.

89. Brandon Mitchener, *Standard Bearers: Increasingly, Rules of Global Economy Are Set in Brussels*, WALL ST. J., Apr. 23, 2002, at A1; Editorial, *Regulatory Imperialism*, WALL ST. J. (Oct. 26, 2007), http://online.wsj.com/article/SB119334720539572002.html (on file with author).

90. *See id.; see also* David A. Wirth, The EU's New Impact on U.S. Environmental Regulation, 31 FLETCHER F. WORLD AFF. 91, 104 (2007). Similarly, multinational restaurant retailers

operating in the EU, including McDonalds, have requested their contract farmers to produce only non-GMO crops to mitigate consumer backlash in the EU. *See* Prakash & Kollman, *supra* note 43, at 632.

91. *U.S. Traders Reject GMO Crops that Lack Global Approval*, REUTERS (May 6, 2016), https://www.reuters.com/article/us-usa-gmo-crops/u-s-traders-reject-gmo-crops-that-lack-global-approval-idUSKCN0XX2AV [https://perma.cc/77L2-6XR7].

92. *Id.*

93. *See* CENTRE DU COMMERCE INTERNATIONAL, DEVELOPPEMENT DES PRODUITS ET DES MARCHES, CACAO: GUIDE DES PRACTIQUES COMMERCIALES, 115 (2012).

94. Regulation (EU) 2015/1933 of 27 October 2015 Amending Regulation (EC) No 1881/2006 as Regards Maximum Levels for Polycyclic Aromatic Hydrocarbons in Cocoa Fibre, Banana Chips, Food Supplements, Dried Herbs and Dried Spices, 2015 O.J. (L 282); *see also EU Commission Updates the Regulation of PAHS in Foodstuffs*, SGS (Nov. 19, 2015), http://www.sgs.com/en/news/2015/11/safeguards-18915-eu-commission-updates-the-regulation-of-pahs-in-foodstuffs [https://perma.cc/D6PY-D6YY].

95. Council Regulation (EEC) No. 315/93 of 8 February 1993 Laying down Community Procedures for Contaminants in Food, 1993 O.J. (L 37).

96. Drying cocoa artificially is one the main issues because when smoke comes into contact with cocoa beans, one risks higher levels of polycyclic aroma to hydrocarbons. *See* Moki Kindzeka, *New European Union Import Laws Hurt African Cocoa Exports*, DEUTSCHE WELLE (May 28, 2013), http://www.dw.com/en/new-european-union-import-laws-hurt-african-cocoa-exports/a-16842178 [https://perma.cc/9MF4-T73Q].

97. Ntaryike Divine, Jr., *European Regulations Worry Cocoa Exporters*, VOICE OF AFRICA NEWS (Feb. 1, 2013, 7:03 PM), https://www.voanews.com/a/european-regulations-worry-african-cocoa-exporters/1595716.html [https://perma.cc/C3JP-7FV8].

98. *Cameroon*, OBSERVATORY ECON. COMPLEXITY, https://atlas.media.mit.edu/en/profile/country/cmr/ [https://perma.cc/RHK7-9PV8] (last visited Apr. 22, 2019); *Top 10 Cocoa Producing Countries*, WORLDATLAS (last updated Sept. 28, 2018), https://www.worldatlas.com/articles/top-10-cocoa-producing-countries.html [https://perma.cc/FEX6-3AL3].

99. *Cameroon*, OBSERVATORY OF ECON. COMPLEXITY, https://atlas.media.mit.edu/en/profile/country/cmr/ [https://perma.cc/RHK7-9PV8] (last visited Apr. 22, 2019).

100. Divine, Jr., *supra* note 97.

101. Kindzeka, *supra* note 96.

102. *EU Tightens Laws on African Cocoa Exports*, VENTURES AFRICA (June 3, 2013), http://venturesafrica.com/eu-tightens-laws-on-african-cocoa-exports/ [https://perma.cc/QY6W-ZK7Y].

103. *Cameroon Refurbishing Cocoa Drying Ovens to Meet EU Rules*, REUTERS (Sept. 4, 2013), https://www.euractiv.com/section/agriculture-food/news/cameroon-refurbishing-cocoa-drying-ovens-to-meet-eu-rules/ [https://perma.cc/UKM3-EUVB].

104. Steve Jaffee & Oliver Masakure, *Strategic Use of Private Standards to Enhance International Competitiveness: Vegetable Exports from Kenya and Elsewhere*, 30 FOOD POL. 316 (2005).

105. Commission Regulation 753/2002 of 29 April 2002 laying down rules for applying Council Regulation No. 1493/1999 as regards the description, designation, presentation, and protection of certain wine sector products, 2002 O.J. (L 118); Council Regulation (EC) No 479/2008 of 29 April 2008 on the Common Organisation of the Market in Wine, Amending Regulations (EC) No 1493/1999, (EC) No 1782/2003, (EC) No 1290/2005, (EC) No 3/2008 and repealing Regulations (EEC) No 2392/86 and (EC) No 1493/1999, 2008 O.J. (L 148), 39.

106. Council Regulation (EC) No 479/2008 of 29 April 2008 on the Common Organisation of the Market in Wine, Amending Regulations (EC) No 1493/1999, (EC) No 1782/2003,

(EC) No 1290/2005, (EC) No 3/2008 and repealing Regulations (EEC) No 2392/86 and (EC) No 1493/1999, 2008 O.J. (L 148), 34; Jacob Gaffney, *European Union Standardizes Wine Labels*, WINE SPECTATOR (May 18, 2002), http://www.winespectator.com/webfeature/show/id/European-Union-Standardizes-Wine-Labels_21288 [https://perma.cc/ZBA6-46HJ].

107. The Liquor Products Act 60 of 1989, art. 10 (S. Afr.).

108. WESGRO CAPE TOWN & WESTERN CAPE RESEARCH, SECTOR: WINE, 16 (2016), http://www.wesgro.co.za/pdf_repository/Wine%20Fact%20Sheet%20-%20Final.pdf [https://perma.cc/532E-2VVT].

109. CITROSUCO, RELATÓRIO DE SUSTENTABILIDADE 2013-2014 [*CITROSUCO SUSTAINABILITY REPORT 2013-2014*], 12 (2014), http://www.citrosuco.com.br/sustentabilidade/relatorio-de-sustentabilidade.html [https://perma.cc/8L6S-RCSP].

110. CITROSUCO, RELATÓRIO DE SUSTENTABILIDADE 2016-2017 [*CITROSUCO SUSTAINABILITY REPORT 2016-2017*], 16 (2017), http://www.citrosuco.com.br/sustentabilidade/relatorio-de-sustentabilidade.html [https://perma.cc/8L6S-RCSP].

111. CITROSUCO, RELATÓRIO DE SUSTENTABILIDADE 2013-2014 [*CITROSUCO SUSTAINABILITY REPORT 2013-2014*] (2014), http://www.citrosuco.com.br/sustentabilidade/relatorio-de-sustentabilidade.html [https://perma.cc/8L6S-RCSP].

112. JBS, "A Maior Empresa Do Mundo, Em Produtos de Origem Animal" [*The World's Largest Company in Products of Animal Origin*], http://jbs.com.br/sobre/ (last visited May 23, 2019) [https://perma.cc/DL9D-AY84].

113. JBS S.A., RELATÓRIO DE SUSTENTABILIDADE 2016-2017 [*JBS S.A. SUSTAINABILIY REPORT 2016-2017*], 115, 116 120 (2017), https://jbss.infoinvest.com.br/ptb/4069/JBS%20RAS%202016%20PT%20170502%20Final.pdf [https://perma.cc/9JDG-PNMP]. For example, the company developed a program, which it called "Origin," to provide consumers the origin of the beef. The program targets the Brazilian market, but it is based on the EU requirement to trace all stages of beef production.

114. Linda Kleemann, Awudu Abdulai & Mareike Buss, *Certification and Access to Export Markets: Adoption and Return on Investment of Organic-Certified Pineapple Farming in Ghana*, 64 WORLD DEV. 79 (2014).

115. Dela-Dem Doe Fianko et. al., *Does GlobalGAP Certification Promote Agricultural Exports?* (Global Food Discussion Papers 112) (2017).

116. *About Us*, AGRICOLA FAMOSA, http://www.agricolafamosa.com.br/agricola-famosa/ [https://perma.cc/MGU3-AZPH] (last visited May 23, 2019).

117. Etsuyo Michida, Vu Hoang Nam & Aya Suzuki, *Emergence of Asian GAPs and its Relationship to GlobalG.A.P.* (IDE Discussion Paper No. 507) (2015); Sam F. Halabi & Ching-Fu Lin, *Assessing the Relative Influence and Efficacy of Public & Private Food Safety Regulation Regimes: Comparing Codex & GlobalG.A.P. Standards*, 72 FOOD & DRUG L.J. 262, 294 (2017); Maya Kaneko, "Apple Exporters Hope to Stay Ahead in Quality Race," JAPAN TIMES (Mar. 24, 2006), https://www.japantimes.co.jp/news/2006/03/24/national/apple-exporters-hope-to-stay-ahead-in-quality-race/#.W7j36C-ZOZo [https://perma.cc/P5QN-3BDQ].

118. Maria Weimer & Ellen Vos, *The Role of the EU in Transnational Regulation of Food Safety: Extending Experimentalist Governance?*, *in* THE ROLE OF EU IN TRANSNATIONAL REGULATION: EXTENDING EXPERIMENTALIST GOVERNANCE? 51 (J. Zeitlin ed., 2015).

119. Agreement on the Application of Sanitary and Phytosanitary Measures, Apr. 15, 1994, Marrakesh Agreement Establishing the World Trade Organization, Annex 1A, art. III, 1867 U.N.T.S. 493 [not reproduced in I.L.M.].

120. Maria Weimer & Ellen Vos, *supra* note 118, at 61–68.

121. In-person interview with Sabine Juelicher, Director of Directorate-General for Health and Food Safety, European Commission (July 18, 2018).

122. Ministry of Agriculture and Supply, Minister's Office, Normative Instruction No. 10, of April 27, 2001 (Repealed by Normative Instruction 55/2011 / MAPA), http://www.agricultura.gov.br/assuntos/insumos-agropecuarios/insumos-pecuarios/alimentacao-animal/arquivos-alimentacao-animal/legislacao/instrucao-normativa-no-55-de-10-de-dezembro-de-2011.pdf/view [https://perma.cc/VFM2-5VCH]

123. Coimma, *A Carne Produzida No Brasil Tem Hormonio? [Does the Meat that Comes From Brasil Contain Hormones?]*, COIMMA BLOG (Oct. 06 2014), http://www.coimma.com.br/balancas-e-troncos/A_carne_produzida_no_Brasil_tem_hormonio.html [https://perma.cc/KX78-HXSX]; Meg Cristina de Campos Pires. *Análise sobre o comércio entre Brasil e União Europeia e as barreiras não tarifárias que o afetam [Analysis on the commerce relationship between Brazil and the European Union and the non-tariff barrier that affects it]*, (Ph.D. Thesis, Universidade Estadual Paulista) 3 (2012).

124. *Brazil Exports Only 20% of Beef Produced and RevenuesReach U.S. $5.9B*, COMEX (Mar. 6, 2016), https://www.comexdobrasil.com/brasil-destina-a-exportacao-apenas-20-da-carne-bovina-produzida-e-receita-chega-a-us-59-bi/ [https://perma.cc/5C9M-N54M].

125. Jale Tosun & Maurıcio de Moraes, *Marcondes Import Restrictions and Food-Safety Regulations: Insight from Brazil*, 7 LATIN AM. POL. 377, 380, 387 (2016).

126. This National Plan refers to a sector-specific version of the Ministry of Agriculture, Livestock and Supply's existing federal inspection and surveillance program to evaluate and monitor food production chains. *Id*. at 385.

127. Regulation (EC) No 178/2002 of the European Parliament and of the Council of 28 January 2002 laying down the general principles and requirements of food law, establishing the European Food Safety Authority and laying down procedures in matters of food safety, 2002 O.J. (L 31).

128. Taiwan lifayuan (台灣立法院), Xingzheng yuan han qing shenyi `shipin weisheng guanli fa xiuzheng caoan'an, *dì 5 tiáo hé dì 9 tiáo (行政院函請審議「食品衛生管理法修正草案」案, 第5條和第9條) [The proposal of Act Governing Food Safety and Sanitation, Article 5 and Article 9]*, Lifayuan guohui tushu guan wangzhan (立法院國會圖書館網站) (May 31, 2014) (Chinese text https://lis.ly.gov.tw/lgcgi/lgmeetimage?cfc7cfcdcfcec8cbc5cdcfcad2cdccc9) [https://perma.cc/N6PF-8NMV].

129. MARIKO KUBO, THE CHANGING WORLD OF FOOD LABELLING REGULATIONS, LEATHERHEAD FOOD RESEARCH WHITE PAPER NO. 23 (2016).

130. European Commission Press Release, European Union and United States Agree to Historic New Partnership on Organic Trade (Feb. 15, 2012), http://europa.eu/rapid/press-release_IP-12-138_en.htm [https://perma.cc/TX3A-2G9P].

131. European Commission Press Release MEMO 17/4686, "Fact Sheet: The New Organic Regulation" (updated Apr. 19, 2018), http://europa.eu/rapid/press-release_MEMO-17-4686_en.htm [https://perma.cc/J7RR-F9HK].

132. Tosun & de Moraes, *supra* note 125, at 390–91.

133. *Id*. at 391.

134. *GMOs Globally*, GMO ANSWERS, https://gmoanswers.com/gmos-globally [https://perma.cc/MUA4-KE8L] (last visited May 23, 2019).

135. Labeling Around the World, Just Label It! http://www.justlabelit.org/right-to-know-center/labeling-around-the-world/ [https://perma.cc/3DZJ-L8E3] (last visited May 23, 2019).

136. Stewart, *supra* note 56, at 9.

137. On the current status of GMO regulation in LatinAmerican countries. *See* Eric Katovish, The Regulation of Genetically Modified Organisms in Latin America: Policy

Implications for Trade, Biosafety, and Development (PhD thesis, University of Minnesota) (2012).

138. Ley No. 29811, Ley que Establece la Moratoria al Ingreso y Producción de Organismos Vivos Modificados al Territorio Nacional por um Periódo de 10 Años, D.O. 09.12.2011, art. 1 (Peru).

139. *See* Ley No. 300, Ley Marco de la Madre Tierra y Desarrollo Integral para Vivir Bien, art. 24(7)–(9).G.O. 15.10.2012 (Bolivia); Constitución Política de Ecuador 2008 art. 401.

140. *See* Brazil, Ministry of Justice Directive No. 2,658/03 (2004), which establishes guidelines for the use of a transgenic logo to label all foods/food products/feeds whenever their GMO-content exceeds 1% tolerability benchmark.

141. *See* Uruguay's Decreto No 34.901, stating in Article D.1774.83 that "[f]oods that have been genetically engineered or that contain one or more ingredients from them, that exceed 1% of the total components, must be labelled." (translation supplied).

142. Katovish, *supra* note 137.

143. Corte Constitucional [C.C.] [Constituional Court], septiembre 8, 2015, Sentencia C-583/15 (Colom.), [http://www.corteconstitucional.gov.co/relatoria/2015/c583-15. htm [https://perma.cc/6229-DTCW].

144. Sentencia C-583/15 (2015), *supra* note 143, at 1.

145. Stewart, *supra* note 56 at 1, 2, 4, 6, 8, and 9.

146. *Id.* at 2.

147. Patrycha Dabrowska-Klosińska, *The EU and Transnational Regulation of GMOs, in* Extending Experimentalist Governance? The European Union and Transnational Regulation 83, 100–01 (Jonathan Zeitlin ed., 2015).

148. *Id.* at 99.

149. S. Res. 764, 114th Cong. § 1 (2016) (enacted) (amending the Agricultural Marketing Act of 1946 by adding a GMO food disclosure standard); National Bioengineered Food Disclosure Standard, Pub. L. No. 114-216, 130 Stat. 834 (2015) (codified at 7 U.S.C. §§ 1639–1639c).

150. *BE Disclosure & Labeling*, USDA, https://www.ams.usda.gov/rules-regulations/gmo [https://perma.cc/66DU-5SKP] (last visited May 23, 2019).

151. *GE Food Labeling: States Take Action*, Center for Food Safety (Jun. 10, 2014), http://www.centerforfoodsafety.org/fact-sheets/3067/ge-food-labeling-states-take-action [https://perma.cc/G7KS-TT4G].

152. 22 M.R.S.A. §§2592(1)(C)(2013) *as enacted by* P.L. 2013, ch. 436, §1 and affected by §2.

153. The Mellman Group, Memo to "Just Label It!" Re: Voters Want GMO Food Labels Printed on Packaging (2015), http://4bgr3aepis44c9bxt1ulx syq.wpengine.netdna-cdn.com/wp-content/uploads/2015/12/15memn20-JLI-d6.pdf [https://perma.cc/MM5F-FC53].

154. *GMOs Part of U.S.-E.U. Trade Negotiations*, Just Label It!, http://www.justlabelit. org/gmos-part-of-u-s-e-u-trade-negotiations/ [https://perma.cc/W3WF-NCJN] (last visited May 24, 2019).

155. Regulation (EC) 1907/2006, of the European Parliament and of the Council of 18 December 2006 Concerning the Registration, Evaluation, Authorisation and Restriction of Chemicals (REACH), Establishing a European Chemicals Agency, 2007 O.J. (L 136) 3 [hereinafter REACH].

156. *See* Melody M. Bomgardner, *Facts & Figures of the Chemical Industry*, Chem. & Eng'g News, July 4, 2011, at 33–67.

157. Council Directive 76/769/EEC of 27 July 1976 on the approximation of the laws, regulations and administrative provisions of the Member States relating to restrictions on

the marketing and use of certain dangerous substances and preparations. *See* DAVID
LANGLET & SAID MAHMOUDI, EU ENVIRONMENTAL LAW AND POLICY 309 (2016).

158. *See* REACH, *supra* note 155, art. 5; Joanne Scott, *From Brussels with Love: The
Transatlantic Travels of European Law and the Chemistry of Regulatory Attraction*, 57
AM. J. COMP. L. 897, 898-99 (2009).

159. *See* Doaa Abdel Motaal, *Reaching REACH: The Challenge for Chemicals Entering
International Trade*, 12 J. INT'L ECON. L. 643, 645 (2009); Scott, *supra* note 158.

160. EUROPEAN ENVIRONMENTAL LAW: AFTER LISBON 452 (Jan H. Jans & Hans H.B.
Vedder, eds., 4th ed., 2012).

161. *Id.* at 453.

162. *See* TFEU art. 191(2); *cf.* Case C-180/96, United Kingdom v. Comm'n, 1998 E.C.R.
I-2269, para. 99.

163. *See Commission White Paper: Strategy for a Future Chemicals Policy*, at 7-8, 28, COM
(2001) 88 final (Feb. 27, 2001).

164. *Id.* at 6. The exception being chemicals that are imported or produced at a rate of less
than 1 ton annually.

165. *Registered Substances*, EUROPEAN CHEMS. AGENCY, https://echa.europa.eu/infor-
mation-on-chemicals/registered-substances [https://perma.cc/C4RJ-RRT8] (last
updated May 17, 2019).

166. Wirth, *supra* note 90, at 102.

167. MITCHELL P. SMITH, ENVIRONMENTAL AND HEALTH REGULATION IN THE
UNITED STATES AND THE EUROPEAN UNION: PROTECTING PUBLIC AND PLANET
26 (2012).

168. *Id.*

169. *Id.* at 35.

170. *Id.* at 37.

171. *Id.* at 38.

172. EUROPEAN COMM'N, SPECIAL EUROBAROMETER 468: ATTITUDES OF
EUROPEAN CITIZENS TOWARDS THE ENVIRONMENT 9 (2017), http://
ec.europa.eu/commfrontoffice/publicopinion/index.cfm/ResultDoc/download/
DocumentKy/81259 [https://perma.cc/8N45-8HJU].

173. *Id.* at 10.

174. *Commission White Paper: Strategy for a Future Chemicals Policy*, 7, COM (2001) 88 final
(Feb. 27, 2001).

175. Lyndsey Layton, *Chemical Law Has Global Impact*, WASHINGTON POST (June 12,
2008), http://www.washingtonpost.com/wp-dyn/content/article/2008/06/11/
AR2008061103569.html (on file with author).

176. Dieter Pesendorfer, *EU Environmental Policy Under Pressure: Chemicals Policy Change
Between Antagonistic Goals?*, 15 ENVT'L POL. 95, 103–04 (2006)

177. SMITH, *supra* note 167, at 41.

178. *Id.*

179. Pesendorfer, *supra* note 176, at 106.

180. SMITH, *supra* note 167, at 42.

181. *See* LAWRENCE A. KOGAN, EXPORTING PRECAUTION: HOW EUROPE'S RISK-FREE
REGULATORY AGENDA THREATENS AMERICAN FREE ENTERPRISE 40-43 (2005).

182. *See, e.g.*, Anne Pouillot et al., *REACH: Impact on the US Cosmetics Industry?*, 8 J.
COSMETIC DERMATOLOGY 3, 5–6 (2009).

183. Henrik Selin & Stacy D. VanDeveer, *Raising Global Standards: Hazardous Substances
and E-Waste Management in the European Union*, 48 ENVIR. 6, 13 (2006)

184. *Id.*

185. *Id.*

186. Pesendorfer, *supra* note 176, at 105.
187. Selin & VanDeveer, *supra* note 183, at 13.
188. Layton, *supra* note 175.
189. *Id.*
190. Frank Ackerman, Elizabeth A. Stanton & Rachel Massey, *European Chemical Policy and the United States: The Impacts of REACH*, 25 Renewable Resources J. 15, 16 (2007).
191. *Id.*
192. *Id.*
193. Pesendorfer, *supra* note 176, at 101.
194. *Id.*
195. Selin & VanDeveer, *supra* note 183, at 64.
196. Smith, *supra* note 167, at 41.
197. Ackerman, *supra* note 190, at 16.
198. *See* Wirth *supra* note 90 at 102-03.
199. *See* Scott, *supra* note 158, at 939-40; Selin &. VanDeveer, *supra* note 183, at 7, 14. This is consistent with David Vogel, Trading Up: Consumer and Environmental Regulation in a Global Economy, 5–8 (1995).
200. *See* Kerstin Heitmann & Antonia Reihlen, Techno-Economic Support on REACH: Case Study on "Announcement Effect" in the Market Related to the Candidate List of Substances Subject to Authorisation 5, 9 (2007).
201. Lyndsey Layton, *Chemical Law Has Global Impact*, Wash. Post (June 12, 2008), http://www.washingtonpost.com/wp-dyn/content/article/2008/06/11/AR2008061103569.html (on file with author).
202. *Preservatives*, Johnson & Johnson, https://www.safetyandcarecommitment.com/Ingredients/Preservatives [https://perma.cc/F8QK-TJWX] (last visited May 23, 2019).
203. *Ingredients*, Johnson & Johnson, https://www.safetyandcarecommitment.com/Ingredients [https://perma.cc/UJB4-WDXG] (last visited May 23, 2019).
204. Layton, *supra* note 175.
205. Vogel *supra* note 80, at 169.
206. Risk & Policy Analysts, Insights on the impact of REACH & CLP implementation on industry's strategies in the context of sustainability: Final report prepared for ECHA 22 (2017), https://echa.europa.eu/documents/10162/13637/echa_css_report_without_case_studies_en.pdf/a0a6f46f-16c8-fbea-8b41-9ff683aafe5c [https://perma.cc/Q5DT-GEGC].
207. Vogel, *supra* note 80, at 217.
208. *Your Questions*, L'Oreal, http://www.loreal.com/sustainability/l'or%C3%A9al-answers/product---ingredient-safety/your-questions [https://perma.cc/7RY9-D5M9] (navigate to "Other Ingredient," "Nanomaterials") (last visited May 24, 2019).
209. *Id.*
210. *Id.*
211. Risk & Policy Analysts, Insights on the impact of REACH & CLP Implementation on Industry's Strategies in the Context of Sustainability: Final Report Prepared for ECHA, 21 (2017), https://echa.europa.eu/documents/10162/13637/echa_css_report_without_case_studies_en.pdf/a0a6f46f-16c8-fbea-8b41-9ff683aafe5c [https://perma.cc/Q5DT-GEGC].
212. Brazilian Association of Public Ministry of Environment, "Reach: Legislation to Control the Entry of Chemical Into the EU Already Affects Brazil," Jusbrasil (Mar. 7, 2013), https://abrampa.jusbrasil.com.br/noticias/100381642/reach-legislacao-para-controle-da-entrada-de-produtos-quimicos-na-ue-ja-afeta-brasil?ref=topic_feed [https://perma.cc/U4G6-Q76Z].

213. THE H&M GROUP, ANNUAL REPORT, 2017, 47 (2017).

214. *Chemicals Management*, H&M Group, https://sustainability.hm.com/en/sustainability/ commitments/use-natural-resources-responsibly/chemicals.html [https://perma.cc/ YHN5-Y6PY] (last visited May 24, 2019),

215. H&M Group, SUSTAINABILITY COMMITMENT (2016), https://sustainability.hm.com/ content/dam/hm/about/documents/en/CSR/Sustainability%20Commitment/ Sustainability%20Commitment_en.pdf [https://perma.cc/KW5G-RKGX].

216. VOGEL, *supra* note 80, at 204.

217. VOGEL *supra* note 80, at 217.

218. *See* Mark Schapiro, *New Power for 'Old Europe,'* NATION, Dec. 27, 2004, at 11, 12; *Chemical Spotlight: The Chemical Industry in the United States*, SELECT USA, https:// www.selectusa.gov/chemical-industry-united-states [https://perma.cc/U5Z8-ASJ2] (last visited May 24, 2019).

219. *See* Lyndsey Layton, *supra* note 201.

220. *See, e.g.* Michael Greshko et al., *A Running List of How President Trump is Changing Environmental Policy*, NAT'L GEO., https://news.nationalgeographic.com/2017/03/ how-trump-is-changing-science-environment/ [https://perma.cc/L25Y-9FH3] (last updated May 3, 2019).

221. Eric Lipton, *Why Has the E.P.A. Shifted on Toxic Chemicals? An Industry Insider Helps Call the Shots*, N.Y. TIMES (Oct. 21, 2017), https://www.nytimes.com/2017/10/21/us/ trump-epa-chemicals-regulations.html (on file with author).

222. Eric Lipton, *The E.P.A.'s Top 10 Toxic Threats, and Industry's Pushback*, N.Y. TIMES (Oct. 21, 2017), https://www.nytimes.com/2017/10/21/us/epa-toxic-chemicals.html (on file with author).

223. *Global REACH?*, EUPHOR, (20 June 2017), http://www.euphoreach.com/global-reach/ [https://perma.cc/8KE6-EKWB].

224. *Id.*

225. European Commission Press Release MEMO/06/488, Q and A on the New Chemicals Policy, REACH (Dec. 13, 2006), http://europa.eu/rapid/press-release_MEMO-06-488_en.htm?locale=en [https://perma.cc/A7KB-37T2].

226. Sorin Burnete & Pilasluck Choomta, *The Impact of European Union's Newly-Adopted Environmental Standards on Its Trading Partners*, 10 STUDIES IN BUS. & ECON. 5, 12 (2015).

227. EUROPEAN CHEM. AGENCY, REPORT ON THE OPERATION OF REACH AND CLP 2016, 111 (2016), https://echa.europa.eu/documents/10162/13634/operation_reach_ clp_2016_en.pdf [https://perma.cc/9XH4-KZD3].

228. Katja Biedenkopf, *Chemicals: Pioneering Ambitions with External Effects in* EUROPEAN UNION EXTERNAL ENVIRONMENTAL POLICY: RULES, REGULATION AND GOVERNANCE BEYOND BORDERS 189, 194–96, 199–201 (Camilla Adelle, Katja Biedenkopf & Diarmuid Torney eds., 2018).

229. Biedenkopf, *supra* note 228, at 199–200.

230. *See, e.g.*, Basel Convention on the Control of Transboundary Movements of Hazardous Wastes and Their Disposal, March 22, 1989, 1673 U.N.T.S. 126, 28 I.L.M. 657 (1989) (entered into force May 5, 1992); Rotterdam Convention on the Transboundary Movements of Hazardous Wastes and Their Disposal, 10 Sept., 1998, 2244 U.N.T.S. 337, 38 I.L.M. 1 (1999) (entered into force Feb. 24, 2004); Stockholm Convention on Persistent Organic Pollutants, May 22, 2001, 2256 U.N.T.S. 119, 40 I.L.M. 532 (2001) (entered into force May 17, 2004).

231. *See* Yoshiko Naiki, *Assessing Policy Reach: Japan's Chemical Policy Reform in Response to the EU's REACH Regulation*, 22 J. ENVTL. L. 171, 178 (2010).

232. Scott, *supra* note 158, at 920–28.

233. *Id.* at 914–20.

234. Scott, *supra* note 158, at 914–20.

235. *Id.* at 910–14.

236. Angela Logomasini, *Trust in Government: A Bad Strategy for the Chemical Industry*, COMPETITIVE ENTER. INST. (Apr. 1, 2016), https://cei.org/blog/trust-government-bad-strategy-chemical-industry [https://perma.cc/VL57-BL88]; Jeff Tollefson, *Why the Historic Deal to Expand US Chemical Regulation Matters*, NATURE (May 25, 2016), https://www.nature.com/news/why-the-historic-deal-to-expand-us-chemical-regula-tion-matters-1.19973 [https://perma.cc/U5DT-ZFJS].

237. Katja Biendenkopf, *EU Chemicals Regulation, in* EXTENDING EXPERIMENTALIST GOVERNANCE? THE EUROPEAN UNION AND TRANSNATIONAL REGULATION 107, 130 (Jonathan Zeitlin ed., 2015).

238. *Id.* at 129–35.

239. *Id.* at 127–28.

240. *Id.* at 130.

241. Tollefson, *supra* note 236.

242. *See, e.g.,* Daniel E. Uyesato & Lucas Bergkamp, *Reformed TSCA and REACH: How do They Compare?,* HUNTON, ANDREWS, KURTH (Oct. 23, 2017), https://www.huntonnickelreportblog.com/2017/10/reformed-tsca-and-reach-how-do-they-compare-2/ [https://perma.cc/5CZU-3ZSL].

243. *Id.*

244. *Id.*

245. Ondrej Filipec, *U.S. Chemical Policy Under Review: How Much Europeanisation*, 5 EAST. J. EURO. STUDIES 159, 2 (2014).

246. Biendenkopf, *supra* note 237, at 125.

247. *Id.* at 126.

248. *Id.* at 127.

249. *Id.* at 126.

250. *See, e.g.,* Leslie E. Kersey, Note, *Trans-Atlantic REACH: The Potential Impact of the European Union's New Chemical Regulations on Proof of Causation in U.S. Federal Courts*, 36 B.C. ENVTL. AFF. L. REV. 535 (2009).

251. *Milward v. Acuity Specialty Products Group, Inc.*, 969 F.Supp.2d 101, 105–08 (D. Mass. 2013).

252. Act on Registration and Evaluation, etc. of Chemical Substances (Act No. 11789, Enactment on May 22, 2013, Enforcement on Jan 1, 2015) (화학물질의 등록 및 평가 등에 관한 법률, 법률 제11789호, 2013. 5. 22. 제정, 시행 2015. 1. 1.) [herein-after "K-REACH"], (English full text available at Korean Law Translation Center (한국법제연구원 법령번역센터): http://elaw.klri.re.kr/kor_service/lawView.do?hseq=31605&lang=ENG; *See also, K-REACH Amendment 2019—Live Updates*, CHEM SAFETY PRO, http://www.chemsafetypro.com/Topics/Korea/K-REACH_Amendment.html [https://perma.cc/AUX8-RD8Q] (last updated 10 Mar. 2019).

253. Biendenkopf, *supra* note 237.

254. For example, Articles 10 and 14(1) of K-REACH impose a materially similar disclosure requirement on both importers and manufacturers as Articles 7, 10, and 14 of REACH.

255. *See, e.g., Differences between K-REACH and EU REACH*, CHEMSAFETYPRO (Jan. 31, 2017), http://www.chemsafetypro.com/Topics/Korea/Difference_between_K-REACH_and_EU_REACH.html [https://perma.cc/FH5L-QQFV].

256. *Compare* REACH, *supra* note 155, Art. 7 and K-REACH, *supra* note 252, Art. 10; *see also How to Comply with Amended K-REACH Regulation 2019*, CHEMSAFETYPRO (Dec. 31, 2015), https://www.chemsafetypro.com/Topics/Korea/Korea_REACH.html [https://perma.cc/CSQ6-MBSV] (last updated Sept. 17, 2018).

257. Environmental Safety & Health Association for High Technology, COMPARISON BETWEEN EU REACH, KOREA REACH AND TAIWAN REACH (2013), http://seshaonline.org/meetings/miniNE2013presentations/Aerssens%20-%20REACH%20comparison%20EU,KOREA,TAIWAN.pdf [https://perma.cc/D6ZF-KNF3].

258. *See Registered Substances, supra* note 165.

259. *K-REACH Registration*, CHEMSAFETYPRO (Dec. 31, 2015), https://www.chemsafetypro.com/Topics/Korea/Korea_REACH_Registration.html [https://perma.cc/4K8D-FUZH] (last updated Apr. 19, 2019).

260. Korea Trade-Investment Protection Agency (대한무역투자진흥공사), Global Business Report 07-031, "Local Responses to EU REACH and Implications" ("EU 화학물질등록승인제도(REACH)에 대한 현지 대응사례 및 시사점"), at 6-7, 06 Aug. 2007, http://125.131.31.47/Solars7DMME/004/81000.PDF.

261. Ministry of Environment (대한민국 환경부), Speech by Man-Hee Lee, the former Minister of Environment (환경부 장관 이만의 연설문) "EU REACH's Effect on Korean Trade and Strategies for Response" ("EU 新화학물질제도(REACH)가 무역에 미치는 영향 및 대응방안"), 15 July 2008, http://www.me.go.kr/minister/web/board/read.do;jsessionid=bczpKrcLn7ik4w1iMBTzt248onK6abYmku1ilJXlfrtT2Csa6InRpojtpFFobDra.mewebivhost_servlet_engine1?pagerOffset=210&maxPageItems=10&maxIndexPages=10&searchKey=&searchValue=&menuId=379&orgCd=&boardId=164642&boardMasterId=15&boardCategoryId=&decorator=.

262. *Id.*

263. K-REACH Legislative Comment (화학물질의 등록 및 평가 등에 관한 법률, 제정.개정이유), Korea Ministry of Government Legislation, National Law Information Center (법제처국가법령정보센터) http://www.law.go.kr/LSW/lsRvsRsnListP.do?lsId=011857&chrClsCd=010102 [https://perma.cc/N59E-KNLM]

264. *Enactment of Act Concerning Registration, Evaluation, etc. of Chemical Substances*, MINISTRY OF THE ENVIRONMENT (Oct. 29, 2013), http://eng.me.go.kr/eng/web/index.do?menuId=167 [https://perma.cc/PKL9-6AQG].

265. Yoshiko Naiki, *Assessing Policy Reach: Japan's Chemical Policy Reform in Response to the EU's REACH Regulation*, 22 J. ENVIRON. L. 171, 191. (2010).

266. The Act on the Evaluation of Chemical Substances and Regulation of Their Manufacture (Kagakubushitu Shinsa Kisei Hou), Act No.117 of 16 October 1973 (as revised by Act No. 39 of May 20, 2009).

267. Naiki, *supra* note 265, at 187.

268. *Id.* at 186–87.

269. *Id.* at 186.

270. *Id.* at 192

271. Katja Biedenkopf & Dae Young Park, *A Toxic Issue?: Leadership in Comprehensive Chemicals Management*, *in* ENVIRONMENTAL LEADERSHIP: A REFERENCE HANDBOOK, 782, 792–93 (Deborah Rigling Gallagher ed., 2012).

272. *Id.* at 793.

273. *Id.*

274. *Id.*

275. *The Strictest Standard by EU Now Put China Produced Toys in the "Desperate Position"?* CIF NEWS (July 22, 2013), http://www.cifnews.com/article/3552 [https://perma.cc/ZXR5-W2TW]; Chen Yu, *Four Mandatory National Standards for the Safety of Children's Toys*, CHINA ECON. NET (May 30, 2014), http://www.ce.cn/cysc/zljd/xfp/201405/30/t20140530_2898420.shtml [https://perma.cc/55P4-JEZ3].

276. Huo Yifu, *The Standard Outline of the "Children's Mat Safety Requirements" is Published in Shanghai*, CHINA QUALITY NEWS NETWORK (Oct. 27, 2017), http://www.cqn.com.cn/zgzlb/content/2017-10/27/content_5032161.htm [https://perma.cc/TXW9-L835].

277. *Id.*

278. Zhou Huiyan, *The New Standard for Floor Mats is Expected to be Released Next Year*, Xinmin Newspaper (Oct. 20, 2017), http://shanghai.xinmin.cn/msrx/2017/10/20/31326884.html [https://perma.cc/5FW5-B8R6].

CHAPTER 7

1. *Index of Legislation, in Manual of European Environmental Policy*, IEEP (2012), https://ieep.eu/publications/2014/10/forthcoming-policy-and-index[https://perma.cc/M85A-WWTC].

2. Diarmuid Torney, European Climate Leadership in Question: Policies Toward China and India 36 (2015).

3. Yumiko Nakanishi, *Introduction: The Impact of the International and European Union Environmental Law on Japanese Basic Environmental Law, in* Contemporary Issues in Environmental Law: The EU and Japan 1, 4 (Yumiko Nakanishi ed., 2016).

4. Jerry McBeath & Jonathan Rosenberg, Comparative Environmental Politics 3 (2006).

5. Treaty on European Union (Maastricht text) art. 130r, July 29, 1992, 1992 O.J. (C 191) 1, 28-29; *Id.* art. 2, at 5.

6. Treaty of Amsterdam Amending the Treaty on European Union, the Treaties Establishing the European Communities and Certain Related Acts art. 3c, Oct. 2, 1997, 1997 O.J. (C 340) 1, 25.

7. Treaty of Lisbon Amending the Treaty on European Union and the Treaty Establishing the European Community art. 174, Dec. 13, 2007, 2007, O.J. (C 306) 1, 87.

8. *Id.* art. 10A, at 1, 23-24.

9. Suzanne Kingston et al., European Environmental Law 70–71 (2017).

10. Case C-176/03, Comm'n v. Council, 2005 E.C.R. I-07879.

11. Case C-441/17 R, Comm'n v. Poland, EUR-Lex 62017CO0441(02) (Nov. 20, 2017).

12. *See* Directive 2002/95/EC, of the European Parliament and of the Council of 27 January 2003 on the Restriction of the Use of Certain Hazardous Substances in Electrical and Electronic Equipment, 2003 O.J. (L 37) 19.

13. *See id.*

14. Directive 2011/65/EU, of the European Parliament and of the Council of 8 June 2011 on the Restriction of the Use of Certain Hazardous Substances in Electrical and Electronic Equipment, 2011 O.J. (L 174) 88.

15. Directive 2012/19/EU, of the European Parliament and of the Council of 4 July 2012 on Waste Electrical and Electronic Equipment (WEEE), 2012 O.J. (L 197) 38.

16. Katja Biedenkopf, *The Multilevel Dynamics of EU and U.S. Environmental Policy: A Case Study of Electronic Waste, in* L'Union Européenne et les États-Unis: Processus, Politiques et Projets 189, 192 (Yann Echinard et al. eds., 2013).

17. *Id.*

18. Council Directive 74/577/EEC, of 18 November 1974 on Stunning of Animals Before Slaughter, 1974 O.J. (L 316) 10.

19. *Id.* The "Five Freedoms" consist of: (1) Freedom from hunger and thirst; (2) Freedom from discomfort; (3) Freedom from pain, injury, and disease; (4) Freedom to express normal behavior; and (5) Freedom from fear and distress.

20. *40 Years of Animal Welfare*, Eur. Commission, https://ec.europa.eu/food/sites/food/files/animals/docs/aw_infograph_40-years-of-aw.pdf (last visited Feb. 7, 2019) [https://perma.cc/V93D-W94S]; Consolidated Version of the Treaty on the Functioning of the European Union art. 12, Mar. 30, 2010, 2010 O.J. (C 83) 47, 54.

21. *EU Animal Welfare Strategy: 2012-2015*, EUR. COMMISSION (2012), https://ec.europa. eu/food/sites/food/files/animals/docs/aw_brochure_strategy_en.pdf [https://perma. cc/3VSC-JJLX].

22. *Milestones in Improving Animal Welfare*, EUR. COMMISSION (2012), https://ec.europa. eu/food/sites/food/files/animals/docs/aw_infograph_milestones_en.pdf [https://perma. cc/33C9-GHUV].

23. *The EU Emissions Trading System (EU ETS) Factsheet*, EUR. COMMISSION (2016), https://ec.europa.eu/clima/sites/clima/files/factsheet_ets_en.pdf[https://perma. cc/7TQ9-CFJN].

24. TORNEY, *supra* note 2, at 39.

25. *Id.*

26. *Id.* at 12.

27. MCBEATH & ROSENBERG, *supra* note 4, at 58.

28. ATLAS OF EUROPEAN VALUES: TRENDS AND TRADITIONS AT THE TURN OF THE CENTURY 119 (Loek Halman, Inge Sieben & Marga van Zundert eds., 2011).

29. Didier Bourguignon & Nicole Scholz, *Chernobyl 30 Years on: Environmental and Health Effects*, EUR. PARLIAMENT: THINK TANK (Mar. 22, 2016), http://www.europarl.europa. eu/thinktank/en/document.html?reference=EPRS_BRI(2016)581972 [https://perma. cc/D3BZ-EHRV].

30. *Introduction to Acid Rain*, ENVIROPEDIA, http://www.enviropedia.org.uk/Acid_ Rain/Acid_Rain_Introduction.php (last visited Jan. 30, 2019) [https://perma. cc/8DCV-MJBT].

31. R. Daniel Keleman, *Globalizing European Union Environmental Policy*, 17 J. EUR. PUB. POL'Y 335, 340 (2010) (citing Jürgen Hofrichter & Karlheinz Reif, *Evolution of Environmental Attitudes in the European Community*, 13 SCANDINAVIAN POL. STUD. 119 (1990)).

32. European Comm'n, Report, *Special Eurobarometer 468: Attitudes of European Citizens Towards the Environment*, OPEN DATA PORTAL 5 (Nov. 2017), http://ec.europa.eu/ commfrontoffice/publicopinion/index.cfm/ResultDoc/download/DocumentKy/81259 [hereinafter *Special Eurobarometer 468*] [https://perma.cc/WV7A-J7RP].

33. European Comm'n, Report, *Special Eurobarometer 459: Climate Change*, OPEN DATA PORTAL 5 (Sept. 2017), https://ec.europa.eu/clima/sites/clima/files/support/docs/ report_2017_en.pdf [hereinafter *Special Eurobarometer 459*] [https://perma.cc/ B6MV-9G4B].

34. *Id.*

35. *Special Eurobarometer 468, supra* note 32, at 5–6.

36. *Id.* at 6.

37. *Special Eurobarometer 459, supra* note 33.

38. Bruce Stokes et al., *Global Concern About Climate Change, Broad Support for Limiting Emissions: U.S., China Less Worried; Partisan Divides in Key Countries*, PEW RES. CENTER 24 (Nov. 5, 2015), http://www.pewresearch.org/wp-content/uploads/sites/2/2015/11/ Pew-Research-Center-Climate-Change-Report-FINAL-November-5-2015.pdf [https:// perma.cc/7NTG-SVXQ].

39. Keleman, *supra* note 31, at 340.

40. TORNEY, *supra* note 2, at 39–40.

41. *Id.*

42. Javier Delgado-Ceballos et al., *Environmental Nongovernmental Organization Coalitions: How the Green 10 Influences European Union Institutions, in* ENVIRONMENTAL LEADERSHIP: A REFERENCE HANDBOOK 254 (Deborah Rigling Gallagher ed., 2012).

43. TOM DELREUX & SANDRA HAPPAERTS, ENVIRONMENTAL POLICY AND POLITICS IN THE EUROPEAN UNION 133 (2016).

44. Delgado-Ceballos et al., *supra* note 42, at 258–59. *See also* for details on each group: DELREUX & HAPPAERTS, *supra* note 43, at 130–32.

45. Delgado-Ceballos et al., *supra* note 42, at 259–62.

46. David Coen, *Environmental and Business Lobbying Alliances in Europe: Learning from Washington?, in* THE BUSINESS OF GLOBAL ENVIRONMENTAL GOVERNANCE 197, 209 (David Levy & Peter J. Newell eds., 2005).

47. Ludwig Krämer, *Environmental Governance in the EU, in* ENVIRONMENTAL PROTECTION IN MULTI-LAYERED SYSTEMS: COMPARATIVE LESSONS FROM THE WATER SECTOR 11, 23–24 (Mariachiara Alberton & Francesco Palermo eds., 2012).

48. DELREUX & HAPPAERTS, *supra* note 43, at 135.

49. Biedenkopf, *supra* note 16, at 203.

50. KINGSTON ET. AL, *supra* note 9, at 27–28.

51. DELREUX & HAPPAERTS, *supra* note 43, at 244.

52. Press Release, European Comm'n, Energy Union: Commission Takes Action to Reinforce EU's Global Leadership in Clean Vehicles (Nov. 8, 2017), http://europa.eu/rapid/press-release_IP-17-4242_en.htm [https://perma.cc/4M6U-EPB7].

53. Keleman, *supra* note 31, at 343.

54. Press Release, European Comm'n, Speech by Commissioner Arias Cañete at the Brussels Europe Power Market Event (Oct. 24, 2016), http://europa.eu/rapid/press-release_SPEECH-16-3526_en.htm [https://perma.cc/8BSG-T24Q].

55. Keleman, *supra* note 31.

56. Press Release, European Comm'n, Environment: Fewer Risks from Hazardous Substances in Electrical and Electronic Equipment (July 20, 2011), http://europa.eu/rapid/press-release_IP-11-912_en.htm [https://perma.cc/4ZW9-UH52]; Otto Pohl, *European Environmental Rules Propel Change in U.S.*, N.Y. TIMES, July 6, 2004, at F4.

57. *RoHS Compliance / Lead Free*, FUJITSU, http://www.fujitsu.com/us/about/local/corporate/subsidiaries/fcai/rohs/ (last visited Jan. 31, 2019) [https://perma.cc/57GD-QFNT]; *Oracle Global Position on Restriction of Hazardous Substances (RoHS)*, ORACLE, http://www.oracle.com/us/products/applications/green/rohs-position-185078.pdf (last visited Jan. 31, 2019) [https://perma.cc/AH65-Q5KY].

58. Katja Biedenkopf, E-Waste Governance Beyond Borders—Does the EU Influence US Environmental Policy? 15 (2010) (unpublished manuscript), https://refubium.fu-berlin.de/bitstream/handle/fub188/19456/Biedenkopf-E-Waste_Governance_beyond_Borders-445.pdf?sequence=1&isAllowed=y [https://perma.cc/HX6P-ERHK].

59. *Id.*

60. Hiawatha Bray, *Tech Firms Face EU Toxics Test: Limits on the Use of Hazardous Materials Pushes US Electronics Makers to Innovate*, BOSTON GLOBE (June 1, 2006), http://archive.boston.com/business/technology/articles/2006/06/01/tech_firms_face_eu_toxics_test/ [https://perma.cc/K5EQ-DZHA].

61. *Id.*

62. *Id.*

63. *The Impact of RoHS—Now and In the Future*, HKTDC (July 1, 2008), http://info.hktdc.com/productsafety/200807/psl_ele_080701.htm [https://perma.cc/V2UP-GBE4].

64. KATJA BIEDENKOPF, INSTITUTE FOR EUROPEAN STUDIES, POLICY RECYCLING? THE EXTERNAL EFFECTS OF EU ENVIRONMENTAL LEGISLATION ON THE UNITED STATES, 241 (2011).

65. *Id.*

66. *Id.*

67. *Hitachi Group to Eliminate 6 Chemical Substances Targeted in RoHS by March 2005 Shifting to Lead-Free Solder by March 2004 in Japan and by March 2005 Worldwide,*

HITACHI (Dec. 1, 2003), http://www.hitachi.com/New/cnews/031201.html [https://perma.cc/N5TA-NANJ].

68. *Id.*

69. *Top 15 Semiconductor Sales Leaders—2018F,* ANYSILICON (Nov. 12, 2018), https://anysilicon.com/top-15-semiconductor-sales-leaders-2018f/ [https://perma.cc/8VB5-6LPS].

70. *Corporate Social Responsibility Report,* TSMC 48 (2017), https://www.tsmc.com/download/csr/2018_tsmc_csr/english/pdf/e_all.pdf [https://perma.cc/FN3K-MNKM].

71. MediaTek is a fabless semiconductor company that provides system-on-chip solutions for wireless communications, HDTV, DVD and Blu-ray, and cell phone. CORPORATE SOCIAL RESPONSIBILITY REPORT, MEDIATEK 139 (2015), https://d8602zu8ugzlg.cloudfront.net/mediatek-craft/reports/CSR/2015-MediaTek-Corporate-Sustainability-Report-Final.pdf (last visited Feb. 7, 2017) [https://perma.cc/E6VX-M4EA].

72. *Overcome ROHS, EU's First Environmental Regulation,* SCI. TIMES (June 6, 2016), http://www.sciencetimes.co.kr/?news=eu%EC%9D%98-%EC%B2%AB-%ED%99%98%EA%B2%BD%EA%B7%9C%EC%A0%9C-rohs%EB%A5%BC-%EB%84%98%EC%96%B4%EB%9D%BC [https://perma.cc/N6W4-V5RS].

73. *Id.*

74. *EU RoHS II (Restriction of Hazardous Substances Directive),* SAMSUNG, https://www.samsung.com/semiconductor/about-us/global-compliance/ (last visited June 3, 2019) [https://perma.cc/ZM4T-YC2Z].

75. Justin McCurry, *Cosmetics Testing: Will Japan Go Cruelty-Free?,* JAPAN TODAY (Oct. 26, 2015), https://japantoday.com/category/features/lifestyle/cosmetics-testing-will-japan-go-cruelty-free [https://perma.cc/A77C-HBPV].

76. *Cosmetics Industry,* COSMETICS EUR., https://www.cosmeticseurope.eu/cosmetics-industry/ (last visited Feb. 8, 2019) [https://perma.cc/X6TK-9GL8].

77. *See Id.*

78. *Id.*

79. David Bach & Abraham L. Newman, *Governing Lipitor and Lipstick: Capacity, Sequencing, and Power in International Pharmaceutical and Cosmetics Regulation,* 17 REV. INT'L POL. ECON 665, 685 (2010).

80. *Id.* at 688.

81. *Shiseido to Abolish Testing Cosmetics on Animals,* JAPAN TIMES (Mar. 2, 2013), https://www.japantimes.co.jp/news/2013/03/02/business/corporate-business/shiseido-to-abolish-testing-cosmetics-on-animals/#.WtO-hq3MzBI [https://perma.cc/QPC6-8PRT].

82. Koa, including Biore, Curel, and Nivea products, halted animal testing in 2015. *Kao Group Confirms Its Policy of "Neither Conducting Nor Outsourcing Animal Testing in Cosmetics,"* ANIMAL RTS. CENTER (June 25, 2015), http://www.arcj.org/en/animals/animaltesting/00/id=608 [https://perma.cc/NDJ7-MHMB]. Kose issued a similar statement in 2014. *Kose Group Promotes Alternatives to Animal Testing,* BEAUTY PACKAGING (Oct. 16, 2014), https://www.beautypackaging.com/contents/view_breaking-news/2014-10-16/kose-group-promotes-alternatives-to-animal-testing/ [https://perma.cc/4SS7-2BTF].

83. *Japan Cosmetics Makers Win OECD Approval for Animal Testing Alternative,* NIKKEI ASIAN REV. (Nov. 2, 2016), https://asia.nikkei.com/Business/Science/Japan-cosmetics-makers-win-OECD-approval-for-animal-testing-alternative [https://perma.cc/YP7X-X3WC].

84. McCurry, *supra* note 75.

85. *Guidelines for Supplier's Assessment,* KAO, https://www.kao.com/global/en/sustainability/procurement/supplier-guidelines/ (last visited Jan. 31, 2019) [https://perma.cc/C343-MA5M].

86. Sophia Yan, *In China, Big Cosmetics Firms are Selling Products Tested on Animals,* CNBC (Apr. 19, 2017), https://www.cnbc.com/2017/04/19/in-china-big-cosmetics-firms-are-selling-products-tested-on-animals.html [https://perma.cc/8FEB-5EPK].

87. Email Correspondence with Shiseido Customer Care Team (Mar.–Apr. 2018) (on file with author).

88. Case C-592/14 European Federation for Cosmetic Ingredients v. UK Secretary of State for Business, EUR-Lex 62014CJ0592 (Sept. 21, 2016), paras. 12–14.

89. *Id.*

90. *Id.* paras. 43, 45.

91. Humane Soc'y Int'l (June 30, 2014), http://www.hsi.org/news/press_releases/2014/06/china-implements-rule-change-063014.html [https://perma.cc/M93W-A4XC].

92. *Report from the Commission to the European Parliament and the Council on the Impact of Animal Welfare International Activities on the Competitiveness of European Livestock Producers in a Globalized World*, at 9, COM (2018) 42 final (Jan. 26, 2018).

93. Cleandro Pazinato Dias et al., The Brazilian Pig Industry Can Adopt European Welfare Standards: A Critical Analysis, 45 Ciência Rural 1079, 1081 (2015).

94. *Id.* at 1085.

95. Council Directive 93/119/EC, of 22 December 1993 on the Protection of Animals at the Time of Slaughter or Killing, 1993 O.J. (L 340) 21.

96. *Id.* art. 5(1)(c).

97. James Moynagh, *EU Regulation and Consumer Demand for Animal Welfare*, 3 AgBioForum 107, 110 (2000).

98. European Parliament Directorate-General for Internal Policies, *Animal Welfare in the European Union*, Eur. Parliament 32 (Jan. 2017), http://www.europarl.europa.eu/RegData/etudes/STUD/2017/583114/IPOL_STU(2017)583114_EN.pdf [https://perma.cc/K4WE-2B8Y]; *see also Beef—Market Report*, Gov't Can., https://web.archive.org/web/20180807135043/http://www.canadainternational.gc.ca/eu-ue/policies-politiques/reports_beef-boeuf_rapports.aspx?lang=eng (last modified Feb. 4, 2014).

99. Directive 97/2/EC first phased out the use of veal crates and regulated the diets of calves, and was replaced by Council Directive 2008/119/EEC, of 18 December 2008. Council Directive 97/2/EC, 1997 O.J. (L 25) 24; Council Directive 2008/119/EC, 2009 O.J. (L 10) 7.

100. *HSUS Report: The Welfare of Animals in the Veal Industry*, Humane Soc'y 8–12 (July, 2012), http://www.humanesociety.org/sites/default/files/archive/assets/pdfs/farm/hsus-the-welfare-of-animals-in-the-veal-industry-b.pdf [hereinafter *HSUS Report*] [https://perma.cc/P8X6-6Y6V]. *See also* Am. Veterinary Med. Ass'n., *Literature Review on the Welfare Implications of the Veal Calf Husbandry*, AVMA (Oct. 13, 2008), https://www.avma.org/KB/Resources/LiteratureReviews/Pages/Welfare-Implications-of-the-Veal-Calf-Husbandry-Backgrounder.aspx [https://perma.cc/E4L2-PWGH].

101. *HSUS Report, supra* note 100, at 1.

102. *Id.* at 2. Arizona legislated 2006, in effect 2012; Colorado 2008, effective 2012; California effective 2015; Maine legislated 2009; Michigan legislated 2009; Ohio legislated 2010, Rhode Island legislated 2012.

103. *Id.* at 2; Animal Care & Housing, Am. Veal Ass'n, http://www.americanveal.com/animal-care-housing/ (last visited Feb. 8, 2019) [https://perma.cc/JGS9-X9WP].

104. *HSUS Report, supra* note 100, at 2.

105. *Id.* at 14.

106. Council Directive 2007/43/EC, 2007 O.J. (L 182) 19.

107. *Poultry Welfare: Matching the New EU Regulatory Framework*, DELACON Dossier 5 (2011), https://www.delacon.com/download/?file=89 [https://perma.cc/U85K-PPMU].

108. European Parliament Directorate-General for Internal Policies, *supra* note 98, at 31.

109. Council Regulation (EC) No. 1/2005 of 22 December 2004 on the Protection of Animals During Transport and Related Operations and Amending Directives 64/432/ EEC and 93/119/EC and Regulation (EC) No 1255/97, 2005 O.J. (L 3) 1.

110. Case C-424/13, Zuchtvieh-Export GmbH v. Stadt Kempten, EUR-Lex 62013CJ0424 (Apr. 23, 2015).

111. David Mahoney, *Zuchtvieh-Export GmbH v. Stadt Kempten: The Tension Between Uniform, Cross-Border Regulation and Territorial Sovereignty*, 40 B.C. INT'L & COMP. L. REV. 363, 364–66, 371 (2017).

112. Clair Gammage, *A Critique of the Extraterritorial Obligations of the EU in Relation to Human Rights Clauses and Social Norms in EU Free Trade Agreements*, EUR. & WORLD, Oct. 10, 2018, at 12.

113. Joanne Scott, *Extraterritoriality and Territorial Extension in EU Law*, 62 AM. J. COMP. L. 87

114. *Id.* at 89.

115. Directive 2003/87/EC, of the European Parliament and of the Council of 13 October 2003 Establishing a Scheme for Greenhouse Gas Emission Allowance Trading Within the Community and Amending Council Directive 96/61/EC, 2003 O.J. (L 275) 32 [hereinafter Directive 2003/87/EC].

116. *See* Directive 2008/101/EC, of the European Parliament and of the Council of 19 November 2008 Amending Directive 2003/87/EC So as to Include Aviation Activities in the Scheme for Greenhouse Gas Emission Allowance Trading Within the Community, 2009 O.J. (L 8) 3 [hereinafter Directive 2008/101/EC].

117. Kati Kulovesi, *Climate Change in EU External Relations: Please Follow My Example (or I Might Force You to)*, *in* THE ETERNAL ENVIRONMENTAL POLICY OF THE EUROPEAN UNION: EU AND INTERNATIONAL LAW PERSPECTIVES 115, 117 (Elisa Morgera ed., 2012); DELREUX & HAPPAERTS, *supra* note 43, at 246.

118. Kulovesi, *supra* note 117.

119. *The European Union's Emissions Trading Scheme: A Violation of International Law: Hearing Before the Subcomm. on Aviation of the H. Comm. on Transp. & Infrastructure*, 112th Cong. 34-36 (2011) (statement of Hon. Nancy N. Young, vice president of Environmental Affairs, Air Transport Association of America, Inc.).

120. *Id.* at 4–5.

121. *See* Directive 2008/101/EC, *supra* note 116, ¶17; *see also* Joanne Scott & Lavanya Rajamani, *EU Climate Change Unilateralism*, 23 EUR. J. INT'L L. 469, 482-83 (2012).

122. *See* Scott & Rajamani, *supra* note 121, at 475.

123. *Id.*

124. *See* Case C-366/10, Air Transp. Ass'n of Am. v. Sec'y of State for Energy & Climate Change, EUR-Lex 62010CJ0366 (Dec. 21, 2011).

125. *See US Aviation Sector Finally Challenges EU Emissions Scheme*, CAPA (July 6, 2011), https://centreforaviation.com/analysis/reports/us-aviation-sector-finally-challenges-eu-emissions-scheme-54825 [https://perma.cc/D9U9-LP5D]. According to the plaintiffs, the ETS Directive violates a number of international agreements, including the Convention on International Civil Aviation (Chicago Convention), the Kyoto Protocol to the United Nations Framework Convention on Climate Change, and the Air Transport Agreement between the United States and the EU and its member states (Open Skies Agreement).

126. Press Release No. 139/11, Court of Justice of the European Union, The Directive Including Aviation Activities in the EU's Emissions Trading Scheme is Valid 2 (Dec. 21, 2011), http://curia.europa.eu/jcms/upload/docs/application/pdf/2011-12/cp110139en.pdf [https://perma.cc/DWP9-WCMR].

127. Kulovesi, *supra* note 117, at 143; TORNEY, *supra* note 2, at 134.

128. TORNEY, *supra* note 2, at 134; DELREUX & HAPPAERTS, *supra* note 43, at 215.

129. TORNEY, *supra* note 2, at 134.

130. *Id.* at 158.

131. *Id.* at 134.

132. DELREUX & HAPPAERTS, *supra* note 43, at 215.

133. *Historic Agreement Reached to Mitigate International Aviation Emissions*, ICAO (Oct. 6, 2016), https://www.icao.int/Newsroom/Pages/Historic-agreement-reached-to-mitigate-international-aviation-emissions.aspx [https://perma.cc/LUW2-Q2UC].

134. *Id.*

135. *ICAO Council Adopts New CO2 Emissions Standard for Aircraft*, ICAO (Mar. 6, 2017), https://www.icao.int/Newsroom/Pages/ICAO-Council-adopts-new-CO2-emissions-standard-for-aircraft.aspx [https://perma.cc/G6RJ-VTDW].

136. *Reducing Emissions from Aviation*, EUR. COMMISSION (Nov. 23, 2017), https://ec.europa.eu/clima/policies/transport/aviation_en#tab-0-0 [https://perma.cc/ZKK6-5LLW]; *See also* Regulation (EU) 2017/2392, of the European Parliament and of the Council of 13 December 2017 Amending Directive 2003/87/EC to Continue Current Limitations of Scope for Aviation Activities and to Prepare to Implement a Global Market-Based Measure from 2021, 2017 O.J. (L 350) 7.

137. Janina Scheelhaase et. al, *EU ETS Versus CORSIA—A Critical Assessment of Two Approaches to Limit Air Transport's CO2 Emissions by Market-Based Measures*, 67 J. AIR TRANSPORT MGMT. 55, 58 (2018).

138. European Parliament, *Environmental Policy: General Principles and Basic Framework*, FACT SHEETS ON EUR. UNION, http://www.europarl.europa.eu/factsheets/en/sheet/71/environment-policy-general-principles-and-basic-framework [https://perma.cc/3KZT-R4M4].

139. Biedenkopf, *supra* note 16, at 194.

140. *Id.*

141. *Proposal for a Directive of the European Parliament and of the Council Amending Directive 2011/65/EU on the Restriction of the Use of Certain Hazardous Substances in Electrical and Electronic Equipment*, at 2, COM (2017) 38 final (Jan. 26, 2017). *See also*, Henrik Selin & Stacy D. VanDeveer, *Raising Global Standards: Hazardous Substances and E-Waste Management in the European Union*, ENVIRONMENT, Dec. 2006, at 6, 14–15.

142. Biedenkopf, *supra* note 16, at 194.

143. *Id.* at 194–95.

144. *Id.* at 202.

145. The United States introduced federal legislation that would amend the Toxic Substances Control Act of 1976 to establish uniform national standards similar to RoHS in 2009 in the Environmental Design of Electrical Equipment Act (EDEE Act), but that bill did not leave the subcommittee. Environmental Design of Electrical Equipment Act (EDEE) Act, H.R. 2420, 111th Cong. (2009).

146. CAL. HEALTH & SAFETY CODE §§ 25214.9–.10.2 (West 2003); *see also* Restrictions on the Use of Certain Hazardous Substances (RoHS) in Electronic Devices, CAL. DEPARTMENT TOXIC SUBSTANCES CONTROL, https://dtsc.ca.gov/restrictions-on-the-use-of-certain-hazardous-substances-rohs-in-electronic-devices/ (last visited Feb. 1, 2017) [hereinafter *What is RoHS*] [https://perma.cc/8YV9-58F9].

147. On September 23, 2003 the California Electronic Waste Recycling Act of 2003 was signed into law. CAL. PUB. RES. CODE §§ 42460-42486 (West 2004) The Electronic Waste Recycling Act establishes a specialized program for recycling such devices by charging consumers a fee upon purchase. See *E-Waste More Information*, CAL. DEPARTMENT TOXIC SUBSTANCES CONTROL, https://dtsc.ca.gov/

ewaste/e-waste-more-information/ (last visited Feb. 1, 2019) [hereinafter *E-Waste More Information*] [https://perma.cc/2LEA-MWCW].

148. *What is RoHS, supra* note 146.

149. *See* Cal. Pub. Res. Code, *supra* note 147. The EU's RoHS Directive is referenced in § 42465.2(b).

150. *How Do the California Restrictions on the Use of Certain Hazardous Substances (RoHS) Law and Regulations Compare to the European Union's RoHS Directive?*, Cal. Department Toxic Substances Control, https://dtsc.ca.gov/how-do-the-california-restrictions-on-the-use-of-certain-hazardous-substances-rohs-law-and-regulations-compare-to-the-european-unions-rohs-directive/ (last visited Feb. 1, 2019) (emphasis in original) [hereinafter *How Does the California RoHS Compare to the EU RoHS?*] [https://perma.cc/4ZZT-MB9Y]. For more on how the EU influenced California, see Biendekopf, *supra* note 64, at 248–55.

151. *See* Cal. Pub. Res. Code, *supra* note 147, at §§ 42463, 42465.2(b); Cal. Health & Safety Code § 25214.10(b) (West 2006); Joanne Scott, *From Brussels with Love: The Transatlantic Travels of European Law and the Chemistry of Regulatory Attraction*, 57 Am. J. Comp. L. 897, 942 (2009).

152. *How Does the California RoHS Compare to the EU RoHS?, supra* note 150.

153. *Covered Electronic Devices*, Cal. Department Toxic Substances Control, https://dtsc.ca.gov/covered-electronic-devices/ (last visited Feb. 1, 2019) [https://perma.cc/Y2DA-AR9B]; Cal. Health & Safety Code, *supra* note 151, § 25214.10.1(a)(1); *E-Waste More Information, supra* note 147.

154. *See* Biedenkopf, *supra* note 58, at 13.

155. *Id.* at 14.

156. S. 981, 217th Leg., Reg. Sess. (N.J. 2016); *See also* State of N.J. Dep't of Envtl. Protection Div. of Solid & Hazardous Waste, E-Cycle N.J., http://www.state.nj.us/dep/dshw/ewaste/ (last visited Feb. 1, 2019) [https://perma.cc/P99H-ZY62].

157. Ind. Code Ann. § 13-20.5-1-1 (c)(6)(A)(ii) (LexisNexis 2017).

158. H.R. 854, 85th Leg., Reg. Sess., at 2(b)(1) (Minn. 2007).

159. 415 Ill. Comp. Stat. Ann. 150/30 §30(a) (LexisNexis 2009).

160. N.Y. Envtl. Conserv. Law §27-2605(1)(f) x (Consol. 2010).

161. *E-Waste*, NYPSC, http://nypsc.org/e-waste/ (last visited Feb. 1, 2019) [https://perma.cc/67L3-9K4Q].

162. Nat'l Inst. of Standards & Tech., *Compliance FAQs: RoHS*, Standards.Gov, https://www.nist.gov/standardsgov/compliance-faqs-rohs (last visited Feb. 1, 2019) [https://perma.cc/54NW-VNBQ].

163. *Restriction of Hazardous Substances*, SGS, https://www.sgs.com/-/media/global/documents/brochures/sgs-cts-ee-global-rohs-brochure-a4-en-10-web.pdf (last visited Feb. 1, 2019) [https://perma.cc/3VCV-XHPW]; *see also* Sorin Burnete & Pilasluck Choomta, *The Impact of European Union's Newly-Adopted Environmental Standards on Its Trading Partners*, 10 Stud. Bus. & Econ. 5, 11 (2015).

164. Burnete & Choomta, *supra* note 163; *Global Regulation of Substances in Electronics*, ChemicalWatch,(Mar. 2013), https://chemicalwatch.com/14164/global-regulation-of-substances-in-electronics (on file with author); *Substance Regulations RoHS and REACH Continue to Expand Globally and Undergo Restriction Updates*, 3BLMEDIA (Aug. 1, 2016), https://www.3blmedia.com/News/Substance-Regulations-RoHS-and-REACH-Continue-Expand-Globally-and-Undergo-Restriction-Updates [https://perma.cc/YB42-TPD8].

165. Burnete & Choomta, *supra* note 163.

166. Directive 2000/53/EC, of the European Parliament and of the Council of 18 September 2000 on End-of Life Vehicles, 2000 O.J. (L 269) 34.

167. *End of Life Vehicles*, Eur. Commission, http://ec.europa.eu/environment/waste/elv/index.htm (last visited Jan. 10, 2018) [https://perma.cc/K3Q6-CTB7].

168. *See* Act on the Recycling of Electrical and Electronic Equipment and Vehicles, Act. No. 8405, enacted on Apr. 27, 2007, enforced on Jan. 1, 2008, , *as amended* (S. Kor.) (전기 · 전자제품 및 자동차의 자원순환에 관한 법률, 법률 제 8405호, 2007.4.27 제정, 2008.1.1 시행). For English summary of the law, see *Korea RoHS/ELV/WEE*, ChemSafetyPro, http://www.chemsafetypro.com/Topics/Korea/Korea_RoHS_WEEE.html (last updated Mar. 2019) [https://perma.cc/D7J5-NMJF].

169. Legislative Comment to Act on the Recycling of Electrical and Electronic Equipment and Vehicles (Act No. 8405, enacted on Apr. 27, 2007, enforced on Jan. 1, 2008, *as amended* (S. Kor.) (전기 · 전자제품 및 자동차의 자원순환에 관한 법률 제정이유, 법률 제 8405호, 2007.4.27 제정, 2008.1.1 시행), Korea Ministry of Government Legislation, National Law Information Center (법제처 국가법령정보센터), http://www.law.go.kr/LSW//lsInfoP.do?lsiSeq=78830&ancYd=20070427&ancNo=08405&efYd=20080101&nwJoYnInfo=N&efGubun=Y&chrClsCd=010202#0000 [https://perma.cc/HC49-DYEY]

170. *ECO-Assurance System*, APEC-VC Korea (July 15, 2016), http://img.konetic.or.kr/apec-vc/xml/img/envdb/16Data-36_ECO-Assurance_System_.pdf [https://perma.cc/59FN-CQMV]. *See also*, Eco-Assurance System for Electrical and Electronic Equipment and Vehicles ("*EcoAs*") (환경성보장제 (EcoAs)), Korea Env't. Corp. (한국환경공단), http://www.ecoas.or.kr/user/system/about.eco (last visited Aug. 5, 2019) [https://perma.cc/J7S2-UE87].

171. *Recycling Policy*, MoE, http://eng.me.go.kr/eng/web/index.do?menuId=143 (last visited Jan. 10, 2018) [https://perma.cc/MS7P-6P2A].

172. *EcoAs, supra* note 170.

173. *Id.*

174. Joon Rae Kim (김준래), *Re-Use of Resources Increases Competitiveness of Manufactures* (폐자원 활용이 제조사 경쟁력 높인다), Sci. Times Korea (Nov. 26, 2014), https://www.sciencetimes.co.kr/?p=130663&cat=40&post_type=news&paged=122 (last accessed Aug 5, 2019) [https://perma.cc/Z5YA-QVR4].

175. John Quick, *Manufacturing Environmental Laws, Directives, and Challenges*, in Handbook of Fiber Optic Data Communication: A Practical Guide to Optical Networking 157 (Casimer DeCusatis ed., 4th ed. 2013).

176. *Id.*

177. Gary Nevison, *Japanese "RoHS" Marking Requirements*, Element14 (July 15, 2010), https://www.element14.com/community/docs/DOC-23360/l/japanese-rohs-marking-requirements (on file with author).

178. Yoshiko Naiki, *Assessing Policy Reach: Japan's Chemical Policy Reform in Response to the EU's REACH Regulation*, 22 J. Environ. L. 171, 182 (2010).

179. See comparative chart in *China RoHS 2 2019*, ChemSafetyPro (Jan. 1, 2016), http://www.chemsafetypro.com/Topics/Restriction/China_RoHS_2_vs_EU_RoHS_2.html (updated Apr. 16, 2019) [https://perma.cc/4C6T-D3VL].

180. *Id.*

181. Biedenkopf, *supra* note 64, at 5.

182. Law No. 14321, Dec. 23, 2011, A.D.L.A 2300 (Arg.).

183. Madeline Kadas et al., *Growing Attention to Product Stewardship Initiatives Seen in Latin America*, 29 Int'l Env't Rep. 596, 600 (2006).

184. *Brazil to Propose RoHS-like Regulation for Electronics*, Chemical Watch (Jan. 4, 2018), https://chemicalwatch.com/62850/brazil-to-propose-rohs-like-regulation-for-electronics (on file with author).

185. Council Directive 1999/74/EC, of 19 July 1999 Laying Down Minimum Standards for the Protection of Laying Hens, 1999 (L 203) 53.

186. European Parliament Directorate-General for Internal Policies, *supra* note 108, at 31.

187. Council Directive 2008/120/EC, of 18 December 2008 Laying Down Minimum Standards for the Protection of Pigs, 2009 (L 47) 5.

188. *40 Years of Animal Welfare, supra* note 20.

189. Wayne Pacelle, *Brazil Adds Its Might to the Movement to End Gestation Crates*, HUMANE SOC'Y INT'L (Nov. 25, 2014), https://blog.humanesociety.org/2014/11/brazil-gestation-crates.html [https://perma.cc/7YJG-XB6F] [hereinafter *BRF Announces Phase-out of Confinement of Breeding Sows*].

190. *Id.*

191. *Call to Follow NZ Lead in Banning Sow Stalls*, SYDNEY MORNING HERALD (Dec. 6, 2012), https://www.smh.com.au/environment/conservation/call-to-follow-nz-lead-in-banning-sow-stalls-20101206-18ltl.html [https://perma.cc/3AYE-DB7T].

192. *Sow Stalls to be Banned*, NAT'L BUS. REV. (Dec. 1, 2010), https://www.nbr.co.nz/ article/sow-stalls-be-banned-134068 [https://perma.cc/7KKB-KSRY].

193. NAT'L ANIMAL WELFARE ADVISORY COMM., ANIMAL WELFARE (PIGS) CODE OF WELFARE 2010 REPORT (2010).

194. Pacelle, *supra* note 189.

195. Lindsay Patton, *9 States That Have Banned Cruel Gestation Crates for Pigs*, ONE GREEN PLANET (Jan. 27, 2015), http://www.onegreenplanet.org/animalsandnature/states-that-have-banned-cruel-gestation-crates-for-pigs/ [https://perma.cc/RXL4-T73C].

196. Interview with Peter Zapfel, European Comm'n DG Climate Action, in Brussels, Belg. (July 17, 2018).

197. Mirabelle Muûls et al., *Evaluating the EU Emissions Trading System: Take it or Leave It? An Assessment of the Data after Ten Years* 3 (Grantham Inst., Briefing Paper No. 21, 2016), https://www.imperial.ac.uk/media/imperial-college/grantham-institute/ public/publications/briefing-papers/Evaluating-the-EU-emissions-trading-system_ Grantham-BP-21_web.pdf [https://perma.cc/ZF99-XCNF].

198. DELREUX & HAPPAERTS, *supra* note 43, at 213.

199. JAN H. JANS & HANS H.B. VEDDER, EUROPEAN ENVIRONMENTAL LAW: AFTER LISBON 435 (4th ed., 2012).

200. *Id.*

201. Nicolas Koch et al., *Causes of the EU ETS Price Drop: Recession, CDM, Renewable Policies or a Bit of Everything?—New Evidence*, 73 ENERGY POL'Y 676 (2014), https:// www.pik-potsdam.de/members/edenh/publications-1/CausesoftheEUETSpricedrop. pdf [https://perma.cc/4SCK-URDN].

202. Interview with Peter Zapfel, *supra* note 196.

203. Kulovesi, *supra* note 117, at 135.

204. *See, e.g., EU and Switzerland Sign Agreement to Link Emissions Trading Systems*, EUR. COMMISSION (Nov. 23, 2017), https://ec.europa.eu/clima/news/eu-and-switzerland-sign-agreement-link-emissions-trading-systems_en [https://perma.cc/G4VP-HRAP].

205. Directive 2003/87/EC, *supra* note 115, art. 25(1).

206. Justin Dabner, *Fiscal Responses to Climate Change in Australia: A Comparison with California*, 31 AUSTRALIAN TAX FORUM 131 (2016).

207. Act on the Allocation and Trading of Greenhouse Gas Emissions Permits (온실가스 배출권의 할당 및 거래에 관한 법률), Act. No. 11419, enacted on May 14, 2012, enforced on November 15, 2012, *as amended* (S. Kor.); Enforcement Decree on the Allocation and Trading of Greenhouse Gas Emission Permits (온실가스 배출권의 할당 및 거래에 관한 법률 시행령), Presidential Decree. No. 24180, enacted and enforced on Nov 15, 2012, *as amended* (S. Kor.). For more details on K-ETS in English, see also, *Republic of*

Korea: An Emissions Trading Case Study, IETA, https://ieta.wildapricot.org/resources/Resources/Case_Studies_Worlds_Carbon_Markets/2016/Korean_Case_Study_2016.pdf (last updated Sept. 2016) [https://perma.cc/5PQJ-5H58].

208. For discussion on implementation of K-ETS, see *What Now for South Korea's Emissions Trading Scheme*, CARBON PULSE (July 5, 2016), http://carbon-pulse.com/22019/ [https://perma.cc/D96U-BSYJ]; *see also Emissions Trading Worldwide: Status Report 2016*, INTERNATIONAL CARBON ACTION PARTNERSHIP 18 (2016), https://icapcarbonaction.com/images/StatusReport2016/ICAP_Status_Report_2016_Online.pdf [https://perma.cc/EK9B-PPD3].

209. *Korea Emissions Trading Scheme*, ICAP, https://icapcarbonaction.com/en/?option=com_etsmap&task=export&format=pdf&layout=list&systems%5B%5D=47 [https://perma.cc/T9NU-5ZPL] (last updated Jan. 25, 2019).

210. Yoojung Lee (이유정), *EU Implements ETS . . . Korean Corporations are Under Pressure* (EU, 탄소배출권 강행... 한국기업 '발등의 불'), HANKYUNG (한국경제) (Jan. 5, 2012), http://news.hankyung.com/article/2012010486891 [https://perma.cc/32G7-KBNX].

211. *Notice of Legislation—K-ETS Enforcement Decree* (온실가스 배출권거래제 시행령 입법예고), MINISTRY OF ENVIRONMENT (환경부) (July 23, 2012), http://www.me.go.kr/home/web/board/read.do;jsessionid=oEzCFbnBeDVwzPXTiIIs9jTkDXKROVfClaf88iDYEowqEjcJOJDEcznJsVFBiZhO.mewebrvhost_servlet_engine1?page rOffset=1890&maxPageItems=10&maxIndexPages=10&searchKey=&searchValue=&menuId=286&orgCd=&boardMasterId=1&boardCategoryId=39&boardId=182166&decorator= [https://perma.cc/3CLC-PTGC] [translation by author].

212. Presidential Committee on Green Growth (대통령직속 녹색성장위원회), Key Questions and Answers Related to K-ETS (온실가스 배출권의 할당 및 거래에 관한 법률」관련 주요 질의.답변 자료) (May 14, 2012), http://17greengrowth.pa.go.kr/?p=51732 [https://perma.cc/U7E8-DHPA] [translation by author].

213. *About the Project*, EU-KOREA ETS PROJECT, http://www.kets-project.eu/en/intrdce/aboutUs.do? menuId=menu21 (last visited Feb. 1, 2019) (on file with author).

214. Joint Press Release, EU-Korea ETS Project, EU and the Republic of Korea Launch € 3.5 Million Emissions Trading System Cooperation Project (July 8, 2016) https://eeas.europa.eu/sites/eeas/files/joint_press_release_final.pdf [https://perma.cc/NXW9-TRCA].

215. EU-KOREA ETS PROJECT, *supra* note 213.

216. TORNEY, *supra* note 2, at 131

217. *ETS Detailed Information: China*, ICAP 1, https://icapcarbonaction.com/en/?option=com_etsmap&task=export&format=pdf&layout=list&systems[]=55 [https://perma.cc/FR8F-FT4K]. (last updated Jan. 25, 2019).

218. TORNEY, *supra* note 2, at 131.

219. Interview with Peter Zapfel, *supra* note 196.

220. Anatole Boute, *The Impossible Transplant of the EU Emissions Trading Scheme: The Challenge of Energy Market Regulation*, 6 TRANSNAT'L ENVTL. L. 59 (2017).

221. *The Introduction of Euro 5 and Euro 6 Emissions Regulations for Light Passenger and Commercial Vehicles*, RSA, http://www.rsa.ie/Documents/Vehicle%20Std%20Leg/Emissions%20regs/Euro%205%20and%20Euro%206%20Emissions%20Reg%20light%20passengercommvehicles.pdf (last visited Feb. 8, 2019) [https://perma.cc/2389-9HDG].

222. Press Release No. 10165/07, Council of the European Union, Motor Vehicle Emissions (Euro 5 and 6) (May 30, 2007), https://www.consilium.europa.eu/uedocs/cms_Data/docs/pressdata/en/misc/94369.pdf [https://perma.cc/BN3H-7ZXX].

223. *Russia: Heavy-Duty: Emissions*, TRANSPORT POLIC'Y, https://www.transportpolicy. net/standard/russia-heavy-duty-emissions/ (last visited Feb. 8, 2019) [https://perma. cc/MXL6-FFKB].

224. Azat Timerhanov, *Krupnejshie napravlenija jeksporta avtomobilej iz Rossii [Russian Car Export Largest Destinations]*, ABTOCTAT [AUTOSTAT ANALYTIC AGENCY] (June 30, 2017), https://www.autostat.ru/news/30558/ [https://perma.cc/43CH-TK7H] [translation by author].

225. Gleb Fedorov, *Russia Gradually Catching Up as It Switches to Euro 5 Fuel*, RUSS. BEYOND (June 17, 2014), https://www.rbth.com/politics/2014/06/17/russia_gradually_catching_ up_as_it_switches_to_euro_5_fuel_37491.html [https://perma.cc/U42B-XEP3].

226. *Id.*

227. *Antidizel'nyj Standart: Chto Nuzhno Znat' o Evro-6* [Anti-diesel Standard: What to Know About Euro-6], AUTONEWS (Mar. 19, 2015), https://www.autonews.ru/ news/58259f779a794747431204b2 [https://perma.cc/VPY9-3EXM] [translation by author].

228. *Discussion Document on the Review of Fuel Specifications and Standards for South Africa*, Suid-Afrika/ Republic of South Africa Government Gazette no. 34089, 8 Mar. 2011, at 26, 29 (These include California, China, India, Japan, Malaysia, the Philippines, and California), http://www.energy.gov.za/files/esources/petroleum/March%202011/1- 34089%208-3%20Energy.pdf [https://perma.cc/62VV-X4HL].

229. SAPIA, ANNUAL REPORT 5 (2017), http://www.sapia.org.za/Portals/0/Annual- Reports/SAPIA_AR%202017_FA_lowres.pdf [https://perma.cc/QL6Q-YBS9].

230. *Repeal of the Amendment Regulations Regarding Petroleum Products Specifications and Standards Published on 1 June 2012 in Notice No. R. 431 Government Gazette No: 35410*, Suid-Afrika/Republic of South Africa Government Gazette no. 40979, 13 July 2017, at 4, http://www.energy.gov.za/files/policies/petroleum/Repeal-of-the-Amendment- Regulations-regarding-Petroleum-Products-Specifications-and-Standards.pdf [https:// perma.cc/B27Y-39JN].

231. SAPIA, *supra* note 229, at 5, 6. The capital investment required to implement Cleaner Fuels II is estimated at R40 billion. *Id.* at 6.

232. SAPIA, *supra* note 229, at 25.

233. *Discussion Document on the Review of Fuel Specifications and Standards for South Africa, supra* note 228, at 21.

234. SAPIA, *supra* note 229, at 25.

235. *See Discussion Document on the Review of Fuel Specifications and Standards for South Africa, supra* note 228, at 9, 23.

CHAPTER 8

1. *See* Leo Cendrowicz, *Is Europe Finally Ready for Genetically Modified Foods?*, TIME (Mar. 9, 2010), http://content.time.com/time/business/article/0,8599,1970471,00.html [https://perma.cc/XK4J-XB4J].

2. *See id.*

3. Frédéric Simon, *Reach 'Monster' will Devour EU Innovation, Chemical Industry Warns*, EURACTIV (Apr. 29, 2016), https://www.euractiv.com/section/science-policymaking/news/ reach-monster-will-devour-eu-innovation-chemical-industry-warns/ [https://perma.cc/EHZ8- H83L].

4. *Oversight on EPA Toxic Chemical Policies: Hearing Before the S. Comm. on Env't & Pub. Works*, 110th Cong. 122–23 (2008) (statement of Jim DeLisi, President, Fanwood Chemical, Inc.).

5. Trade Barriers that US Small and Medium-Sized Enterprises Perceive as Affecting Exports to the European Union, Inv. No. 332-541, USITC Pub. 4455, at 3–5 (Mar. 2014) (Final).

6. The survey targeted CIOs, CISOs, General Counsels, CCOs, CPOs, and CMOs in companies with more than 500 employees.

7. *Pulse Survey: US Companies Ramping Up General Data Protection Regulation (GDPR) Budgets,* PwC, https://4foimd322ifhg1y4zfwk3wr7-wpengine.netdna-ssl.com/wp-content/uploads/2018/03/pwc-gdpr-series-pulse-survey-1.pdf (last visited Mar. 30, 2019) [https://perma.cc/TJC2-4HQ4].

8. Videoconference Interview with Riccardo Falconi, Legal Dir., Uber (Sept. 21, 2018).

9. *Amendments by the European Parliament to the Commission Proposal for a Directive of the European Parliament and of the Council on Copyright in the Digital Single Market and Amending Directives 96/9/EC and 2001/29/EC,* A8-0245/2018 (June 29, 2018).

10. Editorial, *EU Copyright Reforms are Harsh but Necessary,* FIN. TIMES (Mar. 26, 2019), https://www.ft.com/content/233528e2-4cce-11e9-8b7f-d49067eof5od. (on file with author).

11. Anthony I. Ogus, *Regulatory Paternalism: When is It Justified?, in* CORPORATE GOVERNANCE IN CONTEXT: CORPORATIONS, STATES, AND MARKETS IN EUROPE, JAPAN, AND THE US 303 (Klaus J. Hopt et al. eds., 2005).

12. *See* Cendrowicz, *supra* note 1.

13. TRAVIS BRADFORD, THE ENERGY SYSTEM: TECHNOLOGY, ECONOMICS, MARKETS, AND POLICY 447 (2018).

14. Interview with John Frank, Vice President, Microsoft, in Brussels, Belg. (July 16, 2018).

15. *Id.*

16. Brad Smith, *Facial Recognition Technology: The Need for Public Regulation and Corporate Responsibility,* MICROSOFT: MICROSOFT ON ISSUES (July 13, 2018), https://blogs.microsoft.com/on-the-issues/2018/07/13/facial-recognition-technology-the-need-for-public-regulation-and-corporate-responsibility/ [https://perma.cc/8DV4-6WZ5].

17. *See* Stephanie Hare, *We Must Face Up to the Threat Posed by Biometrics,* FIN. TIMES (Aug. 8, 2018), https://www.ft.com/content/b4d47e04-9727-11e8-95f8-8640db9060a7. (on file with author).

18. John C. Coffee, Jr., *Racing Towards the Top?: The Impact of Cross-Listings and Stock Market Competition on International Corporate Governance,* 102 COLUM. L. REV. 1757 (2002).

19. For example, Microsoft views its pro-privacy stance as a source of competitiveness. Interview with John Frank, *supra* note 14.

20. See Jun Le Bao Zai Wei Xian Zeng She Xue Sheng Nai Sheng Chan Xian, Zhi Li Yu Wei Geng Duo Hai Zi Ti Gong Xin Xian You Zhi De Hao Niu Nai (君乐宝在威县增设学生奶生产线 致力于为更多孩子提供新鲜优质的好牛奶) [Jun Le Bao Recently Sets Production Line of Student Milk in Xingtai City, and Aims to Produce Fresh and High-quality Milk for More Children], JUNLEBAO DAIRY (Jan. 2018), http://www.junlebaoruye.com/content.aspx?id=1172 [https://perma.cc/9EV8-FNG9].

21. *See Post Hearing Information Pack, China Shengmu Organic Milk Limited,* HKEXNEWS at 151-152 (June, 2014), http://www3.hkexnews.hk/listedco/listconews/sehk/2014/0715/ltn20140715042.pdf [https://perma.cc/67EY-AW2A].

22. *See* Sun Jie (孙杰), *2016 Ru Ye Wan Li Xing Shang Ban Cheng Shou Gong Wo Guo Sheng Ru Zhi Liang Wen Ding Ke Kao (2016乳业万里行上半程收官 我国生乳质量稳定可靠) [First Half of Quality Promotion of Dairy Industry in 2016 has Completed, and the quality of raw milk in China is stable and reliable],* PEOPLE'S NETWORK (Nov. 28, 2016), http://yuqing.people.com.cn/n1/2016/1128/c210117-28904115.html. [https://perma.cc/9SBC-6USM]

23. *See* LAWRENCE A. KOGAN, EXPORTING PRECAUTION: HOW EUROPE'S RISK-FREE REGULATORY AGENDA THREATENS AMERICAN FREE ENTERPRISE 101–02

(2005), http://www.wlf.org/upload/110405MONOKogan.pdf [https://perma.cc/3TUJ-46KH].

24. Editorial, *Tax Affairs of American Tech Groups Come Under Fire*, FIN. TIMES (Oct. 3, 2017), https://www.ft.com/content/8cdba452-a779-11e7-ab55-27219df83c97. (on file with author).

25. *Why Big Tech Should Fear Europe: To Understand the Future of Silicon Valley, Cross the Atlantic*, ECONOMIST (Mar. 23, 2019), https://www.economist.com/leaders/2019/03/23/why-big-tech-should-fear-europe [https://perma.cc/47Y3-3VZU].

26. Philip Stephens, Opinion, *Europe Rewrites the Rules for Silicon Valley*, FIN. TIMES (Nov. 3, 2016), https://www.ft.com/content/5596e92c-a04d-11e6-86d5-4e36b35c3550. (on file with author)

27. Mark Scott, *E.U. Rules Look to Unify Digital Market, but U.S. Sees Protectionism*, N.Y. TIMES (Sept. 13, 2016), https://www.nytimes.com/2016/09/14/technology/eu-us-tech-google-facebook-apple.html. (on file with author)

28. Interview by Kara Swisher with Barack Obama, in Silicon Valley (Feb. 13, 2015), https://www.recode.net/2015/2/15/11559056/white-house-red-chair-obama-meets-swisher [https://perma.cc/9UD7-5HNF].

29. Jonathan Golub, *Global Competition and EU Environmental Policy: Introduction and Overview, in* GLOBAL COMPETITION AND EU ENVIRONMENTAL POLICY 1, 19, 23 (Jonathan Golub ed., 2013).

30. Fredrik Erixon, *The Rising Trend of Green Protectionism: Biofuels and the European Union* 2 (European Centre for Int'l Political Econ., Occasional Paper No. 2/2012, 2012), https://ecipe.org/publications/rising-trend-green-protectionism-biofuels-and-european-union/ [https://perma.cc/26A5-BW2K].

31. Lawrence A. Kogan, *Trade Protectionism: Ducking the Truth About Europe's GMO Policy*, N.Y. TIMES (Nov. 27, 2004), https://www.nytimes.com/2004/11/27/opinion/trade-protectionism-ducking-the-truth-about-europes-gmo-policy.html. (on file with author)

32. *See, e.g.,* Dr. Bernard D. Goldstein, Opinion, *The EU's Distortion of Public Health Unfairly Hurts US Agricultural Produce*, HILL (Jan. 29, 2018), http://thehill.com/opinion/healthcare/371236-the-eus-distortion-of-public-health-unfairly-bans-us-agricultural-produce [https://perma.cc/8R3Y-RGP3]; THE NEW TOOL AGAINST FORESTRY IN DEVELOPING COUNTRIES, WORLD GROWTH 3 (2010), http://worldgrowth.org/site/wp-content/uploads/2012/06/WG_Green_Protectionism_Forestry_Report_6_10.pdf [https://perma.cc/Y8EL-Q9XQ].

33. *See Communication from the Commission to the European Parliament, the Council and the European Economic and Social Committee: A Strategic Vision for European Standards: Moving Forward to Enhance and Accelerate the Sustainable Growth of the European Economy by 2020*, at 2-3, COM (2011) 311 final (June 1, 2011).

34. *See, e.g.,* Emma Tucker, *Plastic Toy Quandary that EU Cannot Duck*, FIN. TIMES, (Dec. 9, 1998), at 3.

35. *See* Commission Decision 2004/134/EC of 3 July 2001, 2004 O.J. (L 048) 1.

36. John R. Wilke, *U.S. Antitrust Chief Chides EU for Rejecting Merger Proposal*, WALL ST. J. (July 5, 2001), https://www.wsj.com/articles/SB99428227597056929. (on file with author).

37. *See, e.g.,* William J. Kolasky, Deputy Assistant Attorney Gen. Antitrust Div., U.S. Dep't of Justice, Address Before the Seminar on Convergence Sponsored by the Netherlands Ministry of Economic Affairs (Oct. 28, 2002), https://www.justice.gov/atr/speech/what-competition [https://perma.cc/4RXX-EC9T].

38. Wilke, *supra* note 36.

39. Commission Decision of 28 June 2000 Declaring a Concentration Incompatible with the Common Market and the EEA Agreement, Case COMP/M.1741—MCI WorldCom/

Sprint, 2003 O.J. (L 300) 1; Commission Decision of 11 October 2000 Declaring a Concentration to be Compatible with the Common Market and the EEA Agreement, Case COMP/M.1845—AOL/Time Warner, 2001 O.J. (L 268) 28; Summary of Commission Decision of 1 February 2012 Declaring a Concentration Incompatible with the Internal Market and the Functioning of the EEA Agreement, Case COMP/M.6166—Deutsche Börse/NYSE Euronext, 2014 O.J. (C 254) 8; Summary of Commission Decision of 30 January 2013 Declaring a Concentration Incompatible with the Internal Market and the Functioning of the EEA Agreement, Case COMP/M.6570—UPS/TNT Express, 2014 (C 137) 8.

40. Press Release, European Comm'n, Antitrust: Commission Fines Google €4.34 Billion for Illegal Practices Regarding Android Mobile Devices to Strengthen Dominance of Google's Search Engine (July 18, 2018), http://europa.eu/rapid/press-release_IP-18-4581_en.htm [https://perma.cc/X7MR-ZU4J].

41. Summary of Commission Decision of 27 June 2017, Case AT.39740—Google Search (Shopping), 2018 O.J. (C 9) 11.

42. Press Release, European Comm'n, Antitrust: Commission Fines Google €1.49 Billion for Abusive Practices in Online Advertising (Mar. 20, 2019), https://eeas.europa.eu/topics/external-investment-plan/60039/antitrust-commission-fines-google-€149-billion-abusive-practices-online-advertising_en [https://perma.cc/C8W4-SJV7].

43. Earlier this year, the Commission fined Qualcomm $1.2 billion for its exclusive dealing contracts with Apple on the computer chips market. *See* Summary of Commission Decision of 24 Jan. 2018, Case AT.40220—Qualcomm (Exclusivity Payments), 2018 O.J. (C 269) 25.

44. In a separate competition action, the Commission also ordered Ireland to recover €13 billion in illegal state aid from Apple. *See* Commission Decision (EU) 2017/1283 of 30 Aug. 2016, on State Aid SA.38373 (2014/C) (ex 2014/NN) (ex 2014/CP) Implemented by Ireland to Apple, 2017 O.J. (L 187) 1.

45. Summary of Commission Decision of 13 May 2009, Case COMP/C-3/37.990—Intel, 2009 O.J. (C 227) 13. In September 2017, the European Court of Justice overturned the fine levied by the Commission in its decision. Case C-413/14 P, Intel Corp. v. Comm'n, EUR-Lex 62014CJ0413 (Sept. 6, 2017).

46. Commission Decision of 24 May 2004, Case COMP/C-3/37.792—Microsoft, 2007 O.J. (L 32) 23.

47. *See* Steve Lohr, *Antitrust Cry from Microsoft*, N.Y. TIMES, Mar. 31, 2011, at B1, https://www.nytimes.com/2011/03/31/technology/companies/31google.html?mtrref=www.google.com&gwh=A598C6EBBF881EE0FCBA67C3037A8078&gwt=pay&assetType=PAYWALL (on file with author); Brad Smith, *Adding Our Voice to Concerns About Search in Europe*, MICROSOFT ON ISSUES (Mar. 30, 2011), https://blogs.microsoft.com/on-the-issues/2011/03/30/adding-our-voice-to-concerns-about-search-in-europe/ [https://perma.cc/E527-TVFJ].

48. *See, e.g.*, Ben Homewood, *Google 'Abuses' Highlighted in the Wake of Record Anti-Trust Fine*, GOOGLE (July 19, 2018), http://www.musicweek.com/media/read/google-abuses-highlighted-in-the-wake-of-record-anti-trust-fine/073231 [https://perma.cc/XV34-FW6W].

49. *See, e.g.*, Richard Smirke, *Europe and Copyright: A Comprehensive Look at the Continent's Digital Plans*, BILLBOARD (Apr. 28, 2016), https://www.billboard.com/articles/business/7349853/digital-single-market-music-business-european-union [https://perma.cc/KUC2-V2MW].

50. *See* Sam Schechner & Stu Woo, *EU to Get Tough on Chat Apps in Win for Telecoms*, WALL ST. J. (Sept. 11, 2016), https://www.wsj.com/articles/eu-to-get-tough-on-chat-apps-in-win-for-telecoms-1473607662 (on file with author).

51. Case COMP/M.7881, AB InBev/SABMiller, EUR-Lex 32016M7881 (May 24, 2016).

52. Summary of Commission Decision of 1 February 2012 Declaring a Concentration Incompatible with the Internal Market and the Functioning of the EEA Agreement, Case COMP/M.6166—Deutsche Börse/NYSE Euronext, 2014 O.J. (C 254) 8.

53. Summary of Commission Decision of 29 March 2017 Declaring a Concentration Incompatible with the Internal Market and the Functioning of the EEA Agreement, Case COMP/M.7995—Deutsche Börse/London Stock Exchange, 2017 O.J. (C 240) 7.

54. Commission Decision (EU) 2016/2326, of 21 October 2015 on State Aid SA.38375 (2014/C ex 2014/NN) Which Luxembourg Granted to Fiat, 2016 O.J. (L 351) 1.

55. Press Release, European Comm'n, State Aid: Commission Opens In-depth Investigation into Italian State Loan to Alitalia (Apr. 23, 2018), http://europa.eu/rapid/press-release_IP-18-3501_en.htm [https://perma.cc/H9NE-F6UQ]; Press Release, European Comm'n, State Aid: Commission Opens In-depth Investigation into measures in Favour of Ryanair at Frankfurt-Hahn Airport in Germany (Oct. 26, 2018), http://europa.eu/rapid/press-release_IP-18-6222_en.htm [https://perma.cc/DP8G-YYCZ].

56. Anu Bradford et al., *Is EU Merger Control Used for Protectionism? An Empirical Analysis*, 15 J. EMPIRICAL LEGAL STUD. 165, 188 (2018).

57. *Id.*

58. DAVID VOGEL, THE POLITICS OF PRECAUTION: REGULATING HEALTH, SAFETY, AND ENVIRONMENTAL RISKS IN EUROPE AND THE UNITED STATES 27 (2012).

59. *Id.*

60. Interview with Cyril Jacquet, Senior Legal Advisor in the Legal Affairs Unit, ECHA, in Helsinki, Fin. (Jan 4, 2018).

61. *See* Regulation (EU) 995/2010, of the European Parliament and of the Council of 20 October 2010 Laying Down the Obligations of Operators Who Place Timber and Timber Products on the Market, 2010 O.J. (L 295) 23.

62. *See, e.g., Communication from the Commission to the Council and the European Parliament: A European One Health Action Plan Against Antimicrobial Resistance,* COM (2017) 339 final (June 29, 2017).

63. Appellate Body Report, *European Communities—Measures Prohibiting the Importation and Marketing of Seal Products,* ¶ 5.203, WT/DS400/AB/R; WT/DS401/AB/R (Apr. 29, 2014).

64. *See, e.g., US Airline EU ETS Case Against the UK to be Referred to European Court as NGO Coalition Joins Actions,* GREENAIRONLINE.COM, http://www.greenaironline.com/news.php?viewStory=1129 (last visited Apr. 2, 2019) [https://perma.cc/2RK2-TXJK].

65. *See, e.g.,* Kimberly Elliott & Janeen Madan. *Can GMOs Deliver for Africa?* (Center for Global Development, CGD Policy Paper 080, 2016) http://www.cgdev.org/publication/can-gmos-deliver-africa [https://perma.cc/KU9S-E77T].

66. Marnus Gouse et al., *Genetically Modified Maize: Less Drudgery for Her, More Maize for Him? Evidence from Smallholder Maize Farmers in South Africa,* WORLD DEV., July 2016, at 27.

67. Ademola A. Adenle, *Response to Issues on GM Agriculture in Africa: Are Transgenic Crops Safe?,* BMC RES. NOTES (Oct. 8 2011), https://bmcresnotes.biomedcentral.com/articles/10.1186/1756-0500-4-388 [https://perma.cc/8PC2-TE9R].

68. Robert Paarlberg, *GMO Foods and Crops: Africa's Choice,* 27 NEW BIOTECHNOLOGY 609, 610–11 (2010).

69. *See, e.g.,* JAN ZIELONKA, EUROPE AS EMPIRE: THE NATURE OF THE ENLARGED EUROPEAN UNION 9–22 (2006).

70. *See* Zaki Laïdi, *The Unintended Consequences of European Power* 9–10 (Les Cahiers Européens de Sciences Po. No. 5, 2007), https://spire.sciencespo.fr/notice/2441/dkt13evdojn1lb09786c100s2 [https://perma.cc/7YL6-F3YF].

71. Jan Zielonka, *Europe as a Global Actor: Empire by Example?*, 84 INT'L AFF. 471, 475 (2008).

72. *Id.* at 477, 483.

73. Raffaella A. Del Sarto, *Normative Empire Europe: The EU, Its Borderlands and the Arab Spring*, 54 J. COMM. MARKET STUD. 215, 222–23 (2016).

74. *Id.* at 227.

75. *Id.*

76. *See, e.g.,* Editorial, *Regulatory Imperialism*, WALL ST. J. (Oct. 26, 2007), https://www.wsj.com/articles/SB119334720539572002 (on file with author); Angelos Sepos, *Imperial Power Europe? The EU's Relations with the ACP Countries*, 6 J. POL. POWER 261 (2013).

77. Mark Scott & Laurens Cerulus, *Europe's New Data Protection Rules Export Privacy Standards Worldwide*, POLITICO (Jan. 31, 2018), https://www.politico.eu/article/europe-data-protection-privacy-standards-gdpr-general-protection-data-regulation/ [https://perma.cc/9LHF-FM7M].

78. *Id.*

79. Lawrence A. Kogan, *Exporting Europe's Protectionism*, 77 NAT'L INT. 91, 99 (2004).

80. *See, e.g.,* Margrethe Vestager, Competition Commissioner, Opening Remarks at the ICN Merger Workshop: Merger Review: Building a Global Community of Practice (June 3, 2016); The Rt Hon Sir Leon Brittan QU, Vice-President of the European Commission, Address at the WTO High Level Symposium on Trade and the Environment (Mar. 15, 1999).

81. *See generally* Ian Manners, *Normative Power Europe: A Contradiction in Terms?*, 40 J. COMMON MARKET STUD. 235, 235 (2002).

82. *See* Consolidated Version of the Treaty on European Union art. 3(5), May 9, 2008, 2008 O.J. (C 115) 13 17. *See also* Ian Manners, *The Normative Ethics of the European Union*, 84 INT'L AFF. 45, 46 (2008).

83. José Manuel Barroso, *Europe's Rising Global Role*, PROJECT SYNDICATE (Dec. 16, 2009), https://www.project-syndicate.org/commentary/europe-s-rising-global-role? (on file with author).

84. Joseph Stiglitz, Opinion, *The EU's Global Role*, GUARDIAN (Mar. 29, 2007), https://www.theguardian.com/commentisfree/2007/mar/29/theeusglobalmission [https://perma.cc/WJ5Z-TQ4N].

85. *See, e.g.,* Press Release, European Comm'n, The Copenhagen Climate Change Negotiations: EU Position and State of Play (Nov. 9, 2009), http://europa.eu/rapid/press-release_MEMO-09-493_en.htm?locale=en [https://perma.cc/Z7HP-3YA6].

86. *See id.*

87. *See Clean-Air Turbulence*, ECONOMIST, July 9-15, 2011, at 16.

88. *See, e.g.,* MARK LEONARD, WHY EUROPE WILL RUN THE 21ST CENTURY (2005).

89. *E.g.,* Kalypso Nicolaïdis & Robert Howse, *'This is my EUtopia . . .': Narrative as Power*, 40 J. COMMON MARKET STUD. 767, 789 (2002); *see also* Thomas Diez, *Europe's Others and the Return of Geopolitics*, 17 CAMBRIDGE REV. INT'L AFF. 319, 325, 330–35 (2004).

90. *See, e.g.,* Oxfam Int'l, *Adapting to Climate Change: What's Needed in Poor Countries, and Who Should Pay* (Oxfam Briefing Paper 104, 2007), https://www.oxfam.org.nz/sites/default/files/reports/Adapting%20to%20Climate%20Change.pdf [https://perma.cc/N95A-83HV].

91. Hosein, Ian, 2004, Presentation at the 45th International Studies Association Convention: International Relations Theories and the Regulation of International Dataflows: Policy Laundering and Other International Policy Dynamics (Mar. 17–20, 2004) (http://citation.allacademic.com/meta/p_mla_apa_research_citation/0/7/3/8/8/pages73882/p73882-1.php) [https://perma.cc/RWX6-TUEY].

92. Julian Schwartzkopff, *Splendid Isolation? The Influence of Interest Groups on EU Trade Policy* (Berlin Working Paper on European Integration No. 12, 2009), https://www. polsoz.fu-berlin.de/polwiss/forschung/international/europa/Partner-und-Online-Ressourcen/arbeitspapiere/2009-12_Schwartzkopff_SplendidIsolation.pdf [https://perma. cc/T5T4-FJE7].

93. Joseph H. H. Weiler et al., 1995. *European Democracy and its Critique: Five Uneasy Pieces* (European Univ. Inst. Working Paper RSC No. 95/11, 1995), http://cadmus.eui.eu/handle/1814/1386 [https://perma.cc/ZW4U-WV3Q].

94. *See* Robert O. Keohane et al., *Democracy-Enhancing Multilateralism*, 63 INT'L ORG. 1 (2009).

95. Citizens United v. FEC, 130 S. Ct. 876 (2010).

96. ANDREAS DÜR ET AL., POLITICAL INFLUENCE OF BUSINESS IN THE EUROPEAN UNION (2019).

97. Joanne Scott, *From Brussels with Love: The Transatlantic Travels of European Law and the Chemistry of Regulatory Attraction*, 57 AM. J. COMP. L. 897, 920–28 (2009); *see also generally* KATERINA LINOS, THE DEMOCRATIC FOUNDATIONS OF POLICY DIFFUSION: HOW HEALTH, FAMILY AND EMPLOYMENT LAWS SPREAD ACROSS COUNTRIES (2013).

98. *See* Alasdair R. Young, *Political Transfer and "Trading Up"?: Transatlantic Trade in Genetically Modified Food and U.S. Politics*, 55 WORLD POL. 457, 474 (2003).

99. Scott, *supra* note 97, at 923.

100. *Id.* at 920–28.

101. *Id.* at 927 (citing News Release, Scientists, Physicians, Health Advocates, Parents to Obama: Chemical Exposure is an Urgent Crisis in the United States (Nov. 20, 2008), https://smartpolicyreform.org/for-the-media/news-releases/ [https://perma.cc/Y35E-6MCZ]).

102. Donna McCann et al., *Food Additives and Hyperactive Behaviour in 3-Year-Old and 8/9-Year-Old Children in the Community: A Randomised, Double-Blinded, Placebo-Controlled Trial*, 370 LANCET 1560 (2007).

103. Elizabeth Grossman, *Banned in Europe, Safe in the U.S.*, ENSIA (June 9, 2014), https://ensia.com/features/banned-in-europe-safe-in-the-u-s/ [https://perma.cc/6YDR-Z3JA].

104. QUICK MINUTES: FOOD ADVISORY COMMITTEE MEETING MARCH 30–31, 2011, U.S. FOOD & DRUG ADMIN. (FDA), https://wayback.archive-it.org/org-1137/20170406211702/https://www.fda.gov/AdvisoryCommittees/CommitteesMeetingMaterials/FoodAdvisoryCommittee/ucm250901.htm (last visited Apr. 3, 2019).

105. Michael F. Jacobsen, *Strong FDA Action on Food Dyes Urged*, CSPI (Mar. 30, 2011), https://cspinet.org/new/201103301.html [https://perma.cc/5JLU-LUYQ]; Gardiner Harris, *Artificial Dye Safe to Eat, Panel Says*, N.Y. TIMES (Mar. 31, 2011), https://www.nytimes.com/2011/04/01/health/policy/01fda.html (on file with author); April Fulton, *FDA Probes Link Between Food Dyes, Kids' Behavior*, NPR (Mar. 30, 2011), https://www.npr.org/2011/03/30/134962888/fda-probes-link-between-food-dyes-kids-behavior [https://perma.cc/V7WJ-L7QY]; Stephanie Gleason, *Artificial Food Dyes Scrutinized by FDA*, WALL ST. J. (Mar. 29, 2011), https://www.wsj.com/articles/SB10001424052748704471904576228550619608050 (on file with author).

106. *Why M&M's Are Made with Natural Coloring in the EU and Not the U.S.*, WBUR (Mar. 28, 2014), http://www.wbur.org/hereandnow/2014/03/28/artificial-dyes-candy [https://perma.cc/7GP4-KKA7].

107. Katie Lobosco, *Kraft Ends Mac and Cheese Fake Coloring. Will It Still Be Yellow?*, CNN BUSINESS (Apr. 20, 2015), https://money.cnn.com/2015/04/20/news/companies/kraft-macaroni-cheese-fake-color/index.html?iid=EL [https://perma.cc/6PA6-CLXB].

108. Amy Kuperinsky, *Mars to Remove Artificial Colors from M&M's and Other Candy*, NJ. COM (Feb. 6, 2016), https://www.nj.com/entertainment/index.ssf/2016/02/mars_to_remove_artificial_colors_from_mms.html [https://perma.cc/JZC2-NEE2].

109. *See* Otto Pohl, *European Environmental Rules Propel Change in U.S.*, N.Y. TIMES, July 6, 2004, at F4 (on file with author).

110. *See* Joseph Turow et al. *Americans Reject Tailored Advertising and Three Activities that Enable It* (Annenberg Sch. for Commc'n, Departmental Paper No. 524, 2009), https://repository.upenn.edu/asc_papers/524/ [https://perma.cc/TPK7-D6E4].

111. *Regulation: The Right Way to Get Rid of It: America Needs Regulatory Reform, Not a Crude Cull of Environmental Rules*, ECONOMIST (Mar, 2, 2017), https://www.economist.com/leaders/2017/03/02/the-right-way-to-get-rid-of-it [https://perma.cc/G87U-UDH2].

112. For California, REACH can be described as having been "both a catalyst and a resource for regulatory reform." Scott, *supra* note 97, at 898.

113. *See Community Waste Prevention Toolkit: Computer Factsheet*, INFORM, https://www.informinc.org/community-waste-prevention-toolkit-computers-fact-sheet/ (last visited Apr. 3, 2019), [https://perma.cc/N395-U8FH]; Scott Cassel, *Product Stewardship: Shared Responsibility for Managing HHW*, *in* HANDBOOK ON HOUSEHOLD HAZARDOUS WASTE, 159, 198–99 (Amy D. Cabaniss ed., 2008).

114. Katja Biedenkopf, E-Waste Governance Beyond Borders—Does the EU Influence US Environmental Policy? 11 (2010) (unpublished manuscript) (https://refubium.fu-berlin.de/bitstream/handle/fub188/19456/Biedenkopf-E-Waste_Governance_beyond_Borders-445.pdf?sequence=1&isAllowed=y) [https://perma.cc/H7DX-6SDP].

115. R. G. Lipsey & Kelvin Lancaster, *The General Theory of Second Best*, 24 REV. ECON. STUD. 11 (1956).

116. Chad Damro, *Market Power Europe*, 19 J. EUR. PUB. POL'Y 682, 689 (2012).

117. Agreement Between the European Parliament and the European Commission on the Establishment of a Transparency Register for Organisations and Self-employed Individuals Engaged in EU Policy-making and Policy Implementation, 2011 O.J. (L 191) 29; TRANSPARENCY REGISTER, http://ec.europa.eu/transparencyregister/info/homePage.do?redir=false&locale=en (last updated Mar. 25, 2019) [https://perma.cc/4RMU-2G2Q].

118. Statistics for the Transparency Register, TRANSPARENCY REGISTER, http://ec.europa.eu/transparencyregister/public/consultation/statistics.do?locale=en&action=prepareView (last updated Mar. 25, 2019) [https://perma.cc/6D7S-55W5].

119. *Id.* (data filtered according to non-EU countries).

120. Adam Satariano, *G.D.P.R., a New Privacy Law, Makes Europe World's Leading Tech Watchdog*, N.Y. TIMES (May 24, 2018), https://www.nytimes.com/2018/05/24/technology/europe-gdpr-privacy.html. (on file with author).

121. Emilia Korkea-aho, *'Mr. Smith Goes to Brussels': Third Country Lobbying and the Making of EU Law and Policy*, 18 CAMBRIDGE Y.B. EUR. LEGAL STUD. 45, 48, 57 (2016). This commitment is manifested in Article 11 of the TEU, which places a proactive duty on the Commission to consult the affected parties. Third party actors subject to, or affected by, EU rules are seen as stakeholders in this process, falling under the TEU Article 11 duty for consultation.

122. *Id.* at 52.

123. *See generally* Bill Wirtz, *EU-Funded Lobbying is Expensive and Undemocratic*, EUOBSERVER (Sept. 21, 2017), https://euobserver.com/opinion/139093 [https://perma.cc/32XB-BA4V]; RINUS VAN SCHENDELEN, MORE MACHIAVELLI IN BRUSSELS: THE ART OF LOBBYING THE EU 319–20 (2002).

124. Eric Lipton & Danny Hakim, *Lobbying Bonanza as Firms Try to Influence European Union*, N.Y. TIMES (Oct. 18, 2013), https://www.nytimes.com/2013/10/19/world/

europe/lobbying-bonanza-as-firms-try-to-influence-european-union.html (on file with author).

125. Korkea-aho, *supra* note 121, at 59.

126. *REACH Background: Internet Consultation on Draft Chemicals Legislation (the REACH System)*, EUR. COMMISSION, http://ec.europa.eu/environment/chemicals/reach/background/internet_cons_en.htm (last updated June 8, 2016) [https://perma.cc/N7H5-SPEX].

127. Korkea-aho, *supra* note 121, at 60.

128. *Id.* (citing H.R. COMM. ON GOVERNMENT REFORM, MINORITY STAFF SPECIAL INVESTIGATIONS DIV., A SPECIAL INTEREST CASE STUDY: THE CHEMICAL INDUSTRY, THE BUSH ADMINISTRATION, AND EUROPEAN EFFORTS TO REGULATE CHEMICALS (2004), https://wayback.archive-it.org/4949/20141031194315/http://oversight-archive.waxman.house.gov/documents/20040817125807-75305.pdf [hereinafter SPECIAL INTEREST CASE STUDY]).

129. Robert Levine, *Laying Down the Law: How the Music Business Came Together to Score Two Political Wins*, BILLBOARD (Sept. 20, 2018), https://www.billboard.com/articles/business/8476196/music-modernization-act-eu-copyright-music-business-unity [https://perma.cc/S2LM-BDA3].

130. *Who We Are*, GGHH, https://www.greenhospitals.net/ (last visited Apr. 3, 2019), [https://perma.cc/P3MG-TNS8].

131. *See Chemicals*, GREENHOSPITALS.NET, https://www.greenhospitals.net/chemicals/ (last visited Apr. 3, 2019), [https://perma.cc/QMT6-X6W4].

132. Korkea-aho, *supra* note 121, at 50–51.

133. *Our Members*, DIGITALEUROPE, https://www.digitaleurope.org (last visited Apr. 3, 2019), [https://perma.cc/UD48-YB3X].

134. DIGITALEUROPE, *Response to European Commission Consultation on the Legal Framework for the Fundamental Right to Protection of Personal Data* (Nov. 20, 2009), https://ec.europa.eu/home-affairs/sites/homeaffairs/files/what-is-new/public-consultation/2009/pdf/contributions/registered_organisations/digital_europe_en.pdf [https://perma.cc/3TYL-SJHD].

135. Dür et al., *supra* note 96.

136. *Id.*

137. Mehreen Khan & Tim Bradshaw, *Apple and Facebook Call for EU-style Privacy Laws in US*, FIN. TIMES (Oct. 24, 2018), https://www.ft.com/content/0ca8466c-d768-11e8-ab8e-6be0dcf18713 (on file with author).

138. *See generally* DAVID VOGEL, TRADING UP: CONSUMER AND ENVIRONMENTAL REGULATION IN A GLOBAL ECONOMY (1995).

139. This is particularly valuable if a chemical company can show that it produces a safer alternative compared to its competitor's "substance of very high concern," as this would lead to automatic denial of the competitor's substance. *See* Scott, *supra* note 97, at 930.

140. *See* SPECIAL INTEREST CASE STUDY, *supra* note 128.

141. *See* Matt Murray et al., *Oceans Apart: As Honeywell Deal Goes Awry for GE, Fallout May Be Global*, WALL ST. J., June 15, 2001, at A1.

142. See the E.C.J. case discussed by Murray et al., *supra* note 141; see also Joshua Chaffin & Andrew Parker, *Blow to US Airlines in Emissions Fight*, FIN. TIMES (Oct. 6, 2011), http://www.ft.com/cms/s/0/36556726-f005-11e0-bc9d-00144feab49a.html#axzz2BZQvmThR (on file with author).

143. Telephone Interview with Anthony Gardner, Former US Ambassador to the EU (July 30, 2018).

144. For instance, the Bush administration preempted California's regulations on GHG emissions. *See* 42 U.S.C. § 7543(a) (2006). The EPA also denied California's first

application for a preemption waiver. *See* Letter from Stephen L. Johnson, Administrator, EPA, to Arnold Schwarzenegger, Governor of California (Dec. 19, 2007), https://www. epa.gov/sites/production/files/2016-10/documents/20071219-slj.pdf [https://perma. cc/5RLR-PSNP].

145. *See* Adam Liptak, *Trump v. California: The Biggest Legal Clashes*, N.Y. TIMES (Apr. 5, 2018), https://www.nytimes.com/2018/04/05/us/politics/trump-california-lawsuits.html (on file with author).

146. *See* Hiroko Tabuchi, Brad Plumer and Coral Davenport, *E.P.A. Readies Plan to Weaken Rules That Require Cars to Be Cleaner*, N.Y. TIMES (Apr. 27, 2018), https://www.nytimes. com/2018/04/27/climate/epa-emissions-california.html (on file with author); *see also* David Sloss, *California's Climate Diplomacy and Dormant Preemption*, 56 WASHBURN L.J. 507 (2017).

147. *See* Young, *supra* note 98, at 458–59.

148. *See, e.g.,* Brian Coleman, *Clinton Hints at U.S. Retaliation If EU Blocks Boeing Merger*, WALL ST. J., July 18, 1997, at A2, https://www.wsj.com/articles/SB869154847949775000 (on file with author).

149. Deborah Platt Majoras, Deputy Asst. Att'y Gen., Antitrust Div., U.S. Dep't of Justice, Remarks Before the Antitrust Law Section State Bar of Georgia: GE–Honeywell: The U.S. Decision 14 (Nov. 29, 2001), http://www.justice.gov/atr/public/speeches/9893.pdf [https://perma.cc/GRN2-3FY9].

150. Daniel Michaels, *Chinese Envoy Backs Shunning of Airbus*, WALL ST. J. (Mar. 9, 2012), https://www.wsj.com/articles/SB10001424052970204781804577271312775663108 (on file with author). However, the EU insisted it would not back down. *See* Joshua Chaffin, *EU Defies Carbon Trade War Threats*, FIN. TIMES (Mar. 20, 2012), https:// www.ft.com/content/10aebc46-72b6-11e1-ae73-00144feab49a#axzz263rsQIP5 (on file with author).

151. TOM DELREUX & SANDRA HAPPAERTS, ENVIRONMENTAL POLICY AND POLITICS IN THE EUROPEAN UNION 133, 215 (2016).

152. Jim Brunsden, *EU Seeks to End Long-Running Row over Curbs on US Beef*, FINANCIAL TIMES (Sept. 3, 2018), https://www.ft.com/content/03ec6d4c-af85-11e8-99ca-68cf89602132 (on file with author).

153. General Agreement on Tariffs and Trade art. XX, Oct. 30, 1947, 61 Stat. A-11, 55 U.N.T.S. 194 [hereinafter GATT].

154. *See* Appellate Body Report, *European Communities—Measures Concerning Meat and Meat Products (Hormones)*, WT/DS26/AB/R, WT/DS48/AB/R (Jan. 16, 1998) (*adopted* Feb. 13, 1998), https://www.wto.org/english/tratop_e/dispu_e/hormab. pdf [hereinafter Appellate Body Report] [https://perma.cc/847R-TC3T].

155. Appellate Body Report, *supra* note 154, at 28.

156. *See id.* at 20–23.

157. *Id.* at 7.

158. Appellate Body Report, *supra* note 154.

159. *See* Press Release, Office of the U.S. Trade Rep., U.S. Files WTO Case Challenging EU Restrictions on U.S. Poultry Exports (Jan. 16, 2009), https://ustr.gov/about-us/ policy-offices/press-office/press-releases/2009/january/us-files-wto-case-challenging-eu-restrictions-us-p [https://perma.cc/SZG9-D4HL].

160. JOHN H. JACKSON ET AL., LEGAL PROBLEMS OF INTERNATIONAL ECONOMIC RELATIONS 367 (5th ed. 2008).

161. *Id.*

162. *See* RENÉE JOHNSON & CHARLES E. HANRAHAN, CONG. RESEARCH SERV., R40449, THE U.S.-EU BEEF HORMONE DISPUTE (2010). The EU has further continued to gather scientific evidence to justify its import ban and challenge US retaliation. After

another round of WTO litigation and a mixed and inconclusive Appellate Body ruling, both the EU's import ban and the United States' retaliation remain in force. *See also* Press Release, Office of the U.S. Trade Representative, WTO's Appellate Body Vindicates Continued U.S. Imposition of Sanctions After the EU Claimed Compliance in the *EU–Hormones* Dispute (Oct. 16, 2008), https://ustr.gov/archive/assets/Document_Library/Press_Releases/2008/October/asset_upload_file626_15173.pdf [https://perma.cc/3J6J-E2MG].

163. *See* Johnson & Hanrahan, *supra* note 162. And even if the EU were to comply, access of GMOs to its markets would remain limited. The WTO only ruled on the EU's moratorium for authorization of GMOs. The EU's strict requirements on traceability and labeling of GMO products remain intact, considerably limiting the producers' ability to penetrate the European market, given EU consumers' distrust of GMO foods.

164. *See* GATT, *supra* note 153, art. III.

165. However, on privacy, see the general exception clause in Article XIV of GATT, which explicitly authorizes states to restrict trade to "protection of the privacy of individuals." *See* Gregory Shaffer, *Globalization and Social Protection: The Impact of EU and International Rules in the Ratcheting Up of U.S. Privacy Standards,* 25 YALE J. INT'L L. 1, 50 (2000) (quoting GATT, *supra* note 153, art. XIV).

166. *See* Anu Bradford, *International Antitrust Negotiations and the False Hope of the WTO,* 48 HARV. INT'L L.J. 383 (2007).

167. Dominique Sinopoli and Kai Purnhagen, *Reversed Harmonization or Horizontalization of EU Standards?: Does WTO Law Facilitate or Constrain the Brussels Effect?* 34 WISC. INT'L L.J. 92 (2016).

168. Understanding on Rules and Procedures Governing the Settlement of Disputes, Apr. 15, 1994, Marrakesh Agreement Establishing the World Trade Organization, Annex 2, 1869 U.N.T.S. 401.

169. *See* Shaffer, *supra* note 165, at 54–55.

170. *See* Jonathan R. Macey, *Regulatory Globalization as a Response to Regulatory Competition,* 52 EMORY L.J. 1353, 1359 (2003).

171. *See generally, Carbon Offsetting and Reduction Scheme for International Aviation (CORSIA),* INT'L CIV. AVIATION ORG., https://www.icao.int/environmental-protection/CORSIA/Pages/default.aspx [https://perma.cc/6U8Z-9LEA]. The US commitment to CORSIA is less certain under the Trump administration. *See, e.g.,* Allision Lampert & Victoria Bryan, *U.S. Airlines Affirm Aviation Emissions Deal After Trump's Paris Pullout,* REUTERS (June 6, 2017), https://www.reuters.com/article/us-airlines-iata-climatechange-idUSKBN18X2WX [https://perma.cc/6G9S-KQ35].

172. Philip Blenkinsop, *EU Deeply Disagrees with U.S. on Trade Despite Détente,* REUTERS (Aug. 30, 2018), https://www.reuters.com/article/us-usa-trade-eu/eu-deeply-disagrees-with-u-s-on-trade-despite-detente-idUSKCN1LF1E0 [https://perma.cc/7VU2-4N63].

173. Sewell Chan, *Greenpeace Leaks U.S.-E.U. Trade Deal Documents,* N.Y. TIMES (May 2, 2016), https://www.nytimes.com/2016/05/03/world/europe/ttip-greenpeace-leak-trade-deal.html (on file with author).

174. At times, the United States may therefore concede and adopt the EU standard, in particular if it faces domestic demand to do so following any lobbying activity by its own export-oriented companies that are already subject to EU rules and that therefore seek to level the playing field domestically.

175. *See* Daniel W. Drezner, *Globalization, Harmonization, and Competition: The Different Pathways to Policy Convergence,* 12 J. EUR. PUB. POL'Y 841, 845 (2005).

176. *See id.*

177. See discussion of the "Better Regulation Agenda" in chapter 2.

178. *Id.*

179. See discussion in chapter 3.

180. For example, the EU's 2012 regulation on the verification of greenhouse gas emissions simplified and even removed many verification procedures for small emitters. Commission Regulation (EU) No 600/2012, of 21 June 2012 O.J. (L 181) 1, art. 33.

CHAPTER 9

1. *See* Dominic Wilson & Roopa Purushothaman, *Dreaming with BRICs: The Path to 2050* (Goldman Sachs, Global Econ., Paper No. 99, 2003), https://www.goldmansachs.com/insights/archive/archive-pdfs/brics-dream.pdf [https://perma.cc/YKL5-T2CC].

2. *GDP Growth (Annual %)*, THE WORLD BANK, https://data.worldbank.org/indicator/NY.GDP.MKTP.KD.ZG?end=2017&locations=EU-US-CA&start=2010&view=chart [https://perma.cc/G2Z6-BFZ6].

3. *GDP Growth (Annual %)*, THE WORLD BANK https://data.worldbank.org/indicator/NY.GDP.MKTP.KD.ZG?end=2017&locations=EU-CN-IN-ID&start=2010&view=chart [https://perma.cc/PV62-T5L9].

4. Jean Fouré, Agnès Bénassy-Quéré & Lionel Fontagné, *The World Economy in 2050: A Tentative Picture*, (CEPII, Working Paper No. 27, 2010), 48 http://www.cepii.fr/PDF_PUB/wp/2010/wp2010-27.pdf [https://perma.cc/M4P4-L9VH].

5. *Report for Selected Country Groups and Subjects,* IMF, https://www.imf.org/external/pubs/ft/weo/2016/02/weodata/weorept.aspx?pr.x=44&pr.y=12&sy=2008&ey=2018&scsm=1&ssd=1&sort=country&ds=.&br=1&c=001%2C998&s=NGDPD&grp=1&a=1 [https://perma.cc/B6GV-XPHQ].

6. *The Long View: How Will the Global Economic Order Change by 2050?*, PwC, 4, 8, (Feb. 2017), https://www.pwc.com/gx/en/world-2050/assets/pwc-the-world-in-2050-full-report-feb-2017.pdf [https://perma.cc/3A2C-6WR8].

7. Fouré, Bénassy-Quéré & Fontagné *supra* note 4, at 4.

8. DIRECTORATE-GENERAL FOR RESEARCH AND INNOVATION, EUROPEAN COMMISSION, GLOBAL EUROPE 2050, 5 (2012), https://ec.europa.eu/research/social-sciences/pdf/policy_reviews/global-europe-2050-report_en.pdf [https://perma.cc/TN2B-7GX5].

9. THE GLOBAL ECONOMY IN 2030: TRENDS AND STRATEGIES FOR EUROPE, CENTRE FOR EUROPEAN POLICY STUDIES, 61 (Daniel Gros & Cinzia Alcidi eds., 2013), https://espas.secure.europarl.europa.eu/orbis/sites/default/files/generated/document/en/The%20Global%20Economy%20in%202030.pdf [https://perma.cc/5T95-Y4Z3]

10. Zhōnghuá rénmín gònghéguó fǎn lǒngduàn fǎ (中华人民共和国反垄断法) [Anti-Monopoly Law of the People's Republic of China] (promulgated by the Standing Comm. Nat'l People's Cong. Aug 30, 2007, effective Aug. 1, 2008), http://english.mofcom.gov.cn/article/policyrelease/Businessregulations/201303/20130300045909.shtml [https://perma.cc/59MS-YQMC].

11. Michael T. Roberts & Ching-Fu Lin, *2016 China Food Law Update*, 12 J. FOOD L. & POL'Y 238 (2016).

12. Zhōnghuá rénmín gònghéguó wǎngluò ānquán fǎ (中华人民共和国王老安全法) [People's Republic of China Cybersecurity Law] (promulgated by the Standing Comm. Nat'l People's Cong., Nov. 7, 2016, effective June 1, 2017), http://www.npc.gov.cn/npc/xinwen/2016-11/07/content_2001605.htm [https://perma.cc/AE5V-DRQ9].

13. Alex L. Wang, *Explaining Environmental Information Disclosure in China*, 44 ECOLOGY L. Q. 865, 882 (2018).

14. BENJAMIN VAN ROOIJ, REGULATING LAND AND POLLUTION IN CHINA: LAWMAKING, COMPLIANCE, AND ENFORCEMENT; THEORY AND CASES, 48 (2006), (citingLindsay Wilson, *Investors Beware: The WTO will not Cure all Ills with China,* 2003 COLUM. BUS. L. REV. 1007, 1020 (2003); Donald C. Clarke, *China's Legal System and the WTO: Prospects for Compliance,* 2 WASH. U. GLOBAL STUD. L. REV. 97, 111 (2003))

15. Wang, *supra* note 13, at n. 101.

16. Dan Harris, *China Business Regulation Rising,* CHINA LAW BLOG, (July 31, 2010), https://www.chinalawblog.com/2010/07/china_business_regulation_rising.html [https://perma.cc/88K3-YRNW].

17. *See* David Vogel & Robert A. Kagan, *Introduction* to DYNAMICS OF REGULATORY CHANGE: HOW GLOBALIZATION AFFECTS NATIONAL REGULATORY POLICIES 9 (David Vogel & Robert A. Kagan eds., 2004).

18. Karen Ward, *The World in 2050: Quantifying the Shift in the Global Economy,* HSBC GLOBAL RESEARCH, 53 (Jan. 4, 2011), https://www.hsbc.ca/1/PA_ES_Content_Mgmt/content/canada4/pdfs/business/hsbc-bwob-theworldin2050-en.pdf [https://perma.cc/JQ5H-3FCV].

19. Ward, *supra* note 18, at 6.

20. Emily Feng, *Northern China Suffers Smog Pollution After Air Targets Relaxed,* FIN. TIMES, (Nov. 15, 2018), https://www.ft.com/content/983ad260-e88b-11e8-8a85-04b8afea6ea3 (on file with author).

21. Martin Wolf, *The future might not belong to China,* FIN. TIMES (Jan. 1, 2019), https://www.ft.com/content/ae94de0e-0c1a-11e9-a3aa-118c761d2745 (on file with author) (discussing a 2018 study "Long-Term Global Economic Outlook" conducted by Capital Economics).

22. *Id.*

23. *China exports, imports and trade balance By Country and Region 2016,* WORLD INTEGRATED TRADE SOLUTION, https://wits.worldbank.org/CountryProfile/en/Country/CHN/Year/2016/TradeFlow/EXPIMP https://perma.cc/4NVG-EQP9].

24. *See* Jean Blaylock, *If you thought chlorine-washed chicken was scary, wait until you see what else Liam Fox has planned for a UK-US trade deal,* THE INDEPENDENT, (July 26, 2017, 10:30 AM), https://www.independent.co.uk/voices/chlorine-washed-chicken-liam-fox-trade-deal-us-ttip-deregulation-a7860706.html [https://perma.cc/VD33-GTBC].

25. Withdrawal of the United States From the Trans-Pacific Partnership Negotiations and Agreement, 82 Fed. Reg. 8,497 (Jan. 23, 2017).

26. Eleven countries that were parties to the proposed TPP concluded The Comprehensive and Progressive Agreement for Trans-Pacific Partnership (CPTPP): Australia, Brunei, Canada, Chile, Japan, Malaysia, Mexico, New Zealand, Peru, Singapore, and Vietnam. *See Comprehensive and Progressive Agreement for Trans-Pacific Partnership,* GOVERNMENT OF CANADA, https://international.gc.ca/trade-commerce/trade-agreements-accords-commerciaux/agr-acc/cptpp-ptpgp/index.aspx?lang=eng [https://perma.cc/2S7X-C2WF].

27. Doug Palmer, *U.S. aims to reshape world trade rules with regional pacts: Biden,* REUTERS (April 5, 2013), https://www.reuters.com/article/us-usa-trade-biden/u-s-aims-to-reshape-world-trade-rules-with-regional-pacts-biden-idUSBRE9340TD20130405 [https://perma.cc/765A-G9WB].

28. The Canadian Press, *Harper hails Trans-Pacific Partnership, promises $4.3B to protect dairy farmers,* LFPRESS.com (Oct. 5, 2013, 5:24 PM EDT), http://www.lfpress.com/2015/10/05/harper-hails-trans-pacific-partnership-promises-43b-to-protect-dairy-farmers [https://perma.cc/RE8J-9DWX].

29. *U.S. not invited to TPP meeting in Chile; ministers to meet again at APEC,* INSIDE US TRADE (Mar. 15, 2017) https://insidetrade.com/daily-news/us-not-invited-tpp-meeting-chile-ministers-meet-again-apec (on file with author).

30. EUROPEAN UNION INTELLECTUAL PROP. OFFICE, GUIDELINES FOR EXAMINATION OF EUROPEAN UNION TRADE MARKS (2017), https://euipo.europa.eu/tunnel-web/secure/webdav/guest/document_library/contentPdfs/trade_marks/draft-guidelines-2017-wp-lr2/24_part_b_examination_section_4_AG_chap_11_article_7(1)(k)_clean_lr2_en.pdf [https://perma.cc/V2YN-CLK8].

31. *Geographical Indications An Introduction,* WORLD INTELLECTUAL PROPERTY ORGANIZATION, 31, https://www.wipo.int/edocs/pubdocs/en/geographical/952/wipo_pub_952.pdf [https://perma.cc/3H3M-UNYH].

32. Comprehensive Economic and Trade Agreement, Canada-E.U., Annex 20-A, (Oct. 30, 2016).

33. EU-Vietnam Free Trade Agreement, Annex 12-A, unsigned.

34. *See TPP Final Text,* OFFICE OF THE TRADE REPRESENTATIVE, arts. 18.30–18.36, https://ustr.gov/sites/default/files/TPP-Final-Text-Intellectual-Property.pdf [https://perma.cc/AN8B-J8UU].

35. *See TPP Final Text, supra* note 34, art. 18.32.

36. *See* Shawn Donnan, *TPP deal lifts hopes for US-EU trade pact,* FINANCIAL TIMES (Oct. 6, 2015), https://www.ft.com/content/5bde5a48-6bda-11e5-8171-ba1968cf791a (on file with author).

37. *See The Third Industrial Revolution,* ECONOMIST, Apr. 21, 2012, at 15.

38. Additive manufacturing is an industrial production technology that builds 3D objects by adding layer upon layer of material (such as plastic or metal) in precise geometric shapes. While traditional manufacturing often requires removing material through milling or carving, additive manufacturing lays down or adds material to create a 3D object.

39. Richard Kelly & Jörg Bromberger, *Additive Manufacturing: A Long-Term Game Changer For Manufacturers,* MCKINSEY, https://www.mckinsey.com/business-functions/operations/our-insights/additive-manufacturing-a-long-term-game-changer-for-manufacturers [https://perma.cc/PMD8-RHFS].

40. Kelly & Bromberger, *supra* note 39.

41. *Id.*

42. *Id.*

43. *Id.*

44. Regulation (EC) 2018/302, 2018 O.J. (L 060I).

45. *See generally Parliamentary report urges Australians to bypass online geo-blocks that can double prices for IT products,* ABC (July 30, 2013, 12:14 AM), https://www.abc.net.au/news/2013-07-29/geo-blocking-mps-committee-price-report-apple-adobe-microsoft/4850484 [https://perma.cc/W3QE-GRSF].)

46. Allison McDonald, Matthew Bernhard, Luke Valenta, Benjamin VanderSloot, Will Scott, Nick Sullivan, J. Alex Halderman & Roya Ensafi, *403 Forbidden: A Global View of CDN Geoblocking,* 2018 Internet Measurement Conference (IMC '18), Oct. 31–Nov. 2, 2018, Boston, USA, 11, https://ensa.fi/papers/403forbidden_imc18.pdf [https://perma.cc/P6NW-AYL5].

47. Regulation 2018/302 *supra* note 44, paras. 22–26.

48. European Commission Press Release IP/18/6844, Antitrust: Commission fines Guess €40 million for anticompetitive agreements to block cross-border sales, (Dec. 17, 2018).

49. Interview with John Frank, Vice President, Microsoft, in Brussels, Belg. (July 16, 2018).

50. Luca Lombardo, *Genetic Use Restriction Technologies: A Review,* 12 PLANT BIOTECHNOLOGY J. 995, 995.

51. Lombardo *supra* note 50, at 995.

52. *Id.* at 1000.

53. *See discussion in* Lombardo, *supra* note 50, at 995.

54. *GDP and main components (output, expenditure and income)*, EUROSTAT, http://appsso.eurostat.ec.europa.eu/nui/show.do?query=BOOKMARK_DS-406763_QID_23BE6D65_UID_-3F171EB0&layout=UNIT,L,X,0;GEO,L,Y,0;TIME,C,Z,0;NA_ITEM,L,Z,1;INDICATORS,C,Z,2;&zSelection=DS-406763TIME,2016;DS-406763INDICATORS,OBS_FLAG;DS-406763NA_ITEM,B1GQ;&rankName1=INDICATORS_1_2_-1_2&rankName2=NA-ITEM_1_2_-1_2&rankName3=TIME_1_0_0_0&rankName4=UNIT_1_2_0_0&rankName5=GEO_1_2_0_1&rStp=&cStp=&rDCh=&cDCh=&rDM=true&cDM=true&footnes=false&empty=false&wai=false&time_mode=ROLLING&time_most_recent=true&lang=EN&cfo=%23%23%23%2C%23%23%23.%23%23%23 [https://perma.cc/VF8Y-8N7T] (last visited Jan. 11, 2019).

55. *See* Richard G Whitman, *On Europe—Margaret Thatcher's Lasting Legacy*, CHATHAM HOUSE (Apr. 9, 2013), https://www.chathamhouse.org/media/comment/view/190655 [https://perma.cc/F3Y9-M8VR]; Gordon Rayner & Christopher Hope, *Cut the EU red tape choking Britain after Brexit to set the country free from the shackles of Brussels*, THE TELEGRAPH (Mar. 28, 2017, 3:19 PM), https://www.telegraph.co.uk/news/2017/03/27/cut-eu-red-tape-choking-britain-brexit-set-country-free-shackles/ [https://perma.cc/EK8F-47U3].

56. *Is the UK a Winner or Loser in the EU Council?*, GUARDIAN, https://www.theguardian.com/world/datablog/2015/nov/02/is-uk-winner-or-loser-european-council [https://perma.cc/K5B3-KA2R].

57. Brexit: Impact Across Policy Areas, House of Commons Briefing Paper No. 07213, Aug. 26, 2016, 24.

58. Bilateral trade between United Kingdom and European Union (EU 28), TRADEMAP, https://trademap.org/Bilateral_TS.aspx?nvpm=1%7c826%7c%7c%7c14719%7cTOTAL%7c%7c%7c2%7c1%7c1%7c2%7c2%7c1%7c1%7c1%7c1 [https://perma.cc/936C-3SP8].

59. *See infra* notes 70–72 and 83–86 and accompanying text.

60. *The Internet Now Contributes 10 Percent of GDP to the UK Economy, Surpassing the Manufacturing and Retail Sectors*, BCG (May 1, 2015) https://www.bcg.com/d/press/1may2015-internet-contributes-10-percent-gdp-uk-economy-12111 [https://perma.cc/7B3S-PMWU]; "Brexit Could Put Data Sharing in Jeopardy," CHATHAM HOUSE (Mar. 10, 2016), https://www.chathamhouse.org/expert/comment/brexit-could-put-data-sharing-jeopardy [https://perma.cc/FYA5-W76X].

61. EUROPEAN UNION COMMITTEE, BREXIT: THE EU DATA PROTECTION PACKAGE, 2017–19, HL Paper 7, at 5 (UK).

62. *Internet Now Contributes, supra* note 60.

63. EUROPEAN UNION COMMITTEE, *supra* note 61, at 5.

64. *On Data Protection Brexit means mirroring EU rules, confirms UK minister*, TECHCRUNCH, https://techcrunch.com/2017/02/01/on-data-protection-brexit-means-mirroring-eu-rules-confirms-uk-minister/ [https://perma.cc/VE8H-PN8H].

65. *On Data Protection, supra* note 64.

66. *EU General Data Protection Regulation (GDPR)*: Regulation (EU) 2016/679 of the European Parliament and of the Council, (Apr. 27, 2016), OJ 2016 L 119/1, Art. 45.

67. Case C-362/14, Maximillian Schrems v. Data Protection Commissioner, ECLI:EU:C:2015:650, (Oct. 6, 2015), 21–22.

68. EUROPEAN UNION COMMITTEE, *supra* note 61, at 50.

69. Investigatory Power Act 2016, c. 4, § 87, (UK).

70. EUROPEAN UNION COMMITTEE, *supra* note 61, at 41.

71. *Id.* at 41.

72. *Id.* at 42.

73. Kate Allen, *UK finance industry dominates European scene*, FIN. TIMES (Sept. 5, 2018), https://www.ft.com/content/88cdec40-b03c-11e8-8d14-6f049d06439c (on file with author).

74. Orcun Kaya, Jan Schilbach & Kinner Lakhani, *Brexit Impact on Investment Banking in Europe*, DEUTSCHE BANK RESEARCH (July 2, 2018), 6, https://www.dbresearch.com/PROD/RPS_EN-PROD/PROD0000000000469527/Brexit_impact_on_investment_banking_in_Europe.PDF [https://perma.cc/3KKX-XAPK].

75. Kaya, Schilbach & Lakhani, *supra* note 74, at 7.

76. *Passporting*, BANK OF ENGLAND, https://www.bankofengland.co.uk/prudential-regulation/authorisations/passporting [https://perma.cc/R6VU-FXRU].

77. *See The Single Rulebook*, EUROPEAN BANKING AUTHORITY, https://eba.europa.eu/regulation-and-policy/single-rulebook [https://perma.cc/R7FQ-B329].

78. This will happen automatically if the United Kingdom exits without a deal. Of course, the United Kingdom could negotiate an agreement to the contrary under some deal with the EU.

79. *Commission Staff Working Document, EU equivalence decisions in financial services policy: an assessment*, EUROPEAN COMMISSION (Feb. 27, 2017), 6, https://ec.europa.eu/info/sites/info/files/eu-equivalence-decisions-assessment-27022017_en.pdf [https://perma.cc/X79K-D2EB]; J. Deslandes, C. Dias & M. Magnus, *Third country equivalence in EU banking and financial regulation*, DIRECTORATE-GENERAL FOR INTERNAL POLICIES, EUROPEAN PARLIAMENT, Mar. 2019, http://www.europarl.europa.eu/RegData/etudes/IDAN/2018/614495/IPOL_IDA(2018)614495_EN.pdf [https://perma.cc/WGM7-LM4R].

80. *Commission Staff Working Document, supra* note 79, at 7.

81. Eddy Wymeersch, *Third-Country Equivalence and Access to the EU Financial Markets Including in Case of Brexit 4*, J. FIN. REG. 209, 212.

82. *Commission Staff Working Document, supra* note 79, at 8.

83. Gavin Finch, Hayley Warren & Will Hadfield, *The Great Brexit Banker Exodus That Wasn't*, BLOOMBERG (last updated Jan. 31, 2019), https://www.bloomberg.com/graphics/2017-brexit-bankers/.

84. Will Hadfield & Steven Arons, *Money Is Flooding Out of London While the U.K. Bickers Over Brexit*, BLOOMBERG (Jan. 23, 2019), https://www.bloomberg.com/news/articles/2019-01-23/while-u-k-dithers-over-brexit-finance-outflows-pick-up-speed.

85. Regulation (EC) No 1907/2006 of the European Parliament and of the Council (Dec.18, 2006), 2006 O.J. (L 396).

86. ENVIRONMENTAL AUDIT COMMITTEE, THE FUTURE OF CHEMICALS REGULATION AFTER THE EU REFERENDUM, 2016-17, HC Paper 912, 3, https://www.publications.parliament.uk/pa/cm201617/cmselect/cmenvaud/912/912.pdf [https://perma.cc/4DLJ-PYHB].

87. *Statistics*, EUROPEAN CHEMICALS AGENCY (last visited June 4, 2019), https://echa.europa.eu/registration-statistics-infograph# [https://perma.cc/Z4AD-5UDL] (last accessed June 4, 2019).

88. Bruce Lourie, *Without EU regulations on chemicals, the UK will be a toxic dumping ground*, GUARDIAN, https://www.theguardian.com/commentisfree/2017/jun/01/eu-regulations-chemicals-brexit-uk-cancer-eu [https://perma.cc/H5HL-MZKU].

89. Susanne Baker, *Initial techUK views on chemical legislation after EU exit*, TECHUK (Oct. 26, 2016), http://www.techuk.org/insights/news/item/9593-initial-techuk-views-on-chemical-legislation-post-brexit [https://perma.cc/V9TY-77Y9].

90. *Cut EU red tape: Report form the Business Taskforce*, PRIME MINISTER'S OFFICE, (updated Feb. 24, 2014), https://www.gov.uk/government/publications/cut-eu-red-tape-report-from-the-business-taskforce/cut-eu-red-tape-report-from-the-business-taskforce [https://perma.cc/G24D-MDFL].

91. *UK Chemical trade bodies: 'soft' Brexit now more likely*, CHEMICALWATCH, https://chemicalwatch.com/56861/uk-chemical-trade-bodies-soft-brexit-now-more-likely [https://perma.cc/VF5D-PZY5].

92. THE FUTURE OF CHEMICALS REGULATION, *supra* note 86, at 5–6.

93. *See* Charles Grant, *How Brexit is Changing the EU*, CENTRE FOR EUROPEAN REFORM (July 15, 2016), https://www.cer.eu/publications/archive/bulletin-article/2016/how-brexit-changing-eu [https://perma.cc/ZW8Y-AE39].

94. *See* Ben Clements, *IEA Brexit Prize: Britain outside the European Union*, INSTITUTE OF ECONOMIC AFFAIRS, 19–20, https://iea.org.uk/wp-content/uploads/2016/07/Clement%20BREXIT%20entry_for%20web_0.pdf [https://perma.cc/94GC-XU6Y].

95. *See* Judy Dempsey, *Judy Asks: Does Europe Have an Alternative to Populism?*, CARNEGIE EUROPE (Aug. 30, 2018), https://carnegieeurope.eu/strategiceurope/77134 [https://perma.cc/R4X9-TGPV].

96. *See* William A. Galston, *The rise of European populism and the collapse of the center-left*, BROOKINGS INSTITUTION (Mar. 8, 2018), https://www.brookings.edu/blog/order-from-chaos/2018/03/08/the-rise-of-european-populism-and-the-collapse-of-the-center-left/ [https://perma.cc/3WT8-7QKU].

97. *See, e.g., Gains and losses of political parties at the German general election on September 24, 2017 in comparison to the previous election*, STATISTA, https://www.statista.com/statistics/753651/german-election-2017-party-gains-and-losses/ [https://perma.cc/HC5J-EDDB].

98. *Population structure and ageing*, EUROSTAT, https://ec.europa.eu/eurostat/statistics-explained/index.php/Population_structure_and_ageing [https://perma.cc/D36L-QNPG].

99. *Better regulation: Why and how*, EUROPEAN COMMISSION, https://ec.europa.eu/info/law/law-making-process/planning-and-proposing-law/better-regulation-why-and-how_en [https://perma.cc/63CX-BEF4].

100. Intelligence Act of July 24, 2015, https://www.legifrance.gouv.fr/affichCode.do;jsessionid=BF72E2C1162C7C49D52DE78D65BEF5B4.tpdila07v_2?idSectionTA=LEGISCTA000030934655&cidTexte=LEGITEXT000025503132&dateTexte=20160309 [https://perma.cc/54WP-TDYW].

101. Atack Patrick, *UK interior minister calls for end to WhatsApp 'hiding place' for terror suspects*, EURONEWS (last updated Mar. 27, 2017), https://www.euronews.com/2017/03/27/uk-interior-minister-calls-for-end-to-whatsapp-hiding-place-for-terror-suspects [https://perma.cc/AJ5V-ZTQM].

102. *See, e.g.,* Joined Cases C-203/15 and C-698/15, Tele2 Sverige AB v. Post-och telestyrelsen, Secretary of State for the Home Department v. Tom Watson, ECLI:EU:C:2016:970, (Dec. 21, 2016).

103. *See* Piotr Buras, *Poland, Hungary, and the slipping façade of democracy* EUROPEAN COUNCIL ON FOREIGN RELATIONS (Jul. 11, 2018), https://www.ecfr.eu/article/commentary_poland_hungary_slipping_facade_of_democracy [https://perma.cc/8MMB-2TKS]; *Italy budget: Parliament passes budget after EU standoff*, BBC (Dec. 29, 2018), https://www.bbc.com/news/world-europe-46710472 [https://perma.cc/37B8-7MR7]; Katya Adler, *Europe's migration crisis: Could it finish the EU?*, BBC (June 28, 2018), https://www.bbc.com/news/world-europe-44632471 [https://perma.cc/DM3Y-3UCH].

104. *See Legal acts—statistics*, EUR-LEX, https://eur-lex.europa.eu/statistics/2018/legislative-acts-statistics.html [https://perma.cc/AZP3-69T7]. The cited figures consist of both new (basis) and amending acts.

105. *Legal acts—statistics, supra* note 104.

106. Higgins and Kanter, *Order of Business for E.U. in Brussels? Weeds, Then 'Brexit,'* N.Y. TIMES (June 28, 2016), https://www.nytimes.com/2016/06/29/world/europe/brexit-eu-summit-agenda.html?_r=0 (on file with author).

107. European Commission Press Release MEMO 18/5715, State of the Union 2018: A fully equipped European Border and Coast Guard—Questions and Answers, (Sept. 12, 2018), https://europa.eu/rapid/press-release_MEMO-18-5715_en.htm [https://perma.cc/4HMP-5TQA].

Index

For the benefit of digital users, indexed terms that span two pages (e.g., 52–53) may, on occasion, appear on only one of those pages.

3D printing, 274
5G telecommunication systems, 88–89, 314n115

acid rain, 210–11
acquis communitaire, 69–70, 71–72
activist pressure, 62.
ADA (azodicarbonamide), 181, 348n72
additive manufacturing, 274, 382n38
adequacy decision, 149, 168
administrative rule making, 38–39, 41
Africa. *See also* specific countries
    agriculture, 186
    Economic Community of West African
        States, 79–80, 312n79
    food safety, 186, 189–90
agriculture. *See also* GMOs
    Africa, 186
    Brazil, 186, 189, 190–91
    Brexit, 282
    Chernobyl, 210–11
    Common Agricultural Policy, 14–15
    competition law exemption, 117–18
    Department of Agriculture, 32
    exports to EU, 184
    exports to EU, US, 180, 192
    Food and Agriculture Organization, 73
    food exports, success, 171–72
    GlobalGAP, 186–87
    Kenya, 189
    single standard, 60
    South America, 186
Airbnb, data privacy, 144
Alesina, Alberto, 28

Alter, Karen, 75
Ammori, Marvin, 162
Amsterdam Treaty (1999), 207–8, 209
Andean Tribunal of Justice (ATJ), 67–76
Anheuser-Busch (AB) InBev, 104,
    127–28, 244
animal welfare
    Australia, 226
    Canada, 226
    China, 216–17
    cosmetics manufacture, 215–17
    de facto Brussels Effect, 215
    de jure Brussels Effect, 225
    European Convention for the Protection
        of Animals, 209
    Five Freedoms, 209, 358n19
    Japan, 216
    Lisbon Treaty, 209
    livestock production, 217–19
    Strategy for the Protection and Welfare of
        Animals, 209
    United States, 226
Anti-Counterfeiting Trade Agreement
    (ACTA), 85–86
AOL/Time Warner merger, 110
Apple
    competition investigations, 104
    data protection, 143
    European Commission cases, 99
    Ireland tax revenue ruling, 99, 242–43,
        315n5, 372n44
    privacy policy adoption, 143
    Qualcomm exclusive dealings, 99, 107,
        242–43, 372n43

Argentina
chicken meat export, 218–19
data protection, 149, 150
motor vehicle emission control
standards, 73–74
REACH, 199–200
RoHS, 223–24
Artegoddam, 45
Asia. *See also* specific countries and topics
assessment, 233–34
Australia
animal welfare, 192–226
climate change and emissions
trading, 227–28
competition laws, 116, 122
EU exports from, 28–29, 94–95
Facebook, 145–46
geo-blocking, 275
GMO regulation, 180
online regulatory stringency, 168–69
REACH-style law, 199–200
Austria
acid rain, 210–11
chemical regulation, 195
GMOs, 176
hate speech online, 166–67
automobiles
additive manufacturing, 274
California Effect, 59–60
emissions standards, 10–11, 229
foreign direct investment, 59–60
RoHS, 214–15
standardized mass production, 63
Aviation Directive, 219–20, 259
aviation regulations
Aviation Directive, 219–20, 259
Carbon Offsetting and Reduction Scheme
for International Aviation, 90, 221, 261
emissions trading scheme, 68, 96, 219, 226,
246, 261
External Aviation Policy, 71–72

Bao, Jun Le, 240
bargaining power, conditional market
access, 69
Barroso, Jose Manual, 249
Basel Committee on Banking Supervision
(BCBS), 72–73
beef
hormone-treated, EU import ban, 260,
378–79n162
origins certification, 186, 350n113
Beijing Effect, 25, 64
replacing Brussels Effect?, 266
Beke, Laura, 85

benefits, Brussels Effect, 235–63
better, defined, 235
cost increases and innovation
deterrence?, 236
vs. costs to achieve, 235
foreign attempts constraining, 253–57
regulations criticisms, 235–36
regulatory imperialism?, 247
regulatory protectionism?, 241
welfare, measuring, 235
Biden Joe, 271–72
Biedenkopf, Katja, 200–1, 203–4, 214
Binding Corporate Rules (BCRs),
149–50
Bing, right to be forgotten, 146–47
bonus caps, bankers', 51
brand equity, 240
branding, global, 61
Brazil
5G, 88–89
agriculture, 186, 189, 190–91
beef exports, 189
competition laws, 122
copycat litigation, 125–26
cosmetics, 198
data protection, 147–48, 153
exports to EU, 28–29
food safety and exports to EU, 186, 187,
189, 190–91
GMO regulation, 180, 191
honey exports to EU, 189, 190–91
motor vehicle emission control
standards, 73–74
pork exports to EU, 217
REACH, 196, 198
RoHS, 223–24, 225
slaughtering conditions, 218
Brexit, xvi
agriculture, 282
on market size, 287
on non-divisibility, 287
on regulatory capacity, 287
on stringent regulations, 287
Brexit, Brussels Effect
regulatory freedom illusion, 277
Brussels Effect, 25–65, 67–70. *See also*
specific countries and topics
benefits, 235–63 (*see also* benefits, Brussels
Effect; *specific benefits*)
de facto (*see* de facto Brussels Effect)
definition, xiv, 7
de jure (*see* de jure Brussels Effect)
EU interests from, x
future, 265–88 (*see also* external
challenges; internal challenges)

global regulatory influence mechanisms, 67–78 (*see also* global regulatory influence mechanisms)

inelastic targets, 25–26, 48

limits, 91

market size, 25–26

normative stand, ix–x

origins, ix

plus, case studies, 95–96

REACH, 49, 74–75, 93–94

regulatory capacity, 25–26, 30

Brussels Effect, non-divisibility, 25–26, 53–58

economic, 58

fundamentals, 53

legal, 56

technical, 57

Brussels Effect, stringent regulations, 25–26, 37–41

administrative rule making preference and precaution tendency, 38–39, 41

fundamentals, 37

markets *vs.* government, 38–39

BSE, 37–38, 172

bureaucracy

EU, quality, 33

EU, size, 32–33

US, 32–33

business. *See* institutional influence

BVO, 181

California

hazardous substances and electronic waste, 223

REACH, 200

ROHS law, 252–53

California Consumer Privacy Act, 146, 154–55

California Effect, ix, 59–60

California Electronic Waste Recycling Act of 2003, 223, 364n146

Cambridge Analytica, 131–32, 141, 155, 158, 168

Cameroon, food safety, 185, 187

Canada

animal welfare, 226

aviation emissions, 219–20

climate change and emissions trading, 227

competition law, 116, 122

copycat litigation, 122–23

data protection, 149

EU-Canada Comprehensive Economic Trade Agreement, 85–86

exports to EU, 28–29

GDPR, 280

Geographical Indications, 272

GMO regulation, 191–92

REACH, 199–201, 203

seal products ban, 246–47

slaughtering, 218

on Transpacific Partnerships, 271–72

treaty partners, EU, 70–71

cap-and-trade. *See* emissions trading scheme (ETS)

capitalism, varieties, 40

capital mobility, international, 51, 304n163

Carbon Offsetting and Reduction Scheme for International Aviation (CORSIA), 221, 261

carbon trading, 226–27, 229

Cartagena Agreement, 75

cartel regulation and enforcement, 105. *See also* merger control

EU, 89–90, 314n122

foreign jurisdiction EU outsourcing, 123–24

investigations, 110–12

remedies, 56

US, 314n122

vitamins, 111, 320n82

case studies, 93–97

Brussels Effect plus, 95–96

digital economy, 93–94, 131–69 (*see also* digital economy)

financial regulation, 95

format, 94

inelasticity, 95, 96

market competition, 93–94, 99–129 (*see also* market competition, case studies)

non-divisibility, 96

policy areas, 93–94

RoHS regulation, 96–97

stringent regulations, 95–96

Cassis de Dijon, 10

Cathode Ray Tubes, 111

Census, 137

central counterparties (CCPs), 50, 51

Cerulus, Laurens, 248

Charter for Fundamental Rights, 132–33, 156–57

chemical safety, 93–94, 193–99

de facto Brussels Effect, 196

de jure Brussels Effect, 199

as imperialism, 248–49

legislation, major, 193

policy, 93–94

political economy, 194

Chernobyl nuclear disaster, 210–11

China. *See also* Beijing Effect

animal welfare, 216–17

competition law, 117–18

dairy industry, EU standards, 240

China (*Cont.*)
  data protection, 153–54
  emissions trading, 88–89
  5 G technology, 88–89, 314n115
  GDP, 267, 268
  GDP, PPP-adjusted, 267
  GDP per capita, 269
  GMO regulation, 180, 191
  hazardous substances and electronic
    waste, 225
  on market size, 287
  motor vehicle emission control
    standards, 73–74
  on non-divisibility, 287
  purchasing power parity, 267
  REACH, 200, 203–4
  on regulatory capacity, 287
  on stringent regulations, 287
chocolate, EU import market, 184–85
citizen activism, 246–47
Citizens United, 250–51
civil law tradition, 79
class action lawsuits, EU, 43, 301n103
Clayton Act, 100–1, 315n15
climate change
  de facto Brussels Effect, 219
  de jure Brussels Effect, 226
  global response necessity, 249
cocoa, 184–85, 349n96
Code of Conduct on Countering Illegal
    Hate Speech Online, 156, 158
  IT company signatories, 161–63
  Twitter, 131, 158, 164–65, 248–49
Codex Alimentarius Commission, 73, 188
College of Commissioners, 7–8
collusive delegation, 250
Colombia
  data protection, 188, 194
  EU norms export to, 75–76
  food safety, 191
  GMOs, 178, 191
  market competition, 191
Colombian Constitutional Court (CCC), 76
commerce. *See also* specific topics
  global, Europeanization of, xiv
Commodity Exchange Act (CEA), 88
Commodity Futures Trading Commission
    (CFTC), US, 88
Common Consolidated Corporate Tax Base
    (CCCTB), 46
community law, direct effect, 75–76
companies. *See* institutional influence
competence maximizers, 17
competences, regulatory, 32–33, 34–35, 36–37

competition, market
  case studies, 93–94, 99–129 (*see also*
    market competition, case studies)
  policy, 93–94
  political economy, 102
Competition and Consumer Commission of
    Singapore (CCCS), 116
competition enforcement, EU
  US companies as targets, 242–43
  winners, other US companies, 243
competition investigations
  high-tech companies, US, 104
  Microsoft, 62–63
competition law, 100
  Apple taxes owed to Ireland, 99, 242–43,
    315n5, 372n44
  cartels, 105, 110–12
  on company nationality, 49
  competition investigations, 62–63
  consumer welfare, 102–3, 316n32
  corporate compliance, 114
  criminal penalties, 101, 315n19
  divisibility of remedies, 112–13
  dominance, 100–1, 112–13
  enforcement, EU, 106–7, 318n57
  EU *vs.* US, 100–1
  exported abroad, from EU, 99–100
  foreign agencies and courts, 76
  foreign parties, 68
  forum of choice, 108
  global regulatory hegemony, EU, 99–100
    (*see also* market competition, case
    studies)
  global regulatory landscape, 121–22
  India, 76–77, 117
  inelasticity, 108–9
  intellectual property rights enforcement,
    69–70, 309n28
  merger control, 109–10
  objectives, 102
  other countries' emulation, 79
  protectionism, 103, 104–5
  regulatory capacity, 106–7
  regulatory competence, 36–37, 106–7
  shared views, 40–41
competition law, legislative borrowing, 115
  China, 117–18
  enforcement institutional model, 122
  Ethiopia, 100–1
  form, 120
  India, 117
  Latin America, 119
  linguistic and historical connections, 121
  preferential trade agreement leveraging, 121

reasons, 119–20
Singapore, 116–17
South Africa, 115–16
competition regulations
EU, goals, 103, 317n36
US, 40–41
compliance, corporate, 114
conditional market access, 69
consumer awareness, 62
Brussels Effect, measuring, 235
consumer health and safety. *See* health and
safety, consumer
consumer need, satisfying, 237–38
consumer welfare
competition law, 102–3, 316n32
costs, 238–39
Cook, Tim, 148
cooperative mechanisms, 68. *See also* treaties
coordinated market economy, 40
copycat legislation, 78
copycat litigation, 77–78
Anheuser-Busch (AB) InBev, 127–28
attraction, 128
definition, 122–23
de jure Brussels Effect, 122
dominance cases, 124
enforcement, foreign jurisdiction EU
outsourcing, 123–24
Google, 125–27
informational benefit, 123
market competition, case studies, 122
merger control, 127–28
Microsoft Windows Media Player, 124–25
SABMiller, 127–28
copyright, 238, 255, 275
Copyright Directive, 238, 243
corporate compliance, 114
corporate law, 49–50
corporate tax, harmonization, 46
cosmetics
activist pressure, 62
animal welfare, 3, 95–96, 209, 215–17, 230–31
chemical safety and REACH, 193, 197–98
Costa/Enel, 75–76
cost-benefit analysis (CBA), 43–45, 235
costs
consumer welfare, 238–39
innovation, 236, 237–38
market entry, 27
REACH, 237
costs, Brussels Effect, 235
distributional, 238
vs. economic benefits, 240
foreign countries on, 236

GDPR, 237
increased, as innovation deterrence?, 236
reduction from, 239
Council of the European Union, 7–8, 32
Council v. Commission, 208
credit default swaps (CDS), 50
Croquet, Nicolas A. J., 84

Damro, Chad, 26
data localization, 146
data protection. *See also* GDPR (General
Data Protection Regulation)
criticism abroad, 140
EU-US regulatory divergence, 140–41
motivations, external, 137
motivations, internal, 136–37
Nazi regime, 136
non-divisibility, 164–68
policy, 93–94
political process, contested, 137
regulation, 19–20
right to be forgotten, 134–35, 146–47,
166–67, 343n291
data protection, case studies, 131, 132–55
de facto Brussels Effect, 142 (*see also*
de facto Brussels Effect, data
protection, case studies)
de jure Brussels Effect, 147
legislation, major, 132
political economy, 136
data protection, legislation, major
Charter of Fundamental Rights, EU,
132–33, 156–57
data protection authorities, 135–36
Data Protection Directive, 133,
134–35, 136–37
ePrivacy Regulation, 133–34
European Courts, 134–36
GDPR, 133
data protection, standards and laws, 152–53
China, 153–54
India, 154
Latin America, 153
South Africa, 152
United States, 151–52
Uruguay, 150
data protection authorities (DPAs), 135–36
Data Protection Directive, 133, 136–37
Article 12, 134–35
Census, as impetus, 137
Debham, Elizabeth, 279
de facto Brussels Effect, 8, 67–68, 82, 83–84
Apple taxes owed to Ireland, 99, 242–43,
315n5, 372n44

de facto Brussels Effect (*Cont.*)
  chemical safety, 196
  corporate compliance, 114
  countries, 96–97
  market competition, case studies, 106
de facto Brussels Effect, competition law
  cartels, 110–12
  divisibility of remedies, 112–13
  dominance, 100–1, 112–14
  forum of choice, 108
  inelasticity, 108–9
  non-divisible remedies, 112–13
  regulatory capacity, 106–7
de facto Brussels Effect, data protection, case
    studies, 142
  Airbnb, 144
  Apple, 143
  California Consumer Privacy Act,
    146, 154–55
  consumer demand, 144–45
  data localization, 146
  Facebook, 143–44, 145–46
  Google and Spain, 145
  LA Times, 145
  Microsoft, 144
  non-divisibility, 142–43
  privacy by design and privacy by default, 144
  recruiting even-handedness, Article 29, 144
  regulatory capacity and stringency, 142
  right to be forgotten, 146–47
  Sonos, 144–45
  strength, 142
  Yahoo!, 145
de facto Brussels Effect, environment, 213–19
  animal welfare, 215
  climate change and emissions trading, 219
  hazardous substances and electronic
    waste, 214
de facto Brussels Effect, food safety, 179
  African agricultural producers, 186
  artificial dyes, 180–82
  Brazil, 186
  chemicals, 181
  divisibility feasibility, 182
  GlobalGAP, 186–87
  Kenya, 185, 187, 191–92
  operational feasibility, 182
  South Africa, 186
  stringent regulatory standards, 179–80
de facto Brussels Effect, merger control, 109–10
  AOL/Time Warner, 110
  divestiture requirement, 110
de jure Brussels Effect, 8, 83–84
  chemical safety, 199

  countries, 96–97
  definition, 114–15
  food safety, 188
  globalization retreat on, 270
  persistence, 129
  proliferation, 114–15
de jure Brussels Effect, data protection
  adequacy decision, 149, 168
  Argentina, 150
  Binding Corporate Rules, 149–50
  case studies, 147
  China, 153–54
  European standard influence, 147–48
  EU-US Privacy Shield, 151–52
  incentives, 150
  India, 154
  Japan, 150
  Latin America, 153
  South Africa, 152
  South Korea, 151
  standards and laws, 152–54
  United States, 151–52
  Uruguay, 150
  US influence, dwindling, 154–55
de jure Brussels Effect, environment, 221–26
  animal welfare, 225
  climate change and emissions trading, 226
  hazardous substances and electronic
    waste, 222
de jure Brussels Effect, food safety
  Brazil, 189, 190–91
  Colombia, 191
  GMOs, 190–92
  Middle East and North Africa, 189–90
  organic food production, 190
  South Korea, 191
  Taiwan, 189–90
de jure Brussels Effect, market competition
  case studies, 114–22
  competition law, 99–100
  copycat litigation, 122
  legislative borrowing, 115
Delaware Effect, 4–5
DeLisi, Jim, 237
Del Satro, Raffaella, 248
Denison, Richard, 201
derivatives, over-the-counter, 50
Derivatives Regulation, extraterritoriality, 68
digital economy, 93–94, 131–69
digital economy, case studies, 93–94, 131–69.
    See also specific topics
  Cambridge Analytica, 131–32, 141, 155,
    158, 168
  Commission's regulatory, 131–32

data protection, 131, 132–55
hate speech online, 131, 155–60
digital tax, 51–52
Directive 2010/13/EU, 157, 339n231
Directorates-General (DGs), 8
distributional costs, 238
Dodd–Frank Wall Street Reform and
Consumer Protection Act of 2010, 47
dominance
competition law, 100–1, 112–14
copycat litigation, 124
downward harmonization, 10–12
Drezner, Daniel, 26
due diligence duties, US importers, 47,
303n148
dyes, artificial food
EU, 180–82
US, 251–52

Eco-Management and Auditing Scheme
(EMAS), 12–13
Economic Community of West African
States WAEMU, 79–80, 312n79
economic non-divisibility, 58
data privacy, 142–43
economic policies. *See also* specific types
pro-regulation ideology, 39–40
social market, 39–40
economic power, xv–xvi. *See also* specific
topics
economy
digital, 93–94, 131–69 (*see also* digital
economy)
digital, case studies, 93–94, 131–69
political, 102
Ecuador, competition law, 119
Egan, Erin, 148
elasticity. *See also* inelasticity
terminology, 48, 304n153
elastic regulatory targets, 48
emissions trading scheme (ETS), 68, 209–10
Aviation Directive, 219–20, 259
aviation regulations, 68
Carbon Offsetting and Reduction Scheme
for International Aviation, 221
China, 88–89
de facto Brussels Effect, 219
de jure Brussels Effect, 226
extraterritorial, suspension of, 221
international resistance, 220–21
non-EU airlines in, countries opposing,
257–58, 377n142
policy, 93–94
Russia, 88–89

South Africa, 89–230
South Korea, 87–229
United States, 86
environmental regulations and policy, 93–94,
207–31. *See also* specific topics
acid rain, 210–11
Chernobyl nuclear disaster, 210–11
citizen perceptions, EU *vs.* US, 37–38
Council v. Commission, 208
Eco-Management and Auditing
Scheme, 12–13
emissions trading scheme, 209–10, 219, 226
on European businesses, 246
Germany and the Netherlands' on, 14
Green parties, 211
hazardous substances and electronic
waste, 208–9, 214, 222
as imperialism, 248
leadership, EU, 212–13
legislation, major, 207
"Limits to Growth," 210
Maastricht Treaty, 35
multilateralism and global treaties, 207
NGOs, 211–12
originating countries, 10–11
political economy, 210
precautionary principle, 207–8
public opinion, 211
purpose, 19
Sustainable Fishing Partnership
Agreements, 71–72
Waste Electrical and Electronic
Equipment Directive, 208–9, 222
environment regulations and policy, de facto
Brussels Effect, 213–19
animal welfare, 215
climate change and emissions trading, 219
hazardous substances and electronic
waste, 214
environment regulations and policy, de jure
Brussels Effect, 221–26
animal welfare, 225
climate change and emissions trading, 226
hazardous substances and electronic
waste, 222
ePrivacy Regulation, 133–34
equity, brand, 240
equivalence regime, 281
Erbakan v Turkey, 157
Ethiopia, competition law, 100–1
EU-Canada Comprehensive Economic
Trade Agreement, 85–86
EU Charter of Fundamental Rights,
132–33, 156–57

EUHACCP certification, 182, 348n74
EU-Korea trade agreement, vagueness, 84,
　　313n97
European Central Bank (ECB), EU power
　　via, 72
European Commission, 7–9
　　bureaucracy, 32
　　as competence-maximizer, 16, 17
　　competition investigations, US high-tech
　　　companies, 104
　　foreign policy power, 17
　　GE/Honeywell, merger control, 103–4,
　　　109, 242
　　GE/Honeywell, United Technologies
　　　complainant, 108
　　governance via regulation, 16–17
　　mergers, blocking and
　　　restructuring, 103–4
　　motivation, commitment to Europe, 33
　　pro-integration agenda, 17
　　pro-regulation agenda, 15
European Commission against Racism and
　　Intolerance (ECRI), 159–60
European Convention, 157
European Convention for the Protection of
　　Animals, 209
European Court of Human Rights (ECtHR)
　　rulings, 157
European Court of Justice (ECJ, CJEU), 9
　　activist court and judicial integration, 36
　　Cassis de Dijon, 10
　　as competence-maximizer, 17
　　Costa/Enel, 75–76
　　Google Spain v. Mario Costeja, 75, 134–35
　　precautionary principle and *Artegodan*, 45
　　pro-integration tendencies, 17, 18
　　right to be forgotten, 134–35, 166–67,
　　　343n291
　　United Brands, 115, 117
　　Van Gend & Loos, 75–76
European Courts
　　data protection, 134–36
　　foreign litigants, 75
　　regulatory capacity, 36
　　regulatory state expansion, 17
European Data Protection Board (EDPB),
　　133, 152
European Food Safety Authority, 76, 174,
　　179–80
European Framework Decision, 161
Europeanization, of global commerce, xiv.
　　See also specific topics
European Merger Control Regulation
　　(EMCR), 100

European Neighborhood Policy (ENP), 69–70
European Parliament (EP), 7–8
　　bureaucracy, 32
　　as competence-maximizer, 17
　　empowerment, 35
　　regulatory state expansion, 17
European regulatory agencies (ERAs), 33, 74
European Securities Markets Authority
　　(ESMA), 51, 88
European Union (EU). *See also* specific
　　topics
　　anti-EU sentiments, rise of, 283
　　demise, predictions, ix
　　global market regulation, xiii–xiv
　　global regulatory hegemon, ix–x (*see also
　　　specific topics*)
　　superpower, influential, xiii–xiv
　　weakness, misperceived, xiii
EU-US Privacy Shield, 151–52
e-waste. *See* hazardous substances and
　　electronic waste regulations
ex ante regulations, 41, 42–43, 44, 120
expertise, decision-making, 13–14
export market, EU as
　　for American corporate giants, 29
　　by country, 28–29
　　by industry, 29
External Aviation Policy, 72–73
external challenges, 266–73
　　Beijing Effect replacing Brussels Effect?, 266
　　globalization retreat on de jure Brussels
　　　Effect, 270
　　technology revolution on non-divisibility,
　　　273
external regulatory agenda, emerging, 18–21
　　external motives: global norm setting, 21
　　fundamentals, 18
　　internal motives: single market, 19
extraterritoriality, 67–68

Facebook
　　Cambridge Analytica, 131–32, 141, 155,
　　　158, 168
　　China blocking, 168–69
　　Code of Conduct on Countering Illegal
　　　Hate Speech Online, 158
　　competition investigations, 104
　　data protection, 143–44, 145–46
　　European Small and Medium Enterprises
　　　market revenue, 160–61, 341n256
　　GDPR support, 148–49
　　geo-blocking, 166
　　geo-blocking, Austria ruling, 165, 166–67,
　　　342n286

hate speech online, 160–61
hate speech online, universal rules, 164–65
privacy policy adoption, 143–44
facial recognition technology,
     regulation, 239
false negatives, 39, 43, 102
false positives, 39, 43, 102
Feryn, 156–57
Feyissa, Hailegabriel, 119
financial passporting, Brexit on, 280–81,
     384n78
financial sector
  regulation, case studies, 95
financial transaction tax, 51, 304n165,
     304n167
firms, foreign. *See also* institutional
     influence; *specific firms*
  response to Brussels Effect, 254
Fisher, Linda, 197
5G telecommunication systems, 88–89, 314n115
Five Freedoms, animal welfare, 209, 358n19
food. *See also* GMOs
  economic importance, 172
  emotional importance, 172
  export market, EU, 184
  import market, EU, 184–85
Food and Agriculture Organization (FAO), 73
food dyes, artificial
  UK, 180–82
  US, 251–52
food safety
  de jure Brussels Effect, 188
  European Food Safety Authority, 76, 174,
     179–80
  history, 171
  legislation, major, 173
  political economy, 175
food safety regulations. *See also* GMOs;
     specific countries exporting to EU
  BSE (mad cow disease), 37–38, 172
  Cameroon, 185, 187
  Codex Alimentarius Commission, 73, 188
  de facto Brussels Effect, 179
  European Food Safety Authority, 76
  on food producers, European, 245
  history, 171
  as imperialism, 248
  policy, 93–94
  regulation, 47
  scandals, 172
foreign attempts constraining Brussels
     Effect, 253
  foreign firms, 254
  foreign governments, 257

foreign countries. *See also* specific countries
  on EU regulation costs, 236
foreign direct investment (FDI)
  in capital-intensive industries, 59
  international capital mobility on, 51, 304n163
foreign direct investment (FDI), in
     technology, 59
foreign government response to Brussels
     Effect, 257. *See also* specific countries
  United States, 257–62
  World Trade Organization challenges,
     259–61
foreign litigants, European Courts, 75
foreign policy, Commission power, 17
foreign sovereigns, regulatory interference,
     250–51
forum of choice
  competition choice, 108
  for foreign company litigation against
     foreign companies, 256
freedom of expression, 155–56. *See also* hate
     speech online
free speech, 155–56. *See also* hate speech online
future, Brussels Effect, 265–88. *See also*
     specific topics
  external challenges, 266–73
  internal challenges, 277–83

gambling, online, 46, 302n131
GDPR (General Data Protection
     Regulation). *see also* data protection
  applications, 133
  cost, 237
  enforcement responsibility, 16–17, 32–33
  European Data Protection Board, 133
  fines, 34
  fundamentals, 133
  as global, unashamedly, 142
  global reach, as imperialism, 248
  as gold standard, 148
  Google Spain v. Mario Costeja, 75,
     134–35
  India, 48
  lobbying, by foreign firms, 255
  motivations, external, 137
  motivations, internal, 136–37
  other countries' emulation, 79
  Parliament support, 17–18
  political process, contested, 137
  single market, legislative history, 20
  technical non-divisibility, 57–58
  territorial reach, 133
  UK mirroring and emulation, 279
  US corporate support, 148–49

GE/Honeywell, merger control, 103–4, 109, 242
United Technologies complainant, 108
General Data Protection Regulation. *See* GDPR (General Data Protection Regulation)
Generalized System of Preferences (GSP) programs, 85
human rights violations, 297n27
genetically modified organisms (GMOs). *See* GMOs
Genetic Use Restriction Technologies (GURTS), 276–77
geo-blocking, 165, 274–76
Facebook, Austria ruling, 165, 166–67, 342n286
Geographical Indications (GIs), 272
Germany
animal welfare, 219
Brexit, 282–83
competition law, 105–6
data protection and privacy, 10–11, 135–36, 137, 159
emissions regulations, 10–11
emissions trading scheme, 209–10
environmental regulations and policy, 10–11, 14, 39–40
food safety, 172
G-20, 72–73
gambling, online, 46
GDP, 269
geo-blocking, 165
GMOs, 10–11, 176, 177–78
Google advertising revenue from, 29
influence on EU, 39–40
Maastricht Treaty, 45
MEPs, 8
Network Enforcement Act, 159
REACH, 196
social market economy model, 39–40
South African wine imports, 186
worker health and safety, 11–12
GlobalGAP, 186–87
global governance, 18
Global Green and Health Hospitals (GGHH), 255
globalization
retreat, on de jure Brussels Effect, 270
unilateral, 89
global regulatory hegemony, EU, ix–x. *See also* specific topics
benign, 249
competition law, 99
influence, 121–22, 294n63

global regulatory influence
mechanisms, 67–78
EU law appeal as template, 78
European Courts and foreign litigants, 75
fundamentals, 67
treaties and institutions, 69
GMOs. *See also* food safety
adventitious presence, 182–83
European resistance, 172–73
GURTS (terminator seeds), 276–77
GMOs, regulation, 12–13
agricultural standards, 60
Brazil, 180
de facto Brussels Effect, 39
de facto Brussels Effect, Australia, 180
on European food producers, 245
on hunger and poverty, 247
legislation, major, 174–75
McDonalds, EU, 184, 348–49n90
non-divisibility, 182–84
political economy, 176–79
precautionary principle, 45
technical non-divisibility, 58
as trade protectionism, 241
WTO ruling, 260, 379n163
Google
comparison shopping rulings, 62–63
competition investigations, 104
copycat litigation, 125–27
data protection, Spain, 145
data storage and business practices, 57
European Commission, cases and fines, 34, 78, 99
geo-blocking, 165
hate speech online, 160–61, 164–65
market importance, EU, 106
market share, 29, 142
privacy protections, 61–62
protectionism, 104
right to be forgotten, 146–47
Google Shopping, 113
Google Spain v. Mario Costeja, C.131/12, 75, 134–35
governance
global, 18
via regulation, European Commission, 16–17
governments, foreign. *See also* specific countries
response to Brussels Effect, 257
government *vs.* markets, 38–39
Gray, C. Boyden, 103–4
Green 10, 211–12

greenhouse gas (GHG) emissions, 209–10. *See also* emissions trading scheme (ETS)
2012 EU regulation, 262–63, 380n180
Greenleaf, Graham, 147–48
Green parties, 211
green protectionism, 241
gross domestic product (GDP), 27, 28
China, 267, 268
EU, future, 267
India, 267
PPP-adjusted, 267
gross domestic product (GDP) per capita, 27–28
China, 269
gross national income (GNI), 27–28
Group of Twenty (G-20), 72–73
GURTS, 276–77

Hachez, Nicolas, 85
Hancock, Matt, 279
harmonization
downward, 10–12
expertise, country, 13–14
issue salience, 13–14
upward, 10–12
wealth, country, 13–14
harmonization, market-driven, 67–68, 86, 90, 91
advantages, 82
harmonization, regulatory
minimum, 10
pursuit, 10
rationale and goal, 9–10
harmonization, treaty-driven, 67–68, 82, 83, 86
definition, 82
multilateralism, persistence, 86
rationale, 88–89
standard setting, 88–89, 90, 314n115
harmonization article, 34
Hart-Scott-Rodino Act, 315n15
hate speech online, regulation, xiii–xiv, 46
Austria, Facebook case, 166–67
Code of Conduct on Countering Illegal Hate Speech Online, 131, 156, 158, 161–63, 164–65, 248–49
digital company regulation, 157–58
European Framework Decision, 161
free speech/freedom of expression, 155–56
geo-blocking, 165
inelasticity, 164
#MediaAgainstHate, 159–60
"No Hate Speech Movement," 159–60
non-divisibility, 164–67

policy, 93–94
Snapchat, 161, 162–63, 341n261
Twitter, xiv, 131, 158, 164–65, 248–49
voluntary commitments and standards, 160, 161–62, 163
hate speech online, regulation, case studies, 131, 155–60
Brussels Effect, 160
Charter for Fundamental Rights, 156–57
Erbakan v Turkey, 157
European Convention, 157
European Court of Human Rights rulings, 157
Facebook, 160–61
Feryn, 156–57
Google, 160–61
legislation, major, 156
participatory and voluntary approach, 158
penalizing requirement, 157
political economy, 159
Snapchat, 161
YouTube, 160–61
hazardous substances and electronic waste regulations, 93–94
de facto Brussels Effect, 214
de jure Brussels Effect, 222
US states' adopting, 252–53
hazardous waste standards, 30
health and safety, consumer, 93–94, 171–206. *See also* specific topics
chemical safety, 93–94, 193–99
de facto Brussels Effect, 196
de jure Brussels Effect, 199
legislation, major, 193
political economy, 194
food safety, 47, 93–94, 171–88
de facto Brussels Effect, 179
de jure Brussels Effect, 188
European Food Safety Authority, 76
history, 171
legislation, major, 173
political economy, 175
Hooghe, Lisbet, 33
human rights violations, WTO on trade limits and, 297n27

impact assessment, 43–44
imperialism, regulatory
chemical safety, 248–49
environmental regulations and policy, 248
food safety regulations, 248
GDPR, 248
REACH, 248–49
regulatory, 247

incidental externalities, 21
India
    competition law, 117
    data protection, standards and laws, 154
    GDP, 267
    GDP, PPP-adjusted, 267
    GDPR effect on, 48
    General Motors withdrawal from,
        60–61
    motor vehicle emission control
        standards, 73–74
    purchasing power parity, 267
inelasticity
    case studies, 95, 96
    competition law, 108–9
    hate speech online, 164
    market, EU regulation, xiv–xv
    terminology, 48, 304n153
inelastic targets, xvii–xviii, 25–26, 48
initial public offering (IPO), stock exchange
    choice, 49–50
Injunctions Directive (2009), 43, 301n103
innovation, Brussels Effect
    costs, 236
    positive effects, 239
innovation, dynamic costs, 237–38
insider trading rules, SEC enforcement, 84
Institute for the Integration of Latin America
    and the Caribbean (INTAL), 76
institutional influence, 72–75
    Codex Alimentarius Commission, 73
    European Central Bank, 72
    Food and Agricultural Organization, 73
    Group of Twenty (G-20), 72–73
    International Maritime Organization, 74
    International Monetary Fund, 72
    Organization for Economic Co-operation
        and Development, 72–73, 88
    UN Economic Commission for Europe,
        73–74
    World Bank, 72
    World Health Organization, 73
    World Trade Organization, 72–73
institutions, regulation-generating, 7
    bureaucratic growth, 32–33
    College of Commissioners, 7–8
    Council of the European Union, 7–8
    Directorates-General, 8
    European Commission, 7–9
    European Court of Justice, 9
    European Courts, 9
    European Parliament, 7–8
integration, European

Commission commitment and preference,
    15–16
    via regulation, 15–16
integration through regulation, European, 9
intellectual property (IP) rights
    enforcement, 69–70, 309n28
internal challenges, 277–83
    anti-EU sentiments, rise of, 283
    Brexit, regulatory freedom illusion, 277
international law. *See also* specific topics
    stagnation, 83
International Maritime Organization
    (IMO), 74
International Monetary Fund (IMF)
    member state coordination, EU, 72, 310n34
    power via, EU, 72
International Organization for Securities
    Commissions (IOSCO), 88
Ireland, Apple tax revenue ruling, 99, 242–43,
    315n5, 372n44

Japan
    cosmetics manufacture, animal welfare, 216
    data protection, 150
    GlobalGAP, 187
    GMOs, 180, 191
    hazardous substances and electronic
        waste, 215, 224–25
    REACH, 200, 203
Jatar, Anan Julia, 119
Jong-hyun, Park, 151
Jourova, Ver, 22
Juncker, Jean-Claude, 212

Kardasheva, Raya, 14–15
Kenya
    agriculture and food safety, 185, 187, 189
    GMOs, 191–92
Khokhlov, Evgeny, 119
K-REACH, 200, 202–3

labor protections, 11–12
labor rights, in trade agreements, 84–85
labor standards, 83
    child labor, 61–62
    exporting, 62, 307n217
    regulation, 62
LA Times, data protection, 145
Latin America
    competition law, 119
    data protection, standards and laws, 153
    hazardous substances and electronic
        waste, 225

Institute for the Integration of Latin
America and the Caribbean, 76
Lavenex, Sandra, 74
leading standard, 54
legal non-divisibility, 56
legislation, copycat, 78. *see also* copycat
litigation
legislation, major. *See also* specific types
chemical safety, 193
competition law, 100
data protection, 132
environment, 207
food safety, 173
GMOs, 174–75
hate speech online, 156
privacy regulation, 135–36
supremacy and direct effect, 36
legislative borrowing
de jure Brussels Effect, 115
EU law as template, 78
market competition, case studies, 115
"Limits to Growth," 210
Lisbon Treaty, 18, 22–23
animal welfare, 209
data protection, 132–33
environmental protections, 207–8
European values, 39
stringent regulation preference, 39
transformative mandate, institutions, 70
litigation. *See* copycat litigation; *specific topics
and types*
livestock production, animal welfare, 217–19
lobbying EU, by foreign firms, 254–56
GDPR, 255
REACH, 255
success, lack of, 255–56

Maastricht Treaty
environmental protections, 207–8
Parliament empowerment from, 35
precautionary principle, 45
Social Protocol, 11–12
voting since, on environmental policy, 35
mad cow disease, 37–38, 172
Majone, Giandomenico, 16, 36
majority, qualified, 13–14, 35, 38
Maledy, Omer Gatien, 185
Manners, Ian, 81
market
EU distrust, xv
vs. government, 38–39
market access. *See also* specific topics
conditional, 69

market competition
policy, 93–94
political economy, 102
market competition, case studies, 93–94,
99–129
de facto Brussels Effect, 106
de jure Brussels Effect, 114–22
de jure Brussels Effect, copycat
litigation, 122
de jure Brussels Effect, legislative
borrowing, 115
legislation, major, 100
political economy, 102
market-driven harmonization, 67–68, 86,
90, 91
advantages, 82
definition, 82
market economy
coordinated, 40
liberal, 40
market entry, adjustment costs, 27
market power, 26
limitations, 29–30
market regulation
EU internal, xiv–xv
global, xiii–xiv
market size, xvii–xviii, 25–26
Brexit, 287
case studies, 94–95
China on, 287
Marx, Axel, 84–85
#MediaAgainstHate, 159–60
MediaTek, 215, 361n71
merger control, 100–1. *See also* cartel
AOL/Time Warner, 110
competition law, 109–10
divestiture requirement, 110
EU protectionism and, US study of, 245
GE/Honeywell, 103–4, 109, 242
GE/Honeywell, United Technologies
complainant, 108
Microsoft
Code of Conduct on Countering Illegal
Hate Speech Online, 158
data protection, 144
pro-privacy stance, competitiveness from,
240, 370n19
Windows Media Player, 113–14, 124–25
military power, xv–xvi
minimum harmonization, 10
multilateralism, xv
environmental regulations and policy, 207
treaties, EU, 68

multilateralism (*Cont.*)
  treaty-driven harmonization, persistence,
    82–83, 86

National Electronics Stewardship Institute
    (NESPI), 376n113
Nazis, hate speech online, 159
the Netherlands
  climate change, 209–10
  environmental regulations and policy,
    10–11, 14
  hate speech online, 157
  REACH and chemicals regulation, 195
  South African wine exports to, 186
  strong government and welfare state,
    39–40
Network Enforcement Act (Germany), 159
Neunier, Sophie, 69
Newport, Peter, 282
New Zealand
  animal welfare, 226
  competition law, 122
  data protection, 149
  massacre, hate-motivated mosque, 131–32,
    168–69
  Transpacific Partnership, 271
Nicolaidis, Kalypso, 69
"No Hate Speech Movement," 159–60
non-divisibility, 25–26, 53–58, 128–29
  Brexit, 287
  case studies, 96
  data privacy, 142–43
  data protection, 142–43, 164–68
  definition, 53
  economic, 58
  fundamentals, 53
  GMOs, 182–84
  hate speech online, 164–67
  leading standard, 54
  legal, 56
  REACH, 196–97
  technical, 57
  technology revolution on, 273
non-divisibliity, xvii–xviii
norm setting, global, 21

Office of Information and Regulatory
    Affairs (OIRA), 44
Olivier, Gerard, 76
O'Neill, Paul, 103
online gambling, 46, 302n131
online hate speech. *See* hate speech online,
    regulation

Organization for Economic Co-operation
    and Development (OECD),
    72–73, 88
over-the-counter derivatives, 50

package deals, 14–15
Park, Dae Young, 203–4
passporting, financial, Brexit on,
    280–81, 384n78
paternalism, regulatory, 238–39
Pauwelyn, Joost, 83
Peifer, Karl-Nikolaus, 140–41, 147–48,
Pescatore, Pierre, 76
pharmaceutical market standards, 29–30
Pichai, Sundar, 161
policy laundering, 250
policymaking, Europeanisation, 36
political economy
  chemical safety, 194
  data protection, 136
  environment, 210
  false negatives and false positives, 39, 43, 102
  food safety, 175
  GMOs, 176–79
  hate speech online, 159
  market competition, 102
Pollack, Mark, 17
precautionary principle, 207–8
  environment, 207–8
  GMO regulation, 45
  Maastricht Treaty, 45
  REACH, 45
  as unsustainable, 236–37
precautionary risk culture, 37–38
precaution tendency, 38–39, 41, 42–43,
    45–46
preferential trade agreements (PTAs), 69,
    70–71, 87
  on competition law legislative borrowing,
    121
  Transatlantic Trade and Investment
    Partnership, 261, 273
  Transpacific Partnership, 271–72
privacy by default, 144
privacy by design, 144
privacy regulation, 19–20. *See also* data
    protection; GDPR (General Data
    Protection Regulation)
  Google, 61–62
  legislation and court rulings, 135–36
privacy rights
  as fundamental, 132, 326–27n4
  US *vs.* EU, 140–41

Privacy Shield, EU-US, 151–52, 154–55
Product Stewardship Institute, 376n113
protectionism
    citizen activism and, 246–47
    competition law, 103, 104–5
    detection difficulty, 104–5, 244
    envy-driven, 241
    Google, 104
    green, 241
    merger control, US study, 245
    regulatory, 241
purchasing power parity (PPP), 267

Qualcomm, 242–43, 372n43,
    competition investigations, 104
    European Commission cases against, 99
qualified majority, 13–14, 35, 38

race to the bottom, 52–53
race to the top, 52–53
REACH, 193–99
    adoption, 193
    Brussels Effect, 49, 74–75, 93–94
    corporate criticisms, 236–37
    cost, regulatory compliance, 237
    de facto Brussels Effect, 196
    de jure Brussels Effect, 199
    foreign company litigation against foreign
        companies, 256
    impact, global, 193
    as imperialism, 248–49
    legislation, major, 193
    lobbying, by foreign firms, 255
    objectives, key, 19
    policy, 93–94
    political economy, 194
    precautionary principle, 45
recruiting even-handedness, 144
Regional Greenhouse Gas Initiative (RFFI),
    226–27
Registration, Evaluation, Authorisation,
    and Restriction of Chemicals.
    See REACH
regulations. *See also* specific types
    Commission governance via, 16–17
    integration through, European, 9
    key institutions generating, 7 (*see also*
        specific institutions
    normative appeal, 81
    origins, member states, 10–11
regulations, stringent. *See* stringent regulations
regulatory capacity, xvii–xviii, 25–26, 30, 36–37
    Brexit, 287

China on, 287
    definition, 30–31
    degree, on global regulatory authority, 31
    stringent rule propagation of, 31
regulatory competences, 32–33, 34–35, 36–37
regulatory freedom, Brexit and illusion of,
    277
regulatory globalization, unilateral, xiv–xv.
    See also specific topics
regulatory paternalism, 238–39
regulatory power. *See also* specific types and
    topics
    relevance, xv–xvi
regulatory protectionism, 241
Regulatory Scrutiny Board, 44
regulatory sovereignty, Brussels Effect on,
    247
reputational benefits, 240
Restriction of Hazardous Substances
    Directive. *See* RoHS (Restriction of
    Hazard Substances) Directive
right to be forgotten, 134–35
    Bing, 146–47
    data protection, 146–47
    European Court of Justice, 166–67,
        343n291
    Google, 146–47
RoHS (Restriction of Hazard Substances)
    Directive, 49, 208–9, 304n155
    on American companies, 214
    case studies, 96–97
    China, 225
    de facto Brussels Effect, 214
    de jure Brussels Effect, 222–24
    Japan, 224–25
    Latin America, 225
    South Korea, 215, 224
    United States, 222–23, 364n145
    US states' adopting, 252–53
Rosen, Jeffrey, 162
ROW (rest of the world) firms, 105
rule making preference, administrative,
    38–39, 41
rules, EU. *See* regulations
Russia
    Chernobyl, 210–11
    competition law, 100–1, 122
    competition law, Google, 125
    data localization, 146
    data privacy, 168
    diamonds, Alrosa, 112–13
    emissions, Euro-5/6 standards, 229–30
    emissions trading, 88–89

Russia (*Cont.*)
exports to EU, 28–29
General Motors withdrawal from, 60–61
GMOs, 191
hate speech regulation, online, 160, 163
right to be forgotten, 75

SABMiller, 127–28, 244
Safe Harbor agreement, 154–55
safety. *See* health and safety, consumer
sanctioning authority, 34
Sandberg, Sheryl, 143–44
Sarbanes–Oxley Act of 2002, 47
scale economies, 58–59
Schrems, 151
Schrems, Max, 139–40, 149–50
Schwartz, Paul, 140–41, 147–48
Scott, Mark, 248
Sherman Act (1890), 100–1
Siemens/Alstrom, 105–6
Singapore
competition law, 116–17, 120–21
RoHS, 223–24
Transpacific Partnership, 271
Single European Act (SEA), 13, 31–32, 34
environmental protections, 207–8
Parliament empowerment, 35
regulatory reforms, 38
single market, 19, 26. *See also* Single
European Act (SEA)
anti-EU sentiments on regulations for,
284, 285, 286
building, consciously, 31–32
chemical safety and REACH, 193, 194, 282
Commission's pro-regulation agents,
15, 17–18
competition law, 100, 102
countries joining EU, 28
data protection, 136–37
Digital Single Market Strategy, 222, 241
environment, 207
externalizing, as imperialism, 247–49
externalizing, citizen activism, 246–47
externalizing, foreign advocacy
groups, 251
financial industry, 280
food safety, 73, 171, 180
GDPR, 256
institutions and regulations for, 7, 26
integration via regulation, EU, 9
law as template, EU, 80
regulatory capacity, EU, 31–32, 33,
34–35, 36–37

RoHS, 222
stringent regulations, 38, 39–40
trade partner access to, 68, 70–71
Treaty of the Functioning of the European
Union, 34–35
Snapchat, hate speech online, 161, 162–63,
341n261
Snowden, Edward, 24, 131–32, 139, 141, 151
Soare, Jadir, 84–85
social market, 39–40
EU commitment, 300n89
Social Protocol, 11–12
soft norms, 84, 313n97
Sonos, data protection, 144–45
South Africa
competition law, 115–16
data protection, standards and laws, 152
emissions trading, 89–230
food safety and labeling, 186
General Motors withdrawal from, 60–61
South America. *See also* specific countries
agriculture, 186
South Korea
data protection, 151
emissions trading, 87–229
food safety, 191
hazardous substances and electronic
waste, 215, 224
REACH, 200, 202–3
Spain
competition law, 79–80, 119
data privacy, 150
GDP, 269
GMOs, 174, 176, 177–78
Google noncompliance with regulations
of, 145
Google Spain v. Mario Costeja, C-131/12,
75, 134–35
labor standards, 11–12
Spolaore, Enrico, 28
standards and standardization. *See also*
specific topics
contracts, benefits, 57, 306n188
leading standard, 54
treaty-driven harmonization and spread,
88–89, 314n115
US accession and adoption, 262, 379n174
Stasi, 136
stem cell research, 52
Stiglitz, Joseph, 249
stock market regulation, 49–50
Strategy for the Protection and Welfare of
Animals, 209

stringent regulations, xvii–xviii, 25–26, 37–41
  Brexit, 287
  case studies, 95–96
  China, 287
  domestic preference, 37
  EU preference *vs.* US, 37
  fundamentals, 37
  ideology: markets *vs.* government, 38–39
  preference heterogeneity on, 46
  process: administrative rule making preference and precaution tendency, 38–39, 41
  wealthy countries, 37
Substances of Very High Concern (SVHCs), 193–94, 197–98, 255, 256, 377n139
supremacy, doctrine of, *Costa/Enel*, 75–76
Sustainable Fishing Partnership Agreements (SFPAs), 71–72
swaps, 50
Szpunar, AG, 146–47

Taiwan
  animal welfare, 226
  food safety, 189–90
  hazardous substances and electronic waste, 215, 222, 223–24
  REACH, 199–200
Tatham, Alan, 81
tax
  Common Consolidated Corporate Tax Base, 46
  corporate, harmonization, 46
  digital, 51–52
technical non-divisibility, 57
  data privacy, 142–43
technology revolution. *See also* specific companies and topics
  additive manufacturing, 274, 382n38
  geo-blocking, 274–76
  GMO cultivation and GURTs, 276–77
  on non-divisibility, 273
  3D printing, 274
terminator seeds, 276–77
territorial extension (extraterritoriality), 67–68
TFEU. *See* Treaty of the Functioning of the European Union (TFEU)
theory, 7–24. *See also* specific topics
  Brussels Effect, defined, 7
  European Commission pro-regulation agenda, 15

  external regulatory agenda, emerging, 18–21
  integration through regulation, European, 9
3D printing, 274
Tiebout sorting, 53
tort liability and litigation, 41–43
Toxic Substances Control Act (TSCA), 194, 200–2
  amendment, 223, 364n145
trade. *See also* World Trade Organization (WTO); *specific topics*
  EU on, xiv–xv
  EU policy, 22–23
  power in and through, 69
trade agreements. *See also* specific types
  Generalized System of Preferences programs, 85
  international, enforcement difficulties, 85–86
  international, EU standards and regulations in, 84
  labor rights, 84–85
  modern mixed, 85–86
  preferential trade agreements, 69, 70–71, 87
trade protectionism, GMO regulation as, 241
trade wars, on markets, xv–xvi
Transatlantic Trade and Investment Partnership (TTIP), 261, 273
Transpacific Partnership (TPP), 271–72, 383n55
Transparency Register, 254, 376n118
treaties, 34–35, 69–71. *See also* specific treaties
  bilateral and multilateral, 68
  enforcement difficulty, 83
  External Aviation Policy, 72–73
  preferential trade agreements, 69, 70–71
  Sustainable Fishing Partnership Agreements, 71–72
  Treaty Establishing the Transport Community, 71–72
treaty-driven harmonization, 67–68, 82, 83, 86, 88–89
  definition, 82
  multilateralism and, persistence, 86
  rationale, 88–89
  standard setting, 88–89, 90, 314n115
Treaty Establishing the Transport Community, 71–72

Treaty of Dakar, 312n79
Treaty of Rome, 312n79
Treaty of the Functioning of the European
    Union (TFEU), 100
    Article 102, 100, 103, 316n32
    competition law, 79, 106–7, 318n57
    harmonization article, 34–35
Treaty on the European Union (TEU),
    Article 11, 254–55, 376n121
Trump, President
    globalization retreat, 270–72
    international treaties/agreements
        withdrawal, xvi
Turing, Dermot, 50
Twitter
    Code of Conduct on Countering Illegal
        Hate Speech Online, 131, 158,
        164–65, 248–49
    GDPR enforcement, 142
    hate speech online, xiv, 164–65
tyranny of alien majorities, 54–55
tyranny of regulated alien minority, 55
tyranny of the majority, 54–55

UN Economic Commission for Europe
    (UNECE), 73–74
unilateralism
    international affairs, US, xv
    regulatory globalization, EU, xiv–xv
United Brands, 115, 117
United States. *See also* specific topics
    animal welfare, 226
    Brussels Effect, government response,
        257–62
    data protection, 151–52
    emissions trading, 86
    hazardous substances and electronic
        waste, 222–23
    REACH, 200
    RoHS, 223, 364n145
universalism, xv
universal principles, 22
upward harmonization, 10–12
Uruguay
    data protection, standards and laws, 149,
        150, 153
    GMOs, 32, 191
    hazardous substances and electronic
        waste regulations (*See* hazardous
        substances and electronic waste
        regulations)

Van Gend & Loos, 75–76
Vestager, Margarethe, 105–6
Veterinary and Food Office (FVO), 188
vitamins cartel, 111, 320n82
Vogel, David, ix, 37–38
vs. other forms of influence, 82–86

Waldfogel, Joel, 54–55
Washington Effect, 25, 53, 64
Waste Electrical and Electronic Equipment
    Directive (WEEE), 208–9, 222
waste management
    California Electronic Waste Recycling
        Act of 2003, 223, 364n146
    hazardous waste standards, 30
    regulation, 52
    repurposing, China, 52, 305n175
    Waste Electrical and Electronic
        Equipment Directive, 208–9
wealth, country, on decision-making, 13–14
Whetstone, Rachel, 165
Wilders, Geert, 157
Wilkish, George, 214
Windows Media Player, 113–14, 124–25
World Bank (WB), EU power via, 72
World Health Organization (WHO), 73
World Trade Organization (WTO)
    dysfunctional, 24
    establishment, 18
    EU power via, 72–73
    foreign government challenges to EU
        regulation, 259–61
    GMO regulation, 260, 379n163
    human rights violations and trade
        limits, 297n27
    scandals, 24
    trade talk problems, xv–xvi

Xiohong, Ma, 118

Yadov, Yesha, 50
Yahoo!, data protection, 145
yoga mat chemical, 181, 348n72
YouTube
    Code of Conduct on Countering Illegal
        Hate Speech Online, 158
    hate speech online, 160–61
    users, by EU country, 160–61, 341n257

Zielonka, Jan, 247–48
Zuckerberg, Mark, 148–49